1992

# ENCOUNTERS
# WITH
# FILMMAKERS

**Recent Titles in**
**Contributions to the Study of Popular Culture**

In Manors and Alleys: A Casebook on the American Detective Film
*Jon Tuska*

National Styles of Humor
*Avner Ziv, editor*

The Sleuth and the Scholar: Origins, Evolution, and Current Trends in Detective
Fiction
*Barbara A. Rader and Howard G. Zettler, editors*

ort and Society in Latin America: Diffusion, Dependency, and the Rise of Mass
ure
*ph L. Arbena, editor*

ouring Whirlwind: Terror and Transcendence in the Cinema of Cruelty
*ll H. Rockett*

ibernian Green on the Silver Screen: The Irish and American Movies
*oseph M. Curran*

Film Directors on Directing
*John Andrew Gallagher*

Seeking the Perfect Game: Baseball in American Literature
*Cordelia Candelaria*

Take One: The Control Room Insights of Ten TV Directors
*Jack Kuney*

A "Brand" New Language: Commercial Influences in Literature and Culture
*Monroe Friedman*

Out of the Woodpile: Black Characters in Crime and Detective Fiction
*Frankie Y. Bailey*

Freaks of Genius
*Daniel Shealy, editor*
*Madeleine B. Stern and Joel Myerson, associate editors*

# Jon Tuska

# ENCOUNTERS

# WITH

# FILMMAKERS

## Eight Career Studies

*Contributions to the Study of Popular Culture, Number 29*

GREENWOOD PRESS

New York • Westport, Connecticut • London

**Library of Congress Cataloging-in-Publication Data**

Tuska, Jon.
      Encounters with filmmakers : eight career studies / Jon Tuska.
         p.    cm.—(Contributions to the study of popular culture,
      ISSN 0198–9871 ; no. 29)
      Includes bibliographical references and index.
      ISBN 0–313–26305–1 (alk. paper)
      1. Motion picture producers and directors.    2. Motion picture
   industry.    I. Title.    II. Series.
   PN1998.2.T8    1991
   791.43′0233′0922—dc20              91–15983

British Library Cataloguing in Publication Data is available.

Library of Congress Catalog Card Number: 91–15983
ISBN: 0–313–26305–1
ISSN: 0198–9871

First published in 1991

Greenwood Press, 88 Post Road West, Westport, CT 06881
An imprint of Greenwood Publishing Group, Inc.

Printed in the United States of America

The paper used in this book complies with the
Permanent Paper Standard issued by the National
Information Standards Organization (Z39.48–1984).

10 9 8 7 6 5 4 3 2 1

## Copyright Acknowledgments

The author and publisher gratefully acknowledge permission to reprint material from the following copyrighted sources.

Excerpts from PECKINPAH: A PORTRAIT IN MONTAGE by Garner Simmons, copyright © 1982, by permission of the author and the University of Texas Press.

Excerpts from SAM PECKINPAH: MASTER OF VIOLENCE by Max Evans. Copyright © 1972 by Max Evans and reprinted by permission of the University of South Dakota Press, Vermillion, SD.

Excerpts reprinted with permission of Charles Scribner's Sons, an imprint of Macmillan Publishing Company from CITIZEN WELLES: A BIOGRAPHY OF ORSON WELLES by Frank Brady. Copyright © 1989 Frank Brady.

Excerpts reprinted with permission of Hodden & Stoughton, Ltd. from CITIZEN WELLES: A BIOGRAPHY OF ORSON WELLES by Frank Brady. Copyright © 1989 Frank Brady.

Excerpts reprinted with permission of Charles Scribner's Sons, an imprint of Macmillan Publishing Company from THE HUSTONS by Lawrence Grobel. Copyright © 1989 Lawrence Grobel.

Excerpts reprinted by permission of Sterling Lord Literistic, Inc. from THE HUSTONS by Lawrence Grobel. Copyright © 1989 Lawrence Grobel.

Excerpts from ORSON WELLES: A BIOGRAPHY by Barbara Leaming. Copyright © 1985 by Barbara Leaming. Reprinted by permission of Viking Penguin, a division of Penguin Books USA Inc.

Excerpts from THE CINEMA OF ROMAN POLANSKI by Ivan Butler. Copyright © 1970 by Ivan Butler. Reprinted by permission of A.S. Barnes, an imprint of Oak Tree Publications, 999 Summer Street, Stamford, CT 06905.

Excerpts from SCARLETT O'HARA'S YOUNGER SISTER: MY LIFE IN AND OUT OF HOLLYWOOD by Evelyn Keyes. Copyright © 1977 by Evelyn Keyes. Reprinted by permission of Citadel Press, Inc., a subsidiary of Lyle Stuart, Inc.

Excerpts from HAWKS ON HAWKS by Joseph McBride. Copyright © 1982 by the University of California Press. Reprinted by permission of the University of California Press.

Excerpts from HELTER SKELTER by Vincent Bugliosi with Curt Gentry. Copyright © 1974 by Curt Gentry and Vincent Bugliosi. Reprinted by permission of W.W. Norton & Company, Inc.

Excerpts from HOWARD HAWKS, STORYTELLER by Gerald Mast. Copyright © 1982 by Gerald Mast. Reprinted by permission of Oxford University Press.

Excerpts from JOHN HUSTON: KING REBEL by William F. Nolan, copyright 1965. Reprinted by permission of the author.

Excerpts from "PLAYBOY Interview: Sam Peckinpah," PLAYBOY 19, no. 8 (August 1972).

Excerpts from ROMAN BY POLANSKI by Roman Polanski. Copyright © 1984 by Eurexpart B.V. Used by permission of William Morrow and Company, Inc./Publishers, New York.

Excerpts reprinted by permission of William Heinemann Limited, from ROMAN BY POLANSKI by Roman Polanski. Copyright © 1984 by Eurexpart B.V.

Every reasonable effort has been made to trace the owners of copyright materials in this book, but in some instances this has proven impossible. The author and publisher will be glad to receive information leading to more complete acknowledgments in subsequent printings of the book and in the meantime extend their apologies for any omissions.

*quamquam ridentem dicere verum
quid vetat*? [what prevents one
jesting in telling the truth?]

Horace

This one is for you
KATHERINE HABER
—wherever you are!

# Contents

Photographs     xi

Introduction     1

H. Bruce Humberstone     9

Henry King     39

Alfred Hitchcock     65

Howard Hawks     95

John Huston     139

Orson Welles     189

Roman Polanski     239

Sam Peckinpah     277

Notes     329

Filmographies by Karl Thiede     343

Bibliography     401

Index     407

# Photographs

*All photographs follow page 137.*

1. Vicki Piekarski on the set of THE DETECTIVE IN HOLLYWOOD pilot film.
2. H. Bruce Humberstone at the time he became a film director.
3. Warner Oland, as Charlie Chan, and Humberstone on the set of CHARLIE CHAN AT THE RACE TRACK.
4. "Lucky" Humberstone between Rosanne Murray and Danny Kaye on the set of WONDER MAN.
5. Henry King when he was an actor as well as a pioneer director.
6. Richard Barthelmess and Henry King while filming TOL'ABLE DAVID.
7. Henry Fonda and Henry King on location for WAY DOWN EAST.
8. Alfred Hitchcock and Margaret Lockwood on the set of THE LADY VANISHES.
9. Hitchcock directing Edmund Gwenn and Mildred Natwick in a scene from THE TROUBLE WITH HARRY.
10. Hitchcock directing Kim Novak in VERTIGO.
11. Alfred Hitchcock and dress designer Edith Head on the set of FAMILY PLOT.
12. Howard Hawks and his dog, "Cap," when he worked with Howard Hughes on SCARFACE.

13. Hawks directing Carole Lombard and John Barrymore in TWENTIETH CENTURY.

14. Hawks, Victor Kilian, and Jean Arthur conferring on the set of ONLY ANGELS HAVE WINGS.

15. A dialogue conference on the set of THE BIG SLEEP.

16. Hawks and John Wayne on location for HATARI!

17. John Huston shaking hands with his father on the set of THE MALTESE FALCON as Bogart and cameraman Oliver S. Garretson look on.

18. Huston fascinates a young visitor to the set of THE MISFITS.

19. Huston in one of his most famous acting roles opposite Jack Nicholson in CHINATOWN.

20. Huston and Ray Stark on the set of ANNIE.

21. Orson Welles ''riding'' the camera in a scene from CITIZEN KANE.

22. Orson and Rita Hayworth in the mirror scene from THE LADY FROM SHANGHAI.

23. Orson on the set of THE DETECTIVE IN HOLLYWOOD with Fred Hutchison and Jon Tuska.

24. Roman Polanski in costume for CHINATOWN.

25. Polanski finally entering the door to ''the'' apartment in THE TENANT.

26. Polanski on the set of TESS.

27. Sam Peckinpah on the set of PAT GARRETT AND BILLY THE KID.

28. Steve McQueen, Ali McGraw, and Sam Peckinpah on the set of THE GETAWAY.

29. Sam directing Vadim Glowna and a stand-in in a scene from CROSS OF IRON.

30. A very old and tired Sam Peckinpah with Rutger Hauer on the set of THE OSTERMAN WEEKEND.

31. Sam and Katy Haber clowning on the set of CROSS OF IRON.

# Introduction

There are eight career studies in this book. Accordingly, I ought best to define what a career study is and what it is not. It is not just an interview; nor is it an attempt at full-scale biography. It lies between these extremes. Ideally, it is a portrait of an artist in terms of his creations. It does not propose to present the whole man. The field of vision is too circumscribed for that. Yet it does make an effort to evoke his personality. Because I knew each of these eight directors and in most cases visited with each over a period of years, I was able to surround the chronology and appraisal of his work in film with an informal portrait.

I have chosen these particular eight directors because, through their careers, I can also address a dimension outside of their lives and films, namely the development and growth of the motion picture industry itself. For example, H. Bruce Humberstone has been included because he was for most of his career a contract director at Twentieth Century-Fox Film Corporation. He began at Fox in the "B" unit and worked his way up to directing "A" pictures with some of the studio's most famous and popular contract players. Yet, what results he was able to achieve were the consequence of having to contend not only with problems on the set or with a script, but also making a film so that it suited both the individual producer and Darryl F. Zanuck, who was at the time head of production.

The *auteur* theory of film direction originated among French critics and during the 'Sixties and 'Seventies enjoyed a certain vogue among American critics. In brief, this theory equates what a film director does with what a novelist does, viewing him as the principal agent and prime mover behind an artistic creation. This entire concept simply cannot apply when it comes to a contract director. Beyond the studio chief, the head of production, and the producer, there may also have been an executive producer, and an associate producer, and beyond even these there were the inevitable pressures from the sales department, the players, the writers, and during a good many decades of this century from the censors. Even with some latitude in casting, a contract director was also subject to additional studio requirements. The studio may have needed another picture from a contract star and so the star was arbitrarily assigned to a film without any attention given as to the appropriateness of that star and the available role. In some cases, indeed, a studio boss may have been attracted to a female player and it became the contract director's responsibility to elicit a stunning performance from her, sometimes even at the expense of the picture and the other players. Moreover, a contract director was required to direct a given number of pictures every year. Only rarely did he have choice of property; more often he had to make the best of what was handed to him. That best, in view of the mediocrity of much of the material, the limitations of contract personnel, the frequently unrealistic production schedules, and budget limitations was finer in many instances than anyone might reasonably have expected.

Henry King, Howard Hawks, Alfred Hitchcock, and John Huston also began as contract directors, yet each in his own way managed to liberate himself to a degree from the exigencies of this highly regulated aspect of the studio system. Just how this was accomplished by each of these men, in very different ways, is still another dimension of the filmmaker's ingenuity. Orson Welles tried, from the beginning, to buck the studio system and in a very real sense it limited, if it did not finish, him as a filmmaker, as it took its toll on the films he did make. Sam Peckinpah and Roman Polanski came on the scene after the studio system and the idea of a contract director had vanished from the scene, but they were by then replaced by a plethora of other difficulties, no less stressful.

Yet, notwithstanding all I have said, there are some virtues in adopting, at least partially, the *auteur* perspective. A filmmaker's personality has always been important to me because it cannot but influence the character of his work. I recall Sam Peckinpah, as we were screening dailies from one of his pictures on an editing screen, pointing at the screen and saying, "The only important thing in my life is up there." Frank Capra once told me that the biggest problem a director has is getting "the hell out of the way of the actors" and John Ford told me that the one thing that stood out in his memory about a number of his films was the time he had spent thinking up pranks to play on Ward Bond. Of course, a lot of the fun has left the business, what you will find so richly represented in films made by Humberstone and King. It is almost too serious today. The spontaneity and affirmation of life true of older pictures is something scarcely found on a modern set. Capra, who was a good friend of John Ford's and who once accepted an award from Marshal Tito of Yugoslavia for Ford, declared that as a person Ford was perverse, nasty, drunk, mean, and funny. "Thank God," he concluded, "that the world has Irishmen!" Whether a filmmaker is functioning as a contract director or as an independent agent on an independent production, his personality will leave its mark on the finished film. Personality, of course, isn't enough to make up for a weak story or indifferent characters; it cannot prevent a box-office failure; but very often, when everything works right, it can invest a film with a bright intensity and assure it of success.

In my experience, there is only so much you can say about a particular film, and especially is this true in a career study. You might provide a brief synopsis of its story-line. You can mention the principals who played in it. If you are privy to somewhat confidential information, you could divulge how much a picture cost to make and how much it earned upon release. Yet I believe it is unfair to treat a filmmaker only in these terms. It is only half the story and, quite possibly, not the most important half. If I am right and one cannot come to any understanding of the filmmaker's craft without at the same time coming to terms with his personality, if a film director cannot wholly be separated from his work, then at least that much of the *auteur* theory is valid and how a director goes about getting the results he wants, and what goes on during this process, may be as important ultimately as the results.

Still, such an approach does have inherent limitations. A film of particular merit may not be emphasized as much as one of little critical or financial consequence. Yet if, in the end, we come to know what it is precisely that a filmmaker looks for from the screenwriters, the players, the cameramen, the multitude of human forces which must combine to produce a motion picture and how, from these, he was able to transform an essentially private conception into the total public impact of a motion picture projected upon a giant screen, then more might be accomplished than monologue or description alone could ever achieve.

I am not one of those who regards his subjective experience of a film as an avenue to philosophize, or as a flimsy platform on which to hang the trappings of a social, political, psychological, or imagistic commentary. It isn't that these areas should be avoided entirely, only that they should be confined to what the director himself has had to say about these influences on his work. The subject of a career study is properly the director and his films. While either or both might be subjected to a critique, it must be limited by the subject at hand.

Maxim Gorky in his stage play THE ZYKOVS (1912) complained that too many Russians were metaphysicians, too few mathematicians. I might say the same about purely aesthetic or financial approaches to the cinema; either, if used obsessively, can prove philosophically barren. Of all the films made, there are some which fill a current need and enjoy immediate popular endorsement; some that please critics but no one else; some that never lose their poignance; many that show their age quickly; and a very few that may have to await audiences some time in the future. I do not presume that it matters greatly to anyone but myself whether or not I happen to like a particular film. In this book, therefore, I am far more concerned with the human mechanics creating an illusion than simply with the impact of that illusion on me.

Altogether too much film analysis written since the Second World War has been unduly dependent on the techniques and procedures of the herd of literary analysts. As Edgar Allan Poe's armchair detective, C. Auguste Dupin, the literary analyst has long preferred the seclusion of his dark rooms to the bright sunlight of the external world. He chooses to spend most of his time ruminating about what an event might possibly mean and what dark forces may have congealed to produce a certain effect. In "The Mystery of Marie Rogêt" (1842), Dupin solves a murder from the confines of his study merely by perusing and analyzing newspaper accounts of the tragedy. Ever since Poe, there have been many detectives who amuse us by making all manner of deductions about characters involved in the commission of a crime by means of a series of fantastic speculations about how such persons might be expected to act in a given set of circumstances, as if human behavior could actually be predicted. I do not know what the reader's reaction has been to detective stories of this kind, but it was my experience while working on THE DETECTIVE IN HOLLYWOOD (1978) and then IN MANORS AND ALLEYS: A CASEBOOK ON THE AMERICAN DETECTIVE FILM (1988), during which I had to read a wide assortment of detective fiction and watch numerous detective films, that the explanation offered by the author, supposedly revealing the logic behind all the startling and macabre events that had occurred, was usually the most far-fetched, the most clumsy, and the most disappointing aspect of the entire plot.

Perhaps because literary analysts behave in a similar fashion, their results are also disconcerting. They select a novel, retell the plot in boring detail, reintroduce the reader to the characters, and then set about analyzing these characters in depth, usually informed by disciplines wholly alien to the novelist himself, consulting with Freudian or Jungian psychology, Marxist ideology, Christian theology, folklore, or making endless references to characters in other novels which the author of the book being analyzed probably had not read. Armed with these observations, these analysts next proceed to elucidate the novel under examination, which is to say they advise us what the novel *really* means and what it was the author was *really* driving at when he wrote it. Now I am not about to say that sometimes very interesting similarities and parallels, symbolic coincidences and imagistic nuances cannot be discerned by use of an alien discipline. They can be and occasionally the level of interpretation can be enhanced by such use, as, for example, the persistent use of water as a theme of almost Protean variety in Roman Polanski's films. However, if the director himself is not using such a symbol consciously, and may even deny its significance, this kind of elucidation is no more than a speculation. It does not deserve to be regarded as a more valid reality than the film itself.

Unfortunately, motion pictures, when they were taken seriously at all, were very early subjected to film analysis employing a similar methodology and with these film analysts prepared to assert that their speculations did indeed have a greater ontological existence than the film or what the director had to say about the film. Take as an instance what happened to Alfred Hitchcock. He was early latched onto by vigorous and aggressive film analysts. Eric Rohmer and Claude Chabrol claimed in HITCHCOCK (1957) that, thanks to Hitchcock's early exposure to Jesuit schools, the director was deeply imbued with the moral outlook of Roman Catholic theology. Their book sought to demonstrate how each Hitchcock film carries a Roman Catholic message about the nature of man and the nature of sin.

For a long time after Hitchcock deserted London for Hollywood, British critics tended to dismiss him as a commercial hack until Raymond Durgnat published a series of interpretive essays about his films in FILMS AND FILMING in 1970 which he subsequently expanded into a book titled THE STRANGE CASE OF ALFRED HITCHCOCK (1974). Durgnat took exception with Rohmer and Chabrol, but he still insisted on a theological orientation. "For Chabrol and Rohmer," Durgnat wrote, "Hitchcock's vision is impregnated by a Roman Catholicism the severity of whose morality evokes Jansenism. This severity may, however, have reached Hitchcock by a different route. Jansenism is the result, in French Catholicism, of the Calvinist influence, and Hitchcock's sense of a blind, implacable, cruel, yet, somehow, just, providence may well have come to him via the influence, in the British middle classes, of that Puritanism which is the English version of Calvinism."[1]

François Truffaut did the intelligent thing: he conducted an exhaustive series of personal interviews with Hitchcock. He questioned Hitchcock about this supposed moral philosophy, whether Calvinist or Roman Catholic, attributed to his films, only to be told by Hitchcock that " . . . my love of film is far more important than any considerations of morality."[2]

One might think that such an univocal statement would be sufficient, but it wasn't. Robin Wood in his book, HITCHCOCK'S FILMS (1969), swept aside everything Hitchcock had said to Truffaut in 1967, or elsewhere, with the observation: "I used to find maddening Hitchcock's refusal to discuss his work with interviewers on any really serious level; I have come to admire it. It seems so much in keeping with the character of the films themselves that their creator should be such a delightfully modest and unassuming man who makes no claims for his art outside the evidence of his films."[3] But this was not to be construed to mean that Wood himself was willing to limit himself to the "evidence of the films." This is how Wood worked it: he provided his reader with a summary of a plot and then speculated on the possible motivation of the characters, more often than not asserting his findings rather than finding his assertions in the films.

Let one instance suffice. In SUSPICION (RKO, 1941), based on Frances Isles' novel, BEFORE THE FACT (1932), Hitchcock had a story to his liking, about a young, inexperienced, and unattractive woman who marries a worldly socialite who has no money and who decides to murder her for her inheritance. Hitchcock later gave out the story that the RKO management felt Cary Grant ill-suited to the role if it would actually call for him to murder Joan Fontaine, cast as his wife, and so Hitchcock was forced to alter the ending. In the released film Fontaine is the victim of her own fantasies and Grant, although a liar and bounder, has no intention of murdering her. In his interview with François Truffaut, Hitchcock even went so far as to claim that the ending he had had in mind would have had Fontaine writing to her mother that her husband was a murderer just before Grant would hand her a glass of milk containing poison.

After her death, Grant would cheerfully post the letter for her. However, Donald Spoto in his book THE DARK SIDE OF GENIUS: THE LIFE OF ALFRED HITCHCOCK (1983) had access to the RKO files and it appears that from the beginning Hitchcock had wanted Grant *not* to be a murderer, that the film instead was about the fantasy life of Grant's wife and her paranoid suspicions. The actual shooting schedule—from 10 February 1941 until 24 July 1941—turned out to be longer than that required either for REBECCA (United Artists, 1940) or FOREIGN CORRESPONDENT (United Artists, 1940), both more elaborate films with much bigger budgets. The reason for the delay was that the picture had no ending. The way the screenplay had it was that Fontaine, who was pregnant, would commit suicide, but the censors objected to this and the only way around it seemed to be to give her an illicit affair which would morally justify her not living to the end of the picture. Prior to FROM HERE TO ETERNITY (Columbia, 1953) no female lead guilty of adultery was permitted to survive the final fade. The version with the illicit affair brought laughter when screened with this ending at a sneak preview in Pasadena. Hitchcock's wife, Alma Reville, and his assistant, Joan Harrison, had been assigned the task of finding an ending to the picture and were in a total quandary, so they went back to the original ending Hitchcock had had in mind: Fontaine's suspicions were wholly the product of her own neurosis and Grant was not a murderer. By this time, Hitchcock was so disgruntled about the possible reception the film would receive that he was prepared to disclaim it. Only when it turned out to be a hit with the public and Fontaine subsequently won an Academy Award as best actress did he expansively accept the film as his own, although he continued to blame RKO for the ending which had been "imposed" on the film. Wood did not choose to contrast the film with the novel—in the novel the husband murders his wife and, even though she knows it while it is happening, she drinks the poison anyway. What Wood did do was to conduct an analysis of characters who actually appear neither in the film nor in the novel. "She is irresistably attracted to the man," he wrote of the Fontaine character, "who represents glamour and reckless, carefree abandon; but he represents also a total rejection of everything her family background and upbringing has stood for: subconsciously, she *wants* him to be a murderer."[4] The emphasis belongs to Wood. He never indicated what dialogue or what scene showed the viewer that Fontaine wanted Grant to be a murderer. It was merely a projection into Fontaine's portrayal which, according to Wood, would tend to heighten our appreciation of the film. How it was supposed to do this, having nothing really to do with the actual film, he did not say. When a decade ago I saw SUSPICION again at a reissue house in Los Angeles, the audience laughed at the right times, and was transfixed by suspense at the right times, so the picture worked as well in 1978 as it had in 1941 and could be enjoyed and apprehended without transforming the characters into persons they are not and never were intended to be.

In preparing these career studies, I felt my approach must be an alternative to film analysis of this kind which is mostly dependent on a critic's subjective

projections. Although an admitted *auteuriste*, Andrew Sarris in THE AMERI-
CAN CINEMA (1968), a book of perceptive, albeit brief, glimpses of the director's particular art, came closest to what I had in mind, but I wanted to go
one step farther, to approach, as I have said, each director in terms of portraiture.
This has been possible because I sought out many of these directors for the first
time when I was researching cinema history for a series of articles for VIEWS
& REVIEWS Magazine and then, later, used this as background material for
my cinema histories. Some of this material is gleaned from these early essays
and cinema histories, some from career studies I did for the Close-Up on the
Cinema series, and some from my experiences subsequent to any of those previous publications. Seven of the eight directors whose careers are studied in this
book are deceased and this has permitted me to bring to what I have had to say
a certain sense of final closure. Beyond this, in all that I have written, my concern
has always been with the experience of living, of finding one's way in the world.
I am inclined, therefore, to place more than the usual emphasis on just how a
man has lived, what he may have learned, what he never foresaw, and how
much life itself diminished him. Whatever I have had to contribute to cinema
history, then, has been told necessarily in terms of the personalities and experiences I have encountered along the way. Perhaps the reader may recall how
Friedrich Klein in that beautiful short novel by Hermann Hesse, KLEIN UND
WAGNER (1920), was accustomed to carrying a volume of Schopenhauer with
him on his travels and how, once, he opened the book at random and read:
" 'When we look back on our life as we have lived it and above all at our steps
where they faltered, and their consequences, fastening it all before our eyes, it
is often inconceivable that we were able to do this or omit doing that; so that it
appears as if a strange force had directed our steps.' "[5] This looking backward,
this *zürucksehn*, has concerned me most of all, but never in isolation, always
in conjunction with milieu. I have tried, accordingly, to make milieu a significant
component of these career studies since, in my view, it often goes a long way
toward explaining the atmosphere of many of the films produced by the directors
with whom I have dealt.

Conversely, in selecting these particular eight filmmakers, as opposed to any
other eight, I have not been guided solely by my liking for their films, but as
well by my liking for them as people. It might be said of me on this account
that I therefore lack objectivity and impersonality. I do not mind this criticism,
because total objectivity in criticism is usually dubious anyway, and I should
not want to write any book in the spirit of impersonality. Rather, I have sought
where I could to illumine the unique, often incomprehensible, sometimes profound individual human soul. When that is the object of study, then we are
confronted by those depths which Heraclitus once called an expanse without
measure. That expanse, frequently fashioned out of prolonged suffering, certainly
from blundering through life as all of us do, crowned occasionally by achievement, often besieged by failures too numerous and probably too painful to
count—that expanse is the counterbalance we all need to hold precious against

the demons which perpetually torment us, the baseless assumptions leading us into inevitable error, the illusions which we create for ourselves. In the best films there is a confrontation with life, accomplished at times with poetry, at others with emotional electricity, that can be as insubstantial as a shadow on a sunny day, as brutally frank as the barbed-wire of a concentration camp, and, for all that, nonetheless liberating because an artist has the capacity to be totally free.

The interviews with these directors conducted over the years were seldom taped. I have found that if your objective has to do with the promotion of a celebrity, or of a film, or of a performance, the artists are comfortable with a tape recorder; but if your objective is to record oral history, much of it perhaps sensitive and some of it even libelous, then a tape recorder is anathema. Instead, as will become apparent in the very first of these career studies, Vicki Piekarski took notes and later transcribed them. She also watched all the films with me; she traveled everywhere with me that the interviews required; she checked all the facts and dates; and she helped sort out all the tangled memories. Without her, this book, as all that I have written on cinema history, would not have been possible.

Karl Thiede, who became associated with me back in 1969 as Research Editor for VIEWS & REVIEWS Magazine, has prepared the eight filmographies to be found at the back of this book. Although now a busy executive with M-G-M/UA, he is also possessed of an encyclopedic knowledge of release dates, of running times, of casts and credits as well as costs and grosses. I have rarely seen him screen a film without a stop-watch and a cast sheet clipped to a board. He wants cinema history to have lasting referential value and to be, above all, accurate. It is well to have him aboard for this return engagement.

All in all, taken as a composite, I can only hope that the eight career studies in this book will make a definite and positive contribution to the way film is regarded in our time. I do know that I have been able to teach a survey of the American cinema focussed just on these eight directors and, in a way, their lives and works encompass the broad panorama of film direction in this country from the silent era to the present time.

# H. Bruce Humberstone

## I

It was in February, 1971 in a screening room on the Warner Bros. lot in Burbank that we had agreed to meet. I had arranged to have projected THE DRAGON MURDER CASE (First National, 1934) and CHARLIE CHAN AT THE OPERA (20th-Fox, 1937), both of which Lucky Humberstone had directed. Keye Luke, who had played Number One Son to Warner Oland's Chan, was working on sound stage seven in a movie for television titled KUNG FU. He had promised to look in on us if he got a break.

Lucky threw down a package of American filter cigarettes.

"You've got me back on these things, thanks to this damned interview."

It was the first remark he ever made to me.

Lucky would make comments here and there as the pictures were screened and his memory was jarred. He had forgotten how THE DRAGON MURDER CASE came out, so he cautioned me not to reveal the murderer's identity. But he did recall that when Darryl Zanuck had seen the dailies from CHARLIE CHAN AT THE OPERA, he had insisted that it was really a musical. It was a prescient observation. Many of Lucky's best films for Twentieth Century-Fox would be musicals.

We adjourned to a restaurant across the street from the lot and continued talking. Lucky then proposed that the interview be concluded at his Beverly Hills apartment. We went there. His daughter, Robyn, was home ill. He had raised her as a single parent since she was six. Lucky had taken over the lease to the apartment from his close friend, Edmund Goulding, after Goulding died. According to Lucky, he knew right where Goulding had been seated when he committed suicide.

We were in the living room and I produced a small tape recorder, placing it on the floor between us.

"What's that?" Lucky asked.

"It's a tape recorder," I said, extending the microphone arm to within a few inches of his face.

"Don't turn it on."

"Lucky, how can I record what you're saying if I don't turn it on?"

"But I don't want you to record what I'm saying."

"You're just afraid of being recorded."

It was the first time in all my years of interviewing that I had attempted to tape a conversation, and it would be the last. We continued to discuss it, but Lucky remained adamant. Finally, we just talked, and I remembered and wrote it down afterwards.

When it came time that I wanted to do a career study on Lucky in the summer of 1975, I went to him fully prepared. Lucky had changed apartments. Robyn had married Spike Jones, Jr. Lucky still looked the same, medium height, graying hair, bright eyes, and he had not lost his energetic manner.

"I'm ready for you this time," I said, as we sat down to drinks in his well-appointed and comfortable living room.

"See," said Vicki, holding up two shorthand notebooks.

"I've had quite a life, honey," Lucky said, grinning. "I hope it'll be enough."

Lucky explained to us about the little horn on the cocktail table in front of where Vicki was sitting. Guests were to honk when they wanted another drink. Vicki gave the horn a trial honk as Lucky mixed drinks for all of us.

"Vicki's afraid, Lucky, that you and I are going to sit around here all night and never get down to the interview."

Vicki then explained why. We had just been out to the M-G-M lot to visit Sam Peckinpah.

"After spending hours together," Vicki observed, "Jon and Sam could only come up with one sentence that was usable."

"And what was that, honey?" Lucky asked, setting down her Scotch.

"Sam said, 'I wonder why the fuck I make movies. Then I watch television, and I know why.' "

Vicki cocked her head at a sharp angle, and smiled.

"Let's start at the beginning," I suggested as Lucky set down my Scotch and took his vodka martini to his own chair, a rocker.

"All right," Lucky said, traversing the room again to bum a cigarette from Vicki's pack. "I haven't had one of these for four months. Then this guy comes to visit me again, and I'm back on them." He lit the cigarette. "Take down what I say. That's okay. But stop writing when I tell you."

I shook my head, no.

"What's wrong with you?" Lucky asked, settling himself in the rocker.

"I'm trying to write film history," I returned, "but almost everything anyone tells me is off the record."

"I can't imagine why," Lucky said, chuckling.

We began.

H. Bruce Humberstone was born at Buffalo, New York on 18 November 1903. He never let anyone know that his first name was Harry. He hated that name. As a youth, he attended public schools in Cleveland and was sent to the Miami Ohio Military Academy. When he was in his teens, the Humberstones moved to Los Angeles. Lucky found work as a prop boy and assistant cameraman at Universal Pictures when he was nineteen. Carl Laemmle was in charge of the studio.

Humberstone's first assignment was on a Hoot Gibson Western directed by John Ford. The unit went on location to the Vasquez Rocks, north of Hollywood. Ford, Gibson, and the rest of the company had mounts. Humberstone did not. He carried the raw film stock in cans under his left arm, the camera under his right, and the tripod on his back. Reaching the crest of a high plateau, the troupe paused and waited for Lucky to catch up to them. Puffing, exhausted, he finally made it.

"Humberstone!" Ford snapped at him. "What do you think of this location?"

"I think," Lucky replied, wanting to impress the director with his perspicacity, "that the top of that plateau over there would be better."

"Okay!" Ford shouted. "You heard the kid. Everybody over to the other plateau."

Once he had lugged all that gear the great distance while the riders watched him, laughing and joking among themselves, Humberstone had come upon a first principle when working on a Ford picture: when the director asked you a question, you kept your mouth shut.

Lucky got a part as a juvenile in a Laura LaPlante picture. He was promoted to a second assistant director. At the time I interviewed him in 1971, I had asked him how he had got his nickname. He told me he was for a time assistant director to B. Reaves "Breezy" Eason at Universal who also directed some of the Hoot Gibson Westerns. " ' . . . One day on the set . . . Breezy invites me to a party Gibson was throwing that night. I was just a kid. "It'll be a lot of fun," Breezy tells me. So that night I get into Breezy's sports car and we drive out to Gibson's house in the hills. It was one of those nude affairs, you understand, with everyone smashed.'

" 'The Hooter loved parties,' I interjected.

" 'You're telling me,' Lucky quipped. 'Well, it was near dawn when Breezy and I pull out. Breezy was lit up. He speeds along Mulholland Drive like he was fleeing from the devil. Coming up the road, as we round a curve, is a large truck. Breezy doesn't see it until it's too late. He turns the wheel and we plunge over the side. The driver pulled us out. He helped me up the steep incline and sat me down in the back of his truck. "What's this?" he asks me, picking up my nose from where it was hanging by a thread on my chest. He stuck it back on my face. "I'd better get you to a hospital," he says. Breezy was out cold. When Breezy could get around, he came to my room, saw my nose, calls me

Lucky. The name stuck, especially when Gibson and the others found out about it.' ''[1]

"This is how it really happened," Lucky now assured me. "After work at night I used to eat at John's Cafe right across Hollywood Boulevard from Musso and Frank's. Breezy Eason and Hoot Gibson occasionally ate at John's. One night as I walked up the Boulevard, I saw an ambulance parked outside John's. Two attendants came out carrying Tom Mix on a stretcher. I went inside. Hoot and Breezy, who was directing Gibson's pictures, were sitting at a table. Mix and Gibson had had a fight. Both of them were drunk. Breezy wanted to get a quart of bootleg Scotch, although neither he nor Hoot needed any more.

"I felt Breezy was too loaded to drive. He asked me to drive his Stutz for him. He knew a bootlegger. We set out but we never got there. Breezy decided he wanted to go to a party instead. We drove up into the Hollywood hills. The lights were out in the house when we got there and everyone, men and women, was naked. They had hooch in huge tubs. I got loaded. I was just a kid. Breezy got loaded all over again. When we left, Breezy drove. We hit a culvert and the car rolled over three times. Breezy and I were thrown clear. When I reported for work the next day, everyone on the lot kept calling me 'Lucky,' having heard the whole story from Breezy. The name stuck."

Which version is one to believe? Breezy Eason died in 1956 and I had not talked to him. Hoot Gibson, whom I did know, had died in 1962 and this story was not one he had told me; he had not, in fact, even mentioned Humberstone. In years of interviewing people, I have found that there are some who have organized their past into a series of anecdotes so consistently told that there is seldom any variation. Others, bored with what happened or seeking to improve on the past, have altered the facts, often times more than once, in conversation. No rule in such a situation is invariable, but George Orwell came closest perhaps to the truth when he suggested that "autobiography is only to be trusted when it reveals something disgraceful. A man who gives a good account of himself is probably lying, since any life when viewed from the inside is simply a series of defeats."[2] In this instance, there was no newspaper account to validate either version and so it became a matter of intuitive choice. Since the second version was being transcribed and Lucky knew that it would be printed as he told it, my inclination then, as now, was to believe it to be the more accurate account.

In 1925, Lucky was promoted to first assistant director. He made a two-reeler titled UNIVERSAL IN 1925 as an exploitation vehicle for the Universal sales staff. It was so good that Universal decided to release it theatrically. Lucky, as a result, was slated to make a series of two-reelers, but Ernst Laemmle wanted to make them also and he had the considerable advantage of being a relative. Lucky lost out. When William Koenig, Universal's production manager, refused to allow Lucky to assist on THE PHANTOM OF THE OPERA (Universal, 1925), he quit.

Metro-Goldwyn-Mayer had gone into production on BEN-HUR (M-G-M, 1925). Fred Niblo was the director. Lucky went out to Culver City to the

M-G-M lot where the crowd scenes were being filmed. He applied for an assistant directorship. Breezy Eason had been hired to direct the second unit work involving the famed chariot race. William Wyler, who directed the remake in the sound era, was also among those assisting on the picture. Lucky was put on to help handle some 3,500 extras. He wore a bright red sweater. Niblo sat on a platform high above the bustle of activity. He was favorably impressed by the young man in the red sweater. By the time production concluded, Niblo placed Lucky under a personal contract as his assistant, increasing his salary from $85 to $175 a week.

THE TEMPTRESS (M-G-M, 1926) with Greta Garbo and Antonio Moreno came next. Following that film Edmund Goulding requested that Lucky be permitted to assist him on the filming of PARIS (M-G-M, 1926) which starred Joan Crawford and Charles Ray. Goulding and Humberstone became friends. At the end of the shooting schedule, Goulding offered Lucky a contract at $400 a week to work for him as his first assistant. When Niblo heard of Goulding's offer, he countered it by raising Lucky to $500 a week. Niblo had signed with First National, which was then still independent of Warner Bros., and was set to direct CAMILLE (First National, 1927), with Norma Talmadge and Gilbert Roland. Lucky told Niblo he would accept his offer but he had to assist Dimitri Buchowetzki first on the film VALENCIA (M-G-M, 1926), which starred Mae Murray. Niblo agreed to wait.

Following CAMILLE, Lucky went to work for United Artists in the capacity of a first assistant director to directors in general who were signed to direct pictures for United Artists' release. This would indicate that his various contracts with Niblo and others had been on a picture-by-picture basis and dependent upon their work schedule. A contract with a studio offered greater security. Humberstone's initial undertaking was TOPSY AND EVA (United Artists, 1927), directed by Del Lord. Location shooting was to be done at Lake Tahoe. Lucky went there with the cast, which included Rosetta and Vivian Duncan (or, the "drunken" sisters, as they were called), Nils Asther, and Noble Johnson. It was a predicament. Vivian Duncan was in love with Nils Asther. Nils was in love with Imogene Wilson. When the troupe was safely checked in at a resort during the off season awaiting Del Lord's arrival, their solitude was interrupted by Harry D'Abbadie D'Arrast who was directing a picture for Paramount. His company showed up and took rooms at the same resort. Lucky's group was composed mostly of blacks. D'Arrast's included mostly women. The groups began pairing off at night. Myron Selznick, later a powerful talent agent, was production supervisor on TOPSY AND EVA. He had a case of Scotch delivered to his room every day, never stuck his head out, and courted various women from both companies. Lucky did not complain and Selznick always retained the warmest regard for Humberstone's discretion. When Lucky's troupe returned to Hollywood, D.W. Griffith, one of the founders of United Artists, personally did the retakes.

MY BEST GIRL (United Artists, 1927) was directed by Sam Taylor. Lucky assisted. Mary Pickford, America's Sweetheart, was the star, Buddy Rogers her co-star. Although Mary was still married to the dashing Douglas Fairbanks, she and Buddy fell in love.

"Writers are still after me to tell what I know about it," Lucky reflected. "I figure it's nobody's business."

He looked crossly at Vicki's empty glass.

"I was going to honk," Vicki responded to the unasked question, "but I didn't want to break your train of thought."

"No trouble at all," Lucky said, jumping up to make another round.

"Vicki's just getting accustomed to film research," I said. "If we have an interview in the morning, she has two or three sociable drinks. Then, if there is another in the afternoon, she may have four or five sociable drinks."

"Which," Vicki chimed in, "only gets me tuned up for the all night interviews."

Lucky laughed as he handed her a refill.

THE DEVIL DANCER (United Artists, 1927) was directed by Fred Niblo. Originally, Samuel Goldwyn had engaged Alfred Raboch to direct it with Lynn Shores as his assistant. Then Shores was made the director with Raboch as his assistant. When Niblo took over, he received sole screen credit. Between THE DEVIL DANCER and Niblo's next picture for Goldwyn, TWO LOVERS (United Artists, 1928) starring Ronald Coleman and Vilma Banky, Lucky assisted Richard Jones in directing Douglas Fairbanks in THE GAUCHO (United Artists, 1928). Fairbanks developed a positive rapport with Humberstone. Henry King, with whom Lucky would clash a decade later at Twentieth Century-Fox, was taken off THE WOMAN DISPUTED (United Artists, 1928) starring Norma Talmadge before Lucky was assigned to assist his replacement. King shared screen credit with Sam Taylor.

Fairbanks requested Lucky to assist Allan Dwan on his next swashbuckler, THE IRON MASK (United Artists, 1929). Dwan was not too pleased with Fairbanks' choice. The first project he gave Lucky was to compute costs and design sets. Lucky went to Palm Springs and worked out an elaborate series of plans. When he reported back to Dwan, the director cast the sheaf of papers aside.

"There are two things a good assistant director of mine always keeps in mind," Dwan said. "He knows I never read papers and he never asks questions."

Once the picture was started, Dwan became more appreciative of Lucky's acumen. When the unit manager irritated Dwan with his excessive questions, Dwan fired him and offered the job to Lucky. Lucky accepted it on the conditions that he would still receive an assistant director's credit and a raise of $100 a week.

COQUETTE (United Artists, 1929) teamed Mary Pickford with football hero Johnny Mack Brown. Sam Taylor directed with Lucky as his assistant. Taylor was a favorite director of Mary Pickford's and there was no question in her mind, when next she was cast opposite Douglas Fairbanks for THE TAMING

OF THE SHREW (United Artists, 1929), that Taylor should be the director. Lucky had been doing a stint on loan-out to Pathé as production manager for BIG NEWS (Pathé, 1929) directed by Gregory La Cava, but he hurried back to United Artists because Fairbanks wanted him as Taylor's assistant. It was a remarkable situation, worse even than TOPSY AND EVA. Mary was openly in love with Buddy Rogers. Fairbanks was in love with Lupe Velez, the Mexican Spitfire. Mary was not talking to Doug and Doug was not talking to Mary. Hollywood's most glamorous marriage was a bust. Sam Taylor concentrated on directing Mary. If Mary was displeased with anything about Doug's performance, she would tell Lucky, who was in the middle, to tell Doug. Doug would only communicate with either Mary or Taylor through Lucky. It was characteristic of Taylor that he credited the story to "William Shakespeare, with additional dialogue by Sam Taylor."

"There's too much familiarity around here," he once reprimanded Humberstone. "I am not Sam to you. I am Mr. Taylor."

Mary Pickford happened to overhear this exchange and told Taylor that he was becoming hopelessly pompous.

Wesley Ruggles was the director of CONDEMNED (United Artists, 1929). Ronald Coleman was the star. Samuel Goldwyn told Lucky that, although only ten days into production, the picture was already behind six. Lucky found out the reason. Wes was having an affair which required long lunch hours and all-night sessions. Goldwyn, when he learned the cause from Lucky, wanted to pull Ruggles off the picture, but Lucky persuaded him instead to have a talk with the director. He did. The film was completed in the next ten days.

Goldwyn's next problem was with George Fitzmaurice. He was signed to direct RAFFLES (United Artists, 1930). Ronald Coleman again had the lead. Harry D'Abbadie D'Arrast took it over. Lucky assisted them both. Goldwyn tried Fitzmaurice once more on ONE HEAVENLY NIGHT (United Artists, 1930). Lucky found the director more bewildering the more he worked with him. Fitzmaurice might have a grand piano in a scene for three days' shooting and, on the spur of the moment, decide to do the rest of the scene without it. Yet, should a book of matches on a coffee table be moved so much as a fraction of an inch, Fitzmaurice would throw a fit. There was a dessert scene coming up and Fitzmaurice told Lucky he wanted very unusual desserts. Lucky knew better than to try anything conventional. He arranged for the best chefs from the Ambassador, from Maxine's, from the Pig and Whistle, and from The Elite to prepare all manner of exotic desserts. Fitzmaurice rejected one dessert after the other. It wasn't until Goldwyn personally stepped in that production resumed. However, Fitzmaurice was still dour. The desserts just weren't right.

Goldwyn was co-producer with Florenz Ziegfeld on WHOOPEE! (United Artists, 1930), using the entire New York cast with Eddie Cantor in the lead. Lucky assisted director Thornton Freeland. Alfred Newman did the songs, Busby Berkeley the choreography. Lucky worked closely with Berkeley in organizing the dance numbers for the camera. As part of the preparations, Lucky ran a newspaper advertisement for girls. He interviewed five hundred who responded. Among those Lucky picked were Betty Grable, Lucille Ball, Virginia Bruce, Barbara Weeks, and Paulette Goddard. Goldwyn approved Lucky's selections.

King Vidor was signed to direct STREET SCENE (United Artists, 1931). Much of the film took place on a New York city street. It had to be shot outdoors. A set was designed. Exteriors could only be filmed during the morning hours. Lucky went to Goldwyn with an idea. Why not build the identical set facing the other direction? In the afternoon, the camera could turn. Shooting would be done from the other side, thus maximizing the sunlight. Goldwyn was excited by the idea and the additional set was erected. The picture was completed in twenty-two days and Lucky received a $6,000 bonus.

After STREET SCENE, Goldwyn summoned Humberstone to his office. He informed him that John Ford had been contracted to direct ARROWSMITH (United Artists, 1931) and Lucky was to assist. Ford was on loan-out from the Fox Film Corporation. If anything went wrong, Humberstone was to report it to Sam even if Sam was sitting on the toilet. Ronald Coleman was the star. Ford told Lucky that he expected his assistant directors to rehearse all the day's scenes before he arrived in the morning. All went well until virtually the last scene to be filmed. It was set in a hotel lobby in which Ronald Coleman was to exit from an elevator. Lucky designed the set and hired several extras to give the scene verisimilitude to a busy hotel. When Ford arrived, he studied Lucky as sardonically as he had when, years before, he had watched him lug film cans in the Vasquez Rocks.

"Run through the scene," Ford demanded.

Lucky had the scene played with people milling about, Coleman leaving the elevator and making his way through the crowd.

"Is that your conception of it?" Ford asked, when it was over.

Lucky said it was.

Ford became dyspeptic. He demanded that everyone get off the set. Coleman was to come out of the elevator and walk through an empty lobby. That was *his* conception of the scene and that was how he filmed it.

When Lucky saw the rushes, he went to Goldwyn's office. Goldwyn had just fired Sam Taylor. Taylor's comment about it was laconic. "There isn't room enough for two Sams on this lot." Goldwyn had a reputation for interference with his directors and especially for firing them. Lucky told Sam he felt Ford was mishandling the elevator scene. Sam had the rushes screened. He seconded Humberstone's opinion and went onto the set to speak to Ford about reshooting the scene. Ford listened in icy silence. When Sam finished, Ford got up and walked off the picture. Goldwyn, somewhat perplexed by Ford's irascibility, suggested that Lucky should telephone Mary, Ford's wife, and attempt to smooth it over. This got Lucky nowhere. Mary told Lucky that Ford was in one of those black moods where he would close himself in the library and not come out for days. She would only open the sliding doors as long as it took to shove in a case of Scotch and otherwise leave him alone. Suddenly, Ford vanished. Not even Mary, apparently, had any idea where he had gone. Lucky was told to film the elevator scene as he had planned it and that is the way it appeared in the released version.

Lowell Sherman was engaged to direct THE GREEKS HAD A WORD FOR THEM (United Artists, 1932). Lucky assisted. After two weeks of shooting, Goldwyn was dissatisfied with the rushes and, henceforth, confined Sherman to directing dialogue and gave Humberstone his chance to direct principal photography. Sherman had been a stage director and Goldwyn thought him to be too inexperienced in terms of the creative use of the camera. Humberstone liked directing far more than assisting.

King Vidor, impressed with Lucky from their association on STREET SCENE, requested him as his assistant on BIRD OF PARADISE (RKO, 1932). David O. Selznick now headed up production at RKO and this film was to receive his personal attention. After making the necessary financial arrangements with Goldwyn to borrow Lucky, Vidor gave Humberstone a copy of the synopsis to read. A conference with Selznick was then set up. It started off poorly when Selznick insisted that Lucky use an RKO crew. Lucky stated that he had his own crew and that they worked well for him on all Goldwyn's pictures. Selznick compromised to the extent that Lucky could bring his own crew along provided RKO supplied him with a second crew, even if the latter group did nothing on the picture.

Lucky had first met Joseph P. Kennedy when Kennedy was producing THE TRESPASSER (United Artists, 1929) and Edmund Goulding was directing it. Kennedy had been quite taken with Gloria Swanson, the film's star. During his thirty-two months in Hollywood, Kennedy managed to accumulate five million dollars. Little of it came from his backing Swanson's pictures or his promotion of Fred Thomson and other Western players at Film Booking Office; rather it was a consequence of a merger he negotiated between Film Booking Office, Pathé Pictures, the Keith-Orpheum theatre circuit, and General Sarnoff's RCA Photophone company. The new firm was called RKO Radio Pictures and Selznick had been hired to create unforgettable and prestigious pictures.

He asked Lucky about suitable locations. Lucky proposed Mazatlan, or Tahiti, or, the biggest gamble, Honolulu.

"You're working with me," Selznick responded, "not Goldwyn. Don't worry about the cost. We're going to Honolulu."

By the time Lucky arrived there with the troupe, Vidor had already been there for some time. When he met Lucky, he complained bitterly. He had hoped to find a location with a quiet surf, white sand, and hundred-foot palm trees. For weeks, now, he had been searching without success. Once Lucky found a quiet beach with white sand, he contacted the chamber of commerce and received permission to cut down fifty palm trees and transport them to the location. The trees, replanted, were held in place by wires. Lucky telephoned Vidor and asked him to come and inspect the location he had found. The wires escaped Vidor's notice. He was astonished.

"Let's shoot," Lucky suggested.

"There's still no script," Vidor returned.

Selznick had several writers working on it, of course. As it stood now, however, there was only one short scene to be filmed. Vidor decided to shoot it. With the camera so close that only eight square feet of sand were visible, Dolores Del Rio and a young Joel McCrea, the stars of the picture, were brought in. Dolores was to lie on her back on the sand, which she did. McCrea came into camera range, fell on top of her, and Vidor yelled: "Cut!"

Then it began to rain. For fifty-five days it rained. Lucky kept calling Selznick back on the Coast. Selznick kept telling Lucky to stay put. Fifty-five days and still there was no script. Finally, Selznick gave in and recommended that the troupe return to the mainland until such a time as a script was actually completed. Everyone packed up.

The day before his departure, Lucky received a cable from Sam Bischoff. He was head of production at Tiffany Pictures, a small independent producing company. The cable indicated that Bischoff wanted Lucky to direct a picture for him. He offered him $1,500 to do it and assured him that he could secure his release to work on the film. Lucky showed the cable to Vidor.

"Why don't you do it?" Vidor asked.

"Because I'm making $25,000 a year as an assistant," Humberstone replied. "Why should I quit to make $1,500 flat?"

"Do it anyway," Vidor said. "It's a chance to direct your own picture."

Lucky thought it over.

"If script meets my approval," he wired Bischoff, "I can get immediate release."

I started closing reference books which I had been opening during the course of the interview.

"What are you doing?" Lucky asked.

"It's late," I said. "We've been at it nearly eight hours."

"Eight hours," Lucky echoed me, "and you haven't even got me past my assistant director days."

"I call a time out," Vicki said, and then honked softly.

"A good idea," Lucky agreed. Soon he was mixing drinks. "You know who I met on the boat on the way back from Honolulu? I was walking along the deck at night and I ran into Mary Ford. 'Mary,' I said, 'what are you doing here?' 'I had to go to the Orient to get Jack,' she said. He hadn't been in Hollywood since he walked off ARROWSMITH."

Lucky laughed.

"And it wasn't a picture he was coming back for," he continued. "Roosevelt was threatening to take us off the gold standard if he was elected. Mary told me Jack had a million dollars in gold in safe deposit boxes. She could only get him to come back out of fear of what Roosevelt might do."

We chatted pleasantly for another half hour before taking our leave.

## II

Almost a week intervened before we saw Lucky again.

"Should we finish tonight," he said as he set drinks before us, "I want you people to come back, just to visit."

"We will," Vicki said.

Lucky placed the small horn in front of her and then asked her where we had left off.

"Aboard ship," she answered.

"Okay," Lucky said, seating himself in the rocker, "find your place, then. Aboard ship. Yes, well, I decided to take Vidor's advice. I wanted to direct. But I was intent on its being the right picture with which to start on what amounted to a new career."

When Lucky's boat docked, Sam Bischoff was waiting for him with a copy of the script. The screenplay was based on Tiffany Thayer's story, "Strangers of the Evening." Bischoff wanted to film it in a Gothic style similar to FRANKENSTEIN (Universal, 1931). Lucky took the script home with him.

The next time they met, Lucky told Bischoff he would do the picture if he could treat it as a comedy.

"You maybe don't remember it," Bischoff said, "but I worked with you when you were an assistant on BEN-HUR. I promised myself then that if I was ever a producer, I wanted you to direct for me."

Bischoff offered Lucky a contract. Lucky got him to concede that should Bischoff sell the contract to anyone else, Lucky was to receive 50% of whatever would be the selling price. Zasu Pitts was given top billing in the film even though she did not appear until midway through and had a relatively small part. Eugene Pallette, who had been portraying Sergeant Heath in Paramount's popular Philo Vance photoplay series, was cast as the police sergeant. It was an offbeat picture, initially released as STRANGERS OF THE EVENING (Tiffany, 1932), and later retitled THE HIDDEN CORPSE when it was reissued. The production schedule was limited to nine days. Some of the humor was obviously intentional, but some of it was not. Although it is a short film, most scenes consist of only master shots with no intercuts, making it seem long when viewed today. Lucky devised the hand pantomime for Zasu Pitts' routines and she retained it as part of her screen persona. Pallette was given an opportunity for genuine comedy, not always at his own expense as it was in the Philo Vance films.

Sam Bischoff, after his work on BEN-HUR, had become a production supervisor at Columbia Pictures under Harry Cohn in 1928. Tiffany Productions, which emerged in 1929, became part of E.W. Hammons' Educational Pictures conglomerate. Bischoff directed several short comedies for Hammons before Hammons made him production manager for the Tiffany subsidiary in 1931. Shortly after STRANGERS OF THE EVENING was released, Bischoff decided to set up his own production company. He went into partnership with Burt Kelly and William Saal and the three called the company KBS Productions after their initials. The films it produced were still physically distributed through the Educational exchanges. Joe Brandt, who had started in the industry as a secretary to Carl Laemmle at Universal, joined Harry and Jack Cohn in founding CBC Productions in 1921 which soon became Columbia Pictures. Disgusted by the perpetual fighting between the Cohn brothers, Brandt finally sold out his interest in 1932 and in May of that year invested in E.W. Hammons' floundering conglomerate. He was given the title of president of WorldWide Pictures and the added title of vice president of Educational Pictures. In November, 1932, Brandt resigned. During his brief tenure with Hammons, impressed with Zasu Pitts' performance in STRANGERS OF THE EVENING, he signed her to make another picture to be called THE CROOKED CIRCLE (WorldWide, 1932). Pitts asked that Lucky direct the film. It was supposed to be a mystery-comedy with Ben Lyon, C. Henry Gordon, and James Gleason as a motorcycle cop, but Gleason, directed by Humberstone, injected so much comedy into his role the haunted house theme all but receded into the background. C. Henry Gordon played a swami who was actually a secret serviceman in disguise. The dialogue was poor. The picture required fourteen days to shoot.

In a desperate move, E.W. Hammons sold off his exchange network to Ray Johnston and Trem Carr. Carr had been producing extremely cheap Westerns for Tiffany-WorldWide release. Carr and Johnston now founded Monogram Pictures. In 1933 Hammons signed an agreement with Fox Film Corporation for Fox to distribute the Educational productions through the Fox exchanges. Sam Bischoff, discouraged by all of Hammons' manipulations, chucked KBS and joined Warner Bros. as a production supervisor. He freed Humberstone from his contract.

This meant effectually that Lucky was out of a job. Paramount then signed him to a short-term contract. It was suggested that perhaps Lucky's first assignment might be Mae West's SHE DONE HIM WRONG (Paramount, 1933). Mae West, however, wanted Lowell Sherman to direct it. Lucky, of course, had once assisted Sherman. After Mae's small part in NIGHT AFTER NIGHT (Paramount, 1932) made her a hit, she got her way from the studio.

Tiffany Thayer was among the contributors to an unusual production to be titled IF I HAD A MILLION (Paramount, 1932). The picture was to consist of several episodes, each directed by a different director from Paramount's roster, detailing what happened to a person selected at random to inherit a million dollars by an eccentric millionaire. The plot would eventually become the basis for a successful radio and then television series. George Raft's physical resemblance to Rudolph Valentino had been emphasized in NIGHT AFTER NIGHT. Paramount wanted to promote him into a matinee idol. He played a check forger in the episode Lucky directed for IF I HAD A MILLION. There was a sense of challenge for Humberstone to have his work judged alongside other contributors to this omnibus film such as Ernst Lubitsch and Josef von Sternberg. Upon release, Lucky's episode was praised and Emmanuel Cohen, currently in charge of production, thought Humberstone ready for a really big picture so he assigned him to direct KING OF THE JUNGLE (Paramount, 1933).

Originally, Cohen had wanted Cecil B. DeMille to direct it, but DeMille wasn't interested. Frightened by the magnitude of the undertaking, Lucky nonetheless consented. The story had a circus setting. Arrangements were made to use the Barnum and Bailey Circus. This required erecting sound stages near the river bottom where the circus was camped. Much of the shooting had to be done at night. The picture ran way over schedule and far exceeded its budget. Paramount was teetering on the brink of financial ruin. Cohen would occasionally summon Humberstone to his office to explain the delays.

"Lions aren't actors," Lucky told him. "Sometimes you have to run through a scene a dozen times before it's right."

The night the picture opened, Los Angeles was hit by a devastating earthquake. Lucky's option was not renewed by the studio. Always a superstitious man, Humberstone made a pact with himself that he would not attempt to direct any picture again which he did not feel was right for him.

When RKO did finally release BIRD OF PARADISE, David O. Selznick had returned to work for Metro-Goldwyn-Mayer. In early 1933, Lucky was signed briefly by RKO as a contract director. He was given the script to THE LOST PATROL (RKO, 1934), but, in keeping with his pact with himself, he declined it. He thought only Henry King or John Ford could do justice to the picture. Lucky did direct GOODBYE LOVE (RKO, 1933), a semi-comedy about female golddiggers, but he was unhappy with it. The studio kept throwing scripts at him and Lucky kept rejecting them. When Warner Bros. offered him a two-picture contract, he accepted. The trades termed Lucky's departure from RKO as a "walk out."

The first picture under the new contract that Lucky directed was MERRY WIVES OF RENO (Warner's, 1934) which had a comic plotline that sought to demonstrate that divorce could be amusing. Hal B. Wallis, in charge of production at Warner Bros., was impressed with the film. He summoned Humberstone to his office and handed him a screenplay titled THE DRAGON MURDER CASE. It was a Philo Vance story which the studio had purchased while William Powell was under contract. Powell had since left and had signed with M-G-M. He had played Philo Vance in all but one of the American photoplays based on S.S. Van Dine's popular detective novels. Now a new Philo Vance would have to be found.[3]

"This is going to be your next picture," Wallis informed Humberstone.

Lucky took the script home and read it. He showed up the next day and told Wallis, no. He knew that Michael Curtiz, Archie Mayo, Mervyn LeRoy, and Alfred Green had all turned down the picture and he was sure he knew why. It was a terrible story. Lucky disappeared from the studio and went out of town. Wallis, however, did locate him and told him over the telephone that the writers had gone to work on the script and had really improved it. He should return to the lot at once. Lucky did.

When he walked into Wallis' office, he was handed the same yellow-covered script he had been given before.

"I won't do it," he protested.

Wallis then made an appointment for Lucky to see Jack L. Warner personally. Once seated in Warner's office, Warner studied the new director.

"How much are you making?" he asked.

"Seven hundred and fifty dollars a week," Lucky replied.

"How old are you?" Warner asked.

"Twenty-nine."

"Do you know how much I was making when I was your age?" Warner asked. "Twenty-five bucks a week, selling meat." He paused for emphasis. "So, why don't you want to make this picture?"

"Because it's a lousy story."

"Listen," said Warner, "I don't care if it *is* a lousy story. You're going to make this picture. Do you think it matters that it's lousy? That picture, with my theatre chain, is going to make me fifty thousand dollars, good story or not. So you're going to make it for me. Or," he paused again for emphasis, "or you're never going to direct another picture in this town."

Lucky agreed to direct the picture.

THE DRAGON MURDER CASE (First National, 1934) proved one of the finest films in the Philo Vance series. Lucky's creative use of tropical fish spurred a national interest in collecting them and even Lucky himself became for a time an enthusiast. Warren William was cast as Vance with Eugene Pallette returning for the role of Sergeant Heath. Margaret Lindsay, who had been in MERRY WIVES OF RENO, and Lyle Talbot provided the love interest. The picture was budgeted at $320,000 and became one of the top releases that year for First National, now a wholly-owned Warner Bros. subsidiary.

For the première, Lucky had his agent invite most of the noteworthy producers then in Hollywood to attend. The picture was very well-received. Jack Warner collared him afterwards, saying, "Humberstone, don't sign with any of these guys. We want you." But a few days later the trades carried a story about how H. Bruce Humberstone had "walked out" of Warner Bros. Lucky was once more without a job.

Months went past and nothing turned up. It was more than half a year after the release of THE DRAGON MURDER CASE when Lucky's agent told him to report for an interview with Sol Wurtzel, head of production at Fox Film Corporation. Wurtzel said he knew all about Lucky's stubborn streak and the problems he had had at RKO and then Warner Bros. However, he was willing to give him a chance on a detective story slated for immediate production. Lucky would be working for Fox on a picture-by-picture basis.

LADIES LOVE DANGER (Fox, 1935) starred Gilbert Roland as a playwright and amateur sleuth. Robert Ellis and Helen Logan, subsequently associated on so many of Lucky's pictures in the years ahead, did the screenplay. VARIETY, in its review, praised Humberstone's direction. Wurtzel then assigned Lucky to direct SILK HAT KID (Fox, 1935). It had a complicated plot with Lew Ayres as a bodyguard for cafe owner Paul Kelly. Compared to LADIES LOVE DANGER, it was a rather pedestrian affair.

Lucky then went to M-G-M to direct THREE LIVE GHOSTS (M-G-M, 1936), with Richard Arlen and Beryl Mercer as Arlen's greedy, gin-drinking mother who turns in Arlen's best friend for the reward money. Lucky had directed Helen Lowell as a somewhat lunatic mother in THE DRAGON MURDER CASE, but Beryl Mercer played the epitome of an unsentimental, if not wholly unsympathetic, *mater familias* in this picture. VARIETY praised Humberstone again for his direction, but another trade complained that it was unsavory to see a screen mother so dependent on alcohol.

"But that was nothing," Lucky commented, "compared to working with Warner Oland, who was only good as Charlie Chan if he was stoned."

Vicki learned forward and honked.

"The lady needs a break," I said.

"I can't get over the fact that you people are whiskey drinkers," Lucky said, standing in front of his built-in bar. "Everyone out here is a vodka drinker. The women started it, in pictures. Vodka doesn't give you a liquor breath."

"With all the drinking I've been doing on these interviews," Vicki said, "it's not my breath I'm worrying about."

Lucky set down our glasses and fixed himself another tumbler of vodka martinis. He bummed a cigarette from Vicki and we resumed.

Twentieth Century Pictures was formed early in 1933. Joseph Schenck, brother to M-G-M president Nicholas Schenck, set up the producing company and recruited Darryl F. Zanuck from Warner Bros. to be head of production. Louis B. Mayer, vice president in charge of production at M-G-M, bankrolled the venture. At lunch at the Brown Derby on 18 April 1933, Joseph Schenck closed the deal by giving Zanuck a check for $100,000, signed by Mayer. Mayer had one son-in-law, David O. Selznick, working for him at M-G-M. He now wanted his other son-in-law, William Goetz, to become involved in film production. Goetz' official position was that of being Zanuck's assistant.

Joseph Schenck was the president of United Artists. The original founders of that company—Charlie Chaplin, Mary Pickford, Douglas Fairbanks, and D.W. Griffith—had organized it primarily to distribute their own pictures. Griffith in 1933 sold out his interest and the other three co-founders had cut way back on their own productions or had ceased altogether. This meant that it was now up to Samuel Goldwyn, who released through United Artists, and Darryl Zanuck and Twentieth Century Pictures to provide the bulk of the pictures to maintain United Artists' releasing schedule. The new set-up worked almost too well. Zanuck's films, with a single exception, were extraordinarily successful, so much so that Schenck, by this time restless at United Artists, approached Sidney R. Kent, president of the failing Fox Film Corporation. Fox had an even finer distribution network than United Artists and superior production facilities. Once the two companies merged, to become Twentieth Century-Fox, Zanuck was placed in charge of "A" picture production and Sol Wurtzel, who had been with Fox in various capacities since 1915, was made supervisor of "B" productions.

The Charlie Chan films with Warner Oland were one of Fox' most successful "B" series. Sol Wurtzel engaged Lucky to direct CHARLIE CHAN AT THE RACE TRACK (20th-Fox, 1936). Robert Ellis and Helen Logan worked on the screenplay. John Stone was the associate producer. Oland had been a heavy drinker for at least the past twenty years. During the race track sequence shot on location at the Santa Anita race track, Oland disappeared and the entire crew was dispatched to find him. He turned up in a dead sleep in the track restaurant. Lucky needed an intercut of Oland supposedly watching the horse race, but Warner kept dozing off. Yet, for all that, Lucky did encourage Oland to remain slightly inebriated throughout all of his scenes. Watching rushes, Oland had to agree that alcohol improved his characterization. When sober, he recited his lines too quickly; but once his memory was slightly fogged by alcohol, it seemed on screen at least as if the Oriental detective he was playing was grappling with a difficult, alien language when he was only groping for the line. Lucky started casting James Flavin regularly in character roles in his films, regarding him as a sort of good luck charm. CHARLIE CHAN AT THE RACE TRACK was so well-received that Wurtzel signed Lucky again to direct CHARLIE CHAN AT THE OPERA (20th-Fox, 1937).

It was Lucky's idea to cast Boris Karloff as an amnesiac opera singer in the film. Initially Wurtzel had resisted the notion because of the added expense, but Lucky finally gained his point and the picture proved a hit. While in production, Lucky had utilized several of the elaborate sets Zanuck had had built for D.W. Griffith's CAFE METROPOLE (20th-Fox, 1937). Griffith had actually shot most of his scenes in extreme close-up. When Zanuck saw the production values these sets brought to CHARLIE CHAN AT THE OPERA, he remarked to both Wurtzel and Bill Dover, Darryl's right-hand man, "This son-of-a-bitch, Humberstone, is making my 'A' directors look sick turning out a 'B' that looks like this. Put him under contract." Wurtzel did.

CHARLIE CHAN AT THE OLYMPICS (20th-Fox, 1937) was Lucky's first picture under his new contract. Once more it was an excellent entry, with varying locales and an expert integration of stock footage of everything from a Zeppelin to the Olympic games in 1936 in Germany.

CHECKERS (20th-Fox, 1938) came next. John Stone, from the Charlie Chan series, was the associate producer and Lynn Root and Frank Fenton, who would later move over to RKO to work on the Falcon detective series in the 'Forties, did the screenplay. The story had a horse-racing background. The trades praised both Stone and Humberstone for saving the picture from banality.

At three o'clock one morning Bill Dover called Lucky at his home to congratulate him. Dover told him that Darryl Zanuck had decided that Lucky was to make no more "B" pictures and he wanted to see him at his office at ten the next day. When Lucky showed up, Zanuck explained through clouds of cigar smoke that Henry King was presently reading the script for a major production to be titled IN OLD CHICAGO (20th-Fox, 1938). Zanuck had also just purchased screen rights for HEIDI. He now wanted to give King HEIDI and put Lucky on IN OLD CHICAGO. Lucky was optimistic. IN OLD CHICAGO was budgeted at nearly two million dollars. Since Irving Thalberg had died, Darryl Zanuck was generally considered the most consistent production chief in the industry. Both Hal B. Wallis and David O. Selznick were brilliant producers of individual films, but Zanuck alone, it would seem in retrospect, could make fine films in quantity. Zanuck was charged with producing one "A" picture every twelve days. Three out of every four of Zanuck's productions made an impressive profit. Lucky was pleased at the prospect of joining Zanuck's inner circle.

Henry King balked. He told Zanuck that unless he was permitted to direct IN OLD CHICAGO, he would walk out on his contract. Zanuck argued and negotiated and finally effected a compromise: King would direct the film until the cow kicks over the lantern; Lucky, from that point on, was to direct the fire sequences and all the special effects. King agreed. Most of the reviews singled out the special effects for high praise. Lucky went on to direct RASCALS (20th-Fox, 1938). At the time both THE HOLLYWOOD REPORTER and VARIETY customarily extracted a substantial portion of their income through advertisements sold to people working in the industry. The pressure was tremendous for one seeking a livelihood in the picture business to buy space. Even reviews were known to improve. Lucky allocated $2,000 a year for each publication. He was coerced into running an ad crediting himself with directing the fire sequence in IN OLD CHICAGO. However, given the degree of his ambition at the time and his rivalry with King over directing the film, he probably did not need to be coerced too much. At the Academy Awards, IN OLD CHICAGO was nominated for Best Picture. Alice Brady was nominated for Best Supporting Actress for her work in the film. Niven Busch was nominated for Best Original Story. E.H. Hanson won an Oscar for Best Sound Recording. Even the assistant director on the film, Robert Webb, won an Oscar. However, in those days the Academy was unable to nominate for Best Director two or more directors who had worked on a single picture. Although Henry King had received screen credit for directing IN OLD CHICAGO, he was convinced that Lucky's ads in the trades were the reason for his not being nominated. Angry and hurt, King tried to get Zanuck to force Lucky to reprint a retraction of his advertisements. This Lucky refused to do. Zanuck did point out to King that, after all, Lucky *had* directed the special effects. One night King followed Lucky all the way out of the studio lot, heaping abuse on him for his obstinacy. The next day King confronted Zanuck, telling him flatly that either Humberstone was to leave or he would.

"I've no choice," Zanuck explained to Lucky. "Henry King is the best director I have working for me."

Lucky was apparently out of a contract and out of a job.

The production schedule had originally called for Lucky to start shooting PASSPORT HUSBAND for Sol Wurtzel on 21 March 1938. Lucky's "suspen-

*14 6,914*

sion'' postponed production until 9 May 1938 at which time it was begun with James Tinling directing. Between CHARLIE CHAN AT THE OPERA and the contract Lucky signed with Twentieth Century-Fox prior to CHARLIE CHAN AT THE OLYMPICS, a number of sources indicate that Humberstone had been hired by Universal to direct BREEZING HOME (Universal, 1937) and that he had been fired shortly after production began. Lucky denied any knowledge of this picture or ever having worked on it. The sources, however, would seem to be correct in this matter. Once production began on PASSPORT HUSBAND without him, Lucky telephoned Bill Goetz and asked him if he could return. Goetz assured Lucky that he would fix the situation with Zanuck. Lucky was indeed allowed to return, but he was again a ''B'' unit director.

His first assignment was the pilot picture for a new detective series, TIME OUT FOR MURDER (20th-Fox, 1938). Irving Rice, who would subsequently produce the first entries in RKO's Falcon detective series, wrote the original story. Michael Whalen was cast as a roving reporter with Chick Chandler as his comic sidekick. June Gale and Jean Rogers, the latter a recent graduate from playing Dale Arden in the serial FLASH GORDON (Universal, 1936), were also in the cast as was Cliff Clark in the role of a dumb cop. The picture proved a success and was rapidly followed by a second entry, WHILE NEW YORK SLEEPS (20th-Fox, 1939). This time Jean Rogers and June Gale switched roles, with Rogers cast as the female lead. Chick Chandler played the same role. Lynn Root and Frank Fenton did the original screenplay, creating the stupid police comedy duo played by Cliff Clark and Edward Gargan who would portray similar roles when Root and Fenton moved to RKO to script entries in the Falcon series. Lucky's direction was singled out in the trades for praise.

When Warner Oland died unexpectedly, the studio mounted a search for a replacement in the Charlie Chan series, finally selecting Sidney Toler. Without Oland, Keye Luke no longer wanted to play Charlie's Number One Son, so he was replaced by Victor Sen Young who, henceforth, would portray Charlie's Number Two Son. Sol Wurtzel, knowing Lucky's track record with Oland, asked him to direct the first entry in this new series, CHARLIE CHAN IN HONOLULU (20th-Fox, 1939). Toler was almost as heavy a drinker as Oland had been, but he was sober on the set. Lucky gave him the same advice: to take a couple of stiff jolts before coming before the cameras. The technique worked and CHARLIE CHAN IN HONOLULU may well be the best film Toler ever made in that role.

PARDON OUR NERVE (20th-Fox, 1939) was third in the studio's ''Big Town Girl'' series, praised by the trades for the laughs and suspense injected through Lucky's adroit direction. Robert Ellis and Helen Logan did the screenplay. Michael Whalen had a featured role with Lynn Bari and June Gale as the female leads. Lynn Bari was back for PACK UP YOUR TROUBLES (20th-Fox, 1939). Critics claimed that the film was the most hilarious farce about the Great War since TWO ARABIAN NIGHTS (United Artists, 1927) which Lewis Milestone directed for Howard Hughes in the silent era.

"I've got something special for you, Humberstone," Sol Wurtzel told Lucky after completion of PACK UP YOUR TROUBLES. "You're going to make a Cisco Kid picture for me. I'm even going to name it after you."

"That would be LUCKY CISCO KID (20th-Fox, 1940)," I said, consulting one of several reference books piled around my chair.

"You've got the title right," Lucky said, "but that can't be the year. I think it was 1938."

"Nope," I said. "The picture was released on 28 June 1940."

"Then that book is wrong," Lucky insisted.

"Cesar Romero was Cisco," I said. "It has to be 1940."

"Well, it can't be," Lucky retorted. He got up and walked over to the coffee table in front of Vicki and picked up her package of cigarettes.

"Don't worry," she said. "I have more in my purse."

Lucky lit a cigarette. He studied her empty glass. "Why didn't you honk?" he asked her.

"I was wondering which to do first," Vicki said, smiling. "Honk, or ask to go to the bathroom."

After some discussion, it was determined that Vicki should go to the bathroom, Lucky would make another round, and I was to find another volume among the reference books that gave a 1938 release year for LUCKY CISCO KID. Ten minutes later, we all had refills and Vicki sat poised with her pen and notebook.

"I dislike having to let everyone down," I said, "but I'm afraid 1940 is the year."

"That can't be," Lucky returned. "All those books are wrong."

"Let's just hope," said Vicki, lifting her drink and sipping from it, "that I'm within ten years of the release date when I come to transcribe these notes."

Lucky's next assignment was on loan-out, THE QUARTERBACK (Paramount, 1940), in which Wayne Morris played twins and Virginia Dale was the leading lady. When he returned to the studio this time, Lucky was permitted to join Zanuck's "A" unit. Sol Wurtzel had become embroiled in personal problems which finally resulted in his termination. The friction with Henry King was forgotten. Lucky was given TALL, DARK AND HANDSOME (20th-Fox, 1941) to direct. It started Cesar Romero, Virginia Gilmore, Milton Berle, and Sheldon Leonard. In it, Romero played a soft-hearted gangster, with Berle as his chief assistant and Leonard as the head of a rival gang. It was one of the films of which Lucky was quite proud. He perfected a camera technique for it he had first used in CHARLIE CHAN AT THE RACE TRACK. The camera would whip from right to left or left to right at the end of one scene and into the next scene. It was an excellent means to accelerate tempo before the use of the jump cut. Zanuck was so impressed by the effect that he invited all of his directors to a private screening to witness the results.

Darryl and Virginia Zanuck went on vacation to Sun Valley. Lucky was invited along as Zanuck's guest. While there, Zanuck came to think the location ideal for a skating picture with Sonja Henie, one of the novelties then under contract.

Zanuck left Lucky behind and dispatched Robert Ellis and Helen Logan to devise a suitable story. Lucky felt it an apt opportunity to make use of Glenn Miller and his orchestra, then the foremost performing ensemble in popular music. SUN VALLEY SERENADE (20th-Fox, 1941), in addition to Miller (it would be his second and final film) and Henie (it was supposed to be *her* last picture), featured John Payne, Milton Berle, and the Nicholas Brothers. The film had seven hit songs of which "Chattanooga Choo-Choo" with a dance routine by the Nicholas Brothers was far and away the show stopper. Some of the plot ingredients for Sonja Henie had previously been developed by Julian Johnson, head of the story department, and associate producer Harry Joe Brown in collaboration with S.S. Van Dine, work which was terminated upon the detective story writer's death in 1939. The most important of these was Henie's ballet on black ice. The picture opened to a heartening box office and set the tone for a whole series of successful Fox musicals. It acted as such a catalyst for Sonja Henie's slumping career that Zanuck, who had hoped to be rid of her, was compelled to send Joe Schenck to New York to negotiate a new three-picture deal with the skater.

Lucky read Steve Fisher's screen story I WAKE UP SCREAMING and wanted to direct it. Zanuck demurred on the grounds that Lucky was best at musicals and this was to be a psychological murder mystery. Lucky persisted and at last Zanuck gave in. Betty Grable and Victor Mature were to be the stars. In the novel, on which the screenplay was based, Fisher had modeled his character of the psychopathic cop Cornell on suspense fiction writer Cornell Woolrich. Lucky cast rotund Laird Cregar in the role. There was still no ending to the picture when it was screened one night for a small group including Zanuck, Virginia, Otto Preminger, Harry Joe Brown, and Humberstone. Zanuck escorted Virginia out to her car and then returned to the screening room. He had had an idea.

"Humberstone," he said, "there are only two things wrong with this picture as it stands. One: it is a Betty Grable picture in black and white. That's bad enough. But, second: the exhibitors will never sit still for a Grable picture where she doesn't sing one song!"

"But, Darryl," Humberstone objected, "you yourself said this was a psychological murder mystery. She can't sing. It wouldn't be consistent with the whole thrust of the picture."

"Listen," said Zanuck, sweeping all that aside with a wave of his cigar, "I've got the perfect ending. The camera, in the last scene, pans into the basement of a busy department store, with dozens of extras running around, buying things, and so on. It tracks in to a close shot of Grable, sitting at a piano, singing a number. She works there, see, and this is the happy ending: her singing a song for the customers."

Lucky went out and shot the scene as Zanuck wanted it. It was spliced into the work print and screened for the same group. Once more Zanuck escorted Virginia out to her car, when it was over, and returned, gloomily shaking his head.

"Humberstone," he said gravely, "Virginia agrees with me. You've got to be crazy to have Grable singing at the end of a picture like this. It's a psychological picture. It doesn't fit. Get a new ending.''

Lucky did not bother with remonstrance. He went home and thought and thought about how to end the picture. Near dawn, he fell asleep and had a dream. The next morning he rushed into Zanuck's office.

"I've got the ending," he announced confidently.

"What is it?" Zanuck asked.

"Laird Cregar is a screwy cop," Lucky began. "He has photos and ads of Carole Landis, the murdered girl, all over his apartment. Vic Mature goes there, to the apartment, at the end of the picture, and he sees this. He meets Cregar, who's coming home with some flowers to put beneath his shrine to Landis. Mature tells him that they've caught Elisha Cook and that he's confessed everything, including how Laird had him cover up. Cregar takes poison and dies. That's how the picture ends, with Laird dying, a suicide, surrounded by all the pictures of Landis. He was in love with her but afraid to say anything once she became a celebrity."

"That's great!" Zanuck exclaimed. "Why didn't you think of this before? You've held up production almost two weeks on this picture."

"Because I just dreamed it," Lucky said.

"You dreamed it!" Zanuck responded sarcastically.

Yet, that is how the picture ended. In life, which is often stranger than fiction, both Carole Landis and Laird Cregar would be dead by suicide within a few years of its release.

When Zanuck bought screen rights to WILD GEESE CALLING (20th-Fox, 1941), he had originally wanted Lucky to direct it. Lucky read the script and told Zanuck it was a lousy story. Zanuck grew adamant and insisted that Humberstone direct the picture. At seven o'clock one morning on the way to the studio, while driving through Coldwater Canyon, a landslide came down on Lucky's car. He skidded. His head went through the windshield. In the process, his nose came off and had to be grafted back onto his face. It is my suspicion that Lucky at times tended to confuse this accident with the earlier one in which Breezy Eason was involved.

"That son-of-a-bitch Humberstone," Zanuck said, "will do anything to get out of a picture."

Months later, after talking to New York, Zanuck told Lucky what a poor showing the picture had had at the box office.

"I did it," Zanuck confessed, "just to meet my quota of pictures."

The property Lucky did want to direct was TO THE SHORES OF TRIPOLI (20th-Fox, 1942).

"But you don't know anything about the Marines," Zanuck protested.

"By the time we finish the picture," Humberstone said, "we'll be at war."

"Okay, Humberstone," Zanuck, who was sceptical of the idea, told him, "I'm going to teach you a lesson. You start shooting in ten weeks."

Lew Schreiber, who was the Fox casting director, informed Zanuck that

Randolph Scott's contract was up. Zanuck was all for letting him go. However, Lucky wanted him for TO THE SHORES OF TRIPOLI and was able to convince Zanuck to renew the contract. Shooting began at Camp Pendleton. The troupe then returned to the studio for a number of interiors before going back to Camp Pendleton to film the equivalent of a West Point graduation. Lucky was given only a six-minute notice one day to clear out because the camp had to be evacuated. Shooting had resumed at the studio for two days when Milton Sperling, the producer on the picture, told Lucky to wrap up the company. Viewing the rushes of men marching this way and that, Sperling was of the opinion that the film would prove a bomb. Lucky walked off the set. Zanuck then summoned him back to the studio for a screening of the assembled rushes. Zanuck loved it. The picture was completed in the next three days. The last day of production was 7 December 1941. Seven months after release, Bill Goetz presented Lucky with a check for $25,000.

"It was decided some time ago by the board of directors," he said, "that the first Twentieth Century-Fox film to gross a million dollars would net its director a $25,000 bonus. TO THE SHORES OF TRIPOLI was the first."

William LeBaron, Mae West's producer at Paramount in the 'Thirties, was Lucky's producer for his next film, ICELAND (20th-Fox, 1942). It starred Sonja Henie and was scripted along the lines of SUN VALLEY SERENADE, this time featuring Sammy Kaye and his orchestra. John Payne was again the male lead with Jack Oakie and Jimmy Flavin among the supporting players.

Two Technicolor musicals followed. HELLO FRISCO, HELLO (20th-Fox, 1943) started out to be a remake of IN OLD CHICAGO, with the great earthquake replacing the catastrophic fire, but it ended up a much lighter type of musical comedy starring Alice Faye and John Payne. Milton Sperling was credited as the producer, but he was already in military service. If PIN-UP GIRL (20th-Fox, 1944) wasn't Betty Grable's best picture, it was nonetheless responsible for a large measure of her war-time fame as a result of the cheese-cake still of her in a white sharkskin bathing suit with her callipygean figure turned so her backside was toward the camera as part of the publicity for the film. American servicemen all over the world took to patting her bottom for luck before dangerous missions, or merely for the fun of it.

Zanuck entered military service and, technically, Bill Goetz replaced him, although Zanuck did try to keep his hand in the operation of the studio. Zanuck wanted Lucky to direct SOMETHING FOR THE BOYS, Mike Todd's Broadway hit, but Lucky refused. Instead, Lucky landed a job on loan-out to Sam Goldwyn directing WONDER MAN (RKO, 1945) starring Danny Kaye and featuring Vera-Ellen in some exceptional tap dance routines. The film proved a hit and Lucky was singled out for praise in the trades. Notwithstanding, both Goetz and Zanuck were becoming irritated at Lucky's pickiness, especially now since his contract was up for renewal. Lucky was offered THUNDER BIRDS (20th-Fox, 1942) and refused it. Zanuck then got William Wellman to direct it, provided Wellman could also direct THE OX-BOW INCIDENT (20th-Fox, 1943), a picture Wellman really wanted to make. Humberstone persisted in being highly selective about what pictures he would and would not direct. To chastise him properly, he was demoted again to the "B" unit until his contract was up. Among the scripts he was offered was WITHIN THESE WALLS (20th-Fox, 1945) for which Lucky chose Mark Stevens, from the roster of Fox contract players, to be the romantic lead. The role established Stevens as a comer. Zanuck, impressed that Humberstone, no matter what the budget, was simply incapable of making a "B" picture that looked to be a "B" picture, gave in with a sigh of resignation and renewed Lucky's contract for three years at $3,000 a week.

After a ten-week stint on loan-out to Columbia to do preliminary work on THE JOLSON STORY (Columbia, 1946), Lucky returned to Fox to direct THE HOMESTRETCH (20th-Fox, 1947). Fate intervened. Zanuck asked Lucky to join him in screening rushes from THREE LITTLE GIRLS IN BLUE (20th-Fox, 1946), by then some forty days in production. Lucky told Zanuck that he thought the problem was not with the director but with the casting. He recommended the picture be started over with a wholly different cast of leading men. Zanuck agreed to a change in casting if Lucky would direct it. Robert Ellis and Helen Logan had worked on the screenplay. Upon release, the film proved such a success that it was remade later as HOW TO MARRY A MILLIONAIRE (20th-Fox, 1953). The trio of women in search of millionaire husbands in Lucky's version of the story featured Vivian Blaine, Vera-Ellen, and June Haver. THE HOMESTRETCH followed THREE LITTLE GIRLS IN BLUE in production back to back. The story had a horse-race setting and it was set in 1938 with Cornell Wilde and Maureen O'Hara as the stars, but Jimmy Gleason, reunited once more with Lucky, nearly stole the picture in the comic role of a trainer.

Zanuck had promised Lucky a vacation if he would get both pictures done consecutively without taking a break. Lucky went to Palm Springs and almost four months passed before George Jessel, then working as a producer for Zanuck, called Lucky and asked him to read the script for a picture to be titled I WONDER WHO'S KISSING HER NOW. When Lucky responded that he was still on vacation, Jessel informed him that he was calling at Darryl's behest and that Zanuck wanted an answer. When Lucky received the script he delayed reading it for some time and, when he finally did, he told Jessel he didn't like it. He had been waiting, he said, for Zanuck to have a screenplay prepared for a different project and only when he mentioned it did Jessel tell him that that project had been scrapped.

Whatever his ingenuity as a producer, Darryl Zanuck's resentments ran very deep. After the success of THE RAZOR'S EDGE (20th-Fox, 1946), Zanuck had signed its director, Edmund Goulding, to a generous contract which required Goulding to make only four pictures during the next five years and for which he would be paid a million dollars at the rate of $200,000 a year. NIGHTMARE ALLEY (20th-Fox, 1947) was the first film under this contract. Zanuck then had had an altercation with Goulding. When he later had heard that Goulding had mimicked the things he had said to him to a number of people at the Palm

Springs Racquet Club, Zanuck as a punishment assigned Goulding to a very small office next to the elevators. Although he continued to honor the contract's financial terms, Zanuck would only route Goulding an occasional script of inferior quality which Goulding would be compelled to reject. It was Goulding's pride that Zanuck wanted to humble. Now Lucky had got up Zanuck's ire. Zanuck kept him idle for a year. Lloyd Bacon, who had long been a director at Twentieth Century-Fox, offered Lucky what he felt to be sage advice as to how to survive in the studio system. Most screenplays were notoriously bad. Lucky's inclination, as was the case with a number of directors, was to change things around until they played better. It wasn't so with Bacon. He would always shoot a script as written. This way the associate producer on the picture would scurry in alarm to Zanuck, change things around after a brain-storming session, and seemingly save the picture coming out looking good. Because Bacon's producers customarily looked so good, his services were much in demand at the studio. Making a favorable impression on a producer, or even on Zanuck, was not as important to Lucky as making a picture of which he could be proud.

"Humberstone," Zanuck declared as they sat together in a screening room after Lucky's enforced hiatus from behind the camera was finally over, "I don't like these dailies, but I don't know why."

The scene was of a troop of cavalry riding along a dusty trail.

"They're not grimy enough," Lucky observed.

"You're right," Zanuck agreed. "I want you to go on location in Arizona and take over this picture."

Shooting was being done in and around the Old Tucson town set which Wesley Ruggles had erected for ARIZONA (Columbia, 1940). Lucky packed his bag and headed for location. The film was a Western titled FURY AT FURNACE CREEK (20th-Fox, 1948) set in 1880 and starring Victor Mature and Coleen Gray with Albert Dekker as the chief villain. Although the plot was rather conventional, with Indians attacking a fort and a wagon train, Lucky handled the action sequences commendably and the shoot-out at the end was properly suspenseful.

Some time after the picture was released Zanuck gave Lucky the bad news. Since FURY AT FURNACE CREEK had been the only production Lucky had worked on for more than a year, his entire salary had to be charged to its budget. This so increased the negative cost of the film that it made breaking even prohibitive. To satisfy the board of directors, Zanuck was compelled now not to renew Lucky's contract. It was a sly variation of what Zanuck had done to Edmund Goulding. This time Lucky's severance from the studio was final. Lucky asked his agent, Lew Wasserman of MCA, to find him free-lance jobs.

Whatever the advantages of being independent, security was not one of them. Lucky's first assignment was for Universal-International. Bill Goetz, when he left Fox, again with the help of Louis B. Mayer set up International Pictures with Leo Spitz. In 1946 International merged with Universal, Spitz and Goetz becoming production managers for the combined facilities. When Lucky was engaged to direct SOUTH SEA SINNER (Universal-International, 1950), the studio was only a year away from its acquisition by MCA. SOUTH SEA SINNER had a complex plot, starring Macdonald Carey and Shelley Winters with Jimmy Flavin in a character role. However, not even the Flavin talisman could save the picture from mediocrity.

It was HAPPY GO LOVELY (RKO-British, 1951) which proved a life saver. It was produced by Associated British in collaboration with N. Peter Rathvon, head of an American financing company. American money paid for the director and the leading stars, David Niven, Vera-Ellen, and Cesar Romero; Associated British paid for the rest, including production costs incurred by shooting the film in the United Kingdom. It was a Technicolor musical comedy that all the trades declared played as a house of fire. In addition to his salary, Lucky also received 15% of the gross receipts of the film upon release. This money supported him for years. RKO bought domestic distribution rights.

Once more, Lucky's career was on the upswing. Warner Bros. contracted him to direct two musicals, SHE'S WORKING HER WAY THROUGH COLLEGE (Warner's, 1952) and THE DESERT SONG (Warner's, 1953). SHE'S WORK-ING HER WAY THROUGH COLLEGE was a bright musical with Virginia Mayo and Ronald Reagan for which Gene Nelson provided the song and dance numbers. THE DESERT SONG was actually the third make of a film which, upon release, proved less successful than either the 1929 or 1943 versions.

It was nearly two years before Lucky worked again. He was hired by Harry Joe Brown, who was than co-producing with Randolph Scott a series of Scott Westerns for Columbia release. Brown wanted Lucky to direct TEN WANTED MEN (Columbia, 1955). It was a cut above the typical high budget Western, but for one reason or another Lucky was unable to achieve the effects with Scott and the storyline that Budd Boetticher would in the splendid entries he would later direct in the Scott series in the late 'Fifties. Westerns somehow did not tap the creative responses in Lucky that musicals and detective stories could.

Lucky next directed PURPLE MASK (Universal-International, 1955), a swashbuckler set in the Napoleonic era starring Tony Curtis. Further work was not forthcoming, so Lucky severed his relationship with MCA, which was getting out of the agency business anyway. It was on Christmas Day, 1956, that Lucky's new agent called him with an assignment in London. TARZAN AND THE LOST SAFARI (M-G-M, 1957) had been in production for six months and had had four different directors. Lucky did not want the assignment, but his agent persuaded him with the argument that he simply had to keep his hand in the game if he wanted more jobs. Lucky went to London and shot the whole picture on three sound stages with only one exterior of the tree house plus stock footage. The British production crew thought him insane when he staged a forest fire indoors at the conclusion of the film. Yet, Lucky's experience on the fire se-quences for IN OLD CHICAGO served him well. The sequence was carried off without a mishap.

Sol Lesser, executive producer for the Tarzan series, was so pleased with the results that he contracted Lucky to direct the next picture scheduled for production, TARZAN'S FIGHT FOR LIFE (M-G-M, 1958). Gordon Scott played Tarzan in both films. In all probability what Lesser liked most of all was how effectively Lucky could shoot outdoor pictures on sound stages without completely shattering the illusion of the African jungle.

MADISON AVENUE (20th-Fox, 1962) was the last film Lucky directed. He was also credited as its producer. It was a moderately budgeted comedy about the advertising industry in which milkman Eddie Albert was transformed into a successful business tycoon.

"How about a night cap?" Lucky proposed, rising from his rocker.

Vicki reached for the horn and honked weakly.

"Come on," Lucky said. "Where's your energy? The night is still young!"

Vicki gave him a pale smile and honked twice more, as weakly.

"The lady is exhausted," I said.

"You know," Lucky said, "I believe you're right."

Everyone was then quiet for a moment, recovering from the pain and intensity it somehow always takes to remember.

## III

We did return for a purely social visit, the night before we had to continue on our travels. Lucky met us at the door to his apartment with a whiskey over ice in each hand. He gave Vicki one and the other to me.

"That's all you wanted anyway," he said playfully and began closing the door.

"Just a minute," Vicki said. "We came for a slightly longer visit than this."

"Oh," said Lucky, opening the door wide. "In that case, why don't you come on in?"

Once we were seated, Lucky eyed Vicki suspiciously. She was dressed in a black body shirt with a beige skirt and a turquoise scarf tied in a knot around her neck. Her blonde hair was fluffed and her blue-green eyes sparkled.

"Did you bring all your notebooks?" he asked. "We can go over them and check the facts."

"I think I did," Vicki said, searching in her leather shoulder bag. "If I didn't leave them in the car."

"In the car!" Lucky exclaimed in mock disgust. "Some secretary!" He turned to me. "How is she in the hay?"

I was in the process of lighting a cigarette and so did not answer at once.

"Here they are," Vicki said, pulling out the notebooks. "And," she added, raising an eyebrow, "tell him, if he's so interested, that you have no idea how I am in the hay, but that I'm fantasic in bed."

"Have you a cigarette, honey?" Lucky asked, chuckling.

"Sure," Vicki said, grinning. "A really good secretary always carries an extra pack."

Lucky and Vicki lit up off the same match.

"If you get bored," Lucky addressed me, "you can always go out and get a sandwich or something while Vicki and I go over this stuff."

"It's an idea," I conceded.

"What he doesn't know won't hurt him, honey."

"He'd probably find out," Vicki returned, "and include it somewhere in the course of your career study."

"Hey," said Lucky, "I want to read this thing before you publish it."

"You will," Vicki promised. "I'll be certain to smuggle you a copy just as soon as it is finished."

"She's a pretty girl," Lucky said, toasting Vicki with his martini glass, but winking at me.

"And I can type, too, right?" Vicki responded.

There was laughter.

"Not only is she liberated," I told Lucky, "but she doesn't want to work in pictures."

"Sam Peckinpah offered me a job any time I cared to try it," Vicki said. "Provided he had a part for a female with small breasts."

"What did you say to that?" Lucky asked.

"Nothing. He chewed on my arm." She stretched out her right arm. "See." Then she smiled. "But I still love him."

Lucky became serious.

"Vicki said over the telephone that you had gone to see ONCE IS NOT ENOUGH."

I nodded.

"Well, maybe you should think of some way to bring that picture in at the end of what you write about me. The last fifteen years have been for me much as they were for Kirk Douglas in that picture. I have spent them raising Robyn by myself."

"I don't suppose it has been easy," I said.

"Never that," Lucky said. "I could measure the days by how much she grew and what she was learning to do. I didn't remarry and I didn't want any women around constantly. She turned out fine."

"And beautiful," Vicki said, sipping her drink.

"Everywhere I went, she came along," Lucky went on. "If I went out socially, Robyn was always invited. We were companions. Now she's married to a traveling musician. It's difficult getting accustomed to being alone."

We talked far into the night. When it came time to depart, amid plans to visit soon again, Vicki put her arm around Lucky and kissed him on the mouth.

"Take care, you two," he said from the doorway.

"Better yet," Vicki said, "I'll see to it that Jon writes, and I will, and I'll send you the typescript as soon as it's ready. You have my word on it."

Jacaranda trees lined the street outside Lucky's apartment house. They were in bloom and the night was alive with their rich fragrance. I had hoped to get a photograph of Vicki standing beneath one of them, but now it was too late and too dark. Vicki pressed my hand reassuringly as we walked in silence to the car.

Once back in Milwaukee, Wisconsin, where we then lived, I set about fashioning a career study of Lucky's screen work. Since he wanted to read it before it was published—a reasonable request, it seemed at the time—I was careful to delete all the extraneous gossip and the numerous sexual anecdotes, many of them explicitly detailed, with which his narrative had been underscored. Lucky said that he was terrified of being sued by either the people about whom he had told these anecdotes or by their survivors. When he was finally sent a copy of the career study, the telephone calls began coming, usually at about three o'clock in the morning. Lucky was beside himself. He insisted that there were numerous errors, but in the end all of this proved to be only a rerun of the altercation about the release date of LUCKY CISCO KID. He insisted that all the dates of his work as an assistant director at United Artists were wrong. I explained to him that I was sticking to the official release dates which could be verified readily, and not to production dates. He declared that Ben Lyon was in the cast of STRANGERS OF THE EVENING and that that must be added. He would not believe me when I told him that we had screened the film and he was not in it. When I sent him a copy of the review from VARIETY which listed the entire cast of the film to show him that Lyon had not been in it and another review from VARIETY for THE CROOKED CIRCLE which listed him as having been in that film, Lucky would have none of it. VARIETY was wrong. He claimed that Eugene Pallette was not in PIN-UP GIRL and even a copy of the original press kit from the picture, with photo illustrations and full credits, would not persuade him that he was incorrect. He obstinately argued that he had had nothing to do with BREEZING HOME despite the fact that two trade sources listed him as having been announced as the original director on that film under its working title, I HATE HORSES. He objected to any reference to the history and mergers of film companies as irrelevant to his career and would not accept my explanation that many readers would need to know this background in order to appreciate the comings and goings of various administrations and producers.

At some length, in a letter, I outlined what a career study was—a special blend of interview and biography. He proposed that his career study be scrapped and that he be permitted to rewrite and embellish the material to make it a biography. He would telephone to read me the embellishments he had written and became nettled when I observed that the prose was a bit florid and the tone entirely too self-congratulatory, to say nothing of the prohibitive length. Although his career study was but one of ten which were to appear in CLOSE-UP: THE CONTRACT DIRECTOR (1976), most of them by other writers, he became adamant that production on the entire book must be held up until he had rewritten his career study. He began to inundate the publisher of the book with telephone calls and letters. When my editor, Eric Moon at the Scarecrow Press, received a copy of some of Lucky's embellishments, he advised me at once that we must proceed with the career study as I had written it. What Lucky had submitted was totally unpublishable. "In the event Mr. Moon . . . stands firm on no major changes or corrections, no embellishments and no deletions," Lucky wrote to me on 15 June 1976, "then my advice to you, as a friend, is to scrap the entire project as of right now."[4] We were about to embark for Europe and the galleys had already been corrected and returned to the publisher.

Yet, when his career study did finally appear, no one was more proud of it than Lucky. It was actually the first extended interview and commentary on his films to be published anywhere. When, late in 1976, Vicki and I moved to Los Angeles, we saw quite a bit of Lucky and he became enamored of the idea of my writing a full-scale biography of him and his film career. Also, in his final years, his conversation became increasingly lewd. Even though the explicit sexual episodes had been excised from what was published, this tendency now only intensified. The very last time we saw him, in 1978, before moving again, this time to Portland, Oregon, he had some advice for Vicki.

"Don't go down on him too often, honey. After a while it begins to affect a man's brain and in time he starts walking around on his knees."

"I won't," Vicki said, smiling.

When Lucky saw that she had her fingers crossed, he leered.

"Smile now," he said, "but, believe me, I know. I gave Robyn the same advice."

One positive consequence of the publication of his career study was that the American Film Institute invited Lucky to participate in its oral history project. He went faithfully to record for posterity his memories of what had happened, what he had seen, and what he could remember. His willingness to discuss the most intimate sexual details about those whom he had known made him particularly attractive to a number of writers preparing biographies on various people, from Goldwyn to Zanuck. My basic problem with this was identical with his confusion of the two automobile accidents he had had: I never knew how much of it could be reasonably believed. Harold Bruce "Lucky" Humberstone died on 11 October 1984.

# Henry King

## I

When we met Henry King in April, 1976 for the first time, I was struck at once by how fine he appeared wearing a hat, even were it only a straw fedora. Once wearing a hat, which shielded his graying, thinning hair, you would never be able to guess how old he was based just on his alertly observant blue eyes and his deeply tanned skin. Although he had been born on 24 January 1888 at Christiansburg, Virginia, his active interest in life in old age belied his years. In 1976 he was still logging 12,000 miles a year flying in his own airplane and he frequently would play a round of golf. His first wife, Gypsy, had died in 1952 and he married again in 1959. He and his second wife, Ida, lived in North Hollywood in Amelia Earhart's former house, bordered in the rear by a golf course with verdant turf spread beneath majestic trees stretching quietly in the Southern California sun.

At the time, he still maintained an office in a building adjacent to Hollywood and Vine. It was here that he preserved all the scripts from his films and the memorabilia from his long career in the industry. He was as meticulous, organized, and professional in his business life in retirement as he invariably had been during his active years as a film director. Probably the most astonishing thing, though, about Henry King in old age was his memory. Unclouded by the passage of time, he was possessed of a staggeringly detailed recall of nearly every picture he had worked on, what the plot line was, who was in it, the time during which it had been filmed, the season of the year, the money involved. Remembering required no special effort. He reminded me of no one so much as the portrait Cicero rendered of Cato Maior, except that he was wholly without need of any Pythagorian system to maintain the astuteness of his recall; and, as

Cato, he had achieved already what his juniors could only yearn after: his life had been long and to some purpose.

Henry King, by that same fickleness of Fortune which led to the irascible John Ford being nearly canonized by serious critics and students of the cinema and whose career spanned a comparable period of time, seemed then as now to have been unconscionably neglected. Yet, his credits are as praiseworthy as his achievement is remarkable. In his finest films he was positive, certain, and inimitable because his sense of story was always thoroughly secure. Whereas Ford frequently got sidetracked by the visual luxury of his images, Henry King, when he faltered, betrayed rather the need for a cogent, well-made story. For King, his style was the telling of his story. He was, therefore, always at his best when his story was without excessive subtlety or indirection.

As a filmmaker, Henry King was by nature an optimist. His view of American life, as depicted in his films, is informed by a pervasive nostalgia, not so much a longing for the past as a persistent tendency to juxtapose its languid ease and less complicated premises with the harsher intricacies of the present. King had been a convert to Roman Catholicism in mid life. Unlike John Ford's desperate frenzy to believe or his sentimental attachment to religious legend and iconography, King's theological persuasions would seem to have been more soberly philosophical, more the unassuming tranquility of St. Francis than the struggling turmoil of St. Augustine. If King's visions of human beings lack an unsettling intensity, nonetheless their very placidity, behind what is often cosmopolitan dialogue and an infinite sensitivity for differences in perspective, evokes a cinematic poetry that somehow assuages the rhythm of life to produce a calming effect. Above all, Henry King in his best films can make you believe that his characters are capable of a devoted, although not necessarily passionate and almost never destructive, love of one another. For the time it is playing, you can honestly believe that Spencer Tracy's Stanley is beguiled by the unassuming charm of Nancy Kelly's Eve Kingsley in STANLEY AND LIVINGSTONE (20th-Fox, 1939) or that Don Ameche's selfless love for Alice Faye in ALEXANDER'S RAGTIME BAND (20th-Fox, 1938) actually makes him prefer to see her fulfilled rather than to hold her to himself.

I believe it was due to King's inordinate prepossession that he was so little a markedly personal intruder in his films as he was in his personal relationships. Perhaps for this reason alone his unique talent has been so indefinable to critics. His singular warmth and humanity conspired to be elusive because his customary soft focus escaped sensibilities more prepared to respond to sharply aggressive etchings. The absence of any real communion with despair left him ill-suited to recreate Ernest Hemingway's THE SUN ALSO RISES (20th-Fox, 1957), though, quixotically, Hemingway was almost effusive in his endorsement of the film. Yet, precisely this temperamental deficiency combined with King's sense of wholly intuitive gentlemanliness and appreciation of a past which was simpler permitted him to create such masterpieces as TOL'ABLE DAVID (First National, 1921), STATE FAIR (Fox, 1933), and THE GUNFIGHTER (20th-Fox, 1950).

Already as a youth, Henry King had begun to act in school plays. He liked make-believe enough to incur the censure of his family with the exception of his mother who supported him even when he elected to pursue the career of an actor. He joined a local stock company. He rapidly gained experience in touring road companies. A new path seemed open before him when Wilbert Melville, manager of Lubin's West Coast studio, suggested King come to Hollywood after seeing him on stage in New York. King turned down the suggestion to accept his first opportunity to direct a play in Chicago. However, his approach to directing struck the players as so untoward that they complained to the management and he was fired. Then he did go to California. King had thought that his blue eyes could not be photographed. Melville had told him that such was no longer the case. The color of his eyes notwithstanding, King's first film role was that of a Mexican in A FALSE FRIEND (Lubin, 1913). Although King did act in a number of short films, he was usually cast as a villain. He found the new industry unstable and financing was a continuing problem. He spent too much time idle rather than before the camera.

It occurred to him that he might try his hand at writing a scenario. WHO PAYS? (Balboa-Pathé, 1915) was the result. Set in King's native Virginia, the story tells of a tragic love affair between a young boy and girl. The action centers around a school commencement. The two lovers are forced by circumstances to separate, but before their parting they cannot say enough to each other in the little time they have together. When the boy leaves, the girl, despondent, commits suicide. King wrote a role in the picture for himself and Ruth Roland was given the feminine lead. Pathé released the picture in twelve three-reel episodes. The film, thus blocked in a chapter-play format, proved a considerable success and the title anticipated the final title card: "Who pays?"

Increasingly, King found that he preferred directing. His last role of any kind in front of the camera was in HELP WANTED—MALE (Pathé, 1920). King left Balboa Studios in 1917, after four years there following his stint with Lubin, and joined the American Film Company, based in Niles, California. At both Balboa and American, King functioned as both producer and director with his own assistant director and cameraman. The studio, after approving a story property, would turn it over to King. American preferred to employ King directing outdoor dramas with its improvident Western star, William Russell. King found directing Westerns great fun and particularly enjoyed staging the fight sequences.

Toward the end of 1919, Thomas Ince invited King to come to see him at his studio in Culver City. Ince's office was on the second floor of a replica of Washington's home at Mount Vernon and it would later become the headquarters for David O. Selznick's studio. Ince was an energetic, hard-driven man with an unnatural pallor. He had a script titled 23½ HOURS LEAVE which he wanted King to direct.

"I'm giving you two punks," he said, "and I want two stars when you're finished."

Ince left on vacation before King had even begun shooting. The picture ran considerably over budget and schedule. In the final editing, King worked directly with the cutter, at the time an unusual practice for a director although Ince himself had been accustomed to doing it. Ince was still out of town when the completed film was ready for release. His studio manager, irked by what he felt to be King's excesses, fired him. The film won critical accolades. Ince returned in an ebullient mood, determined to place King under contract. When he learned what had happened, he fired his studio manager. It was for naught. King rejected Ince's offer.

Instead, at the behest of Robertson-Cole, he went to New York to talk to the principals. They offered to pay his expenses, but King said he preferred to pay his own way. He had a long talk with Cole. Apparently, the firm's backers had gone bankrupt. Robertson was out trying to raise new capital. After meeting with Robertson, King agreed to a one-year contract. The firm would provide him with scripts, or approve scripts he came up with on his own, much as had been the case all along, and the rest would be up to King. However, the firm's financial solvency did not improve. Money was always running out. After his contract was up, King quit. He had a better proposition from Charles H. Duell. Richard Barthelmess, who had built a substantial following acting in D.W. Griffith productions, was Duell's partner in a new company called Inspiration Pictures and King was given a fifty-percent participation. The first film would be based on a story by Joseph Hergesheimer.

" 'We had a writer on the picture, Edmund Goulding, who became a director later,' " King once told Kevin Brownlow. " 'He was an Englishman, and he didn't know too much about Virginia. There were things in the story I disagreed with. It didn't develop. I talked to Eddie about this. I talked about the boy, the type of person he was, the family he came from. I talked about the family kneeling around the chairs each night, saying their prayers, which was done in my home for as long as I can remember. But Eddie didn't quite understand what I was talking about. I took my secretary down to Virginia, and I rewrote the middle of the story and some of the things pertaining to the end. I rearranged the conflict between the girl and the boy and the intercutting of the girl escaping and the boy fighting. When I got back to New York, Eddie Goulding was very much afraid I had ruined the story. But Hergesheimer thought I had enhanced it. . . . Eddie was unhappy until the picture opened and then he found himself author of the screenplay of the best picture of the year.' "[1]

TOL'ABLE DAVID is a film that has withstood the passage of time and can still be viewed with pleasure. Its vision of pastoral America, its gentle nostalgia, and its magical images of rustic life are imperishable. The film reinforced Richard Barthelmess' popularity and it made Inspiration Pictures a viable entity. Five more pictures with Barthelmess followed, but King felt that none of them was quite the equal of the first, an attitude that was reflected at the box office.

While King was at work on what would prove his final film featuring Barthelmess, FURY (Inspiration, 1923), Charles Duell was taken with the idea of making a picture with Lillian Gish. FURY was a sea story and King had chartered a ship for sixteen days in order to get the footage at sea. When the ship docked, Duell met him with Lillian Gish. Edmund Goulding had done the scenario for FURY and he wanted to write the scenario for the Gish film which was titled THE WHITE SISTER (Inspiration-M-G-M, 1923) upon release. Goulding claimed he could complete the job in ten days. When King saw Goulding's treatment, he threw it out. Fortunately, King bumped into George V. Hobart, a Broadway playwright, and King told Hobart that he was willing to pay $1,000 a week for a *good* screenwriter—something of an indication as to his growing opinion of Goulding's abilities as a screenwriter. Hobart joined King in a short trip to Atlantic City to talk about the story line. A week later they had twelve pages of a story that King liked.

When King returned to New York, he encountered Edward Small, who was a talent agent at the time. Small said there was a good play on Broadway at the 39th Street Theatre and that King should take a look at the actor in the second act. The play was a starring vehicle for Ruth Chatterton. Ronald Coleman was the actor Small had had in mind. King was impressed and arranged to meet with him. He wanted him for the role of Giovanni, the male lead in THE WHITE SISTER. Coleman told King that he had come from England with the hope of appearing in films, but that he photographed poorly and, having been given a role in the play, felt he could not leave. King insisted on doing a screen test anyway. He slicked down Coleman's pompadour and drew a moustache on him. The four-hundred-foot test was shot three times. THE WHITE SISTER had been inspired by Lillian Gish's desire to play a nun. It was to be the first film she would make after leaving D.W. Griffith. Gish had seen Coleman in the play with Henry King and she was enthusiastic about Coleman's rushes in the screen test. The picture was to be filmed in Italy. Coleman agreed to play in it. He was signed at $450 a week. Gish was getting $1,000 a week.

"Officials of the Church advised us on every religious scene," Lillian Gish wrote in THE MOVIES, MR. GRIFFITH, AND ME (1969), "to ensure its authenticity, and arranged for me to visit more than thirty cloistered orders before I decided on the one that we would use for THE WHITE SISTER—the Order of Lourdes."[2] The same order would figure prominently also in King's later film, THE SONG OF BERNADETTE (20th-Fox, 1943). Gish appears in her customary role of that era, the sainted, vestal heroine D.W. Griffith had first seen in her. According to the screenplay, Gish falls in love with Coleman. Then, believing him killed in the Great War, she decides to enter a convent. Coleman shows up after she has taken her vows and, however waveringly, Gish successfully resists him. "Perhaps King's greatest strength as a director," Clive Denton wrote, "is that constant ability to make us really believe that two people are in love."[3] I would go farther. In THE WHITE SISTER, as in THE SONG OF BERNADETTE, King could make a viewer believe in the power of faith and religious devotion in a convincing way whereas with Cecil B. DeMille in a film such as THE TEN COMMANDMENTS (Paramount, 1923) these emotions merely devolved into spectacle and sentimentality.

First National, which had been distributing Inspiration's features, declined to distribute THE WHITE SISTER on the grounds that it held little box-office promise. The film was then offered to Nicholas Schenck, president of Loew's, Inc., the theatre chain which owned Metro-Goldwyn-Mayer. Schenck was willing to distribute the picture. The picture proved a commercial success. It had cost only $300,000 to make in spite of its location shooting in Europe. King had found the Italians easy to work with and not at all the difficult and lazy bunch they were according to Fred Niblo when he was working in Italy on BEN-HUR (M-G-M, 1926).

Ronald Coleman so liked working in pictures he asked King if there were a part for him in King's next production. King wanted to make ROMOLA (Inspiration-M-G-M, 1924) based on the George Eliot novel. The location was again to be Italy. It was to be a costume drama, a much more expensive film to make with its Fifteenth-century setting, albeit once more with a religious motif, a romantic drama played out against the ravings of the fanatic Savonarola. Lillian and Dorothy Gish were to be the heroines. William Powell and Ronald Coleman were the male leads.

When Henry King returned to the United States, he signed a two-picture deal with Paramount. Both films were mediocre love stories, although the second one, ANY WOMAN (Paramount, 1925), did make some feeble attempts at comedy. ROMOLA was released after the two Paramount films and bombed at the box office. However, the picture did bring Ronald Coleman to the attention of Samuel Goldwyn. Goldwyn offered Coleman a contract, but Coleman was undecided. He felt he should stay with Henry King. King, on the other hand, urged him to accept Goldwyn's offer since, with the failure of ROMOLA, Inspiration was in financial straits. In the end, Goldwyn also offered King a contract to direct Ronald Coleman in what would prove one of his most successful pictures for Goldwyn, STELLA DALLAS (United Artists, 1925). In retrospect, it was a pathetic story, with the screenplay by Frances Marion, about a socialite, played by Coleman, who in a fit of despondency marries a woman far beneath his station played by Belle Bennett. After they have a daughter, played by Lois Moran, Coleman deserts. He falls in love again with Alice Joyce. Bennett wants her daughter to go and live with her father and his new bride so she will have greater social advantages. After some arguing about this, Moran agrees. By the fade, she is making a good society wedding and her real mother is standing outside the church in the rain looking in at the proceedings.

King remained with Goldwyn for three more pictures, a comedy titled PART-NERS AGAIN (United Artists, 1926) and two more starring Ronald Coleman, THE WINNING OF BARBARA WORTH (United Artists, 1926) and THE MAGIC FLAME (United Artists, 1927). The story is quite well known, I suppose, of how Gary Cooper came down from Montana, intent on a career in pictures. He wanted to play Abe Lee in THE WINNING OF BARBARA WORTH. King spotted him on the Goldwyn lot and hired him as a rider to go out on location to the Black Rock Desert in Nevada. When problems developed in casting the role of Lee, King thought he would give Cooper a chance. He rehearsed him in the scene where he knocks on a cabin door after having ridden for twenty-four hours, only to collapse, falling to the floor once Coleman opens the door. Goldwyn, overseeing the filming, peeked through the canvas backdrop of the exterior while the scene was being rehearsed. He told King subsequently that he thought Cooper a great actor and he wanted to sign him.

Vilma Banky played opposite Coleman in THE WINNING OF BARBARA WORTH and she was again cast opposite him in THE MAGIC FLAME. Studio publicity played up a torrid romance between them. In THE MAGIC FLAME Coleman had a dual role, as a prince in pursuit of Banky and as a clown whom Banky is pursuing. After TWO LOVERS (United Artists, 1928) directed by Fred Niblo, Goldwyn split up this duo. For one reason, Banky had married Rod La Rocque; for another, her salary when combined with Coleman's made their joint vehicles too expensive; and, for a third, Goldwyn wanted to work on Banky's thick Hungarian accent in preparation for talking pictures. However, Banky wearied of the kinds of roles Goldwyn was assigning to her and finally quit. Coleman went on to become a major star in the early sound era and still had a wide following when he died in 1958. For a time, in the late 'Twenties, Ronald Coleman and Vilma Banky were among the screen's great love teams and surely some degree of their popularity was owed to Henry King's sensitive direction, his facility to depict romantic love poetically and convincingly.

Joseph Schenck, in charge of United Artists, produced a certain number of pictures himself every year for United Artists release. He was aware of the fine work King had been doing for Goldwyn and asked him to direct a picture with Norma Talmadge, THE WOMAN DISPUTED (United Artists, 1928). Schenck took an extremely proprietary interest in any film he produced but nowhere so much as when one starred Norma Talmadge. The screenplay concerned a self-sacrificing heroine who gives up her life for the sake of Austria and her true love. King directed the film for Schenck and then agreed to return to Inspiration for a new three-picture deal, even though these films would have lower budgets than had his previous films for the firm. United Artists would release the films. King began directing the first of them, SHE GOES TO WAR (United Artists, 1929), when Schenck got in touch with him. Schenck was unhappy about the ending of THE WOMAN DISPUTED and wanted King to come back to the set to reshoot the concluding scenes. King read over the new scenes Schenck gave him and then begged off because of SHE GOES TO WAR. Schenck called in Sam Taylor, who was under contract to Goldwyn, to finish the film the way he wanted it. Taylor brought along his first assistant director, Lucky Humberstone. After Taylor shot the new scenes, they were screened for Henry King. King did not like them and an altercation arose. Taylor alleged that his few scenes were so vastly superior to anything King had contributed to the picture that he should be given sole screen credit for direction, a position King could have scarcely been expected to endorse. Schenck decided the matter by assigning them co-directing credits.

Although SHE GOES TO WAR had some part-talkie sequences, Henry King's first complete sound film was HELL HARBOR (United Artists, 1930). It was made on location in Florida with Lupe Velez cast as the head-strong descendant of a pirate. It was cheaply made but not as much a disaster as the third and final picture for Inspiration, EYES OF THE WORLD (United Artists, 1930), which had Sol Lesser as the production supervisor. Lesser was already then one of Hollywood's low low-budget producers.

After a dispute while on loan-out to Samuel Goldwyn, John Ford walked out on his contract with the Fox Film Corporation and took off for the Orient with his close friend, George O'Brien. Fox had scheduled him to remake LIGHTNIN' (Fox, 1925) which he had made as a silent film. The remake would be a sound film. Henry King was hired to direct it instead.

"I didn't like those last three Inspiration pictures," Henry King said, as we relaxed in a spacious booth at the Hollywood Brown Derby after having left his office a block away. "The budgets were very low. I took my money and went to work for Fox."

It was but the beginning of what would prove an uninterrupted thirty-year association between that studio and Henry King.

## II

LIGHTNIN' (Fox, 1930) was a far more elaborate production than the Ford version had been. Will Rogers was aptly cast as Lightnin' Bill Jones, a man who loves to drink, married to Louise Dresser. Together they own a hotel which happens to be built on property that is slated for a right of way for the railroad. Joel McCrea was cast as a lawyer in love with Helen Cohan, playing the Jones' adopted daughter. When two confidence men try to buy the hotel, Lightnin' refuses to sell. They then convince Dresser to divorce him so she can get the hotel as a settlement and sell it to them. The casting was very appealing and the picture opened to favorable notices and a good box office.

Sol Wurtzel was general manager of the studio. Winfield Sheehan was in charge of production. Fox decided that the studio would now embark on an extensive program of sound remakes of silent films which had been successful. When George O'Brien and John Ford returned from their travels, O'Brien, who was under contract, was put at once into a new Western series based on scripts from Tom Mix films from the 'Twenties, many of them adapted from novels by Zane Grey. Ford wanted more independence. Never again would he be loaned out to anyone. While he would make more films for Fox than any other studio over the next twenty years, the best he would agree to was a split contract. Henry King was assigned a series of remakes by Wurtzel and by agreeing to go under an exclusive contract he and not John Ford was now regarded as the leading director on the Fox lot with, increasingly, his choice among the top properties acquired by the studio.

MERELY MARY ANN (Fox, 1931), King's second picture for Fox, had been made twice before, in 1916 and 1920. This newest version starred the popular romantic team of Janet Gaynor and Charles Farrell. Although the film was not produced on a scale comparable to King's romances with Banky and Coleman, he was able to bring to the portrayals of his principals the same secure sense of tenderness and warmth in a story about a composer and the hard-working girl who is in love with him. OVER THE HILL (Fox, 1931) harked back to STELLA DALLAS with its theme of motherly devotion, starring Mae Marsh and James Kirkwood as a middle-aged couple, James Dunn as their son, and Sally Eilers as the female love interest. THE WOMAN IN ROOM 13 (Fox, 1932) was a murder mystery.

All of these films were merely a prelude to one of Henry King's best pictures of the decade, the original and, to my way of thinking, finest version of STATE FAIR (Fox, 1933). Upon completion of THE WOMAN IN ROOM 13, King had been given three months off. He was told by Wurtzel to read Phil Strong's STATE FAIR (1932) because the Fox office in New York wanted to know if it were suitable for screen adaptation. King read the story and loved it. He urged Sheehan in New York to buy it. He went so far, in the telegram that he sent, to say that he was willing to purchase the rights if Fox did not. King waited a month without a reply. The Fox Film Corporation was in all manner of difficulties because of the recent stock manipulations of its president and founder, William Fox, in his effort to seize control of Loew's, Inc., and Metro-Goldwyn-Mayer. For a time, it appeared as if he would be successful, but then came the economic panic of the Depression, the unsecured credit, the questionable stock issues, the suits charging monopoly and unfair trade, all of which involved Fox in a long series of court battles which would finally result in his imprisonment. In addition to the studio, Fox owned an extensive theatre network and a series of exchanges throughout the world. To maintain a full release schedule, a distribution contract was signed between Fox and E.W. Hammons to distribute for a period of five years all of the independent films that Hammons released from a number of small independent companies, such as Tiffany and WorldWide. The George O'Brien Western series, although successful, was subcontracted to Sol Lesser with Lesser financing and Fox releasing. True, Fox Film Corporation had contracted Shirley Temple as a consequence of her work in one of Hammons' Educational Pictures short subjects and she would prove an overnight sensation, doing for the studio in the 'Thirties what Tom Mix had done for it in the 'Twenties, but in 1933 that was still a year away.

Sheehan went to Europe and then came out to the West Coast. He told King that he had bought STATE FAIR, but he wondered what they were to do with it. King said he wanted to star Will Rogers in the picture. Sheehan objected that Rogers' last two pictures had been poorly received and that he would probably be disastrous to the enterprise. Why not feature unknowns, which would also be less expensive? Rather than argue further, King and Sonya Levien, of the Fox story department, went to work on a treatment. One Sunday, King got a call from Sheehan instructing him to report the next day to talk about STATE

FAIR. It turned out that Sheehan had just seen GRAND HOTEL (M-G-M, 1932), a star-studded extravaganza directed by King's former scenarist, Edmund Goulding. Sheehan wanted Fox to make a picture that would outdo M-G-M. King could use Will Rogers if he would also produce a screenplay that would have substantial roles for Janet Gaynor, Robert Montgomery, and Spencer Tracy.

"You have until tomorrow to give me your answer," Sheehan said.

King knew that in order to accommodate Sheehan's notion the entire script would have to be rewritten. Spencer Tracy proved unavailable, so studio casting substituted Lew Ayres in his place. Jack Gardner, in casting, brought Victor Jory to King's attention. King felt Jory to be ideal. It marked his debut. Because Louise Dresser had been so good with Will Rogers in LIGHTNIN' and since *that* film had proved a viable Will Rogers vehicle, King again cast her opposite Rogers. Norman Foster played their son and Sally Eilers was cast, again as in Jory's case, at the recommendation of Jack Gardner. In the meantime, the screenplay was bogged down. Paul Green had been a professor of English at the University of North Carolina who, on the basis of a stage play he had written, had been hired by Warner Bros. to do an original screenplay. King ran into Green and brought up the problems he was having. Green agreed to work ten days on the screenplay, during which time he rewrote the opening. King was able to give Janet Gaynor the finished script to read just at the time when she was going to Palm Springs for the weekend. He warned her that it was still in need of considerable polishing. She telephoned him on Saturday to tell him, "I'll be the best Margy."

"And she was terrific in the role," King commented to us.

Best of all, though, was Will Rogers. The part of Abel Frake who takes his prize hog to the fair won Rogers such popularity that all of his later films, until his untimely death, were box-office triumphs.

"Will Rogers never tried to act," King said. "He was very intellectual. But he had a genuine ability to fall in love with that hog, Blueboy. I went to lunch one day while we were shooting and when I came back I found Rogers in the pen with Blueboy, sleeping, using the hog as his pillow."

When the film was premièred, Rogers sent Norman Foster a telegram declaring that Foster and Blueboy played the only believable characters in the picture.

A string of modest programmers followed, the most notable of which was perhaps ONE MORE SPRING (Fox, 1935) based on Paul Green's stage play THE HOUSE OF CONNELLY. It starred Janet Gaynor, Lionel Barrymore, Robert Young, and Shirley Temple in a small part with Lincoln Perry, who had adopted the screen name of Stepin Fetchit, cast as Scipio. Both John Ford and Henry King made effective use of Stepin Fetchit at Fox as is evidenced by this film and Ford's STEAMBOAT 'ROUND THE BEND (Fox, 1935) which starred Will Rogers. Even Louis King, Henry King's brother, assigned Perry a notable role in CHARLIE CHAN IN EGYPT (Fox, 1935). These performances run counter to the belief promulgated at the time that Stepin Fetchit's characterizations on screen were a disgrace to his race. Instead, his portrayals were actually caricatures of white prejudice.

WAY DOWN EAST (Fox, 1935) was Henry King's last film for the old Fox regime. It was, of course, a remake of the D.W. Griffith classic from 1920. King regarded the film as a great challenge. Unfortunately, Fox was financially strapped. The Shirley Temple musicals, the Will Rogers comedies, and the Charlie Chan detective series were the only consistent money-makers the studio was producing. King could not afford, as Griffith had, to film the exteriors of crossing a river on ice floes during a blizzard on location. Rather, he was confined to the back lot at Fox' Western Avenue studio. King wanted to simulate frozen eyelashes, such as Lillian Gish had had in the original. He could not. Henry Fonda was able to jump around on cakes of phony ice, but he was sweating when he did it.

"You can't act cold, if you aren't," King summed it up. "You just can't outdo nature."

Joseph Schenck, who had resigned his position with United Artists to head up a new company named Twentieth Century with Darryl F. Zanuck in charge of production, decided now to merge with the floundering Fox empire. Winfield Sheehan resigned all his offices. Sol Wurtzel stayed on as production manager for the budget unit. Henry King was able to renegotiate his contract so that for every two pictures he might direct for Twentieth Century-Fox, he could make one picture on the outside. Between the signing of this contract and his retirement, he only exercised this option once. Such proved to be the case because of the amazing professional and personal rapport which soon developed between King and Zanuck. There has been a tendency, however, to read more into this relationship than there was. "Henry King worked more years for Zanuck and made more pictures for him than any other director," Mel Gussow wrote in DON'T SAY YES UNTIL I FINISH TALKING (1971). "He was at Fox even before Zanuck, joining the company in 1930 to direct LIGHTNIN', remaining through the merger with Twentieth Century, and lingering to direct more than forty films. It was his destiny to direct many of Zanuck's personal productions. The result was that . . . there was no Henry King. He became Zanuck's alter ego, with no definable personality of his own."[4] Gussow then went on to contrast King with Ford, quoting Zanuck as having said that John Ford was the greatest visual artist who ever worked in film. This seems too extreme. There is no denying that King lacked Ford's passion and his intoxication with visual art. Perhaps a Henry King picture, as a Somerset Maugham story, can never move you to emotional extremity. Yet, art to be art need not of necessity provide you with an emotional peak. In the end, it is all a matter of the artist's predisposition and his objectives. It is possible to enjoy a film devoid of emotional peaks. Ford achieved his most stunning effects by means of his use of the camera. His most successful stories are those which tell of the fragmenting of the family, the disappearance of a way of life, an overwhelming sense of loss. Such sentiments were, for the most part, alien to Henry King. He was fundamentally an optimist, whereas Ford was often a bitter pessimist. Even when King was filming a story such as THE GUNFIGHTER, which is rife with themes common to Ford's films, there is an element of dignity and resilience that remains unscathed, an element that in a Ford film usually transformed itself into sentimentality.

From the start, Zanuck did at Fox what he had done at Warner Bros. He would screen all the rushes on all the pictures produced by his ''A'' unit, conferring with his directors, telling them of changes he thought should be made. Zanuck was fond of fast pacing. He insisted on tight editing on all his pictures. He made much of Lucky Humberstone's pacing in CHARLIE CHAN AT THE RACE TRACK (20th-Fox, 1936) and Humberstone owed a measure of his success at the studio to his penchant for rapid pacing. Henry King was a director of grace and moderation. ''If on several projects King was able to slow down the inexorable Fox machinery,'' Clive Denton wrote, ''in other instances the sweeping hand of Zanuck seems in evidence. . . . If we can agree that King's career has not been only under-rated but insufficiently evaluated on any terms, then how strange it is that such adulation as he has received should have centered on work not fully characteristic of the man. Both TWELVE O'CLOCK HIGH (20th-Fox, 1949) and THE GUNFIGHTER possess elements of tautness and suspense more native to Zanuck than to King.''[5] (This is, of course, conjectural, but their respective records before and after this period surely bear out the opinion.) This may, indeed, be true, for Zanuck's zeal for speed in narrative development and rapid editing may have begun to affect both the length and character of Henry King's films, but, by way of contrast, John Ford's films, also submitted to Zanuck for screening, still managed valiantly to sag in the middle! King commented to me that he often found Zanuck's criticisms and comments a valuable adjunct. Moreover, Zanuck, in King's opinion, tended to favor the way in which King directed films and, consequently, it was on this basis that Henry King was generally assigned to pictures that were among the studio's best properties. It was in terms of personal taste that the two men were closest.

Zanuck rarely visited a director's set because he wished to keep his mind clear when he screened rushes to all hours of the night and morning. It was possibly this trait, more than any other, which kept Ford with Zanuck for over a decade. Ford detested interference of any kind. The only time he appreciated Zanuck's physical presence on one of his sets was when Ford was pouting over some insult, real or imagined, and would sullenly chew on his handkerchief off in a corner until Zanuck could bring about a reconciliation between Ford and a troublesome actor who might have dared to have an original idea about how a role should be played and to have voiced it to Ford. There is no question that Zanuck exercised a certain control over Ford's pictures. When I related to Ford that Zanuck had told me that the one scene which proved what a great visual artist Ford was occurs at the very end of MY DARLING CLEMENTINE (20th-Fox, 1946), Ford snapped back that he wasn't surprised to hear it since that was the ending Zanuck had wanted for the film and not the one he had wanted. If King proved more malleable when it came to Zanuck, it wasn't merely a matter of temperament. King tended to listen to Zanuck because he respected his cinematic perspectives and felt that his opinions were valuable. Zanuck, after all, differed from Samuel Goldwyn and David O. Selznick, who upon occasion could make far better pictures as has already been said, in that he could make *more* fine pictures at greater speed and in larger quantities than they ever could have. In King's estimation, Zanuck was in a class with Irving Thalberg, in his capacity to put a film together, to work creatively with a director, and to comment from a distance on what the director might have been too close to on a daily basis to assess properly. Since Zanuck and King liked the same kinds of stories—and both were in accord on the pre-eminent importance of a strong storyline—and since they both knew how a finished picture should look, it was only natural they should collaborate to get a result they both wanted.

## III

RAMONA (20th-Fox, 1936) was Henry King's first film under Zanuck. It was a remake of a film D.W. Griffith first made in 1910 and which was then remade by Donald Crisp in 1916 and by Edwin Carewe for Inspiration Pictures in 1928. It was a project that had already begun before Winfield Sheehan resigned and it was to be the studio's first film in the Technicolor process. King's version is perhaps no more notable than its predecessors, but the fault was not entirely his. Zanuck first pressured King to complete the film and then to interrupt production on it. A woman in Ontario had just given birth to quintuplets and Zanuck was convinced that this made for the greatest possible love story. For ten days after it was highly publicized in the Hearst papers, Zanuck could talk of nothing else. He told Nunnally Johnson to get some kind of story on paper and had Sonya Levien hold regular story conferences with King. They all worked from eleven at night until two in the morning, dictating to two stenographers in order to get out a screenplay. Once the screenplay was finished, Zanuck wanted the film to go into production at once. He signed the Dionne quintuplets to appear as themselves in the picture. Dr. Allan Roy Dafoe, who had delivered the quintuplets, served as technical advisor on the film which upon release was titled THE COUNTRY DOCTOR (20th-Fox, 1936). Jean Hersholt starred as Dr. John Luke, a role which served as the beginning of his portrayals of small country doctors, most notably in the Dr. Christian programmers. In view of the havoc and how much he spent on it, Zanuck was indeed fortunate that the film did show a small profit. King then returned to RAMONA, with some of the impetus gone. It had a negative cost of $600,000 because of the expense of the color film stock.

The studio had acquired a story by Steven Bush titled "Mrs. O'Leary's Cow" and Zanuck assigned Lamar Trotti and Sonya Levien to fashion a screenplay based on it. King, who had followed RAMONA with LLOYDS OF LONDON

(20th-Fox, 1936) and SEVENTH HEAVEN (20th-Fox, 1937), saw in this property his chance to win an Academy Award and his enthusiasm mounted when Zanuck informed him that he was willing to spend as much on the picture as it would require to make it a first-rate production. King wanted there to be a musical number in the picture and both he and Zanuck were so pleased with the result—"In Old Chicago"—that it was decided to make it the title of the film. King went to Honolulu to work on the screenplay. While he was gone, Zanuck got the idea in his head that Henry King would be the ideal director for HEIDI (20th-Fox, 1937), a perfect vehicle for Shirley Temple and Jean Hersholt and for Henry King given its inherent family values and pastoral setting. Lucky Humberstone who worked in the Fox "B" unit had also been badgering Zanuck for a chance at a really big picture. Since IN OLD CHICAGO (20th-Fox, 1938) would be a semi-musical, something for which Henry King was not particularly known but something which seemed perfect for Humberstone, Zanuck wired King that it was his intention to take King off IN OLD CHICAGO so he could direct HEIDI. King was deeply distressed and returned at once to the studio. He told Zanuck that he wanted Clark Gable for IN OLD CHICAGO and that he had every intention of directing the film. Zanuck was obviously in a quandary. He conceded that King could still direct the picture, but no Gable. King then proposed Tyrone Power as an alternative. Zanuck balked. It was probably a strategy. If King could not get whom he wanted, he might surrender the film. It didn't work. King walked off the lot and stayed away for ten days. Zanuck and Kenneth MacGowan, associate producer on IN OLD CHICAGO, then had King back for a meeting. Zanuck said King could have Tyrone Power.

"He's younger than Gable," was how he put it.

However, after the meeting, Zanuck took King aside and told him how he thought Lucky Humberstone was a director who showed promise. He had assured Humberstone that he could work on a big picture. Would King agree to letting Humberstone assist him? In this, King was willing to co-operate. He proposed that Humberstone supervise the second unit work which would be filmed on location in Yuma, Arizona.

"I've known Lucky Humberstone for some years now," I once said to Henry King as we sat in the study of his North Hollywood home, sunlight streaming in at the windows. "He has his own interpretation of what happened."

"Well," King responded, his tanned face benign and relaxed, "I can only tell what I remember. I told Lucky to do whatever the cinematographer, Fred Sersen, told him to do. As I recall, Lucky had no part in the actual fire sequences. He was instructed by Sersen to shoot the scene with Mrs. O'Leary riding along in her buggy. A fire wagon runs into her and the buggy tips over. I was informed that Lucky had requested a hundred extras to be included in that scene. I talked him out of it. We were filming on the back lot by this time, both of us. Lucky was rehearsing this one scene all day long. I was farther down the street where the fire had broken out and buildings were burning. Tyrone Power was searching for his brother and found him. The set was so hot we had to sprinkle it with water. A lot of the fire was a result of optical printing and special effects. I shot all of the fire scenes in one day. The next day the production manager screened our rushes. He thought Humberstone's footage didn't fit. He was all for firing him. I felt Lucky should be kept on the picture. After all, the big scenes had already been filmed. Lucky was only to handle the scenes of going to the fire, nothing of the fire.''

''According to Lucky,'' I said, ''you were angered when he ran advertisements in THE HOLLYWOOD REPORTER and VARIETY naming himself as having directed the fire in IN OLD CHICAGO. He said you called him every dirty name there is because you thought his attitude cost you the Academy Award on the picture, that his claim amounted almost to a co-director's credit.''

''We were heated, both of us, that's true,'' King replied.

''He alleges you had him kicked off the lot,'' Vicki said softly.

''I was nettled at his egotism. What irked me about the whole business was that he had nothing on which to base the claims he made at the time. But he had talent and he showed it later in his own films.''

On balance, IN OLD CHICAGO is a deeply flawed film. The first half seems, with its elaborate production numbers, to be almost a musical; the second half, with the spectacular fire sequences, is a sheer action picture. Tyrone Power, cast as an O'Leary son, falls in love with dance hall queen Alice Faye and somehow manages to come up with enough money to build the most ostentatious dance hall in Chicago. Despite his youthful appearance, combined with a rather ingenuous screen presence, Power is able to manipulate elections and control all the powers there be in the toughest city in the Midwest. Don Ameche was cast as Power's rather stiff and proper brother whom Power has elected mayor on a reform ticket only for Ameche to include Power and his establishment in a general clean-up. Ultimately, Power's character is an ambivalent one, especially when he has his brother marry him to Alice Faye only to announce afterwards that his reason for doing it was so she could not testify against him. Ameche is killed in the fire and, of course, Power has a change of heart by the fade, and Faye takes him back. The most visually striking scenes come at the very opening of the film when the O'Leary wagon is moving across the plains. This is sheer poetry and the kind of thing at which Henry King was best. In having wanted Clark Gable for the leading role, undoubtedly King had in mind an unofficial remake of SAN FRANCISCO (M-G-M, 1936) in which Gable played a character very similar to that played by Power in IN OLD CHICAGO, a film that also ends with a catastrophic disaster.

The same principals were back for ALEXANDER'S RAGTIME BAND, a musical with lyrics and music by Irving Berlin. Tyrone Power was cast as Alexander whose band fares poorly until Alice Faye joins it as its headline singer. She marries Don Ameche, the band's piano player, and it isn't until Ameche comes to realize that she really loves Power that he is willing to step aside so, after a few more complications, the two can be finally united at the end. It was an enjoyable entertainment, but it only set the stage for Henry King's next two films which, I think, rank among the best of his work in the sound era: JESSE JAMES (20th-Fox, 1939) and STANLEY AND LIVINGSTONE. While it is true that Zanuck was very partial to historical and biographical films and both of these fall into that category, King did leave his personal stamp upon them. Tyrone Power was cast as Jesse and Henry Fonda as Frank James with Randolph Scott as a sympathetic lawman and Nancy Kelly as Jesse's wife. Henry Hull was cast as a rambunctious newspaper editor who felt the James brothers were victims of all manner of conniving, in particular on the part of Donald Meek in an off-beat role as the head of a railroad. John Carradine played Bob Ford who shoots Jesse at the end. King insisted to me that he had had the subject thoroughly researched before work on the screenplay was begun and that Nunnally Johnson had derived most of his screen story from actual newspaper accounts. However, when I asked why, in the bombing episode, Jesse's mother was shown as having been killed rather than merely maimed he shook his head and confessed that he honestly could not remember why that had been included. Yet, in viewing the film, the reason is somewhat evident. It was King's intention to engender sympathy for Jesse and this fictitious event, along with a number of others which have no basis in historical reality, tends to have precisely that effect. Such a posture, of course, would have been daring a decade earlier. Fred Thomson's career as a movie cowboy was virtually ruined when in 1927 in one of his films he tried to portray Jesse James in a favorable light. The public outcry at the time was amazing. However, more recently Roy Rogers had played a member of Jesse's gang in a "B" Western and audiences accepted it with equanimity. In fact, it was a trend in the middle decades to make heroes out of traditional Western villains, a tendency which over the years since then has reversed itself a number of times.[6]

King found an ideal location for the picture on the border of Missouri and Arkansas and it was here that he filmed one of the unforgettable sequences, along a strip of railroad track which paralleled a road with only forty feet between them. In the sequence, at twilight the members of the James gang jump one after the other on top of a moving train, silhouetted against the darkening sky as they scurry along the tops of the lighted cars. The whole scene had to be shot in fifteen minutes. The interiors of the Pullman cars were illumined by very intense lights. The images of the passengers were cardboard cutouts. The train had to be paced. King was on the train. The first night, from the train, he signalled the camera car to start. The cameraman signalled the engineer in the locomotive. The train was rolling at 35mph when King inadvertently fell off. That was a wrap for that day. The next day the scene was filmed in a single, long take. All interiors and some exteriors were filmed in Hollywood. It cost $900,000 to make but it did so well at the box office that Zanuck followed it with a sequel, THE RETURN OF FRANK JAMES (20th-Fox, 1940), directed by German Expressionist director, Fritz Lang. While on location, King gave Tyrone Power flying lessons.

What is most personal to Henry King in JESSE JAMES has to do with the sense of family and the domestic scenes. When the film was still in preproduction, King had flown to the James farm and talked to Robert F. James, Frank James' son, a retired lawyer. They had sat in the backyard and talked. King got the impression that the James family had been a good one; the stepfather had been a minister, reminding him no doubt of how his own family had wanted him to study for the Methodist clergy. He saw the window where the bomb had been thrown in during the trouble with the railroad detectives and he saw where Frank James was buried, next to a cherry tree, although tourists had whittled away the headstone. It was King's custom, when preparing a screenplay, to go into seclusion and he did so with the partially completed script for JESSE JAMES. He rented a house on the beach near Tampa, Florida, for $35 a month. He would run in the morning, then swim, before driving to a tea room for breakfast. He would work two hours, swim again, work till five o'clock, eat dinner, work until nine, then swim, and go to bed. In ten days, the script was ready. In Jesse's longing for a family life much as he had had when growing up is that characteristic King nostalgia, a longing that cannot be fulfilled, as increasingly came to be the case in King's films beginning with JESSE JAMES. The facile happy endings so typical of King's Fox films in the 'Thirties were replaced by endings far more ambiguous.

Zanuck had wanted King to direct STANLEY AND LIVINGSTONE before JESSE JAMES, but King had objected on the grounds that the script was terrible. It was totally rewritten by the time JESSE JAMES was completed. Spencer Tracy was excited about the part of Henry M. Stanley. Sir Cedric Hardwicke was cast as Dr. Livingstone and Walter Brennan was just as sagely cast as Jeff Slocum, Stanley's guide and comrade. Nancy Kelly played Eve Kingsley, the woman with whom Stanley falls in love in one of the most touching of King's screen romances only for her to end up married to Richard Greene while Stanley carries on Livingstone's work in Africa. All of the African location work was filmed by the second unit which neither King nor the principals accompanied. Tracy's added narration contributed significantly to the universally fine characterizations by all the players and provided the finished film with almost a symphonic quality, a picture that can be viewed repeatedly without diminishing the beauty of its effects, although the biographical elements are as romanticized as those in JESSE JAMES.

Henry King made three more films before he directed a film based on a screen story by Zanuck, A YANK IN THE R.A.F. (20th-Fox, 1941). It was followed by REMEMBER THE DAY (20th-Fox, 1941), an evocative film about a female schoolteacher's life in the middle America vein so dear to King. THE BLACK SWAN (20th-Fox, 1942) was the last film King directed before he, as Zanuck, joined the Armed Services. However, his military career didn't last very long. The same progressive, even aggressive, political spirit which led Zanuck to produce a propaganda film such as A YANK IN THE R.A.F. congealed into a tempestuous idea for the cinematic biography of Woodrow Wilson. Zanuck believed it an extremely topical notion to depict near the end of one war the tribulations of a President of the United States at the end of a previous war. He became so obsessed with his concept he even managed to get Henry King released from service to work on the picture.

During the time King had been away from the studio, a great many tests had been conducted, trying to cast THE SONG OF BERNADETTE. King found himself assigned to this picture before he could even commence work on WIL-SON (20th-Fox, 1944). He favored Linda Darnell for the title role, but Joseph Schenck suggested that before King come to any final decision he should see the screen tests Jennifer Jones had made for David O. Selznick. King screened her tests and invited the Selznick *protégée* to the studio. He wanted to do an additional test with her. He placed her in front of a painted backdrop with stones on the stage in front of her. Since the part would require of her that she talk and act as if she were addressing somebody no one else could see, he felt by testing how effectively she could pretend to put water around the rocks he would get some idea of her abilities at imaginative projection. Jones made it seem credible. There were further tests. King tried testing the apparition, first with Jones and Roman Bohner, then with Jones alone with the Virgin. There was quite a bit of argument about whether or not the apparition should actually be shown. King was inclined *not* to photograph the Virgin. Zanuck, when he returned to the studio for a brief visit, questioned this decision. King pointed out to Zanuck that if the audience believed Jennifer Jones saw the apparition, that should be sufficient. Zanuck finally acceded but Bill Goetz, in charge of studio operations during Zanuck's absence, didn't want Jones in the picture at all, apparition or no apparition. After all, prior to Selznick's "discovery" of her all she had done in pictures was to appear in low-grade Republic Westerns and a Dick Tracy serial. King assembled Jones' tests and asked Goetz to screen them all. After seeing the tests, Goetz gave his approval. Ten minutes after Jennifer Jones was told that Henry King had selected her, Selznick telephoned King to thank him. The role would win an Academy Award for her.

"Jennifer was peculiar to work with," Henry King said, sitting near the small shrine he had constructed in his home showing Jones in the role of the visionary. "She really listened. She only required one take to do a scene. You could feel her during rehearsals—you could feel her build. You could tell when she was ready to do the scene. She was so enraptured with being in the picture that she seemed in a trance—which was a good thing for that particular role."

George Seaton did the screenplay, based on a novel by Franz Werfel who was among the German political refugees then living in the United States. He had married Gustav Mahler's widow and, I imagine, was encouraged as much in high-blown, grandiloquent statements by his wife, as she had once similarly encouraged Mahler. Seaton went to the extreme of incessantly blessing the Virgin throughout the script. King deleted all the recreations of the visions. When Werfel was told that the Virgin would be nowhere in evidence, he wanted the scenes put back. Zanuck, when consulted, suggested that to keep peace King should try shooting the visions with Linda Darnell as the Virgin, dressed in blue.

Seaton was so displeased with these scenes that he had them screened for Werfel. They incensed the author even more and he threatened to damn the whole enterprise in a letter to THE NEW YORK TIMES if the scenes were not deleted at once. King still did not want *any* scenes of the Virgin. Now Werfel wanted different ones. King proposed, as a compromise, that only the Virgin's feet be shown, and filmed it that way, with an extra suspended over a bush photographed from her ankles down. This strategy pleased no one. In the final release version, the full figure of the Virgin was back.

In the meantime, Zanuck was becoming extremely impatient. He wanted King to quit the picture altogether so he could get on with WILSON. When he looked at a rough cut of THE SONG OF BERNADETTE, he thought the film much too slow, filled with static, tedious scenes, such as Jones endlessly scrubbing floors. A film that slow would fail, visions or no visions. So he undertook to edit the picture, speeding it up. However, when Jones won her award, she would show her knees and claim that it was all that scrubbing of floors which had done it for her!

Zanuck was a progressive, perhaps, but he wasn't a Democrat. He prided himself on his friendship with President Roosevelt but no one had worked more arduously for the election of Wendell Willkie than had Zanuck. Zanuck was a fighter who believed that American involvement, militarily and economically, in the world at large was the thing that would bring peace and he regarded Willkie as the greatest potential peacemaker in national politics since Wilson. Henry King may have been credited for the direction, but most of the credit—or, should I say, discredit?—for WILSON belongs to Zanuck. For the first time, Zanuck was constantly on the set, watching every scene as it was filmed. He was continually conferring with Lamar Trotti, who did the screenplay, changing the action or altering the dialogue. He was perpetually discussing with Henry King how each sequence should be directed. Zanuck spent three and a half million on the film. Upon release, it died not so much bitterly as suddenly, even though Zanuck had gone all out to promote it. As part of the publicity campaign, Zanuck arranged a visit to his hometown of Wahoo, Nebraska, loading a train with Hollywood celebrities. It was all for naught. "Why," Zanuck's hometown physician had said to him, "should they pay seventy-five cents to see Wilson on the screen when they wouldn't pay ten cents to see him alive?" Three years later Zanuck was still so irritated by the indifference to WILSON that, upon receiving an award from the Academy for GENTLEMAN'S AGREEMENT (20th-Fox, 1947), he told the audience that he should have got the Oscar for WILSON—and he wasn't joking.

King's most exceptional post-war films, other than the moody A BELL FOR ADANO (20th-Fox, 1945) with John Hodiak, Gene Tierney, and William Bendix, were three pictures he directed, all starring Gregory Peck. They were TWELVE O'CLOCK HIGH, THE GUNFIGHTER, and THE SNOWS OF KILIMANJARO (20th-Fox, 1952).

The opening of TWELVE O'CLOCK HIGH is still compelling. Dean Jagger, alone in England after the war, visits again the airstrip from which American bomber planes were dispatched daily across the channel. The airstrip is deserted, the cement cracked; water stands in pools; the sky is overcast. Quietly on the track the voices of American fliers are heard singing the songs they were accustomed to sing in the canteen. Then the propellers are heard, the engines revving up for take-off. The rest is flashback to the time when Gregory Peck, as an air force general, was appointed to command the station, replacing Gary Merrill who allowed himself to become too emotionally involved with the fate of his men. As such, the story isn't exactly new. Howard Hawks, among others, dealt with a similar theme in DAWN PATROL (Warner's, 1930). What is novel and fresh is King's approach. He had trouble with Peck and found himself having to shoot several scenes over because Peck had some difficulty playing a general. He tended to overact or otherwise behave in a way that a general would not be expected to behave. The extra time and care paid off. It was one of Peck's most convincing roles.

Millard Mitchell, who had given a fine account of himself as Peck's commanding officer in TWELVE O'CLOCK HIGH, was back for THE GUN-FIGHTER, this time as a sympathetic sheriff. Although he received no credit, the basic idea of the film was due to Nunnally Johnson. The story concerns an aged gunfighter who would like to divest himself of his reputation and no longer have to prove himself to every young upstart whom he meets. Peck liked the story and he wanted Henry King to direct the picture, convinced that King could make him better in the role. Also, unlike TWELVE O'CLOCK HIGH, this story would concentrate on him alone, not on several stories. Zanuck insisted that it be filmed in black and white. He felt that the drab background would enhance the bleakness and tragedy of the story line, much as it had William Wellman's THE OX-BOW INCIDENT (20th-Fox, 1943). Zanuck then left for Europe. King told Peck to grow a moustache for the part. Nunnally Johnson objected to this innovation. He said that a hero in a Western could not wear a moustache. King responded that Peck had last played a general.

"You can't just take off a uniform and become a cowboy," he told Johnson.

When Zanuck returned and screened the finished picture, his comment to King was "it's a Rembrandt, but I don't like the moustache." Zanuck was certain Peck's fans would resent it, but he needn't have worried. The film had both a reassuring box office and a warm critical response. It still stands as somewhat unique in that eccentric trend, beginning with LAW AND ORDER (Universal, 1932), in which the hero does not triumph at the end. Other classic Westerns of the decade, HIGH NOON (United Artists, 1952) and SHANE (Paramount, 1953) prominently among them, were still firmly couched in a traditional ending. While he made very few Westerns, in THE GUNFIGHTER and later in THE BRAVADOS (20th-Fox, 1958), also with Gregory Peck, Henry King penetrated behind the usually brittle veneer of clearly defined heroes and villains which was such a convention in Westerns and sought to reveal the interiors of the characters. In a Western, a viewer is accustomed to watch the action, never really questioning it and, therefore, never suspecting it of possessing any depth beyond its surface. It is not so in Henry King's two Westerns of the 'Fifties. When it came to innovations, he was still in the vanguard and it would not be until the 'Seventies that Westerns generally would deal so harshly with accepted story lines and conventions.

Twentieth Century-Fox brought more of Ernest Hemingway's stories to the screen than any other studio and Henry King worked on two of them, THE SNOWS OF KILIMANJARO and the jinxed THE SUN ALSO RISES. In retrospect, the two films are especially noteworthy for spanning that period during which Darryl F. Zanuck's inspired leadership of the studio and the life-style he had defined for himself began to undergo major fragmentation. He became, as a Hemingway protagonist, a man increasingly alienated from his surroundings and went off in search of vague answers to questions he could not quite formulate.

Casey Robinson, who did the screenplay for THE SNOWS OF KILIMANJARO, expanded the story to include more than a writer's struggles with physical illness and spiritual malaise. He incorporated a number of flashbacks which were suggestive of the narrative of A FAREWELL TO ARMS (1928) and, possibly also, touches from THE SUN ALSO RISES (1926). Hemingway had once felt that Africa, relatively unplundered as it was when he first went there, was wild, extravagant, brutal, uncomplicated, a place where a man could come to terms with himself. Gregory Peck, who was to star, read the screenplay and reacted negatively to it. He particularly did not like the flashbacks. He was concerned because he couldn't believe the story as Robinson told it and, if he couldn't believe it, would anyone else? King began to rewrite the story as it was being filmed and perhaps for this reason it ultimately misses the mark attained by TWELVE O'CLOCK HIGH and THE GUNFIGHTER. Hemingway was concerned with human defeat. He saw the world as a challenge in which the winner takes nothing but who, in winning, inexorably causes others to lose. Such a view was probably too alien to potential audiences, if not to King and Peck in making the film.

It was back to remakes with KING OF THE KHYBER RIFLES (20th-Fox, 1953), a film based on John Ford's THE BLACK WATCH (Fox, 1929). Although it was supposed to take place on the hot plains of British India, it was filmed on location at Lone Pine, California. Tyrone Power was the star, as he was in Henry King's next film, UNTAMED (20th-Fox, 1955), another chapter from the history of the British Empire, this time set in South Africa during the Boer War.

Henry King retained a personal affection for LOVE IS A MANY-SPLENDORED THING (20th-Fox, 1955). It was based on an autobiographical book by Han Suyin, telling of a love affair between a Eurasian and an American war correspondent. As Zanuck was spending more and more time in Europe, the studio was increasingly under the administration of Buddy Adler. Zanuck had freed himself from responsibility of having to do a set number of pictures every year and now only produced those films in which he took a personal interest.

He no longer oversaw every "A" production on the lot. When King heard that Buddy Adler would be producing the film based on Han Suyin's book, he wrote a note to Zanuck that no one could do the picture as well he could. Zanuck telephoned King and asked him if he really wanted to do the picture. "Do I usually lie to you?" King asked him. When Adler got in touch with King, it was only to tell him that he had had him in mind all along to direct the picture.

King told Adler that he wanted to go to Hong Kong to get some location footage. Adler argued that such a trip would be unnecessary. The studio already had more than sufficient footage as out-takes from Edward Dmytryk's SOLDIER OF FORTUNE (20th-Fox, 1955) which had been months shooting on location in the British Crown Colony. King disagreed. As he saw it, in his picture Hong Kong itself was to be a character, not merely a setting. Adler reluctantly gave his permission. King divided filming between Hong Kong and the Pacific Palisades. Jennifer Jones played Han Suyin. William Holden was the correspondent. King had to match one scene where Jones' footage was shot in Hong Kong with her mounting a flight of steps while Holden in the Palisades waited at the top, but it was so well executed no one could detect the difference. For her performance Jennifer Jones was nominated for an Academy Award.

THE SUN ALSO RISES was really very much Zanuck's picture, as WILSON had been. The fact that Henry King directed it was almost incidental. Howard Hawks owned screen rights to the novel. Zanuck purchased the rights from Hawks, engaging Peter Viertel, a friend of Hemingway's, to prepare the screenplay. When the script was completed, apparently without reading it Zanuck sent it on to Henry King at the studio. King read the script and wrote to Zanuck that he thought it was very bad. He did recommend, though, Ava Gardner for the role of Lady Brett, if Zanuck insisted on going ahead with the project. Zanuck had already offered the Lady Brett part to Jennifer Jones but when Jones turned it down he sent the script to Ava Gardner. She was living in Spain, close to where Hemingway himself was at the time. Ava showed the script to Hemingway and he sent Zanuck a telegram informing him that he would sue the studio if it put his name on the picture. Zanuck responded by calling a story conference in New York. Henry King was more uncertain than ever about the picture but Adler telephoned him, asking when Zanuck might expect him to be at the St. Regis Hotel in New York. The film was now to be an independent production, with Fox releasing but not financing. Zanuck was spending his own money on it. Zanuck tried a new writer on the script but they could agree on nothing and Zanuck fired him. This left him again with Viertel. When Henry King arrived in New York, Zanuck asked him what they could do to improve the script. King said that in his opinion the opening was all right but from that point on it just didn't stand up. He said if Zanuck would let him he would take the script back to California and work on it there. Once he finished with it, he proposed sending it to Zanuck and Zanuck could send it on to Viertel. King returned to Hollywood and set to work.

He decided to follow the novel and every page of his revised script had a page reference to the book. He had been working on the script for ten days when Buddy Adler called from the studio to say that Zanuck was now in England and wanted to know when he might expect the finished screenplay. The next day King sent Zanuck what he had. As soon as Zanuck received it, he summoned King to London for a story conference with Viertel. Viertel met with Hemingway and discussed the screenplay. Henry King flew to London and, once Viertel arrived, they completed it. When he read it, Hemingway commented that "finally somebody understands what I'm saying."

Zanuck began casting the picture. To play the bullfighter, he selected Robert Evans whom he had seen dancing at El Morocco. Evans had formerly been in the clothing business until Norma Shearer picked him to play her first husband, Irving Thalberg, in MAN OF A THOUSAND FACES (Universal, 1957). Evans had a shapely figure in toreador pants but acting was not his strong suit. He returned to the clothing business briefly before he became a procurer of women for Gulf & Western executives and then head of production at Paramount Pictures, a position from which he was finally fired in 1976.

Yet, the most fateful casting of all was that of the French singer Juliette Greco as Georgette. Mel Ferrer had a role in THE SUN ALSO RISES and his wife, Audrey Hepburn, who accompanied him on location to Mexico, suggested Greco for the part to Zanuck. Tyrone Power was cast as Jake Barnes and the theme of Barnes' impotence, which Hawks felt could only be dealt with comically, was treated with solemn gravity. Errol Flynn and Eddie Albert were cast as Barnes' buddies. Interiors with Greco were filmed at a rented studio in Mexico City. Zanuck and Greco were immediately attracted to each other and a tempestuous romance ensued during which Zanuck declared his total independence, becoming a producer at large, spending money without seeming limit and terming this a release from bondage. Failures, love affairs, fights with his son Richard Zanuck, a battle for control of Twentieth Century-Fox, and a return to Fox management were all in the future for Zanuck, as were his eventual return to his Palm Springs home and his wife Virginia, and his suffering from severe malnutrition. In 1957, the first of the big failures came. Upon release, THE SUN ALSO RISES was not a success even with critics.

Following THE BRAVADOS, for the first time since he had gone to work for Fox Henry King exercised his right to direct a picture for a rival company. The film was THIS EARTH IS MINE (Universal, 1959) with Jean Simmons and Rock Hudson. Casey Robinson had done the screenplay and was co-producer on the picture.

King chose Gregory Peck to play F. Scott Fitzgerald in BELOVED INFIDEL (20th-Fox, 1959), once he was back at his home studio. Deborah Kerr was cast as Sheilah Graham. In order to get Peck to play a drunk scene effectively, King had him take several drinks before shooting, enough to thicken his tongue but not enough to interfere with his ability to act. No doubt it was on the basis of this film that Spyros Skouras, who had succeeded Buddy Adler as head of the studio, asked King to direct the screen version of Fitzgerald's most problematic novel, TENDER IS THE NIGHT (20th-Fox, 1961). It would prove to be Henry King's last theatrical film. Ten years earlier David O. Selznick had wanted King to direct a picture based on the novel. King had turned him down because he felt the story in bad taste. Fox had purchased the screen rights from Selznick and Jennifer Jones was to star. With both the studio and Jones wanting him to direct it, King acquiesced. However, Ivan Moffat, in doing the adaptation, deleted the scenes to which King had most objected in the novel. In Moffat's version, the Jennifer Jones character is the villain. When Selznick, who was in Europe at the time, heard about the changes he called the studio collect and declared that he would sue Fox if anybody altered *his* concept of the novel. Skouras, Moffat, and King had a meeting with the legal department but it turned out Selznick was right. The contract the studio had with him virtually gave Selznick dictatorial control over what the studio could do with the story.

King wanted the scene where the child and her nurse both get drunk to be the nurse's fault and to show her to be negligent. Selznick, however, continued so to fret about this story twist that he pressured Jennifer Jones, by this time his wife, to exert what influence she could on King. Selznick also sent King an irate letter. Jones suggested to King that perhaps he and David should get together to talk about it. Selznick, when he returned to California, set up a meeting with King and had two writers present. King explained to Selznick that he thought it an error to deviate so far from the novel as to make the picture really the nurse's story which was Selznick's basic conception of the film. Selznick countered that he would have the two writers completely rework the script. King resisted and, through shrewd diplomacy and some help from Jennifer Jones on the home front, he finally was able to assuage Selznick's worries. King also deleted some two hundred feet from the rough cut before he would allow the picture to be released. Selznick liked the film, but King felt it no more than "got by."

Much of the challenge and joy of filmmaking seemed to disappear for Henry King in these last films—from THE SUN ALSO RISES to TENDER IS THE NIGHT—and he felt, increasingly, the time had come to depart. There was some discussion of his directing THE SOUND OF MUSIC (20th-Fox, 1965), but it was Zanuck who discouraged him by saying that musicals were dead at the box office! Back in 1915, when he was working at Balboa Studios, Henry King had written in an article for MOTOGRAPHY that working there was "more like one big family than anything else. Directors, actors, and all other employees work harmoniously to the common end of producing good pictures for their employers."[7] With Zanuck gone from Fox, and the organization he had built all but vanished, the sense of family which he had at this studio for so many more years than he had been at Balboa now had disappeared.

I might well describe Henry King's life-style in retirement as graceful. He had none of the bitterness of John Ford, who had managed to drink himself out of pictures completely, none of the dissipation of Darryl Zanuck which finally left him a physical wreck, none of the creeping senility which at last claimed

Alfred Hitchcock. Instead, Henry King had found an inner tranquility which permitted him to contemplate the past with no sense of regret whatsoever. He was affected by the past events in his life much the way Dean Jagger is affected at the end of TWELVE O'CLOCK HIGH when he mounts his bicycle again and peddles off into the peaceful English countryside. Henry King was the pastoral poet of the American cinema. He died in his sleep at the age of ninety-four on 29 June 1982.

# Alfred Hitchcock

## I

Vicki and I had occasion to screen the majority of Hitchcock's British films while living in London during the summer of 1976. It was with the keenest anticipation that every morning we boarded the tram in front of our hotel overlooking Hyde Park and rode the distance to Piccadilly. The British Film Institute, a few blocks from Piccadilly, had not only Hitchcock's British films but he had also been so well disposed that he donated to the Institute prints of some of his American theatrical features and also those episodes from his television series which he personally directed.

I cannot claim to be totally conversant with the British cinema, but many of Hitchcock's British films are sufficiently impressive still that it is easy to believe that he was regarded as the foremost British director in the 'Thirties. Many of the themes which figure so prominently in Hitchcock's later American films were anticipated, and even varied, in his melodramas after 1933, the crucial turning point in his career. More than that, the British films constitute a very different perspective than that of Hitchcock's Hollywood films and even greater than the similarities in thematic material are the differences in lighting and plot development, of setting and orientation.

Alfred Joseph Hitchcock was born 13 August 1899 in London, the son of a grocer and fruit importer. Very little of Hitchcock's childhood is known and much that was told and retold by him was found, upon investigation, to be inaccurate. For example, he often told how, as a child, his father had sent him as a punishment to the constabulary with a note requesting that he be placed in the lock-up. According to Hitchcock, the emotional effects of this incident were traumatic. Terror over his predicament and an overbearing sense of the injustice of it carried over into his adult life. Donald Spoto in his biography of Hitchcock can find no evidence to support this recollection, but that does not mean that it did not have a psychic reality quite as real and imposing as if it had actually happened. After all, as C.G. Jung once observed, "everything unconscious is projected."[1] What we do know of Hitchcock's childhood is that he was a solitary boy, much given to quietude and fanciful games in which he was the lone participant.

Hitchcock's parents, who were Roman Catholic, enrolled him in Jesuit schools and he was in mortal fear of corporal punishment. He was fascinated by geography and, even as a youth, he kept a chart of British merchant ships as they sailed about the globe and he was equally absorbed by railway time tables. After studying electrical engineering at the University of London, Hitchcock secured employment with the Henley Telegraph Company while simultaneously he studied art. When he read a newspaper advertisement that Famous Players-Lasky, later Paramount, was seeking to staff a British operation, he applied for a job in the art department, after readying a number of sketches he felt would be suitable for use on title cards illustrating silent films. He was hired and eventually became head of the title department.

When Famous Players-Lasky decided the studio at Islington was unprofitable, the installation was abandoned to a number of British companies. Hitchcock applied at Gainsborough, one of the domestic firms, and was hired in the capacity of an assistant director. Michael Balcon was head of the company. During the next two years, Hitchcock worked in various areas of film production, when not as art director or assistant director then as a production manager. He was first credited in the dual capacity of art director and assistant director on WOMAN TO WOMAN (Gainsborough, 1923) directed by Graham Cutts. It was on this picture that Hitchcock met Alma Reville, an editor and script clerk. They became engaged.

After having had Hitchcock assist him on some five pictures, Graham Cutts informed Michael Balcon in 1925 that he no longer wanted Hitchcock's services. Obviously, he felt threatened by Hitchcock's evident talent. Balcon's response was to propose to Hitchcock that he should direct a film on his own. The company had an arrangement with a German production firm for a co-production that was titled upon release THE PLEASURE GARDEN (Gainsborough, 1927). Hitchcock agreed to direct it. Virginia Valli and Carmelita Geraghty, two Hollywood actresses, had been signed to star in order to provide an American market for the film. The production had a niggardly budget and Hitchcock, among his other duties, had to manage the expense money while on location. Costs were so great in Italy that Hitchcock had to borrow money from Miles Mander, who was cast as the bounder who marries Valli. However, Mander soon wanted his money back. Alma Reville was dispatched to Paris to oversee the arrival of Valli and Geraghty. Hitchcock, to solve the problem, asked for an advance on his own salary and induced his fiancée to borrow two hundred dollars from Valli. However, she was to keep it secret that this was Hitchcock's first directorial effort.

In interviews on a number of occasions Hitchcock claimed that he was very naive about sexual matters even at twenty-five years of age. In one scene Mander was to carry out of the water the drowned body of his mistress. The actress Hitchcock engaged to play the mistress had her period and this made shooting the scene impossible. However, Hitchcock apparently had been unaware until this incident about menstruation! The substitute Hitchcock did hire to do the scene was too heavy for the diminutive Mander to carry out of the water, resulting in his dropping her several times and in numerous retakes. The German producers declared the film brutal, but Michael Balcon thought otherwise. "The surprising thing," Balcon told Hitchcock, "is that technically it doesn't look like a continental picture. It's more like an American film."[2]

Unquestionably, Hitchcock had a native genius for the medium. He also developed quickly attitudes which would remain with him. John Russell Taylor has pointed out that already while at Famous Players-Lasky, Hitchcock had come to regard actors as "merely counters in this game of chess . . . taking on significance from the way they were moved around in the course of the game. And this practical lesson came, be it noted, some three years before Kuleshov carried out his famous experiments with audience-manipulation."[3] What Kuleshov would demonstrate was that emotions in a viewer could be manipulated depending on what shot was juxtaposed with another, that the same shot of a man juxtaposed with a bowl of soup and then with a child would elicit entirely different responses, responses that were actually projections of the audience and not of the filmmaker. Following THE PLEASURE GARDEN, Hitchcock continued to work in Germany with UFA, the largest of the German producing companies. "I met all sorts of technicians while I was at UFA," he told me subsequently, "and I was forced to learn German. The first day at UFA I remember I communicated with a draftsman by drawing pictures. My first German words were, '*Wo ist mein Hut?*' I learned enough conversational German to get by, but not enough to work on dialogue. I worked on two silent films in Germany. But German films were not as good as English films." What obviously impressed Hitchcock the most about the German cinema while he was at UFA, or Universum Film Aktiengesellschaft, was the use of lighting and camera angles to provide an added dimension to straight film narrative, along with advice F.W. Murnau once gave him. What you can see on the set does not matter, Murnau assured him. The only truth that counts is what appears on the screen. In terms of theme, the German impact was also great. In the so-called German "street films," the plot was supplied by "the theme of security at home against outer social chaos . . . ," and as Donald Spoto observed "Hitchcock's films (from RICH AND STRANGE [British International, 1932] through NORTH BY NORTHWEST [M-G-M, 1959]) make it clear that he felt a spiritual kinship to this motif."[4]

Hitchcock's second British effort as a director, THE MOUNTAIN EAGLE (Gainsborough, 1927), was unremarkable, but in his third, THE LODGER (Gainsborough, 1927), he made a film that contributed significantly to his reputation and which bears all the marks of what would later become known as a "typical" Hitchcock thriller. Based on a novel by Mrs. Belloc Lowndes inspired by the Jack the Ripper murders and which also had a successful run as a stage play, THE LODGER deals with suspicion, fear, and human irrationality. When a man comes to stay at a London boarding house during a series of murders perpetrated by someone calling himself The Avenger, he is soon suspected by everyone, including the viewer, of being the culprit. Already apparent this early in his career is Hitchcock's tendency to limit story perspectives in such a fashion that the viewer becomes profoundly involved in the unfolding drama. Human behavior is observed from the *outside* so that we are free to draw certain definite, almost instinctive conclusions about its probable meaning which turn out to be all wrong, demonstrating that even the greatest certainties in life are based on the most absurd emotional responses. Brian Moore, who was the writer on TORN CURTAIN (Universal, 1966), insisted that Hitchcock was totally ignorant of human motivation. I believe that in the conventional sense he was. As Aristotle pointed out long ago, motivation is the logic which makes a drama accessible and on this basis he preferred the plays of Sophocles in which motivation can always be discerned in contrast to the dramas of Euripides in which the universe is too often perceived as being fundamentally irrational and, therefore, motivation seldom clear or decipherable. If Hitchcock was akin to either, it would be to Euripides and much that happens in his films is only comprehensible if the premise is embraced that the universe is irrational and human motivation almost always obscure. In retrospect, Hitchcock expressed regret that Ivor Novello, cast as the lodger, was a star of such substantial magnitude that he wasn't permitted to make a murderer of him. Yet, the film is effective precisely because the lodger is innocent. Hitchcock experimented with lighting and achieved an impressive mood when the shadows of lorries, trams, and cars passing the lodger's windows are reflected in suspicious movements across the ceiling and again when the lodger's fretful pacing, photographed through the transparency of a plateglass floor with the lodger walking back and forth, registers on those on the floor below, puzzled and troubled by his ceaseless movement. Almost fifteen minutes of screen time is devoted at the opening of the picture to clarifying in the viewer's mind via an interesting series of communicative devices exactly the type of women The Avenger preys upon and the viciousness of his methods. What, then, is a viewer to conclude when he watches the lodger standing silently in the hall outside the water closet, listening intently as the heroine takes a bath? The helplessness of a victim engaged in such an activity occurred to Hitchcock as early as this film although the notion would not be fully developed until PSYCHO (Paramount, 1960). "Enough indications are planted to suggest that Novello may be 'The Avenger' who goes around killing girls with golden curls," John Russell Taylor wrote, " . . . for us to consider his guilt as a serious possibility, and to find, by a typical Hitchcock switch, that we sympathize with him and want him to get away with it long before we are clearly told that he is not guilty."[5] If Hitchcock had any reason for wanting to make the lodger guilty, it could only have been his desire to manipulate the audience into wanting a murderer to escape.

Hitchcock made his first cameo appearance in THE LODGER. Over the years, it became a superstition with him, then a gag; finally, after he became a familiar figure world wide due to his television program, it proved troublesome because viewers began to wait for him to show up. He then had to appear early in the picture so as not to distract audiences from the progress of the story. The distributors were dissatisfied with THE LODGER as Hitchcock had shot it and, for a time, it was not put into release. Many changes were recommended of which Hitchcock agreed to two. When THE LODGER was released, critics hailed it as the finest British film produced to that time. It was perhaps this circumstance which persuaded him that film critics, rather than audiences, producers, or distributors, were the ones for whom he made his films. Surely, he began at this time the courtship of the press which he practiced throughout his career until after FAMILY PLOT (Universal, 1976) when he refused to see virtually anyone.

Even before THE LODGER was released, Hitchcock was approached by a rival producing firm and offered a multi-picture deal at the princely salary of thirteen thousand pounds a year. With this financial security, he and Alma Reville were married. As a contract director with Balcon, he still had two pictures left to go, both of which were rather routine. DOWNHILL (Gainsborough, 1927), which again starred Ivor Novello, suffers from a weak storyline and EASY VIRTUE (Gainsborough, 1928), while based on a play by Noel Coward, is disagreeably sentimental. THE RING (British International, 1928) was Hitchcock's first film under his new contract. Although he continued to like it, possibly because he had personally written the screenplay, the plot and its treatment seldom rise above the conventional. The film does attempt, however, to illustrate the fickleness and insubstantiality of love and the ludicrous romantic notions about love which, despite repeated experiences to the contrary, seem to preoccupy and exert a persistent influence on the popular imagination.

I suspect I may be almost alone in having enjoyed THE FARMER'S WIFE (British International, 1928). For me, it was one laugh after another because Hitchcock's ingenious sense of satire and the absurd could transform a trite and sentimental drama into a comedy reminiscent of Aristophanes. A farmer's wife dies and her last wish is made to the housekeeper to be sure to air out the farmer's pants. Once the farmer begins looking for a new wife, he naturally overlooks the housekeeper completely. The three women he does propose to all reject him, the hilarity increasing proposal by proposal. It was while screening this film that a member of the British "B" Western Film Society paid me a visit and he happened to watch the last half with Vicki and me. When we did have a chance to speak, he pointed out that it was films such as this one which perhaps best explain why British movie-goers, as in his case, preferred "B" Westerns.

CHAMPAGNE (British International, 1928) was another, largely comedic effort dealing in a general way with the troubles that can come from imbibing too much champagne. In addition to his love of eating, which could lead him to eat as many as four steaks at a sitting, Hitchcock enjoyed drinking, sometimes to excess, and smoking cigars. In many of his later films, one character offering another character a drink is very much a persistent motif, in which alcohol is regarded as Hitchcock himself regarded it: if not as medicine itself, as a very strong palliative in a frequently unpredictable and chaotic world. In contrast to CHAMPAGNE, THE MANXMAN (British International, 1930) was intended as a serious film, although the highly sentimental treatment accorded its subject— a woman marrying a man she thought she loved only to live in misery until her true love agrees to take her away from it all—is done in so serious a manner as to appear laughable to modern viewers. The film is perhaps most notable for the casting of Anny Ondra as the unhappy woman who sits around for most of its duration looking profoundly sad. Hitchcock was so impressed with Ondra's performance that he cast her as the female lead in what was to be his first sound film, BLACKMAIL (British International, 1929). He made a test take with her before the camera and microphone which survives. Ondra became so self-conscious that she giggled nervously. Hitchcock's voice is recognizable on the sound track urging her not to be alarmed which only causes Ondra to giggle more convulsively. Hitchcock later commented that Ondra's problem was that she spoke with a thick foreign accent and knew little English and that it was for this reason that he had Joan Barry dub her voice in the actual film, but the test take indicates that these were only part of Ondra's problems. I suspect that what Hitchcock liked about her enough for him to use her anyway was her ability to appear sad and anxious which had served her so well in THE MANXMAN.

BLACKMAIL is an important film not because it was a talking picture so much as its plot called on Hitchcock's ingenuity in depicting fear and guilt on the screen, creating much the same oppressive atmosphere he had achieved in THE LODGER. He was not permitted to film the story as he had conceived it. He had wanted to show a police detective going on a date with his girl. They have a tiff and the girl takes up with an artist. The artist seduces the girl and then she, in a frenzy, stabs him to death. Her detective friend is assigned to the case and by the fade he is seen routinely booking her. When asked by an older policeman if he plans to see his girl that night, the detective replies, "No, not tonight." What the distributors insisted on was for the girl to escape and wind up in the detective's loving arms. This altered the plot but it did not detract from its essentials. By interpolating a blackmailer into the scheme, threatening at every turn to expose Ondra's black deed, dramatic tension could be carefully built to an almost painful extreme. Hitchcock already by this time would shoot a picture in tiny little sections according to the editing scheme he had in mind and every shot was planned on an individual story board. In one scene in BLACKMAIL, Ondra is holding a bread knife at the breakfast table the morning after the murder and the table conversation turns to the stabbing of the artist. The sequence is broken up into small parts, the montage effect Hitchcock was to master so completely. Ondra's hand holding the knife tells one story while the dialogue tells another. This was one major liberation which the sound medium brought to Hitchcock, the ability to disassociate what characters say with what they do without the distraction of a title card. Ondra is particularly good in her role as the girl because of her nervousness. Much of this was no doubt due to the fact that the dubbing had to be done directly onto the sound track while she was acting her scenes with her only mouthing the words. It gave her precisely the edginess Hitchcock wanted. In terms of Ondra's character in the film, it is also worth noting that her sudden burst of murderous activity is not inspired by any desire to preserve her virtue. Her action is without *apparent* motivation, spontaneous, sudden, consuming, impulsive, *un acte gratuit* in André Gide's sense, as much a surprise to the girl as to her victim and, therefore, all the more terrifying. In the act of murdering the artist, a hidden side of the girl's personality, a little suspected proclivity toward brutal violence takes possession of her, and she is made helpless by it. The addition of the blackmailer creates a situation in which the legal consequences of Ondra's act are not so terrible as the horror represented by the blackmailer's knowledge which, with a word, could shatter illusions and lies which several of the characters desperately need as their shields from reality. Hitchcock was thus able to contrast the dullness of everyday life with the powerful, primitive passions which, without warning *and without reason*, can and suddenly do erupt, driving the emotions of an otherwise conventional existence into a paroxysm of frenzy.

Hitchcock's whole life, even in 1930, was totally absorbed in filmmaking. Howard Hawks loved a rugged life as much as film direction. John Huston was more intent on living out his personal fantasies than he was in directing any film. For Hitchcock, nothing else was of any consequence. Hawks could achieve the moments Hitchcock did only when his characters were confronted with the irrational, pervasive finality of death. Death, negation was the energizing force that released the dark side of the personality. For John Huston, the violence and perversity of his personality brought his characters to life and to a confrontation with the demiurge. Hitchcock, conversely, relied on the melodrama of crime in which the extinguishing of life is present but of secondary importance. The crime plot enabled him to amplify unusual aspects of human behavior, almost obsessively: fear of exposure, fear of smashing life-sustaining illusions, greed, power, sexuality, and vanity. Yet, he was scarcely in a position, as a contract director, to pursue these notions uninterruptedly and probably at this time he was not yet aware that this was his true *métier*. His next two assignments are disappointing. He directed a segment from ELSTREE CALLING (British International, 1930), a compendium film, and then a faithful, if not really cinematic, rendering of Sean O'Casey's stage play JUNO AND THE PAYCOCK (British International, 1930). It was not until he directed MURDER (British International, 1931), based on a screenplay by Alma Reville, that he could return to the kind of story for which he had a true penchant and utilize more than ever before the techniques he had learned during his apprenticeship in Germany.

MURDER would be Herbert Marshall's first talking picture and it was also the first detective story in the classical form that Hitchcock directed. The objection he had to detective stories as a genre was the emphasis that is automatically placed on the surprise at the end when you learn the identity of the murderer. Just so, even in a conventional detective story Hitchcock refused to be completely conventional. A woman is found dead and another woman is nearby, stupefied and unable to tell the police what happened. She is arrested. Hitchcock's portrayal of the police shows them to be both lazy and unimaginative. Although it is commonplace today, it was somewhat unique in 1930 to stress that in the prosecution of a crime it matters little whether a man is innocent or guilty, but rather how his actions can be made to appear in court. Hitchcock also managed to involve the viewer with the victim to a degree that one's natural lethargy had to be abandoned. Herbert Marshall is on the jury when the woman is sentenced to death. He doubts she committed the crime but he lacks the courage to battle his fellow jurors. Only after sentence has been passed does he set out to investigate the crime on his own. He is working against time because the impersonal machinery of human justice, however capricious in spirit, is inexorable in practice. The solution turns out not to have been so simple as the prosecutor made it out to have been; but then, it had to be simple enough so that the least intelligent juror could perceive the incontestable logic of the imputation. The real murderer, it turns out, was forced to silence the woman for fear she would betray his homosexual inclinations to his fiancée.

The films that followed MURDER, Hitchcock himself later admitted, represent him at his lowest ebb. THE SKIN GAME (British International, 1931) was another filmed stage play, this time by John Galsworthy. RICH AND STRANGE (British International, 1932), based on a story idea concocted by Hitchcock and Alma Reville while on their honeymoon, is a loosely fashioned travelogue which today seems dull and tiresome. NUMBER SEVENTEEN (British International, 1932) was a story of the old, dark house variety. It has its interesting moments, particularly in the miniature work utilized in a chase between a bus and a train, but with the fluctuations of identities between villains and heroes much of it is confusing. Hitchcock confessed that he was bored and became careless in its direction. He next acted as production supervisor on LORD CAMBER'S LADIES (British International, 1932) directed by Benn W. Levy. It was filmed, as Hitchcock remarked to me, "on a low budget and was of a lower order. Nigel Bruce was in it. He played the same old part which was built into the script for him. But I liked Bruce because you could always count on him to be Nigel Bruce."

It was while directing WALTZES FROM VIENNA in 1933 on loan-out to Gaumont-British that Michael Balcon, who was now associated with this new firm, approached Hitchcock and asked if he had any screen properties ready to be put into production. Hitchcock had prepared a screen treatment of THE MAN WHO KNEW TOO MUCH for John Maxwell, head of production at British International, but nothing had been done with it. Balcon liked the script. Hitchcock purchased it from Maxwell for two hundred and fifty pounds and turned around to sell it to Gaumont-British for twice that sum. With the profit he made from the transaction, he commissioned the sculptor Jacob Epstein to fashion a bust of Balcon which he later presented to him. Hitchcock was always especially generous to people he felt could be of assistance to him and his professional or financial aspirations. " . . . Whatever happens in the course of your career," Hitchcock told François Truffaut, "your talent is always there. To all appearances, I seemed to have gone into a creative decline in 1933 when I made WALTZES FROM VIENNA, which was very bad. And yet the talent must have been there all along since I had already conceived the project for THE MAN WHO KNEW TOO MUCH, the picture that reestablished my creative prestige."[6]

## II

Following the release of FAMILY PLOT, Hitchcock became almost a recluse. No one outside his intimate circle had much suspicion why this was so. He had hired Suzanne Gauthier as his secretary while at Paramount in 1956 preparing the remake of THE MAN WHO KNEW TOO MUCH and she stayed with him until that fateful day in 1979 when he closed up his office on the Universal lot for good, leaving her without any provision for further employment or financial recompense. His last words to her would be: " 'Leave me alone. I am . . . I . . . a sea of . . . alone.' "[7] In those last years, as Donald Spoto described it, "Suzanne Gauthier was unsure how much of his illness she could endure—how many more scenes of lunatic rage and inconsolable weeping and sudden, unusually childish tenderness alternating with senile obscenities."[8]

I was at work on my book on the history of the American detective film and I had a number of anecdotes from Peter Lorre the veracity of which only Hitchcock could confirm or deny. Of course, Hitchcock himself was well known for his rather malicious practical jokes over the years and, since Lorre's anecdotes had more than a little to do with pranks he supposedly played on Hitchcock, I did not foresee a problem in discussing them. For example, during his contract days in the United Kingdom, he had once bet a property man a week's salary that he would be too frightened to spend a whole night chained to a camera in a dark and deserted film studio. When his challenge was accepted, before departing Hitchcock offered the man a beaker of brandy which he had drunk. It contained an extremely powerful laxative and when the man was found in the morning he was weeping, exhausted and humiliated by his ordeal. On 7 July 1928 Hitchcock's only offspring, Patricia, was born. Thirty years later when he was filming STRANGERS ON A TRAIN (Warner's, 1951), Pat had a role in the picture. While shooting the carnival sequence, Pat begged to have a ride on the Ferris wheel. Hitchcock agreed. However, when she reached the top, Hitchcock ordered the machine shut down and all lights were extinguished, while he went elsewhere on the location to film a scene. An hour later, when he ordered that the machine be started again and she was lowered, she was hysterical with fear.

Suzanne Gauthier arranged for Vicki and me to interview Hitchcock at his Universal office bungalow.

"You cannot bring a camera in here," he announced as we entered. He stood in front of his desk and beamed pleasantly. He had lost some weight and his face was ruddy, especially his cheeks, but his weight always did fluctuate. At forty, he had weighed 365 pounds and he was invariably retreating from that figure or advancing upon it. His wisps of hair now were white. He moved with an extraordinarily slow step as he walked toward an easy chair, but not without grace.

"I haven't got a camera," I said.

He had seen my hands when we entered and he knew very well that I didn't have a camera.

"I have just got off the 'phone," he said, reclining gently into the chair. "I have a pacer in my heart. I have to dial in to a computer. Then I rest the receiver in a special box and hold a microphone to my heart. My heart beat is transmitted over the telephone wire to the computer and the computer calculates if it is beating too fast or too slow, or if it's normal. It's an interesting device. When they put it in, they extended a long wire up through one of the arteries of my arm until it reached the heart, and it was then connected to the pacer. The computer evidently approved of my present condition."

Hitchcock again smiled benignly.

Peter Lorre had made his English-speaking debut in THE MAN WHO KNEW TOO MUCH (Gaumont-British, 1935). Fritz Lang had originally hired him from the Berlin stage to appear as the child murderer in M (Nerofilm, 1931). Then, fleeing the Nazis, he had worked briefly in Austria before arriving in Paris where, despite his deplorable French, he had been engaged to dub Paul Lukas' voice onto a French voice track. Times were bad and became worse, so Lorre emigrated to the United Kingdom, having no money and speaking no English. Sidney Bernstein, a producer, introduced Lorre to Hitchcock and Hitchcock cast him as the principal anarchist in THE MAN WHO KNEW TOO MUCH. Cecilia Lvovsky, whom Lorre had met in Berlin, played a Russian aristocrat in the film and they were subsequently married.

Years later, Lorre recalled his initial meeting with Hitchcock. "Hitch talked," he said, "and I leaned forward, looking intelligent but not understanding a word. By following his gestures, I'd guess when he was coming to the gag-line and I'd laugh out loud. I got the role and it was two weeks before Hitch found out I spoke no English. I must say he got a big kick out of it."

I related Lorre's account of their first meeting to Hitchcock.

"I had no idea at all," he drawled, "that Lorre was Hungarian, so, when we met, I spoke to him in German. I had to learn German when I worked in Germany as an art director." Hitchcock smiled demurely. "When, in 1931, I made an Anglo-German talking picture, it was done without changing lighting or anything, using the English cast in one set-up and then substituting a German cast to do the scene in German. The translator I had working on the film, who told me what the Germans were saying to one another, was a Yugoslavian."

Hitchcock did not have occasion to cast Lorre again in a film until THE

SECRET AGENT (Gaumont-British, 1936) based on a stage play by Campbell Dixon which drew upon characters and an amalgam of the plots of two of the stories contained in W. Somerset Maugham's ASHENDEN, OR THE BRITISH AGENT (1929). The role Hitchcock assigned Lorre was that of the hairless Mexican and then, somewhat as an inside joke, had him coiffured with wildly curly hair. Since working on THE MAN WHO KNEW TOO MUCH, Lorre had gone to the United States where he had been cast by Josef von Sternberg as Raskolnikov in the film version of Dostoyevsky's CRIME AND PUNISHMENT (Columbia, 1935). Yet, before production even began on that film, Lorre was signed by M-G-M to play a bald maniac in MAD LOVE (M-G-M, 1935) directed by Karl Freund, a German emigré director, as was von Sternberg himself. Doubtless, the latter role suggested to Hitchcock that he cast Lorre in THE SECRET AGENT. Years after, Lorre recalled that on his way back to the States, once the picture had been completed, he had purchased an entire pet shop of canaries and had them shipped to Hitchcock's London flat. According to Lorre, Hitchcock took immediate revenge. He began cabling Lorre aboard ship every fifteen minutes, night and day, telling him what he had named each of the canaries and giving him a moment-by-moment account of what each canary was doing. The cables were so incessant that Lorre was unable to sleep. I asked Hitchcock, as we talked, if that had indeed happened.

"No," he said.

With answers as succinct as that, taking notes on this interview would present no special problems for Vicki, but now the conversation turned to Hitchcock's own career and about this he had much more to say.

The plot of the original THE MAN WHO KNEW TOO MUCH concerns a young couple, played by Leslie Banks and Edna Best, who learn while vacationing in Switzerland of a plot to assassinate an official during a concert at Royal Albert Hall in London. Their little girl is kidnapped by the conspirators to assure their silence. Hitchcock managed to create maximum anxiety in the scene of the attempted murder, by having the spies rehearse the cantata to be performed so that both the expert rifleman and the viewer know exactly when to expect the cymbal crash which is to cover the discharge of the bullet and by parallel cutting between Edna Best's efforts at the hall to warn the official and the monitoring of events back at the hide-out via a wireless broadcast of the concert. The visual contrast between the snow-covered Alps and congested London streets had first come to Hitchcock while honeymooning in Switzerland and it is quite as strikingly innovative as the effective use of sound to heighten tension. The picture became, upon release, the most impressive financial success of all Hitchcock's British films to that time and it won him a wide following even in the United States where British films were held in generally low esteem.

Hitchcock's next film was THE THIRTY-NINE STEPS (Gaumont-British, 1935), based on a character and using the title of a thriller by John Buchan. In simplifying the plot for the screen, Hitchcock retained only the notion of the central character's pursuit by the police, who suspect him of murder, and a ring of spies anxious to prevent him from divulging his supposed knowledge of their activities. This supposed knowledge in the film was what Hitchcock came to call a MacGuffin. The thirty-nine steps described a place in the novel; in the film, if they mean anything, they are a code name for a subversive organization. A MacGuffin, by definition, need not be explained. It is quite enough that it should be sufficient to excite most of the characters to desperate and extreme behavior. Robert Donat was the suave hero, Madeleine Carroll the first of Hitchcock's many blonde heroines. Consistent with what would become a recurrent theme, Donat and Carroll commence their relationship in hostility and, after undergoing a long ordeal, they become lovers. Increasingly, Hitchcock used the camera as point-of-view, insinuating the viewer into the scene by witnessing events through the eyes of one or another of the characters. In one scene, Donat looks out his bedroom window and, in the street, standing just outside the illumination cast by the street lamp, he sees the conspirators. It is a classic image, with the camera acting as his eyes. Hitchcock merely reversed this sequence totally when, in NORTH BY NORTHWEST, he placed Cary Grant in similar jeopardy only with all enclosures stripped away, the vacant street replaced by a deserted country road, the darkness punctuated by street lamps replaced by bright sunlight, and the telephone ringing in Donat's apartment replaced by the revving engine of a crop-duster where there are no crops. THE THIRTY-NINE STEPS is a pursuit picture in grand style, with one scene cutting right into the next, achieving a fluid exposition both stirring and upsetting. Again the denouement occurs in a public place, the Paladium, disrupting a stage performance, as in BLACKMAIL, where sight-seers are disrupted at the British Museum, and in THE MAN WHO KNEW TOO MUCH, where violence erupts during a concert.

Hitchcock cast John Gielgud as Ashenden in THE SECRET AGENT, with Madeleine Carroll back as the blonde heroine. Lorre's role is that of a brutish and indifferent murderer, assigned to be Ashenden's assistant in carrying out an assassination, but often behaving against type as in his first scene in which he seems more a gnome-like and impish comedian as he chases a maid. Carroll is courted by amusing and debonair Robert Young. Lorre is to do the assassination under Gielgud's supervision. A single organ note reverberates through a Swiss valley when their contact, an organist in a church, is murdered, his body falling forward onto the organ. Once the execution has taken place, Ashenden is chagrined to learn that the wrong man has been killed. Lorre regards this as a trivial oversight. Ashenden, however, is paralyzed and unable to act even when it becomes clear that Robert Young is the man that was supposed to die. Only after Ashenden and Carroll have fallen in love and Carroll is kidnapped by Young can Ashenden act; yet it is a train wreck which dispatches Young, although not before he shoots Lorre.

Charles Bennet, who had worked on the scenario of every Hitchcock film since THE MAN WHO KNEW TOO MUCH, adapted Joseph Conrad's novel, THE SECRET AGENT (1907), the title changed for obvious reasons to SABOTAGE (Gaumont-British, 1937). Hitchcock cast Oscar Homolka as Verloc, the anarchist, and Sylvia Sidney, imported from the States to provide the film with American appeal, as his wife. The story was updated and Verloc's occupation in the film is that of a theatre-owner. Walt Disney designed the cartoon sequence which is projected on the screen when the action requires the camera to track the characters through a theatre while a film is in progress. In Conrad's story, as in the film, Verloc's wife murders him when she learns that her little brother, on an innocent errand, was killed by a bomb prepared by Verloc. Hitchcock expressed his regret to us that he had taken this element from the novel since audiences proved hostile at such a senseless death. Yet, he could not really have avoided it. The boy's death gives Sidney her reason to kill Homolka and the story its substance. Hitchcock anticipated the explosion of the bomb in the film, hidden in two film cannisters the boy is transporting on a tram, by showing clocks constantly recording the passage of time. It is effective and perhaps it works better with contemporary audiences more familiar with the caprices of terrorism than were British audiences at the time the film was released. "What I like to do always," Hitchcock wrote in an article titled "Direction" published the year after SABOTAGE, "is to photograph just the little bits of a scene that I really need for building up a visual sequence. I want to put my film together on the screen, not simply to photograph something that has been put together already in the form of a long piece of stage acting."[9]

SABOTAGE was the last British film directed by Hitchcock that was produced by Michael Balcon. Balcon went to work briefly for the British M-G-M facility and then went into independent production. Hitchcock himself signed a new contract with Gainsborough, although Gaumont-British would continue to distribute his films. YOUNG AND INNOCENT (Gainsborough, 1938) was the first project under these new auspices. Charles Bennett collaborated with Alma Reville on the screenplay. After completing work on this picture, Bennett signed a contract with David O. Selznick in the United States. Hitchcock's agent was Myron Selznick, David's brother, and he, too, began to explore possibilities of moving to Hollywood.

YOUNG AND INNOCENT at the very opening restates the skepticism Hitchcock increasingly felt toward due process, especially when a case depended on circumstantial evidence and supposed eye-witnesses. Cutting swiftly from a fight between a man and woman, the viewer next sees her body washed ashore. The young man, played by Derrick de Marney, who discovers her body is accused of being the murderer by those who come on the scene later. So air-tight is the case made to seem in court that conviction is certain before he escapes. In his efforts to outwit his pursuers, the young man is helped by Nova Philbeam, the local constable's daughter. The MacGuffin in this case is a raincoat which de Marney must find to prove his innocence. Hitchcock used a long tracking shot of one hundred and forty-five feet from the entrance of a *thé dansant* past the tables and the dancers into the orchestra until it pauses on a close-up of the murderer's twitching countenance, a drummer in black face. The culprit does not realize that the police are there to arrest de Marney and his own guilt causes him to give himself away, but the viewer isn't fooled. A bit more self-possession on his part and, because of unimaginativeness and sloth, due process would have enthusiastically convicted the wrong man.

Perhaps the masterpiece from Hitchcock's British period is THE LADY VAN-ISHES (Gainsborough, 1938). The picture still has about it just the right mixture of comic situations which stem naturally from the characters as they are established at the outset in a few deft strokes which are then played out contrapuntally in the exposition of the complex plot. The whole setting of the picture, opening to some fine, if obvious, model work of a Balkan village establishes a comic tone as the strong personalities of the cast are played off, one against the other, amid a charming satire on the very insular British at large in the outer world. Produced on one of the smaller stages at Islington, with the train set a mere ninety feet long consisting of one coach and all the other cars transparencies, the intimacy of the camera work, the viability of the characters, the crispness of the dialogue, and the engaging relationship which develops, following the requisite moments of initial hostility, between Michael Redgrave and Margaret Lockwood as they search the train to find Dame May Whitty who has been secreted by spies congeal to fashion a film that can be viewed repeatedly without significant diminution of enjoyment. Even the comedy of the situations and the dialogue are such as to withstand repetition.

While THE LADY VANISHES was in production, Hitchcock received a cable from David O. Selznick asking him to come to Hollywood to direct a picture based on the sinking of the *Titanic*. It was Hitchcock's first trip to the United States and, while he pursued other possibilities, no one would pay him what Selznick was offering. He signed a contract that commenced in April, 1939. Upon his return to the United Kingdom, Hitchcock's agent suggested that in the interim he should direct JAMAICA INN (Mayflower, 1939). It was to be produced by a company in which the German producer, Erich Pommer, and Charles Laughton were the principals. Hitchcock, who had met Pommer previously in Germany and who had lunched occasionally with Laughton, needed money and so he accepted the advance of several thousand pounds with alacrity. Then he read the script. He felt the property unworkable. It dealt with a gang of ship-wreckers working off the Cornish coast in the Eighteenth century. Laughton was to play Sir Humphrey Pengallon, an insane squire and justice of the peace who is the actual leader of the gang. Hitchcock told Laughton frankly that his popular identification with screen villains was so well known that no one would be in much suspense for very long. He wanted to bow out of the project. Since the money had already been spent, Hitchcock revealed his plans to sell his London flat in order to pay back the advance. Laughton would hear nothing of it. His inflated acting style and amateur theatrics had for some reason caught the fancy of the public and, confronted now by a number of personal monetary woes including a tax investigation, he needed a successful picture and this would be it. Besides, if all that were not enough, did Hitchcock want to be personally responsible for putting a German refugee like Erich Pommer out of work? Hitchcock acquiesced, but remained exceedingly uncomfortable.

During our conversation, I asked Hitchcock again to clarify his position regarding the role of actors in a film.

"It isn't necessary," he said slowly, "to depend on an actor's virtuosity or his personality to create tension. The chief requisite for an actor is his ability to do nothing well. That is not so easy as it sounds. He must be willing to be used by the director and the camera. It is the camera which must decide what to emphasize and what is most dramatic."

Given that conviction, it is easy to understand how much of an ordeal it must have been to work with Laughton and his persistent lack of professionalism. He insisted that he be photographed only in close-up or stationary until he got down just the right tempo for Pengallon's walk which he only improvised after ten days of listening to Weber's "Invitation to the Dance" on a gramophone on the set. When the script required Laughton to tie up heroine Maureen O'Hara, he was incapable of even attempting it until he found just the right mood. He sulked in a corner until it occurred to him that he must play the scene as a boy of ten who had just wet his pants!

All of this notwithstanding, JAMAICA INN proved sufficiently popular with audiences that both Laughton and Pommer made an easy transition to Hollywood once war broke out, but it did not earn quite enough to save their Mayflower production company. Hitchcock, pleased it was finally over, sold his London flat and the home he had purchased in Surrey where he had been accustomed to spend his weekends and, with his family, set sail for the United States. He had been trained, he felt, by an American film company when he first entered the industry and he had always retained his admiration for American films. Hollywood would, in fact, bring him huge international success. He would become independently wealthy and, more importantly, for a time he would achieve total independence as an artist. Yet, in the end, his own frugality, his fear of total independence which ultimately would overpower his desire for complete freedom, his unrequited longing finally to consummate in the flesh a union with the cool, graceful, blonde woman who would continue to haunt his finest films, his carefully constructed social *persona* proved insufficient to withstand the power of the deep turmoil within and would lead to a shattered existence, resembling in personal terms more defeat than success. "A human being," C.G. Jung wrote, "cannot do away with himself in favor of an artificial personality without being punished."[10] Hitchcock may once have believed that *extra ecclesiam nulla salus*, but, as Pat grew older, his interest in the church evaporated, leaving only film as his profession and his place of worship. "The paradox of Alfred Hitchcock," Donald Spoto wrote, "was that his delight in his craft could never be liberated from a terrible and terrifying heritage of desire and its concomitant guilt."[11]

REBECCA (United Artists, 1940), like JAMAICA INN, was based on a Daphne du Maurier novel; it was Hitchcock's first film for Selznick. In mounting the film, Selznick went out of his way to engage a predominantly British cast for a film set in England, starring Laurence Olivier, Dame Judith Anderson (from Australia), George Sanders (born in Russia of British parents), and in supporting roles C. Aubrey Smith, Reginald Denny, Nigel Bruce, Leo G. Carroll, and Gladys Cooper. Joan Fontaine, cast as the young heroine, seemed apt to play someone cringingly intimidated by a hostile environment. When Evelyn Keyes, who was cast in GONE WITH THE WIND (M-G-M, 1939), was introduced to Hitchcock, he said to her: " 'I have one pa-ht left to cah-st, the vil . . . lage i . . . di . . . ot. Wou . . . ld you li . . . ke to play it?' "[12]

Some critics have claimed that REBECCA wasn't really a picture suited to Hitchcock's talents, despite the fact that it would be the only film he directed which would receive an Academy Award for Best Picture. To the contrary, I feel that the direction was remarkably fine and that the psychological orientation of the film is a precursor for the atmosphere of his best films of the 'Fifties. The technique of delayed revelation, by which the plot is revealed in all its twists and permutations, is precisely the structure which came to characterize Hitchcock at his most effective. I asked him how it came to be that he was possibly the only director who worked amicably with Selznick on a number of pictures despite Selznick's penchant to address himself to all aspects of any production and, especially, to the direction.

"Selznick always used to say that Irving Thalberg was great with a finished picture." Hitchcock grinned devilishly. "To think like that is equivalent to putting up a building and then taking it down again. I never had a problem with Selznick. I was, of course, told that I couldn't shoot a scene unless Selznick was on the set to oversee it. So I would rehearse the actors and then tell one of the messengers to go get Selznick. He would come on the set and I would begin the scene. If he saw something he didn't like, he would lean over and whisper in my ear, 'Don't you think he or she should do this?' I would look straight at him and tell him that if that's what he thought should be done he should go and tell him or her himself. Selznick never would. That may be why we got along so well. I wouldn't fight with him and he wouldn't talk to the actors himself."

Following REBECCA, Hitchcock went repeatedly on loan-out, Selznick paying him his contracted salary but charging the borrowing studio considerably more. FOREIGN CORRESPONDENT (United Artists, 1940) was made for Walter Wanger. Charles Bennet was teamed again with Hitchcock for the screenplay and the film has much in common with the British pictures the two had collaborated on in the previous decade. Once Wanger approved the script, Hitchcock had relative autonomy, something which he had not had, his comments to the contrary notwithstanding, in working for Selznick. One of the reasons Hitchcock had most looked forward to working in Hollywood was the pool of top stars that he would have at his disposal. However, the kinds of cinematic stories he preferred at first worked against this ambition. He had wanted Gary Cooper for FOREIGN CORRESPONDENT but Cooper turned it down, convinced that it was beneath him to appear in a thriller. Hitchcock wound up with Joel McCrea.

Laraine Day, less than a top star, played the heroine. However, Herbert Marshall, playing a part quite the opposite from the one he had had in MURDER, helped assuage the disappointment, and George Sanders was again cast effectively.

"I liked Sanders," Hitchcock told us. "He was a good actor, if a trifle audacious. I remember once he rang the doorbell at my Bel-Air home and told the maid he was a close personal friend of mine. I wasn't at home at the time. Sanders said all he wanted to do was borrow a book by George Bernard Shaw and he went in the study and got it. But, I must say, he did return it."

MR. AND MRS. SMITH (RKO, 1941) is a screwball comedy starring Carole Lombard and Robert Montgomery as a couple who discovers that their marriage of some years' standing is not legally valid. Critics have complained that the film gives no indication of any of Hitchcock's usual trademarks, yet there was no reason why Hitchcock should have tried to confine himself exclusively to one kind of film. Indeed, among his attempts at pure screen comedy, this may be his finest achievement. Cary Grant had been among the celebrities who had met Hitchcock on his first trip to the States and he found the rotund director such a delight that, despite his usual parsimony, he did not even object to being slipped the check when they dined at expensive restaurants. Grant met Hitchcock again at Alexander Korda's house while he was directing MR. AND MRS. SMITH and he had no difficulty agreeing to play the bounder in SUSPICION (RKO, 1941). Since the husband, as played by Grant, was innocent ultimately of any wrong-doing, Joan Fontaine seemed perfect to portray his highly susceptible and easily intimidated new wife. However, in her personal life Fontaine was in the midst of a melodrama as compelling as that in REBECCA and it caused her to be erratic and absent occasionally from the set. Grant had not liked working with her in GUNGA DIN (RKO, 1939) and working with her again, and under these circumstances, only made him all the more testy and disgruntled. Yet, in him, Hitchcock had found one of the leading men with whom he would make some of his most memorable films.

Hitchcock subsequently declared that Robert Cummings was all wrong for SABOTEUR (Universal, 1942) because "he has an amusing face, so that even when he's in desperate straits, his features don't convey any anguish."[13] Yet, he willingly enough cast him a decade later as Grace Kelly's distraught lover in DIAL M FOR MURDER (Warner's, 1954). He was even more nettled by Priscilla Lane being cast as the heroine. "She simply wasn't the right type for a Hitchcock picture."[14] In many ways, the film is a remake of THE THIRTY-NINE STEPS with Cummings and Lane hostile toward one another until, learning of his innocence, Lane falls in love with him. In one sequence, during their dash across the country, Cummings is still half-manacled (resuming the handcuff theme from the earlier picture). However, there is no question that Hitchcock was bored and indifferent, so that his direction tended to sabotage any effort Lane might have made for him. Wandering in the desert, Hitchcock had her dressed in skirt, suit coat, and high heels.

SHADOW OF A DOUBT (Universal, 1943) was more successful. It may have lacked anything approaching the spectacular scene in SABOTEUR where Cummings and his Nazi opponent struggle atop the Statue of Liberty, but it more than compensated with carefully drawn psychological portraits and a tense, suspenseful plot in which Joseph Cotten plays a psychopath preying on lonely widows who returns to the small town home of his niece, played by Teresa Wright, who loves and admires him until her ardor turns to horror as she learns the truth. The longing to see small town America and to use it as a background in a film inspired Hitchcock to engage Thornton Wilder as the writer on this picture and, for a time, the two of them lived in Santa Rosa, California, where the film was set. Eventually, Hitchcock bought himself a country home at Santa Cruz where he could go on weekends.

It was while making LIFEBOAT (20th-Fox, 1944) that Hitchcock encountered Darryl F. Zanuck. They meshed badly from the start, and perhaps that is why it turned out to be the only film Hitchcock ever made at that studio. Zanuck, screening Hitchcock's rushes, complained that many of the scenes were too static and he wanted to find some way to speed them up. Hitchcock resisted, feeling Zanuck's recommendations were of questionable merit. The plot concerns a group of survivors from a ship that has been torpedoed by a German U-boat that is also sunk. Walter Slezak, cast as the U-boat captain, proves in the course of the film to be a competent and masterful person, especially since he is aided by water and drugs which he takes when the others are not looking. At the time, the film was criticized for showing a Nazi in such a positive fashion. However, such criticism overlooks the basic conclusion to which the film comes, one that in its cynicism is beyond any issue of who is right and who is wrong. The survivors finally turn on the Nazi and kill him, as had been their intention in the beginning. It may be argued that Hitchcock was speaking out against appeasement but I suspect if he was making any kind of statement it was more akin to the observation that anyone, given the proper circumstances, is capable of murder. What is particularly fascinating about the film, even today when its rhetoric is tired and hackneyed, is the way in which it is capable of sustaining interest no matter how confined its visual scope is to the interior of a single lifeboat. Following this assignment, Hitchcock returned to the United Kingdom and directed two propaganda films intended for use by the Free French and the Resistance to win support for the Allies after the Normandy invasion. The dialogue was in French and Hitchcock employed French advisors, but only one film, dealing with Gestapo spies, was found acceptable and put into circulation.

During these years, Hitchcock was scarcely alone in being perpetually on loan-out from Selznick. Selznick himself produced no pictures between REBECCA and SINCE YOU WENT AWAY (United Artists, 1944). All of his contract personnel were exploited and packaged in the same fashion Hitchcock was. Joan Fontaine, for example, made ten pictures while under contract to Selznick but only REBECCA was produced by Selznick. The man was constantly torn between his urgent desire to join the war effort in an executive governmental capacity and his stormy love affair with Jennifer Jones. For a welcome change it turned

out that SPELLBOUND (United Artists, 1945) would be the second film Hitchcock directed for him in the first five years of their seven-year contract. The
background of the film was psychoanalysis and, while the novel on which Ben
Hecht's screenplay was based was surfeit with the wildest lunacies, Hitchcock
wanted to treat the subject more sensibly. In working on SHADOW OF A
DOUBT, Teresa Wright had occasion to perceive how Hitchcock "really scored
the sound effects the way a musician writes for instruments."[15] For the dream
sequence, Hitchcock proposed that Selznick hire Salvador Dali to design the
entire episode, creating visual images as menacing out of everyday objects as
he had formerly achieved with sounds. Selznick thought the suggestion an excellent publicity gimmick, but nothing more. He vetoed any additional expenses,
such as filming the episode outdoors to capture the intense sunlight effects
Hitchcock wanted. The result was that the picture got the publicity but Hitchcock
got considerably less than he had wanted. "Selznick predicted," Donald Spoto
wrote, "that Hitchcock's attitude toward production costs and efficiency would
alter when he became his own producer, and no prophecy could have been more
accurate."[16]

Perhaps Hitchcock's finest American film following REBECCA was NO-
TORIOUS (RKO, 1946). More by accident than intention he had decided—a
full year before Hiroshima—that the McGuffin the Nazis would be after in the
picture was to be Uranium–235. When he explained this idea to Selznick, Selznick thought it was ridiculous. He had never heard anything about uranium and
bombs. Ben Hecht was at work on the screenplay and, on the basis of a story
outline, Hitchcock was able to interest both Cary Grant and Ingrid Bergman in
playing the leads. Selznick did some rapid figuring, projecting what the finished
picture would cost against what he had invested so far, and then sold the entire
package of Hitchcock, Hecht, Grant, and Bergman to RKO for $800,000, or
three times what he had in it at that point. In a way, it was type-casting all down
the line. The plot required the character Grant played to be a cynical, callous,
exploitive instrument of American foreign policy. Ingrid Bergman, who was
promiscuous in her personal life, played the daughter of a traitor, a sensuous
tramp with a fondness for alcohol and parties. Bergman, of course, had been a
Nazi sympathizer before the war, although later she repudiated the Nazi philosophy publicly. Grant had been involved in spy activities for the British government. Grant's character name was T.R. Devlin, Bergman's was Alicia
Huberman. "NOTORIOUS also illuminated an aspect of Cary's sexual character," Charles Higham and Roy Moseley wrote in CARY GRANT: THE
LONELY HEART (1989). "At the beginning, he says, 'I've always been scared
of women.' When Devlin kisses Alicia, it is either to inveigle her into a plot
that would involve her sexual betrayal of him or as a cover when they are
discovered by her husband in an act of espionage. Having scarcely protested,
and indeed aided, the FBI's manipulation of a beautiful woman into bed and
marriage with a man she detests, Devlin criticizes her for what is in fact his
own moral failure. His possessiveness, sexual ambiguity, and deep-seated guilt

and fear are from the beginning to end Cary Grant.''[17] Perhaps it was just as well that Selznick sold off this property since it is doubtful that he would have endorsed the great liberties Hitchcock took with the script, while the RKO front office was satisfied by the circumstance that Devlin and Alicia end up in each other's arms by the fade.

Although Hitchcock was contradictory on the subject of Selznick, complaining about him at times, and at others insisting that Selznick left him alone most of the time, the worst and best of it came together on the last film that he directed while still under contract to him. It also marked the beginning of a new slump, far more devastating in many ways than the previous hiatus in his career in the United Kingdom. Alma Reville adapted THE PARADINE CASE (Selznick International, 1947) for the screen, but Selznick cast it, employing for the most part his own contract players. He had quarreled with United Artists and was, by now, distributing his films himself. To keep his exchanges occupied and his contract personnel earning money for him, he had to produce pictures himself and abandon his packaging routine. Consequently, Gregory Peck was uncomfortably cast as an English barrister, the cold, self-possessed Alida Valli had to play a sensuously passionate and even murderous woman, and Louis Jourdan was a down-at-the-heels groom and Valli's secret lover. Possibly it would be more accurate to say that these contract players *tried* to portray these roles and even had their characters rewritten to fit their physical appearance, but the part each had to play was determined by the plot and that could not be altered. The result was a dismal film. Hitchcock, given this script and this casting, had very little to direct, and even a minor role, such as the lascivious judge played by Charles Laughton, only confronted him with a situation he had already encountered before on JAMAICA INN. Hitchcock, who condemned Selznick for his long-term contracts and lavish productions, would, however, fall heir to the same mistakes later on in his own career.

Sidney Bernstein, who had introduced Peter Lorre to Hitchcock, had recently founded his own production company and he made Hitchcock a partner in the venture, thinking that Hitchcock's reputation in Hollywood could only make Transatlantic Pictures all the more viable. ROPE (Warner's, 1948) was the first film, shot at Warner's Burbank studio and released by Warner Bros. Hume Cronyn, who had appeared in LIFEBOAT, adapted a stage play which dealt with two homosexual men who commit a murder and James Stewart was cast as the man who finds them out. Farley Granger played one of the homosexuals and this casting may have suggested to Hitchcock his later use of Granger in a role that had latent homosexual undertones in STRANGERS ON A TRAIN. ROPE did poorly and the next film, UNDER CAPRICORN (Warner's, 1948), did even worse. Set in Australia, it was a period piece (the last Hitchcock would ever do), filmed at the M-G-M studio in the United Kingdom. Hitchcock thought that by signing Ingrid Bergman—then the most sought-after actress in the world—his triumphant return to filming in his native country would be assured. Whatever might be said about the somewhat confusing screenplay, the basic problem with

UNDER CAPRICORN was something that had not been evident in a Hitchcock film since WALTZES FROM VIENNA: it was dull.

Hitchcock told François Truffaut that his innermost tendency, when confronted by a project engendering vagueness or doubt, was to run for cover. Running for cover after UNDER CAPRICORN meant a full-fledged return to the kind of picture typical of his pre-war British thrillers. However, in directing STAGE FRIGHT (Warner's, 1950), Hitchcock had to indulge himself with another gimmick. In making ROPE, he had tried to film entire reels without a break or cut. Instead of accelerating the pacing, it had retarded it. Now in STAGE FRIGHT he tried to deceive the audience by the use of deliberately inaccurate flashbacks. Unfortunately, viewers had come to rely on flashbacks as a clarifying device, even if contradictory or personally stylized as in CITIZEN KANE (RKO, 1941). However, the most evident problem with the film was that neither the story nor the performances were especially remarkable. Hitchcock had reached another nadir.

## III

Raymond Chandler was a difficult man with whom to work. His association with Billy Wilder in co-authoring the screenplay for DOUBLE INDEMNITY (Paramount, 1944) had been fraught with strife and he didn't find working with Hitchcock adapting Patricia Highsmith's novel, STRANGERS ON A TRAIN (1950), any improvement. He was guaranteed $2,500 a week for five weeks' work. He was then living in a home in La Jolla, California, and Hitchcock would be driven down for story conferences. Chandler was antagonistic from the start. He once remarked to his secretary so loudly that Hitchcock overheard it that she should look at the fat bastard trying to get out of his car. Hitchcock, for his part, found his meetings with Chandler singularly unrewarding, not only because of Chandler's customary rudeness but also because Chandler could not get the idea of a co-operative venture through his head.

"We'd sit together and I would say, 'Why not do it this way?' and he'd answer, 'Well, if you can puzzle it out, what do you need me for?' " Hitchcock looked steadily at us. "A cobbler should stick to his last," he said then.

Chandler only proved Hitchcock correct when he complained morosely that the director was "full of little suggestions and ideas, which have a cramping effect on a writer's initiative. . . . This is very hard on a writer, especially on a writer who has any ideas of his own, because the writer not only has to make sense out of a foolish plot, if he can, but he has to do that and at the same time do it in such a way that any kind of camera shot or background shot that comes into Hitchcock's mind can be incorporated into it."[18]

Chandler ended up having to share screen credit with Czenzi Ormonde, a writer who worked as one of Ben Hecht's assistants. He didn't like it and he didn't like the fact that the picture proved a success upon release. "I don't know why it's a success," he wrote to his English publisher, Hamish Hamilton, "perhaps because Hitchcock succeeded in removing almost every trace of my writing from it."[19] Hitchcock had always felt that the writing of a complete screenplay with every camera angle, every set-up detailed was essential in putting a picture together. The actual shooting of the screenplay was almost anticlimactic. Finding screenwriters with whom he could successfully collaborate proved his most persistent difficulty.

The plot narrates a chance meeting between two men on a train, played by Farley Granger and Robert Walker. Granger is a professional tennis player unhappily married who wants a divorce so he can marry another woman. Walker is the psychopathic son of a wealthy man. Walker proposes that they should exchange murders and, in this fashion, escape detection. The theme of the transference of guilt, so heavily stressed by the French in writing about Hitchcock's films, receives its most powerful evocation to date in STRANGERS ON A TRAIN. To this psychological parallelism was added a tense, dramatic parallelism achieved by cross-cutting between Granger, desperately trying to win a tennis match quickly so he can prevent Walker from planting his cigarette lighter at the scene where Walker murdered Granger's wife, intercut with Walker's frantic efforts to retrieve the incriminating lighter from the manhole into which he accidentally dropped it. In the best Hitchcock tradition, the film concludes with spectacular shots of a carrousel gone haywire, accomplished through the use of a miniature.

I CONFESS (Warner's, 1953) had many of the same themes as the previous film but here they did not quite work. Montgomery Clift was cast as a parish priest who is being blackmailed. The blackmailer is murdered by a parishioner and the parishioner confesses the crime to Clift, thus effecting a variation on the theme of the transference of guilt since the priest was likely to have been similarly tempted. The most memorable aspects of the film remain Clift's subtle performance in which his fear and distress are conveyed only by his eyes and not through any facial expression or bodily movement. Perhaps believing that the plot had insufficient tension to carry the story, Hitchcock again added a spectacular finish, but not even this could save the enterprise from seeming unduly mechanical.

Of the four films Hitchcock made for Warner Bros. release, DIAL M FOR MURDER is quite probably the best. Hitchcock was convinced that he had found in Grace Kelly the ideal actress to embody and epitomize the varied traits of the Hitchcock heroine: a reticent, cool, majestic exterior concealing an impassioned, frenzied sexual abandon. It was not entirely a subjective fantasy. Hitchcock, who loved gossip, undoubtedly had heard of Kelly's promiscuity and numerous romances before he cast her. He apparently also thought enough of Robert Cummings to use him again, this time as an American mystery novelist with whom Kelly was once involved. Ray Milland played the rich Kelly's husband, a former tennis champion, very much the kind of person the character Farley Granger had portrayed might have turned into after years of marriage to a woman he had married for her money. Milland hires a man to kill Kelly. When Kelly foils the scheme by stabbing her assailant with a pair of scissors, Milland is able to construe the evidence to make it appear deliberate homicide rather than self-defense, thus returning to the theme of how prone to error due process can be. Kelly is tried, convicted, and sentenced to death before, at literally the last minute, Milland is exposed.

At this point everything in Hitchcock's life and career finally came together. Following Myron Selznick's death, Hitchcock became one of the premier clients of MCA where, in rather short order, he was represented by Lew Wasserman, president of the talent agency since 1946. Wasserman negotiated a contract with Paramount which gave Hitchcock virtual independence in the producing and directing of his films and which, after distribution by Paramount for a period of seven years, granted Hitchcock a total reversion of rights on several titles, even though the films themselves were all to be financed by Paramount. In 1949, an enterprising editor at Dell Books had approached Hitchcock with a proposal to use his name for a paperback collection titled SUSPENSE STORIES (1949) for which an introduction was prepared by a ghost writer over Hitchcock's signature. In 1955, Hitchcock signed an even more lucrative contract with Richard E. Decker who then began publishing ALFRED HITCHCOCK'S MYSTERY MAGAZINE and followed it with a long series of anthologies and story collections with ghostwritten introductions. At about the same time, Wasserman negotiated a generous television production contract which resulted in the long-running series, ALFRED HITCHCOCK PRESENTS. All of the shows were introduced by Hitchcock although he directed only a handful of the actual episodes. The combination of this multiple media exposure, however, was enough to make Hitchcock for the rest his life the most widely recognizable film director anywhere in the world.

With REAR WINDOW (Paramount, 1954), the first of Hitchcock's films under his new contract, he began his association with screenwriter John Michael Hayes with whom he would collaborate on a total of four films in which, in Donald Spoto's words, "there is a credibility and an emotional wholeness, a heart and humor to the characters that other Hitchcock films—like STRANGERS ON A TRAIN and I CONFESS before, and others after—conspicuously lack."[20] Hitchcock's preoccupation with psychological and physical claustrophobia became more pronounced than ever in his Paramount productions and REAR WINDOW is certainly no exception. Based on a short novel by Cornell Woolrich, the plot contains all the elements of macabre suspense and tense entrapment which characterize Woolrich's best fiction. The story also gave Hitchcock the opportunity to throw back the curtain and reveal his view of human beings, how they live, or try to live, and how selfishly and sordidly they interact with each other. He had begun this process in LIFEBOAT but had been restricted by the times and the prevailing political mood. In REAR WINDOW he was able to cast James Stewart as the central character and yet stress his rather disagreeable personality.

He could cast Grace Kelly as Stewart's fiancée and show her to be brittle and possessive. Raymond Burr, as the brutal wife murderer, played his role of calculated villainy with a consummate, affable sadism.

TO CATCH A THIEF (Paramount, 1955) had Cary Grant back, this time playing a retired jewel thief, certainly not a novelty when you reflect on the myriad "B" pictures that had already been made about similar characters such as the Lone Wolf and Arsène Lupin. Grace Kelly was cast as a society girl fascinated by the possibility that Grant may actually have come out of retirement to commit a whole new series of daring thefts. The only way Grant can clear his name is to apprehend the real thief. Hitchcock intended the film as a comic thriller with no pretensions beyond that, although critics at the time seemed disappointed that it was not another picture in the same vein as REAR WINDOW.

Hitchcock continued the trend toward comedy in THE TROUBLE WITH HARRY (Paramount, 1955). It is an experiment in black humor in which several of the characters in the story, thinking themselves implicated in Harry's demise, move his body about, interring and disinterring it. Apparently any humor in the film was lost on most viewers at the time of its release, much in the fashion that Hitchcock would later claim that an audience would react to one of the stories supposedly he could not produce for television in which a man murders his wife, grinds up her bones and feeds them to the chickens, only to roast and feed the chickens to the law enforcement officers searching for her body. Yet, being Hitchcock, he *did* film this story eventually. THE TROUBLE WITH HARRY, even when it was re-released after Hitchcock's death, proved problematical with viewers.

Hitchcock decided to remake THE MAN WHO KNEW TOO MUCH (Paramount, 1956) partly because he needed a story for James Stewart and the old screenplay was near at hand, partly because he wanted to make the picture again with all the massive forces now at his disposal which he had not had in the United Kingdom during the Depression, and partly because there would be a lot of location shooting paid for by Paramount. Yet, in many ways the remake is less successful. The Albert Hall sequence is considerably longer, but to no real benefit. Hitchcock was able to have the cantata lavishly orchestrated and stunningly performed so that the camera could follow along in the conductor's score and the audience could see the percussionist prepare to sound the fatal cymbal crash. However, Switzerland was gone, as was the siege in the street and that strange scene in the dentist's office where those who threaten the cause are dispatched. Gone, also, was Peter Lorre's softspoken treachery. The gender of the kidnapped child was altered and Doris Day, as the aggrieved mother, was simply not convincing, nor were matters improved by having her sing her hit song, "*Que Sera Sera*."

Hitchcock still owed Warner Bros. a picture and so he made THE WRONG MAN (Warner's, 1957). The film again focused on the inept machinery of the law when Henry Fonda, in a case of mistaken identity, is arrested for a series of robberies he did not commit. The camera follows him through his torturous agony, sees his wife driven insane by the stress, and Fonda nearly destroyed by the system before the true culprit is exposed.

In a decade of highpoints, VERTIGO (Paramount, 1958) may be at the top of the list for depth and subtlety, while NORTH BY NORTHWEST clearly transcends any previous treatment he had ever given the theme of an innocent man embroiled in a network of nearly fatal circumstances which propels him into ceaseless and helpless flight. Hitchcock had intended the dual role in VERTIGO for Vera Miles and he was apprehensive, when she proved unavailable, about casting Kim Novak opposite James Stewart. Novak's role was so intricate that it is entirely possible she would not have been as effective as she was had Hitchcock not blocked out every nuance and shading of her characterization in the screenplay and dissected the interpretation she had to project down to the smallest detail, a living montage as complicated and elaborately constructed as any series of camera positions or interlocking cuts of film. Bernard Herrmann composed the score for THE WRONG MAN and Hitchcock retained him in that capacity through the production of MARNIE (Universal, 1964), which would be Hitchcock's last significant film. However, in the end, Hitchcock would treat Herrmann very badly, just as he would John Michael Hayes. People in a human sense never mattered very much to him and he tended in retrospect to discount much of their value to him and to the pictures on which they worked.

In VERTIGO, James Stewart played a former policeman who resigned from the force due to a fear of heights. He is hired by an old acquaintance to shadow the acquaintance's wife who is thought to be suicidal. Novak was cast as the wife and, from afar, Stewart falls in love with her. Because of his disability, he is unable to prevent her from jumping to her death from a mission belfry. His failure plunges him into a deep depression. He is suffering from acute melancholia and a guilt complex is how the screenplay explains it and, according to Donald Spoto, this was more than a little a self-diagnosis on Hitchcock's part. Stewart does not completely recover until, some six months later, he encounters a woman on the street who looks to be the reincarnation of the dead wife. As becomes apparent, the whole episode was a plot in which Stewart was the dupe. Novak, it turns out, was actually the old acquaintance's mistress who joined him in murdering his wife and deceiving Stewart into thinking her death a suicide. By sharing this knowledge with the viewer before the denouement, it is possible to appreciate more fully the complexity of Novak's characterization of a woman who loves one man enough to conspire with him to murder and who, twice, is the object of Stewart's love and, to an extent, returns it sufficiently to demonstrate that a woman can not only love two men at once but also keep a part of herself still hidden from view and to withstand such a contradiction with relative insouciance. When it is noted that the viewer never actually sees the wife and that, therefore, it is not even certain that Novak resembled her in the least, the ambiguity of the plot is further enhanced.

Cary Grant was the ideal choice in NORTH BY NORTHWEST to play the glib executive for whom both life and success have become predictable and routine only to be thrust into a Euripidean *malaise* where every certitude becomes a doubt, every freedom an imprisonment, everything sensible, absurd, everything normal, abnormal and contradictory. The psychological effect is similar to James Stewart's haunting acrophobia in VERTIGO. Probably the suggestion of a homosexual attraction between the chief Soviet agent, played by James Mason, and his assistant was a veiled reference to Cary Grant. Ray Austin, who would become a director, was present on the set at one point and he was able to hear Hitchcock mutter, in reference to him, " 'Here comes Mr. Grant and his man,' "[21] although there was no truth to the allegation. Grant, for his part, had worked enough for Hitchcock to trust him implicitly on every detail of the film. The spectacle at the conclusion was a fight atop Mount Rushmore which Hitchcock was not allowed to film on location. " 'They objected to a chase sequence up the nostrils of Lincoln's nose,' " Hitchcock later told Charles Higham. " 'Maybe they were afraid he would sneeze at this desecration of the shrine of democracy?' "[22] Eva Marie Saint gave a highly credible performance as a double agent and the sudden jump cut at the end, from the terrors of Mount Rushmore to Grant and Saint united again in a railway sleeping compartment makes the entire chase seem to be more a dream than a reality.

PSYCHO was Hitchcock's last film for Paramount before he signed a new contract with Universal which had been acquired somewhat recently by MCA. It remains Hitchcock's most important box-office success and the only film he financed personally. It is surely his *magnum opus* in the terror and suspense genre and it broke what had been a film convention prior to its release. The first point of view character is played by Janet Leigh. Her sudden, ridiculous chastity, inspired by her frustrated desire to legitimize her sexual liaison through marriage, leaves her more emotionally barren than before, and her questionable solution to her predicament, while garnering a viewer's tacit acquiescence, runs her into a totally unforeseen collision with the savage caprice often governing human behavior. She is lost to the viewer one third of the way through the film. Searching, then, for another point of view with which to identify, a viewer is provided the private detective investigating Leigh's theft of $40,000 or the unbalanced Norman Bates played by Anthony Perkins. When the detective is murdered, the viewer then is left with Perkins or Leigh's former lover who has now allied himself with Leigh's sister, played by Vera Miles, trying to learn what happened to Leigh. At the conclusion, however, a viewer is left where life frequently leaves all of us: with no one wholly admirable, no point of view capable of being indiscriminately embraced, and no fantastical day-dream which doesn't have its dark, nightmarish side, threatening to ensnare us. Instead of comforting fantasies, PSYCHO reminds us of human finitude. Hitchcock belongs to that tradition in the cinema that draws no moral conclusions but rather chooses to expand our consciousness to encompass the improbabilities of existence and the ingenious facility with which human beings deceive each other and themselves.

It was in this emotional climate that Hitchcock began work on THE BIRDS

(Universal, 1963), his third film based on a Daphne du Maurier story and his first under his new contract with Universal which was so generous, at least initially, that he could make what proved to be his most costly film to date. Hitchcock had placed women under a personal contract in the past, hoping to build each one into the prototype of the Hitchcock heroine, but with Tippi Hedren, a former model whom he saw in a television commercial, he was convinced that he had found—literally—the woman of his dreams. He chose her wardrobe and intended to script even her personal life. She was a divorced woman with a young daughter and, unbeknownst to Hitchcock at first, in love with her agent. He cast her as the heroine in THE BIRDS. " 'With any other director it would have taken fifteen years,' " Hedren later recalled, " 'but he had me involved in every part of the film—script completion, wardrobe design, special-effects work, dubbing. It was his film from start to finish, and he wanted me to learn how to put it together.' "[23] Rod Taylor was given the male lead, an actor with Cary Grant's ease but without his special charm and screen charisma.

THE BIRDS was fantasy in purest form. Hitchcock deserted his former dependence on classical unity in plot construction and occupied himself instead with a strictly thematic approach which, henceforth, became his principal mode of operation. In the wild, savage behavior of the birds he wanted to show the menace which surrounds us everywhere, although we are seldom aware of it. For the first time on a picture, he actually improvised several scenes on the set, changing the story and adding incidents as he was shooting. His emotional involvement in the subject matter was stronger than it had ever been before and the picture proved a completely exhausting experience for him. The final scene of Tippi Hedren, Rod Taylor, Jessica Tandy, and Veronica Cartwright making their way through the assembled flocks of birds, poised to attack but not yet ready to do so, brought the only resolution the film was to have, an outlook both bleak and unpromising. It is, indeed, Hitchcock's darkest vision of the inadequacy of humans to deal with the environment in which they find themselves. The final irony—which reveals that the resolution is no resolution at all, so much as it is despair in any resolution—comes when the little girl, played by Veronica Cartwright, asks to take the caged love birds along with them in the car as they pass through the low-humming congregation of birds of every description unified in their common hostility to man.

Hitchcock had hoped to tempt Grace Kelly back to the screen for MARNIE. She had met Prince Rainier of Monaco while filming TO CATCH A THIEF and now married and a mother she found, possibly to her dismay, that her subjects preferred to have her bounce royal children on her knee. Instead, and fatefully, Tippi Hedren was assigned the role of an emotionally disturbed thief who is married to Sean Connery whose motivation seems to be his attraction to a woman possessing abnormal criminal tendencies, sort of a reversal into the opposite of the polarities in TO CATCH A THIEF. At the time of its release, the film was greatly criticized for its poor technical details, from obvious painted backdrops to inadequate rear-screen projection. Some critics of Hitchcock tried to defend these slips and even deduced the most profound psychological inferences from them. The truth of the matter, however, is that Hitchcock simply lost all interest in the project once Tippi Hedren flatly refused his proposal that they sleep together. Hitchcock had said on several occasions to the press that he had been celibate for thirty years. Whether true or not, his attempt to achieve in reality that which before had only been possible through sublimation onto film shattered him. Universal, confronted by the poor showings of the film at the box office, retaliated by seizing control of his films from that point forward. Whatever he might choose to do in the future, he would have to use big name stars—often selected by the studio—and submit all details of story, script, production budget, and set design to the studio for its approval. Wasserman, who remained a close personal friend, arranged for Hitchcock to trade his interest in the television series and PSYCHO for a large block of MCA stock, which made him a multimillionaire, but the contract he had with Universal cost him most of his artistic freedom. " 'He became a different man,' " Bernard Herrmann subsequently reflected. " '[MCA] made him very rich, and they never let Hitch forget it.' "[24]

Hitchcock had signed Tippi Hedren to an exclusive seven-year contract. He had told her that if she would not accede to his demands, she would be finished in Hollywood. She chose to sit out her contract. Universal cast Paul Newman and Julie Andrews to star in TORN CURTAIN. Except for a relatively brief scene in which Hitchcock demonstrated that it is not so easy to murder an unwilling victim, TORN CURTAIN has little to recommend it and conveys the impression of patch-work and haphazard production. Universal nixed a script Hitchcock developed with Howard Fast, saying it was not a Hitchcock picture, an action which reduced him to tears, but he did not, or could not, fight it. TOPAZ (Universal, 1969), which appeared three years after TORN CURTAIN, was, if anything, worse. Hitchcock was so undecided about how to end the picture that, even after its previews, it was still released with two alternative conclusions. " 'He didn't have the strength to stand up against the company powers when it came to money . . . ,' " Samuel Taylor, the screenwriter who came to Hitchcock's rescue, recalled. " 'TOPAZ was a dreadful experience because Hitchcock threw out the screenplay entirely and had me writing scenes a few days—and in many cases a few hours—before they were shot.' "[25]

There is no question that these persistent failures began to undermine Hitchcock's confidence in himself. Increasingly, he turned for advice to those he would once have readily ignored and almost willingly refused to take a step without thoroughly discussing every aspect of it with the Universal management. In a last ditch effort to regain what he was convinced he had lost he resorted once more to the formula of the British thriller in FRENZY (Universal, 1972). It was filmed on location in the United Kingdom and was more than an echo of THE LODGER insofar as the plot concerned a strangler preying upon women whose crimes are blamed on an innocent person. The murders are shown in far more graphic detail, however, with the point clearly made that the strangler's thrill comes from having an orgasm while choking his victims. Jon Finch, having just appeared in Roman Polanski's MACBETH (Columbia, 1971), was cast as the innocent man and he proved both unlikeable and unsympathetic in the role. FRENZY was "magnificently structured, crisply acted, smoothly edited—and utterly devoid of any positive human feeling," is how Donald Spoto summed it up.[26]

FAMILY PLOT (Universal, 1976) was four years in the making and, reputedly, the strain was such that it was the cause for Hitchcock's pace-maker having had to be implanted, although his weight and increased drinking probably also contributed to the situation. It is an entertaining, comical, but implausible film. Hitchcock did not want it to be his final picture. Yet, as the months passed, and then years, even he finally recognized that it indeed would be.

Vicki closed her notebook. We had come to the conclusion of our conversation. Hitchcock observed the perplexed look on my face and responded with an inquiring glance.

"It's that Peter Lorre anecdote," I said, "the one about sending you the canaries. It's such a fine story, I wish it were true."

Hitchcock appeared genuinely regretful.

"Then say it is true. Just say that I can't remember it having happened, but as I get older there are many things I can't remember."

On the way out of his office we paused before a painting on the wall which reproduced the presidents' faces on Mount Rushmore in which Hitchcock's familiar countenance, at once beaming and leering in diabolical jest, had been interpolated. In its way, it symbolized the private jokes he loved to play on audiences, the eruption of the disconcerting or dangerous into the mundane, a ghoulish discord in the midst of complacency, the infinitely capricious turns life can take when we least expect it and are least prepared to cope with it. Nothing was said. We just all smiled at one another.

Alfred Hitchcock died on 29 April 1980.

# Howard Hawks

## I

It was hot in Palm Springs. The sand from the white dunes swept across the highway, blown by a hot wind. The heat rose in silent eddies from the city streets. It radiated everywhere. It was here that Howard Hawks had finally come to live. The French were the first to recognize him as one of the great directors of Hollywood films. He was also a gentleman.

He was dressed in light blue shorts and a white shirt as he opened his front door that day in late spring, 1975. The effect of the heat was profound. It made you feel almost light-headed. It clouded your mind and obscured your memory. You walked as if in a daze. Yet, Howard was accustomed to it. He walked very slowly. His legs were still tender with blisters from cactus poison.

"I've been in the hospital for the last three days," he remarked, lowering himself into a leather reclining chair and propping up his legs. He was being careful. "I was out motorcycling with my son." Gregg Hawks, Howard's youngest son from his third and final marriage, had been named after the cinematographer Gregg Toland. Now in his teens, Gregg was living with his seventy-nine-year-old father. "I made the mistake of riding through a clump of poisonous cactus. I'll be laid up at least another week, maybe ten days."

There were two dogs in the room, one of them a golden shepherd, the other a hound. There were no rugs, only cool stones bordered by masonry. The hound collapsed on the floor near Howard's chair. The shepherd came over to me, laid his head on my leg, and regarded me with sad eyes. I petted him briefly and then he sauntered philosophically away. The heat was everywhere in the room, heavy and lethargic.

I recalled something French director and film critic Jacques Rivette had written about Hawks' MONKEY BUSINESS (20th-Fox, 1952) in LES CAHIERS DU

CINÉMA. "But now the enemy creeps within man himself: the subtle poison of the Fountain of Youth. After all, for a long time we have known the temptation of youth is the not very subtle temptation of the Devil—now a monkey, now a hound—when held in check by a rare intelligence. Hawks with a bit of cruelty is dead-set against that most baneful of illusions: adolescence, infancy are barbarous states from which only education saves us. The infant is scarcely distinguishable from the savage whom he imitates in his games. Should he drink of the precious liquid, even the most dignified old man will fall prey to imitating an ape. In this we recognize a classic conception of man who is unable to be great except by acquired knowledge and by maturity. At the end of his journey, a man's old age will be his judge."[1] Now Howard Hawks was an old man.

"I will tell you a story I have never told anyone," he said. The shepherd got up, shook himself, and found a new, cooler spot on which to slumber as Vicki opened her notebook. Hawks looked at us for a moment. His eyes were distant. So often in his films, he ignored dialogue and concentrated on eyes. "It's a sequel, really, but I have to tell you the whole story first, for it to have any meaning. Lauren Bacall's coming to Hollywood was a mistake on my secretary's part. I only wanted to find out about her and my secretary sent her an airplane ticket instead. She showed up in a sweater and gabardine skirt, very excited, with a high nasal voice. I couldn't use her. I told her it was her voice. She asked me what she could do about lowering it. I repeated what I had heard from other people. For two weeks I didn't see her. She went back to the apartment where she was staying and worked on it. When she saw me again, I was amazed. Her voice had become deep, husky.

"I began to invite her to my home for the Saturday night parties I gave. I always ended up having to drive her home.

" 'Betty,' I told her, 'this isn't going to work. I don't always want to take you home. Can't you interest one of the others in escorting you?'

" 'I've never been very good with men,' she said.

" 'Why not try being insolent?' I suggested.

"The next Saturday night she came over to me and said she had found a ride home.

" 'How'd you do it?' I asked.

"She said, 'I just walked up to him and asked him where he bought his tie. He asked me why I wanted to know. I told him so I could tell people not to go there. He laughed, and now he's driving me home.'

"It was Clark Gable.

"I got so to like her insolent style that I went to Jules Furthman when I was back on the Warner lot. We were preparing Ernest Hemingway's TO HAVE AND HAVE NOT [Warner's, 1944]. Furthman and Bill Faulkner were doing the screenplay."

I interrupted.

"Duke Wayne told me that originally you had done all the preparation work on CASABLANCA [Warner's, 1942], but that at the last minute you went off the picture and Michael Curtiz directed it in your place. Duke said you only have to look at CASABLANCA to see how much of a Hawks picture it really is. I wouldn't bring it up, except a number of critics have claimed TO HAVE AND HAVE NOT was an imitation of CASABLANCA.''

"Well, Wayne's right. I did most of the preparatory work on CASABLANCA. When it came to doing TO HAVE AND HAVE NOT, I wanted the picture to be different. Ernest had given me screen rights on the novel some years before, but I just couldn't come up with the right treatment for it. With Betty, I thought I might have it. I asked Jules if he could write in a part for an insolent girl. He didn't see why not. I gave Betty a screen test opposite Bogart. I even wrote that line for her, 'All you have to do is whistle. You know how to whistle, don't you? Just put your lips together and blow.' Betty was great.''

"They fell in love," I said. "Did you try to capture that in the picture, or, later, in THE BIG SLEEP [Warner's, 1946]?''

"No. I tried to keep it out. I had told Bogie that I had a challenge for him, a girl as insolent as he was. I didn't figure he would fall in love with her. But he did. Of course, that helped Betty. Bogie played all his scenes for her. Under other circumstances that would have been an almost impossible thing for anyone to get Bogie to do.''

Howard grew quiet. Outside the sun blazed mutely. Its light glared on the white stone fence.

"Did it occur to you that Bogart was falling in love with someone who was to a certain extent your creation?" I asked.

Howard nodded. "I even took Betty aside and warned her. 'Bogie is falling in love with you, Betty. He doesn't know it's just a role.' " He smiled. "That's what brings me to the sequel. This last year I was invited by the Academy to receive a special award. Wayne was going to give it to me. Betty was there. She came up behind me and kissed me. She said, 'I'm still playing the same role, Howard.' ''

"He was not a demonstrative, relaxed sort of man," Lauren Bacall wrote about Hawks in BY MYSELF (1978), published a year after Hawks' death. "He was inscrutable, speaking quietly in a fairly monotonous voice. He seemed very sure of himself.''[2] She confirmed that "Howard had thought everything out very carefully indeed. He was tailoring everything to complement what he wanted me to be, and out of that would come his dream realized, his invention—emerging perfectly out of his mold after the proper baking time of all the right ingredients.''[3] Hawks had married his second wife, Nancy Raye Gross, in 1941. He called her Slim and she called him Steve. These became the pet names by which Bogart and Bacall referred to each other in TO HAVE AND HAVE NOT. However, the reality was somewhat different than the cinematic fantasy. As Gerald Mast put it in HOWARD HAWKS, STORYTELLER (1982): "Unlike the men in so many of his films, Hawks was never able to find a woman who could be simultaneously his vocational and sexual partner.''[4]

It seemed an incongruity to me that Hawks, who placed human relationships first among his elective affinities, should have found himself friends with two such divergent personalities as Hemingway and Faulkner. Hemingway had early perceived the inevitable losses life extracts from you and was preoccupied by how to deal with them, but Faulkner was light years removed from such ruminations. When he wrote for Howard, however, he worked, I suspect, by assignment, submerging any of his own concerns in order to give Howard what he wanted.

"You knew Faulkner rather well."

"Yes, I did. I was in New York working on SCARFACE [United Artists, 1932]. I read Faulkner. He was employed as a clerk in Macy's book store. I later bought his short story, 'Turnabout,' and made it the basis for the picture TODAY WE LIVE [M-G-M, 1933]. Faulkner by then was living back in Mississippi. I sent him a check and invited him to come to Hollywood to M-G-M, where I was under contract, to assist on the screenplay."

Howard rolled his head to one side to see me better. The heat in the room seemed to dry you up so that you were actually chilled by it.

"He came to my office. 'I'm Howard Hawks,' I told him. 'I know,' he said. 'I saw your name on a check.' He sat there and smoked his pipe while I took a couple of hours to explain what I wanted. He said nothing until I finished. Then he stood up. 'Where are you going?' I asked him. 'I'm going to write your screenplay,' he said. 'It should take me no more than a week.' He didn't know anything about screenwriting. 'Wait a minute,' I said. 'I want to know something about you.' He hesitated. 'Have you got a drink?' he asked. I pulled out a bottle and we began to talk. When we finished that, we went out and visited a few saloons. By three in the morning, when the last cigarette was drowned in a whiskey glass, it was the beginning of a relationship. We were friends from that day until his death."

I remembered, as we sat about in easy chairs, the air in the room yawning then falling wearily to dozing, that Faulkner had sent Howard a letter after he had returned to Oxford, Mississippi following his stint at Metro. "I'm sitting on the porch with the rain dripping off the eaves, drinking bourbon, and I hear a wonderful sound—the toilet, and it's due to you."[5]

Throughout his career as a filmmaker in his quiet fashion Howard Hawks managed to assemble some extraordinary talent around him, all of it to put forth a consistent, cogent point of view. I knew better, however, than to say it because he would probably deny it. "He took me to lunch and told me about his directing experiences with various actresses," Lauren Bacall wrote. "It was always what he said to them, or to Howard Hughes, to Jack Warner—he always came out on top, he always won. He was mesmerizing and I believed every story he told me."[6] According to Bacall, Hawks enlisted Slim in his efforts to keep her and Bogart apart. In Hollywood, everyone prefers to live by illusions, and, when you come down to it, not just in Hollywood. What Bacall did not tell was that she had set her hat for Bogart and, if it took playing the Hawksian woman off screen as well as on to accomplish her goal, she would do it. But Bogart did not respond as swiftly as she hoped. He continued to delay divorcing Mayo Methot, his third wife, and this circumstance so depressed Bacall that she became awkward and flat in her scenes in THE BIG SLEEP which went into production next. So much was this the case that Jack L. Warner, who had bought half her contract from Hawks, decided to hold up release of the picture for six months and to try Bacall in another film, and with another director, Herman Shumlin, whose first Warner's vehicle, WATCH ON THE RHINE (Warner's, 1943) had earned Paul Lukas an Academy Award. Titled CONFIDENTIAL AGENT (Warner's, 1945), Bacall played opposite Charles Boyer but her performance was even more flat and wooden than it had been in THE BIG SLEEP. It was therefore in a state approaching desperation that Warner insisted Hawks write additional scenes for Bogart and Bacall to capture some of the magic they had had in TO HAVE AND HAVE NOT. The strategy worked, in more ways than one. Bogart finally did go through with his divorce from Mayo and on 21 May 1945 he and Bacall were married. Hawks, however, could see what was going on. He had turned down an offer of $75,000 from another studio for a loan-out of Bacall while THE BIG SLEEP was in production. Now he sold his half of her contract to Warner.

Once married to Bogart, whatever her career would hold for Bacall, the special Hawksian charisma vanished. She lost virtually all interest in sailing on the *Santana* which was where Bogart's heart and soul were truly at peace. It wasn't too long, in fact, after Bacall stopped coming to the boat that Bogart resumed his affair with Verita Thompson, whose last name was then Peterson and whom he called Pete. A former make-up artist, eventually she became Bogart's executive secretary and remained his mistress for a number of years. In one intimate conversation, as recorded in BOGIE AND ME: A LOVE STORY (1982), Bogart confessed to her, " 'I got drunk and I got married and I don't even know how the hell it all happened! But now I'm locked in again, and I gotta figure a way out of it.'

"It was a non sequitur if I'd ever heard one. To put it quite simply—and it's an oversimplification—I was stunned.

" 'Out of your *marriage*?' I said.

" 'Yeah,' Bogie said. 'What the hell do you think I'm talking about?'

" 'I don't know *what* the hell you're talking about,' I said. 'Are you saying that you don't even love her?'

" 'I don't know what the hell I'm saying, Pete. She's a great broad, she really is, but . . .'

" 'But do you love her?'

" 'What the hell's love?' Bogie said.

" 'Don't toy with me, Bogie. I don't give a damn how you define love. I want to know if you love her, however you define it.'

" 'All I know is that it's not like with you and me,' he said. 'Christ! I've really done it up good this time. An actress again, and an ambitious one. We haven't a damn thing in common, and she's young enough to be my daughter.'

" '*I'm* young enough to be your daughter,' I said.

" 'In years, yeah. But that's not what I'm talking about. She really needs someone more her age. And she's an actress, and with this goddamned Hollywood and its Casanova leading men. I've really done it this time.'

" 'So that's what's *really* worrying you. You're afraid she'll go running off with a Casanova and make you look like an ass!'

" 'No,' Bogie said. 'Well, the thought has crossed my mind, but that's not what I'm talking about. Look, I just want you to know that I still love you and that everything I've ever said in the past about us still stands. Please, Pete, don't hold this against me. I didn't do this to *you*; I did it to *me*.'

" 'And to Betty,' I said.

" 'Christ! And to Betty, yes. I really screwed up. But I'll work it out, Pete. I've got to.' "[7]

If George Raft used his marriage-in-name-only to protect himself from ever having to marry again, Bogart was a person too deeply divided, with patterns too deep seated, with contradictory needs too great to live a conventional life. I shall have more to say about Bogart's obsessive anxieties and self-doubts later on, in the career study of John Huston who did so much to help create the Bogart persona, but for now let it suffice that in the end Hawks was right, Bogart, no less than the movie-going public, had fallen in love with a woman who was very much a Hawks creation, a woman whom he had named Lauren for the world and Slim for TO HAVE AND HAVE NOT.

## II

A descendant of wealthy paper manufacturers, Howard Hawks was born 30 May 1896 in Goshen, Indiana. He was the eldest of three brothers. All three would enter the motion picture industry. In Jack L. Warner's words, Kenneth Hawks, "who became a comedy director, was killed in an airplane crash just as fame was within his grasp, and Howard went on to the pinnacle...."[8] Kenneth died in 1930. William Hawks was a Hollywood producer for many years. The Hawks family moved to Neenah, Wisconsin when Howard was two and again to California when he was ten. Howard attended elementary and high school in Pasadena. In 1917 he graduated from Cornell University with a degree in mechanical engineering. During his summers, he worked as a property man at Famous Players-Lasky, long before it became Paramount, and was eventually promoted to an assistant director. He joined the Army Air Corps once the United States entered the World War and was stationed in France. At the signing of the Armistice, he held the rank of a second lieutenant. After the war, he built airplanes and drove race cars until 1922 when an inheritance permitted him to re-enter the picture business as an independent producer and writer of short comedies. Howard and Ken Hawks scripted five Monte Banks comedies for Jack L. Warner's fledgling production company which were sold to the CBC Company in New York. CBC would become Columbia Pictures and through his work on

these comedies Howard made the acquaintance of Harry Cohn, one of the founders of the company and eventually head of production at Columbia. The comedies
cost about $3,000 to make and were sold to CBC for $6,000. When Jesse L.
Lasky offered him a better opportunity at Paramount, Howard ended his association with Warner and went to work in the Paramount story department. During
his time with Lasky, he was involved in some way in the production of more
than forty films, and on several received screen credit for the scenario. In other
cases, he wrote titles cards for the films. "It is interesting," Gerald Mast wrote,
"that a director like Hitchcock, who began as a designer, storyboards his films—
sketches the look of shots on cards—while a director like Hawks, who began
in a story department, writes the narrative sequences down."[9]

By 1924, Howard was convinced that he wanted to direct films. He signed
on at Metro-Goldwyn-Mayer, shortly after it was formed, in the hope of realizing
this ambition, but after two years, when the hope still had not materialized, he
quit. Sol Wurtzel in charge of production at Fox Film Corporation had previously
heard of the fine work Hawks had done while at Paramount and put him under
contract with the definite promise that he would be given a picture to direct.
That film turned out to be THE ROAD TO GLORY (Fox, 1926) which starred
May McAvoy and Rockliffe Fellowes. Hawks' screenplay for the picture was
based on an experience he had had when a girl at a party he gave went blind as
a result of drinking bootleg liquor. While she was waiting for the doctor, she
said, "Just because I'm blind doesn't mean I'm not good in bed." Hawks admired
her spirit and, while not daring to use such a line in his scenario, he did tell a
story about a young girl's reaction to going blind. In talking with him many
years later, Hawks made certain that it was understood that Wurtzel was "a very
astute and wise man," but that THE ROAD TO GLORY was appreciated by
only a few critics. " 'Look,' " Howard quoted Wurtzel as having said,
" 'you've shown you can make a picture, but for God's sake go out and make
entertainment.' So I went home and wrote a story about Adam and Eve waking
up in the Garden of Eden and called it FIG LEAVES. It got its cost back in one
theatre. And that taught me a very good lesson. From that time on, I've been
following his advice about trying to make entertainment."

Hawks followed FIG LEAVES (Fox, 1926) with a comedy titled THE CRA-
DLE SNATCHERS (Fox, 1927) which was given the fast pacing that would
come to typify Hawks' treatment of comic material. The picture was based on
a stage play by Russell Medcraft and Norma Mitchell and featured Arthur Lake
and Sally Eilers. PAID TO LOVE (Fox, 1927) came next, with Virginia Valli,
George O'Brien, and William Powell. F.W. Murnau had just completed directing
SUNRISE (Fox, 1927) and the Fox executives were taken with his use of trick
photography. Being of a mechanical frame of mind, Hawks tried several trick
techniques in this picture but no sooner had he tried than he abandoned them.
He felt that simple expression is preferable to all manner of complexity and he
came, for the most part, to keep his camera at eye level. Anything else, unless
it was required for emphasis, tended to be a distraction and therefore interfered

with the ability of the viewer to remain oblivious to the mechanics by which personality and incident were being projected on the screen.

Howard wrote the screenplay for A GIRL IN EVERY PORT (Fox, 1928) and it proved "the beginning of a relationship I have used in a number of pictures. It's really a love story between two men." The story concerns two sailors, played by Victor McLaglen and Robert Armstrong, who share the same girls in port. At the end, the two renounce women forever and go off together. The story moves from port to port and given the women these two meet their attitude seems justified. What is uppermost in the film is that what unites men in friendship is alien to the predatory and exploitative instincts of women. Hawks married for the first time the year the picture was released, to Athole Shearer Ward, Norma Shearer's sister, and adopted Athole's son Peter Ward from her prior marriage. While such an action in his personal life may seem at odds with the view of women in A GIRL IN EVERY PORT, the truth would appear to be that Hawks was just beginning to detail the complex and tenuous bonds which hold human beings to one another rather than concentrating on the isolation and separateness of so many relationships. Most of his subsequent films deal in one way or another with a love affair between two people, a man and a woman in many cases, but also, as in RED RIVER (United Artists, 1948), between two men.

Peter Bogdanovich remarked once that in perspective and viewpoint he found Hawks most closely related to Ernest Hemingway. Gerald Mast went even farther to draw a parallel between them when he observed that "both told stories of men in action, and that action was a personal assertion of existential meaning in a universe of potential cosmic meaninglessness. Both had a special fondness for stories of 'Men Without Women' and of men who tried to find and make a place for those necessary women. Both preferred characters who did more than they said, felt more than they spoke. Both built their narratives upon moral systems based on personal definitions of honor and integrity, rather than the societally accepted and acceptable ones, which their works overtly, or covertly attacked. Both developed a style—either verbal or visual—which was distinguished for its spare, bare understatement."[10] However, what is missed in all of these similarities is what ultimately separated the two men. Hemingway was haunted by visions of the utter futility of all human endeavor. This posture Hawks could never endorse, just as he would later bitterly condemn Hemingway's suicide as an act of cowardice. Without being aware of it, or even the consequences of his logic, Mast came to much the same conclusion when he reflected on the difference between Harry Morgan as Hemingway drew him in TO HAVE AND HAVE NOT and Hawks' film version of the character. "Hemingway's Harry passively suffers a lot of bad luck; he is precisely the kind of loser Hawks did not like. Hawks would convert this loser into a loner who finally rebels against his luck by taking action against it. He becomes the master, not the slave of his fate."[11] The option Hawks purchased on Hemingway's THE SUN ALSO RISES (1926) soon after it was published he never exercised because he could not conceive how it might possibly be made into a comedy and he had no desire to treat impotence tragically. Joseph McBride in HAWKS ON HAWKS (1982) insisted that "Hawks misunderstood Jake Barnes' problem."[12] To validate his point, he quoted what Hemingway had told A.E. Hotchner in PAPA HEMING-WAY (1966) when Hotchner confirmed that Barnes had not lost his testicles. "No," Hemingway replied. "And that was very important to the kind of man he was. His testicles were intact. That was all he had, but this made him capable of feeling everything a normal man feels but not able to do anything about it. That the wound was a physical wound, and not a psychological wound, was the vital thing."[13] Yet, Hawks' major problem with the story as Hemingway wrote it was not whether Barnes' impotence was physical or psychological in origin, but rather how such a disability could be portrayed on screen so that it would be acceptable to the censors. Beyond this, Hawks could not bring himself to treat this subject tragically, as Hemingway had, precisely because of his tem-peramental opposition to the despair at the center of Hemingway's world-view. For Hawks, THE SUN ALSO RISES would have to be a comedy since, if he could find a way to introduce Barnes' impotence, it would only have been in such a way that Jake Barnes could be seen to overcome it. Hawks did tell McBride how, six months after he had sold the property to Darryl Zanuck, Zanuck had telephoned him: " 'Howard, how were you gonna make that?' I said, 'Darryl, I'll be glad to tell you for $100,000.' "[14] Henry King opted to treat Barnes' impotence tragically and the film proved unsuccessful.

Hawks' last three films for Fox were all made as a result of existing contractual obligations by the studio. FAZIL (Fox, 1928) was a routine affair and THE AIR CIRCUS (Fox, 1928) was not much better, although in the latter Howard did have an opportunity to develop a story about two novice fliers overcoming their fear of the air. TRENT'S LAST CASE (Fox, 1929) was based on a mystery novel by E.C. Bentley and proved to be Hawks' first cinematic detective story. The studio was unable to acquire rights to make a talking version of the novel, so it had to be filmed as a silent. Hawks, who found the plot preposterous (a man plans his own death so as to implicate his young wife's lover), changed much in the story and filmed it as a comedy.

Persuaded that being a contract director unnecessarily constricted his ability to make pictures the way he wanted to make them, Hawks left Fox and became a freelance director. Henceforth he would contract to individuals or to studios to make one picture or several after his own fashion on terms which would allow him to have control over stories and casting. Occasionally, as in his work for Samuel Goldwyn, he would compromise this freedom, but he was never entirely happy with the results and those films are not generally regarded to be among his best work. The fact that he had an extraordinary talent for making financially successful pictures permitted him over the years to retain a degree of artistic freedom with virtually every studio that was almost unique in the entire industry. Since this freedom also meant that he would have to make a living on what his films earned by way of profits, it made him as keenly conscious of costs and grosses as any film distributor.

Hawks' first talking picture was THE DAWN PATROL (Warner's, 1930) which he contracted to make for Jack L. Warner. He worked on the screenplay and was able to choose his own players. The story permitted Hawks to introduce themes which he was to vary, invert, and transmute over the next four decades. The film deals with the fraternity of men at war, the excitement of mechanical flight, and the confrontation with mortality. It was a time for war pictures. William Wellman had directed WINGS (Paramount, 1929). Lewis Milestone was directing ALL QUIET ON THE WESTERN FRONT (Universal, 1930) and Howard Hughes was at work producing HELL'S ANGELS (United Artists, 1930). Hawks hired for his picture some of the same fliers Hughes had previously used in preparing certain aerial sequences for HELL'S ANGELS. When Hughes learned that the pilots had been interrogated by Hawks about what they had done for Hughes, he grew worried lest the Warner Bros. film copy identical scenes from a picture in which he had invested heavily. Hughes questioned the pilots himself and learned that there was at least one striking similarity between the two films: the bombing of an enemy ammunition dump. Hughes became even more alarmed when he realized that THE DAWN PATROL would precede HELL'S ANGELS into general release.

When THE DAWN PATROL was screened at a San Francisco theatre, Reggie Callow of the Hughes organization and Joseph Moncure March, story editor on HELL'S ANGELS, flew up to see it. They thought it an excellent film but were struck by similarities it bore to a stage play that had been successfully directed by James Whale and had done much to establish his reputation. Returning to Hollywood, the two contacted Whale who, in turn, notified the copyright holder for JOURNEY'S END, the stage play in question, and a few days later the copyright holder for the play joined Hughes in a joint suit against Warner Bros. for plagiarism. The screenplay for THE DAWN PATROL had been written by Hawks, Don Totheroh, and Seton I. Miller, based on an original story by John Monk Saunders titled "The Flight Commander." Hughes very much wanted to obtain possession of the screenplay. One day a private detective Hughes had hired showed up at Joseph Moncure March's office and told March that he had arranged with one of the secretaries at Warner Bros. to get a copy of the screenplay and to show it to them at her apartment. March was to accompany the detective. They went. It was a plant. They were both arrested. Eventually the plagiarism suit was heard and the motion denied. Shortly thereafter the charges against March and the detective were dropped.

Hawks felt all the fuss idiotic. He had made, he was convinced, a good film with Richard Barthelmess, Douglas Fairbanks, Jr., and Neil Hamilton. The story did have certain superficial similarities to JOURNEY'S END which was filmed by Gainsborough in the United Kingdom and distributed in the United States by Tiffany Productions and critics did not hesitate to point these out, along with making a suggestion that perhaps the genre should die out quickly. THE DAWN PATROL, as Hawks had filmed it, was a lean, straightforward story of British pilots who in a spirit of hopelessness encounter the inevitability of death as they systematically prepare for bombing missions over enemy territory. Hawks at times piloted a camera plane and many of the aerial sequences are truly remarkable. If Hawks had had any shortcoming, it was learning how to direct actors in a sound film. "I saw the rushes after the first day of shooting," Jack L. Warner recalled in MY FIRST HUNDRED YEARS IN HOLLYWOOD (1965), "and the actors looked like wooden soldiers glued to a board.

" 'Howard,' I asked, 'have you ever directed a talking picture before?'

" 'Well . . . no,' he said, and his face looked like a bad case of sunstroke.

" 'Howard,' I said crisply, 'in a talking picture the people talk. Please have them talk and move around a little more. That's why my brothers and I created sound and talking films. You remember—*don't you*?' "[15]

Years later, and after many more very successful films for Warner Bros., after Jack L. Warner had sold out and was working on his memoirs, he ran into Hawks again and, after telling him about his projected book, he started to recall some of their early experiences together. "He walked away," Warner recalled, "and I could have caught pneumonia from the cold shoulder I got."[16] Hawks' reaction is comprehensible because he had taken Warner's advice to heart but, without any mention of it or his having needed it, he had since developed his own version of what had happened. "When I was making THE DAWN PATROL . . . ," he told Joseph McBride, "I got forty letters from the front office . . . saying that I'd missed chances of doing good scenes because I'd underdone them so much. I've saved the letters just for fun. The dialogue before that reminded you of a villain talking on a riverboat, UNCLE TOM'S CABIN or something like that. They hammed it up. And I stopped them from doing that in DAWN PATROL. They weren't used to normal dialogue. They weren't used to normal reading. They wanted to have somebody beat his chest and wave his arms. But when Thalberg saw the picture, he said, 'You son of a bitch. Everybody'll be trying to do that, and they won't know how to do it, and we'll get into more goddam trouble.' It was the biggest grossing picture of the year. And then they decided I knew dialogue."[17] THE DAWN PATROL did make a respectable profit, but it is questionable that it was the most successful picture at the box office in 1930. What is characteristic in all of this, beyond the pardonable hyperbole, is Hawks' insistence that it was he who always knew exactly the right thing to do and that he persisted in doing it despite all the wrong-headed objections with which he was constantly bombarded.

Hawks was hired by Harry Cohn at Columbia Pictures to direct THE CRIMINAL CODE (Columbia, 1931) which starred Walter Huston and Constance Cummings. The story was based on a stage play that had failed because of its ending. It concerns a district attorney who brilliantly secures a number of convictions. When his political fortunes reverse, he ends up as warden of the prison where many of those he once prosecuted are serving time. "I got together with ten convicts and said, 'How should this end?' " Howard related, "and they told me in no uncertain terms." Four decades later, he still felt that Walter Huston, cast as the district attorney, was one of the greatest actors Hollywood had ever had. "His character was based on a district attorney we had here in California," he continued, "who was finally tried and sentenced to prison, and they put him in the prison hospital to protect him because the place was full of men he had sent there. Finally he said, 'I can't take this any longer. I want to go out into the yard.' He went out into the yard, and the scene we did in the picture was just what he did. Things like being shaved by a man he had sent up for cutting someone's throat were all true." Hawks learned something important while directing THE CRIMINAL CODE, that tragedy can be made amusing and that to perceive the humor and folly in human tragedy is to experience a sudden, surprising sense of freedom.

Considering the fact that Howard Hughes put nearly three million dollars into HELL'S ANGELS and had tinkered with it for months, it cannot have pleased him that it lost $357,807.07 upon release. Hughes thought most highly of Lewis Milestone, but when it came to making SCARFACE he wanted the director of THE DAWN PATROL, a film which, upon release, had showed a profit of $400,000. Hughes negotiated a contract with Hawks whereby the former would produce and the latter direct any property the two agreed on and which could be broken by nothing more than a verbal dissent. Hughes also guaranteed Hawks control of the picture. Hawks was intrigued with the idea of making a gangster film, but he wanted to alter the treatment. Films such as LITTLE CAESAR (Warner's, 1930) and PUBLIC ENEMY (Warner's, 1931) had stressed that social conditions were the major cause of criminal violence in the United States. Hawks was more Calvinistic. He told Ben Hecht when he began work on the screenplay that he wanted to tell the story of Al Capone but so stylized that it would take in the whole family in such a way that it would seem that the Borgias had been set down in modern Chicago. Paul Muni was cast as Scarface and George Raft, making his film debut, played Guino, for a time Scarface's hit man. Hawks had become acquainted with John Ford when they both worked at Fox and one important cinematic element he learned from Ford was how to select a single physical action to indicate the interior sensations of a character. Two or three gang killings in Chicago had involved a victim with a nickel clenched in a palm. Hawks had Raft flip a nickel in SCARFACE as his trademark. Gerald Mast observed an even less obvious use of a physical action in the scene where Raft sits in Muni's chair cutting out a string of paper dolls. Ann Dvorak, cast as Cesca, Muni's sister, is attracted to Guino. "The identical, symmetrical dolls (neither the object nor the business appears in the script) is perhaps a metaphor for Guino's love life—a series of faceless, identical, flat physical objects, each of them different but all of them alike. Cesca manages to lure Guino's attention away from these dolls with her provocative humor: 'The one on the end is cute.' "[18]

"We were influenced a good deal by incestuous elements in the story of the Borgias," Howard told us. "We made the brother-sister relationship clearly incestuous. But the censors misunderstood our intention and objected to it because they thought the relationship between them was too beautiful to be attributed to a gangster. We had a scene in which Muni told his sister that he loved her, and we couldn't play it in full light. We wound up playing it in silhouette against a curtain with the light coming from outside. It was a little bit too intimate to show faces—you wouldn't dare take a chance.''

Hawks regarded Paul Muni as a fine actor but he was unaccustomed to fist-icuffs. In the picture, he had to hit a man. Hawks engaged a friend of his who was a prizefighter and had him work with Muni. Every time Muni threw a punch, the fighter blocked it with a hand. When the scene was filmed, the fighter took the blow straight on and was knocked over a table. Muni was so petrified by what he had done that he became nonplussed. ''Act!'' Hawks shouted at him. Muni acted.

Capone heard about SCARFACE and sent several of his associates to see Hawks, requesting a preview of the picture. Hawks told them when it was released Capone could buy a ticket. However, once it was completed, Hawks did screen it for a few of Capone's friends. They thought it was great and related their sentiments to Capone. When Hawks came to Chicago, Capone wanted to meet him and sent a car for him.

''They met me at the train,'' Howard recalled. ''They were late. One of the fellows said, 'There was a killing last night and we had to go to the funeral.' I said, 'Do I have to ride with you if there was a killing last night?' They said I could ride in a different car. But when we went into a cafe, they would sit with their backs to the wall and I had my back to the door. We had some damn good-looking girls with us, a bit brassy but very pretty. When I saw Capone, we had tea and he was dressed in a morning coat, striped trousers. I was with him for two or three hours.''

Capone liked SCARFACE so much he went to see it five or six times and finally got a personal print of it. Capone's enthusiasm may seem a little curious particularly in view of the end the screenplay indicates for the protagonist. Yet the censors were sufficiently concerned that they felt it was not enough to show the gangster gunned down. They wanted a scene added in which Muni would be shown mounting the scaffold. The scene was actually shot and added, although it was later dropped. Problems such as this held up release of the film for nearly two years.

Hawks returned to work for Jack L. Warner on a brace of pictures. THE CROWD ROARS (Warner's, 1932) is a transition film. It embodies a love of danger and excitement. Hawks knew race cars as he knew airplanes and he knew the men who drove them as he had known wartime fliers. James Cagney had the lead. He was tough, really tough, but he was also capable of an amazing degree of sensitivity. Hawks made use of that. Indeed, he may even have had Cagney in mind when he wrote the original story.

TIGER SHARK (Warner's, 1932) was more modest in social impact than SCARFACE, but it was as thoroughly Hawksian, varying the theme of A GIRL IN EVERY PORT by adding the tension of a romantic triangle. Hawks was always interested more in the personalities of actors and actresses than just simply the plot and what the characters were supposed to do in the plot. And it is to Edward G. Robinson's personality that TIGER SHARK owes whatever merit it may have. "When we started TIGER SHARK," Howard said, "it was written about a very dour man. At the end of the first day I said to Eddie, 'This is going to be the dullest picture that's ever been made.' Eddie said, 'What can we do?' I said, 'Well, if you're willing to try it with me, let's make him happy-go-lucky, talkative. You're going to have to keep talking all through the picture.' Eddie said, 'Fine, let's do it.' So every day I gave him a sheet of yellow paper and said, 'Here's your lines.' "

Years before, when Howard's brother-in-law, Irving Thalberg, had first met him, they would talk film stories and Thalberg had come to regard Hawks as the best storyteller he knew. This may be one reason why Hawks' films do not really age: they consist of compelling stories told through the actors' personalities and the interrelationships between those personalities. Gerald Mast, who studied the scripts to Hawks' films in their various stages, found that "when reading any script for a Hawks film—even the one marked 'final shooting script'—one repeatedly observes the film's scripted story evaporate as the narrative progresses, dissolving into that other fuller and richer story which the film became. Hawks constantly reworked his ideas, both on the set and at home, as his filmed narration took shape, until he had reached a narrative conclusion that frequently bore no relationship at all to the one in the script with which he began shooting."[19] The same with all those little bits of business. Once, when Howard was hunting with Hemingway, Hemingway challenged Hawks to hit him. Howard hit him. He broke the back of his hand. Hemingway just laughed and stayed up half the night working a tomato can into a splint so Howard could go shooting the next morning. This, for Hawks, demonstrated a closeness between them better than words could. In A GIRL IN EVERY PORT, the one friend pulls the other friend's finger. It is a sign of intimacy and yet one superior to back-patting which Hawks thought inane. In TIGER SHARK, Richard Arlen was cast as Robinson's friend. Their intimacy is conveyed when Robinson frequently scratches Arlen's back.

The film opens to a chilling scene of a shark surfacing and snatching off Robinson's hand which is hanging overboard from a life boat. For the remainder of the picture, he has a hook. He is mutilated. When he marries Zita Johann and she, in turn, falls in love with Arlen, there is a sequence in which the sound of Robinson's shooting sharks crazily from the forecastle is heard while the camera records Arlen and Johann in a clinch. They don't stop even when the shooting ceases. The suspense becomes agonizing in anticipation of Robinson's opening the door and discovering them.

Hawks' pictures have a way of growing on you and I suspect the reason for this is that each one seems to advance and deepen the perspectives of previous films. This continues to be the case throughout the films of the 'Thirties and 'Forties and only when you come to the later films, where less and less is added and more and more is just repetition, does it decrease significantly.

"Jack Warner was a showman," Hawks told Joseph McBride. "Harry Cohn was a showman. They let you alone. But Thalberg would let you make a picture and then would get you in very nicely and say, 'Look, we've got the sets, we've got all the people, everybody's under contract. Now, I think you could do a little better with this.' And he'd make about ten days' work over again and make a whole different picture out of it. He didn't do that with any of mine. We were good friends. We used to talk things over before we made it."[20] Hawks signed on at M-G-M after TIGER SHARK, this time as a director, but his association with this studio, notwithstanding what he told McBride, proved no more satisfying than it had been before when Thalberg had preferred to keep him in the story department rather than to let him direct. TODAY WE LIVE was based on one of Faulkner's few slick magazine stories. It had run in THE SATURDAY EVENING POST where Hawks had read it. Hawks sold the rights to M-G-M and then convinced the studio to let him bring in Faulkner himself to work on the screenplay. Faulkner never did achieve an easy prose style nor the ability to produce a well-made narrative in his fiction, but he had a marvelous imagination and Hawks openly admired Faulkner's considerable facility for creative story-telling. The story was about the friendship between two men in England during the war. Hawks wanted to elaborate on this, but that was not what the studio decided it wanted done. Louis B. Mayer, head of production, was intent on saving Joan Crawford's popular image after the adverse effects of her role as Sadie Thompson in RAIN (United Artists, 1932). Hawks was informed that TODAY WE LIVE was henceforth to be moulded into a Joan Crawford come-back vehicle. This meant the screenplay had to accommodate her character and the original concerns had to be set aside. However, Hawks and Faulkner did become friends and they did continue to work together, thus providing Faulkner with a source of income he could never hope to earn from the unpopular novels he preferred to write.

Matters became worse on VIVA VILLA! (M-G-M, 1934) which starred Wallace Beery as the Mexican bandit. It was produced by David O. Selznick and Ben Hecht was called in to assist on the screenplay. Hawks cast Lee Tracy in the film as the sympathetic American. When, some years earlier, Neville Brand had urinated on a bus load of tourists being escorted around Universal City Studios, the incident excited little more than a casual laugh in Hollywood gossip columns. Lee Tracy wasn't so fortunate. While on location, Tracy got drunk and urinated from a balcony on the Mexican army. Louis B. Mayer was outraged by the episode when he heard about it and summoned both Tracy and Hawks back to Culver City. Mayer informed Hawks that he expected him to bear witness against Tracy. He was determined that the man would never again work in pictures. Hawks refused to comply and Mayer took him off the picture, replacing him with Jack Conway. Although Hawks had done the story preparation and all the exteriors and those interiors filmed in Mexico, he received no credit when the picture was released. Hawks had contributed to the screenplay for RED DUST (M-G-M, 1932) and subsequently contributed story ideas for CAPTAINS

COURAGEOUS (M-G-M, 1937) and TEST PILOT (M-G-M, 1938), all directed by Victor Fleming, Howard's good friend and his roommate prior to Hawks' marriage to Athole Shearer Ward, but VIVA VILLA! would be the last film Hawks would ever direct at M-G-M. Mayer later contended that Hawks was fired from VIVA VILLA!, not because of the Tracy incident, but because he worked too slowly, the same reason he had been replaced by W.S. Van Dyke as the director of THE PRIZEFIGHTER AND THE LADY (M-G-M, 1933). John Lee Mahin, the screenwriter who had written the script for THE PRIZE-FIGHTER AND THE LADY, insisted that the dispute in both pictures had been over Hawks' slowness in production and, while Hawks would later add GONE WITH THE WIND (M-G-M, 1939) to the list of Fleming pictures to which he made creative contributions, Mahin, who was Fleming's frequent collaborator, denied that Hawks contributed anything to any of the four films. Whatever, the fact remains that Lee Tracy was fired from VIVA VILLA! and replaced by Stuart Erwin. Moreover, of the three M-G-M films on which Hawks had worked, only VIVA VILLA! showed a profit.

Harry Cohn, on the other hand, had made money on THE CRIMINAL CODE and he told Hawks he could direct a film at Columbia any time he wanted. Hawks now went to Cohn and told him he wanted to film TWENTIETH CEN-TURY (Columbia, 1934) based on a stage play by Ben Hecht and Charles MacArthur who also were hired to do the scenario. It was to be Carole Lombard's first comedy role and, although she did not know it at the time, she was to become the first full-fledged Hawksian woman. Lombard was brash, fun-loving, empathetic, caustically outspoken. While standing around on the set of another picture, chatting with male cast and crew members, she quipped when she saw the ingenue of the film arrive an hour late after a visit to the producer's office, "I'll bet she sucks a beautiful cock. She can't act." Yet, when Lombard came to work opposite John Barrymore whom Hawks had signed for the male lead and who was well in his stride following his successes in BILL OF DIVORCE-MENT (RKO, 1932) and GRAND HOTEL (M-G-M, 1932), she was terribly at sea.

"She rehearsed and tried to act," Hawks recalled. "Barrymore started holding his nose where she couldn't see him. 'Look,' I told him, 'until four o'clock in the afternoon I don't want to hear a peep out of you. After that, you can say anything you want.' I took Carole out and told her she was doing very well. She knew all her lines. I asked her how much she was getting paid, and she told me.

" 'That's pretty good,' I said. 'What are you getting paid *for*?'

" 'Acting, of course!'

"I said, 'You've earned all that money today, and I don't want any more acting.' I knew Carole pretty well. We'd both grown up in the same little town in Wisconsin. I think she was a second cousin. 'Carole,' I said, 'what would you do if a man said lick my dick to you?'

" 'I'd kick him right in the balls.'

" 'What would you do if a man said fuck you?'

"She made a typical Lombard gesture.

" 'Well,' I said, 'you didn't kick Barrymore.'

"She just stared at me.

" 'Why didn't you wave your arm like that? Look, you go back in there and forget about acting. Kick him right where you said you were going to. Do anything to him you want, just don't act any more.'

" 'You're serious, aren't you?'

" 'If you don't do it,' I said, 'I'm going to fire you.'

"So we went back.

" 'Let's try a take,' I said.

" 'We're not ready,' Barrymore said.

" 'Who's boss?' I asked.

" 'You are,' he said.

"We started the scene. Barrymore read his line. Carole made a kick at him. He started to dance around. She kept on waving her arms and kicking him. That was the first and only take. We had three or four cameras on it because I didn't know what was going to happen. Barrymore made his exit. Then he came back.

" 'That was so perfect,' he said to Lombard. 'That was marvelous. Have you been kidding me all this time?'

"She burst into tears and ran off the stage. He turned to me.

" 'What the hell is going on here?'

"I told him.

" 'The girl is simply marvelous,' he said. 'She's a cinch to be a star.'

" 'Okay,' I said, 'but you've got to help.'

"We made that picture in three weeks. Those two people—all I had to do was turn them loose."

The plot has it that Barrymore, playing theatrical entrepreneur Oscar Jaffe, took Mildred Plotka, the girl played by Lombard, and turned her into a star named Lily Garland. Now Lily has decided that she no longer wants to be Lily Garland but instead wants to go back to being just plain Mildred Plotka. The action is set on the Twentieth Century Limited, the train running between Chicago and New York. Hawks so played the dialogue that sentences overlapped and characters seemed to be talking at once, as they do in life, constantly moving about while speaking. Not even Jack L. Warner could have complained now that Hawks was not a master of the sound medium. The pacing and rapid-fire dialogue gave the film a sense of almost frantic pacing, the comedy constantly building in a crescendo. In an apt analysis of the film's ideological content, Gerald Mast noted that "first, the film's storyteller assumes it is better, more interesting, more exciting, to be Lily Garland than Mildred Plotka. . . . Second, Lily Garland really is Lily Garland and not Mildred Plotka. She has the soul of Lily Garland in the body of Mildred Plotka. And Jaffe releases that soul. . . . Finally, to sentence Lily Garland to a lifetime of Oscar Jaffe is not to imprison her but to allow her to be most fully and most completely what she is."[21] The ideology works splendidly in the film. It would again and again in the future. Only when Hawks in his way, as Hitchcock eventually in his, tried to recreate his screen fantasy in his own life would he find that the formula did not work.

During the next two years, although Hawks kept working regularly, he did not create any particularly notable films. He directed BARBARY COAST (United Artists, 1935) for Samuel Goldwyn, a film about which I shall have something to say a little later on, and returned to Warner Bros. to direct James Cagney in CEILING ZERO (Warner's, 1936), the plot of which concerns mail pilots and the dangers they face in their profession. THE ROAD TO GLORY (20th-Fox, 1936) bore no relationship to Hawks' film by the same title for Fox a decade before. In a way it is a weak reprise of THE DAWN PATROL, probing the question of what it is in war that keeps men going. It is notable primarily because Hawks was able once more to engage Faulkner to work on the screenplay and Gregg Toland was in charge of principal photography.

COME AND GET IT (United Artists, 1936) was Hawks' second film for Goldwyn, with Jules Furthman working on the screenplay and Gregg Toland again the cinematographer. Frances Farmer had the lead, although she was a contract player getting paid only seventy-five dollars a week. "I don't think there's any doubt that Frances Farmer was the best actress I ever worked with," Hawks subsequently told Joseph McBride.[22] According to Hawks, Farmer was not the actress Goldwyn intended to have the lead, but Goldwyn had had to go into the hospital for prostate surgery and he put Hawks in charge of the production. Hawks wanted Farmer in the role. He also rewrote much of the story in the last half of the picture, retaining, however, the strong ecological theme from the original Edna Ferber novel in which loggers are chastised for ruining the environment and saw mills for polluting the streams, decades before this kind of criticism became commonplace. Hawks had Farmer play both mother and daughter and the mother role he changed from a lame waif to a lusty wench. He also cast Walter Brennan again, as he had in BARBARY COAST, this time as an old man who must speak with a Norwegian accent. When seen today, Brennan is anything but convincing using this accent, but notwithstanding in spring, 1937 he won his first Oscar as Best Supporting Player for his work in this picture.

When Goldwyn recovered from his operation and the emotional blow of Irving Thalberg's death which had occurred while he was in the hospital, he had rough cuts of the two films he then had in production, DODSWORTH (United Artists, 1936) directed by William Wyler and COME AND GET IT, run in the projection room at his home. He flew into a rage at the rewriting which had been done on COME AND GET IT and he sent for Hawks, demanding an explanation. " 'Directors are supposed to direct, not WRITE!' " he yelled at Hawks when they met. He insisted that Hawks reshoot the entire last half of the film following the original script. He was also displeased about Frances Farmer's having been cast in the role he had intended for Virginia Bruce and he did not share Hawks' conviction that Farmer was another Carole Lombard. Hawks was committed to begin shooting BRINGING UP BABY (RKO, 1938) the next day and he did not have the time to reshoot the picture the way Goldwyn wanted it. Hawks grew quite heated, and so did Goldwyn, who finally summed up the matter to Wyler: " 'That's the trouble with directors. Always biting the hand that lays the golden egg.' "[23] Goldwyn had Wyler shoot the final half of the film again. He wanted Hawks' name taken off of the picture entirely, but this Wyler would not tolerate. Wyler finally won out with a compromise, Hawks' name first and his second as the director, although Wyler never counted COME AND GET IT among his credits. VARIETY reported that the reshooting cost Goldwyn an additional $900,000. That is probably an inflated figure, but the negative cost was $1,291,934.27 and, upon release, the film lost nearly $500,000. However tempestuous their parting may have been on COME AND GET IT, Hawks would return to work for Goldwyn twice more in future years, obviously for the money as would also be the case at Twentieth Century-Fox. For, while other studios permitted Hawks the freedom both to produce and direct his films, obviously there were times when Hawks, quite frankly, needed money more than he needed total freedom although, certainly, he never told it that way.

Hawks was both producer and director on BRINGING UP BABY. He cast Katharine Hepburn to play the wealthy heiress who sets her cap for a naive paleontologist who wears horn-rimmed glasses played by Cary Grant. His technique working with Hepburn was different from that he had used with Lombard and Farmer, but it proved no less effective. In this film, the comedy was to arise from the silly situations in which the characters found themselves and, therefore, required that Hepburn play the most absurd moments in complete dead-pan. The plot was complicated by a leopard which required an early use of special effects, so that the leopard would seem to be in the back seat of a car with Grant and Hepburn in the front seat, or to be following them down a hallway when in fact the sequences were filmed separately and superimposed later. " . . . Hawks delights in revealing the distance his story has traveled from everyday probability with a scene that juxtaposes those observers who are innocent of the comic circumstances with those participants who are entangled in them," Gerald Mast observed.[24] In BRINGING UP BABY—Baby is the leopard—there is one such scene which particularly stands out. Grant is dressed in a fluffy nightgown and encounters Hepburn's aunt who is the patroness to whom Grant is looking for an endowment to continue his researches. "Do you dress like that all the time?" she demands. "No," Grant replies, "I've gone gay all of a sudden!" Hawks was very strict about one thing, however. In no case was Grant's behavior while in drag *ever* to appear effeminate.

Fritz Feld was cast as a psychiatrist in the film. He later described what it was like to work with Hawks on a picture. "Life in Hollywood in those days was easy," he recalled. "Howard Hawks would come in in the morning and say, 'It's a nice day today. Let's go to the races.' And Cary, who loved horses, was especially delighted when we would pack up and *go* to the races. Kate Hepburn also amused Cary by serving tea, as was her custom, every afternoon on the set at four o'clock. After one scene Hawks had especially liked, he delivered the cast two cases of the best champagne. Those were the days!''[25] Although it became a cult classic in later years, following its initial release BRINGING UP BABY lost almost as much money as COME AND GET IT had.

ONLY ANGELS HAVE WINGS (Columbia, 1939) is one of Hawks' best pictures, perhaps the only one he made in the 'Thirties which can be grouped with the finest films he made in his entire career, all of which would be produced in the next decade. It was based on a true experience. Hawks did a lot of flying in these years. One night he had dinner with some Mexican bush pilots who told him of their work. He wrote it down on a piece of paper. Shortly later, when he went to the Columbia lot to visit Frank Capra, Harry Cohn heard about it and sent for Hawks. He was in a bind. He needed a story for Cary Grant and Jean Arthur and he didn't have one. Hawks told him about his idea of a bush pilot mail service.

"When can you start?" Cohn asked Hawks.

"What do you mean? I haven't got a script written."

"You've got to start ten days from now."

Howard paused after narrating this conversation to us. He smiled.

" 'Okay,' I told Cohn, 'but it's going to cost you a lot of money.' "

The story concerns an expatriated group of characters in a Central American banana republic where aviation was still in a primitive state. Hawks wanted Jean Arthur to play a Hawksian heroine, tough, filled with wisecracks, aggressively pursuing Cary Grant who was cast as the man in charge of the mail service and who played a character obviously based in part on Howard Hughes. Hawks had a lot of trouble getting Arthur into her character and related, with some amusement, how it wasn't until years later when Arthur saw Bacall in TO HAVE AND HAVE NOT that she really understood what it was that Hawks had wanted from her. Comradeship among the pilots is what supports the group since they are constantly faced with death in their work. Rita Hayworth was cast as Grant's lost love. This was before Cohn began her star build-up. In ONLY ANGELS HAVE WINGS, Hayworth shows up married to Richard Barthelmess, himself a pilot who must overcome a cowardly act in his past and for whom this job will be a proving ground.

As much as Hawks admired Howard Hughes for his accomplishments, he also wanted to impress Hughes with the fact that he was a better filmmaker than Hughes could ever hope to be. Hawks persuaded Harry Cohn to let him remake THE FRONT PAGE (United Artists, 1931) as a romantic comedy. It was originally based on a stage play by Ben Hecht and Charles MacArthur. Hughes had produced the earlier film which Lewis Milestone directed. The picture made a profit of $164,859.36. Hawks hired Hecht to work on a new screenplay with him. "See, THE FRONT PAGE was intended as a love affair between two men," Hawks told Joseph McBride. "I mean, they *loved* each other. There's no doubt about it. And it was a lot easier for me to make a love story with a man and a girl and make some better scenes."[26] Hawks cast Cary Grant as the shrewd newspaper editor and former husband of star reporter Rosalind Russell who has now decided that she ought to quit doing what she is best at and settle down to a quiet married life with fiancé Ralph Bellamy. What we have here is only a variation on the plot of TWENTIETH CENTURY. Hawks by this time had worked out a basic narrative structure for his films, best articulated by Gerald Mast. " . . . Hawks builds every story in an identical four-part structure. The first part is a prologue that either (1) establishes the conflict in a past or present close relationship of the major characters (this is the usual pattern of Ben Hecht's scripts for Hawks) or (2) initiates a conflict by the collision of two apparently opposite characters upon their initial meeting (this is the usual Furthman-Faulkner pattern). The second and third parts develop the central conflicts established in the first, either by letting one of the conflicting characters or lifestyles dominate in the second part, then the other in the third, or by letting one of the characters work alone in the second part, then both of them together in the third. And the fourth section resolves the central conflict, often by a return to the original physical setting of the prologue but in which setting the warring characters now see themselves and one another in a new light. Occasionally Hawks adds a very brief epilogue or 'tag' to return the narrative full circle to its beginning."[27] As such, this narrative structure is essentially the same as that which the ancient Greeks devised for the romance in which the *agon*, or conflict, is followed by the *pathos*, or a life-and-death struggle, followed by the final stage, the *anagnorisis*, or the recognition. The recognition in TWENTIETH CENTURY is that Lily Garland is best off being Lily Garland because that is who she most truly was all along. In THE FRONT PAGE, Russell as Hildy comes to recognize that by not working at what she loves to do and does extremely well she is betraying herself and cannot really be herself. This recognition brings her full-circle by the fade, doing the same job and married to the same man, but with an awareness of why this must be so.

While in Mexico, Hawks had once heard a legend that Pat Garrett had shot off the face of someone else so that Billy the Kid could escape. Hawks was convinced that this story could make an excellent Western and he went to Howard Hughes with the idea. Hughes, happy for an opportunity to work again with Hawks, was anxious to produce the picture. Hawks claimed that it was he, and not Hughes, who had first discovered Jane Russell working in a dentist's office, and he wanted to try her out in the film. Whether true or not, Hughes was immediately taken with Russell and a torrid affair began between them. Hawks also cast new-comer Jack Beutel to play a very boyish Billy the Kid. Then fate intervened.

Since Adolph Zukor had forced Jesse L. Lasky out of Paramount, times had been hard for Lasky. He was now trying to peddle to the various studios a story about Sergeant York, a pacifist who became a war hero during the Great War. Lasky had given Hawks his first important job in the industry, as he had Gary Cooper. Hawks contacted Cooper, sold him on the idea of playing York, and then the two of them approached Jack L. Warner about making the picture.

Warner agreed. Ultimately, Lasky would make two million dollars from the deal. Yet, a commitment now to make SERGEANT YORK (Warner's, 1941) at Warner Bros. meant that Hawks would not be able to continue work on THE OUTLAW, the title of the Billy the Kid picture Hughes was financing. Hawks suggested to Hughes that, since he wanted to be a director anyway, he should finish the picture himself. Hughes responded positively to Hawks's proposal but the nature of the picture was changed. Intrigued by Russell's figure, Hughes had a special brassiere fashioned for her and played up her steamy sexuality in the film. He even shot two versions of the picture, one (not for release) with Russell topless. This, combined with censorship problems for the version Hughes wanted to release, held up the picture in production and resulted also in its being yanked from release in 1943 so a line could be dubbed in at the end to the effect that the Kid and the Russell character, instead of simply riding off together, would in fact be married. Other suggestive material also had to be excised. It was rereleased in 1946 at 116 minutes and again in 1950 at 103 minutes.

Cooper won an Academy Award for SERGEANT YORK and Hawks was nominated for one. The picture proved to be Hawks' greatest commercial success, due in large measure to the timeliness of the subject, just on the eve of the Second World War. Hughes may have buried the hatchet with Hawks to work with him on THE OUTLAW, but he resented Hawks' pulling out of the film when he did and he would try, years later, to get back at Hawks.

# III

It is impossible for me at this point to continue in a chronological fashion to detail Hawks' films. With SERGEANT YORK he did more than complete a cycle; he established his orientations and outlined the basic genres and narrative structure in which he was henceforth to do his finest work. Hawks' brilliance as a director is not to be found, however, in his iconoclasm nor in his innovative daring. It is rather in the novelty and uniqueness combined with variations upon a consistent point of view which he brought to bear on making distinctly generic films: comedies and musicals, crime and adventure films, and Westerns. Perhaps his work in each group is best illuminated by dealing with those specific films within a particular genre.

Hawks directed AIR FORCE (Warner's, 1943) to assist the Allied war effort. It was the story of the *Mary Ann*, a B–17 bomber, and the men who flew her in the early days of the Pacific theatre of the war. In a way, it was a reworking of THE DAWN PATROL, with far more sophisticated aerial action footage. Perhaps the most moving episode in the film was the death scene which Faulkner wrote. Hawks wisely chose to direct it by ignoring what the characters were saying, even what they were doing, and concentrating instead on the emotions reflected in their eyes. The characters by this time had the true Hawksian philosophy of life. As John Belton pointed out in an essay on Hawks, his "characters face the world head-on, never faltering for a moment or pausing to worry about their limitations. Their adaptability enables them not only to live with the surrounding world, but to use what they have to master it. Their unquestioning commitment to the world of positive action reveals Hawks' profound belief that energy and vitality, no matter what the odds, will ensure ultimate triumph.''[28] He also observed that ''we know, even though it is never consciously articulated, that Hawks' characters behave with a sort of inner-directed, self-dictated consistency that precludes their domination by external forces.''[29] Occasionally a character might lose this orientation, as Dude played by Dean Martin in RIO BRAVO (Warner's, 1959), but the screen story also shows us how he is able to win back the character which for a time he had lost.

For years Hawks had been trying to convince Ernest Hemingway to write for pictures. After all, he had been successful in a similar attempt with William Faulkner. Hemingway resisted.

'' 'Howard,' '' Hawks quoted Hemingway as saying, '' 'I don't want to. I don't know enough about writing for pictures. I'm good at what I'm doing and I don't want to go to Hollywood.' ''

Hawks assured Hemingway that he need not come to Hollywood. They could go hunting and fishing together and work on a story. Hemingway was not sure. Maybe he suspected that what interested Hawks most was his inner personality and how it influenced the kinds of stories he chose to tell.

'' 'Ernest,' '' Hawks continued, '' 'I can make a picture out of your worst book.'

'' 'What's my worst book?' ''

'' 'TO HAVE AND HAVE NOT is a bunch of junk.' ''

Hemingway shrugged the novel off as something he wrote because he needed money. It was not a valid assessment. He was also positive that Hawks could not turn it into a good film. For ten days the two of them talked about the two principal characters in the book and how they first met. If Hawks was critical of the novel's structure, he had a case, but TO HAVE AND HAVE NOT is not Hemingway's worst book insofar as it articulates better than much of what he wrote how really beat up we are by the course of our lives and the hopelessness of one man being alone in the modern world. Hawks opted to avoid this perspective. He wanted to dwell instead on the love story between Harry Morgan and Marie, the former whore to whom Harry is married at the time of the novel. Harry Morgan loses everything he values in life and finally he loses his life, too. When Johnson charters Harry's boat and then skips out without paying him, he inadvertently triggers a series of disasters. Hawks reversed this chain of events at the outset by having Humphrey Bogart as Harry Morgan get the best of Johnson.

Hawks learned that Howard Hughes had purchased the screen rights to the novel for $10,000. Here was another chance to show up Hughes. Hawks bought the screen rights from Hughes for $80,000 and then sold them to Warner Bros. for half the profits of the picture above his salary to make it. Hawks later bragged to Hemingway that what Hemingway had sold for $10,000 had earned Hawks well over a million dollars. Understandably, Hemingway was extremely angry about it for some time.

Hawks had discovered Ella Raines and introduced her to the screen in COR-VETTE K-255 (Universal, 1943), which he produced and Richard Rosson directed. Raines was effective as the boyish heroine which, ideally, is the embodiment of the Hawksian woman, but it was Lauren Bacall who came to project precisely what Hawks wanted, smoky passion, a sharp tongue, and an insolent sexuality. In every scene in TO HAVE AND HAVE NOT, she walks out on Bogart.

"It is difficult to imagine," Gerald Mast wrote, "how Hawks would have been able to solve his narrative problem—to get Bogart and Bacall into this Hemingway story—without the shift from Havana to Martinique."[30] In contrasting TO HAVE AND HAVE NOT with CASABLANCA, Mast also noted that the latter "film has always been more popular, perhaps because Rick-Bogart's climactic self-denial is more unabashedly romantic and hence more comforting than Harry-Bogart's refusal to betray his code and his self."[31] Yet as Hawks told us, it was because he had worked on CASABLANCA in its development stages that he wanted to negate it with TO HAVE AND HAVE NOT, just as RIO BRAVO would be intended to negate HIGH NOON (United Artists, 1952). To effect an equivalence in time and circumstances, the setting had to be changed and the only French possession in this hemisphere that would be suitable and which was under Vichy control was Martinique. If TO HAVE AND HAVE NOT has never been as popular as CASABLANCA because of the termination of their respective plots and narrative structures, that is nonetheless exactly the way Hawks wanted it to be.

TO HAVE AND HAVE NOT was Hawks' first time working with Bogart. Hawks was fascinated by the fact that Bogart had lost the use of his upper lip so he could not smile. Bogart tried to see what he could get away with, returning to the set one day after lunch in an intoxicated state. Hawks knocked him against a wall and warned him that if it happened again he would take him to Warner and see that he was taken off the picture.

John Huston had worked on the screenplay for SERGEANT YORK. It was in his contract that he would be able to direct a picture and, when the time came, Huston asked Hawks if he had any ideas of the kind of screen story he should write. " 'Don't write anything,' " Hawks told him. " 'It's hard enough to direct your first picture. There's a story that Warner's owns that I've always been going to do called THE MALTESE FALCON.' He came back again and said, 'It's been made twice,' and I said, 'It's *never* been made. Always some idiot thought he could write better than Dashiell Hammett. You go and make MALTESE FALCON exactly the way Hammett wrote it, use the dialogue, don't change a goddam thing, and you'll have a hell of a picture.' "[32] When Huston's version appeared in 1941, it proved a solid critical and commercial success. In view of the fine reception TO HAVE AND HAVE NOT received, when Jack

L. Warner proposed to Hawks that he should make another film with Bogart and Bacall while they were still a hot item, Hawks wanted to try his hand at a hard-boiled detective story but found that virtually all of Hammett's properties had been used and re-used. Talking it over with Faulkner, Hawks found that Faulkner agreed that, if you couldn't have Hammett, Raymond Chandler was the next best. Hawks purchased screen rights to Chandler's first novel, THE BIG SLEEP (1939), for $25,000. He intended to do a similar turn-around with the property as he had done with TO HAVE AND HAVE NOT.

Leigh Brackett had written a hard-boiled crime novel and Harry Wepplo of Martindale's book store saw to it that a copy found its way into the pile of thrillers Hawks was regularly accustomed to buy. Hawks liked Brackett's dialogue and called her agent. He thought she was a man because she wrote as if she were one. Despite his surprise on learning the truth, Hawks signed her for $125 a week. According to a subsequent conversation we had with Brackett, when she was first introduced to Faulkner he was immaculately attired in country tweeds and greeted her in a gentlemanly manner. "We will do alternate sets of chapters," he told her. "I have them marked. I will do these; you will do those." In a very short time, the script was completed.

Actually as written, THE BIG SLEEP was unfilmable in 1945. You could not deal on the screen as openly with homosexuality as Chandler had in the novel, or with nymphomania. Yet, Hawks was not going to get himself into the kind of confusion that had resulted when KING'S ROW (Warner's, 1941) was brought to the screen and the incestuous relationship of the character played by Claude Rains had to be circumvented and all the consequent action, including Charles Coburn's amputation of Ronald Reagan's legs, really is left without sufficient motivation. The one way out that Hawks could see was to explain absolutely nothing and, instead, to concentrate on individual scenes. Only the vaguest suggestions of Chandler's original plot were allowed into the film, such as the scene where Bogart in a bit of business he himself devised speaks in a swishy, effeminate way when entering Steiner's book store. Faulkner, perhaps using his own experiences working in a book store, added a wholly extraneous scene in which in another book store Bogart seduces a willing Dorothy Malone, a sequence which nonetheless obviates the sexual squeamishness the detective, Philip Marlowe, possesses in the novel.

In book form THE BIG SLEEP also has serious structural problems due to the fashion in which Chandler put the narrative together out of unrelated short stories he had written earlier. When Hawks was filming the sequence where Owen's car is pulled out of the water on Warner's tank sound stage, Bogart asked him who killed Owen. After all, Bogart insisted, if he was the detective and point-of-view character, he ought to know. Hawks wasn't certain, but he said he would ask Faulkner. Faulkner said he didn't know. So Hawks wired Chandler at his home in La Jolla. Chandler replied facetiously that the butler had done it. In the novel, it is not at all clear, although it is probable that Joe

Brody, played in the film by Louis Jean Heydt, killed Owen. However, the way Hawks was making the film, so that nothing is explained, the solution to this mystery is no longer important.

There is a particularly engaging scene in the novel. Marlowe is taken out to a greenhouse to meet General Sternwood, who hires him. In the short story version, the scene runs approximately 1,100 words, whereas Chandler expanded it to 2,500 words in the later novel. Chandler also made palpable the claustro-phobic reality of the humid heat and physical decay. It took Hawks' sensitivity to human relationships, however, to get the characters beyond talking tough and revealing momentary affection for one another. Throughout the picture Marlowe is able to relate to people in a way he never can in any of Chandler's novels. The loneliness in which Marlowe perpetually dwells is lifted. This also allowed Hawks to increase the emphasis on the elder Sternwood daughter, Vivian, played by Bacall and thus, in Gerald Mast's words, "by making Marlowe's professional quest a partial blur, Hawks throws the Marlowe-Vivian personal relationship into sharp foreground focus."[33]

In THE MALTESE FALCON (1930), Hammett described Sam Spade as a blond Satan. Spade, as every other character in the book, is out only for himself. Hemingway, based on the run-ins he had had with Hammett, didn't like him and in TO HAVE AND HAVE NOT he described Harry Morgan as a blond Satan. Hemingway was out to show that not even a hard-boiled blond Satan had a chance. In casting Bogart in these roles, neither John Huston nor Howard Hawks retained very much of the original conceptions of the characters. The violence that both Hammett and Hemingway perceived as an indigenous by-product of the American system of values—something on which they *did* agree—and the pained isolation in which their characters live could not, apparently, be translated on screen into the Bogart persona, although it was decidedly a part of Bogart's own temperament off screen. In THE BIG SLEEP, he was in love. It was the affirmative electricity of his relationship with the Hawksian Bacall that, in the film, works effectively to offset the despair derived from being constantly lied to by everyone. It was through Bacall, most of all, that Hawks could again project his fantasy of a forthright and honest woman, one who prefers the company of men, a woman whose virtues are in being outspoken and loyal, a companion more than a wife, independent but not without affection, capable of feeling and expressing lust but in a light-hearted manner. When Warner asked Hawks to add the extra scenes with Bogart and Bacall, he had been racing his horses at Santa Anita at the time. He wrote the humorous dialogue himself about race horses which Bogart exchanges with Bacall, filled with sexual in-nuendo and culminating in Bacall's jocular comment that how good she is in the home stretch depends entirely on her jockey.

Hawks' later adventure films reveal the same surge of even-tempered optimism that infiltrated his treatment of criminal violence in THE BIG SLEEP, as opposed to the lingering images of social decay which haunt SCARFACE. John Ford's profound disillusionment with life and his cognizance that his values were increasingly out of place is an experience that Hawks escaped. However, as he aged, the pace of Hawks' films did slow down and they lost much of the tension which had once held them together so tautly. Leigh Brackett did the screenplay for HATARI! (Paramount, 1962), but much of it was improvised on location in Africa because action involving the capture of wild animals cannot be scripted. John Wayne was the star and Hawks had no one against which Wayne's screen persona could be played. Hawks was convinced that only he and Ford could handle Wayne before the camera, but this is not altogether true since Henry Hathaway managed quit ably. Hawks confessed years later to Joseph McBride that HATARI! "was weakened by not having anybody that had any strength in there at all except Wayne. There wasn't anything there; it just became nothing. There was no fight; there was no argument."[34]

Hawks tried again. He reversed HATARI! in RED LINE 7000 (Paramount, 1965). From familiar actors, the picture went to unfamiliar actors. Instead of being able to identify positively with men who love danger, a viewer becomes estranged. The setting is a race car track. Hawks used the story as an opportunity to vary again plot ingredients from what they had been back in THE CROWD ROARS, but it was an experiment that was not successful. No one can be right all the time. Hawks persisted in repeating what had proven successful in the past, by using it in variation. Yet, if the variation should fail, he never made the error of trying it again. Except, that is, when it came to casting Wayne without anyone to stand up against him. That happened in RIO LOBO (National General, 1970), Hawks' last Western and his final film.

## IV

I have mentioned that for a time Hawks roomed with Victor Fleming. He told us how they met. When he was driving race cars, in one race Hawks forced another driver coming up rapidly behind him into a fence. Racing then was a rough sport. It looked for a time as if there would be a fight, but the two had a drink instead and became friends. Hawks invited the driver over to his house and, since he had no place to stay, Hawks invited him to stay with him, which Fleming did for the next five years. Hawks helped him become a film director. Even after they had gone their own ways, Fleming would still seek out Hawks' advice. When directing Vivien Leigh in GONE WITH THE WIND, Fleming complained to Hawks that, try what he might, he couldn't get her past being precious rather than a flirty bitch. Hawks suggested that Fleming have Leigh bend over and then kick her as hard as he could in the derrière. Fleming tried it. He was overjoyed with the results. It worked as nothing else had.

Hawks himself was not a sentimental man and probably for this reason his characters lack sentimentality. He would have surely agreed with Marcus Aurelius in the book known as THE MEDITATIONS that "the god within you should preside over a being who is virile and mature, a statesman, a Roman, and a ruler; one who has held his ground, as a soldier waiting for the signal to retire from life's battlefield and ready to welcome his relief; a man whose credit need neither be sworn to by himself nor avouched by others. Therein is the secret of cheerfulness, of depending on no help from without and needing to crave from no man the boon of tranquility. We have to stand upright ourselves, not be set up.''[35] Hawks, in the stories he told about himself, never sought the advice of others; rather, as John Huston prior to THE MALTESE FALCON or Victor Fleming when directing Vivien Leigh, others invariably came to him. Sometimes, as in the Tom Dunson character played by John Wayne in RED RIVER, this aggressive stoicism can be taken too far; but sometimes, as in the John T. Chance character in RIO BRAVO, all the humors as it were are in balance and we are intended openly to admire it.

In his Westerns, above all, Hawks charted the course of his stoic hero, from a man who found fulfillment in male camaraderie and female companionship to a man who was increasingly isolated and stood alone, detached but never indifferent. "I decide to make a film whenever the subject interests me," Hawks told Jacques Rivette and François Truffaut in an interview published in CAHIERS DU CINÉMA. "It may be on auto racing or on aviation; it may be a Western or a comedy, but the major drama for me is the one which has as its subject a man in danger. . . . When I made RED RIVER, I thought it might be possible to make an adult Western, for and about mature people, and not one of those about mediocre cowboys. And at that time, everyone was looking to make intelligent Westerns. . . . ''[36]

RED RIVER is commonly regarded as Hawks' first Western although, technically, BARBARY COAST preceded it as did THE OUTLAW. Both of these projects were less than successful. However, in view of how Hughes took over THE OUTLAW, it is perhaps specious to impute Hawks with either credit or blame for any part of it. BARBARY COAST is another story. Set in San Francisco around 1850, the plot concerns Miriam Hopkins who arrives on a boat from the East, finds that her betrothed is dead, and decides matter-of-factly that she will become a gold-digger. Edward G. Robinson runs the largest gambling establishment in town and, upon meeting Hopkins, remarks, "I hope you like San Francisco. I own it." In the motion picture shorthand of the day, they evidently sleep together, but Hopkins is less than enthusiastic, regarding their association as purely a business arrangement while Robinson becomes obsessed, first with Hopkins' fidelity, and second with making her love him. Joel McCrea was cast as a prospector who likes poetry and, when he encounters Hopkins on the trail one day while she is out riding, he gives her a volume of Shelley's poems which causes Robinson to fly into a paroxysm of jealousy and suspicion. McCrea has divided women into those who are innocent and those who are tainted. He regards Hopkins as one of the former until he sees her in Robinson's casino. He proceeds to lose all his hard-earned gold to her at her roulette table.

Walter Brennan, cast for the first time in a Hawks film as a grizzled old timer, assures McCrea that "things'll be simpler in the East." To which McCrea responds, "Sure will . . . for poets and failures." In the name of law and order, the vigilantes waylay Robinson's right-hand man, played by Brian Donlevy, and string him up. This may be democracy in action, but from the looks of the vigilantes democracy seems almost mob rule. Some critics have said that, based solely on the characters played by Hopkins, McCrea, and Robinson, one might not be certain how it will come out; but the formulary plot structure—a sensitive miner, a basically innocent, family-oriented heroine whatever her pretensions to the contrary, and a greedy villain—makes the outcome inevitable.

I would underscore this point because in making RED RIVER Hawks was far more concerned with consistency of character than he was with plot conventions. Indeed, he turned around Borden Chase's ending of BLAZING GUNS ON THE CHISHOLM TRAIL (1948), the novel on which the film was based. Chase had the Dunson character die at the end. For Hawks, such an ending was unacceptable. Matt, played by Montgomery Clift, originally at fourteen years of age threw in his lot with Dunson and has too much regard for him to kill him, just as Dunson, in his own way, has too much regard for Matt to carry through his threat to kill him. The way Chase drew Dunson, he was the stereotype of the tyrannical big rancher who must die in order to give the next generation, in Chase's words, "the promise of a new day."[37] Donald C. Willis probably put it best in THE FILMS OF HOWARD HAWKS (1975) when he wrote that "the extent of Matt's feeling and respect for Dunson is measured by the difference between the tentative acts of defiance he does commit and the absolute acts he could and probably should commit. His action here is little more than the equivalent of Groot's [Walter Brennan] 'You was wrong, Mr. Dunson.' Matt and Groot disagree with Dunson but, unlike him, aren't so sure of themselves that they want to interpose their own will."[38]

John Ford contended that STAGECOACH (United Artists, 1939) made John Wayne a star, but RED RIVER proved him to be an actor. "I didn't know that big sonofabitch could act," was how Ford put it. He himself began henceforth to cast Wayne as an older man and Wayne, as he grew older, found that the public preferred him this way. Gerald Mast is of the opinion that "once Wayne had played this unbendingly hard (yet vulnerably insecure) male for Hawks he would play variations on it forever. . . ."[39] To an extent this is true, but with one big difference: Wayne as Dunson is wrong whereas the post RED RIVER Wayne persona is invariably right! "He read the script for RED RIVER," Hawks told us, "and said, 'I don't know whether I want to play an old man.' I said, 'you're going to be an old man pretty soon, and you ought to get used to it. And you also better start playing characters instead of that junk you've been playing.' So he said, 'How do I show that I'm old?' and I said, 'Did you ever see me get up? Just do it that way.' So he did it and he saw the film and he said, 'Lord, I'm old.' He didn't have to do a lot of damn silly things to get that impression across."

"What was it that first impressed you about Walter Brennan?" I asked. "You've used him in so many films."

"When I was casting BARBARY COAST, they brought in Walter Brennan.

I looked at him and laughed. I said, 'Mr. Brennan, did they give you some lines?' And he said, 'Yeah.' I said, 'Do you know them?' And he said, 'With or without?' I said, 'With or without what?' He said, 'Teeth.' I laughed again and said, 'Without.' He turned around and read the lines. I said, 'You're hired.' When we were going to do RED RIVER, there was a line in the scenario; it said, 'The cook's name was Groot.' He said, 'What are we going to do?' I wasn't worried. I said, 'Remember how we met, that with or without teeth? Well, I got an idea that you're going to lose your teeth in a poker game with an Indian. And every night he makes you give them back.' 'Oh,' he said, 'we can't do that.' I said, 'Yes, we can.' "

The Indian who wins Brennan's teeth was played by Chief Yowlachie, a Yakima who had appeared in the first two-color Western, WANDERER OF THE WASTELAND (Paramount, 1924), based on the Zane Grey novel by the same title. Hawks, working at Paramount at the time, urged the studio to film at least two or three Grey stories a year. His interest in Westerns was apparent already this early in his career. Noah Beery, Sr., was the chief heavy in WANDERER OF THE WASTELAND. For RED RIVER, Hawks cast Beery's son, Noah, Jr., known as Pidge, as well as Harry Carey and Carey's son, Harry, Jr., known as Dobie, thereby making the film, among other things, a generational tribute to decades of Western filmmaking.

For Montgomery Clift it was the first on a five-picture contract he had signed with Hawks. He was enthusiastic about his part and waited with anticipation for what he felt would be his big scene, when he takes the herd away from Wayne and leaves Wayne behind, wounded, on the trail. After the scene was shot, Clift went to Hawks and complained that it had not turned out to be so big, after all. Wayne never even looked at him. While Clift spoke his lines, Wayne continued to stare over the saddle of his horse into the distance, with his back more or less to Clift. Finally, Wayne said simply, "I'm gonna kill you." Hawks laughed and chided Clift for thinking he could best Wayne in any scene.

It was Wayne's opinion that Borden Chase had rewritten MUTINY ON THE BOUNTY (1932) as a Western with the Tom Dunson character a surrogate for Captain Bligh. "When Hawks bought the story," Wayne told me in a conversation prior to our first visit with Hawks, "I felt I could play an old man. He wanted to have Cooper. What he was aiming at was Cooper and Cary Grant to play Cherry. That was what he wanted. Now, his idea of the old man was that he was becoming senile and he was afraid. In the last scene, there was a great chance for me to play a coward. This was how he conceived of it. He had Walter Brennan in and I sat there and listened to them. Hawks is a very easy man to talk to, but Brennan evidently had been giving him the thing, 'I'll teach this guy to play an old man,' because Brennan was playing that part when I first met him and he was about thirty years old. He really always was an old codger. He said, 'I'll fix it, Mr. Hawks. We'll get some springs and his legs will do this.' I listened. 'Oh, Christ,' I thought, 'what have I got myself into?' Hawks said, 'Yep, that's good, sounds very good.' He sent for a prop man. I didn't want to say anything with everybody together. I waited until the following morning and then I went to see Howard. 'Mr. Hawks,' I said, 'you been down to Texas lately?' 'Yes, Duke,' he said, 'I've been down there a little.' I said, 'Have you ever noticed how the older these strong men are, the top ranchers, how much straighter they get and how much more personality and power they have as they reach maturity?' He said, 'I get it, Duke.' I never had any more trouble. There was another scene. Two fellas stand up to me. Howard said, 'This is Academy Award stuff, Duke. Show you're afraid.' I told Howard that it might be Academy Award stuff to show that I was afraid, but I wasn't gonna be no goddamn coward. I'd been strong all through the picture. The kid, Clift, loved me because I was a man he *could* love. But, sure, I told Howard I could be afraid, but not a coward. That's the way we played it.''

No opportunity would be better than the present one, so I repeated this conversation to Howard.

''Sure,'' he said, snapping out the word, and then smiling. ''How do you think I got that big sonofabitch to act? He performed better when he was angry or stubborn or determined and that was what the character he was playing was supposed to do. I got Wayne to do what I wanted by getting him mad.''

''Dunson travels a rough course in which human obstacles, removed by him with a rare violence, count for more than physical obstacles,'' Jean-Louis Rieupeyrout observed in LA GRANDE AVENTURE DU WESTERN (1964). ''From murder to brawling, he arouses a singular antipathy, as opposed to the traditional characterization of the hero one is fond of following in this film genre, and yet appearances are misleading. Dunson winds up convincing and pleasing us because even his rudeness is brought about through his intent to force a superhuman task to its rightful conclusion.''[40] Hawks changed the Dunson character because he regarded his determination as a virtue taken to an almost insane extreme and the structure of the film was also changed so that Dunson could retain his integrity and the viewer's esteem for his determination, if not for his methods. This reduces to absurdity Borden Chase's complaint in FILM COMMENT (Winter, 1970–1971) that the ending to Hawks' film is inconsistent with everything leading up to it. Chase may have written the original story and worked on the screenplay, but he did not grasp that the structural change in the ending was made necessary because of the very different way that Hawks conceived of the Dunson character.

The cattle drive in RED RIVER *is* brought to its rightful conclusion even though it is in Kansas and not, as Dunson intended, in Missouri. Surely one of the reasons Dunson would not kill Matt, even had he been able to bring himself to try it, is because Matt was successful: he achieved what he set out to do. This is a value for the Dunson character which supercedes all other values and it was this same value which, at the very beginning of the picture, prompted Dunson to leave the wagon train he was with and the woman he loved. Dunson could scarcely be anything but pleased to see the same value holding true for Matt.

Hawks during our conversation confirmed that the reason he pared back the role of Cherry, the gunfighter played by John Ireland, was because Ireland drank heavily while on location and became difficult to manage. It had initially been Hawks' intention to create tension between Matt and Cherry during the second half of the film when Wayne was off the screen most of the time, a threat to be sure but one in the future when he should catch up and not one in the present. The romance between Matt and Tess, which also occurs during the second part of the film, was also supposed to keep the story from flagging. Hawks had cast Margaret Sheridan in the role and then, at the last minute, had had to replace her with Joanne Dru because Sheridan was pregnant and production was about to commence. During shooting, Hawks did not like Dru's screen presence and so he also cut back her role. These circumstances would tend to negate Gerald Mast's proposal that "Hawks' narrative sense convinced him that anything in his story that did not relate directly to its Dunson-Matthew love-friendship center was indeed peripheral and inessential, and ought to remain vestigial."[41] It was only a series of happy accidents which brought about this situation and which, therefore, makes it a stronger, more unified film. What definitely weakened the picture upon its release was that Hawks had staged the final confrontation between Dunson and Matt according to the way in which he had conceived of the ending to THE OUTLAW when Garrett and the Kid confront each other in the desert. The Kid is being sided by Doc Holliday and it is Doc whom Garrett shoots in almost a homosexual frenzy, afterward letting the Kid escape. Instead of Dunson and Matt killing each other, Cherry was supposed to get killed, allowing the two men to become friends once again. Hughes objected to this ending and brought suit against Hawks, holding up release of RED RIVER. To satisfy Hughes, Hawks had his cutter, Christian Nyby, meet with Hughes and cut the ending to whatever degree would satisfy Hughes' objection. Only now, after all of these years, has the original version of RED RIVER been placed into general release, with the climactic battle as Hawks intended it to be staged. Mast is absolutely correct in stating that if a viewer has not seen this restored version he has not seen RED RIVER. Again, it was a case of Hawks' having wanted to show up Hughes which led to a less than satisfactory conclusion.

In John Ford's films about superhuman tasks, all the way from THE IRON HORSE (Fox, 1924) to CHEYENNE AUTUMN (Warner's, 1964), although they might be successful in their terminations, the feeling at the end is one of ambivalence, concern over whether it was worth it. There seems to be an acute awareness of what the effort has cost and what has been lost irretrievably. Ford's answer to T.S. Eliot's question in "The Love Song of J. Alfred Prufrock," "And would it have been worth it, after all . . . ,"[42] was less optimistic and assuring than was Hawks'. A.B. Guthrie, Jr., has written that "I believe all of us become better citizens, better and richer human beings, through a familiarity with the dreams and deeds of the men and women who went before us in this adventure that we call the United States of America."[43] Hawks was far more in accord with this sentiment than Ford as is made clear in THE BIG SKY (RKO, 1952). In the novel as Guthrie wrote and structured it, Jourdonnais' daring trek up the Missouri ends with him and most of his men being killed by the Blackfeet.

The novel is divided into five parts, spanning the years 1830–1843, but Hawks confined the screenplay to only the second part, that concerned with Jourdonnais. It was, Hawks told us, the most dramatic moment in the novel and, therefore, of still more significance is the fact that Hawks' film, while showing Jourdonnais' men undergoing even more hardships than in the novel, has a successful termination and the journey is thus brought to what, for Hawks, was its rightful conclusion. His sympathies were more Roman than Greek; he preferred satisfying terminations to tragedies culminating in frustration or resignation. However much Hawks' stories and characters might demonstrate a stoical attitude, *he* was not a Stoic.

The spoken narration at the beginning of the film version tells of the first white men to venture through 2,000 miles of hostile Indians to open up the Great Northwest. Kirk Douglas was cast as Jim Deakins and Dewey Martin as Boone Caudill. As with Tom Dunson, the Boone Caudill character in the film is altered from its literary prototype. "I wanted to show the mountain man . . . for what he was," A.B. Guthrie, Jr., wrote of the creation of Boone Caudill, "or what he seemed honestly to me to have been—not the romantic character, the virtuous if unlettered Leatherstocking, but the engaging, uncouth, admirable, odious, thoughtless, resourceful, loyal, sinful, smart, stupid, courageous character that he was and had to be."[44] Such a character was of no interest to Hawks. Boone Caudill, for Hawks, was a man much as Matthew Garth as played by Montgomery Clift in RED RIVER: his initiation into manhood comes about as a result of his participation in a superhuman task. As in the earlier Western, the men are given a choice by Jourdonnais, played by Steven Geray, of either quitting or sticking it through to the end. Desertion is not so much of an issue, however, as is the necessity of the men to control their lustful impulses toward the Indian maiden being taken on the journey. She is Teal Eye, played by Elizabeth Threatt, the daughter of a Blackfoot chief who, Jourdonnais hopes, will make the Indians friendly and willing to trade. Arthur Hunnicutt was cast as Uncle Zeb, an uncle of Boone's, and in a moving soliloquy he characterizes the white man's sickness as "grab," first grabbing everything they can grab and then grabbing from each other. Poor Devil, a demented Blackfoot from a different part of the novel, was interpolated into the film. As played by Hank Worden, he becomes integrated and vital to the group. Hawks always joked that he borrowed extensively from John Ford. In the case of this film, Hawks created a sequence during which the Indians follow the men on the boat for a long time riding ominously on both shores before, finally, they attack. Ford used a similar scene in THE SEARCHERS (Warner's, 1956).

"The undercurrent of homosexuality in Hawks' films is never crystallized," Peter Wollen wrote in SIGNS AND MEANING IN THE CINEMA (1969), "though in THE BIG SKY, for example, it runs very close to the surface. And he himself described A GIRL IN EVERY PORT as 'really a love story between two men.' For Hawks men are equals, within the group at least, whereas there is a clear identification between women and the animal world. . . . Man must strive to maintain his mastery. It is also worth noting that, in Hawks' adventure dramas and even in many of his comedies, there is no married life. Often the heroes were married or at least intimately committed to a woman at some time in the distant past but have suffered an unspecified trauma, with the result that they have been suspicious of women ever since. Their attitude is 'Once bitten, twice shy.' ''[45] I believe Wollen's point to be exaggerated. Hawks' view was not so much homosexual as asexual. "He doesn't like losers, or antiheroes," Leigh Brackett once said of Hawks. "He values bravery, strength, expertise, loyalty, all the 'masculine' virtues (though Lord knows I've known women who had a damned sight more of them than some of the men I've known; it isn't sex, it's the individual). So why should he give his women a position of equality—often, indeed, dominance—in a genre that usually relegates them either to being decorative in the hero's relaxed moments, or to looking doleful as the hero goes off about his business? I suspect that it's because Hawks doesn't like women in their *negative* aspect, and until he can accept a female character, as the hero must, as another man, or an asexual *human being* with the attributes he respects, he can't like her. And if he didn't like her, he wouldn't know what to do with her. Hawks has to like all his people (the villains are kept down to a minimum) and this is why such a great deal of affectionate good humor comes through in films like RIO BRAVO and HATARI!''[46]

In the final analysis, Elizabeth Threatt, as an actress, was not much better portraying a Hawksian heroine than Joanne Dru had been. Physically, and in terms of her costume in the final scenes, she was clearly a Pocahontas stereotype. Yet the structure of the film, as well as the way her character was drawn, required that she be universally respected among the members of her tribe, not only because of her status as a chief's daughter but even more because of her fortitude, her moral strength, and her downright ability to know her own mind and proceed accordingly. Such characteristics may be regarded as "masculine" in a certain cultural setting, but for Hawks they were simply virtues that had nothing to do with a person's gender.

After seeing Sam Peckinpah's THE WILD BUNCH (Warner's, 1969), Hawks was convinced that Peckinpah "doesn't know how to direct. I can kill four men, take 'em to the morgue, and bury 'em before he gets one down to the ground in slow motion. All I saw was a lot of red paint and blood running. I don't think a good director has to utilize that stuff."[47] He also felt that "Peckinpah and I believe in exactly the opposite thing. I like it when it's so quick that you say, 'My God, did it really happen?' ''[48] No doubt this antipathy was due to the very significant differences in the way the two men approached the Western. "The Western," according to Peckinpah, "is a universal frame within which it is possible to comment on today."[49] For Hawks, as he told us, "a Western is gunplay and horses. It's about adventurous life and sudden death. It's the most dramatic thing you can do."

HIGH NOON was released almost a decade before Peckinpah directed his first theatrical Western but it might nonetheless be said to embody his viewpoint.

Neither Hawks nor John Wayne particularly liked the film. They felt it lies about what they perceived as the frontier spirit. Hawks felt that Gary Cooper's role in HIGH NOON showed him to be less than a professional, indeed very nearly a loser. He recalled what he had wanted Tom Dunson to represent in RED RIVER and in scripting RIO BRAVO he wanted a story about a sheriff threatened by a lawless element who is not afraid, who does not ask anyone for help, but who gets it anyway because of the kind of man he is and because he has the kind of character that inspires loyalty in others. If Hawks had once played TO HAVE AND HAVE NOT off against the premises of CASABLANCA, he did the same here. Those inspired by the Wayne persona are Dean Martin, cast as a deputy driven to drink by a relationship with a woman but who now is struggling to regain his self-esteem; Walter Brennan in his customary role as a feisty old timer; and, instead of the younger man, played by Lloyd Bridges in HIGH NOON, who tries to move in on the sheriff's old girl friend, Ricky Nelson was cast as a youngster who has to prove himself in order to be accepted by men whom he admires. Ward Bond was cast as a freighter whose offer of assistance is rejected because he is too old and has other people who depend on him. Unlike the cowardly townspeople in HIGH NOON, Bond declares his intention to take a hand anyway and is killed. This incident is similar to the situation confronting the character played by Thomas Mitchell in ONLY ANGELS HAVE WINGS and I tend to agree with Donald C. Willis' conclusion that "RIO BRAVO is almost the same movie as ONLY ANGELS HAVE WINGS, only longer, more loosely structured, and imperfectly cast."[50] Angie Dickinson played Feathers, perhaps the best portrayal of a Hawksian heroine in his Westerns, but somehow the lines—only slight variations in some cases of those uttered by Bacall earlier—sound hollow and not entirely persuasive. She and Wayne express their affection for each other mostly through aggressive banter that does not work as effectively as it did when Bacall and Bogart were playing such scenes together.

"In RIO BRAVO Dean Martin had a bit in which he was required to role a cigarette," Hawks told Peter Bogdanovich in an interview. "His fingers weren't equal to it and Wayne kept passing him cigarettes. All of a sudden you realize that they are awfully good friends or he wouldn't be doing it. That grew out of Martin's asking me one day, 'Well, if my fingers are shaky, how can I roll this thing?' So Wayne said, 'Here, I'll hand you one,' and suddenly we had something going. . . . "[51] In the final release print, Wayne only hands Martin one cigarette paper, but by this gesture we know they are friends, that Wayne respects Martin too much to do it for him. It aptly sums up Hawks' personal code and, in fact, the point of the whole film. Having Dean Martin and in particular Ricky Nelson in the picture added to what it grossed at the box office, although some critics subsequently find them less than credible in these roles because of their activities outside and beyond the characters they are playing. However, if judged only in its own terms as a film, Dean Martin probably gave his finest performance in any motion picture in RIO BRAVO and Ricky Nelson at least physically supplies that contradiction in stereotypes in Westerns which Montgomery Clift managed far more effectively: the slender young man with a pretty face who is just as capable and deadly as any of his more brawny and substantial peers.

It is a different matter when it comes to racial stereotypes. Robin Wood in HOWARD HAWKS (1968) sought to justify, on rather shaky grounds, Hawks' images of French-Canadians in THE BIG SKY (to which I would add Poor Devil and Teal Eye) and the Mexican played by Pedro González-González in RIO BRAVO. "One can say that the very existence of such stock figures is itself insulting, and this is fair enough," he argued; "one can, I suppose, go on from that to complain that Hawks is unthinkingly helping to perpetuate the insult; but that is rather different from finding actual racial malice in his attitude. He is simply—and very characteristically—making use of the conventions (and the actors) that are at hand, and not questioning their initial validity. He takes the stock figure of the comic, cowardly, gesticulating, garrulous Mexican and, by eliminating the cowardliness while playing up the excitability, builds up a character whose dauntlessness and determination win our sympathy and respect even as we laugh at him."[52] To me, at best this is being mincing, at worst, an exercise in apologetics. The truth of the matter is that Hawks, no less than John Ford, was a racial elitist and a viewer just has to accept this attitude in his films and, albeit disapproving of its presence, move on to other considerations. However, this should not be done so swiftly that one forgets that in the world of Hawks' films the white man self-evidently belongs to a master race and that, in quieting our objections, we are expressing our willingness to endorse tacitly this racial bias in order to participate in other, more pleasant aspects of Hawksian fantasy.

In an essay in FOCUS ON HOWARD HAWKS (1972), Peter Bogdanovich claimed that "Hawks' vision of the world is tragic: his men are gallant, brave, reckless, but it is the façade for a fatalistic approach to a world in which they hold a most tenuous position."[53] This may apply to the "marked men" in Hawks' films, the ones who do not listen to the protagonists and who die, but for Hawks' protagonists and heroes it is utter nonsense. One is never in doubt during RIO BRAVO that the sheriff will come out of it alive; nor do doubts arise concerning the fate of the characters played by John Wayne in either EL DORADO (Paramount, 1967) or RIO LOBO. Hawks' alteration of the conclusion Borden Chase intended for RED RIVER was indicative of his basic attitude toward his heroes. In EL DORADO a gunfighter played by Christopher George is on the side of big rancher Bart Jason, played by Edward Asner, and calls it "professional courtesy" when he prohibits his men from shooting Wayne in the back. At the end of the film Wayne finishes off George with a rifle. "You didn't give me a chance," the George character complains before he dies. "You're too good to give a chance to," Wayne tells him. What in this is tragic?

In Hawks' final Westerns, the aging characters played by John Wayne take on an increasing significance as for him too, to echo Jacques Rivette's words, "a man's old age is his judge" and in the process the judgement of old age is brought to bear on the values of the Hawksian hero. "As Wayne declines in years and physically deteriorates," Gregg Ford wrote, "director Hawks, in compensatory fashion, insistently endows him with greater apparent dignity and self-respect."[54] Ford also recognized that while RIO BRAVO, EL DORADO, and RIO LOBO are thematically very closely related, structurally they represent a graduated return to the journey and search theme of Hawks' earlier Westerns. The focus in RIO BRAVO is on the jailhouse and the surrounding urban world is one of great danger, typical of the paranoia of so many so-called "town Westerns." EL DORADO is partially a town Western and is partly set outside of town. In RIO LOBO, the story embodies a revenge theme and is structured in the form of a quest. In Hawks' journey films, according to Gregg Ford, male adventurers are denied the "prefab shielding of any inviolate womb-like redoubt" and they are sent out "wandering, desultorily, exposed to the transcience and chaos and unknown of a genuine ordinary social milieu. In RIO LOBO, Hawks toys with topography to evolve a fleetingness, an elusiveness, an impermanence. . . ."[55]

In EL DORADO Robert Mitchum, cast as a drunken sheriff whom Wayne decides to help out, serves as a good balance to Wayne's powerful screen presence. Not only is there no such balance in RIO LOBO, but Jennifer O'Neill, as the heroine, proved to be so neurotic and awkward that Hawks rapidly lost interest in her and she virtually drops out of the film before the end.

The heat outside the house drifted upwards in silent but intense shimmerings.

"Do you plan to make another Western?" I asked.

"You know, Wayne called me just the other day and said, 'Howard, we should make another picture together.' " Hawks paused and then shook his head. "But he's too old and too fat."

He said no more, but it struck me at once that Wayne had been in every Western he had ever made, except for THE BIG SKY and BARBARY COAST, and that if he could not have Wayne, he could not really conceive of a Western that he could possibly want to make.

While John Ford was frequently given credit for directing RED RIVER, and wasn't above graciously accepting it, Ford could never have made that picture any more than he could have made any of Hawks' subsequent Westerns. Hawks in his Westerns concentrated too much on alternatives to the family as a basic unit; the relationships in them were necessarily more nebulous, more a reflection of men striving toward some common goal of moderate behavior rather than spiritual fulfillment. Romantic love really goes begging. Yet, by concentrating on the personalities of the actors and merging them into one with the characters, Hawks managed within the parameters of his philosophy to produce Westerns that balance action with meaning in such a manner as to avoid the disasterous pitfall of what is termed social significance.

# V

Hawks collaborated with Billy Wilder and Charles Brackett to make BALL OF FIRE (RKO, 1942) for Samuel Goldwyn. Gary Cooper played a professor at work on a comprehensive encyclopedia of the world's knowledge whose perspectives undergo a severe alteration when he is exposed to an erratic show girl played by Barbara Stanwyck. "He was a hell of a cameraman," Hawks said of Gregg Toland who was the cinematographer on the picture. "We had a marvelous scene where Cooper had to come in to say something to the girl. She was in bed, you couldn't see her face, you could just see her eyes. I said to Toland, 'How the hell can I do that? How can I light her eyes without lighting her face?' And he said, 'Well, have her do it in blackface.' So the next day I saw her and said, 'Barbara, tomorrow don't bother making up. I want you to play in blackface.' She said, 'What the hell kind of scene is that?' Oh, God, it was a good scene."[56]

Howard told us that, in general, he was dissatisfied with the comic pacing in BALL OF FIRE and for that reason did not do another comedy until 1948 and, then, ironically, it was the same picture! "Goldwyn pestered me and pestered me," Howard recalled. "He offered me $25,000 a week to remake BALL OF FIRE as A SONG IS BORN. I finally gave in. There was a way I thought we could do the picture, but Goldwyn wouldn't let me do anything. It was a horrible experience. Goldwyn kept interfering no matter how much I insulted him. Danny Kaye and his wife were separating and he was a basket case, stopping work twice a day to see a psychiatrist."

Perhaps because of his frustration at not being able to make A SONG IS BORN the kind of comedy he wanted it to be, Hawks next tried another comedy, I WAS A MALE WAR BRIDE (20th-Fox, 1949). Cary Grant was cast as a French army captain who has a hostile relationship with WAC Ann Sheridan only to discover midway through the film that he is in love with her and she with him. From this point on the tension arises from just how, once they are married, Sheridan can get Grant into the United States and the only possible way is for Grant to qualify as a "war bride." The role required him to dress in drag. The film would be shot in Germany and on the way Grant stopped at the Shepperton Studios in London to talk with Hawks. "Cary acted out a scene in a WAC uniform," Charles Higham wrote, "but Hawks, always cold, hard, and detached, though with a wry, sharp sense of humor, was not amused. He told Cary to set aside his effeminate gestures; he must not pretend to be a woman but must walk and talk like a man. Cary protested that this was ridiculous: no one could possibly mistake an aggressively male figure in a skirt; much of the comedy sprang from the misunderstanding, and this approach would destroy the movie. Hawks won. His macho hang-up about homosexuality was such that he would not tolerate even an inkling of gay behavior on any of his sets, even when, as in this instance, the script unquestionably called for it. As for Cary, he knew that his large female audience so completely worshipped him as a sex symbol that nothing he did would risk his reputation."[57]

Hawks doubtless took both the job of directing A SONG IS BORN and I WAS A MALE WAR BRIDE, the latter produced by Sol C. Siegel who only recently had come to Fox from Republic Pictures where he had been a production supervisor, because he needed the money. RED RIVER was held up in litigation until September, 1948 when at last United Artists was able to release it. As a consequence of Nyby's efforts with Howard Hughes, Hawks was able to re-establish his relationship with the eccentric tycoon who now also owned RKO. He persuaded Hughes to finance THE THING (RKO, 1951) which would be produced by Howard through his Winchester Productions and which Nyby would direct. After this film, Nyby went back to work for Hawks as a cutter. Subsequently Hawks denied any credit for the film, although Nyby was only too ready to admit that he frequently consulted Hawks and that Hawks both sat in on all the rehearsals and worked extensively on the script. The screenplay was based on "Who Goes There?"—one of the finest short stories of science fiction that John Campbell, long-time editor of ASTOUNDING SCIENCE FICTION, wrote under his Don A. Stuart pen-name. Russell Harlan, who photographed RED RIVER, was the cinematographer. THE THING became a pace-setter among science fiction films and with its closing line about the necessity to keep watching the skies, a harbinger of the paranoia which characterized this genre in the 'Fifties. James Arness played the terrible vegetable creature from a distant world who crashes in a flying saucer into the frozen wastes of the North Pole only to be discovered and brought to life by a group of naive scientists. Nyby and Harlan worked again with Hawks, with Hughes financing and Hawks directing and producing, on THE BIG SKY.

Hawks' apparent contempt for scientists, evident in the way they are treated in films from BRINGING UP BABY to THE THING, had a field day in his next major film, MONKEY BUSINESS. Originally Hawks had been invited back to the Fox lot to direct one of the five episodes included in the compendium film O. HENRY'S FULL HOUSE (20th-Fox, 1952) as well as MONKEY BUSINESS. The screenplay for the latter was by Ben Hecht, Charles Lederer (who had married and divorced Orson Welles' first wife), and I.A.L. Diamond. Diamond would later become Billy Wilder's collaborator and would script a vicious parody of Cary Grant in Wilder's SOME LIKE IT HOT (United Artists, 1959) where Tony Curtis pretends to be sexually impotent while doing a Cary Grant impersonation in order to seduce Marilyn Monroe. In MONKEY BUSINESS, Grant was cast as a scientist seeking an elixir that will rejuvenate aging human tissues. Ginger Rogers was cast as Grant's wife, principally according to Hawks because Grant refused to be shown married to a younger woman. It is more a bitter satire than a comedy. Although it did business, it also marked a significant departure for Hawks. When a chimpanzee actually concocts the elixir and it is transferred to a bottled water dispenser, both Grant and Rogers regress, but in so doing they become younger not really physically but mentally, betraying in their behavior the mindless idiocy of adolescence among teenagers in the 'Fifties.

MONKEY BUSINESS is not highly regarded generally among many American critics, but here I tend to agree with the French critics who esteem it as perhaps Hawks' best comedy precisely because its wit and satire are so pointed in their condemnation of American popular culture which, at that time, was spreading throughout Europe. The film is also memorable for the brief but effective performance of Marilyn Monroe. Darryl F. Zanuck was so impressed by Monroe's performance that he decided to give her full star treatment.

"They gave her about four stories," Howard told us, "and they were all failures. Zanuck wanted to know why. 'Because,' I said, 'you did real pictures, and she isn't real. She's just a complete fantasy. There isn't one real thing in her. She ought to do a musical comedy.'

" 'But she can't sing!'

" 'Yes she can.'

" 'How do you know?'

" 'She goes to cocktail parties in Palm Springs. Nobody will take her home, so she comes around and asks if I will. And then she doesn't talk. One time I said, "If you can't talk, can you sing?" and she said, yes. We turned on the radio. She sang along. So, I know she can sing.'

" 'Okay,' Zanuck said, 'make the picture.'

" 'Only if I can get someone like Jane Russell to back up Monroe.'

" 'You can't get her.'

"I told him I thought I could. I had got her started in pictures. Zanuck got her on the 'phone.

" 'Jane,' I said, 'I've got a picture for you.'

" 'When do we start?'

" 'Wait a minute. There's a part in it that may be better than yours.'

" 'Well, you want me, don't you?'

" 'Yes.'

" 'Okay, I'll do it.'

"She was more help than anybody else could have been because she would explain to Marilyn what I wanted. Marilyn would say, 'Well, why didn't *he* say that?' after I'd just explained it all to her six or seven times. The camera liked Monroe. The camera made her sexy. But if you worked with her, she could be sitting around with practically nothing on and no one would give her a second look. If a good-looking girl all dressed up would pass by, everybody would whistle. They never did that with Marilyn. She could never get anyone to take her out."

GENTLEMEN PREFER BLONDES (20th-Fox, 1953) permitted Hawks to cast the two chief sex symbols on the screen at that time. Heavy of breast and buttocks, they make a striking contrast to Bacall's Slim, or Sheridan's WAC, or Ginger Rogers in MONKEY BUSINESS and Angie Dickinson later in RIO BRAVO. The humor was often biting and usually at Monroe's expense, especially when her heavily endowed body constantly and clumsily gets in her way.

Although neither MAN'S FAVORITE SPORT (Universal, 1964) nor RED LINE 7000 (Paramount, 1965) rank among Hawks' better screen efforts, LAND OF THE PHARAOHS (Warner's, 1955) may well be the least satisfying film Hawks ever made. He knew from the beginning that it would be problematical because he had no conception of how a Pharaoh speaks. William Faulkner was at last having some literary impact on the reading public and had given up screenwriting. He had certain commitments to Random House, the publisher which had stuck with him for twenty years, but when Hawks asked him to come and help bail out the picture Faulkner consented at once. Faulkner, Harry Kurnitz, and Hawks worked on the script in Paris, Stresa, St. Moritz, and Cairo. When Faulkner kept asking Hawks how Pharaohs talk, Hawks had no better answer than he had had before Faulkner had joined him. Faulkner left the picture somewhat ahead of schedule and made some needed alterations in a manuscript which Donald Klopfer, his editor at Random House, had insisted upon. Making the alterations in Paris, Faulkner gave an interview in which he described LAND OF THE PHARAOHS as "the same movie Howard has been making for thirty-five years. It's RED RIVER all over again. The Pharaoh is the cattle baron, his jewels are the cattle, and the Nile is the Red River. But the thing about Howard is, he knows it's the same movie, and he knows how to make it." Then Faulkner did what for him was a very unconventional thing. He helped promote the film in Memphis at a sales meeting a month before the picture went into release. His assessment of Hawks' film contrasted with his promotional activities is only indicative of the ambivalent and contradictory attitude he had come to have about Hollywood. " 'There's some people who are writers who believed they had talent,' " he once summed up his Hollywood years, " 'they believed in the dream of perfection, they get offers to go to Hollywood where they make a lot of money, they begin to acquire junk swimming pools and imported cars, and they can't quit their jobs because they have got to continue to own that swimming pool and the imported cars. There are others with the same dream of perfection, the same belief that maybe they can match it, that go there and resist the money. They don't own the swimming pools, the imported cars. They will do enough work to get what they need of the money without becoming a slave to it . . . it is going to be difficult to go completely against the grain or the current of a culture. But you can compromise without selling your individuality completely to it. You've got to compromise because it makes things easier.' "[58]

"I think a director's a storyteller," Howard said, now that the interview was over, "and, if he tells a story that people can't understand, then he shouldn't be a director. I don't care what they do as long as they tell it well." He paused for a moment. Vicki had almost closed her notebook. "It's been a lot of fun," he said then, "but it has been a long fight for directors like Ford, Capra, myself. We fought to get credit and the way we did it mostly was by not going under contract. Never agree to do something until you have things your own way."

On the trip back to Los Angeles, the wind was sharper, blowing across the flat lands and swirling around the dunes. A fine sand beat against the windshield. Actors, actresses, even topgraphy, I could not help reflecting, are so much more recognizable to American filmgoers than the names of directors.

We visited several times more with Howard. When an earlier version of this career study appeared, I sent a copy to him. When next we saw him, he had a sardonic expression on his face.

"Some sonofabitches maybe can't think in the heat," he snapped. "I can."

Of course, he was right. John Ford had come to the desert to die. Howard had been at his side. But for Howard the desert, the unceasing heat, the dry, unstirring air had preserved him.

In his final years, Howard Hawks lived alone, although he had a housekeeper during the week and his son Gregg technically was staying with him when he was not gone motorcycling. He was not anywhere around when Vicki and I paid our last visit to Howard shortly before his death for the purpose of recording an interview on video tape. Howard knew his stories well. He had reduced his life to a vast number of finely chiseled anecdotes which he delivered for the camera with animation and authority. He was also home alone in December, 1977 when he tripped over one of his dogs, striking his head upon the stone floor. He lay unconscious for well over twenty-four hours before he was discovered and an ambulance summoned. Hawks spent two weeks in the hospital but the concussion and the complications arising from it proved too great a shock for his system. When John Ford was dying, he would invariably watch old Westerns on television, the really old Westerns from the early 'Thirties made on small budgets and with primitive sound-recording equipment. Howard spent his final days watching football games on television and drinking martinis. He wasn't yet in such dismal shape he could not play out a dramatic scene with his daughter Barbara, however. "He told her he loved her," Gerald Mast has recorded, "and she began to cry. It was the first time she'd heard him say it. Then Hawks tossed off one of those flippant, comically defensive comments that always undercut the sentimental force of such moments in his films: 'Oh, get on with you.' "[59]

During our video-taped interview, Howard told me that Peter Bogdanovich had got it wrong in his article, "Taps for Mr. Ford," in NEW YORK MAGAZINE (October, 1973). Ford had not said, "Goodbye, Howard" once followed by a "I mean really goodbye." He had said goodbye to Hawks seven or eight times.[60] There is no question that the men had a high regard for each other. But this is not to say that, however much they might have borrowed bits of business from each other, their films had many common or shared themes. Even if Ford had not said that he admired Hawks for the austerity and stoicism of his films, albeit certainly not in these words, putting it instead that his own films were "only corn" compared to Howard's, it could be deduced by comparing the films themselves. "Where Ford's long shot/close-up editing idealizes his characters," John Belton observed, "the same sort of cutting in Hawks' films humanizes his."[61]

John Wayne always spoke the most highly of John Ford while Ford was still alive and he once sent me an eloquent letter about what he felt Ford to have been as a director, shortly after Ford died. However, the last time I spoke with Wayne he insisted that Hawks was the best director with whom he had ever worked and who had had the greatest impact on his career. Howard Hawks died on 26 December 1977.

If John Ford was a painter and Henry King was a poet, Howard Hawks, more than King, more even than Ford, and despite his patrician spirit had a quality of the people about him. At his very best, he still entertains. He tells us little about the times in which we live, nor was he a visionary. Instead, he tells of men and women who are not losers and therefore are exceptional enough to attract our interest and who are human enough to engage our sympathies. Above all, he never lost his sense of humor, his amused cognizance that almost nothing in life deserves to be taken seriously for very long, lest it be our most personal fantasies. Nothing provides a more significant contrast of Hawks and Ford in their "forced" retirement than their trophy rooms. Ford had an entire room in his Palm Desert home devoted to all the awards he had received from his work in motion pictures and in military service and the room was literally filled to overflowing. Hawks instead in his den had displayed Gregg's many trophies from motorcycle races. John Kobal perhaps put it best. "Talking of the son," he wrote, "you saw the proud father, and more, for in his son's exploits you saw the shape of the Hawks hero."[62]

1.  Vicki Piekarski on the set of *The Detective in Hollywood* pilot film. *Photo by James Metropole.*

2. H. Bruce Humberstone at the time he became a film director. *Photo courtesy of H. Bruce Humberstone.*

3. Warner Oland, as Charlie Chan, and Humberstone on the set of *Charlie Chan at the Race Track* (20th-Fox, 1936). *Photo courtesy of H. Bruce Humberstone.*

4. "Lucky" Humberstone between Rosanne Murray and Danny Kaye on the set of *Wonder Man* (RKO, 1945). *Photo courtesy of Movie Star News.*

5. Henry King when he was an actor as well as a pioneer director. *Photo courtesy of the Museum of Modern Art Still Archive.*

6. Richard Barthelmess (left) and Henry King (right) while filming *Tol'able David* (First National, 1921). *Photo courtesy of the Museum of Modern Art Still Archive.*

7. Henry Fonda and Henry King on location (briefly) for *Way Down East* (Fox, 1935). *Photo courtesy of the Museum of Modern Art Still Archive.*

8. Alfred Hitchcock and Margaret Lockwood on the set of *The Lady Vanishes* (Gainsborough, 1938). *Photo courtesy of the British Film Institute Still Archive.*

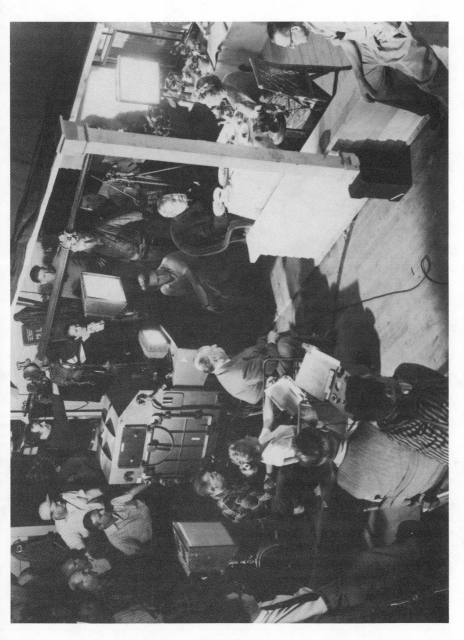

9. Hitchcock directing Edmund Gwenn and Mildred Natwick in a scene from *The Trouble with Harry* (Paramount, 1956). *Photo courtesy of MCA-Universal.*

10. Hitchcock directing Kim Novak in *Vertigo* (Paramount, 1958). *Photo courtesy of MCA-Universal.*

11. Alfred Hitchcock and dress designer Edith Head on the set of *Family Plot* (Universal, 1976). *Photo courtesy of MCA-Universal.*

12. Howard Hawks and his dog, "Cap," when he worked with Howard Hughes on *Scarface* (United Artists, 1932). *Photo courtesy of the Wisconsin Center for Theatre Research.*

13. Hawks directing Carole Lombard and John Barrymore in *Twentieth Century* (Columbia, 1934). *Photo courtesy of Columbia Pictures Industries.*

14. Hawks, Victor Kilian, and Jean Arthur conferring on the set of *Only Angels Have Wings* (Columbia, 1939). *Photo courtesy of The Memory Shop.*

15. A dialogue conference on the set of *The Big Sleep* (Warner's, 1946) with Hawks, Sonia Darwin, Margaret Cunningham (Hawks' secretary), Bacall, Bogart, and Louis Jean Heydt. *Photo courtesy of the Museum of Modern Art Still Archive.*

16. Hawks and John Wayne on location for *Hatari!* (Paramount, 1962). Note the *Red River* belt buckles. *Photo courtesy of the Museum of Modern Art Still Archive.*

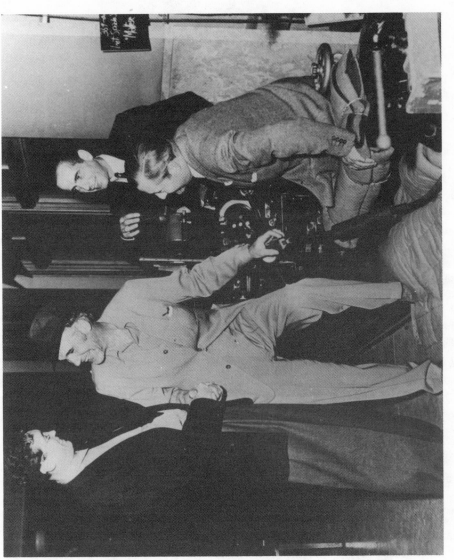

17. John Huston shaking hands with his father on the set of *The Maltese Falcon* as Bogart and cameraman Oliver S. Garretson look on. *Photo courtesy of the British Film Institute Still Archive.*

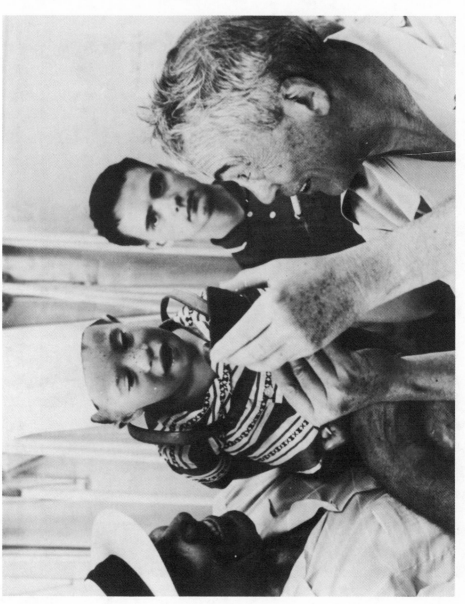

18. Huston fascinates a young visitor to the set of *The Misfits* (United Artists, 1960). *Photo courtesy of United Artists.*

19. Huston in one of his most famous acting roles opposite Jack Nicholson in *Chinatown* (Paramount, 1974). *Photo courtesy of Paramount Pictures.*

20. Huston and Ray Stark on the set of *Annie* (Columbia, 1982). *Photo courtesy of Columbia Pictures Industries.*

21. Orson Welles "riding" the camera in a scene from *Citizen Kane* (RKO, 1941). *Photo courtesy of Eddie Brandt's Saturday Matinee.*

22. Orson and Rita Hayworth in the mirror scene from *The Lady from Shanghai* (Columbia, 1948). *Photo courtesy of Columbia Pictures Industries.*

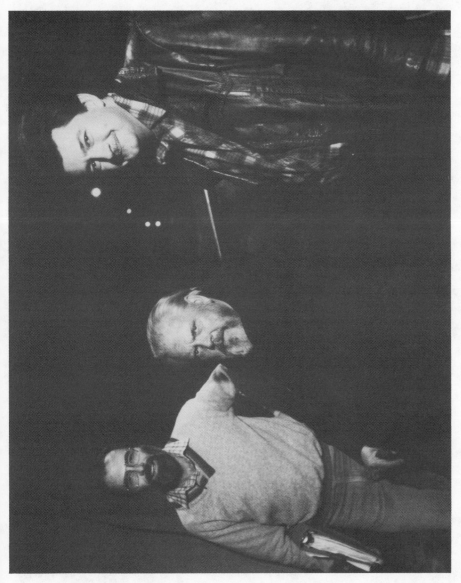

23. Orson on the set of *The Detective in Hollywood* with Fred Hutchison (left) and Jon Tuska (right). *Photo courtesy of James Metropole.*

24. Roman Polanski in costume for *Chinatown* (Paramount, 1974). *Photo courtesy of Paramount Pictures.*

25. Polanski finally entering the door to "the" apartment in *The Tenant* (Paramount, 1976). *Photo courtesy of Paramount Pictures.*

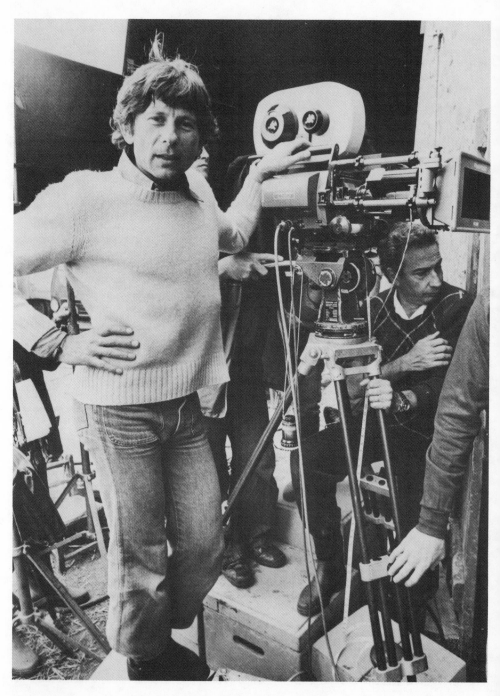

26. Polanski on the set of *Tess* (Columbia, 1980). *Photo courtesy of Columbia Pictures Industries.*

27. Sam Peckinpah on the set of *Pat Garrett and Billy The Kid* (M-G-M, 1973). *Photo courtesy of Metro-Goldwyn-Mayer.*

28. Steve McQueen, Ali McGraw, and Sam Peckinpah on the set of *The Getaway* (National General, 1972). *Photo courtesy of National General.*

29. Sam directing Vadim Glowna and a stand-in in a scene from *Cross of Iron* (Avco-Embassy, 1977). *Photo courtesy of Avco-Embassy.*

30. A very old and tired Sam Peckinpah with Rutger Hauer on the set of *The Osterman Weekend* (20th-Fox, 1983). *Photo courtesy of Twentieth Century-Fox Film Corporation.*

31. Clowning on the set of *Cross of Iron* (Avco-Embassy, 1977). Katy Haber, dressed in a nurse's uniform, wheels Sam Peckinpah about in a wheelchair. She was a good and loyal friend to Sam and on one occasion saved his life. *Photo courtesy of Katherine Haber.*

# John Huston

The first important book in English to appear on John Huston was William F. Nolan's JOHN HUSTON: KING REBEL (1965). There are two and a half pages of acknowledgments ending with Huston's name in bold-faced type. I brought the book with me as a reference when Vicki and I met with Huston for the first time at the suite he occupied at the Beverly Hills Hotel. It was in late spring, 1975. Huston was on his way back to Las Caletas in Mexico, near Puerto Vallarta, and we were *en route* to Europe. A television commercial for RCA had brought him to Los Angeles and, since we were also there at the time, this happy coincidence made an interview possible.

Huston had long said that acting in motion pictures, as opposed to directing them, was strictly a lark; but it did make him a familiar figure to audiences. The thin gray hair, the brown eyes, the drooping lines of his face were now augmented by a gray stubbly beard and a bristly moustache. The drawl was no different than it had been when he played the dissolute cowboy star Buck Loner in MYRA BRECKINRIDGE (20th-Fox, 1973) and the assurance of his carriage had about it that same confidence he exhibited as Noah Cross in CHINATOWN (Paramount, 1974).

"I thought KING REBEL was rather favorable toward you," I said, "although the title struck me as curious."

"I've heard about that book," Huston replied, relaxing in an imitation Charles chair and puffing blandly on a cigar. "I've never read it. I never read anything written about me." He paused to exhale a huge puff of cigar smoke. "Maybe if its author had ever talked to me, he mightn't have been so favorable." Huston's mouth fell into a lop-sided smirk and his eyes glinted.

Three years later Stuart Kaminsky would publish JOHN HUSTON: MAKER

OF MAGIC (1978) also without interviewing Huston; but, in his case, it would not be for want of trying.

"THE MALTESE FALCON [Warner's, 1941] was the first picture you directed?"

"Yes. I was under contract to Warner Bros. as a writer. My option was coming up for renewal. I told them I would stay on if they would let me direct. I was told to pick a property I wanted to direct. They were surprised when I chose THE MALTESE FALCON."

"Howard Hawks has told me that you talked over the project with him because Jack L. Warner wasn't too keen on it."

Huston nodded in agreement. "They'd already made the picture twice, once in 1931, and then again in 1936."

The 1936 film was titled SATAN MET A LADY and starred Warren William and Bette Davis. It only loosely followed Hammett's plot with some drastic character changes. According to Allen Rivkin, who worked with Huston on the screenplay, prior to writing anything a secretary at Huston's suggestion recopied Hammett's book, breaking the book itself down into shots, scenes, and dialogue. According to both Rivkin and Huston, when a copy of what the secretary had done made it to Jack Warner's desk, he read it, liked it, and informed Huston to start shooting the picture in a week.

"Did you have a hand in the casting?"

"Some. I wanted Geraldine Fitzgerald for the part of Brigid O'Shaughnessy. I was voted down on that choice in favor of Mary Astor. At that time, Mary was producing her own pictures at Warner Bros. The studio liked her and insisted she be given the role. I wanted George Raft for the lead."

"I talked to Raft about that."

"What did he tell you?"

"He said Myron Selznick was his agent then and Selznick thought the picture would hurt him. 'You've got three dames in this picture,' Raft quoted him as saying, 'and none of them is box office. The picture has already been made twice before, so it can't come to anything. And you have an untried director.' "

"Well, how much of that do *you* think was right?"

"He was wrong about the picture's not being superior to its predecessors. That's certain. Many film critics have come to regard your version of THE MALTESE FALCON as the finest detective film ever made. As for casting, that surely was part of the magic. Peter Lorre remarked that casting was the secret to the film's success. Everything just seemed to click. The three women were quite apt in their respective roles."

Huston coughed. "The only objection Raft ever gave me was that I was a brand new director. But if you want my honest opinion, I think he was afraid of the script."

"How so?"

"George never liked his lines to be too long. He always wanted everything shortened. Sam Spade had a lot of dialogue. There was no getting around it. I think that scared Raft.''

I recalled the conversation we had with Raft, as we sat together at his customary table in the Beverly Hills Brown Derby. ''I wasn't too smart when I came to Hollywood,'' he said. ''I didn't know very much. So I hired guys who were supposed to be smarter than I was to tell me what to do. I guess they weren't so smart. I learned how to read in a Catholic school. You know what they're like. So when I didn't understand a part, or what I was supposed to be saying, I turned the part down.'' Raft, for a long time, was so concerned about his screen image that, although he customarily smoked four packages of Lucky Strike cigarettes a day, he would not allow himself to be photographed smoking because it might tarnish the clean-cut image he wanted very much to maintain. Even when we knew him, in his seventies and eighties, he made repeated references to the fact that he did not drink. He came, however, both to drink and smoke on screen.

''But,'' Huston went on, ''Raft would have been good as Sam Spade.''

I could not help but comment on how George Raft, in a way, had been responsible for Humphrey Bogart's becoming a major star in the 'Forties, primarily because Bogart accepted roles that Raft rejected, from DEAD END (United Artists, 1937) and HIGH SIERRA (Warner's, 1941) to THE MALTESE FALCON and CASABLANCA (Warner's, 1942).

''Raft always played hard guys,'' Huston said, nodding. ''But Bogie had personality. We had to adjust the Sam Spade role a little for him, for his personality, rather than the dialogue, which we would have had to adjust for Raft had he taken the part. But I think Bogie made a damned good Sam Spade.''

Huston had just finished breakfast when we arrived, in the company of two women who were his friends. They had told us not to expect too much from him since, it seemed, his fifth marriage was in trouble. There was a large pot of fresh coffee and we all replenished our cups.

''Norman Foster, who directed Peter Lorre in the Mr. Moto series, told me that he found Lorre, before they made the first picture, recuperating in a sanitarium from drug addiction.''

''Now,'' said Huston, dusting cigar ash in a saucer he had taken from among the breakfast dishes, ''Peter Lorre was wonderful to work with. He was in very good health when we were doing THE MALTESE FALCON. He was intelligent and yet a consummate actor. He'd do a scene, and it would look good. But on screen it was fantastic, elusive, mobile. Peter Lorre was a beautifully educated man. I was very fond of Peter. He had a fluid wit and he loved obscenities. When Peter knew there were going to be visitors to our set, he would go to Mary Astor's dressing room, wait until the visitors were outside the dressing room door, and then time it so he would be coming out of her dressing room buttoning his fly just as the visitors were passing.'' Huston had to laugh as he remembered.

"Did you meet Dashiell Hammett?" I asked.

"I knew him very well," Huston responded. "He was the most attractive man I have ever known, a fine gentleman, unique, austere. But I had the feeling that behind that gentleman, that controlled exterior, there was a wild man. It wasn't until Hammett would have his second or third drink that fireworks would start. He was exactly like Ned Beaumont in THE GLASS KEY [1931]. He wore gloves, carried a cane. There was an elegance about Dash Hammett. I knew he was a radical, but he lived by his own code and I respected him for that. He loved THE MALTESE FALCON the way we made it."

"Did you keep in touch with him after the war?"

"Yes, through all of his life. When he was called before the House Un-American Activities Committee, he told them that 'words can't express the contempt I feel for you.' They sent him to jail and then, for the rest of his life, they took away all his money and any possibility he might have to make money. He never complained. The last time I saw him he was living in a cottage by a lake in the East, about a two-hour drive from New York City. He would fish a lot. The walls of the cottage were covered with anatomical drawings of the human eye. That's what he was studying at the time.

"Willy Wyler brought him out here again to write the screenplay to DETEC-TIVE STORY [Paramount, 1951]. Willy knew what the IRS had done to Hammett, and what the Committee had done, and that Hammett was blacklisted, but he knew Hammett, if anybody, could do a good job on the script. Hammett was given a suite at the Beverly Wilshire Hotel. Willy gave him a check for the script before he started. Willy would visit Hammett every other day, just to talk the story over with him. About two weeks after he arrived, Dash handed Wyler back the check he'd given him. 'I can't do it any more,' he told Willy. 'I'm sorry.' It was sad."

"But he had quit writing long before that, in the mid 'Thirties. Have you any idea why?"

"He fell in love with Lillian Hellman, you know," Huston said, rolling the cigar about and then drawing in on it. "She took him East and introduced him to all her intellectual friends there. And they didn't think much of detective story writers, and that's what Hammett was, what he did best. And then Lillian herself wanted to write plays and Hammett would help her. It made him want to write something else, something different from what he had been writing. And he couldn't do it. I think that's the real reason he quit writing.

"But I'll tell you something more about him. Dash was a man whose word meant more to him, ten times more than anybody's bond. When his doctor told him that he would have to quit drinking or it would kill him, Dash gave his word that he'd quit. Lillian Hellman, who was living with him, went to put the liquor away. Dash told her not to bother. He'd given his word." Huston paused again to puff on his cigar. "And he kept it."

"What were your thoughts on THE MALTESE FALCON as you went into it?'' I asked, lighting a cigarette and pouring some more coffee for Vicki and myself.

"THE MALTESE FALCON was a classic form of the detective story. I don't know, maybe it's the best one ever written. Everything comes together in it. The plot is astonishingly precise, but not without a surprise at the end. Sam Spade is a character with his own code, and he sticks to it. You might not like his code, but it's his, and it's all he's got. The story has a moral ending.''

"In the film, there's a moral ending,'' I put in, "but I get the impression from the novel that Hammett had gone farther than you did in the film. Nobody wins in the novel, just as nobody really wins in life. They just think they do.''

"There were certain conventions we had to respect then,'' Huston said.

"But don't you find it disturbing that in THE MALTESE FALCON Bogart's Sam Spade comes out something of a winner, whereas in CHINATOWN everything was different?''

Huston sighed. "I liked working with Polanski,'' he said. "He's a great director with a little bit of a poet inside.''

"In CHINATOWN, you play the character who has money and power; who has successfully swindled the people of Los Angeles so you can make millions more; who has conceived a granddaughter incestuously with your own daughter. You own the police and the courts. And, at the end, you get your daughter/granddaughter to go away with you, with every expectation that her child will also be kept 'in the family.' The detective is no match for the corruption of the courts, the judges and policemen on the graft. He is told to stay out of it, or be jailed. There is no justice, and there is definitely no 'morality,' as they say, in such an ending. The detective film had come a long way since THE MALTESE FALCON in 1941.''

"Not at all,'' Huston protested, "not at all. It was the same in 1941.'' He leaned forward in his chair toward us. "Only we were less able to accept it then.'' He reclined again, puffing on his cigar, his features leering in a radiant grin.

## II

Walter Houghston was born in Toronto, Canada, in 1884. When he later went on the stage, he changed the spelling to Huston. His first theatrical appearance was in 1902. He joined a road company, despite objections from his parents, particularly his father who was a contractor and urged him to pursue a career in engineering. In 1905, while in New York, he met Rhea Gore. She was a domineering newspaper woman who enjoyed playing the horses. Huston was twenty-one years old. For the sake of his bride, he quit the stage and he and Rhea relocated to Nevada, Missouri where Walter became an engineer in charge of power and light for the small community. On 5 August 1906 John Marcellus Huston was born. Walter would amuse his son with all manner of vaudeville skits. Family life was running smoothly and might have continued indefinitely in the same routine if Walter hadn't mistakenly turned off the town's water supply one night during a fire. Half the town was destroyed. Before morning, the Hustons were on their way to Weatherford, Texas.

The Hustons relocated again, this time to St. Louis. Walter met an actress named Bayonne Whipple. Disgusted by the tedium of engineering, Walter and Bayonne teamed for a vaudeville act. John Huston's concept of married life must surely have been influenced by his own perception of his parents' failed marriage. "He went, and that was the end of the marriage," Huston recalled in AN OPEN BOOK (1980). "He wrote frequently and sent us money, but he never returned home after that."[1] Following the separation of his parents, John found himself spending time with each of them, always in a different part of the country. His mother's love of gambling kept her broke much of the time and Walter's career for some years did not pay well. John had been in and out of several schools when, at twelve, it was discovered that he suffered from an enlarged heart and kidney ailment. Huston developed a confident disregard for his apparent physical frailty and chose to ignore his condition completely. Indeed, pressing forward in the face of physical adversity became a way of life for him. He was transferred to a military school in California in 1918. His health showed considerable improvement by that summer when he visited his father in New York. Walter Huston had finally got a break, winning high praise for his role in Eugene O'Neill's DESIRE UNDER THE ELMS.

When he returned to California, John attended Lincoln Heights High School in Los Angeles where he became interested in boxing. He started to box at little clubs for money, eventually contending as a light-weight in some twenty-five bouts, winning twenty-three and breaking his nose in the bargain. It was also at this time that John became interested in painting and made the acquaintance of Stanton MacDonald-Wright, co-founder with Morgan Russell of the Synchronism school of painting. In his autobiography, Huston tended to glamorize his relationship with Wright.[2] I knew Wright very well during his last years when he lived in the Pacific Palisades and was still actively painting. He was the brother of Willard Huntington Wright who wrote the Philo Vance detective novels under the *nom de plume* of S.S. Van Dine and Stanton had nothing but contemptuous things to say about Huston, particularly after Huston came to visit him and was at work on what would become AN OPEN BOOK. One of the most vivid memories I have of Stanton is sitting talking with him in his studio surrounded by the brilliant splashes of color in his paintings. Years later, in Gladys Hill's apartment in Puerto Vallarta, I saw one of John's large canvases. It was, for me, almost *déjà vu*. Although the painting was clearly signed John Huston, that marvelous flood of colors and light reminded me of nothing so much as Stanton's own paintings.

John spent his time increasingly with his father and the two developed a friendship that would endure until Walter's death, perhaps the deepest friendship that John would ever have in his life. John even landed a few acting jobs before

Walter suggested that John might like to get out of New York for a month or two and John hit on the idea of going to Mexico. He even joined the Mexican cavalry briefly before his mother was able to persuade him to return to California. Once back in Los Angeles, John continued his courtship of Dorothy Harvey, by that time a philosophy major in college who wanted to become a poet. Huston himself claimed that "she was the first girl to whom I had ever made love that I had any feeling for other than carnal."[3]

Huston wanted to paint. Dorothy would read philosophy while John painted. When his mother went to Europe, she returned with a copy of James Joyce's ULYSSES, which Dorothy read aloud as John painted. They had no money. To start them off in marriage, Walter had sent them a check. The couple lived on what money Walter would send them. When John married his third wife, Evelyn Keyes, she recalled in her autobiography Walter's advice to her. " 'When he married for the first time,' " Walter told her, " 'he was twenty and broke and I gave him five hundred dollars to set up housekeeping. That was a lot of money then. He spent the entire amount on a chandelier. I haven't worried about him too much since then. Perhaps you had better do the same. . . . ' "[4] John also tried his hand at writing fiction. What little there is of it concentrates on the defeated, the losers, as would the preponderance of his later films. One of these stories, "The Fool," John sent to Walter in New York who showed it to Ring Lardner who in turn showed it to H.L. Mencken who bought it for publication in THE AMERICAN MERCURY. John was paid $200 for it. That was enough to convince him that his future lay in writing, not in painting, and he and Dorothy went to New York where now John's mother was also working. With Rhea's help, he landed a job reporting for the NEW YORK GRAPHIC. He wasn't very good as a reporter, apparently, since he was frequently fired and rehired until his termination became permanent after he wrote up a New Jersey crime story in which he switched the names of the victim and the accused. By this time, Walter had split with Bayonne Whipple and was married for the third time to Nan Sunderland.

While John was on and off at the GRAPHIC, he wrote a marionette show for Ruth Squires which was produced in 1929 under the title FRANKIE AND JOHNNIE. Sam Jaffe, with whom John had worked during a brief stint as an actor, composed a musical score for the show. It proved sufficiently successful that Boni and Liveright paid John $500 against royalties to publish the play in book form. On a trip to Saratoga, John got into a crap game and ran up the advance to $11,000 which he would eventually lose in the same way. He had inherited his mother's love for gambling.

Walter had been appearing in motion pictures since 1928, including THE VIRGINIAN (Paramount, 1929) directed by Victor Fleming and ABRAHAM LINCOLN (United Artists, 1930) directed by D.W. Griffith, when Howard Hawks cast him to star in THE CRIMINAL CODE (Columbia, 1931). With his father in California, John decided to return there once his termination from the GRAPHIC became final. He negotiated himself a writing job working for Samuel

Goldwyn who was vitally concerned about talking pictures and, accordingly, always on the look-out for playwrights. Huston was given a writing job at Goldwyn because his play had not only been produced but it had also been published as a book.

When no writing assignments were forthcoming after six months, John changed his affiliation from Goldwyn to Universal. His father was by now a major motion picture star. John received credit for working on the dialogue of MURDERS IN THE RUE MORGUE (Universal, 1932), a film based very, very loosely on the story by Edgar Allan Poe, and on the screenplay of LAW AND ORDER (Universal, 1932) which was one of his father's starring vehicles and one of the most unconventional and revolutionary Westerns of the 'Thirties. The picture was so successful that Universal reversed its company policy against the production of sound Westerns and signed Tom Mix to star in what would prove an outstanding series of Western features. RIDER OF DEATH VALLEY (Universal, 1932), the second entry in this series, sufficiently impressed John that it stayed with him. Tom Mix, Lois Wilson, two heavies, and Tom's horse Tony are stranded for more than half the picture in the desert without food or water. The effects of thirst on all of them produce a high state of dramatic tension. John would have his own opportunity to treat this theme in THE TREASURE OF THE SIERRA MADRE (Warner's, 1948).

Probably as a consequence of John's unstable lifestyle during these years, Dorothy turned increasingly to drink for solace. "I contended with it for some months," Huston later wrote; "then the day came when, despite all my feelings of guilt and responsibility, I decided to cut and run."[5] Humphrey Bogart used to sum up marriage this way: " 'I sometimes wonder if the fucking you get is worth the fucking you *get*.' "[6] It would not be that way for John Huston. " . . . She filed suit for divorce, asking nothing of me, not alimony—nothing," Huston stated.[7]

John was restless and the problems with Dorothy did not help. He left for Europe and later claimed that in London he was able to negotiate a job for himself in the story department at Gaumont-British Films. The position did not work out, but Huston concocted a story he called THREE STRANGERS about three individuals who acquire a winning lottery ticket but cannot cash it in because it becomes a clue in a murder investigation. Angus MacPhail liked the idea enough to have Huston narrate it to Alfred Hitchcock who also liked it; but Michael Balcon did not and it went nowhere. Dorothy was in England at the time in an effort to put her life together. She and John began seeing each other again and finally she moved in with him. Her drinking problem had become so severe that Huston agreed, once she was hospitalized, to let her be treated with strychnine which was believed to aid in the cure of alcoholism. It nearly cost Dorothy her life. Once she was out of the hospital, she left John with a vast number of bills which, since he had been let go by Gaumont-British, he was unable to pay. Huston did manage, however, to win a hundred pounds in the Irish sweepstakes and used the money to send Dorothy back to her parents in California.

John then took a flyer with Edward Cahn, the director of LAW AND ORDER, who was in England seeking work. The job did not pan out but Cahn was able to get five hundred pounds as an advance from an automobile company to produce a film about racing. This film project did not work out either, but the money was sufficient to buy tickets back to the United States. Reunited with Walter in New York, John's father was greatly relieved to find his son well. John stayed in New York only long enough to try his hand at editing THE MID-WEEK PICTORIAL. When that failed, he went on to Chicago to play the role of Abe Lincoln in Howard Koch's play THE LONELY MAN which was presented at the WPA Theater there. The theme of the play was what might have happened if Lincoln were to return to free the industrial workers as he had the slaves. It amused John to be playing the same role his father had earlier in the decade for D.W. Griffith. Whatever its liberal orientation, THE LONELY MAN seems to have caused none of the controversy Orson Welles and John Houseman encountered when they tried to stage Marc Blitzstein's THE CRADLE WILL ROCK for the WPA Theater Project in New York, a play with much the same kind of sentiments. While in Chicago, John met an Irish girl named Lesley Black. A few weeks before THE LONELY MAN was to close, Huston wrote a screen treatment of THREE STRANGERS. He called Willy Wyler, who was then working at Warner Bros. on JEZEBEL (Warner's, 1938), and arranged to stay with him. John was able to sell his treatment to Warner Bros. for $5,000 and with the money felt he could afford to marry Lesley. Following their marriage, Huston went to work for Warner Bros. to prepare a finished script for THREE STRANGERS and also ended up working on the script for JEZEBEL. Henry Blanke was producing JEZEBEL and he and Huston became friends. Blanke proceeded to champion John at the studio.

"I knew that Johnny had potential," Blanke later recalled, "but when I first met him out here with his father he was just a drunken boy, hopelessly immature, without an ounce of discipline in his makeup. You'd see him at every party, a drink in his hand and a monkey on his shoulder. Marrying Lesley was probably the best thing that ever happened to him. She gave him standards to live by and the incentive to work."[8] The relationship obviously also helped John withstand any repercussions he may have felt when his mother, who had also moved to California and with whom he was on the friendliest terms, died while on the operating table for brain surgery.

During his first year at Warner Bros., in addition to his work on JEZEBEL, John also contributed to the screenplay of THE AMAZING DR. CLITTERHOUSE (Warner's, 1938) which starred Edward G. Robinson as a medical man who turns into a jewel thief to test his criminal theories. Humphrey Bogart was a featured player in this latter film and a friendship and rapport developed quickly between him and Huston that would last until Bogart's death.

In 1939, Huston contributed to a number of screenplays, most notably to JUAREZ (Warner's, 1939), a Paul Muni vehicle directed by William Dieterle which, in its time, seemed such an important film only for it to appear today to be exaggerated and pretentious. John also taught a workshop on screenwriting, to earn extra money, and got permission to take a leave of absence from Warner Bros. to direct his father on Broadway in the play A PASSENGER TO BALI. It closed after only four performances but the experience reinforced John's conviction that what he wanted most was to direct.

John's script for DR. EHRLICH'S MAGIC BULLET (Warner's, 1940) won him his first Academy Award nomination. Huston disliked working in the morning hours and was usually hung-over anyway. His erratic schedule even prompted a reprimand from Jack L. Warner personally, but all such concern was dispelled when Huston's work on the screenplay for Howard Hawks' production of SERGEANT YORK (Warner's, 1941) earned him a second Academy Award nomination. Yet, in terms of John's future career, the most important screenplay he worked on was his adaptation of W.R. Burnett's crime novel which was filmed under the same title, HIGH SIERRA. It was intended as a George Raft vehicle but Raft refused adamantly to die in any more pictures. Bogart got the role and, with Huston's help, he was able to give his most moving screen portrayal since appearing as Duke Mantee in THE PETRIFIED FOREST (Warner's, 1936), the role which had brought him to Hollywood for a second time from the New York stage and then only because the star of the film and the play, Leslie Howard, refused to make the picture unless Bogart was part of the package. His performance in that film had landed him a Warner Bros. contract which he was still under. At the time Bogart was married to his third wife, Mayo Methot. "She was totally unpredictable, and Bogie liked that," Verita Thompson described Mayo; "she worshipped him and was jealous of him, and Bogie thought that was cute; she was easily provoked into argument, which was Bogie's favorite pastime; she matched him drink for drink (and then some), and Bogie admired her for that; and she had a fiery nature, and that totally captivated him."[9] Huston had come to know Bogart so well that he could tailor his lines for him. In the picture, Ida Lupino weeps apologetically for being such a shrew and Bogart forgives her with the line: "My mother and father always used to fight. I wouldn't give you two cents for a dame without a temper."

It was this film coupled with the subsequent THE MALTESE FALCON which created the public persona for Bogart that won him an increasing box-office appeal and established the mold from which all the characters he would play henceforth were fashioned. Huston was as important to Bogart's later career in terms of the Bogart persona as Howard Hawks would be in creating the John Wayne persona in RED RIVER (United Artists, 1948). The Bogart persona was a man who had come from nowhere and who was going nowhere, who was successful on a short-term basis with women but who, in the end, became a victim to their predatory scheming or who for one reason or another would henceforward be alone. The character was a man who, fortified by alcohol and tobacco, managed with their aid to preserve his own inner integrity, however acute his personal suffering and intense the reversals in his life. In time, added dimensions would be given to this basic character, especially after Bogart's spectacular marriage to Betty Pesky following her screen debut as Lauren Bacall in TO HAVE AND HAVE NOT (Warner's, 1944). This romance, so much the creation of film vehicles and Hollywood gossip columns, gave the Bogart screen persona an option that was wholly new to him: the possibility of an abiding love. The Bogart persona enabled Bogart to turn his back once for all on ''B'' pictures and to become one of the brightest stars of the next two decades and to accrue a fame and glamour that would actually increase after his death. Virtually everything written about Humphrey Bogart since THE MALTESE FALCON is about this Bogart persona and somewhere, in all of this verbiage, the real Humprey Bogart has been obscured, probably forever.

It was due primarily to his promising record of achievement as a screenwriter and the chance his father had given him to direct in New York that the Warner management acceded to John's desire to direct a film. To play Gutman, the fat man in THE MALTESE FALCON, Huston imported Sydney Greenstreet from the Broadway stage. For thirty years Greenstreet had played everything from Shakespeare to butlers, but this was his first film. Henry Blanke was the associate producer on the picture and he advised Huston to shoot every scene with infinite care. Huston followed this advice, even to sketching all the scenes beforehand. He had Mary Astor run around the set to keep her breathless when she had to deliver all the lies in her dialogue. The film was completed for $375,000 and was immediately hailed by the critics as a classic. It also made a huge profit. According to Stuart Kaminsky, Huston's version of Hammett's story ''emphasizes the marginal existence of Spade, his cynicism, commitment to principle, near-madness, and enjoyment of irony. Huston further suggests an admiration for those who can accept defeat. Another important element . . . is his emphasis on the world of lies and masks through which Spade must move, masks that Spade must penetrate to get to the truth while he himself is proving to be a master at deception.''[10] While Huston was so concerned with feminine duplicity on the screen, his second marriage was also in trouble.

Lesley had suffered a miscarriage and it was, again, the same story as with Dorothy's drinking. Or, in the words Hammett gave Sam Spade when unloading on Brigid in THE MALTESE FALCON (1930): '' 'All we've got is the fact that maybe you love me and maybe I love you. . . . It's easy enough to be nuts about you. . . . But I don't know what that amounts to. Does anybody ever? But suppose I do? What of it? Maybe next month I won't. I've been through it before–when it lasted that long. . . . I'll have some rotten nights—but that'll pass.' ''[11]

Once THE MALTESE FALCON was completed, Huston and Howard Koch, caught up in the political temper of internationalism as opposed to isolationism, co-authored a Broadway play titled IN TIME TO COME which dealt with Woodrow Wilson's struggle for the League of Nations following the First World War. It closed after only forty performances but not without winning the New York Drama Critics' Circle Award and suggesting to Darryl F. Zanuck that the life of Wilson was of sufficient interest for a motion picture to be based on it.

Back at Warner Bros., Huston hired Koch as the scenarist on his second directorial effort, IN THIS OUR LIFE (Warner's, 1942), which starred Bette Davis,
Olivia de Havilland, and George Brent. Although still married to Lesley, Huston
began an affair with Olivia that for a time was well publicized. In terms of its
plot, the film was right in the Huston tradition. Davis and de Havilland were
cast as sisters, Stanley and Roy. Stanley steals Roy's husband but in the end
drives him to suicide. Her uncle, played by Charles Coburn, who stole the family
business from the girls' father welcomes Stanley back into the fold and has
evident sexual designs on her which Stanley encourages. However, Stanley's
major objective is to win back her former lover, played by George Brent, who
now is in love with Roy. When Brent rejects Stanley, in her fury she recklessly
hits a child with her car and attempts to lay the blame for the act on a young
black man. Walter Huston, "for luck" as he termed it, had a bit part in THE
MALTESE FALCON and appeared briefly in this film as a bartender who positively identifies Stanley as the driver of the car that killed the child. By this
time her uncle is too sick to care and Stanley dies in a wild car chase with the
police. The film was even more successful at the box office than THE MALTESE
FALCON.

Primarily because of how well IN THIS OUR LIFE did, the studio dropped
the idea of a sequel to THE MALTESE FALCON and instead gave Huston
ACROSS THE PACIFIC (Warner's, 1942) to make in its place, but with many
of the same principals: Humphrey Bogart, Mary Astor, and Sydney Greenstreet.
It had actually been Huston's intention to remake MOBY DICK with Walter
Huston cast as Captain Ahab. No one was much interested in this idea. When
John received his commission as a lieutenant in the Signal Corps, he was in the
middle of directing ACROSS THE PACIFIC. He left the picture incomplete
with Bogart in a nearly inescapable death trap.

In the Signal Corps, John would be charged with filming documentaries to
help in the war effort. During a furlough, he returned to Hollywood and Warner
Bros., still talking about MOBY DICK. Despite what he had done to ACROSS
THE PACIFIC, the studio had forgiven him since Vincent Sherman had been
able to complete the film and it showed a healthy profit upon release. What
management wanted Huston to do was to contribute to the screenplay for BACK-
GROUND TO DANGER (Warner's, 1943), the vehicle that Raft had decided
*was* right for him and in which he would be teamed with what had come to be
considered the diabolical Laurel and Hardy of crime, Sydney Greenstreet and
Peter Lorre. Ezra Goodman subsequently described Huston's response to this
assignment, "sitting there in his uniform with his long legs propped up on the
desk, cap pushed back on his head, sketching and listening. . . . [He] finally stood
up, yawned, adjusted his cap and said, 'Gentlemen, I am going to the Aleutians'
and walked out."[12]

What Huston had worked out in these early years was a preference for shooting
a picture in sequence. Later, when writing AN OPEN BOOK, he stressed that
because Roman Polanski had filmed CHINATOWN in sequence he was able,

as an afterthought, to add the sequence where Jack Nicholson, playing the detective, gets his nose slit and not have to worry about a lot of scenes having been filmed that would show Nicholson without the sutures in his nose. It was this technique which he brought to filming documentaries.

Dashiell Hammett, although in his late forties, had been able to get into the Army and was stationed in the Aleutians. He was present during the late summer in 1942 when Huston arrived with his six-man camera crew to film a documentary on military operations there. Hammett had long been a heavy drinker while a civilian, but now he appeared pleasantly sober and quite happy in the service. Huston visited him during the shoot. John's REPORT FROM THE ALEUTIANS (1943) was favorably received and he was promoted to the rank of captain.

Where Huston first encountered resistance was in filming THE BATTLE OF SAN PIETRO (1943). It was shot on the Italian front, showing how the Allied armies hammered their way to Rome. Huston was unsparing in his depiction of the senseless slaughter of war, the wasted suffering, the anguish. By filming in sequence, he was able to interview for the camera young American soldiers and record their idealism when stating their personal objectives as to why they were there and then loop these words in juxtaposition with the dead faces on the corpses of these same men following the battle. Huston, who also wrote the script, commented on the closing scenes of the documentary which pictured Italian civilians, mostly old people and children emerging from hiding once the Germans had retreated, that in a few years "they'll have forgotten there ever was a war." He wasn't altogether correct. American school children know very little about the Second World War or even what and who were involved, but in Italy casual reference is still made to the various battles on bus tours outside of Rome, the tone of course varying with the nationality of the tourists occupying the bus.

THREE STRANGERS (Warner's, 1945) was produced while Huston was still in the Signal Corps' documentary unit. The final screen version had been written by Howard Koch but Huston had polished it. Geraldine Fitzgerald, Sydney Greenstreet, and Peter Lorre starred as the ill-fated threesome. The greed of these three turns each against the others until they are totally frustrated in their hopes for enrichment.

Huston's final documentary was titled LET THERE BE LIGHT. It deals with the rehabilitation of veterans, shot again in sequence, showing the condition of the men before and after therapy. It was considered to be such an indictment of the effects of war that the War Department would not permit it to be shown anywhere.

Once again a civilian after four years, Huston collaborated with Anthony Veiller on the screenplay for THE KILLERS (Universal, 1946) based very loosely on the Hemingway short story by the same title. However, he took no credit for his work on this picture, not wishing to create a conflict with Warner Bros. where he was still under contract. Before returning to Warner Bros., Huston also took time out to direct the American version of Jean-Paul Sartre's stage play, HUIS-CLOS, translated as VICIOUS CIRCLE in the United Kingdom and as NO EXIT in the United States. As a result, I imagine, of his war-time experiences, from being actually under fire in Italy to the mental wards back home, Huston felt himself rather in sympathy with the French Existentialist philosopher who wrote for a generation compelled as few others before it to come to terms with the ultimate meaninglessness of life and yet who was unwilling to surrender all semblance of personal meaning, no matter how tenuous. The play closed after only thirty-one performances but not without winning the New York Drama Critics' Circle Award for best foreign play of the year.

While Huston had been away from Hollywood, Humphrey Bogart's stature had continued to grow as a screen personality. CASABLANCA had involved movie audiences as no film before it in the Bogart persona, the vision of his idealistic and romantic loss of the only woman he had ever loved moving patrons to tears. Then Howard Hawks had added a new dimension. In TO HAVE AND HAVE NOT the Bogart persona was rewarded with romance. " 'Not only does she soak up everything you tell her, but also she absorbs things by just walking through a room,' " Hawks had commented about Bacall during production. Bogart voiced a similar sentiment when he observed that " 'she's like a chameleon. She takes on the color of things around her.' "[13] Bacall wanted to marry Bogart, but Bogart dragged his feet. He was in his mid forties and very set in his ways. He had learned to control his drinking so that he would know "when he was running dry and would supply himself with just the right amount of replenishment to keep a glow-on all the time while still being able to function."[14] While working with Hawks, Bogart switched his customary drink from martinis to Scotch whiskey and, except for bloody Marys in the morning and beer with meals, Scotch remained his drink for the rest of his life. He recognized that the amount of alcohol he consumed constituted a potential danger. His father had died of morphine addiction and a sister was constantly in and out of mental hospitals. Bogart was a haunted, highly tense man and alcohol made it easier simply to exist. To counteract its effects, he had regular injections of vitamin-B. His throat was extremely sensitive and to assuage the whiskey Bogart took to mixing it with soda. The five packages of cigarettes he smoked a day, however, was another excess that he could neither curb nor assuage. " . . . I think it was characteristic of him to feel somewhat obligated to wed those he bedded," Verita Thompson said of him. "His flaw, then, if one can call it that, lay in being attracted to and bedding women who, for one reason or another, were incapable of offering the stability he needed."[15] His three wives prior to Bacall had been similarly actresses and he had taken up with each one of them while still married. When in New York to promote TO HAVE AND HAVE NOT, Bogart and Bacall occupied different suites at the Gotham Hotel. Bacall herself had sixty-two interviews scheduled for one week. "During a particularly lengthy press session, Bogie phoned to inform her of his annoyance at being deserted. Immediately Betty cut the conference short and rushed to his room. When she entered, he burst into tears for the first time since she knew him, and exclaimed, 'I didn't think you'd come.' "[16] Once they were married and Bogart carried Bacall across the threshold of their suite at the Garden of Allah, the same hotel that had been the scene of his surreptitious affair with Mayo Methot while still married to Mary Phillips, Bogart quipped, " 'You weigh a ton.' "[17] This was symptomatic of the needling which came to characterize Bogart and Bacall, as it characterized every close relationship Bogart had ever had, a serious struggle for supremacy, probably because he wanted to dominate another human being as he had been unable ever to dominate his cold and self-obsessed mother.

Because Bacall was under contract, the studio tried to salvage her career by starring her with Bogart in a third film, DARK PASSAGE (Warner's, 1947), written and directed by Delmer Daves; but she appeared flat and lifeless on screen. " 'I slid down the ladder so fast that it was all I could do to catch myself midway,' " Bacall said in an interview for McCALL'S at the time. " 'I hadn't the training I needed to protect myself. As a compensation, though, I was Bogie's wife. And was thought of as Bogie's wife by my friends and my friends were producers and directors and writers. I was Bogey's wife first and an actress second and as a result I gradually had fewer and fewer opportunities to find a place for myself. I had terrible frustrations about my work. I chose always to have my marriage come first. If I had the choice to make over again, I'd do it the same way. But I felt moments of frustration and anger because people didn't think of me the way I thought they should . . . as an actress.' "[18] In the meantime, Bogart also gave out incessant interviews in which he would customarily talk about his new wife. " 'Class,' " he would say about her, " 'that's what she has—real class.' " He would also add, " 'She's great in the sack!' "[19] It was quite conscious and intentional on the parts of both Bacall and Bogart in all of these interviews to keep themselves and their relationship in the public eye, to project personae that were consistent and which also provided the public with the images the public wanted to see and hear.

The same year he made DARK PASSAGE, Bogart signed a new contract with Warner Bros. It had a term of fifteen years and called for him to be paid $300,000 a picture. He was required only to make one picture a year for the studio and he reserved the right to free-lance for other production companies. Bogart, who was a man in actuality very much to himself and who rarely confided in anybody ever, seemed to be acutely aware of the age difference between himself and Bacall and he was convinced from the outset that she would outlive him. Reputedly, he purchased a 16mm print of A STAR IS BORN (United Artists, 1937) and would be reduced to tears at the end when the aging actor takes his own life, having become useless to the highly talented star to whom he is then married and not wanting to interfere with her career.

John Huston had fallen in love with Marietta Fitzgerald in New York. She was unhappily married. He wanted her to divorce her husband and to marry him. This she refused to do until she had entered psychoanalysis. Ultimately, it would seem, she did not want to be married to Huston, knowing that he could never be faithful to a woman. Back in Hollywood, Huston began dating actress

Evelyn Keyes, known principally for having been Scarlett O'Hara's younger sister in GONE WITH THE WIND (M-G-M, 1939) and currently under contract to Columbia Pictures. Keyes had previously been married twice, most recently to film director Charles Vidor. On her second date with Huston, Keyes went to bed with him, waking him up and forcing him to leave her apartment before morning. "He came back for more, though," she recalled. "Charles had taught me well. He had shown me what a man likes, and I was a good pupil."[20] The two were married. Huston in his autobiography claimed that Keyes proposed marriage to him and Keyes in hers insisted that Huston had proposed to her. In the event I do not suppose it mattered much, since being married at this point mattered so little to Huston. "Walter Huston . . . laughed loudest of all at his son's latest caprice," Keyes wrote. "Even John's girlfriends didn't take his matrimonial step seriously and continued to call, send notes, and sometimes even flowers. I had married a very popular man."[21] That was in Hollywood. In New York, according to Keyes, and no doubt as a result of his work on the Sartre play, "John . . . was the darling of . . . Truman Capote's gang. They were well-born, moneyed, intellectually and artistically inclined. They gathered artists about them in their elegant houses and apartments—writers, painters, designers, directors and actors. But only the best, mind you."[22]

Huston had overcome being an invalid as a youngster and he had been in a shooting battle in war and had lost the fear of death. It was this fact of life which had given Sam Spade an edge over all of the others in Huston's film version and now it was John Huston's edge in life because, if you do not fear death, there is no threat that can be effective since every threat in the end must reduce itself to the threat of death or go begging.

"Eddie Dmytryk," I said to Huston during that first interview, "told me that when he directed Bogart, Bogie would stand to one side of the camera and cough his lungs out before doing a scene so he wouldn't cough before the camera."

"Well, now, I wouldn't know about that," Huston drawled, grimacing and inhaling deeply from his cigar, "because I was probably coughing on the other side of the camera."

"John drank," Keyes wrote. "I mean *a lot*. No alcoholic, just a person who could—and did—put a monumental amount of booze away on occasion (with accompanying monumental hangover). Something to do, he firmly believed, with his Irish background."[23]

Bogart's response to the incessant inquiry, "Do you drink any more?," became standard: " 'Not any more. The same amount.' "[24] However, this was mostly for the press. "His reputation as a drinker never diminished," Verita Thompson wrote, "but he cut down a good deal during the last ten years of his life. He never stopped drinking his 'smashes,' as he called them, of loudmouth, but he drank them in tall glasses, with plenty of soda and ice, and he would often make two or three of them last an entire evening. He always had a glass in hand, though, and the size of the drink made it appear that he was drinking much more than he actually was. Of course, sometimes he *did* drink as much as his reputation warranted, but not as often as people thought.''[25] Bogart's binges were covered by the tabloids throughout his career and so the prevailing impression was somewhat contrary to the everyday fact.

Keyes also recalled that Huston's drunken irregularities would often tax even his closest friends. ''Even Bogie. Once at their house, high as a kite, John decided for no apparent reason except mischief to slip his hand under Betty's skirt, crying out, 'I'm going up the Amazon!' Said Bogie, 'Oh no you're not!' and leaped upon him (although he came only to John's shoulder).''[26] While Bogart was still alive and Bacall was giving out the image-building kind of interview she knew would please Bogart, and also hold him to her, she pretended friendship with Huston. As late as 1953, she said in a LOOK magazine interview, concerning her preference for older men, that John Huston was one of the men she admired most because ''he lives life the way many of us would like to but don't. . . . John has left his friends' bodies strewn all over the world. When you are with him you have his undivided attention—until he feels the need to move on. Then there you are with egg on your face.''[27] In her autobiography, it was somewhat different, even though Huston was still alive. ''It was mostly good fun,'' she wrote, recalling those years, ''except for the moments John displayed his disdain for women—his wife in particular. Poor Evelyn would say something and John would say, 'What? What was that, Evelyn? Now, wait a minute—I want everyone to hear this' and Evelyn was on the block. Any casual, innocent, occasionally thoughtless remark was magnified and she was made to look like a fool. It was humiliating. . . . I didn't envy her, married to John. He was brilliant, he was fascinating, he was fun—but stay a friend. Better still, a friend's wife.''[28] Bacall would be cast in the last film in which Huston was to act, a role that he ultimately did not play because his death intervened. Only later, when appearing in a documentary about Huston's life, would Bacall express herself even more candidly. ''I don't think John liked women very much. . . . I don't think he respected them. I think he respected the mothers of his children as the mothers of his children . . . but I would hate to have been in love with him.''[29]

Huston returned finally to Warner Bros. intent on incorporating his wider perspectives into a motion picture. The themes of human greed and the inevitable futility of all that we do were teeming in his brain. He set about contacting B. Traven's agent. He had written to the reclusive author during the war. But now he had arranged definitely to bring THE TREASURE OF THE SIERRA MADRE to the screen. Warner Bros. had purchased the property some years before and Henry Blanke saw to it that it wasn't filmed until Huston was free to do it.

## III

No one had ever seen Traven and he had managed to elude photographers. He sent Huston a twenty-page letter giving his views on how his novel should be filmed and how the sets were to be constructed. Huston wrote back to him, requesting a meeting. "I can guarantee nothing," Traven replied, "but if you will come to the Hotel Reforma in Mexico City, early in January, I will try to meet you there. I make no promises."[30]

Huston thought it worth a try. He followed Traven's instructions and nothing happened. He was preparing to return to Hollywood when a thin, short man dressed in faded khaki accosted him in the lobby of the hotel, handing Huston a card which identified him as being H. Croves, a translator from Acapulco. He showed Huston a typed note from Traven claiming that Croves knew Traven's work better than he did. Croves said that when Traven found he couldn't make it, he had authorized him to answer any and all questions Huston might have. Huston hired Croves as a technical advisor for those portions of the picture to be shot on location in Mexico.

After a lengthy scouting trip, Huston selected as his site the rough, mountainous terrain surrounding the little inland village of Jungapeo. Huston asked the studio to grant him at least two months on location. He felt the duration justified in terms of his experiences in filming for the War Department. Blanke went personally to see Jack L. Warner to talk him into it. Although he finally acceded, Warner began at once to worry about rising costs.

For his three central characters, men in pursuit of gold, Huston selected his father to play the old prospector (and even convinced him with some effort to play the part without his false teeth), Bogart to portray the more brutish and paranoid of the three, and John Garfield to play the youth accompanying them. A change in casting substituted Tim Holt in the role intended for Garfield.

"Holt's acting was limited for some roles," Huston told us, "but he was ideal for this picture."

Bogart took over as director of the film briefly while Huston did a cameo as an American tourist when the troupe was in Tampico. He managed to raise Huston's ire by forcing him to do the scene over and over until he thought it right. Huston would eventually have his revenge.

Croves joined them as the troupe began the long trek into the mountains. It was here, in Mexico, that Huston discovered pre-Columbian art and collecting it became one of his passions. Evelyn Keyes and Betty Bacall came along for the trip. For Bacall, it would be the first time she would have been separated from Bogart and neither, apparently, wanted that. For Keyes, she was a new wife and intended to be a good one.

John and Walter were having such great fun working together and John was so in love with the Mexican ambience that he seemed almost to be losing interest in the picture itself. It would become an intensely serious problem, especially in later films, when the director's boredom became altogether too transparent. Bogart wanted to race the *Santana* in the Fourth of July sprint to Honolulu and he began needling Huston to hurry up and make the picture. " 'Out to make a fuckin' masterpiece, right, John?' " he would ask after several drinks. This went on for days until one night Bogart growled, " 'For crissake, John, . . . just how much longer is this miserable picture going to take?' " Smiling all the while,

Huston reached across the table and took Bogart's nose between two fingers, twisting it hard, so hard tears came to Bogart's eyes, but he neither flinched nor pulled away. He just never brought up the subject again and the boat race went on without him.[31]

Keyes was the first one to leave. She was still under contract to Columbia Pictures and she was offered a part she did not want to turn down as the female lead opposite Glenn Ford in THE MATING OF MILLIE (Columbia, 1948). During his second marriage, John had designed and built a house near Tarzana in the San Fernando Valley where he had enough land to keep horses. This was where he and Evelyn now lived and where Walter came to stay following completion of his work on the picture. John switched locations to Bakersfield in California where for two weeks he shot scenes of Bogart searching for water in hot and dry weather. The rushes were sent back to the studio in Burbank for Blanke and Warner to screen. Bogart searched and searched and searched.

" 'If that son of a bitch doesn't find water soon,' " Warner remarked to Blanke, " 'I'll go broke.' "[32]

Obviously, Bogart was not the only one who had become worried about the time the picture was taking.

While they had been in Mexico, Huston continued to send letters to Traven in hope that he would visit the set. His letters had gone unanswered. Croves, on the other hand, had been constantly around rendering advice, although he seemed to share Traven's dislike for being photographed. After they had left Croves in Mexico City and were on their way back to the States, Huston had showed Bogart a rare photograph he had found of B. Traven.

" 'Do you recognize this guy?' " he had asked Bogart

" 'Sure,' " Bogart had said. " 'That's old Croves. I'd know him anywhere.' "[33]

By the time he came to write his autobiography, Huston claimed that he doubted "that Croves and Traven were the same man. I believe that B. Traven was two or more persons who worked in collaboration."[34] Conversely, in her autobiography Keyes detailed how Huston sought at every opportunity to humiliate and ridicule Croves. Years later, when she and John were divorced, Croves once paid her a visit and wanted to talk about what a terrible man John Huston was and was evidently not pleased when Keyes sought to defend her former husband. If Croves and Traven were actually one and the same—and Traven's wife in the introduction to the 1976 edition of THE BRIDGE IN THE JUNGLE attested that Traven did pose as Croves—he had more to complain about, if he were at all serious about what he had written, than John Huston's efforts to belittle him. Traven's Bolshevik sympathies and anti-Catholicism, so manifest in the novel, were nowhere in evidence in the film Huston made. Traven's concerns about human social conditions were replaced by an interest only in the dimensions of the personalities of the three prospectors and the final emphasis was on the futility of the quest for wealth from which only the character played by Walter Huston was able to escape unscathed.

Bogart discovered a whole new aspect of the Bogart persona. He could effectively project the cynical pessimism and paranoid fears which haunted him in his personal life on the screen and still be accepted, even liked, by viewers. Huston won the New York Film Critics' Award for best direction when the picture was released in January, 1948, FILM DAILY voted him best director for 1947–1948, and the film was nominated for four Academy Awards, with John winning the Oscar for Best Direction and a second for Best Screenplay and Walter winning an Oscar for Best Supporting Actor. John Huston toasted Henry Blanke when he accepted his awards. Walter Huston, putting his arm around his son, told the audience, " 'A long time ago I brought up a boy. When he became a writer I told him one thing: "Some day you write a good part for your old man." Well, by golly, he *did*!' "[35]

Henry Blanke could recall the fight he had had with Jack L. Warner about the necessity of Bogart's having to die at the end of the picture. Warner's argument was that Bogart was now a major star, not at all the same man who had replaced George Raft in HIGH SIERRA. Blanke finally won his point. The scene with Bogart surrounded by Mexican bandits, holding off and savoring the inevitable murder, is still one of the most powerful images Huston ever created. Warner had something to be happy about also, beyond the critical recognition, and that was the fact that the picture turned a profit. Bacall, however, remembered something else, something that had happened one night when at the Bakersfield location. John and Bogart had been drinking and talking and Huston confessed to Bogart how much he envied him his life. " 'The trouble with me is that I am forever and eternally bored.' "[36]

Bogart, flushed with his new success, set up his own production company which he called Santana, a partnership which included his business manager, Morgan Maree, and Robert Lord, a former M-G-M producer who came in as a replacement for Mark Hellinger who died suddenly during negotiations. Evelyn, too, got a dividend, only one for which she had not bargained. John arranged for the thirteen-year-old Pablo Albarran, who did not speak English and had served as the water boy while on location in Mexico, to come to live with him and Evelyn. It was a noble gesture, but for Huston it was possibly no different than any of the various animals he adopted and let roam about his home. He soon lost all interest in the boy and Evelyn ended up spending a lot of time with him. "At every opportunity," she recalled, "he would snuggle close and flick my nipples with his finger, grinning at me the while." In the end, given their doomed marriage and the lack of love either felt for the youth, Evelyn wondered "if John—we—really did him any good?"[37] Huston was even more adamant when he thought back about the incident. "Pablo was educated in the United States and eventually married a lovely Irish girl who bore him three children. Then his life turned sour. He deserted his family, returned to Mexico City and became a used-car dealer. Perhaps I should have left him in Jungapeo."[38]

In characteristic fashion, Huston reacted violently to the House Un-American Activities Committee, calling it an obscenity. He helped form the Committee for the First Amendment and together with Bogart, Bacall, William Wyler, Paul Henreid, Danny Kaye, and others, chartered a plane to Washington to lodge a group protest against the hearings. " 'It didn't do much good,' " Huston commented later, " 'but it gave us a secure feeling to be in there fighting for what we believed was justice.' "[39] Keyes was somewhat more realistic. "When the investigation of the motion picture industry first began, John was very courageous. (He became less so later when the watchdogs of patriotism got to him, threatening him, too, with oblivion.)"[40]

I suppose it is possible to read a political message into KEY LARGO (Warner's, 1948). Huston certainly gave that impression after it was made in an interview for TIME when he claimed that Johnny Rocco, the gangster played by Edward G. Robinson in the film, " 'was supposed to represent a sort of evil flower of reaction. In other words we are headed for the same kind of world we had before, even down to the gang lords. . . . ' "[41] Bacall had been placed on suspension six times by Warner Bros. for refusing roles in proposed films; once she and Bogart both walked out rather than appear together in STALLION ROAD (Warner's, 1947). By casting the two of them in this picture, Huston was doing Bacall a favor—her career was in a total eclipse—and Warner Bros. as well. Lionel Barrymore was cast as Bacall's father who owns a resort in Florida. The action takes place during the off-season when Robinson and his gang hole up. Barrymore was in a wheelchair. Knowing how much he hated President Roosevelt, Huston saw to it that Barrymore had one bit of dialogue in which he had heroically to stand up out of his wheelchair in order to defend Roosevelt's memory.

The film was based on a play by Maxwell Anderson but Richard Brooks and John Huston in their screenplay altered the whole thrust of the story. Claire Trevor won an Academy Award for her portrayal of a middle-aged alcoholic, a former mistress of gangster Johnny Rocco.

" 'You're the kind of drunken dame,' " Huston told her, " 'whose elbows are always a little too big. Your voice is a little too loud; you're a little too polite. You're very sad, very resigned. . . . ' " He himself slouched at the bar as he spoke, his elbows sticking out. " ' . . . Like this. Got it?' "[42]

At one point in the film, Barrymore asks the group held hostage by Robinson what it is that Robinson wants.

"He wants more," Bogart responds laconically.

"Yeah!" Robinson exclaims, pouncing on the idea. "More. I want *more.*"

"Will you ever get enough?" he is asked.

"No," Robinson replies, suddenly perplexed. "I don't think so. I haven't yet."

It was this scene Roman Polanski had in mind in CHINATOWN when he had Jack Nicholson confront John Huston, a man guilty of incest, murder, bribery, theft, and betrayal of the public trust.

"How much money do you have?" Nicholson asks the Huston character. Huston shrugs his shoulders.

"A million dollars?" Nicholson asks.

Huston nods.

"Ten million?"

Huston grins his affirmation.

"Well, then, why do you want more?"

Huston becomes philosophical. "Because you've got to think of the future."

In real life, Huston's attitude was scarcely so clutching, even as far back as the making of KEY LARGO. Keyes has recorded how he would drop his entire salary of $5,000 a week gambling and come back for more. "It just doesn't exist," Huston said of money. "You get this colored paper and you give it to someone and he gives it to someone else and that someone gives it to someone else—so where is the money? It's just smoke in your hands. Nobody can get a grip on it."[43] Needless to say, Keyes who was trying to build some kind of stable life with Huston, who was trying to have a child with him, did not appreciate his capriciousness.

Bacall was flat in the film, standing around most of the time with a quiet smile, obviously contented. To get a pained reaction out of her at one point Huston went to the extreme of twisting her arm. The shoot-out between Bogart and Robinson in which Bogart finally got his chance, after Robinson had done him in so many times in years past, to plug Robinson was filmed aboard Bogart's boat, the *Santana*.

Once the film was completed and opened to good business, Huston went to Jack L. Warner personally to ask for a personal loan of $50,000 which he felt was what he needed to get him out of his gambling debts. Warner refused. Huston reminded Warner that he had been with the studio for ten years and that Warner had invested two and a half million in THE TREASURE OF THE SIERRA MADRE and had made it back. Warner, while conceding all that Huston said, remained obdurate.

At a Beverly Hills cocktail party, Huston ran into Sam Spiegel for whom he had worked colloraborating on the screenplay for THE STRANGER (RKO, 1946) and which Spiegel had even hoped Huston would direct before Orson Welles usurped that job. Huston told Spiegel of Warner's unreasonable attitude. Spiegel told Huston he would get him the money if Huston would agree to direct a picture for him. Huston accepted gleefully. The next day, Spiegel had the money for him and in New York was eventually able to arrange a loan of $900,000 from Bankers Trust Company with which to make the picture. The production firm Spiegel and Huston formed was called Horizon Pictures.

Spiegel, who had changed his name to this from S.P. Eagle, had worked for Universal Pictures' Berlin office prior to the rise of Hitler. He had tried everything from operating a cotton brokerage to draining a swamp in Palestine before entering the American motion picture industry. He got Columbia Pictures to agree to distribute the film. It was titled WE WERE STRANGERS (Columbia, 1949) and starred John Garfield, Jennifer Jones, and Gilbert Roland as three revolutionaries in Cuba digging a tunnel in a cemetery as part of a plan to assassinate a government official. Huston shot much of the film in the tunnel itself, imbuing it with a claustrophobic atmosphere. Just as the black bird turned out to be a fake and gold was lost in the desert sands so here the plot is foiled when the official cancels his visit to the cemetery and the revolutionaries engage in a gun battle with the Cuban police. THE HOLLYWOOD REPORTER labeled the film as "Communist-inspired" while the Communist paper THE DAILY WORKER termed it "Capitalistic propaganda." Huston thought the flurry amusing. It proved less so for John Garfield who had been a founding member of the Committee for the First Amendment. His later career, and his life as well, were shattered by the endless investigations into his political beliefs and the subsequent attempts at blacklisting. Huston, who could see what was happening, adeptly avoided for more than a decade making any film which might seem to have any political connotations whatsoever.

Warner's refusal to assist Huston had nothing to do with his approval or disapproval of how John spent his money. The studio, terrified by the impact television was having on its market, was in the process of dropping all contract artists. Bacall was allowed to buy out of what remained of her contract only to learn later that the studio would gladly have let her go for nothing. Even Bogart, although he would continue to make films for Warner Bros., was eventually let out of his contract. Not that any of this mattered much to Bacall or Bogart. Betty gave birth to Stephen Humphrey Bogart, named after Steve, the character Bogart had played in TO HAVE AND HAVE NOT. About the name, Bogart commented, " 'We wanted our son to be part of our happiness at having met.' "[44] During Bacall's pregnancy, Bogart's friends had held a comic stag baby party for him at Romanoff's. "The highlight," Howard Greenberger wrote, "was a mock baby delivery that had John Huston using fire tongs to wrest an imaginary baby from a pseudo-pregnant and prone Bogey. Later the actor was touched to receive all the baby gifts his friends presented to him and he tried to describe his feelings about becoming a father in a speech, but the booze made him blubber."[45]

At about the same time, John Huston's third marriage was coming to an end. Huston, in writing about it later, attributed the failure not to his perpetual philandering and often drunken indifference but to Evelyn's allergies.[46] In the event, Huston had actually fallen in love with Enrica Soma whom he had first met when she was a small child. "Is there something appealing about a girl-child growing up to a fuckable age under your nose?" Keyes asked aloud in her autobiography. It wasn't until Huston told Evelyn that Ricki was pregnant that she began to understand. Knowing the difficulty she had had getting pregnant, Keyes asked Huston if he was sure that he was the father. " 'It doesn't matter,' he said. A light bulb went off in my head. I hadn't been paying attention at all. He wanted progeny any way he could get them. It was he who had brought back Pablo."[47] However, Huston was in such a rush to marry Ricki that he did not think of the consequences. Evelyn not only got half of his pre-Columbian art collection, "she'd got everything: ranch, livestock, paintings, works of art—

and, on top of that, alimony.''[48] Some years later, Huston proposed to Evelyn that they flip a coin for the other half of the pre-Columbian art collection, and Evelyn won.

Strapped for money and unlikely to realize any corporate profit on WE WERE STRANGERS for some years, if ever, Huston readily accepted an offer from M-G-M to direct a new and more spectacular version of QUO VADIS? in which Walter Huston would be cast as St. Peter and in which Gregory Peck and Elizabeth Taylor would star. Huston signed for $3,000 a week. Production was to commence on location in Rome in July, 1949, but Gregory Peck developed an eye infection. Arthur Hornblow, Jr., the associate producer on the picture, suggested to Huston that, while they were waiting, they should work on another project, an adaptation of W.R. Burnett's novel THE ASPHALT JUNGLE (1949). Huston remembered Burnett from when they collaborated on the screenplay of Burnett's HIGH SIERRA (1941). The plot had to do with a major heist. Huston cast Sterling Hayden as a hoodlum besieged by liquor and bad luck. M-G-M was not particularly pleased with Huston's choice. Hayden had a drinking problem in real life and was then under the care of a psychoanalyst, but Huston prevailed.

When it came to the part of Angela, a young girl who was at once innocent and cunning, Huston was stumped. Lucille Ryman, in M-G-M's casting department, recommended Huston try an actress named Marilyn Monroe who, as yet, had had no speaking lines in a picture but who looked ideal. Huston interviewed her in Hornblow's office. She was extremely nervous. Huston tried to reassure her, gave her a copy of the script, and told her to return in three days' time. When Marilyn returned, she looked around the room. The scene was supposed to be done reclining on a divan.

'' 'I'd like . . . to . . . read the first scene on the floor,' '' she improvised, blinking at Huston.

'' 'Sure, dear,' '' he mused aloud, '' 'any way it feels right to you.' ''

Kicking off her shoes, Monroe got down on the carpeted floor and did the scene. Then, before Huston could comment, she did it again. She stood up, fidgeting as she looked at him.

'' 'You didn't have to do it twice, honey,' '' he said, in his honey-toned voice. '' 'You had the part on the first reading.' ''[49]

Huston gave Monroe the break she needed, to get her foot in the door, and it was enough to bring her to the attention of Howard Hawks who helped her the rest of the way. THE ASPHALT JUNGLE (M-G-M, 1950) earned Huston two more Academy Award nominations and he won the Screen Directors' Guild Award. The picture concluded with the frustration of all ambition and with death. This was now becoming known as a "Huston ending."

Huston did not resume QUO VADIS? Instead, he turned to another project, a screen adaptation of Stephen Crane's Civil War novel THE RED BADGE OF COURAGE (M-G-M, 1951). Gottfried Reinhardt, an M-G-M producer, brought the property to Huston's attention and the two of them took it to Dore Schary who was in charge of production and locked in a battle with Louis B. Mayer for control of the studio. It had been Mayer's flare for organization, promotion, and star value which had made M-G-M all it ever was—which was, quite frankly, the most successful studio in Hollywood—but Mayer belonged to a different generation than post-war filmmakers. He still regarded film as a medium for escape from reality, a lavish flight into fantasy, amid singing and dancing. The Mayer type of movie always had a happy ending. He looked upon a film such as THE ASPHALT JUNGLE as unseemly and even unworthy of the studio. Schary, on the other hand, had worked for Mayer's one-time son-in-law, David O. Selznick, and subsequently at RKO. He had been terrified when he screened the rough cut of Edward Dmytryk's CROSSFIRE (RKO, 1947) and he held up release of the picture for months only to do an about-face when at last it was released and won critical and popular acclaim, proud then to accept congratulations for his courage in making the film and displaying the various awards the film earned on the walls of his office. Schary was particularly enthusiastic about THE RED BADGE OF COURAGE because he knew Mayer hated it. Now that he was at M-G-M and not at RKO, he wanted to consolidate his position and that meant Mayer must be put in his place. Schary sent the script to Nicholas Schenck in New York. He wanted Schenck, who was company president, to back him in overriding Mayer's objections, and Schenck did. Huston's salary was increased to $4,000 a week with an additional $28,000 guarantee for the screenplay. Huston, however, asked Schary for an advance of $150,000, which was the sum he needed to get him out of his marriage to Evelyn Keyes and free to marry Ricki. Schary reluctantly gave it to him.

A birthday party was arranged at Romanoff's for Walter Huston, with Sam Spiegel, Spencer Tracy, and a number of other well-wishers in attendance. Walter, however, could not make it due to severe abdominal pains. John rented a room across the hall from his father's at the Beverly Hills Hotel. Walter had been stricken by an aneurysm of the aorta. The next morning, with John at his bedside, he died. It was a condition that a few years later would not be fatal. John Huston would also suffer from an aneurysm only in his case to be saved by a surgical procedure. To the public, he showed himself totally in control. " 'What the hell can you say?' " he remarked. " 'Except that Dad was too tough to get sick. He just *died*, that's all. He went fast, the way he wanted to go.' "[50] Walter Huston was probably the one person, except later, much later, his own children, about whom John Huston really cared. " 'I've been around actors all my life,' " he once said, " 'and I like them, and yet I never had an actor as a friend. Except Dad. And Dad never thought of himself as an actor.' "[51] Henceforth, John Huston's behavior became more savage, his struggle for realism on the screen made his direction increasingly virulent and unbridled. He lost what little respect he once had had for life and, through others as well as through himself, if he didn't court death, he spurned it, mocked it, defied it. Huston's films now themselves, behind the camera as much as before it, became battlegrounds in which he and his crews and his players were the combatants. When his fifth marriage was virtually over, during that first interview, I asked him what kept him going, only for him to give me an answer that he had given out before.

"Before I go to bed at night, I pour out a glass of bourbon and put it beside the bed." He inhaled deeply on his cigar and continued. "Then, in the morning, I open one eye. I see that glass. Then I am glad to open both eyes and start the day."

Huston chose Audie Murphy to play the lead in THE RED BADGE OF COURAGE. Dore Schary didn't like Murphy, but Huston persisted. He was, after all, the embodiment of a war hero, the kind of man he had drawn for Howard Hawks in the screenplay for SERGEANT YORK (Warner's, 1941). " 'He's a gentle-eyed little killer,' " was how he put it. " 'Why, in the war, he literally went out of his way to find Germans to kill.' "[52] Huston particularly enjoyed the battle scenes. When he had completed the picture, it was only four days over schedule and only $200,000 over budget. Pablo was at Huston's side during much of the filming and Ricki was secluded at the home John was renting at Malibu Beach. On 16 April 1950 she gave birth to Walter Anthony Huston.

The M-G-M management was displeased with what Huston had done. There was no story. Huston was told to shoot more scenes to give the picture some body. In the meantime, Sam Spiegel had cleared financing for them to begin their second Horizon production, THE AFRICAN QUEEN (United Artists, 1952), which was to be filmed on location in Africa. Huston became so excited by this new venture that he lost all interest in THE RED BADGE OF COURAGE. James Agee, an eminent film critic, had made the mistake of being a Huston admirer. Huston contacted him. He wanted him to assist on the screenplay for THE AFRICAN QUEEN. Once he and Agee started work, Huston rousted the fragile, heavy-drinking and heavy-smoking critic out of bed every morning for three vigorous sets of tennis. Huston was a heavy drinker and smoker and he could do it. Agee ought to be able to do it, too. Presently Agee collapsed on the court of a heart attack, an ailment which would bring about his early demise in 1955.

Huston was invited to attend a sneak preview of THE RED BADGE OF COURAGE. The scene with the Tattered Soldier walking around, mumbling, then falling over and dying caused the audience to laugh. The preview was a disaster. Huston advised Reinhardt somewhat cavalierly to have the picture cut any way the studio wanted it. He was on his way to Africa.

Mayer and Schary grew more and more heated in their antipathy for each other. Mayer telephoned New York to inform Nicholas Schenck that it had come to a choice, Mayer or Schary. Schenck chose Schary. Mayer found himself fired from the studio he had put together with nothing but guts, ingenuity, promotional flair, and total confidence in the future. Now, after twenty-seven years, he was out. He shook his head in bewilderment. Schary went about house-cleaning, releasing M-G-M contract players such as Clark Gable and Spencer Tracy until, finally, he was also released and bought out of his contract. The dissipation of

Metro-Goldwyn-Mayer which began with Schary took until the 1980s to be completed when the company even abandoned the lot and moved out of the Irving Thalberg building. THE RED BADGE OF COURAGE died at the box office. In its severely edited version, it is not a very good picture, but it remains a testament to the corporate strife which produced it.

Huston wanted Humphrey Bogart for the male lead in THE AFRICAN QUEEN although it would be a radical departure from the Bogart persona the two had worked so hard to create in the previous decade. He would play opposite Katharine Hepburn. Bacall went to Africa with Bogart. As she put it, "you're going with your husband, who believes in no separations in marriage, who is working."[53] Their young son would stay behind. The script retained the absurdity to be found in the C.S. Forester novel on which it was based, namely the mistaken idea that in Africa rivers run inland toward lakes rather than outward toward the sea. Also in the novel, the leading characters live. Huston wanted them to die. He wanted them to die even if it doomed the picture at the box office. When Spiegel's financing ran into problems, Bogart, who by this time was totally committed to the new role, invested in the picture. Huston went to London to purchase an entire wardrobe for the adventure. He would now be living the life of a Hemingway protagonist in the flesh. He contacted his friend, Peter Viertel, in Switzerland and asked him to come to London to polish the final scenes. They had worked together before on the script for WE WERE STRANGERS. Spiegel and Viertel became allies about the ending Huston wanted and finally they prevailed. If there was one thing alone to which the subsequent success of this film may be attributed, it would be this change in the disposition of its conclusion. Viertel went on to write an unflattering account in novel form of the making of the film, joining Lillian Ross' PICTURE (1952) which would tell the story of the unmaking of THE RED BADGE OF COURAGE, and more books by various authors would follow over the years inspired by Huston's various productions.

" 'I simply *had* to do this film on location,' " Huston commented. " 'I wanted these characters to sweat when the script called for it. On a sound stage you fake it, but in Africa you don't have to *imagine* that it's hot, that it's so humid and wet that cigarettes turn green with mold; it really is hot and clothes *do* mildew overnight—and when people sweat it isn't with the help of a make-up man. Africa was the only place to get what I was after.' "[54] More and more Huston wanted utter realism on the screen.

Huston, Bogart, and Katherine Hepburn all agreed to having their salaries deferred to cut down on expenses. Hepburn got into the spirit of roughing it, even to dressing out in the bush, and her enjoyment of the total experience was made obvious in the memoir she wrote many years later. When she started doing her scenes with Bogart, a humorous byplay developed spontaneously.

"I had no idea this would happen," Huston told us. "It just grew up between them, a comic element that wasn't in the book or in the screenplay, and I just let it develop."

Bogart confined himself to a diet of Scotch, even brushing his teeth with it.

When the tropical rains came, Huston and Bogart would sit around drinking for hours. They tried to get a rise out of Hepburn but failed at it. When the troupe went to Uganda, it was challenged by the colonial British to a game of cricket. Although the Americans lost 51 to 160, Bogart proved to be the star of the losing team.

The picture opened to a tremendous box office. Huston was nominated for Best Director and as co-author of the Best Screenplay. Bogart won an Academy Award as Best Actor. However, they weren't receiving any money. Spiegel kept coming up with excuses for the delay. Bogart told Huston that if he were not paid immediately, he intended to sue Horizon. Morgan Maree, Bogart's business manager, came to Paris to talk matters over with Huston. The result was a friendship between the two men with Maree's becoming Huston's business manager as well. Maree's advice to both of his clients was to get what they could and get out. In Huston's case, this meant severing his relationship with Horizon and his participation in all future profits. Bacall was pregnant again. Leslie Bogart was born on 22 August 1952, named after Leslie Howard who had given Bogart his decisive break in motion pictures.

While basking beneath the hot African sun, Huston had read Pierre La Mure's fictional biography of Henri de Toulouse-Lautrec. The life of the famous French painter conjured within him vivid memories of his own attempts at painting. He obviously saw himself in the artist—in fact, the character that emerges on the screen is far more a stylized John Huston than it is anything having to do with Lautrec. Instead of a heart condition, Lautrec had stunted legs, the result of a fall in early life. As Huston at that time, the Lautrec in the film prefers to keep himself full of alcohol. All that matters to him in his entire existence is his painting. However much he may be wounded and scarred in his dealings with other humans, his art never deserts him. It is always there to engage his interest, consume his emotions, bury his anxieties, salve his bruises, explain his consciousness, justify his continuance. These are difficult emotions to depict. You have to be an artist of exceptional talent who has been drinking heavily for years before you can even approach the proper perspective in which the crucifixion of anguish, the pain of regret, the stigma of rejection are transfigured into strokes of a brush, a flush of color, a refraction of light, a timid fall of a shadow, a dumb play whereby figures and objects take on an emotional life of their own. José Ferrer wanted to adapt the novel for the stage, but Huston convinced him to act in it for the screen. The film was titled MOULIN ROUGE (United Artists, 1953). Through special and intricate use of filters, light, and color in the processing of the film Huston found that he could almost make Lautrec's paintings come to life.

To reproduce Lautrec's dwarfish figure, a rig was prepared for Ferrer, painful to wear but effectively reducing his stature from five feet ten to a stunted four feet eight. The British producer on the film selected Zsa Zsa Gabor to play Jane Avril, the cafe singer who inspired one of Lautrec's best posters. Huston didn't like her, neither her exaggerated accent nor her narcissistic insulation. He kept her part at a minimum and it never taxed her very limited scope in dramatic projection. However, when Huston learned of her love of horses, he became much more friendly and even wound up driving her to the airport when her part in the film was completed. He was profoundly attracted to Suzanne Flon who was also cast in the picture. Although only recently married, his attentions to other women became even more flagrant than they had been in the past. Photographs of Ricki taken about this time already show the tense strain and disillusionment at play in her very youthful countenance. Huston's bitterness over his divorce from Evelyn can be found in all the finely etched portraits of women as accomplished predators in this film.

Huston nearly lost his life when a man who had helped Suzanne Flon and her family during the war and who had appointed himself her guardian jumped Huston one night as he escorted Suzanne home and actually fired a gun at his heart only for the hammer to fall on a faulty cartridge. Huston returned the next night to give the man a proper beating after which the man tried to commit suicide. Although they never married, Huston would later call Flon the best of his wives. Nevertheless, in AN OPEN BOOK he lied about her and said she was engaged to photographer Robert Capa when MOULIN ROUGE was in production.

While on location in Havana filming WE WERE STRANGERS, Huston had got Peter Viertel to introduce him to Hemingway who lived there with his fourth wife, Mary. One day, on Hemingway's boat, the author handed Huston a rifle and asked him if he would try his luck. Huston shot an iguana on shore, but only wounded it. Hemingway, joined by Huston and Viertel, jumped into the water and waded ashore to find the creature. After a time, Huston and Viertel tired of the quest, but Hemingway was relentless and searched for two hours in the scorching midday sun until he found it. It had died. Huston was there with Evelyn, Viertel with his wife. One night both men took off and, after gambling and losing, went to a whorehouse. "His and Peter's big joke the next day," Evelyn recalled, "was how one of the girls smoked a cigarette with her sweet little cunt, and when John offered her a cigarette later, she said, 'No thank you, I don't smoke.' "[55] In his autobiography, Huston in writing about Hemingway told his version of the iguana story, only in his version Hemingway found the creature still alive and killed it. Huston praised Hemingway for his persistence and his determination. Yet, the story he told at greatest length is one that Robert Capa told him about why it was that he and Hemingway had become enemies. It happened during the war when he and Hemingway were on their way to Paris and encountered a German tank. Both ducked, but Capa saw the tank wheel and vanish over a hill before Hemingway looked up. He snapped a picture of Hemingway's ass as he lay crouched and then refused to surrender it. Hemingway never spoke to him again.[56]

The way Huston viewed life and lived it was what he wanted to get onto film, but that was not possible in a film such as MOULIN ROUGE. It "got mixed reviews and was successful at the box office, but I didn't like it," he confided in an interview more than a decade after its release. "It was kind of interesting physically. It just wasn't Toulouse-Lautrec, that's all. You could put him on the screen today; you couldn't then. He was sentimentalized. Actually, he was a clinically cold little realist, with the courage to look life in the teeth. He was sardonic, not bitter. There's never been another like him in life."[57] I suspect Huston admired that realism most and sometimes fancied that in this at least he resembled Lautrec. Yet, Huston's most deceptive quality was his ability to be utterly beguiling. Orson Welles told me that no one could be as charming as Huston, by which he meant subtly manipulative. It was a trait Welles would notice since it was also so much a part of his own personality. At the time of MOULIN ROUGE, Huston fell in love with Ireland. Once the film was released and making money, he decided to live there, setting himself up as a country gentleman joining in fox hunts and drinking a strong brew. Ricki presented John with their second child, Anjelica, but she resented Suzanne Flon and she never particularly liked it in Ireland. Although, once Huston began to renovate the big house of the estate he purchased, she would live in the small house with the children for nearly a decade, she was Huston's wife in name only.

While in Africa, Huston had given Bogart a copy of a novel by James Helvick which, he said, had the makings of another MALTESE FALCON. Bogart took the bait. He telephoned Huston in Paris to inform him that he had purchased screen rights to the novel and wanted John to work up a screenplay. Huston promised to contact Helvick and have him collaborate, but in the end he engaged Peter Viertel. Huston and Viertel sent versions of the script back and forth in the mail. After three months, Huston sent the final draft to Bogart who thought it was terrible. This was something of a challenge for Huston. He was able not only to persuade Bogart to come to Italy at once to start production but to invest in the film. Before he was done, Bogart would sink more than half a million dollars into the picture, a substantial investment from which he never received a cent in return. Huston promised to call in Truman Capote to slap the script into shape. Capote had just written dialogue for Jennifer Jones in her forthcoming film, INDISCRETION OF AN AMERICAN WIFE (Columbia, 1954), and David O. Selznick had especially high praise for him. Now Jennifer was to be cast opposite Bogart in BEAT THE DEVIL (United Artists, 1954), as the production was titled. Later Huston said of Selznick that "everything he did was for Jennifer. His whole life centered upon her, to the detriment of his good judgment. David never did anything worth a damn after he married Jennifer."[58] Huston knew that to support the lifestyle he envisioned in Ireland he would have to keep working and he would work no matter what. With the exception of MOBY DICK (Warner's, 1956), Huston seems to have cared nothing about any of the pictures he directed after MOULIN ROUGE until FREUD (Universal, 1962). Bogart invested in the film because he felt in Huston's debt due to the acclaim AFRICAN QUEEN had brought him and because he regarded Huston as a friend. Huston, for his part, probably did not particularly want Jennifer Jones in it but he knew that Selznick was getting ready to resume film production and he surmised there might be a job in it along the way. Huston would even endure Selznick's endless memos if there was money in it. Bogart, conversely, had become increasingly insecure and restless in his marriage to Bacall, now especially since her career had started again in earnest. While BEAT THE DEVIL was being filmed in Italy, Bacall was working in HOW TO MARRY A MILLIONAIRE (20th-Fox, 1953). It would mark their longest separation: four and a half months. Bogart took Verita Thompson with him to Italy where Huston intended to film at the villa where, before the war, Greta Garbo and Leopold Stokowski had sought refuge during their much publicized affair. Robert Capa was hired to take promotional photos.

Peter Lorre was added to the cast, an obvious reference to THE MALTESE FALCON, but the picture that Huston filmed never even came close to his earlier classic. What he ended up with was a complex parody of the genre about which the nicest thing you could say was that it appears no more confusing to the viewer than it was to the cast while it was being made. Bogart had always been somewhat indifferent to his physical surroundings and had blanched when, after the birth of Leslie, Bacall had insisted on the purchase of a hundred and sixty thousand dollar home, a mansion as Bogart termed it. The purchase caused him mounting anxiety, as did the sumptuous lifestyle Bacall wanted them to lead. He was increasingly unsure about how long he could keep making films, how long his popularity would last, how long he would continue to make money. Lorre and Bogart were not only good friends; they frequently met at Romanoff's. His presence on the set was intended to be reassuring, but I question Huston's assertion in his autobiography that, when he warned Bogart that BEAT THE DEVIL might well be a disaster, that the penurious Bogart sloughed it off with a crooked grin, saying, " 'Why, John, I'm surprised at you. Hell, it's only money!.' "[59] I believe he was too obsessed with the prospect of financial security in the future, especially for his children, ever to have made such a remark.

Bogart knew the end was coming long before it came. He kept punishing his body with alcohol and tobacco. Since the predisposition to cancer seems to have a genetic basis, the chances are he would have died of this disease in any case. About two years before his always sensitive throat became affected, Verita Thompson discovered that he had skin cancer. " 'Hell,' " he once said to her about his children, " 'I'll never see them grown. . . .' "[60]

I do not doubt that Frank Sinatra genuinely admired Bogart, never more so than when his attention was increasingly turned toward acting in films. However, it cannot have been too long after he and Bogart became friends that Sinatra also felt himself attracted to Bacall. Had Bogart not fallen ill when he did, it is an open question as to just how this triangle would have worked itself out. As it was, close friends of Bogart's were convinced that in his last year the knowledge that Bacall and Sinatra were in love would have proven more devastating to him than the realization that his condition was terminal.

In Hollywood with the rough cut of BEAT THE DEVIL in final editing, Huston managed to interest Warner Bros. in producing a new version of MOBY

DICK. The studio had already made the film twice, both times with John Barrymore, but that was ancient history. Huston engaged Ray Bradbury to work with him on the screenplay, which they wrote in six months in Ireland. The final script did manage to project the multiple levels of ambiguity which give the Herman Melville novel its sustaining quality: the madness of Ahab, the utter irrationality of the universe, the unity in God of both benignity and evil, the notion that since in the beginning there was only God, only God could have created good and evil in equal portions. When I recall Walter Huston in his final scene of Lewis Milestone's RAIN (United Artists, 1932) and the close-up of his tormented eyes, nearly black holes in his skull, or his diabolical ebulliance as the Sin-killer in David O. Selznick's DUEL IN THE SUN (Selznick, 1947), I can readily imagine him capturing for the camera the righteous fanaticism, Faustian striving, and maniacal hatred which infuses Ahab's very soul and blazes in his eyes. Huston had cast Gina Lollobrigida in BEAT THE DEVIL because, despite Bogart's objections, he was convinced that her large breasts would pay off at the box office. Now Huston felt, and so apparently did Warner Bros., that Gregory Peck would attract audiences to see MOBY DICK if he were cast as Ahab.

Huston appeared utterly oblivious to Peck's difficulties with the role and concentrated instead on what went on around Ahab: the harpooning of whales, the typhoon sequence which he insisted on shooting aboard a facsimile of the *Pequod* during an actual storm at sea, drying off the camera lenses with an air hose, and the final sequence where Ahab arises from the sea, drowned, caught in the harpoon cords on Moby Dick's back. In all of this, Huston demanded utter realism and he got it, although numerous men in the cast and crew including Peck were injured in the process. The film did good business and Huston received the New York Film Critics' Award for best direction and the National Board of Review voted Huston the best director of the year. Huston obviously felt that the personal battle he had fought getting the story on film was more important than any artistic failings that may be attributable to casting. He was especially pleased with Orson Welles' brief performance.

He was still at work on MOBY DICK, staying in New York before going on to Ireland, when Bacall and Morgan Maree called him to tell him that Bogart's condition was hopeless and that they wanted him to compose the eulogy. Huston did get to see Bogart after a stopover in Ireland and he went along with Bacall's fiction that Bogart was certain to recover. Bacall was convinced that Bogart did not know the truth. Huston was more cautious. "He seemed to accept it," was all he would say about the way Bogart responded to all the lies that he would get better.[61] Yet, Bogart did sell his interest in Santana Productions so Bacall and the children would have the money. He did encourage Bacall to go to Las Vegas for Sinatra's opening at the Sands Hotel and the birthday party that Sinatra threw for Bacall while she was there. Bacall was working regularly now. Bogart, as long as he could, went sailing with his son, enjoying his Scotch and cigarettes, studying sea and sky and occasionally dozing.

What impressed Huston most, he said in his eulogy, was the courage with which Bogart had faced death. Beyond that, however, I think Huston was most deeply affected by Bogart's stubborn resolution to go on living precisely the way he had been living until he passed into the final coma from which he never awoke.

Bacall continued the courtship with Sinatra, using newspaper and magazine interviews in quite the way she had when courting Bogart. Once Sinatra finally did propose to her, she managed to let it leak to the press. Yet, the scenario did not play out the way she had expected. Sinatra shied away. Later there was bitterness on her part; and still later there was only philosophical indifference.

MOBY DICK did so well at the box office that Huston was considered highly bankable. Twentieth Century-Fox hired him on a three-picture contract. Although plagued by incipient heart disease and chronic emphysema, he forged right ahead, living life as he wanted to live it. He had learned well from his father and from Bogart. "He stood behind his choices," Bacall wrote of Bogart, "and, persuasive as Frank could be, he could never make Bogie forget who he was. That intractable sense of self was Bogie's greatest strength and certainly one of his greatest attractions for his men friends—to say nothing of his women, to say nothing of future generations."[62]

## IV

As early as 1956, Huston wanted to film Rudyard Kipling's "The Man Who Would Be King." He even went to India to scout suitable locations. The picture didn't materialize at that time. What did was the first film on his new contract, HEAVEN KNOWS, MR. ALLISON (20th-Fox, 1957), upon which he worked while Bogart's life slipped away from him. In it, Robert Mitchum was cast as a G.I. stranded on a Pacific island with a nun, played by Deborah Kerr who, eventually, would marry Peter Viertel. The studio wanted the film to be financed out of funds frozen in Great Britain so Huston chose as his location Tobago, a British colony approximately twenty miles from Trinidad. All the speaking roles in the picture, other than the two principals, were Japanese, but with few Japanese at that location Huston had to settle for Chinese actors for all but eight of the roles.

While in production on this film, Huston's strategy with Selznick paid off. Selznick contacted him. He intended to remake A FAREWELL TO ARMS (20th-Fox, 1957). Ben Hecht had written the screenplay based on the Hemingway novel and Selznick wanted Huston to direct the picture. He offered him $250,000 to do it. Huston got Fox' permission to do the film. After completing HEAVEN KNOWS, MR. ALLISON and returning to Los Angeles to deliver his eulogy at Bogart's funeral, Huston flew to Paris to meet with Hemingway and discuss how to film A FAREWELL TO ARMS. Hemingway seemed pleased with Huston's ideas and he said he liked the screenplay Huston had contributed to for THE KILLERS. Selznick, however, had not produced a picture since POR-

TRAIT OF JENNY (Selznick, 1949) and he wanted to be certain from the start that Huston would be willing to follow orders. Selznick insisted that his films be made his way and his overall success as a producer was such that his artistic supervision seemed justified. Given Huston's independence of mind, a clash was inevitable. Yet, what ultimately and irrevocably separated the two men was this: Selznick wanted to use Hemingway's story as the basis for a love story between Jennifer Jones and Rock Hudson and Huston wanted to be the first to bring to the screen a story that Hemingway had written that embodied as much of Hemingway as he could get into it. Selznick's response to this was that he was prepared to throw Hemingway's book out entirely if he felt convinced that he could get a better picture without it. Huston ended up resigning from the production.

The accumulated grosses of recent Huston films were becoming impressive with the exception of BEAT THE DEVIL. Fox, therefore, decided to gamble on Huston's proposal of filming a fantasy treatment of Townsend Harris' diplomatic mission to Japan which led to trade with the West and an exchange of ideas. It was Huston's notion for John Wayne to star as Harris. To get Wayne, Fox had to guarantee him a salary of $700,000, the highest salary paid out to an actor up to that time. Along with Wayne, however, came the plethora of problems which hiring Wayne after 1955 always seemed to bring. Wayne, even more than George Raft, was zealously protective of his screen image and he wanted it to be kept sacrosanct. It may have amused Huston to think of the Wayne persona representing a roughneck American a hundred years ago, towering over the Japanese, self-confident and righteous, only for him to be flipped around in a humiliating match with a Judo expert who was much smaller, but Huston had underestimated his protagonist. THE BARBARIAN AND THE GEISHA (20th-Fox, 1958) was filmed on location in Kyoto, Japan and, from his first scene, Wayne began making objections.

"It was no marriage made in heaven," Huston commented to us. "To this day, I hold Wayne responsible for its not being a good picture. Wayne didn't approve of the story or the way I wanted to direct it. I heard even more complaints second-hand from Wayne than those he gave me face-to-face. Buddy Adler was in charge of production at Twentieth at the time. Wayne didn't like the way he appeared in scenes. He thought his eyes were too red. He bellyached so much that the studio agreed to reshoot those scenes he didn't like once we returned from location. I felt it was important that Wayne and the Japanese girl *not* sleep together. Wayne had his own ideas. Even that part of the script was changed back at the studio with the new scenes Wayne had them shoot." Huston paused to light a new cigar. "If Buddy Adler hadn't been dying of a brain tumor," he continued, exhaling smoke, "I would have insisted that my name be removed from the picture. Right from the outset Wayne came to me and told me that John Ford was an especially close friend of his and he had a little request to deliver to me from Ford: Ford wanted me to do what I could to help Wayne look good. When I asked Wayne what that was supposed to mean, he began telling me what to do, that I should only photograph his right profile, all that sort of thing.''

Between Wayne's salary and Huston's, Fox had nearly a million dollars invested in the film before shooting began. None of this made Huston cost-conscious. He spent money even more freely than usual, recklessly getting the shots he wanted. The blazing inferno with which the film concludes was quite real and Huston kept his actors in the center of it through three separate takes, quitting only after Wayne had scorched an arm and Sam Jaffe, playing Wayne's interpreter, found his pants were smoking. Upon release, even with all the scenes Wayne had done again, the film was poorly received, critics and public alike in agreement that this was not what they expected from a John Wayne picture. It probably occurred only to Huston that in this picture he had tried to critique the Wayne persona rather than glorify it. It was a critique no one was much interested in seeing.

It was unfortunate that Huston's third picture on his Fox contract should have been Darryl F. Zanuck's second independent production following the disastrous release of THE SUN ALSO RISES (20th-Fox, 1957). The story of THE ROOTS OF HEAVEN (20th-Fox, 1958) was set in Equatorial Africa and Zanuck, aware of Huston's success with THE AFRICAN QUEEN, concluded that he was the obvious man to direct it. The plot is concerned with an idealist who sets out to save the elephants from greedy ivory hunters. What no one had figured on, perhaps Zanuck least of all, was the arduous working conditions presented by temperatures ranging between 140 degrees during the day to 100 degrees at night. Liquids were sweated out before they reached the stomach. Disease was rampant. Trevor Howard had the lead, replacing William Holden who had been Zanuck's first choice and who, years later, would become a crusader to preserve African wild life. Also in the cast were Errol Flynn, Orson Welles, Eddie Albert, and Zanuck's latest, and hottest, romantic interest, Juliette Greco, whom Zanuck had introduced in THE SUN ALSO RISES. Her acting hadn't improved. However, after weeks in the heat, some of the company prostrate, others driven to madness or delirium, it really didn't matter.

Huston tried at first to alter the shooting schedule, beginning at dawn and quitting by noon. Notwithstanding, the troupe was preyed upon by malaria, dysentery, heart attacks, and diseases of unknown genealogy. Eddie Albert, when he arrived, announced that he had lived and worked in the Mexican desert and that the experience had made him a sun-worshipper. He dropped on his second day and was out of his mind for three weeks. Juliette Greco developed a rare blood disease and nearly died. Errol Flynn came armed with what he felt was a perfect antidote, fruit juice and several cases of vodka. He drank constantly. Huston and Flynn, when they both worked at Warner Bros., had had a fistfight one night at a Selznick party. By now they were friends.

'' 'He would sit all night with a bottle of vodka,' '' Huston recalled, '' 'and an open book, and a Coleman lantern, and never look at the book. He was never drunk when working but whenever we shifted to another location he would drink too much, and to recover he needed drugs. Errol was on his way out, of course. He was dying.' ''[63]

In less than a year, Flynn would be dead. Huston and several of the others stuck to Scotch and consumed so much of it that cases had to be sent in by airlift. Zanuck stayed with beer, drinking ten to twelve bottles a day. When the heat finally got to him, Zanuck lapsed into mild lunacy, telling everyone that he intended to make several more pictures in Africa, writing out projected scenes in long-hand and giving them away. By the time the troupe made it to Paris to finish shooting, Zanuck had contracted a case of shingles. Flynn, despite his dietary precautions, was forced to enter a Paris hospital with a severe case of malaria. Huston, typically, suffered from nothing, not even a hangover. The same was true for Orson Welles but in his case that was because he had not gone to Africa. His scenes were all shot in Paris.

Huston and Zanuck vied with each other to shoulder the blame for the film's failure. With it, Huston's Fox contract was up and he signed with Hecht-Hill-Lancaster to make a Western, his first unless you are inclined to believe the Warner Bros. publicity that THE TREASURE OF THE SIERRA MADRE is a Western. THE UNFORGIVEN (United Artists, 1960) starred Burt Lancaster as a white man, eventually marrying Audrey Hepburn who, it transpires, is of Indian blood. Much about the film is inept, especially the Indian attack at the end. Huston denounced it as the film he disliked most of those he directed. ''. . . I wanted to turn it into the story of racial intolerance in a frontier town, a comment on the real nature of community 'morality.' ''[64] That he was not allowed to do. In fact, the screenplay retains the ideology of the Alan LeMay novel on which it is based in which the Indian way of life, and not their biological and genetic make-up, is what is at fault in their brutish and savage dealings with the white man.

THE MISFITS (United Artists, 1961) was a modern Western. It was also a film fraught with tragedy. Playwright Arthur Miller had come up with a story about modern mustanging while waiting out a divorce near Reno so he could marry Marilyn Monroe. Miller published the story in ESQUIRE and some months later discussed with Huston the possibility of turning the story into a film. Miller eventually did a screenplay which Huston liked. Russell Metty, Huston's cameraman, recommended the picture be filmed in black and white so as to retain the harsh lines of the story. With all the problems that beset THE MISFITS in production, it became one of the most expensive black and white films in history.

"Monroe was in terrible shape," Huston told us. "But there was a magic about her that the world could respond to. She could turn on and off like nobody else. She took drugs, drugs to go to sleep and drugs to stay awake. Her future seemed hopeless. The drugs were destroying her. She had a huge fear of no longer being beautiful. When she had to go to the hospital, the picture closed down for two weeks. She returned and was right back on drugs."

THE MISFITS was Monroe's last picture and the last picture for Clark Gable. He had been a contract player for years at M-G-M, accustomed to early morning calls, priding himself on being prompt and always knowing his lines. He seethed at Monroe who refused to work before noon, and then would only work if she was feeling in the mood. Gable had gone on a crash diet for the picture, shedding thirty-five pounds. Huston worked him hard in action sequences, in one scene demanding take after take with Gable running hard behind a pickup truck.

"I've heard it from quite a few sources," I said, "that you were responsible for killing Gable."

Huston winced. "Now, that just isn't the truth," he replied. "I had stunt men doing all the hard stuff, dragged or wrestling with the stallion. The intercuts that Gable had to do seemed to require little effort. But he had been drinking heavily for years and he shook almost like he had Parkinson's disease."

There would seem to be more than a little truth in this. Edward Dmytryk, who had directed Gable several years before in SOLDIER OF FORTUNE (20th-Fox, 1955), confirmed that Gable was a very heavy drinker but that it was kept a secret. He would sometimes have the shakes so bad he would have to go to his room. This was in direct contrast to Bogart who *did* have a reputation as a heavy drinker and who might even have a drink during the shooting day if he didn't have much more to do but who never had the shakes. It is too often forgotten that different metabolisms respond quite differently even to the same stimulus.

Huston found that he got on well with Montgomery Clift. He found the actor to be a deeply introspective person.

"Funny thing about Clift," Huston rambled on. "He only propositioned men when he was drunk. There was nothing abnormal about him when he was sober. I found him a delight to work with, which is why I put him in FREUD."

THE MISFITS came out topping four million dollars in costs. The film was a failure. Miller's marriage to Monroe was finished by the time production began and Gable felt ill-at-ease in his love scenes with her. Monroe, on the other hand, gushed about how fine an artist John Huston was and what a pleasure it was to be working again with the man who had given her career its real start. Whether because of what happened to Gable or not, henceforth the passion and, to an extent, the brutality (at least on screen) vanished from Huston's films and they became increasingly eloquent intellectual statements that somehow lacked the primitive intensity of raw emotion and honesty in portrayal which had so clearly marked his films of the 'Forties and 'Fifties.

In 1959, Huston sent Gladys Hill a cable soon after her divorce: " 'Since you like to travel and since your job is temporary, why not come to Ireland and work for me forever and ever?' "[65] She did come and she remained with him, as his assistant and collaborator, until her death. Huston's fourth marriage was over by this time. Ricki had held on longer than any of the others, probably because of the children. Eventually, the womanizing, the long absences on film projects, Huston's preoccupation with the hunt and other local female attractions did take their toll. Keyes had become involved with producer Mike Todd. Knowing that the marriage to Ricki was a bust, Keyes called Huston where he was staying at the Beverly Hills Hotel when she left Todd for what would be the last time and asked to stay with him. Keyes declared Huston a splendid fellow in emergencies as a result, apparently unable to perceive any of the perverse delight Huston would have derived from such a situation. Nothing came of it, but some years later she did visit him for a last time in Ireland where he greeted her dressed in a Japanese robe. " 'How are you, honey?' he said in melted caramel. That hadn't changed. Over Irish coffee polite conversation was exchanged. 'Did you have a pleasant trip? The weather isn't at its best.' As if I were a perfect stranger who had wandered in out of the bog. I suppose I was. But then, who was this white-haired gentleman in the flowing Oriental robe talking to me? Apparently everybody but me knows you can't go home again.''[66]

They had been separated a decade when, in 1969, Ricki died in an automobile accident in France. By that time Huston had had a second son, Daniel Huston, with Zoë Sallis who continued to live in Rome and Ricki had had an illegitimate daughter, Allegra, born in London in 1964. In his old age, Huston drew both of them into his inner circle.

The original script Huston commissioned from Jean-Paul Sartre for FREUD was many times too long and had to be severely edited and reworked before shooting could begin. Why Huston had gone to an anti-Freudian for a script in the first place remains a mystery. Sartre's treatment has since been published as he wrote it. FREUD was released under the title THE SECRET PASSION in an effort to attract viewers. However, Huston's rendering of Freud's psychological investigations into the unconscious were made superficial by all that had to be omitted and what was left struck audiences and critics alike as too coldly intellectual. During production Montgomery Clift was in a hopeless physical and psychological condition and for years afterward Huston had to defend himself against charges that he had only intensified Clift's decline in the way he had worked with him.

He next directed THE LIST OF ADRIAN MESSENGER (Universal, 1963), starring George C. Scott and Kirk Douglas. Perhaps the most interesting aspect of this picture had to do with the famous stars who appeared only in disguise and who were for the most part unrecognizable. Huston's career as a film director was, in fact, at its lowest ebb up to this point when Otto Preminger came to his rescue by hiring him to portray Cardinal Glennon of Boston in THE CARDINAL (Columbia, 1963), for which role Huston was nominated for an Academy Award as Best Supporting Actor. He took on whatever project was offered to him, no matter what the property, whether from a small, independent producer or from a large studio, simply in order to keep working. He had actually run out of things to say. Following THE NIGHT OF THE IGUANA (M-G-M, 1964), everything was only repetition. Whether the theme was the pursuit of an elusive goal or an impossible objective, or the hopeless duplicity of women, in every case he had done it all before, and done it better.

THE NIGHT OF THE IGUANA possessed undoubtedly the most bizarre cast Huston had ever assembled. Richard Burton was the star. Elizabeth Taylor tagged along with three children from previous marriages to be at Burton's side on location at Puerto Vallarta in Mexico. She was still married to Eddie Fisher and Burton was not yet divorced. Ava Gardner, a Huston favorite, was in the cast. She had once been married to band leader Artie Shaw and Shaw was by then married to Evelyn Keyes. Ava, who had dumped Sinatra just before Sinatra began his courtship of Bacall on the rebound, now had an entourage of young men around her and Huston incorporated this aspect of her private life into her screen character perhaps because it amused him to see a woman pursuing a way of life that he had adopted long ago when it came to sexual relationships. Deborah Kerr had married Peter Viertel who had fallen hopelessly in love with Ava Gardner while Henry King was directing THE SUN ALSO RISES. Michael Wilding, one of Elizabeth Taylor's ex-husbands, was Richard Burton's publicist. Sue Lyon carried on her romance with Hampton Fancher III whose wife at the moment had mistakenly come to the location and ended up quartered with Lyon's mother. Tennessee Williams, on whose stage play the film was based, had never married, although he was also there with his boy friend and a tiny pet dog. Because the picture was being filmed in Mexico, a Mexican director had to be included in the crew and Huston hired Emilio Fernández, a favorite of Sam Peckinpah's, who already had a bad reputation for having once shot his producer. Only after extreme pressure was brought to bear on him would Huston compel Fernández to take off the sixgun that was part of his regular apparel.

Much to Williams' dismay, Huston altered the ending of the play. Burton was cast as a defrocked, drunken minister who is attracted to teenage girls. He is destroyed in the play. Huston decided to imitate what he had done in THE AFRICAN QUEEN and let the minister settle down with Ava Gardner in her run-down hotel. I believe Huston strongly identified with the character Burton was playing, a character who had much, although highly romanticized, in common with himself and, in a way, the attraction of the minister for the nubile young woman played by Sue Lyon was not all that different from the attraction Huston had once felt toward Ricki Soma. To symbolize the breakthrough at the conclusion of the film, Huston wanted a captive iguana to dart to freedom following the death of the world's oldest poet, played by Cyril Delavanti, who is accompanied on his travels by Deborah Kerr. The iguana refused to take his liberty until Huston came up with the idea of touching him with a 110-volt shock stick. Whatever the picture's difficulties, it was a solid artistic and commercial triumph. I do not think I am entirely alone in ranking it second only to THE TREASURE OF THE SIERRA MADRE and among Huston's most consummate cinematic achievements.

The same decidedly could not be said for THE BIBLE . . . IN THE BEGIN-NING (20th-Fox, 1966). It was one of those typical Dino De Laurentiis extra-vanganzas which started out, as more recently De Laurentiis' KING KONG (Paramount, 1976) did, with years of preparation, exploitative publicity and chest-thumping, only to turn out to be vulgar, inconsequential, and unconvincing. Huston, however, was amused at the idea of creating the heavens and the earth and went so far as to cast himself as Noah, a role which in view of his lifelong love of animals of all kinds was rather apt. He had found a new home in Las Caletas, inaccessible except by boat from Puerto Vallarta, and he had reached a nadir as a director from which he would never quite recover. He worked as one of several directors assigned various segments of CASINO ROYALE (Columbia, 1967), an elaborately unfunny spoof on the James Bond pictures, and both REFLECTIONS IN A GOLDEN EYE (Warner's, 1967) and SINFUL DAVEY (United Artists, 1969) were artistically disappointing and box-office disasters. A return to Fox found Huston directing A WALK WITH LOVE AND DEATH (20th-Fox, 1969), notable only perhaps in that it marked the first time he directed his daughter Anjelica, and THE KREMLIN LETTER, a pseudo spy drama in which George Sanders had his final screen role before he decided to end it all.

Orson Welles then hired Huston to act in THE OTHER SIDE OF THE WIND, which was begun in 1970 and which would not be taken completely out of Orson's hands until 1984. I did not say finished in 1984. There seems to be some speculation about that. Orson insisted all it needed was his final editing. The plot of this picture concerns a homosexual film director who has come to the end of the line. "Orson denied that it was autobiographical in any way," Huston later wrote, "nor was it biographical as far as I was concerned."[67] What troubled Huston most of all was that there was no script and Welles simply wanted him to say whatever he thought appropriate. It proved difficult to say lines, indeed long speeches, *ad libitum* and doubly so when the lines were directed at a character played by Lilli Palmer who was not on the set but with only Orson standing in for her. Huston first realized that Orson had run out of money once Orson began borrowing cigars from him.

Huston walked off the set of THE LAST RUN (M-G-M, 1971) and was replaced by another director. When he was again behind the camera for FAT CITY (Columbia, 1972), the downward trend continued with a story involving only losers, losers who are never shown to have even a chance of winning. Similarly, Huston's next two films, both with Paul Newman, proved a calamity for director and star. Huston's script for THE LIFE AND TIMES OF JUDGE ROY BEAN (National General, 1972) had Bean alive a good many years after the historical Bean was long dead, Yet, this is scarcely the major drawback. The major drawback is that the film is dull, irremediably dull from beginning to end, and not even Ava Gardner's brief cameo as Lily Langtry can spark it up.

"I think one of the biggest problems on THE LIFE AND TIMES OF JUDGE ROY BEAN," Huston remarked near the end of our visit, "was due to the fact that I had to cut out several scenes. That was a mistake. As a result, the picture was misunderstood by the critics. They thought I was in favor of capital punishment, when I just wanted to show the hypocrisy behind our whole judicial system. I was taken to task over showing a hanging. Well, hell, you shouldn't hide a thing like that. Bring it out into the open. There wouldn't be capital punishment if people could watch it.''

There is a movement afoot to televise state executions. Knowing human nature, I rather suspect that seeing capital punishment may not have such a prohibitive effect as Huston thought. Notwithstanding, Newman got on so well with Huston, and was so charmed by him as a person, that he requested Huston as the director for his next film, THE MACKINTOSH MAN (Warner's, 1973). Here, again, Newman played a rather unsavory character. He projects the sheerest violence in one scene where, after a severe beating, he gets back at his captors, setting fire to their house and kicking a woman in the groin. Of course, Newman had played bounders in the past, but Huston's concentration on blood lust and brutal sadism in these films made them seem to delight in the presentation of malice. They also seem to contain a nihilistic element that probably derived more from Huston's direction than it arose spontaneously from Newman's interpretation of the roles he was assigned. THE MACKINTOSH MAN was Newman's sixth consecutive commercial failure. It was Huston's ninth, and he went on to his tenth, although it has since acquired the status of a classic.

Originally Huston had wanted to film Rudyard Kipling's short story ''The Man Who Would Be King'' with Clark Gable and Humphrey Bogart. By the time he got his chance to make the film, he had outlived them both and so cast Sean Connery and Michael Caine instead. It proved a better picture than Huston had made in a long time with what now was definitely *the* Huston ending: men in defeat, a defeat that is ironic rather than pathetic, and certainly not tragic.

The last thing Huston told us before we left him was that whatever I might want to write about him he did not want to read it. Mike Romanoff had once said of him: ''He does not really live; he just plays the part of John Huston . . . and his entire life has been a magnificent performance.''[68] When you consider that Romanoff was himself a phony Russian prince, I suppose the same could be said of him. I ignored what Huston had told me. I had already sent him a copy of THE FILMING OF THE WEST (1976) and sent him a copy of his career study when it appeared and, as well, a copy of THE DETECTIVE IN HOLLYWOOD (1978). In retrospect to have done this was a mistake. He did not like the image which emerged of him in the career study. In a way, he wrote AN OPEN BOOK to plead his own case against what William F. Nolan, Evelyn Keyes, and dozens of others, myself included, had said about him. However, he was also honest enough to admit, when confronted by those who knew him best, that AN OPEN BOOK was only for the public. '' 'I'm not going to expose my personal life,' ''[69] he blithely remarked. Unfortunately for me when, in THE DETECTIVE IN HOLLYWOOD, I addressed the question of why Hammett had quit writing I mentioned—without naming names—what Huston and a number of others had told me had been the reason: the social and intellectual sphere Hammett entered when he began his relationship with Lillian Hellman. THE TORONTO STAR decided to make much more of this issue than I had ever intended and contacted both Hellman and me in an effort to create a stand-off in the paper's literary section. I wanted no part of it and I told the paper as much. When we went into production on the documentary I wrote based on THE DETECTIVE IN HOLLYWOOD, I wanted to interview Huston for the camera. I hoped to get him to reminisce about Hammett as he had known him, to talk about what his objectives had been in filming his version of THE MALTESE FALCON and, if possible, to draw the lines of comparison between that film and CHINATOWN which he had done in our conversation with him. I telephoned Gladys Hill at her apartment in Puerto Vallarta and asked her to get a message to Huston in Las Caletas about what we proposed to do. Gladys cautioned me at once that it would be impossible to do any kind of an interview at Las Caletas because of its inadequate power supply. When she got back to me, she had bad news. Huston did not want to do the interview. Lillian Hellman had telephoned him and had advised him to have nothing to do with my project. This put me in a quandary. Huston's comments, I felt, were vital to my intention and I did not want to miss this opportunity. I discussed the matter with the unit director, Fred Hutchison, who suggested the thing to do was to fly to Puerto Vallarta and camp there with all our gear. He proposed going on ahead, taking a boat to Huston's home, and doing his best to persuade him. Oregon Educational and Public Broadcasting Service had put up the money and, whatever we did, the PBS affiliate must not be told of the problem. So, off we went, Fred in advance, Vicki as production supervisor, our sound man, our lighting expert, a production assistant, and myself as the producer/writer following in his wake.

Getting to Puerto Vallarta by air, of course, was not so much a problem as getting through customs. The Mexican authorities x-rayed our film stock and so there was a delay while we had to acquire new stock. Our Mexican guide met us at the airport. As we entered Puerto Vallarta the amazing thing was how what had once been a sleepy village when Huston had gone there to film THE NIGHT OF THE IGUANA had since become a resort town. Wealthy Americans had built magnificent villas along the coast and there were also posh hotels for the tourists, this opulence standing in stark contrast to the poverty and squalor of the original village which continued to loom in grim criticism of such social and economic inequity. Huston only occasionally came to town. Mostly he stayed in his compound at Las Caletas on land he leased from the local Indians and which, upon his death, would revert to being a wilderness. Since completing THE MAN WHO WOULD BE KING (Allied Artists, 1975), he had done nothing very notable. He had directed a short film celebrating the Bicentennial commissioned by the National Park Service and had been replaced on a low-budget, modern-day shoot-em-up titled LOVE AND BULLETS (A.F.D., 1979), starring Charles Bronson and Jill Ireland. WISE BLOOD (New Line Cinema, 1980) had just been released, a modest little picture for the art theatre circuit. PHOBIA (Paramount, 1980), his major studio effort, would be released by the end of the year and would prove so bad that it would have a domestic gross of $21,000.

AN OPEN BOOK had just appeared and several of the crew members had copies, hoping that Huston would autograph them after the shoot—if there was to be a shoot. I asked our guide what she had heard from Fred. She said he had managed only that morning to charter a boat to take him to Las Caletas. I had not, as yet, read Huston's autobiography but since Orson Welles had agreed to participate I looked up what Huston had had to say about him. Although he had known and worked with Orson for years, when it came time to comment on him, Huston could do nothing but project once more the legend of Orson Welles and tell nothing at all about him as a human being. Years later, I would be struck by an observation writer Edna O'Brien would make about Huston following her experience of living for a time in the compound at Las Caletas and working on a screenplay for a film titled THE RACK which would never be produced. " 'He once told me that he hated physical cowardice,' " she remarked. " 'Well, he went into the physical terror zones, but not the psychological ones. In many ways, for all the bravura, he was a lost man. Alone, coughing, in that white shirt, looking at television at four A.M., you wondered what went on in there.' "[70]

After checking into our hotel and with still no word from Fred, Vicki and I took the opportunity to wander a bit around Puerto Vallarta. Entering a chapel, we were struck by the statuary, especially the realistic blood which seemed to pour from the wounds of the saints with the stigmata. Perhaps when the sufferings of life are less assuaged by media distractions, the wounds can be shown to be more real. Television was not so ubiquitous and the one set we encountered, in a bar, was tuned in to a prize fight. Once we got back to the hotel, Fred was there with news. Huston had agreed to the interview. It would be done at Gladys Hill's apartment. However, Huston would only agree to the interview provided he could say for the camera how happy Dashiell Hammett had been once he met Lillian Hellman and that he was happier with her than he had been at any other time in his life. This did not bode well. Huston, I was certain, did not believe that any more than I did. Hammett had not been a happy man before or after he met Lillian Hellman and had nearly drunk himself to death before he had sworn off liquor forever. He had been sent to prison for what he believed was right. His last words to Lillian, as she herself had admitted, as he was being taken to the hospital for the last time was to express astonishment that Lillian was intent on coming along. I shrugged my shoulders. It did not matter. The question as to why Hammett had quit writing was not even addressed in the script. I was concerned instead with the view of American society which Hammett had set forth in his fiction and how that view had been translated to the screen.

Huston was cordial when we arrived for the shoot. He had THE FILMING OF THE WEST and THE DETECTIVE IN HOLLYWOOD displayed prominently on a bookcase and he was only too willing to sign copies of his book for the crew. To get enough electric current to operate the lights, camera, and sound equipment, we had to string extension cords to adjacent apartments. The tripod camera locked and would not budge above a knee-high position. I sought to distract Huston by talking about Stanton MacDonald-Wright and he warmed to the subject. Fred had positioned Huston in front of one of his own giant canvases and it was then that I perceived the similarity of his color scheme with that of Wright's. However, in just the past few years his emphysema had worsened considerably. His speech was slower than ever because his breathing was so impaired. Once the filming began, I was to ask him questions off camera and he was to respond on camera. Orson's narration would tie it all together. Virtually every question I asked him about Hammett led him inevitably back to how happy Hammett had been with Lillian and how much she had done for him. In response to a query as to what he had been about in THE MALTESE FALCON, he side-stepped entirely the intense pleasure the viewer is supposed to feel as Spade tells Brigid that he's sending her over because he won't take the fall for her and insisted, to the contrary, that THE MALTESE FALCON is a morality tale and that it celebrates the triumph of virtue at the end. Moreover, he absolutely refused to say anything about the view of corruption in either his film or in CHINA-TOWN. In fact, much of what he did say amounted to almost patriotic platitudes, even when the talk bordered on Hammett's imprisonment or his own involvement in protesting the HUAC hearings.

Once we were back in Los Angeles, Orson asked me how the interview had gone. I could only voice my frustration at getting not even one straight answer from Huston. "I can understand that," Welles said. "He isn't saying anything about anything or anybody that is likely to get him in trouble because he wants to receive the Life Achievement Award from the American Film Institute." When I responded that I could wish I had known that going in, Orson only chuckled, puffed on his cigar, and sipped champagne.

No one in Hollywood would offer Orson a film because, after repeated op-portunities, he had proven himself totally unreliable. During John Ford's last years, no one would offer him a film primarily because of his drinking. Howard Hawks had greater and greater difficulty putting the money together, despite his record of hits, because of his independent spirit. When Frank Capra could no longer get anyone to let him make a film his way, he wrote his autobiography instead which even he admitted, as we once joked about it, read as if it were the prototype of all the films he had made. Huston, because of the persona he had set out to create in his last years, because of his charm, because of the successes he had had early in his career, and because he was willing to direct virtually anything he was offered, managed to keep working. VICTORY (Par-amount, 1981) was scarcely a notable film, nor was the only musical Huston ever directed, ANNIE (Columbia, 1982). However, Ray Stark wanted Huston to direct the latter film because he knew Huston needed the money and he figured anyone could make a hit film from what was already a hit on the stage. Originally, Stark had wanted Huston to play Daddy Warbucks in the picture but his health had deteriorated too much for that and so Albert Finney was given the role and was asked to play it as if he were Huston doing it. Huston was so impressed with Finney's impression of him that he cast him in the role of the Consul in UNDER THE VOLCANO (Universal, 1984), a role which in a way was a surrogate for Huston's image of himself, a drunken, querulous, rambunctious man who cannot reconcile with a woman who loves him but who does manage to form a friendship that is binding with his son.

Yet, of all of the films of Huston's last decade, the only true commercial and critical success was PRIZZI'S HONOR (20th-Fox, 1985) which had him again directing Anjelica, this time opposite her long-time lover Jack Nicholson. In the somewhat grotesque triangle in this film, there is almost a reprise of THE MALTESE FALCON and what might have happened to Spade had he married Brigid. In this case both Nicholson and Kathleen Turner play professional killers. The Mafia family to which Nicholson belongs wants and expects him to stay with its choice for a mate, Anjelica, but Nicholson opts for Turner. Her last contract is to kill Nicholson but he is able to send a knife through her neck before she can accomplish the deed. Anjelica had grown considerably as an actress and her Academy Award for her performance in the film continued what was now a Hollywood dynasty. Huston's final film as a director was THE DEAD (Vestron, 1987) based on a completely unfilmable short story by James Joyce for which Tony Huston co-wrote the screenplay and in which Anjelica starred.

In an effort to get publicity for the film, Huston gave out interviews, the most interesting of which was with Cleveland Amory. Huston's physical condition had deteriorated further. He was now confined to a wheelchair although he would occasionally try climbing a flight of stairs just to see if he could do it. The emphysema which had troubled him for forty years had become so severe that he had to have a plastic tube leading from his nose to a tank of oxygen. He could not be away from an oxygen machine for more than twenty minutes or he would die. Even so, he frequently had to gasp for air or would have a paroxysm of coughing. Defiant to the end, after recent bypass surgery Huston had been found smoking a cigar. He was grateful, he told Amory, that he still had his vision and his hearing was fine. Actually, his eyes could not focus sufficiently for him to be able to read. His fifth marriage to Celeste Huston he had described in AN OPEN BOOK as "tantamount to putting my finger in the sea-snake's mouth"[71] and he made certain Amory understood that, while he accepted responsibility for the failure of his first two marriages, Evelyn Keyes had proposed to him and that she had taken everything with her when she left. Such comments always tended to make Keyes laugh derisively. Huston's doctors had forbidden him to return to Las Caletas and so now he was, in a sense, homeless. At the time of the interview, he was staying with Burgess Meredith. They had been friends from the time Meredith was married to Paulette Goddard and Huston to Keyes. Amory asked Huston if he had ever been in love over a long period. He said, yes, with Marietta Fitzgerald. " 'When I met her,' " Huston told Amory, " 'she was still married. And then I got married, and after that, when we were both free, she wouldn't have me. She said I would have been the perfect husband too—as long as I could have a harem.' "[72] Huston went on to tell how Marietta had come to visit him on the set of THE MISFITS and how Clark Gable had been so struck with her that he had insisted she be assigned a small part that was being cast. The impression Huston gave was that there *had* been one love in his life, the one that he was destined not to have. It gave to his life the sense of neatness and defeat typical of the Huston ending to a film.

He once said that "for me the point of MOBY DICK as Melville wrote it is that Ahab hated God, and in essence felt that he was bringing the Judge Himself before the bar of judgment and condemning Him. This theme of blasphemy was missed by most people who saw the picture, and who think of Ahab simply as a madman. Hence Gregory Peck's performance as Ahab didn't coincide with their preconceived notions of the story.''[73] Although he could see no consistency in his films, no thematic unity, perhaps this was due to the number of films he directed simply for the money as opposed to those which he made because he really wanted to make them. In all that he did, his technical proficiency was usually there, his penchant for editing in the camera, his refusal to make master shots, and his insistence that two setups could serve as well as five.

Huston's strategy in AN OPEN BOOK worked. He had wanted to be accepted in the new role of the grand old man of film with mostly good things to say about everybody except, at times, himself. In 1982 the Directors' Guild devoted a weekend as a tribute in his honor and in 1983 Orson Welles proved a prophet: he became the eleventh recipient of the American Film Institute's Life Achievement Award. Welles injected the only skeptical note into the congratulatory proceedings in his inimitable baroque manner when he noted how Huston had played Svengali to Humphrey Bogart, and Marilyn Monroe and called him " 'an epicurean, an amiable Count Dracula.' " Probably the most telling remark of all was when Welles declared that " 'John is also Mephistopheles to his own Faust.' "[74] Nowhere is this borne out more than in Huston's agreeing to let Lawrence Grobel write a truthful biography of him and his family and even going so far as to encourage intimates to tell Grobel everything as honestly as possible. The benevolent Burgess Meredith in Cleveland Amory's article was somewhat less than that when he presented Huston with a bill for $13,000 for his stay at his home, a bill which Huston reluctantly paid. The preponderance of testimony which Grobel gathered supported what Jeanie Sims, Huston's secretary from the 'Fifties, had told him: "Huston needed to destroy those who loved him, that 'he had a compulsion to make people—especially women—love him, and then, once having secured their love, an equal compulsion to spurn them.' "[75] John Milius, who wrote the script for THE LIFE AND TIMES OF JUDGE ROY BEAN, had once discussed women with Huston and John had given him his philosophy: " 'Be anything they want. Mold to their caresses. Tell them anything. Just fuck 'em! Fuck 'em all!' "[76] Celeste had sought to give Huston what he wanted, constant sexual excitement, but in the end she found the work too difficult, the task too taxing, and the final straw before their break was when Tony Huston told her that he had seen his father fucking Celeste's maid, Maricela Hernández. When Huston left Cici, as Celeste was called, he took with him his silverware, his wine, and her maid. THE DEAD is dedicated to Maricela, who remained with Huston for his final years and who was with him when he died. Yet, if Lawrence Grobel is correct in THE HUSTONS (1989), it wasn't Maricela, or Marietta Tree, or any of the other women in Huston's life who ultimately mattered so much as Gladys Hill who died at sixty-one in New York just as ANNIE was about to go into production. Huston wept at her funeral, as he had at that of his father, and Grobel concluded that "he was chilled by the sudden loss. . . . She had put up with so much of his foolishness, with his disastrous last marriage, his dalliances, his faults and weaknesses that only she knew. She had meant more to him than any of his wives."[77]

At the time of his death, Huston was slated to act in a film that was to be directed by Danny Huston, a film which Huston had co-written. Eloise Hardt MacNamara, known as Cherokee, had been John's maid when he first went to work for Warner Bros. and she stayed a friend over the years. " 'To this day Tony breaks my heart when I'm with him,' " she confided to Grobel, " 'because I can still see him crawling on the floor in Chantilly. Those kids had no love at all. Ricki was spending all her time chasing John and John couldn't care. It was a horrible marriage, a classic example of kids caught in a crossfire between two people who were so involved with themselves.' "[78] In his final decade Huston tried to be as close to his own children, and as helpful to them, as his own father had been to him in his youth. He may have come to feel this concern very late in life, but he did come to it, and for that he deserves recognition. After Ricki's death, he let Allegra take his name and, while he did little to nurture her, he did what he could to see that she was cared for and repeatedly urged her real father, who refused to acknowledge her legally, to look after her materially. Zoë Sallis, Danny, Allegra, and Anjelica were all on hand to celebrate John's eighty-first birthday with him. He was saved the fragmented, even absurd end, to which Orson Welles would come.

Grobel came to blame Rhea Huston for John's inability to relate to women in any permanent way. "She may have believed she had never failed him, but he believed that she had nearly suffocated him. All those quarrels, all that yelling. If he had problems relating to women for any length of time, it was as much because of her over-bearing personality as anything else."[79] However, I am always troubled by how far one should go in affixing blame to others when an individual proves inept at self-overcoming, to put it in Nietzschean terms. Doris Lilly, one of John's New York girlfriends at the time of his marriages to Lesley and Evelyn, felt that " 'John didn't like women very much. I can't help but think that. I hate to even say it, but he might have had homosexual feelings.' "[80] Dr. David Stafford-Clark, the psychiatric consultant on FREUD, thought Huston had "developed a love/hate relationship"[81] with Montgomery Clift on the picture. Huston himself confessed to Clift's biographer, Patricia Bosworth, that what had soured him on Monty was what had occurred during his visit to St. Clerans when Clift took the reporter who was interviewing him to bed with him for the night. " 'The incident seemed trashy—I felt Monty had insulted me,' " Huston said. " 'I wish he'd considered my family and how I felt about it. I can't say I'm able to deal with homosexuality.' "[82]

Huston would have no more to do with Pablo after he left his wife. " 'I think he would have felt better if he had,' " Pablo told Grobel, " 'but he taught me never to crawl. And that is the best lesson anybody could teach you.' "[83] If Huston had been unwilling to tell the story of his life honestly in AN OPEN BOOK, he nonetheless allowed Grobel to do it. And so we have the image of the director who enjoyed the complications of playing women he had gone to bed with off of one another, as at the Academy Awards in 1941 where, "if the evening was awkward for Olivia de Havilland, it was also strange for Mary Astor, who was still fond of John. As for John, who was there with his wife, blowing kisses at Olivia and beaming his gracious smile at Mary, it was all part of the Hollywood circus that he could thoroughly enjoy. . . . "[84]

At ten in the evening on 28 August 1987 on location for MR. NORTH (Heritage Entertainment, 1988), Tony shared a brandy with John and his father asked him for a massage. John then complained that Tony was hurting him. Tony told his father, " 'You're too grumpy, old man.' "[85] He cut the massage short and left the room, turning out the light as he went, leaving his father in the dark. Huston regarded the gesture as symbolic. He began to shudder as his face turned ashen and tears came to his eyes. He rang the bell that stood on his night table, summoning Maricela. It is not known what happened after that moment. Maricela was alone in the room with him. She was alone with him hours after he was already dead. She claimed that he had asked for her hand and then looked into her eyes.

" 'How many express rifles have we got?' " he is supposed to have asked her.

" 'Thirty, John,' " she answered.

" 'How about ammunition?'

" 'Oh, we've got plenty of ammunition.'

"Then he squeezed her hand and raised it up over his head like a prize-fighter. 'Just give 'em hell,' he said.

"His hand dropped and Maricela held him tight."[86]

This is Huston's death as Maricela later told it. However, this is the same Maricela who also later said that she did not care if the family did not believe her when she insisted that John's Oscars and awards had been accidentally thrown out in the garbage and then changed that story to say they were put in a box and given to one of the film academies where they were lost.

Huston's last battle was with Ted Turner, in an effort to prevent Turner from desecrating what there was of art in what is otherwise only a manufacturing industry in his efforts to colorize black and white films, a battle he was destined to lose. Ironically, a documentary both highly complimentary and even at times a bit sentimental on Huston's life directed by Frank Martin would have its première on Turner's TNT network. For its conclusion, the documentary told Maricela's version of Huston's death. Danny Huston was more realistic. " 'If you start to look at the horrors that might have occurred during the last week of my father's life . . . and dissect Maricela's behavior, you might begin to perceive differently the past two years of Dad's life. A little friction or conflict between my father and Maricela a year ago I thought was kind of cute. Here he was having a relationship and it was keeping him alive. But if you look at Maricela as somebody who's slightly evil, then it takes on a whole new light. And it's hard to deal with the horror of that. Maybe I didn't want to see it.' "[87]

*Vir recte vivere, quis non*? Horace asked. Does anyone not wish to live well? For me, no contrast could be more significant than that between Howard Hawks and John Huston when old age became their judge. Hawks was a man of moderation. He smoked and drank in moderation and, but for a freak of fate, was in sufficiently good health to live many years longer than he did. Huston drank and, especially, he smoked with a compulsive excessiveness. Once in his late years, when he was about to be operated on, his doctor asked him how many cigars he smoked. All I had, he responded. When asked if he inhaled, he replied, all I can. He resented others who had not been debilitated by smoking as he had been, but then who with emphysema would chain-smoke cigars, inhaling deeply, other than someone with Huston's contempt for moderation? As Hawks lived his life, he became more and more sure of himself. As Huston aged, he became increasingly insecure. I suspect that the turn his life took in his final years was greatly influenced, at least when it came to his children, by the experience of writing his autobiography and reflecting on his own relationship with his father and what had happened to Pablo. Yet, when it came to a burial plot, Huston chose to rest next to his mother, and not next to his father. Hawks has been described as having had an insufferably high opinion of himself. However, Hawks never thought enough of himself and his life to write an autobiography. In none of his films would Hawks have been capable of the self-indulgent excess of Huston's UNDER THE VOLCANO, much less have welcomed a documentary being made about such a picture the way Huston did. Huston's mode of living found him—in Burgess Meredith's words—having " 'every operation known to man and then some' " and left him gasping at the end.[88] Hawks was virtually always in control, stoical and self-possessed. He did not merchandise himself as Huston did. Still, Huston knew what he was doing. He knew that if you set out to create a legend about yourself it might survive you. Hawks cared nothing about legends. He regarded himself as a professional and was pleased if others judged him strictly in these terms. " 'We all surrender, little by little, parts of our freedom,' " Huston said near the end, " 'and we're all hostages one way or another—mine is to this machine.' "[89] Hawks was able to retain his freedom and mobility. Above all, Hawks dealt with winners and winning, Huston with losers and losing. It is mostly a matter of predisposition and inclination whose philosophy a viewer will embrace. Film is a medium that can accommodate both.

# Orson Welles

## I

We did not meet Orson Welles in the same way we did the other filmmakers with whom I am concerned in this book, because I wanted to talk to him about his career or about someone with whom he had once worked. We got to know him because I wished to engage his services. I had appeared in all ten episodes of THEY WENT THAT-AWAY (PBS, 1970), the documentary series I produced and wrote on the history, growth, and development of the Western film. When the time came to adapt THE DETECTIVE IN HOLLYWOOD as a television documentary on the development of the detective film, I did not want to do it the same way. I wanted to have a narrator say what I could not show, a narrator who would be consonant with this most Gothic and baroque of literary genres, a narrator well known to the audience and who could speak with a natural authority. I wanted Orson Welles.

Of course there would be problems with this, some of which I could anticipate, some of which I could not. Dr. Donald S. Bryant, Executive Director of Oregon Educational and Public Broadcasting Service, had given the project a green light and placed in charge Tom Doggett, Director of Television and Radio Programming. OEPBS had production facilities in Portland and in Corvallis and since Tom was headquartered in Corvallis, a city in the center of the state, he wanted the videotaping of interviews to be conducted there in the KOAC-TV studios on the campus of Oregon State University. Fred Hutchison, whom Dr. Bryant had designated to be the director/cameraman on the project, disagreed from the outset on the use of videotape. He wanted to film the documentary in 16mm. As the producer/writer, I agreed with Fred but felt it was prudent at least to try it Tom's way. I contacted Edward Dmytryk, one of the Hollywood Ten who had directed entries in the Boston Blackie and Lone Wolf series as well as having worked as the cutter on the Bulldog Drummond pictures before he moved to RKO where he directed such classic detective films as MURDER, MY SWEET (RKO,1944). I had first met him in Hollywood when Vicki and I lunched with him at the Hollywood Brown Derby while I was researching the book and we had stayed in contact over the years. Presently he was teaching film direction at the University of Texas in Austin and agreed to make the trip to Corvallis.

Vicki and I met Eddie at Portland International Airport and were to transport him the ninety miles to KOAC in my Datsun B-210. Eddie sat in the passenger seat and Vicki sat in back, leaning forward to converse.

"Who are you planning on to host this thing?" Eddie asked, once we were under way.

"Orson Welles," I replied.

"You knew him, didn't you, when you were at RKO?" Vicki put in.

"Actually I saw him in New York for the first time, a year or two before he came to RKO. I wandered into a bar one night and the only person there was Orson Welles. He was sitting alone and drinking and muttering over and over so loud anyone could hear him, 'I'm the greatest actor in the world. I'm the greatest actor in the world.' Some years later I saw him again in New York. I was with N. Peter Rathvon, who was then president of RKO, and he saw Welles in the lobby of the St. Regis Hotel and went over to talk with him. When he came back, he was smiling. 'Welles has cost us a few million dollars,' he said, 'but he's such a charming bastard that, with a little push, I'd sign him again tomorrow.' "

"You know," I said, "even if we get Welles to agree to be the host, it'll still be ticklish. Among the people I want to have for on-camera interviews is John Houseman and they've been enemies for years. Houseman had the temerity once to tell me that no one has prevented Orson Welles from making one CITIZEN KANE after the other, except Orson Welles."

"What's wrong with that?" Eddie asked. "It's pretty much the truth. You know, when Orson first came to RKO, he had a wonderful contract. He could make exactly the film he wanted to make. But I've seen this sort of thing happen more than once. Welles got the support of every member of a very experienced crew to make CITIZEN KANE. He was particularly lucky to get Gregg Toland as his cameraman and Robert Wise as his head cutter. Then, when the film was finished and it proved a success, his head became inflated. From that point on, anyone offering him advice was considered a threat to his authority. When that happens, failure is assured."

"But there's no denying he made a great first picture," Vicki said.

"Certainly not," Eddie agreed. "There's no question that he freed motion pictures. Before CITIZEN KANE, where you set the lights was determined by where the microphone was placed. The sound mixer and the cameraman were always at odds. The sound mixer generally won until Orson Welles came along. With his radio background, he was able to cut the shackles to the microphones and photography was again as free as it had been during the final days of silent films."

Eddie pulled out his pipe and began filling it with tobacco.

"If you do get Welles to agree," he asked, "how are you going to get him to Corvallis?"

"By car," I answered.

"This one?"

"We drove Robert Altman around Palm Springs in this car when he was filming THREE WOMEN [20th-Fox, 1977]."

"Yes," Eddie said, nodding, "but Orson Welles is a lot bigger than Robert Altman."

"You've got a point," I conceded.

OEPBS had never undertaken so ambitious a venture as this documentary, which would have to be of network quality. Unfamiliar with the PBS pay scale for talent, Tom Doggett had asked me how much Dmytryk should be paid. Recently I had worked as the special film consultant on IMAGES OF INDIANS (PBS, 1980) produced by KCTS-TV in Seattle and I had called one of the producers there to find out what the going rate for talent was. I had been told between four and eight hundred dollars, information which I conveyed to Tom after he welcomed us at KOAC and Eddie was being lit for the cameras. Although I would be asking Dmytryk questions for the camera, I was not to be photographed. The narration of the host would be intercut with the interview segments and film clips during the final mix. On the way back to Portland, following the videotaping, Eddie was deeply disgruntled.

"It isn't a question of the money," he said sharply. "That isn't important. I would have been willing to do it for nothing. It was just the way it was put to me."

"Uh-oh," Vicki said.

Tom had handled the talent fee negotiations in private just before we departed.

"What were you told?" I asked.

"Well, Tom said that the scale of reimbursement at PBS was between four hundred and eight hundred dollars. Then he said I was going to be paid four hundred. It would have been all right, as I said, no matter what I was paid, it's just that I don't like knowing that I'm being paid absolutely bottom dollar."

By the time we reached Portland International Airport, the matter had been forgotten. However, I did discuss it later with Dr. Bryant who decided that, henceforth, he would take over as executive producer. He also acceded to Fred's desire that the documentary be filmed rather than videotaped. We were free to go on location to interview the talent rather than flying everyone to Oregon. This would mean interviewing Eddie again, this time on film and in Austin, but he would be paid again, and that meant he would be receiving top dollar!

Orson Welles never had an agent. From the time in the late 'Thirties when he was part of the Mercury Theater, L. Arnold Weissberger had been his attorney and he continued over the years to handle all of Orson's contracts. I had written to Weissberger initially on 11 April 1979, proposing just to interview Orson on *film noir*. In subsequent correspondence and telephone conversations, it turned out that Welles would be more interested in acting as the host than to be merely one of the many persons whose comments would be integrated into the final product. After Dr. Bryant had given us more mobility, I wrote to Orson at his home in Las Vegas, Nevada, where he lived with his third wife, Paola Mori. I had broken the three-hour documentary down into six half hour units. There was an outline for each episode and a completed script for that unit which was to deal with the emergence in fiction and on the screen of the private detective. This unit was to be filmed first, as a pilot, in order to attract additional financing. I sent Orson a copy of the book along with the outlines and the completed script. After giving the matter some thought, the documentary, as it was presently conceived, would follow the path blazed by IMAGES OF INDIANS in its six units. In addition to narration, film clips, and interview segments, there would also be some dramatizations of episodes from the history of the detective story. Also, to make it all work better, I toyed with the idea of using the first person camera, so that Orson would be heard but only seen in reflection or in silhouette. Robert Montgomery had used the technique in LADY IN THE LAKE (M-G-M, 1946). My missive was dated 6 March 1980. Orson's response was swift in coming.

"I enjoyed your book very much," he wrote, "but am rather worried about your plans for the TV shows. For starters, the subjective camera has to rule me out because I'm about to use it in a feature film. If I'm involved in anything like it as a performer on somebody else's television program, it's got to look as though I stole the idea, or at least borrowed it from my own movie. This would be doubly unfair since the original idea happens to be mine. I first came to Hollywood to make Conrad's 'Heart of Darkness' in which the principal actor (whose name, by the way, was Marlowe [sic]) would be played by the camera. This was ditched when we couldn't get the budget down to where RKO felt comfortable, but there was a lot of publicity about the first person singular use of the camera, and a lot of talk about it around Hollywood. Montgomery deserves credit for going ahead with the idea but not for thinking it up. . . . So now that I'm finally going to employ this device, I'm sure you'll appreciate my many-layered reluctance to participate in a sort of TV preview.

"Aside from that, I think you're too heavily [sic] ballasted with 'production.' 'Poe's life is briefly dramatized and he is shown writing the first detective story. . . .' Shots of the drinking and drugging? The child bride on her death-bed? Poe scratching away at his desk, and maybe, if PBS will spring for the cost, a tame raven flapping on the pallid bust of Pallas? All that kind of stuff looks good in a 'presentation,' and encourages the notion that 'production values' will 'open things up' and keep the show from being a 'mere' documentary. But I've never seen it help, in fact, it always hurts.

"Television is a story-teller's medium, and loses its impact when it ceases to be simple. You have film clips and still photographs plus a talking head. Add one more dimension: brief dramatizations, and the mixture is too rich. The *original* visual material and the originality of what you'll have to say about that material is what will make the programs; more is not better.

"I know what makes horse races, but I also know what will make me want to be a part of your project. Anyway, and in case I haven't managed to convince you—all best wishes for much success. Yours, Orson Welles."[1]

Raymond Chandler once complained that W. Somerset Maugham, in an essay on the detective story, consistently misspelled the name of Chandler's detective, Philip Marlowe, dropping the "e" whereas Conrad's character from "Heart of Darkness" and other stories spelled his name "Marlow." John Houseman, who knew and worked with Chandler at Paramount, would recount for the camera the symbiotic relationship he felt there existed between Conrad's character and Chandler's detective. At any rate, it seemed obvious to me, first, that Orson's objections had definite validity, and, second, that he very much wanted to be on camera. Jonathan Rosenbaum had run a part of the revised estimating script, the script that Welles had originally prepared for RKO on HEART OF DARK-NESS from which a budget could be made, in FILM COMMENT in 1972. In a commentary accompanying the script excerpt, Rosenbaum concluded that "an obvious drawback to the [first person singular] technique for Welles is that it would have restrained the use of the camera as an independent expressive device—a central aspect of his later style."[2] I wrote again to Orson on 17 March 1980, assuring him that I had no problem with his suggestions and that a representative from OEPBS would be in touch with Arnold Weissberger concerning contractual matters. I did not think one way or another, then, about whether, despite Rosenbaum's reservations and speculations about the first person singular technique, Orson actually intended to make a film or television program using it. Only later, when I got to know him better, did I realize that Orson always had a dozen projects going at once, most of which never got past the talking stage.

At the time, Orson was appearing regularly in television commercials for Paul Masson wines. In making these, Orson was working very closely with a man named Marty Roth, who had been the film editor on a documentary Orson had himself made for German television on his filming of OTHELLO (United Artists, 1955). Weissberger suggested that in the preliminary stages I should work matters out with Marty, such as scheduling a script conference with Orson in either Los Angeles, where Orson did own a home, or in Las Vegas, and decide on a production date for Orson's narration. There was also the matter of a suitable set. Roth introduced a whole new array of problems. First, there was Orson's weight. He currently weighed 420 pounds and he could not stand by himself unaided for more than five minutes. Welles had been asked to deliver the funeral oration for Darryl Zanuck and, unfortunately, those responsible for making the arrangements had located Orson alone on a stage with only a lectern in front of him. About seven minutes into his address, his entire body started to protest the strain and he began to tremble. At the end of ten minutes, the lectern was shaking and rocking as Orson struggled to remain standing. Therefore, Marty insisted during a visit with him at his Screen Images office in Hollywood, whatever set might be used, Orson would have to be photographed sitting. This did not suit Fred Hutchison at all. If Orson was to be on camera during his narration, he wanted for him at least to be able to move about among various props and settings.

"I'm telling you, it can't be done," Marty said. "Orson is too heavy to move around, much less to stand. But, then, what do you expect when he eats sixteen course lunches at Ma Maison every day that he's in town, to say nothing of what he eats and drinks for dinner?"

Marty did have a further suggestion. There was an iron chair on his premises that Orson occasionally used when making commercials. It was high enough that Orson could lean back on it and appear to be standing, if the camera were kept to a head and shoulders shot. This didn't sit particularly well with Fred either, since it quite definitely limited camera movement to zoom shots at a static pose. When Fred voiced his concern, Marty not only reaffirmed that that was indeed a necessary limitation but he predicted, with prescient accuracy, that Orson himself would demand all shots be confined to head and shoulders since he would not want any attention called to his girth.

There was one more hurdle: money. Paul Masson was paying Welles $300,000 a year for his commercials. What we could afford was $3,000 a half hour unit, or one percent of what Orson was getting from Paul Masson, $3,000 for what would amount to a full day's work. At this point, Orson himself entered the picture. He was sufficiently enamored of the project to agree to that salary. Had this been another time, say before the Paul Masson commercials, one of those periods during which Orson was looking for work because he needed it, accepting this kind of salary limitation would have been comprehensible as a necessary evil. To accept it now, however, when he did not need the work but because he believed in the project and, as it proved, liked the script sufficiently not to demand any significant changes, was indeed gratifying and reassuring. A script conference with Orson was arranged for 16 September 1980 and the projected filming date for the pilot program would be in the early part of November.

In retrospect I must confess that, even had the opportunity availed itself (and, really, it did), I should not have wanted to interview Orson for the camera or for publication. " 'I don't want *any* description of me to be accurate,' " Welles once said, " 'I want it to be flattering. I don't think people who have to sing for their supper ever like to be described truthfully—not in print anyway.' "[3] In a very basic way, Orson Welles was incapable of telling the truth about anything. Anything and everything he might say was said to achieve the effect he wanted, and the events of his life which he might call upon to achieve that effect would change from day to day according to what end he had in mind. His most fundamental motive as a conversationalist was to entertain. Perhaps, though, conversationalist is a misleading word in this context. Orson was incapable of conversation in the sense of an exchange of ideas. Kenneth Tynan, in preparing a magazine article on Welles, found that "on this occasion as on all previous ones, I automatically assumed the role of stooge."[4] Whenever Orson was with anyone, he invariably had to dominate the proceedings. Because he actually despised the truth, especially when it came to himself, he would contradict himself from one interview to another and, when questioned about something he had said, would almost automatically reverse his story and declare that the interviewer had misunderstood him or deliberately distorted what he had said.

When it came to the past, no two individuals could have been more opposite from each other than John Houseman and Orson Welles. When he felt the time for house-cleaning had come, Orson simply had boxed up all the scripts, correspondence, letters, proposals, and scrawled notes he had accumulated since the days of the Mercury Theater and sent them off to the University of Indiana where they are now housed in the Lilly Library. Houseman, on the other hand, had shelf upon shelf of letter boxes in his study, indexed by year and content and all in chronological order. He sorted out his past and respected each scrap of paper as a document to be weighed and balanced with the sharp scrutiny of an historian. If you were to ask Houseman a specific question about an event or person in the past, he would know right where to go to find any documentation he might have on it. For Orson, the past was fluid, something that was to be altered according to one's present mood and the demands of the occasion as he would perceive them. The result is, for the most part, that Orson's life became almost the same as that of the fictional Charles Foster Kane, the only difference being that most of the variations in perspective came originally from Orson himself. Houseman was quite definite that this aspect of CITIZEN KANE, the ambiguity of all the testimony about the man by those who knew him, had been Welles' conception of the film's internal story treatment from the beginning. The consequence, when it comes to Welles' life and career and above all to the many biographies about him, is that there is much that is disputed, much that is inaccurate, and a series of profiles dependent upon which of his many versions happened to appeal to a particular writer. Tynan, in the article he wrote on Welles, pointed out that Welles "is also alleged to have improvised Harry Lime's famous observation [in THE THIRD MAN (Eagle-Lion, 1950)] that after centuries of democracy the Swiss have produced nothing more inspiring than the cuckoo clock; falsely attributed to Orson, the line was actually written by Graham Greene."[5] Conversely, Frank Brady in CITIZEN WELLES (1989) wrote that "Welles has claimed that the line was not entirely original on his part but stolen from, or based on, a fragment of an old Hungarian play."[6] What actually happened would seem to be this. The line is to be found in Graham Greene's book but was not in the original screenplay. Welles had read the book and so proposed the line be added to his dialogue. Henceforth, Sir Carol Reed, who apparently had not read the novel or had forgotten the line by the time he came to direct the film version, publicly attributed the genesis of the line to Orson and Orson, on one occasion when asked about it, fabricated the tale of the "old Hungarian play."

Only when it came to certain anecdotes about his past did Orson manufacture a fantasy about an actual event and then stick to it, making only minor embellishments. One of the problems I foresaw working with him on the *film noir* unit had to do with THE LADY FROM SHANGHAI (Columbia, 1948). Orson had his own version about how he came to direct this film with Rita Hayworth, his estranged wife at the time. Welles claimed that he had run out of money financing his stage version of Jules Verne's AROUND THE WORLD and that, in desperation, he telephoned Harry Cohn, head of production at Columbia Pictures, and got Cohn to agree to send him $25,000 as an advance against his payment to direct a film for the studio starring Rita Hayworth and based on a thriller by Sherwood King titled IF I DIE BEFORE I WAKE (1938). Cohn, happy at the chance to get Welles to direct and to have a picture for Rita, agreed and wired Welles the money. Orson's various embellishments of this story would alter the amount of money Cohn sent him or he would laugh at the episode because supposedly he had not so much as read the book, merely seen the cover of a paperback edition. In reality, Welles was craftier than that. He knew that Harry Cohn would be dubious in the extreme about hiring him to direct any picture, much less one with Rita Hayworth who was the one star under contract to Columbia.

The first thing that put me onto the truth of the matter was an article by John Kobal on Rita Hayworth's career which appeared in FOCUS ON FILM (Summer, 1972) in which he claimed that Hayworth was originally slated to play the *femme fatale* in DEAD RECKONING (Columbia, 1946) opposite Humphrey Bogart but that, in the end, she turned down the role in favor of playing opposite Orson in THE LADY FROM SHANGHAI. Lizabeth Scott replaced Hayworth in DEAD RECKONING. Since the latter film had long been of great interest to me, the matter led to the one and only occasion on which I spoke to Rita. My question was: why did she turn down DEAD RECKONING? Her answer was that Orson had telephoned her and spoken highly of a story he had read which would be a natural for both of them to do together. Rita had always believed in Orson as a film director and agreed to support him in his efforts to get Harry Cohn to finance the picture. This is certainly consistent with a cable dated 26 April 1946 from Richard Wilson, then Orson's business manager, to Lolita Hebert at the Mercury office in Hollywood instructing her to " 'try desperately to get IF I DIE BEFORE I WAKE to Harry Cohn immediately. Perhaps Franchot Tone has book. Tell him we need it for picture deal.' "[7] William Castle, then under exclusive contract to Columbia as a director, supplied another piece of the puzzle in his autobiography published in 1976. It was he who first came across IF I DIE BEFORE I WAKE and saw in it the potential for an outstanding thriller. Harry Cohn was out of the office and so Castle prepared a ten-page treatment and took it to Columbia's story editor who turned it down. In his frustration, he sent a copy of his treatment to Welles, who had suggested to Castle during the period prior to AROUND THE WORLD in a telephone conversation that they should do a picture together, with Welles producing and Castle directing, or the other way around. In his letter to Welles accompanying the treatment, Castle informed Orson that "if he was serious about working with me, I'd like him to consider IF I DIE BEFORE I WAKE."[8] Orson wrote back to Castle, about a month later, and stated his enthusiasm for the story. "I have been searching for an idea for a film," he remarked, "but none presented itself until IF I SHOULD DIE and I could play the lead and Rita Hayworth could play the girl. I won't present it to anybody without your O.K. The script should be written immediately. Can you start working on it nights?"[9]

Rita's contract with Columbia was up for renewal. She had only one more picture to make on her old contract. " 'Honey, I knew it was a classic while we were making it,' " Rita told John Kobal when he was preparing his full-scale biography of her. " 'Harry didn't think so though.' "[10] Castle, according to his account, was rather shocked when Cohn called him to his office and informed him that, although he might have anyone in Hollywood, Welles had chosen Castle to be the producer on the picture! Here Castle had wanted to direct the film himself and had gone to Orson hoping to win his support and through him perhaps to enlist Rita, and now Orson had closed the deal with himself as the male lead and the director as well as scenarist. As for Welles' version, which he retold once again for a British documentary on him and his films, speaking to the camera from his home in Las Vegas, there it was all again, right down to the lurid paperback cover. It was televised for the first time in the United States under the title, A LIFE ON FILM, on TNT in 1990, long after Welles himself was dead. No one thought to check into the matter as Charles Higham did when preparing ORSON WELLES: THE RISE AND FALL OF AN AMER-ICAN GENIUS (1985). Higham found that "no paperback edition existed until 1962."[11]

Since THE LADY FROM SHANGHAI and DEAD RECKONING would be two of the *films noirs* I intended to focus upon in my own documentary, how could I have Orson narrate facts so in conflict with his own cherished version? My choices, it would seem, were only two: either skip THE LADY FROM SHANGHAI, which Orson certainly wanted to include, or dispense with Orson as the narrator, at least for that unit, which would damage the continuity seriously, maybe even decisively. Nor were contradictions such as this, or the problem of including John Houseman among those interviewed, the only problems with Orson once we got down to work. In the unit we were going to do first, Raymond Chandler was one of the authors whose work would be highlighted. James Naremore in THE MAGIC WORLD OF ORSON WELLES (1978) had found a parallel in Chandler's world-view and that of Welles in a film such as TOUCH OF EVIL (Universal, 1958), commenting that the words and imagery given to Marlene Dietrich in her final comment in the film matched "almost exactly the elegiac sentiments in the last paragraph of Raymond Chandler's THE BIG SLEEP [1939]. . . . "[12] I thought Orson would be pleased with the comparison, but such was not the case. He insisted that he had never read Chandler's fiction and knew nothing about him other than what I had written for him to say as the narrator. Dashiell Hammett was another matter.

"I met Hammett on only one occasion," Orson said. "I was in a bar in Philadelphia, trying to raise money for a play. I have spent most of my life trying to raise money for one thing or another. And I almost had a commitment from the backer when Hammett walks over and, without even introducing himself, says to the backer, 'Don't trust this guy. You'll lose your shirt.' " As he told it, Orson couldn't help laughing. "And that," he added, "was that."

When on camera, Orson insisted that he be shot from a low angle upwards, framing his head and shoulders. He was very often photographed in this manner in films and so a viewer had the impression of height, whereas he was not a tall man. He walked with a cane and said that he was suffering from gout, which with a smile he attributed to an excess of rich sauces. A few years hence, he was even less mobile and was usually transported in an oversized wheelchair. He customarily dressed in black, especially for the camera, because it had a "slimming" effect. Much of his weight he carried in his stomach which was a concentrated protuberance, and in his thighs which were so thick he could no longer really bend his legs. He seldom went anywhere without a box of Havana cigars. Often he would only smoke half a cigar before flinging it away and lighting another.

The script was to be transferred to giant "idiot cards" which had to be made by the same typographer Bob Hope customarily used. When I praised his delivery, Orson was quick to comment that Margaret Carrington had been his voice teacher.

"She was also John Barrymore's voice teacher," he remarked with unmistakable pride.

In this he was correct. Margaret Carrington was John Huston's aunt and she had worked many long hours with Barrymore prior to his Broadway appearances in RICHARD III and HAMLET. In Orson's case, however, she had only worked with him for five weeks. Yet it was sufficient for him to learn from her the art of breathing when speaking. Breath control became exceedingly important for Orson as the years passed and his weight increased since he would generally be out of breath from the mere exertion of standing up or standing in one place.

Of course he would not be caught dead drinking a Paul Masson wine. In presenting a radio adaptation of Conrad's "Heart of Darkness" on the Mercury Theater of the Air in the early days, Welles had played both Marlow and the murderous Kurtz. When at the end of the show the time came for Orson to give his usual farewell to the listening audience, he had a special announcement to make: in four weeks' time the program would have a sponsor, Campbell's Soups. Even then his overt hatred of the money-making aspect of show business and his anti-commercialism were so strong that he made this announcement in the degraded voice of Kurtz! When we discreetly inquired at Ma Maison, which was on Melrose Avenue and which Orson frequented because he loved the food and he was allowed to dine with his small dog in a private booth, as to what wine we should serve Orson on the set, it came as no surprise that he preferred a French champagne which retailed at $60 a bottle.

The impression that stole upon me was that Orson Welles' greatest illusion was not to be found in CITIZEN KANE or in any of the string of failed "masterpieces" or incomplete films which followed it, but rather in the design and perpetuation of the legend of Orson Welles, a brilliant genius who could have continued to make one magnificent film after the other if only he had been given a chance. Over the years, publishers had been after Orson to write his memoirs, one going so far as to send him an advance only for Welles to return it when, after much time, nothing whatsoever was forthcoming. Film directors Peter Bogdanovich and Henry Jaglom each spent years in recording exhaustive interviews with Welles, only for nothing to come of it. The reason, I suspect, is that what Orson had to tell them simply could not be used as the basis for anything since what he said was either preposterous albeit unverifiable or incontrovertibly false. When a biography finally did appear that presented Orson Welles' perspective on his life and did so at the expense of any relationship to factual realities, it was Barbara Leaming's ORSON WELLES: A BIOGRAPHY (1985). In Leaming Orson found precisely the person he needed as a biographer: one who combined a fundamental gullibility with a fanatical determination to attribute to Orson's every statement the reverence and devotion usually reserved for sacred texts. As DAILY VARIETY put it in a review of her biography, "even though Leaming's book was not officially authorized, Welles could not have cooperated with it more than he did and Leaming must have been so anxious not to cross her friend in any way that what she has written cannot qualify on any level as a serious biography. It is inconceivable that anyone writing a life of Welles would not speak with John Houseman, Lea Padovani, Peter Bogdanovich, or Gary Graver, but Leaming has done so; astoundingly, Padovani, one of Welles' great passions, and Bogdanovich, a loyal disciple throughout the 1970s, are not even mentioned. Unfairly, Leaming instantly adopts Welles' startlingly poisonous attitude toward Houseman, and almost every line she writes about the director's partner at the Mercury is infused with contempt. . . . It is ironic that it is Leaming, or rather, Welles himself, who proves the biggest gossip around. Welles seems intent upon proclaiming himself Hollywood's greatest ladies' man of the 1940s . . . dropping tantalizing—and entirely unverifiable—tidbits about dalliances with Judy Garland, Marilyn Monroe, and many others. Welles also freely airs the flip side of the Don Juan syndrome, stating that 'queens' were chasing him practically from the time he learned to walk. . . . Leaming makes Welles appear as obsessed with the subject of repressed homosexuality as he is with achieved heterosexuality. . . . In the end, then, Leaming has delivered Welles as perhaps he would have liked the public to see him, but her work must be taken with a grain of salt as large as the book itself due to her refusal to do a biographer's real job."[13] Leaming's book is dominated by Orson's voice, narrating everything, even directing her how to write the book and how to characterize him, right down to the difficulty she had getting in contact with him, since even though Arnold Weissberger was dead by the time Leaming came to write her book anyone wanting to contact Welles was still instructed to write to the attorney! It would also be through Leaming that Welles, who had used and abused and humiliated Rita Hayworth so much while he was married to her, would be able—from the grave—to humiliate, reduce, attempt to distort her memory, to assure that only his wretched caricature of her would survive, much in the manner of Ahknaton who sought to destroy his father's soul in eternity by defacing every existing image of him as he had been in life. Yet, that is to anticipate.

" 'Orson *seduces* you in a marvelous way,' " Charlton Heston said of him. " 'You know he's one of the most charming men in the world, if it's important to him to be charming. . . . If it's important to him to enlist your support and cooperation, he is as charming a man as I have ever seen.' "[14] Yet, for all his charm, Orson could also be harshly rude upon occasion. I recall having to telephone him to set up a meeting. He instructed me to call him at home at two o'clock in the afternoon, not a minute before, not a minute after, but precisely at two. We did not synchronize our watches but I must have been within seconds of the exact time. When he picked up the 'phone, no sooner had I identified myself than he rasped, "Not now," and slammed down the receiver. That was the other side of his personality. When Orson did get back to me, it was as if nothing had occurred at all; he was utterly beguiling and totally winning.

It was Charles Higham, first in THE FILMS OF ORSON WELLES (1970) and then at even greater length in his full-scale biography of Welles, who diagnosed in Welles a "fear of completion" which supposedly explained his long string of failed enterprises. Leaming, no doubt at Welles' instigation, quoted him at length rationalizing each one of these failures, intruding herself only to support each assertion that Welles made, even ignoring or misrepresenting facts when necessary. For example, she blamed Welles' failure to complete THE DEEP on the death of the film's leading man, Laurence Harvey, in 1973 when principal photography had actually been fully accomplished three years prior to his death. William Johnson in his essay, "Orson Welles: Of Time and Loss" (1967), put his finger on the single greatest pitfall of virtually all Welles criticism: "With a filmmaker as vigorous and idiosyncratic as Welles, it's temptingly easy to find some justification for nearly everything he does. [MR.] ARKADIN [Talbot, 1962] is based on an exciting and fruitful idea; some of the sequences in the film are excellent; many others are exciting or fascinating—and so I could go on, justifying the film piece by piece to the conclusion that it is all good. But here I'd be falling into the same trap as those who deny the originality of KANE. . . . It's the total effect that counts, and . . . the total effect of ARKADIN falls far short of its piecemeal felicities."[15]

Orson complained on numerous occasions that critics tended to use each new film project as an excuse to review him and his failures rather than the film itself. In large measure, Orson had only himself to blame. He personalized everything. He was the most self-obsessed man I have ever known and, whether it was his past or his future that might be preoccupying him at the moment, nothing else existed except his own feelings, his own sensations, and he warmed to you, or he did not, depending on the extent to which you would allow yourself to be involved by him in the only subject that was ultimately ever of interest to him: the legendary Orson Welles.

## II

Today there are streets and houses in Kenosha, Wisconsin as quaint and provincial in a Midwestern fashion as most of them were on 6 May 1915 when George Orson Welles was born in his parents' home at 463 Park Avenue, the younger son by a decade of Richard and Beatrice Welles. Orson's older brother, Richard, Jr., would suffer from mental problems all his life and would spend many years in and out of institutions. As a child, Orson was unruly, peevish, fawned over by his parents and from the time he was eighteen months old by Dr. Maurice Bernstein, an orthopedist who had a yen for art and Orson's mother and who, at one point in his life, would live in a *ménage à trois* with Chicago Opera singer, Edith Mason, and her former husband, conductor Giorgio Polacco. As a youngster Orson would spend vacations with Bernstein at Edith Mason's home on Lake Shore Drive in Chicago. In his later years, Orson, too, would maintain his own *ménage à trois*, one somewhat more stable than Bernstein's which lasted only two years before Mason divorced him and remarried Polacco.

Years before this, when Orson was six, his parents separated. Orson's father had become despondent over the way in which Dr. Bernstein had insinuated himself into the lives of his wife and youngest son and he had taken to drinking heavily and traveling alone. Beatrice established a salon in Chicago and entertained extensively, inviting people associated in one way or another with the arts. Her young son was permitted to participate in these social gatherings provided he was amusing, charming, and entertaining. Leaming perceived that this would prove "a vital factor in shaping what would become the classic Welles persona,"[16] but did not recognize that in having to be constantly interesting to highly cultivated adults the path Orson chose was to let his fantasies predominate. Reality was something that required perpetual embellishment if it were to attract and retain the attention of others.

Beatrice fell ill. When Orson was eight, she had a birthday party for just the two of them in her Superior Street apartment in Chicago. " . . . Beatrice spoke to him of her approaching end, quoting Shakespeare, her shining eyes appearing dark by the light of the candles on his birthday cake. Eyes that had been green were now almost black with suffering; her flesh was yellow and flabby with sickness. She told Orson to blow out all the candles on the cake, and as he did so, for there was no other light in the room, it became utterly dark. In this charged and symbolic way, she told him what death was. . . . "[17] Death would become one of the major themes in Orson's films, maybe *the* major theme.

Dr. Bernstein and Richard Welles vied with each other in their efforts to be a guardian to the young Orson. When Orson was eleven, his father sent him to the Todd School at Woodstock, Illinois. This was in 1926. Three years later, on 6 October 1929, when Dr. Bernstein married Edith Mason, the couple on their wedding night took Orson to Kenosha to put flowers on Beatrice's grave. Orson traveled with his father and vacationed with him, but he was deeply troubled by the latter's hopeless alcoholism, finally rejecting him. Richard Welles died on 28 December 1930. He left the bulk of his estate, $37,000, to Orson to be held in trust for him until he was twenty-five. Bernstein was designated as the executor and this amount was later to be adjusted downwards to $20,000. John Houseman was absolutely certain that Richard Welles' death was a suicide, but he based this on what Orson had told him, and already at the Todd School Orson was notorious for the fanciful stories he would tell about his aunts, one of whom he declared was actively engaged in witchcraft. Dr. Bernstein, who signed the death certificate, claimed death was due to chronic myocarditis and chronic nephritis resulting in cardiac failure. Houseman should have known better. However, he was neither the first nor the last who would be seduced by the power of Orson's fantasies and the totally persuasive way in which he could make them seem real.

At the Todd School, Roger Hill, better known as Skipper, the son of the school's head master, became Orson's new mentor and Roger and his wife, Hortense, were the closest instance the young Welles would encounter of a successful marital relationship. Only many years later would Orson confess openly and publicly to Roger Hill, " 'I'm the boy you could have had.' "[18] With Roger Hill's support, Orson became involved in staging plays at the school and eventually the two of them would prepare acting editions of Shakespeare plays. Orson was convinced that he wanted most to be an actor. Upon graduation, Orson chose to take a trip to Ireland during which he would decide whether or not he would follow Hill's advice and enroll at Harvard. Although he was only sixteen, he managed to wangle employment from the two partners who operated the Gate, a theatrical company in Dublin, Hilton Edwards and Micheal Mac-Liammoir. However short-lived this association, and however stormy, for many years afterwards Edwards and MacLiammoir would become involved in various projects with Welles. The first such project occurred once Orson had returned to the United States and had found himself confined to minor roles in a thirty-four state tour with Kit Cornell's company. It was in preparation for this tour that Welles studied briefly with Margaret Carrington. Orson wanted to direct himself and to be the leading player and that wasn't going to happen for years, if ever, were he to satisfy himself with merely working up through the ranks in established theatrical companies. Just as he would later say that the only really good roles he got in films were those he wrote for himself, so already in 1934 he got Roger Hill to agree to sponsor a summer theatre festival at the Todd School. Three plays were to be staged. Edwards and MacLiammoir were invited to direct one apiece; Orson would direct the third. It was during this summer session that Orson met and fell in love with Virginia Nicholson, who came from a socially prominent Chicago family. Also, in this heady atmosphere, Orson with Virginia and William Vance produced, directed, and starred in a short four-minute film titled THE HEARTS OF AGE.

Orson went to New York that fall to appear in a production of ROMEO AND JULIET, in the role of Tybalt, and Virginia followed him. They married in November. " 'We really only married in order to live together,' " Welles later told Leaming. " 'It wasn't taken very seriously by either of us.' "[19] In a script Welles wrote for an autobiographical film to be called THE CRADLE WILL ROCK, Orson depicted Virginia as a young woman intent on escaping her family, with exalted ambitions for a stage career, a zealous, single-minded, hard person who used him as a convenient way to get out of town. Not only does this image of Virginia stand in bold contradiction to that supplied by all her other contemporaries, including Houseman who felt the couple was deeply in love with each other, but it overlooks who did the using. Frank Brady, in preparing his biography of Welles, did something Leaming (who even misspells Virginia's surname) of course did not bother to do: he talked to her. "Virginia was forced to pawn a matching fur scarf and muff," Brady wrote, "and then, one by one, virtually all of her best dresses, simply to pay the rent."[20]

Orson, of course, wanted a stage career, but his greatest initial success was on the radio, where his fabulous voice lent itself perfectly to commercials, voice-overs, and even dramatic parts. In fact, it is highly questionable if he would have got anywhere on the stage as a director and a leading player, at least as early as he did, had John Houseman not seen him perform. Houseman approached Welles and subsequently involved him in the Federal Theatre Project. Even with all his work on radio, Orson was living hand to mouth, continually borrowing money from Roger Hill to make ends meet after Virginia's wardrobe had been exhausted. It was Orson's association with Houseman which gave him his first real chance to show his significant talent as a director and as an actor, which brought him national notoriety and critical praise, and which raised the level of awareness among radio executives so that Orson was able to advance himself rapidly in that medium as well. " 'Houseman started out being in love with me,' " Welles told Leaming, " 'and then turned to hate.' "[21]

In interviewing Houseman for the camera, I told him beforehand that I had Orson Welles in mind as my host/narrator. In what Houseman had to say about Welles, there was objective evaluation, as between one person and another who had worked together for a number of years and who knew each other's strengths and weaknesses. If Houseman had any concern, it was not that Orson would be the host, but rather what Orson's reaction might be when he found out that Houseman would be among those whose comments were to be included. In this Marty Roth concurred and even went so far as to caution against discussing the matter with Weissberger since, in that case, it would be certain to get back to Orson. In 1935, Orson had hired Augusta Weissberger, Arnold's sister, as his secretary, and the next year he engaged Arnold to represent him in forcing Dr.

Bernstein to turn over what was left of the trust his father had left him. The two had worked hand in hand ever since.

The idea for making the all-black MACBETH a voodoo version, based on the character and career of Henri Christoph, king of Haiti, who set up his court in the mountains, was Virginia's, and the production became Orson's first un-qualified stage success. Orson got on splendidly with Jack Carter, the black cast as Macbeth, and the two would leave the theatre every night after midnight, drinking and whoring together in brothels until dawn. In adapting Shakespeare's play, Welles telescoped the action down to a single act and Macbeth, rather than having a flaw in his character which would motivate his downfall, was depicted instead as a man driven by Fate and a victim of black magic. It was Hecate's curse which doomed Macbeth, rather than his ambition. This theme would continue to obsess Welles later in his films, never really to be resolved, whether it was a man's temperament which determined his failure, or some force outside of himself which victimized him.

Welles and Houseman finally ran amok with the WPA Theatre Project when they decided to stage Marc Blitzstein's play with music, THE CRADLE WILL ROCK, which was a blatant condemnation of the evils of capitalism and suffi-ciently inflammatory to cause a stir among conservatives in Washington who did not propose to see tax dollars spent in support of a property that was subversive to what they considered the American way of life. However, in addition to MACBETH, the WPA financing had also permitted Welles and Houseman to stage a brilliant version of Christopher Marlowe's DOCTOR FAUSTUS in which Welles could put to effective and dramatic use his radio experience in producing the most chilling sound effects, such as the bell tolling, summoning Faustus to his doom. What emerged from the ruins was a wholly independent theatrical company, managed jointly by Houseman and Welles, named the Mercury Theater after the Roman god of fleetness and daring as well as THE AMERICAN MER-CURY magazine. Its first offering, a modern dress version of JULIUS CAESAR in which the Roman characters were dressed in the garb of Fascists and made more sinister by a thrillingly dramatic use of creative lighting, proved an out-standing critical and popular success. It secured the Mercury Theater as a viable company and it led, the next year, 1938, not only to four more stage productions but also to the advent on radio of the Mercury Theater of the Air, presenting classic stories adapted as radio dramas, hosted by Orson Welles who would also star in one or more of the leading roles.

On radio, the Mercury productions were titled "First Person Singular" and it was as an April Fool's prank in 1938 that the company broadcast its adaptation of H.G. Wells' WAR OF THE WORLDS. It caused a sensational panic and made the name of Orson Welles a household word. It is the only one of the CBS radio broadcasts that really took on a life of its own, being issued subse-quently on phonograph recordings and cassette tapes. In the early 'Fifties Welles even edited a volume titled INTERPLANETARY STORIES published by Dell Books, although he may have had no more to do with the actual selection of the stories than Gene Autry did with the two Dell paperback collections of Western stories supposedly "edited" by him. Thanks to an elaborate contract with the network which Arnold Weissberger had drafted, Welles could not be held personally liable for any damages which might result as a consequence of the broadcasts so he was able to enjoy the notoriety of the public furor without being troubled by any lawsuits.

Welles had put together a good group to assemble these weekly broadcasts, both in terms of players and in terms of personnel, with John Houseman acting as the supervising editor and the young Howard Koch, who was responsible for the adaptation of WAR OF THE WORLDS among other notable broadcasts, as one of the principal writers. In his later years, Orson tended to be more generous in assigning credit to those who worked with him, but at the time he tended to be quite the opposite, claiming for a time that it was *he* who had adapted the Wells story.

In the meantime, the Mercury theatrical productions were in constant financial trouble due to Orson's tendency to spend money freely without keeping to a strict budget. His second "film" was a silent sequence, running approximately forty minutes, which he produced and directed to be integrated into a stage performance of the play TOO MUCH JOHNSON by William Gillette. In the event, he could not use the footage because it turned out that Paramount Pictures owned the film rights. However, Orson had spent so much money and so much time on the film, that the play was under-rehearsed and had a disappointing box office.

The Mercury Theater probably would have vanished from the scene even if Orson had not signed the generous motion picture contract he did with RKO Radio Pictures. In fact, Mercury was in such severe straits that to stage FIVE KINGS, Welles' compendium of Shakespeare historical plays, was possible only because of a co-financing deal with the Theatre Guild. Mercury put in $5,000 toward the estimated budget of $40,000, with Welles and Houseman putting up an additional $5,000 in their services, respectively, as director and producer; the rest of the money would come from the Theatre Guild. There were two stars in this hybrid: Welles as Falstaff and the complicated revolving stage that he had had designed for the production. However, the play proved a failure in large part because of Welles' intemperate dissipation. He was now drinking between one or two bottles of whiskey or brandy a night and his sexual affairs, which had begun at the time of MACBETH, had by this time become an obsession. He had a penchant for prostitutes, as much now as would later also be the case when he was in Brazil or later, in Hollywood, when married to Rita Hayworth. While FIVE KINGS was in its death throes, Welles purportedly fell in love with two women, both ballerinas, Tilly Losch, an exotic dancer from Austria fourteen years his senior, and Vera Zorina. In neither case was he able to advance these relationships beyond the platonic stage, but the experience prompted him to announce to Virginia that he wanted a divorce.

Virginia, as Charles Higham aptly put it, "was beautiful, stylish, gifted, with a first-class mind—and perhaps in his heart of hearts Welles would have preferred a mindless and submissive wife whose domesticity and lack of competitiveness would allow him to express himself without contradiction at every turn of the conversation.''[22] Virginia confided to Frank Brady that the problem with the marriage was that '' 'it was always another woman coming between us.' ''[23] They were legally separated in December, 1939, five years after they had married.

Leaming, relying only on what Welles had to tell her about the RKO contract, claimed that he was to receive $100,000 plus 20% of the profits on his first picture after RKO had recouped $500,000 and $125,000 plus 25% of the profits on his second picture after a similar sum had been recouped. Frank Brady, who troubled himself to read the actual contract, found that Welles was guaranteed the sum of $35,000 as producer and $30,000 as actor plus 20% of the net profits of the first film and, for the second, he was to receive a slightly smaller advance—$25,000 as producer and $35,000 as actor—but more of the net profits: 25% after the picture broke even. After the FIVE KINGS fiasco, Orson definitely needed the money and so he moved the headquarters of Mercury to the West Coast. At first he could not get Campbell's Soups to agree to let him broadcast his weekly programs from Los Angeles so for a time he was obliged to commute between the two cities on a weekly basis. Eventually, he was permitted to broadcast from Los Angeles, but by then the quality had fallen off considerably since Welles seemed to have lost interest. The program was finally cancelled in March, 1940. Diana Bourbon, the Campbell's representative on the program's staff, said of Welles: '' 'Orson sings a siren song to anybody that will listen. . . . Don't be hypnotized by him. He's dangerous.' ''[24] This may seem unduly biased, but it is to be remembered that he had just cost the Theatre Guild $30,000 and was about to cost RKO close to two million dollars.

Many years later, Pauline Kael would stir up quite a controversy when she claimed that Herman J. Mankiewicz, who worked on the screenplay of CITIZEN KANE along with Houseman and Welles, should be credited as the sole author of the film. It was a senseless debate. The Academy had long ago resolved any possible misunderstanding of the authorship when it determined to award an Oscar to both Orson Welles *and* Herman J. Mankiewicz for Best Screenplay. Other major contributions came from Gregg Toland, who offered his services to Welles to be the cinematographer on the picture and who had been working on deep-focus photography for years, and Bernard Herrmann, who composed the score and who had been working with Orson as music director of the Mercury radio broadcasts, as well as Robert Wise, who became chief film editor. It was the combination of all of these talents, along with the skilled RKO crew, and the cast, made up of Orson's own people who had never before been in front of a camera, that combined to produce a motion picture masterpiece. Welles' unique contributions, of course, are not to be taken lightly. First, it was he and he alone who assembled this highly talented group. Second, he brought with him the use of superrealistic sound which he had pioneered in radio drama. Finally, and most importantly, there is the highly stylized theatricalism of the entire production, the vitality of the acting and the energetic direction which makes every set-up and every shot memorable and exciting. However, Houseman did have a point in RUN-THROUGH (1972), when he observed that it was not a denigration of Welles' ability to recognize that throughout his career "he . . . functioned most effectively and created most freely when he was supported by a strong text. . . . Writing was a particularly sensitive region of Orson's ego. It was a form of creativity in which he had never excelled but in which he refused to concede defeat. His ability to push a dramatic situation far beyond its normal level of tension made him a great director but an inferior dramatist. His story sense was erratic and disorganized; whenever he strayed outside the solid structure of someone else's work, he ended in formless confusion."[25] Orson conceded that the idea for Rosebud as the "key" to CITIZEN KANE, which turns out actually to be an ambiguous symbol at best, came from Mankiewicz. To the rather naive Leaming, Welles alleged that Rosebud was the name William Randolph Hearst used when referring to Marion Davies' genitalia. Leaming repeats this allegation without even raising the question of how Welles, or Mankiewicz for that matter, could possibly have been privy to such information.

Welles had proposed both Conrad's "Heart of Darkness" and other potential properties before the idea for CITIZEN KANE was chosen as his first film. In those days, it was customary for a cinematographer to learn what his next assignment would be a few days before production was set to begin. It was George J. Schaefer, then head of RKO and the man responsible for bringing Welles to Hollywood on a contract that more or less gave him total control over the films he was to make, who backed Orson in such unconventional strategies as keeping Gregg Toland on the payroll for a half a year, during the time of preparation as well as during the actual shooting. Toland found in Welles one wholly sympathetic with his view that photography should fit the story. Toland's experiments with photography and lighting were, in a way, variations on techniques developed by the Weimar cinema, with the camera shooting directly into lights, or in which characters were isolated in light and surrounded by darkness, and in a John Ford film such as THE LONG VOYAGE HOME (United Artists, 1940), on which Toland had worked, he had used ceilings made of muslin to provide the settings with a claustrophobic effect. " . . . Before actual shooting began," Toland recalled, "everything had been planned with full realization of what the camera could bring to the audience. We arranged our action so as to avoid direct cuts, to permit panning or dollying from one angle to another whenever that type of camera action fitted the continuity. By way of example, scenes which conventionally would require a shift from close-up to full shot were planned so that the action would take place simultaneously in extreme foreground and extreme background."[26]

Because all of the actors were new to the camera, no one could tell Orson he didn't know what he was doing, or it couldn't be done the way he wanted to do it. By the same token, he was freed from tradition and could permit his dramatic and staging fancies full rein. Beyond this, both director and fellow actors were comfortable because they had been working together now for years. Welles wanted a film that had fluid visual images and, while he took no interest in the cutting of the film, he did supervise the sound track at every stage. Unquestionably, one of the most influential aspects of CITIZEN KANE was Welles' novel use of sound, something which would influence other filmmakers at the time and others in the future, including Roman Polanski who was most impressed with this aspect of the picture when he first saw it at the Lodz Film School many, many years after its release.

CITIZEN KANE was over two years in progress and with the cancellation of his radio program Orson was in constant need of money. He made Arnold Weissberger his financial advisor and Weissberger was perpetually after him to cut down on his personal extravagances which were costing him $800 a week. While CITIZEN KANE was being filmed, Orson would disappear for a few days without telling anyone, neither studio executives nor his closest associates, where he was going. Sometimes he would sneak away for a rendezvous with Dolores Del Rio. He had finally succeeded in having an affair with a glamorous older woman. Sometimes production had to shut down because Orson had a radio engagement. One such was his appearance on the "Rudy Vallee Show" where he was teamed for the microphone with his idol, John Barrymore. The two men sang a duet and concluded with a scene from JULIUS CAESAR with Welles as Brutus and Barrymore as Cassius. "When Barrymore spoke the line, 'Must I endure all this?' in a sound barely above a whisper, it was as if he were commenting on his own life situation," Frank Brady wrote, "recognizing the reduction of his talent to that of buffoon having to play on a comedy show. Brutus' last line of the sketch also seemed to be an awareness of the veiled lament by Barrymore, when he takes Cassius' hand 'and my heart, too.' "[27] The way Welles behaved was typical of a man who regarded himself as the center of his universe and everyone and everything must wait upon his whim. Mark Robson, one of the RKO editors on CITIZEN KANE, saw in this instead Orson's personal need to fail. CITIZEN KANE as a motion picture ultimately did not fail because all of those working on the picture were fanatically intent on seeing to it that it did not fail.

" 'I'm still suffering ... ,' " Kenneth Tynan quoted Welles as saying, " 'from the traumatic effect of being forbidden to do what all my friends were doing.' "[28] By this Welles meant, of course, his having been passed over by the draft. However, the truth of the matter was exactly the reverse. Welles was constantly after Weissberger to do everything he could in a legal way to keep Orson from being drafted. Orson had had his first daughter, Christopher Welles, on 28 March 1938 with Virginia Welles. Although at the time of his legal separation from Virginia he had promised to pay child support, none had been forthcoming. Virginia continued to press him for what he owed and was constantly summoning him to court. She did so even after she married a second time, to screenwriter Charles Lederer. Obviously, her conduct was not that of a woman who considered her marriage to Welles as merely a ticket out of town.

Nonetheless, because he could not claim support of Christopher as a reason for deferral, Weissberger and Schaefer worked out a plan whereby Welles received a 2-B deferment based on the fact that his continued employment by RKO assured seven members of the Mercury team a livelihood. After Welles' second film for RKO was almost completed, he managed to negotiate himself a deal, with RKO's backing, to go to Brazil to make a good will documentary, something about which I shall have more to say presently. For now, just let it be said that he probably would have remained in Brazil whoring and drinking and eating at RKO's expense while producing nothing that was useable indefinitely had the studio not shut off his funds. Shortly after Welles returned to the States and was fired by RKO, he was reclassified 1-A. Welles was terrified. He was convinced that he was temperamentally incapable of military life with the discipline that would be required of him, to say nothing of the privileged existence he now had come to expect and the career he was making for himself. He finally managed to get a 4-F on medical grounds, quite possibly with the collusion of Dr. Maurice Bernstein who had followed him to the West Coast and had set up a practice in Beverly Hills. The reasons provided for his medical deferment were " 'chronic myo[car]ditis and original syndrome arthritis, bronchial asthma, high fever, and inverted flat feet,' "[29] to which were added angina and bifida of the spine.[30] Ignoring them all save the angina and chronic myocarditis, it must be concluded that, although Welles' heart was presumably in this condition when he was not yet thirty, he would go on for more than forty years, most of them spent carrying avoirdupois of between three and four hundred pounds while living under the perpetual strain of excessive eating, drinking, and stress, all of which would make his life span seem, assuming these early diagnoses to be accurate, no less miraculous than even the most sensational feats attributed to the lives of certain medieval saints.

The release of CITIZEN KANE was held up by the controversy surrounding the picture, most of it generated by people around William Randolph Hearst who insisted that Charles Foster Kane was based on Hearst. Louis B. Mayer, a close friend of Hearst's, even went so far as to offer to buy the negative from RKO at cost. In due course, RKO came to think that all of this publicity would only encourage a strong box office. When the film was given its world première at the Palace in New York on 1 May 1941, Orson Welles experienced his finest hour. Times Square was jammed with people and a four-story neon sign announcing the film flashed above the throng. Welles attended with Dolores Del Rio. This was indeed his big moment. He could not realize that there would never be another like it. Predictably, he had denied that Kane had anything to do with Hearst, and then, when the Hearst newspapers refused to run advertisements for the film or to review it, he blamed Hearst for its problems at the box office. CITIZEN KANE lost $154,000 once all the hoopla was over.

Welles went to work on his next film, THE MAGNIFICENT AMBERSONS (RKO, 1942), but without a number of people who had helped make CITIZEN KANE at least a *succès d'estimate*. After numerous quarrels, he and Houseman parted for good. After the contretemps over sharing a writing credit with Herman J. Mankiewicz, Welles alone was credited for the screenplay based on Booth Tarkington's novel. Gregg Toland had another assignment so he was replaced as chief cinematographer by Stanley Cortez, who by comparison worked very slowly and was often wont to impress anyone who would listen with his knowledge of the history of art. Also, for the first and last time in his career, Orson Welles would produce a film that was not a personal, one-man show. He gave himself no role. The plot is concerned with the decay of a family in the face of industrial progress, a family in a small town much as Kenosha was when Orson was growing up.

Welles' consuming notion was to have the camera move in long, uninterrupted shots through the Amberson house, creating a symphonic effect. Doubtless François Truffaut was correct when he surmised that "in shooting CITIZEN KANE Orson Welles was more anxious about the medium, while in AMBERSONS he seems to have been excited primarily by the characters."[31] The uninterrupted shots, the symphonic camera movements are always secondary in this film; the focus is the characters and what happens to them. What is perhaps most disconcerting, as well as indicative of future Welles films, are the lapses, the slipshod quality of some scenes. Welles had begun the actual filming of CITIZEN KANE even before the script was completely approved, shooting what he called test shots, but actually staging for the camera the scene in the projection room where a newsreel summarizing Kane's life is run for a group of reporters. Joseph Cotten and other members of the cast, who should not have been in this scene, are clearly discernible. In this case, however, Welles had an excuse. He had none in THE MAGNIFICENT AMBERSONS when he came to shoot a montage sequence of the years passing prior to George Minafer's birth and we see George, fully grown, with his mother in a boat, his mother looking no older than in the rest of the film. Moreover, Agnes Moorehead, cast as Fanny Minafer in the film, is also to be seen among a group of townspeople commenting on the Minafers. Welles evidently did not care, or opined that no one would notice.

At about the same time, Welles also acted as producer and prepared a screenplay in collaboration with Joseph Cotten for JOURNEY INTO FEAR (RKO, 1942), based on a novel by Eric Ambler and to be directed by someone else. Welles was to star as Colonel Haki, with Joseph Cotten as the young protagonist, Howard Graham, and Dolores Del Rio as the slut, Josette. Both of these films were left in various stages of incompleteness, THE MAGNIFICENT AMBERSONS in need of final editing and lacking most of the scenes of JOURNEY INTO FEAR, because Welles became involved in the documentary to be filmed on location in Brazil titled IT'S ALL TRUE. His motives were complex. Since the project had been proposed by Ourival Fontes, the Brazilian minister of propaganda and popular culture, and had the sanction of the U.S. Department of State in the person of Nelson Rockefeller, who was a major stockholder in RKO, Welles saw in the opportunity a sure way to retain his 2-B deferment since, following the completion of THE MAGNIFICENT AMBERSONS, he could no longer claim to be responsible for the livelihood of the Mercury players who had worked in his two films; they would be going their own ways. He had no regular radio series. RKO would obviously wait to see how AMBERSONS did at the box office before signing a new production agreement with him and, possibly, Welles realized that AMBERSONS might not do well at all upon release. The proposal was one of a kind and another one would not likely be coming along. Finally, leaving the States meant he could break off his affair with Dolores Del Rio who wanted them to marry. Rockefeller committed the U.S. Government to back the film if RKO would agree to pay up to $300,000 of its cost which was estimated at a million dollars. Welles departed for Rio de Janeiro after convincing George Schaefer and Robert Wise that he could supervise the final cut of THE MAGNIFICENT AMBERSONS from abroad if he was provided with a movieola and leaving JOURNEY INTO FEAR in Norman Foster's hands, who had been pulled off a documentary he was filming in Mexico, assuring Foster that any additional scenes he might need with Welles in his character Welles could shoot in Brazil.

In all, Orson spent six months in Brazil during which time he exposed thousands upon thousands of feet of Technicolor film in takes that appeared disjointed and repetitive and ultimately unuseable. Most of his research was done in nightclubs and boudoirs and his frequent absences from shooting locations were blamed on massive hangovers. About half way through the project, for which there was no script, Orson decided that he would focus on the blacks and other social outcasts and he shot quite a bit of footage of those living at the poverty level before it became manifest to those funding the project that this approach was antithetical to the propagandistic intent of the documentary. By 7 April 1942 Tom Petty of RKO, in Brazil with Welles, wrote to an executive at RKO that " 'if all the film we've shot was laid end to end, it would reach to the States, and there would be enough left over to serve as a marker for the Equator. As for film story, only God and Orson know; Orson doesn't remember.' "[32]

In order to control JOURNEY INTO FEAR, Orson withheld certain revised segments from the screenplay so that often Norman Foster did not know why he was filming certain scenes or even what the picture was about since, prior to leaving, Orson had instructed him not to bother with the book since the screenplay didn't follow it and Orson was holding onto the revised segments only because they needed more work. THE MAGNIFICENT AMBERSONS was cut initially according to Orson's indications but, when it was previewed, the audience laughed at scenes intended to be painfully serious and many walked out on the film. There was a war on, a war Orson had so far been able to avoid, but movie audiences were looking for escape and laughter. What Orson gave them instead was a story about death, decaying lives and families, a spinster's sexual frustration, and the impudent cruelty of a young boy, a film of shadows and dark scenes, scarcely reassuring to American family values since it was intended to be an attack on the hypocrisy of those values. The studio had the film recut. New scenes were filmed and interpolated. The story was given a happy ending.

Yet, THE MAGNIFICENT AMBERSONS could not be saved. After its release, it lost $674,000. Far from sticking to the original guarantee of $300,000, Welles had also been able to persuade Schaefer to advance him more than three times that sum only for Orson to return to Hollywood with absolutely nothing to show for the money. Orson promised to do what he could with JOURNEY INTO FEAR, but it, too, upon release was a box-office bomb, with a loss of $195,000.

The legend of Orson Welles, as Orson created it, claimed that here was a filmmaking genius whose creativity and natural talent were defused by the studio system and almost destroyed, as the pictures he made were with the exception of CITIZEN KANE almost destroyed. It is instructive to contrast, therefore, Welles' early career in Hollywood with Alfred Hitchcock, who came to Hollywood at about the same time Orson did, and John Huston, who began directing films at about the same time as Orson. Alfred Hitchcock's REBECCA (United Artists, 1940) had a profit of $700,000. It was followed by FOREIGN CORRESPONDENT (United Artists, 1940) which lost $55,000, MR. AND MRS. SMITH (RKO, 1941) which had a profit of $73,000, and SUSPICION (RKO, 1941) which had a profit of $425,000. Huston's first four theatrical films comprise an even more spectacular record: THE MALTESE FALCON (Warner's, 1941) with a profit of $845,000, IN THIS OUR LIFE (Warner's, 1942) with a profit of $1,282,500, ACROSS THE PACIFIC (Warner's, 1942) which was completed by Vincent Sherman had a profit of $1,105,250, and THE TREASURE OF THE SIERRA MADRE (Warner's, 1948) which had a profit of $397,250. George J. Schaefer was replaced by N. Peter Rathvon who, in his comment to Edward Dmytryk, put Welles' cost to RKO at two million dollars. Is it any wonder that Orson had difficulty in finding another directing assignment in Hollywood, especially one which would give him total control over the picture? What is more, no picture that Orson Welles ever directed showed a profit upon its release. The experience at RKO would only be repeated again and again in picture after picture.

This is not to say that Orson was not a highly talented and innovative filmmaker. That can never be denied him. Rather, he was a tremendously gifted filmmaker who, to function properly, effectively, *and* profitably, would have had to have someone else in charge to oversee what he did, and that is something, after his parting with John Houseman, he would never again tolerate. Welles, of course, was not prepared to admit publicly his failure in Brazil. He took the role of Edward Rochester in JANE EYRE (20th-Fox, 1944) directed by Robert Stevenson and used part of the money he was paid to develop some of the IT'S ALL TRUE footage at a laboratory, proposing that he would write a script, cut the film himself, and sell the finished product to a studio other than RKO. Rathvon saw in this a way for the studio to get back the profit percentages that Welles, by contract, held on CITIZEN KANE and THE MAGNIFICENT AMBERSONS and so, in exchange for an additional loan of $195,500 and access to the footage, Welles signed a promissory note whereby if he did not complete the project and meet a specified schedule of payments his percentages would be forfeited as well as all right, title, and interest in the Brazilian footage. Even though his backing of Orson Welles had cost him his job, George J. Schaefer thought he might at least have Welles' sympathy. Instead, Orson made no effort ever to contact him. He was no longer important to Orson so he ceased to matter. Orson tried to interest Darryl F. Zanuck in purchasing IT'S ALL TRUE, but the deal turned sour, perhaps as a consequence of Zanuck's refusal to allow Orson the title of associate producer on JANE EYRE in recognition of his creative influence on the picture whereas, in reality, his egotism and clashes with the director had hindered rather than helped in making the film. Just before the time for Orson to do anything to salvage IT'S ALL TRUE ran out, cameraman Russell Metty offered to arrange all the available footage for potential backers to see. Welles was to be on hand to provide a coherent spoken narrative for the film segments. The screening was set up, the backers arrived, but Orson never showed up. The footage went back to RKO. By that time, probably, saving the footage and his reputation were no longer important to Orson because he had moved on to better opportunities. He had married Rita Hayworth, had access to her money, and through her influence and financial backing was able to direct two more films.

## III

Margarita Cansino was born on 17 October 1918, the oldest child and only daugther of Eduardo Cansino and Volga *née* Haworth. At the time Eduardo was still touring the country, teamed with his sister, Elisa, as "The Dancing Cansinos," bringing to audiences a highly Americanized version of the dances of their native Spain. It wasn't until a year and a half after Rita's birth, when Eduardo, Junior, was born, that the elder Eduardo decided the time had come to settle down. Volga had been with the Ziegfeld Follies when he met her but soon after the marriage she gave up her career to handle Eduardo's business affairs and the bookings as well as accommodations. Eduardo bought a home in Jackson Heights, Queens, where the family lived, although he continued to tour. Another son, Vernon, was born. Eduardo hoped to keep the family more closely together by involving the children in his dancing act, but of the three only Rita showed any aptitude for dancing. This does not mean she liked dancing, only that she had an aptitude for it and was sufficiently acquiescent that the choice was made for her. Eduardo and Elisa danced in a Warner Bros. Vitaphone short in 1926 and Eduardo could see tremendous possibilities in the coming of sound to the movies. He moved to Los Angeles with his family, opened a dance school, and free-lanced for work in films, while Elisa more or less retired from the stage.

What interfered with Eduardo's plans was the fall of the stock market and the onset of the Great Depression. Eduardo lost what he had been able to save and his dance school fell on hard times. In his frustration, he proposed to revive the idea of a dancing act, this time with Rita as his partner. There were a number of clubs at the Mexican border where it was easy to get bookings, Agua Caliente prominently among them, eighteen miles below San Diego, especially at the Jockey Club there which was frequented by motion picture executives and screen personalities. Rita told John Kobal, to date her only reliable biographer, what her schedule was like in those days when she was only fifteen years old. " 'When I was dancing with my father in Agua Caliente,' " she said, " 'I'd have a tutor between shows. I did four shows a day; at noon and at 2P.M. After that I went back to school for three hours in Santa Monica. Then I'd drive back to the club, which was about three hours away and do the ten o'clock and half eleven shows. By the time it was over it was 12:30, we'd get home around 3A.M. and then I'd have to get up and rehearse. That was the routine. I'd also be taking lessons with my father between rehearsals in the morning and the next show. It was quite a heavy schedule.' " [33]

James Hill, who would become Rita's fifth husband, was a youth of fifteen when he encountered Rita for the first time on a trip to Agua Caliente with his parents. He saw Rita and her father dance and he overheard a conversation between them where Eduardo was demanding to know from Rita if a boy she had seen had spoken to her and she replied, " 'No, father. . . . ' Then his tone got even colder and angrier as they moved off. 'I've told you *never* to call me father down here. . . . I have also told you never to leave the club without me. I don't want to have to discipline you, so make sure it doesn't happen again.' " [34] Eduardo's reluctance to bill Rita as his daughter had to do mostly with his desire to keep men away from her; instead, he gave the impression that they were married, although Volga always accompanied them and stayed with Rita when the time came to go back and forth to school. In a conversation with Hill, after they were married, Hill asked Rita what she thought about when she thought of her father. " 'Someone stern. A disciplinarian,' " she said. " 'And your mother?' 'She was the opposite,' Rita said. 'Very gentle.' " [35]

Rita's break into motion pictures came about as a result of her appearances at the Jockey Club. After fleeting interest was shown in her by others, she was actually put under contract by the Fox Film Corporation where, billed as Rita Cansino, she appeared in a dance sequence in DANTE'S INFERNO (Fox, 1935) and as a mysterious Egyptian house servant in CHARLIE CHAN IN EGYPT (Fox, 1935). When Fox merged with Twentieth Century, Darryl F. Zanuck, the new head of production, decided to drop Rita from the contract roster. However, while at Fox, Rita and her father had made the acquaintance of Edward Judson, a middle-aged second-hand auto salesman who posed as an agent for Texas oil money seeking investment opportunities. Judson persuaded Eduardo that he should be permitted to take over managing Rita's career. He said he knew his way around the studios and he believed that he could make Rita into a star. Judson proved as good as his word when he landed Rita the part of a bootlegger in MEET NERO WOLFE (Columbia, 1936), her first film after leaving Fox, and followed this up with getting her parts as the heroine in two Tom Keene Westerns produced by Nat Levine under the Crescent Pictures brand name.

Levine had founded Mascot Pictures in 1927 and by 1935 it had been merged to form Republic Pictures with Levine as the head of production. Judson knew Levine from having sold him an automobile. They might have been only Westerns, but Rita was playing the female lead. She also appeared opposite George O'Brien in a Western at RKO. Even years later, O'Brien would recall Rita's movements before the camera as poetry in motion. In Westerns such as HIT THE SADDLE (Republic, 1937) with the Three Mesquiteers and TROUBLE IN TEXAS (Grand National, 1937) with Tex Ritter, Rita might be paid only $200 a picture, but she had usually second billing and exposure on all the one-sheets and advertising. Judson also insisted on taking Rita, very fashionably dressed, to all the best night spots so that she was seen by the right people. When, in 1937, Judson negotiated a new contract for Rita at Columbia Pictures, he proposed that they marry. Four months after the contract was signed, they eloped. " 'My mother never could take that marriage,' " Vernon Cansino, Rita's youngest brother, told John Kobal. " 'Judson was as old as my father and Mom could not stand him. It seemed to me that he used to come over to the house just to torment Mom because he knew she didn't like him. She even slapped him on several occasions in my presence. It made for a very bad relationship while Rita was married. After Rita left him, things eased up. 'Course Rita was in love with him and when she was married to him she had to take his side. But that's Rita, she's very loyal. Once she makes a decision she really sticks it out, no matter what the guy's like or what people say.' "[36]

It was Judson who decided that Rita had to change her image if she wanted to get away from playing Spanish roles. He convinced Harry Cohn at Columbia to help finance an expensive electrolysis process which would move back Rita's hairline and then her hair was dyed red.

Jack Cole, who choreographed Rita's pictures at Columbia, told John Kobal in a conversation published in PEOPLE WILL TALK (1985) that " 'Rita did not have a good figure. She had beautiful breasts, *beautiful* arms, the most beautiful hands in the world and shoulders . . . if you wanted to do a portrait of a Spanish lady, she was it. The close-up would be extraordinarily beautiful, and she was always this young woman who was more beautiful than she photographed. . . . And the hair was always a problem because it was real Spanish-growing hair, baby, and it had to be done practically every other day. The day it was done, it was red. The day after, it had just the slight mark of black which photographed marvelously, made it very strong. By the third day the black was *there* and it was a real Spanish lady. . . . There were problems in dressing her. No ass and no waist: her legs went right into her rib cage. The legs were perfectly good legs, but not extraordinary. It was just the top of her that was very beautiful.' "[37]

Rita's big break at Columbia came when Howard Hawks cast her as the second female lead in ONLY ANGELS HAVE WINGS (Columbia, 1939). When Kobal was researching his biography of Rita, he made the mistake of telling her on the telephone that he was on his way to Palm Springs to talk to Hawks. Rita was rather upset by this, wondering why talking to Hawks was even necessary, and finally confessing that she didn't like him very much. Kobal went anyway. In reproducing his entire talk with Hawks in PEOPLE WILL TALK, Kobal noted that "Hawks' voice, as so often, trails off with his pipe smoke; he doesn't finish the sentence, but comes back in the middle of another one."[38] Vicki, in transcribing her notes, closed up Howard's sentences to give them coherence. Kobal used a different technique. " 'Rita . . . at her best, was slightly . . . unreal,' " Hawks told Kobal. " 'She belonged in a kind of . . . fairy-tale story. Because she was so beautiful . . . and because that's what people liked to see her as. . . . But then, I couldn't ask for things that were beyond her. That just doesn't happen to be my way.' "[39]

It was Rita's role in ONLY ANGELS HAVE WINGS which convinced Harry Cohn that he had a potential star and, Hawks would later claim, it was he who told Cohn how to promote her. Yet, Cohn gloried in being vulgar, and he always treated Rita poorly. He would leave the door to his private water closet, near his desk, open when he urinated while discussing business with Rita. James Hill recalled the first time he saw Cohn and Rita interact with each other. By then, Rita was at the end, rather than only at the beginning, of her long contract with Columbia. Cohn wanted Rita to come to his desert home for the weekend. " 'So get your goddamn diaphragm and get your ass in my car,' " he told her. "I thought for sure she was going to break then, because of the way her lower lip trembled," Hill reflected. But, instead, she said, softly, for Rita almost always spoke softly, on her breath as it were, " 'I'm busy, Mr. Cohn.' "[40]

If Rita had married Judson to escape the stern discipline of her father, she found Judson an even more demanding master. It was Judson who insisted that Eduardo and Volga provide him with an accounting of all of Rita's earnings prior to their marriage and he insisted that Eduardo pay back whatever Rita had coming. It was Judson who spent most of Rita's contract salary on clothes for her and nights out on the town, so she would be seen and photographed, while at home they lived only modestly because there was only so much money. Whereas Eduardo had pretended to be married to Rita to keep potential suitors away and forestall any possibility of dalliance, Judson encouraged Rita to sleep with producers and motion picture executives to help along her career. In this Rita resisted. She would not do it. She refused to sleep with Harry Cohn, no matter what his importunities, no matter even when Judson bowed out at the last minute and let her go boating with Cohn without his being along. In all her relations with men, Rita's loyalty would extend well beyond what anyone would expect, but then a point would be reached where enough was enough. She finally reached that point with Judson. He threatened to disfigure her if she went through with a divorce. He kept all her money and sued her for more. He did his best to damage her image in the press and to endanger her viability as a star. Rita stayed the course, with only her mother offering her sympathy and support.

Rita's divorce from Judson occurred in 1941, just as her career was on the upswing, especially because of films she made on loan-out from Columbia for

Warner Bros. and Twentieth Century-Fox. By 1943, she was not only Columbia Pictures' only major star, she was perhaps the most popular female star on the screen. Kobal, in his biography, correctly assessed what about her screen persona made her so attractive: " . . . she was desirable, yet could be a sex symbol for servicemen without offending the women back home; she possessed an air of romance that made it possible for her to exude those elements of mystery, formerly the stock-in-trade of foreign *femmes fatales*, without reminding the wives and sweethearts of the sort of women their men might find overseas; furthermore, she was an American classic, a heady mixture that enthralled the world."[41]

Orson Welles told Leaming that he decided to marry Rita Hayworth, whom he did not know except from her photographs, when he was returning to the United States from Brazil. In the event, he met her at a dinner party at Joseph Cotten's home. Rita, beyond her beauty, had a truly sweet nature. She was quiet. She was generous. Co-workers at Columbia would recall how she would stick up for members of the cast or crew, even though she let herself be trampled on by the same people. She had about her a purity and an innocence. Being quiet, she was also an avid listener, and always interested in learning something new. These qualities, particularly that of being a good listener, appealed to Welles. Rita, for her part, regarded him as a genius, and a great filmmaker. Yet, all of this notwithstanding, as Dorothy Dumont would tell James Hill about Rita, " 'I've stood in for her, and I've worked on sets with her. The voice may be soft, but there's steel underneath.' "[42] Hill himself reflected that "for such a slight and feminine person, she had pure steel running down her spine."[43] That was a quality her father, and Judson, and Orson Welles as well, became aware of only later, only when their relationship with Rita had reached that point where enough was enough. Ultimately, even Harry Cohn found Rita impervious. It was this aspect of Rita's personality which, I suspect, Welles came to resent and to hate, so much so that he exaggerated it even to caricature in the character he created for her to play in THE LADY FROM SHANGHAI.

In the middle of filming COVER GIRL (Columbia, 1944), on 7 September 1943, Rita and Orson were married at Santa Monica Superior Court. Orson had long ago set his sights to marry a glamorous movie star, beginning with Dolores Del Rio, and now he had done it. He also spent her money. The home the couple bought at 136 South Carmelina Drive was purchased in her name and most of the money that went into furnishing it was hers. To bolster his financial position, Orson borrowed $30,000 from Rita at no interest and spent it freely pursuing his own projects. No offers to direct motion pictures were forthcoming, although there were numerous radio appearances and film roles which came Orson's way. He even managed to convince THE NEW YORK POST to hire him as a syndicated columnist. Orson told Leaming that he was intent on a political career at this time, with ambitions to become an U.S. Senator, either from California or Wisconsin. This is highly improbable in a real sense, although he may have entertained such fantasies about himself as a potential candidate. He used his column, for which he hired researchers to garner information for him, to attack the sense of moral superiority among Americans, totally hypocritical in view of racism, the tendency to support dictators, the American desire for economic domination, and the persistence of reactionary tendencies. He also lambasted what he called a "phony" fear of Communism. The column would have died a natural death, so out of touch was it with what Americans in any numbers were thinking and feeling, were it not that, once again, Orson sabotaged himself, falling behind in his deadlines and finally missing them altogether. Six months after it started, the column was canceled. As a matter of fact, Orson found in Rita perhaps his most avid pupil. She read the books he told her to read. She listened to him for hours as he told her what he thought and believed and, as was her nature, for the time she, too, thought and believed as he did. Otherwise, in public and in private, he treated her with an utter lack of courtesy and even friends had to remark on his brusque way with her and asked Rita why she put up with it.

Welles hated Judson because he was still after Rita for money and he began, once Rita became pregnant, to hate himself. More than once, passing through the living room, Shifra Haran (Welles' secretary who had a bit part in JOURNEY INTO FEAR and who would stay on as Rita's secretary after Rita was separated from Orson) would hear him grumble, " 'That's the couch where I lost control.' "[44] Orson busied himself giving public lectures and stumping for Franklin D. Roosevelt's re-election, so much so that he was seldom home. Rita hoped that the child would bring them closer together. Instead, it drove Orson farther away from her. Orson was in New York on 25 January 1945 when Volga Cansino died. Orson's customary way of dealing with Rita when they traveled together and he had a meeting with other men to talk business was to tell her to go have her hair done. Often, she would throw a fit upon being ignored when she returned, and Orson would have to go off with her to quiet her. Now she was in Los Angeles and heart-broken. She wanted Orson with her. He refused to return. Only a month or so before, on 17 December 1944, their daughter Rebecca had been born, and Orson had been quite indifferent. Now Rita needed him, even more. Lee Bowman who was working with Rita at the time filming TONIGHT AND EVERY NIGHT (Columbia, 1945) recalled how, once, Rita " 'just grabbed me and held me in her arms for some time, and cried. I don't think that deep emotion, showing it in public, was something that came easily to her. No doubt but her mother's death shook her very hard.' "[45] Leaming, taking her usual gentle posture toward Welles, did comment that even Orson "had to admit that he had made a dreadful mistake in failing to fly to Los Angeles for Volga's funeral."[46]

Rita's father took the loss equally hard. By this time his dance studio was again well established and he was making money. They had been married for thirty years. "Sometime later," John Kobal wrote, "he sold the house on Sterne Drive where they had lived since first arriving in town, but which was now too full of memories. He moved in with his daughter until he found a small apartment suitable for himself on South Vermont Avenue, adjoining his new dance studio. At Rita's he slept in the library, but moved to his own place after a few weeks since Orson's habit of working late nights, with friends and secretaries coming and going at all hours, gave him little rest."[47]

William Goetz was managing production at Twentieth Century-Fox while Zanuck was involved with helping the war effort. When Zanuck increasingly took charge once again, Goetz convinced his father-in-law, Louis B. Mayer, to finance him in setting up his own production company. International Pictures was the result. Sam Spiegel, who wanted to produce films, formed an alliance with Goetz and had John Huston and Anthony Veiller develop the script for THE STRANGER (International-RKO, 1946). Spiegel's idea originally was for Huston to direct the film but Huston had a contract with Warner Bros. which would not allow that. Spiegel wanted Orson Welles to play the Nazi in the film who changes his identity and hides in a small American town. Welles proposed that he should direct the film. Spiegel was uncertain. He had got to know Welles rather intimately. He regularly had parties at his home the chief attraction of which was a constant bevy of prostitutes and Welles, although supposedly happily married to Rita, seemed to prefer their company and sexual favors. Goetz had a talk with Welles. He would pay him $50,000 to act in and direct THE STRANGER, provided Welles would sign an agreement whereby, if he did not complete the film, he would pay back the studio's investment from any income he would make over $50,000 a year and provided he would have Rita co-sign the agreement to pay back the money in the case that Welles was for any reason unable to pay. Rita's friends at Columbia were telling her about the way Orson was carrying on with other women. Shifra Haran, commenting on Welles' attitude toward Rebecca, said " 'I don't really think Mr. Welles ever paid any attention to her—just not in the cards,' "[48] an attitude that was not too surprising considering how he had reacted to Rita's pregnancy. Somehow Orson must have persuaded Rita that the source of his difficulties in the marriage derived from his inability to find a film to direct, or perhaps Rita came to this conclusion on her own. At any rate, she signed the agreement and Welles went ahead with THE STRANGER. Goetz promised Orson additionally that, if he could bring in the film on schedule and within its budget, he would be willing to sign him to a four-picture deal. It may have been a ploy to hedge Goetz' bet.

THE STRANGER, François Truffaut observed, was "very clearly influenced by Hitchcock's SHADOW OF A DOUBT. The same realistic and everyday portrait of a small town in America; the same succession of peaceful, familiar, and familial scenes presented in contrast to the central character's terrible secret; the same construction on the principle of the vise closing in."[49] The direction is disappointing to those who prefer Welles' flamboyance, but, then, he was too closely watched to attempt any novelties. Many of Welles' critics, of course, try to defend the film, but even Frank Brady, who purposely skirts anything controversial, personal, or derogatory in the spirit of de mortuis nil nisi bonum, had to mention the others who found Welles' "acting 'boyishly bad,' 'weak,' and suggested that 'Director Welles might have hinted to actor Welles once or twice that he was inclined to overdo the glaring eyes and the other bogeyman tricks.' ''[50]

Orson's frustration by this time was probably at an all time high. He was getting vitamin injections daily on the set of THE STRANGER because he was on a severe diet. His weight had been hovering above two hundred and fifty and he actually became slimmer than he had ever been since the very early days in New York with Virginia and slimmer than he would ever be again. He resented all authority other than his own, and he certainly resented the close scrutiny he was receiving from Goetz and Spiegel. He resented the power Harry Cohn exerted over Rita. Cohn had opposed their relationship from the beginning, forcing Rita to withdraw from her appearances with Orson in the magic act in which he sawed her in half in a show he had put on for servicemen prior to their marriage. Cohn continued to keep a tight rein on Rita because he wanted to protect her earning capacity and perhaps that earning capacity Orson resented most of all. Once THE STRANGER was completed and it did not appear that the film would make any money, Goetz backed away from his four-picture deal.

Orson managed to interest Mike Todd in financing a stage production of Jules Verne's AROUND THE WORLD, only for Todd to back out. Orson decided to finance the play himself, putting into it the money he had received from RKO to salvage the IT'S ALL TRUE footage, the money he had got from Goetz, the money he got from Alexander Korda on the basis of his being back at work again in films intended to develop new properties, and what money he could borrow from Rita. His overwhelming desire to make AROUND THE WORLD a one-man show found him revamping the script and creating so many roles for himself that he was on stage as much as Arthur Margetson who was cast in the lead as Phileas Fogg. The play was dying a bitter death when he got Rita to support him in his efforts to direct THE LADY FROM SHANGHAI for Columbia. His financial losses were such on the play, which he charged off as personal expenses and which the IRS then refused to recognize as business expenses, that for the next two decades he would owe a tremendous amount in back taxes that he often could not, and when he could, did not want to pay.

Rita, who was by this time estranged from Welles and preparing to divorce him, was evidently won back by him, in what may have been a forlorn hope that he would become the loving husband and father she wanted him to be. There was talk of a reconciliation when the company went on location in Mexico, but Welles used the opportunity to humiliate Rita once again. He had placed a young starlet named Barbara Laage under a personal contract and had even hinted publicly that he wanted her to star in the film, rather than Rita. When Laage showed up in Mexico with Orson, Rita must have known for certain that the marriage was over. She persisted, however, in making the film because, as she herself would later say, she felt it would become a classic. Among Orson's resentments, surely, was the success Rita had had internationally in GILDA (Columbia, 1946). To create the *femme fatale*, the lady with a spine of steel, the image of her he wanted to project, he began by chopping off her hair and having it dyed blonde.

Vinicius de Moraes, a Brazilian poet whom Orson had first met when in Rio, was currently at Columbia studying production techniques and, incidentally, had a chance to watch Welles and Rita working together. " 'They called each other "Momma" and "Poppa," ' " he later recalled. " 'It sounded very artificial. With Orson she was just able to put a word in here and there because he would hold the reins of the conversation. She seemed to be impressed by him. He would direct her very little, he was mainly concerned with other people on the set. When you saw them together, on the set or socially, you had the impression that she was effacing herself for him. Orson wasn't very delicate about women, you know. He once told me that women were things that you had to use.' "[51] Not only is this misogyny typical of Welles' treatment of Rita's character in THE LADY FROM SHANGHAI, but it is typical of the roles assigned generally by Orson to women in his films. He would later tell Maurice Bessy, a French critic and friend until he started writing about him, that women are stupid, that he had known some who were less stupid than others, but he assured him they are all stupid. Bessy concluded that in THE LADY FROM SHANGHAI Orson was settling his account with Rita. In this, I concur, but he also made one of the most notable films of his career and one of the finest examples of *film noir*.

As early as 1955, Raymond Borde and Etienne Chaumeton concluded in PANORAMA DU FILM NOIR AMÉRICAIN(1941–1953) that "Orson Welles resumed in a certain sense the expressionistic tradition of [DAS CABINET DES DR.] CALIGARI [German, 1920]. The setting is always, by contrast or by analogy, in rapport with the psychological situations."[52] Moreover, building on his techniques from CITIZEN KANE, in this film Welles made sound as expressionistic as the visual style. "Throughout the film," Charles Higham and Joel Greenberg observed in HOLLYWOOD IN THE FORTIES (1968), "the feral shrieks and neurotic whispers or giggles of the cast, the sneezes, coughs, and chatter of the trial scene extras, give the listener the impression of being trapped in a cage full of animals and birds."[53] Rita, cast as Elsa, while married to Arthur Bannister, a brilliant trial lawyer (played by Everett Sloane who, of course, had appeared as Bernstein in CITIZEN KANE, the character based on Dr. Maurice Bernstein), also dallies with Welles as Michael O'Hara, an aspiring author who is also an experienced navigator. O'Hara is embroiled in murder and mayhem and, at the end, it turns out that Elsa was behind all the wrongdoing. Elsa and Bannister shoot each other to death in a hall of mirrors in a deserted fun house. In the original ending to the script, O'Hara was supposed to stand over Elsa's dead body, waiting for the police to arrive while, in the background, an approaching siren is heard. Instead, Welles rewrote the ending and the two have a brief conversation, Elsa lying on the floor, O'Hara standing over her.

Elsa (dying): You can fight, but what good is that?

O'Hara: You mean we can't win?

Elsa: No, we can't win. Goodbye. Give my love to . . .

O'Hara: We can't lose, either. Only if we quit.

Elsa: And you're not going to do that.

O'Hara: Not again.

Walking away from her and from everything, O'Hara believes that his innocence will be proven. "But innocence is a funny word. Stupid's more like it. The only way to stay out of trouble is to grow old, so I guess I'll concentrate on that. Maybe I'll live so long that I'll forget her—maybe I'll die trying."[54]

James Naremore felt that Welles was "a major contributor to the misogynistic tone of 'Forties melodrama. In [THE LADY FROM SHANGHAI] . . . he gives a bitter farewell to his wife and portrays her as a woman 'kept' by rich businessmen. Later he suggested MONSIEUR VERDOUX to Chaplin, and after THE LADY FROM SHANGHAI he turned to Lady Macbeth."[55] André Bazin, citing critic Jacques Doniol-Valcroze, agreed that "the average American moviegoer couldn't forgive Welles for killing off Rita. Even worse, he let her die like a bitch on the floor of a hellish chamber while he walked out indifferently, eager to have things over and done with, without even the courtesy of dying in the arms of the rugged sailor. For some years, the misogyny of the American cinema has become a commonplace of intellectual criticism. Rita Hayworth was undoubtedly one of its first victims, and remains, through Welles' genius, its most glorious martyr."[56]

To achieve the effects he wanted in the aquarium scene, Welles had tanks of sea creatures shot separately at the Los Angeles Zoo. These shots were then enlarged and matted into the frames of O'Hara and Elsa kissing and whispering in the darkness. Later, in an interview for CAHIERS DU CINÉMA, Welles suggested that "the scene in the aquarium was so gripping visually that no one heard what was being said. And what was said was, for all that, the marrow of the film. The subject was so tedious that I said to myself, 'This calls for something beautiful to look at.' Assuredly, the scene was very beautiful."[57] Yet, visually, this scene is also the center of the film's complex symbolism. "Anyone who's seen THE LADY FROM SHANGHAI will remember the squid that pulses up and down in the aquarium as Mike and Elsa kiss," William Johnson wrote. "In isolation this might be an overemphatic comment on Elsa's predatory nature, but it works because Welles has imbued the whole film with visual and verbal imagery of the sea. The Lady herself comes from one seaport and has settled in another (San Francisco), and many scenes take place on or by the water. The squid is one of several images involving dangers that lurk beneath the surface, just as they lurk behind Elsa's alluring exterior: there are shots of a water snake and an alligator, and Mike relates a parable about sharks that destroy one another. Even the hall of mirrors connects with the pelagic imagery: the multiple reflections are like waves receding row after row, and when the mirrors are smashed Mike can finally step out onto terra firma, ignoring Elsa's last siren call."[58]

Yet, this is to ignore what Welles had accomplished in terms of Rita's screen image. As John Kobal wrote in an article for FOCUS ON FILM, "THE LADY FROM SHANGHAI . . . is one with which she's pleased, and she's pleased with few of her films. It is also her only film to have a critical cachet because of its director. But to me, it seems a flawed work. Welles' perverse use of his star's qualities rejected the opportunities they offered. . . . Her platinum blonde bob was used to turn Rita into a lethal weapon; it gave her features the fine cutting edge of crystal. . . . Hayworth was more than adequate but Welles ignored the things that GILDA had shown she could do better than any of her contemporaries, suggesting to me at least, that he was unable or unwilling to deal with a force on screen as strong as his own and in whose creation he had had no part."[59]

In the back of her mind maybe Rita had hoped that working together with Orson would open up a new dimension in their relationship. It was not to be. On 10 November 1947 at her divorce hearing she testified that " 'Mr. Welles showed no interest in establishing a home. Mr. Welles told me he never should have married in the first place, as it interfered with his freedom in his way of life.' "[60] When, subsequently, THE LADY FROM SHANGHAI was released, it was no longer in the condition Orson had wanted it to be. He had filmed the entire picture without any close-up of Rita. Harry Cohn insisted that close-ups of her be inserted. Welles wanted little music, in order to emphasize other sounds. Cohn had wall-to-wall music composed and a theme song with a scene inserted of Rita singing it.

Earlier the night he died, Orson appeared on THE MERV GRIFFIN SHOW together with Barbara Leaming, ostensibly to discuss but actually to plug her biography of him. Since Orson was already ashen and in great pain before the program was taped, and the pain only increased when Welles, Leaming, and Welles' friend Alessandro Tasco had dinner later at Ma Maison, I suspect he knew the end was near. He had been for so long obsessed with death, had died so often on screen, and he lived so completely in his own world of fantasy that I do not doubt for a moment that, when the conversation on the program had got around to Rita and he declared that he was still deeply in love with her, he was only playing out again his final scene with her from THE LADY FROM SHANGHAI. The image he intended to leave behind that night was of a man who had spent his life getting old and who still had not forgotten her. But he had done more. In justifying his treatment of Rita to Leaming, he had told her on 23 July 1983, more than two years before, what I regard as a vicious, and yet wholly characteristic, lie: he had claimed that the reason ultimately that they could not make a go of the marriage was that Rita as a teenager had been repeatedly raped by her father. When he had told Leaming this, Rita was still alive, albeit a victim of Alzheimer's disease and closely protected by her daughter from her marriage to Aly Khan, Yasmin Aga Khan. In the same conversation, Welles had asserted that Eduardo Cansino, contrary to his claims of being a Spaniard, was actually a Gypsy and that, therefore, Rita was " 'half gypsy, not half Spanish.' "[61] John Kobal in his biography of Rita had traced her family geneology back for generations in Spain and had even reproduced the family crest, yet Leaming never questioned Welles about this assertion, either. Now, with the lie about incest, Orson had planted the seed which would spring to life after he was gone, and Rita was, again, made into a caricature, no less a fabrication than his vision of her as Elsa Bannister, in Leaming's IF THIS WAS HAPPINESS: A BIOGRAPHY OF RITA HAYWORTH (1989). Leaming, using Orson's lie as a nucleus, then proceeded to flesh out Orson's caricature to the full span of Rita's life. This "horrifying secret" which Rita presumably had revealed to Orson and never to another soul, to none of her longtime friends, none of her intimates, neither to her daughters nor to her other husbands, but only to Orson was that during their days at Agua Caliente "her father had repeatedly engaged in sexual relations with her."[62]

After first presenting this preposterous notion to the reader, Leaming did become equivocal, stating that "even if one were still inclined to doubt Margarita's disclosure to her husband about what her father had done to her in private, there can be no question whatsoever of the very public exploitation to which Eduardo subjected his daughter."[63] In view of the strident partiality she had shown to Orson in writing his biography, it is not surprising that Leaming should not even have engaged in the most rudimentary effort to find some sort of corroborative evidence. In fact, she bent over backwards to suppress evidence that openly contradicted Orson's assertion. Rita had told John Kobal what her schedule had been when she was dancing with her father at Agua Caliente. Leaming could have checked on school records. She did not. When Volga died, Eduardo moved in with Rita and Orson. Leaming skirted this issue entirely by pretending it never happened. " . . . Rita was confronted with a new crisis: her father's attempts to visit her now that Volga was dead. Orson always managed to head him off. 'He was a terrible man,' Welles recalled. 'And she really hated him. She couldn't deal with him at all.' At times like these Rita felt so safe with Orson."[64]

Following THE LADY FROM SHANGHAI, Rita's agent negotiated a new contract for her with Columbia whereby Beckworth Pictures was formed (the name an anagram for Rita's surname and Rebecca's praenomen) which would receive a quarter of the profits from her pictures. Her very next film was THE LOVES OF CARMEN (Columbia, 1948) for which Eduardo Cansino was hired to assist Rita in the dance numbers, another fact that Leaming overlooked; and, of course, Orson was not around to protect her at this time. The truth of the matter is that Rita did not need protection. The studio also hired Antonia Morales, a Flamenco specialist, who had once been one of Eduardo's students. Morales told John Kobal how it was working with the two of them. " 'So I would have to teach the Flamenco steps to Eduardo and he would then teach them to Rita . . . ,' " she recalled. " 'First I'd tell Eduardo and then I'd get Rita on the side to tell her. Of course Eduardo was bitter, after all he'd been my teacher, but there was never any row on the set.' "[65] From everything we know of Eduardo, he was an extremely proud man and he had great difficulty in adjusting to the changed circumstances in his relationship with Rita. "She was no longer the obedient pupil,'' as Kobal pointed out, ''but the star and Eduardo's employer.''[66]

Leaming was not the least bit equivocal when it came to an interview for PEOPLE Magazine about her biography. '' 'I felt a tremendous sense of responsibility writing this book . . . ,' '' she said. '' 'Perhaps it can do something—not only to make Hayworth better understood, but to let us know a bit more about the devastating effects of incest.' ''[67] I suspect her primary sense of responsibility in writing the book was not to its subject at all, but rather to Orson. Just as Orson's narrative voice so dominates her biography of him, so his voice dominates her biography of Rita, in the events having to do with their marriage and throughout the remainder of Rita's life. When Rita met Aly Khan and fell in love with him, it must somehow have been particularly unsettling to Orson since it prompted him to another elaborate fabrication. '' 'She sent me a telegram in Rome,' '' Orson told Leaming concerning Rita's forthcoming marriage to Aly. '' 'I couldn't get any plane, so I went, stood up in a cargo plane to Antibes.' Rita was waiting for him there in a hotel. 'There were candles and champagne ready—and Rita in a marvelous negligée,' Welles said. 'And the door closed, and she said, ''Here I am. Marry me.'' ' ''[68] I believe that Orson wished that this fantasy had been the way it happened. The reality is so much more mundane. Rita was finished with him. Aly fawned over Rebecca and played with her with all the enthusiasm that Rita had hoped Orson would have felt for their daughter, and which Welles did not. What Welles sent to the wedding was not himself, but rather a spaniel puppy which he had named ''Pookles,'' the pet name Dr. Bernstein had given Orson when Orson was a child.

As the events of Rita's life cascade past, there is always Orson's voice, evaluating, judging, assessing, concluding. '' 'After Aly, Rita was on a downward path, a steep, steep toboggan slide,' said Orson Welles.''[69] These words better describe what happened to Orson after *his* marriage to Rita than what happened to Rita. Leaming also tried to win sympathy for Welles as a parent: ''As Orson would admit years later, he had always felt intense guilt about his own blatant failures as a parent, but as long as Rebecca was with her mother he could tell himself that everything was all right.''[70] Leaming wrote these words after Orson was dead and his will had been read. There is in that final document no indication of any such guilt. He left $10,000 each to his three daughters from his three marriages while dividing the bulk of his estate between his third wife and his mistress of many years, Oja Kodar, with an additional provision that should Paola die, then all that remained of his estate was to go to Oja.

Fortunately, Leaming's collaboration with Welles on Rita's life has so far had little effect. In answer to an inquiry about whether or not Rita had been the victim of childhood incest, Walter Scott wrote in his popular column in PARADE that ''Rita's father was the Spanish dancer Eduardo Cansino, who enlisted his daughter . . . as a dancing partner. There is no conclusive evidence, however, that he abused her sexually or insisted that she service various Hollywood executives. Such horrors have been attributed to her first husband, Ed Judson, who reportedly placed her on starvation diets, had her face and figure reshaped, urged her to exchange casting-couch favors for film roles.''[71]

If there was anything sad about Rita's life, it was that she had been denied a normal childhood because of economic exigencies and that most of her career decisions were made for her by exploitive men who never had her best interests at heart. Her father had instilled in her an awe for a father figure and an attitude of subservience so that she gravitated toward strong-willed men against whom her only defense was her back of steel. When at a relatively early age she found herself an important movie star, she realized only slowly and only in time that that is not what *she* wanted for herself; and, in the end, it was all she would have, except for the love of her children, Yasmin especially. Vincent Sherman who directed her in AFFAIR IN TRINIDAD (Columbia, 1952) found an elemental sadness in Rita which seeped into the film. He once had an intimate conversation with her over dinner. '' '. . . She's not very articulate,' '' he recalled, '' 'but she had been opening up, unburdening herself, and I really felt for her. It was about 9 P.M. when I realized that I had to go . . . and I told her so. . . . That beautiful woman looked at me and said, 'I'm boring you.' . . . From that moment my heart broke for her. I tried to be as gentle and loving as I could while we were working together. This beautiful, lovely creature who thought she was boring when she talked.' ''[72] Such is the way Rita was for those who knew her. For Leaming, however, even—to use André Bazin's words—Orson's letting ''her die like a bitch on the floor of a hellish chamber'' had its *raison d'etre* and its justification. '' . . . When Rita confronts the multiple fragments of her divided self, no matter where she turns she also unavoidably sees the father-husband's reflection staring back at her, trying to destroy her. For the incest victim this vision of the destroyer in the mirror, in oneself, may be the ultimate horror.''[73]

## IV

As part of her divorce action, Rita sued Orson to pay back the $30,000 he had borrowed from her. She also expected Orson to pay for Rebecca's support, but in this regard she would have no better luck than Virginia had had. To make some quick money, Welles was able to persuade Herbert J. Yates at Republic Pictures to let him direct and star in a film version of MACBETH (Republic, 1948) to be made on a very low budget: an estimated $884,367 for a twenty-one day shooting schedule.

Orson began work on this film very soon after THE LADY FROM SHANG-HAI was completed, but it was held up in release, as was the former, due to problems with it. In MACBETH's case, these had to do with post-production since Welles did manage to complete principal photography in the time allotted. However, the film needed a final edit and the sound track, which had all the characters speaking in a heavy Scots burr, made what they said totally incomprehensible. Welles was in Europe, appearing as an actor in BLACK MAGIC

(20th-Fox, 1949), and so the work was postponed again and again. So many costs were run up in final editing and dubbing that the budget had been far exceeded by the time of release and this circumstance, coming on top of the RKO and Columbia debacles, effectively finished Welles' opportunities to find employment as a director in Hollywood.

In terms of Welles' treatment of Shakespeare's play, much was carried over from his stage production of the voodoo MACBETH. Magic is the potent force which rules the destinies of the characters and the witches, shown fashioning a clay figure of Macbeth, literally take possession of his soul. The violence was more explicit than in the play itself, but it is still rather tame compared to Roman Polanski's later version. In one regard, however, Welles and Polanski were in agreement: in the manner in which they changed the ending of the play. Welles, as Polanski would subsequently, leaves no doubt in the viewer's mind that Macbeth's death is *not* a relief from tyranny. Indeed, in dying, Macbeth has the shattering recognition that there is no way out for anyone. Given the shadows, the claustrophobic effects of sound stage sets, the expressionist lighting and sometimes surreal compositions, Welles' MACBETH is quite in the *film noir* style and employs a *film noir* narrative structure. Yet, as Charles Higham observed, the film is flawed and this "chiefly in the performances. These, Welles' included, seldom rise above the amateur. . . . "[74] There is also the disturbing presence which would become a dominant factor in all of Welles' future films of shoddiness, from a zipper clearly visible on Lady Macbeth's gown to Macbeth's costume which seems a forerunner of those used in RADAR MEN FROM THE MOON (Republic, 1952), a twelve-chapter serial later made by the same studio.

In the interim between the completion of principal photography on MACBETH and going to Europe where he would for the most part remain for the next two decades, Welles moved in with Charles Lederer in the latter's Santa Monica home now that Lederer and Virginia were separated. Following BLACK MAGIC, Welles began preliminary work on his next film production, OTHELLO, and he was hired to appear in PRINCE OF FOXES (20th-Fox, 1949) directed by Henry King. " 'He was the most cooperative actor I've ever worked with,' King said at the film's end."[75] However, Welles did find a way to undermine the film. He announced in the press that he didn't find many anti-Nazis in Germany, something which offended the German people. Welles refused to retract the statement and the studio estimated that the comment cost it a quarter of a million dollars in lost revenue in the German market.

With OTHELLO, Welles began what became sort of a tradition in a number of his films: casting his paramours as his leading ladies, whether or not they could act. Virginia, following her divorce from Lederer, took Christopher and went to live in South Africa where she eventually married for the third time, a businessman named Jack Pringle. Welles, on the continent, fell in love with the Italian actress Lea Padovani, an affair about which he later said that " 'during the nine months that I spent with her I paid for everything I'd ever done to women in twenty years. . . . ' ''[76] Notwithstanding her execrable English, Orson cast her opposite him as Desdemona.

According to Alexandre Trauner, Welles' art director and set designer on OTHELLO, Orson was an artist who was determined to destroy his creations. Even when all would go well, he would find a convenient excuse to bring the whole film into question and tinker interminably. When his falling out with Padovani became final, he hired Suzanne Cloutier to portray Desdemona, using some of Padovani's footage interchangeably with Cloutier's, figuring perhaps that audiences would not notice the difference or the many interpolated shots of Moroccan stand-ins who would be summoned to the set when Cloutier was unavailable. The intermittant filming schedule on and off over three years, shooting when Orson had found more money, disbanding temporarily when he ran out of money, certainly did not help the production maintain any consistency. Welles was always rather proud of how he had improvised a scene in a Turkish bath when his actors were without proper costumes. In post-production, he hired Gudrun Ure to dub Cloutier because he had come to despise her almost as much as he despised Padovani. '' 'We'll have Ure dub the entire Desdemona,' '' he told film editor Bill Morton. '' 'I can't wait to see what Cloutier's reaction will be when she attends the première and finds out it's not really her, at least not her voice, and in many shots not her body—on the screen.' ''[77] Humiliating Cloutier and Padovani, however, must have been more important than producing a masterpiece, or even a comprehensible film, since what Welles ended up with was a highly expressionistic screen style, full of extraordinarily striking shots and dark moods, but a jumbled story which even a foreknowledge of the play would not make wholly decipherable.

One of the acting roles Welles accepted, albeit reluctantly, while trying to complete OTHELLO was that of Harry Lime in THE THIRD MAN. His appearance in this film is notable because he played the part without makeup, without even a false nose which he almost invariably wore, and managed for perhaps the first time in his career and, certainly, for the last to create convincingly a character who was someone other than Orson Welles. After the première of OTHELLO at Cannes in 1952, Welles wrote a short novel, UNE GROSSE LÉGUME [THE BIG SHOT], which appeared only in French translation with an Introduction by Maurice Bessy who articulated the legend of Orson Welles with a persuasive vividness that would provide a welcome band wagon for members of the international critical community. Welles is depicted as an artist of enormous stature utterly unappreciated by the moneymen and *arbitri gratiae* of his time, a lonely eagle, restless, constantly in motion, seeking to satisfy his cravings for good food, good drink, beautiful women, but most of all to do his great work, an American abroad who in his glorious exile was intent on becoming a citizen of the world.

It was a role which Orson came to prefer to the exclusion of all others and one which he could play with consummate artistry long before some spectators became aware that a tremendous gulf often separates the powerful projections of the media from the rather prosaic reality. After all, being foremostly an illusionist had invariably appealed to Orson. He wrote a rather baroque and superficially stylish novel published first in France, MR. ARKADIN (1954), and it was this which he used as the basis for a film initially titled CONFIDEN-TIAL REPORT (Warner's, 1955) when it was released in Great Britain, seven years prior to its American release. His sycophants declare that MR. ARKADIN, as it was titled in the United States, is Welles' second attempt to film CITIZEN KANE, but it does one well to bear in mind William Johnson's admonition about the "pitfall" of Welles criticism. There is no denying that the film has brilliant moments, although it ultimately lacks coherence and tends to confuse rather than clarify anything. Yet, in his role as Arkadin, Welles did find a suitable parable for his fundamental conviction that human nature, a person's essential character, is immutable, a parable far more effective than the fictitious Chinese proverb he had inserted into the dialogue of THE LADY FROM SHANGHAI. "A scorpion, who could not swim, begged a frog to carry him to the other side," the viewer is told. "The frog complained that the scorpion would sting him. This was impossible, said the scorpion, because he would then drown with the frog. So the pair set forth. Halfway over, the scorpion stung the frog. 'Is that logical?' asked the frog. 'No, it's not,' answered the scorpion, as they both sank to the bottom, 'but I can't help it, it's my nature.' "

Arkadin hires Guy Van Stratton, played by Robert Arden, to find out as much as he can about his past and what he was before he emerged as one of the wealthiest men in the world. With each witness that Van Stratten unearths, the viewer gets another piece of the puzzle which reveals the utter wickedness of Arkadin, only for that witness to die, presumably murdered by Arkadin who is only using Van Stratton to cover his past so deeply that no one will ever find it. Paola Mori, with whom Welles had fallen in love, was cast as Arkadin's daughter, Raina, but in the reality of what she does and says on the screen, what we are actually seeing is Kane's trying to make something out of Susan Alexander that she could never be, for which she has no talent, in this case Welles' attempt to make Mori into a credible actress. Yet, in a way, MR. ARKADIN seems to have been created primarily as a vehicle for Mori. The sloppiness of Welles' makeup is particularly noticeable, since in some scenes the matting is clearly visible where his wig was attached, in others the wig, beard, and mustache are so obvious as to appear amateurish, while his false nose distracts utterly from his credibility. Already in OTHELLO, Orson had begun dubbing the voices of other males in the cast, a procedure that he took to an even further extreme here, so that his voice is almost as ubiquitous as it is throughout Leaming's biography. In fact one of the few places where Welles' persistent monologue is interrupted is when, in connection with this picture, Leaming had occasion to quote Robert Arden who felt that " 'once Orson had written the script of the film and got it done in his head and on paper, he then lost interest in the actual filming . . . and then, to maintain his flagging interest, he would keep changing things, always saying that any discrepancies could be fixed up in the dubbing. Hence the

occasions when the lips aren't saying what the sound track is saying.' ''[78] Added
to this is the jumble of scenes which heightens the sense of the bizarre while
obscuring meaning. Perhaps the only admirable performance is Suzanne Flon's
as a world-weary aristocrat. Louis Dolivant, who financed the picture, ended up
suing Welles for $700,000 and accusing him of being most often drunk while
in production and failing to deliver anything resembling the film he had promised.

In addition to his brief appearance in John Huston's MOBY DICK, Welles
put on his own stage production in 1955 in which there were few props other
than an empty stage and the lighting reduced most of the other actors to silhouettes
while a spotlight shone on Orson as he held forth. About this same time Welles
began filming his version of DON QUIXOTE which he was destined never to
finish and most of the footage from which was apparently destroyed in a fire at
the home he had in Spain after he and Paola Mori were married. What footage
does survive was screened at Cannes in 1986, mostly outtakes and unrelated
shots, with Welles' voice on the track having dubbed both Quixote and Sancho
Panza.

It was Charlton Heston who used his influence to secure for Orson his last
directing job for a major Hollywood studio. Heston was the first to realize that,
as he had rewritten the script for TOUCH OF EVIL, the best part was that which
Orson played. '' 'TOUCH OF EVIL is about the decline and fall of Captain
Quinlan,' '' Heston said in an interview. '' 'My part is a kind of witness to
this.' ''[79] Welles was so secretive during production of the film that the Universal
executives became somewhat jittery and their worst suspicions were confirmed
when they finally had a chance to screen what Orson proposed as his final cut.
Harry Keller, who was called in to repair the film before it could be released,
told Frank Brady of the rather basic problems with which he had to contend.
For example, '' 'the line, ''That's the second bullet I took for you, partner''
made no sense,' '' Keller told Brady, '' 'unless it could be explained in an earlier
scene, which is why I included a new scene of Menzies telling Susan that *en
route* to the motel.' ''[80]

Yet, curiously, after going to all the effort to shoot new scenes and dialogue
to make the film internally consistent and comprehensible, Universal then released a hybrid version without many of the new scenes, the result being that
there now exist two versions of the film, the original hybrid version and the
long version which has many scenes in it for which Orson was not responsible.
What is probably most significant about TOUCH OF EVIL is that although
appearing relatively late in the *film noir* cycle—1958—it still evokes all of the
more basic icons of the style, both in visual and narrative terms. Welles as
Captain Quinlan plays a detective in a border town who has earned his reputation
as a policeman by framing those he intuitively suspects. Heston was cast as
Vargas, a Mexican detective married to an American, Susan, played by Janet
Leigh. Later Leigh would contrast Welles with Hitchcock, commenting on the
greater freedom Welles gave his actors to improvise, something that Hitchcock,
who had worked out everything beforehand, would never have tolerated. When

a new turn in the script would contradict dialogue in scenes that had already been filmed, Orson would counter that he could always loop in new dialogue later. This, of course, led to discrepancies in synchronization which Welles ignored in his own films but which Keller was expected to repair prior to release. Vargas keeps interfering with the way Quinlan wants to conduct an investigation of a double murder. Susan is first gang-raped and then Quinlan tries to frame her as a drug addict. One memorable scene was the continuous tracking shot with which the film opens, culminating in an explosion; another was the sequence in a seedy hotel room where Welles strangles to death Joe Grandi, played by Akim Tamiroff, whom he had also cast as Sancho Panza. When Susan regains consciousness, she becomes aware of the corpse as a light outside the window flashes on and off, grotesquely illuminating it. Welles got Marlene Dietrich to play a cameo role as a fortune teller. She is given a moving piece of dialogue when Quinlan asks her: "Read my future." She replies: "You haven't got any." Quinlan's world crumbles; not even his friendship with Menzies, his partner played by Joseph Calleia, can survive his final exposure. In the darkness of the night, as the net closes around Quinlan, the camera rises and falls with the motion of an oil pump. Quinlan's wife was killed and her murderer is the last killer ever to get away from him. Quinlan is a good detective, but he is also a bad cop. To this ultimately negative image are added others. Vargas hates his work and he hates *gringos*. Susan with the exception of her husband hates Mexicans— which makes her gang-rape by them twice as repulsive. Quinlan ends up losing his life, but the kinds of lives led by the other characters are scarcely more desirable. Once again Orson was trying to lay bare the corruption and hypocrisy he saw as rampant in American society, with predictable consequences. Also once again, and not for the last time, he showed himself a director capable of brilliant moments but incapable of sustaining continuity or consistency.

With Welles back in Hollywood, Lucille Ball, who had known him when they were both under contract to RKO, gave Orson a chance to direct a half-hour pilot for television. Welles shocked her and Desi Arnaz by taking a month to film it, rather than the ten days that were allotted, and then, as Ball told Charles Higham, he threw an elaborate wrap party so that it seemed that " 'all the money went into the party and none went into the pilot.' "[81]

What followed was that Welles resumed his pilgrimage through the capitals of Europe endeavoring to find financing for a new film venture. THE TRIAL (Astor, 1963) was the film. Ostensibly it is based on the novel by Franz Kafka, although visually what is depicted in the film is quite the opposite of what is described in the novel. Notwithstanding, Peter Cowie concluded in THE CINEMA OF ORSON WELLES (1973) that THE TRIAL "remains Welles' finest film since KANE and, far from being a travesty of Kafka's work, achieves an effect through cinematic means that conveys perfectly the terrifying vision of the modern world that marks every page of the original book. . . . "[82] Welles did this, however, in spite of the viewer, or perhaps by using the viewer in an unconventional manner. Dubbing the voices of almost a dozen of the actors,

THE TRIAL is not only a personal *tour de force*, but the somewhat muffled track only adds to the dull and mundane scenes, creating the desired mood by deadening receptivity, so that the viewer becomes an unwilling participant in the pervasive sense of dreadful blandness.

All of Orson's most egomaniacal traits came to the fore in CHIMES AT MIDNIGHT (Peppercorn-Wormser-Saltzman, 1967), his final reworking of the basic fabric of FIVE KINGS so as to yield the full story of Falstaff, whom he regarded as one of Shakespeare's most enduring creations. His tendency toward improvisation intensified while his contempt for the technical crew became unbounded. He had music on the set to relax his actors but refused to let the sound engineer ask him any questions, above all if a scene should be done again. If there were problems with the sound, the standard answer now applied: they would be resolved in the dubbing. No one was to come to him about anything, simply do their jobs. The upshot was that for long stretches this film is incomprehensible. A viewer simply cannot make out what the characters are saying, including Welles as Falstaff, Shakespeare without Shakespeare's words ever being totally audible. Actors speaking on a cold day have puffs of breath coming out of their mouths and their lips moving when they are not speaking. What alone saves the film is the scene of Falstaff's expulsion. Joseph McBride, no doubt correctly, felt that "it is unlikely that Welles as director or actor will achieve again so moving a scene"[83] and Frank Brady concluded that "so perfectly does Orson capture the meaning of the confrontation . . . that it's difficult to tell where Falstaff begins and Welles ends. It is probably Orson's finest moment on the screen."[84]

Orson's affair with Olga Palinkas began while THE TRIAL was in production. Palinkas was a sculptress who Welles decided, much as he had with Paola, ought to be an actress and his co-star. He renamed her Oja Kodar. While THE DEEP was in production during the years 1967–1969, Welles at one point contacted Roger Hill who was by then living in retirement in Florida and engaged him to film some scenes for the picture to be shot in the Bahamas, notwithstanding the fact that Hill was scarcely a professional cinematographer. THE DEEP was never completed but the occasion permitted Orson to introduce Hill to Oja, as he had to the women whom he had married in the past. The difference in this case was that, unlike Virginia and Rita, Paola was willing to tolerate Welles' having a mistress with whom he traveled, with whom he appeared in public, and whom he cast in his various film ventures. Leaming, as might be expected, supplied the *apologia pro sua vita*, explaining that Paola and their daughter Beatrice meant *home* to Welles, wherever they might be living, his permanent address, while Oja presumably appealed to his creative, artistic spirit. "For many years Orson would divide his time between the two women in his life," she explained, "so that, in its own way, his relationship with Oja was every bit as stable as that with Paola."[85]

Oja Kodar, it has been said, was responsible for bringing an awareness of the erotic into Orson's films. He received financing from French television to make a small-screen film based on a story by Karen Blixen, who wrote in English under the name Isak Dinesen, a film which retained the title and the basic plot of its source, THE IMMORTAL STORY (Altura Films, 1968). It was Orson's first completed film in color, a medium he had generally avoided, and he starred as the old rich man who wants to make a story told by sailors about a night of love into a reality. Charles Silver, while insisting that THE IMMORTAL STORY remains "one of the most poignantly personal works in all cinema," could not at the same time deny that "the sound, at least in the English-language version, is rather bad. The lighting, sets, props, and makeup have a decided air of cheapness and haste, reflecting the fact that this was, after all, only a television production. The continuity and editing tend toward a certain sloppiness, and the acting and *mise-en-scène* appear stolid, completely antithetical to the wild Welles we have known."[86]

THE IMMORTAL STORY really marks the end of Orson's long European sojourn. Increasingly, the focus for the rest of his life became finding work in the United States, appearing as a guest on television talk shows, voicing commercials for radio and television, and picking up what acting and narration jobs he could. I have already quoted what Joseph McBride had to say about Welles' CHIMES AT MIDNIGHT. He had begun working on his biography, ORSON WELLES (1972), about the time that Orson was preparing THE IMMORTAL STORY. In the nearly four years he was at work on it he was not given an opportunity to interview Welles. As would later be the case with Barbara Leaming, Welles had to assure himself first that McBride would be willing to tell his story the way Orson wanted it told, embodying the sycophancy and tone of high praise suitable for the Orson Welles legend. Welles settled his family, wife Paola, daughter Beatrice, and his mother-in-law, in a home in Sedona, Arizona from which he would make his business trips to Los Angeles. He also rented a house in Los Angeles for his use while there and, of course, for his visits with Oja. Once Welles perceived that McBride, with a little encouragement, would write about him in the fashion he wanted, he agreed to a series of interviews in his Los Angeles home. I suspect Orson also hoped to use McBride's book as a vehicle with which he could dispel the attacks on his legend being perpetrated by his former friend, Maurice Bessy. In verbal statements and then for the written record, Bessy had implied that Welles was a repressed homosexual. As part of his rationale, he cited the powerful male relationships in Welles' films, from that between Iago and Othello to that between Prince Hal and Falstaff.

Welles also began work on THE OTHER SIDE OF THE WIND in 1970. He was still at it when he had the interviews with McBride. The controversy about the authorship of CITIZEN KANE was then at its height and, after having had Weissberger read what Pauline Kael had written only to conclude that a law suit could not suppress what was essentially a matter of opinion, he also hoped that McBride's book would argue his case. Nor was he wrong. McBride went even further with an article in Orson's defense for FILM HERITAGE titled "Rough Sledding with Pauline Kael." Bessy's ORSON WELLES appeared in English translation in 1971, McBride's biography the next year. Why not transpose this contretemps into the plot of THE OTHER SIDE OF THE WIND? It was easy enough to do. In an interview incorporated into André Bazin's appreciation of Welles, Orson had commented that shooting a film without a script is "a very special method of work which is impractical for commercial films."[87] Yet, that is precisely what he now intended to do in THE OTHER SIDE OF THE WIND. He hired McBride to play a character based on himself in the film. Not only was there no script, but matching shots were ignored, so that over the years, when parts of the film were occasionally shot, Orson would call back people such as McBride, oblivious apparently that their apparel was different and that they had obviously aged. Orson never really completed this mess and it is perhaps better that it was left unfinished. Although Orson claimed that the film was just about complete when he was forced to turn the negative over to the Iranians who had financed a good deal of it, Oja Kodar was still trying to get the negative back from the Iranians after Orson's death and even approached John Huston at the time of THE DEAD (Vestron, 1987) to see if he would be willing to direct its completion. When Orson became a recipient of the Lifetime Achievement Award of the American Film Institute in February, 1975, he did show some clips from THE OTHER SIDE OF THE WIND in hope that he could garner additional financing. When that did not work, he arranged to screen selected scenes at the Screen Directors' Guild, the most substantial of which was a frenetic episode of Oja Kodar performing oral sex on one of the male characters.

Kodar also appears as an erotic presence in F IS FOR FAKE (Specialty Films, 1977) completed in 1973. For the most part, this film consists of documentary footage Orson collected concerning art forgery, but, as Frank Brady noted, the high point of Welles' interpolations into the miscellany may be Oja's "seductive wiggle filmed from every possible angle, much to the delight of the male audience and onlookers in and outside the film."[88]

Orson made the move to Las Vegas in part because of his mother-in-law's respiratory problems but also because he hoped to get bookings for his magic act in the casinos and actually made a videotape on gambling which was shown on closed-circuit television in hotel rooms. He purchased the home on Stanley Avenue in Los Angeles as his residence when working and it was in the yard there that he paid for a brief scene to be filmed based on another Dinesen story titled "The Dreamers," in which Oja as Pellegrina says good-bye to her oldest and closest friend, Marcus, played by Welles. He was never able to raise money for this project.

In a sense, Charles Higham, who was among those pilloried in THE FAR SIDE OF THE WIND, had it right and, as Orson's waistline expanded, his career contracted, "almost as though eating and drinking were substitutes for creativity."[89] A year or so after we had filmed him, perched on his iron chair, he found that he was feeling poorly virtually all the time. He consulted a physician and after numerous tests learned that his heart was in a weakened condition, his liver severely damaged, and his blood pressure phenomenally high. He announced that he intended to lose 125 pounds, which sounded more ambitious than it actually was since that would only put him at 300 pounds, where he mostly stayed until his death.

His last completed film project was released shortly before we met, FILMING OTHELLO (Independent Images, 1979), the documentary financed by German television. Orson appears on camera as the narrator and the Orson Welles legend is given its most eloquent statement yet in his portrayal of himself as a beleaguered filmmaker. In the discussion scenes about filming the play, Orson must have found that others were saying more memorable or profound things than he was since he cut in very badly matched shots of himself, obviously from an entirely different location, expounding his customary combination of witticism and philosophy more brilliantly than anyone else. At the end, he elaborately lights a cigar with a wooden match and turns off the movieola. It was a farewell gesture made by the Orson Welles legend to all those who were willing to believe him.

It was Michael Fitzgerald, the producer of WISE BLOOD (New Line Cinema, 1980) and UNDER THE VOLCANO (Universal, 1984), who in the interim between these two John Huston bombs proposed that Orson write and direct a film to be titled THE CRADLE WILL ROCK, which would tell the story of his early years as he wanted it told. Discussing the project at Ma Maison, Orson declared that Amy Irving would be perfect in the role of the young Virginia Welles. He even arranged to have lunch with her and her husband, Steven Spielberg, and was disillusioned when Spielberg let Orson pay the check! The project fell through because of Fitzgerald's financial problems.

Henry Jaglom was another of the true believers in the Orson Welles legend. He came up with the idea that Orson should write something that was frankly commercial and he would get it produced. With that done, then, Jaglom opined, Welles would find it easier to get financing for THE DREAMERS. The basic problem with this strategy was that it was blind to the real Orson Welles. The screenplay that Welles wrote was titled THE BIG BRASS RING. The plot concerns a Texas U.S. Senator who had just lost a presidential election. The Senator, named Blake Pellarin, leaves his wife in order to have a rendezvous with his former Harvard professor, lover, and mentor, Kimball Menaker, who was to be played by Welles himself. A woman journalist sets out to expose the love affair between the two men and hopes by this means to destroy what is left of Pellarin's political career. None of the major studios in Hollywood felt that this story, with its obsessive homosexual overtones, was likely to be big at the box office. Whether Bessy's claim about Orson's repressed homosexuality was true or not, there is no question that in the last decade of his life Orson was increasingly transfixed by the subject, a tendency that had already begun with the basic idea for THE OTHER SIDE OF THE WIND with its tale of a homosexual film director who comes to the end of his rope.

In 1985, Orson was diagnosed a diabetic. His heart condition also continued to plague him. He spent more time at his home in Las Vegas, less with Oja in Los Angeles and at Ma Maison. A deep melancholia set in and in an absurd effort to lose weight so that he might appear in a film version of KING LEAR that he would also direct, he began swimming twenty laps a day in his swimming pool. Although he was approached to play Santa Claus in a motion picture, he turned down that role. His last screen appearance was as the Orson Welles legend in Henry Jaglom's SOMEONE TO LOVE (International Rainbow Pictures, 1987) where he said: "We're born alone, we live alone, we die alone. Only through our love and friendship can we create the illusion for the moment that we're not alone." He went home to Stanley Avenue on the night of 9 October 1985 after dining with Barbara Leaming and Alessandro Tasco at Ma Maison. Alone before his typewriter, Orson Welles died that night of a massive heart attack.

Other than the cash bequests to his three daughters, Oja received the Los Angeles home and all its contents, Paola the home in Las Vegas, its contents, and whatever money would be left. Paola contested the will, in large measure I believe because of the provision that upon her death everything would revert to Oja rather than to Beatrice. A hearing was scheduled for 14 August 1986. Two days before, on 12 August 1986, Paola was killed in an automobile accident a short distance from her home in Las Vegas. Oja Kodar got everything by default.

On 4 November 1986 a tribute to Orson Welles was held in the auditorium of the Directors' Guild of America. Oja Kodar made a brief appearance during which she did her best to perpetuate for all time the legend of Orson Welles. "She talked," Frank Brady wrote, "of the 'dreary little selves whose fingers are still sticky from plucking at his wings.' Lowering her voice for a moment, she told them that Orson, being generous, would have forgiven those who plucked a feather or two in their attempts to stop *him* from defying the force of gravity. Despite all the defamation against Orson, and the lack of cooperation he received from the film community, she continued, her voice rising now, almost strident— 'I promise you it didn't make him bitter.' "[90] For those in the room who had last seen her in the clip from THE OTHER SIDE OF THE WIND, this was a new role for Oja, even if her message was the same one they had been hearing over the years from that loyal legion, men such as Peter Bogdanovich, Joseph McBride, and Henry Jaglom. In a way it was fitting, since the legend of Orson Welles alone justified a life which otherwise would seem to be too much what it was: a profligate immersion in obsessive self-indulgence.

I could go no farther than I had with Orson Welles. Accurate reportage would forever be at odds with my narrative script whenever and wherever it touched upon the Orson Welles legend and, truthfully, too much of it touched. Orson Welles was in a most graphic sense the architect of his own downfall, as is *not* the case with the mighty characters he played in his own films who were shown as the victims of irrational forces clearly outside of their control. In this vision, he was one with Euripides, who articulated so eloquently the dread that accompanies recognition that the world of human endeavor, indeed the whole universe, is at base irrational. Yet, for all of that, Orson Welles did leave behind CITIZEN KANE, and in bright flashes from THE MAGNIFICENT AMBERSONS, THE

LADY FROM SHANGHAI, and TOUCH OF EVIL he produced a legacy that must always assure him of a place of honor in the history of film in the Twentieth Century. Only when his achievement on film is at last separated from the man will our full appreciation of it be possible. The legend was designed to hide the failures of the man. I doubt that it will outlive his films.

# Roman Polanski

**I**

Some years ago in a magazine article I had occasion to use the word "aloneness" and a reader wrote to advise me that there is no such word in the English language. Technically, that reader was incorrect. According to the OXFORD ENGLISH DICTIONARY, the word has been around at least since 1382 and it is defined as "the quality or state of being alone." Yet, in the present context, I am dissatisfied with that definition. Ivan Butler gave a better definition in THE CINEMA OF ROMAN POLANSKI (1970) when he observed that "all his characters convey a powerful impression of 'aloneness'—something considerably stronger than loneliness and not accurately described as isolation."[1] Proust may still have been wide of the mark when he suggested "*nous sommes irrémédiablement seuls*" but Cicero seems to have come closest when he wrote "*in animi doloribus solitudines captare*": in anguished souls solitudes are captured. For me, as for Ivan Butler, aloneness comprises the inner lexicon of all Polanski's films, those he made prior to 1970 and those which he has made since.

Just before we met for the first time in Paris in the spring of 1976 at the Studios de Boulogne, Vicki and I had been to Chartres. It was a good thing, not because Chartres today is so much as it was during the Middle Ages with its majestic cathedral and its medieval dwellings, but because it brought to mind Bernard of Chartres who wrote in the Twelfth Century that we have nothing that we are not given and because in this century we have often chosen to reject all that we have ever been given so as to exist in a self-imposed vacuum amid feelings of indeterminate loss.

Polanski was in the midst of dubbing his most recent film, LOCOTAIRE (THE TENANT), into English. The scene projected on the giant screen was the one where Polanski climbs the stairs alongside Melvyn Douglas while he is being told how to act properly in Paris. The French term this the "rock and roll" sound system because it permits the sound tracks being mixed to flow back and forth remaining synchronized. Up the stairs, backwards, up the stairs, backwards, up the stairs—each time some new sound effect was added; each time the bands indicating the various sound tracks running horizontally on the screen beneath the picture took on different markings. Shapes were sounds. Polanski was giving directions in French and with every success, every "*Bon!*" from him and triumphant murmurs of endorsement from the technicians, a feeling of increasing eerieness stole over the sequence, not visually save on the sound tracks, but aurally, suggestive and macabre. Up the stairs, backwards. . . .

After a time, Polanski walked over to where we were sitting opposite the control panel.

"*Parlez-vous français?*" he inquired.

"*Oui,*" I replied, "*mais ma campagne ne le parle pas.*"

"Will you have a cigar?" he asked, switching to English and picking up a box of Havanas.

"*Non, merci,*" I said, knowing Vicki's feelings about cigar smoke in confined areas.

"This is my new picture," he said, addressing Vicki. "It is about a man who comes to live in Paris. He becomes a naturalized French citizen. But the French, they do not accept him. He is made to feel an outsider. He may be a French citizen, but he is not French. And his mind, he is beginning to lose his mind."

He left the sentence hanging and resumed working. Up the stairs, backwards. I began to think that Polanski and Douglas would never make it. Then they did. Douglas opened the door to his apartment. A clock began to chime. "*Dix heures!*" Polanski proclaimed, followed by a "*Bon!*" Then, suddenly, backwards, up the stairs, backwards, up the stairs.

Time passed and, while it did, I thought of how fondly the French had once treated Polanski, in his early years as a new force in the international cinema, of the respectful portrait of him which had been drawn by Michael Delahaye and Jean-André Fieschi in the February, 1966 issue of CAHIERS DU CINÉMA. Now, quite the same as the character Trelkovsky whom he was playing in the film, Polanski was a naturalized French citizen. After all, he had been born in Paris. Suddenly, he popped up again in our midst.

"Have you ever had couscous?" he asked.

"No."

"It's a dish from Northern Africa. Come, I know a restaurant nearby. Try some."

He escorted us out of the editing room.

"Posters all over Paris are announcing the opening of LOCOTAIRE," I told him as we made our way along a narrow passageway.

"Yes, but the French critics don't like it. It was entered at Cannes, one of the two French entries. I don't give interviews. That was a mistake. In France, you must give interviews, or you'll pay for it. I'm paying for it now.''

We began descending a long flight of steps.

"Did you ever interview Adolph Zukor?'' Polanski asked me, pausing at the midway landing.

"Yes. He was nearly a hundred and had what I thought to be an incredible memory.''

"Let me tell you a story.'' We resumed our descent. ''When I was at Paramount in New York, I would see him every day at lunch time. He always hid his mouth with his hand, as if he didn't want anyone to see that he was shoveling the food in, you know? When he had a mouthful, he would take his hand away. Every day one of the publicity people would take me over to his table and introduce me. 'Mr. Zukor, this is Roman Polanski. He is directing a picture for us.' ''

Polanski giggled light-heartedly as we came out into the grayish light of day. It had been raining. Water stood in pools in the street.

"And every day he would nod at me as if we were meeting for the first time. 'Good,' he would say, 'that's good.' ''

We paused in the middle of the sidewalk at the studio entrance. It appeared as if it might rain again.

"This way,'' Polanski directed. "It isn't far.''

I felt a drop or two of rain. Some lines of Rilke's, memorized long ago, came back to me.

> *Regnet hernieder in den Zwitterstunden,*
> *wenn sich nach Morgen wenden alle Gassen,*
> *und wenn die Leiber, welche nichts gefunden,*
> *enttäuscht und traurig voneinander lassen;*
> *und wenn die Menschen, die einander hassen,*
> *in einem Bett zusammen schlafen müssen:*
> *dann geht die Einsamkeit mit den Flüssen . . .* [2]

"What's wrong with him?'' Roman asked Vicki.

"Oh, nothing,'' she quipped. "It's just that he spent several hours yesterday walking around Paris trying to find a bottle of Scotch, and, when he found one, it was of the lowest grade and cost him a hundred francs.''

"This is Paris, you must remember,'' Polanski said, laughing.

Once we arrived, Roman held the door. We were shown to a booth. Polanski ordered couscous. We had whiskey; he had wine.

We had with us a book of screenplays from Polanski's first three feature films. There were many candid illustrations of him directing.

"Have you seen this?'' I asked.

"No,'' he said, taking the book at once and avidly paging through it, intrigued by the illustrations. "You know,'' he said after a time, ''it is strange, I was so unhappy when I made these pictures, but when I look at these photographs, I feel nostalgic.''

"I understand from John Huston that you were responsible for changing the ending of CHINATOWN?''

"Yes,'' he said, putting down the book.

"Keep it,'' Vicki said.

"When I was given the script,'' he went on, acknowledging the gift as he spoke, "it was about 250 pages. Many of the characters were unfilmable. I worked on the script for eight weeks just to get rid of unnecessary characters. The script had it that Huston died at the end. I didn't want that. I wanted him to live.''

"Why?'' Vicki asked.

"Because there is no justice in the story. You want the audience to be perturbed because justice *isn't* done. Hollywood likes to tease the audience, but the hero always comes along at the end and kills the bad guy. It's not that way, and I didn't want to film it that way. I wanted Huston for the role of Dunaway's father. He was perfect. And Nicholson. The script was written with him in mind. Ask Bobby Evans at Paramount to show you the original script I was first handed. You wouldn't believe it.''

Couscous was brought. Roman gave instructions in how it was best seasoned.

"Now, what do you think?''

We both nodded our accord.

"Don't go anywhere else in Paris but here,'' he cautioned.

"The detective loses in the end,'' I said.

"Well, he had to lose, didn't he? Detectives are losers to begin with. Theirs is a dirty business, peeping and spying, getting photographs of what people do in hotel rooms. That's not a profession. A detective is a loser.''

"What amazes me about the film,'' Vicki remarked, "is how little violence there is in it.''

"Yes,'' Polanski nodded vigorously, "and the critics attacked it, saying it was full of violence. But there is none, really. Violence shouldn't be drawn out. It's there in the scene where I cut Nicholson's nose. It happens so fast, you aren't aware of it. Then it's over. That's how violence is. They want to cut that scene when they release the film to television. Even when Dunaway gets shot, the violence is quick. Audiences like sensations. So if you have to include violence, if it's quick, it is also sensational.''

When we were nearly finished eating, Moroccan tea was served, in glasses, drawn from a samovar which was brought to our table and left there. For a moment at least, Roman seemed at home in Paris. Roman, for whom life was being constantly active, at work, or skiing, or exercising frantically, or bedding women, was comfortable. He stretched out in his booth seat.

"CHINATOWN didn't have a very happy ending,'' I taunted him.

"Happy endings make me puke, don't they you?''

"But audiences like happy endings.''

"I don't believe in giving people what they want, or what they think they want. When I was little I saw OF MICE AND MEN [United Artists, 1939]. That didn't have a happy ending, did it?'' He knew I hadn't been serious, but he persisted. "Think about successful stories. They're usually unhappy. Happiness doesn't give you intrigue, no suspense; and if you don't have conflict, you don't have a movie."

"Can I ask you something?" Vicki put in.

"Anything, dear. You can ask me anything."

"What's WHAT?"

"What?"

"WHAT? What is WHAT?"

"What? Do you mean WHAT? Oh, WHAT?!'' Roman broke into laughter and drew himself together in his seat. "WHAT? Dear, WHAT? is like a *rondo*. You know? Tra-la-la-la, tra-la-la-la, and then la-la, and then it comes back again, tra-la-la-la, tra-la-la-la. WHAT? is a *rondo*."

"But it doesn't make any sense."

"*Rondos* don't make any sense. They are *rondos*, that's all. It's a theme you keep coming back to, that repeats. I wanted to do a movie that was like a *rondo*."

It was time to go. Roman threw two hundred francs on the table and we walked out of the restaurant. His spirits were jubilant. He began to whistle as we walked; or, I should say, as *we* walked and he skipped along the curb.

I could not help thinking of Hawks' TO HAVE AND HAVE NOT, the way he gave the story a happy ending and allowed Humphrey Bogart, one man supposedly alone, to triumph over his situation. The Harry Morgan character Bogart was playing had nothing to do with Hemingway's character.

" 'A man,' Harry Morgan said, looking at them both. 'One man alone ain't got. No man alone now.' He stopped. 'No matter how a man alone ain't got no bloody fucking chance.'

"He shut his eyes. It had taken him a long time to get it out and it had taken him all his life to learn it."[3]

That was how Hemingway had written it. He had told how Harry Morgan had to lose his boat, because in life, when somebody wins, somebody else has got to lose. And lying on the deck of his boat, gut-shot and bleeding to death, Harry Morgan lost his freedom and his self-reliance, and was even losing his life. When Paramount would film ISLANDS IN THE STREAM in 1977, with George C. Scott in the starring role, Denne Bart Petutclerc ignored the third part of Hemingway's posthumous novel and went back to Harry Morgan's story from TO HAVE AND HAVE NOT, but for the fade . . . for the fade he went back to Howard Hawks!

Criminal corruption, by the time CHINATOWN was made, could as John Huston reflected be shown for what it was, something that is indigenous to the American way of life. The "future" for Huston in the film is possession of his daughter/granddaughter whom he incestuously conceived with Faye Dunaway playing his daughter. Jack Nicholson's detective J.J. Gittes would prevent that future from happening; he would have Huston brought to justice. Dunaway and the daughter/granddaughter are about to escape from their hiding place in Chinatown. Huston arrives there with Nicholson. Nicholson's men were supposed to wait for him there, but the police have shown up in the interim and now Nicholson's men are handcuffed. When Dunaway makes a break for it, she's shot through the eye by one of the policemen. Huston embraces his daughter/granddaughter and leads her away from this terrible sight.

"He owns the police," Dunaway as Evelyn Mulray screams at Nicholson's Jake Gittes as he would struggle and object to what is about to happen.

"As little as possible," he mutters beneath his breath once Dunaway is dead.

"C'mon, Jake," he is comforted. "It's Chinatown."

Mike Wilmington in an article shortly after the film was released found that "CHINATOWN is basically a lament. It mourns the death of a hero: the symbolic hero who stands at the end, stripped of his defenses, revealed as a man paralyzed and defeated by the 'system.' Jake is a small-time detective, out of his depth; Evelyn a doomed neurotic who couldn't save herself. But the revelation does not really diminish them. They still retain, perhaps through the sympathy evoked for them, perhaps through the whole supporting iconography of the genre, a stature which earns them something more than pathos."[4] In the same article, Wilmington also made an important distinction between Polanski's CHINATOWN and Robert Altman's attempt to satirize Raymond Chandler in THE LONG GOODBYE (United Artists, 1973). "Rather than try to explode the genre from inside, like Altman, he [Polanski] and scenarist Robert Towne try to make a 'perfect model,' the 'ideal' private eye film. If THE LONG GOODBYE shows the private eye as an anachronism, his values made absurd; Polanski, instead, recreates the world which made those values."[5] It is because I completely endorsed this view of CHINATOWN that I dedicated THE DETECTIVE IN HOLLYWOOD "for Samuel Dashiell Hammett, who brought contemporary America to the detective story—and for Roman Polanski, who brought the vividness of Hammett's vision to the screen." Andrew Sarris, in his review of my book in THE NEW YORK TIMES BOOK REVIEW, took exception to that dedication. "One can understand the homage to Hammett," he wrote, "but one would expect the second dedication to devolve on John Huston or Humphrey Bogart for bringing Sam Spade to life in the 1941 production of THE MALTESE FALCON. One might expect even a nod to Raymond Chandler and Howard Hawks for THE BIG SLEEP. But Roman Polanski for CHINATOWN is a perverse choice by any standards. . . . The deep pessimism and antic absurdism that typify both CHINATOWN and THE LONG GOODBYE actually correspond with Mr. Tuska's cynical conception of 'truth' in the detective film. Evil, according to Mr. Tuska, flourishes at all levels of our society, and the detective film indulges in the purest fantasy when it follows the dictates of the censor in punishing malefactors with 100 percent efficiency."[6]

Sarris had missed the whole point of what I had tried to say in that book. Later, when I adapted what I had written for film, I had Orson Welles sum up what had been my essential view of the matter. "No doubt, as the years passed," Orson said on camera, "it became increasingly difficult for anyone to believe in a private eye as a savior. But with such disillusionment came something else, more important. It became possible in the detective film to depict *American society* the way Hammett and Chandler had depicted it in their fiction. Law is where you buy it. Politicians are more often corrupt than honest and the police are most often brutal or indifferent. Finding out the truth—when and if the detective could find it out—didn't make any difference, and it certainly didn't mean that a criminal would be brought to justice—not if that criminal happened to have power, and money, and political influence. In THE MALTESE FAL-CON, the way Dashiell Hammett wrote it and *not* the way it was filmed, the detective was as corrupt in a small way as most of the other characters were corrupt in a big way. The one basic principle of life was that everyone—including the detective—used everyone else for selfish and personal ends. When that view of American society and of the private eye was brought to the screen, the detective was named J.J. Gittes and he was portrayed by Jack Nicholson. Hammett had nothing to do with that film or with that character, but it was a slice out of life the way he had seen it."

All of that, of course, was in the future. At the moment, as I watched Roman Polanski skipping along, it occurred to me that relatively soon now, in the States, a made for television movie would be broadcast exploiting the sensation that the murder of his wife had caused.

"CHINATOWN didn't have a very happy ending," I said again.

Polanski moved back to the sidewalk and walked beside us.

"When people leave a theatre," he said, "they shouldn't be allowed to think that everything is all right with the world. It isn't. And very little in life has a happy ending." He stopped in his tracks and faced us. "And CHINATOWN was a popular film, wasn't it?"

"You needn't be so smug about it," I returned. "All you're saying is that you were lucky—once—and got away with telling the truth."

We were at the entrance to the Studios de Boulogne. Polanski put his arm around me.

"Let's go back inside and work on LOCOTAIRE, shall we?"

## II

It was Friedrich Nietzsche who observed that "in conversation deep thinkers always appear as comedians because in order to be understood they must first simulate a superficies."[7] Polanski, who remarked once to Ivan Butler, "I am not a pessimist, I am just serious,"[8] had sufficient provocation to simulate a comic superficies at eight years of age when he was left very much to his own resources. That was in 1941 during the German occupation of Poland. He had been born in Paris on 18 August 1933 where his father, a native of Cracow, Ryszard Polanski, had immigrated several years before after divorcing his first wife in Poland. There, Ryszard met a married woman, a Russian Jewess named Bula Katz. They fell in love and Bula Katz divorced her husband so she could marry Ryszard. She retained custody of her young daughter. In 1936, the Polanski family returned to Poland, to Cracow, leaving Bula's daughter from her first marriage behind in France. Because they were Jewish, Roman's parents became part of Hitler's *letzte Auflösung* to the Jewish question.

There remains some mystery about the exact events of Roman's life since he has been thoroughly willing over the years to use them himself, depending on the responsiveness of his audience, to further his own ends. This situation has not been helped by the fact that Barbara Leaming's first effort at writing film biography was her book, POLANSKI: THE FILMMAKER AS VOYEUR (1981), the degree of personal spite perhaps intensified by Roman's unwillingness to grant her an interview. Roman himself did not really help clarify the facts much when he published his autobiography, ROMAN (1984), since his objective was quite definitely to engender sympathy for his plight as a consequence of the rape charge to which he pled guilty in Santa Monica Superior Court. However, I would give credence to the first sentence in ROMAN in which Polanski confessed that "for as far back as I can remember, the line between fantasy and reality has been hopelessly blurred."[9]

At first, Roman lived with his parents in the Cracow ghetto. During the day, he stayed with a Gentile family named Wilks. "My mother took me out, on her pass, to the Wilks'," he wrote in ROMAN. "When the time came for me to go back, it was my father, not my mother, who collected me on his way from the factory in town where he was employed as a metalworker. . . . As we were walking back across the Padgorze bridge toward the ghetto, he started weeping uncontrollably. At last he said, 'They took your mother.' I said, 'Don't cry, people are watching.' I was afraid his tears might advertise the fact that we were Jews, unescorted and off limits."[10] Leaming, naturally, has her own version. One day a truck came to the ghetto to collect Jews, Roman's mother among them, who "according to the testimony of a survivor, hurled her eight-year-old son from the truck that was taking her away. This was 1941, and Romek fled into the ghetto to his father."[11] Roman was named Raymond in Paris, which can best be pronounced Roman in Polish. Throughout her biography, Leaming chose to refer to him by the Polish diminutive of his name, Romek. Typically, she cited no source for the "survivor's" testimony. Had the incident actually happened, I cannot imagine why Roman would not have told it that way, since it *plays* better than the version he did tell, and throughout ROMAN he constantly condensed scenes, characters, and conversations to make them more immediate and even cinematic.

One day, Roman saw his father in a line of men being marshaled about by German soldiers. As they were marching out of the ghetto, Roman followed, trying to get his father's attention. Ryszard sidled over toward his son and "then, out of the corner of his mouth, he hissed, 'Shove off!' Those two brusque words stopped me in my tracks. I watched the column recede, then turned away. I didn't look back."[12]

Roman's mother was taken eventually to Auschwitz, where she would be gassed. His father would be taken in time to Mauthausen, where he would survive. Before he was seized, Ryszard had made arrangements for Roman to be cared for should he be taken away and he was sent to a small farm near the tiny village of Wysoka where he lived in a hovel with a couple named Buchala and their three children.

In 1977, Polanski began providing various versions of this story to members of the press, to garner support during his rape case. "As the Germans sealed off Cracow's Jewish ghetto, Polanski and his parents were taken to Auschwitz concentration camp where his mother later died," Lee Grant wrote for THE LOS ANGELES TIMES syndication service. "Polanski, however, escaped: 'My father cut the wires,' Polanski later recalled, 'and I was off.' "[13] In an interview with PEOPLE magazine, Polanski had a similar story to tell. " 'Even when the Nazis showed antisemitic propaganda films, I'd be glued to the barbed wire,' he said. 'There was a magic about movies, though I was fully aware of the content.' "[14] When we talked that first time in Paris, there was not the need to reprise the past and force it to serve an objective. "The real source of human character is genetic and what you've experienced in the first three years of your life," he told me in response to my inquiry about his life during the war. "I was raised with gentleness and care and love." I believed that at the time and I still regard it as more accurate than anything which has been written about those years since. Roman pretended to be Roman Catholic while living in Wysoka and even for a while after the war. This subterfuge was easy since he did not look particularly Jewish. "They were great people," Roman told me of the Buchalas, "even though they couldn't read or write. Having to do farm chores made me think for myself." Roman also admitted that he willingly exchanged Roman Catholicism for Marxism with the arrival of the Red Army. "They were the avengers who brought us freedom," was how he put it, much as any Pole would have said of Napoleon a century before when the French "liberated" Poland from Russia.

When Ryszard returned to Cracow, he was reunited with his son. He enrolled Roman in a technical school while resuming work himself as the manager of a small plastics factory. When Ryszard began a relationship with a Christian woman, Wanda Zajaczkowska, Roman objected violently and never again would he live with his father, although his father did pay both room and board for him to live elsewhere in Cracow. Bored with school, already at fourteen Roman secured work as a child actor. This led in time to acting in films and he appeared, most notably, in THREE STORIES in 1953 and in director Andrzej Wajda's first important production, A GENERATION, in 1954. Not wanting an education in a technical school, Roman persuaded his father to assist him in attending the Cracow Art School where he studied graphic arts and sculpture. His Marxism evaporated commensurately with his disinclination to enter military service. Encouraged to do so upon graduation, Roman underwent the grueling examination required of applicants to the National Film School at Lodz, hoping to be accepted as an acting student but instead, because of his previous training, he was accepted by the directing school. Polanski's early student film, THE BIKE, was left unfinished, but it was based on an actual incident. In his early days in postwar Cracow, he had wanted to purchase a racing bike and had been lured by a young thug to an abandoned German bomb shelter where he was nearly murdered. He survived the beating, however, and the thug was later apprehended and executed for other crimes he had committed. He did complete a short film titled BREAK UP THE DANCE in 1957, which incorporates the plot in the title, and in 1958 he filmed TWO MEN AND A WARDROBE, the first of his student films destined to be seen outside Poland.

Polanski felt that dialogue had little place in a short film and therefore concentrated on telling visually the story of two men who emerge from the sea carrying an old-fashioned wardrobe. No one wants any part of the men or their burden. When a girl is about to be molested by a gang of thugs, she sees their reflection in the wardrobe mirror and runs to safety. In retaliation, the thugs fall upon the two men and beat them up. Polanski cast himself in a cameo role as one of the thugs. Finally, in despair, the two men decide to return to the sea, still carrying the wardrobe between them. In making the film, Polanski adhered to Flaubert's admonition, *"il ne faut jamais conclure."* He has never really retreated from this principle, nor has he done much to change his orientation since this early propaedeutic exercise. I think it is a mistake to pillory Polanski because he does not embrace moralistic conclusions, thereby faulting him for amorality. His stubborn refusal to grow in personal perspective has been a far more serious flaw. The music for TWO MEN AND A WARDROBE was composed by Krzysztof Komeda who, until his death in 1968, composed the music for nearly all of Polanski's films. "Though symbolically one regards the two men as a single entity," Ivan Butler observed, "in actual fact they have at least the companionship of each other, a friendship that stands all the strains of their dilemma, and which later solitaries . . . will not know."[15]

In 1959 Polanski directed THE LAMP, never seen outside Poland, and WHEN ANGELS FALL, his diploma work which, after his fame in the West, was occasionally blocked with one or another of his features in American art theatres. WHEN ANGELS FALL tells of an old woman who works as a matron in a public lavatory. Her present is filmed in black and white, whereas her memories of the men in her past, the cavalry officer who seduced her, the son to whom she gave birth, the death of her lover during a war (with Polanski in a bit part), are filmed in color. She is constantly reminded of the present through the sordid incidents happening in the urinal until, magically, her lover crashes through the skylight in the form of an angel with comic wings and a wired-on nimbus, setting her free in death. To play the old woman in the scenes of her youth, Polanski cast Barbara Kwiatkowska who was already relatively well known in Polish films. In 1959, Polanski had completed all of his course work except for his thesis, which he never wrote and so he never technically graduated from Lodz. However, he married Barbara Kwiatkowska and she would prove his ticket to the West. In Poland, there was not a great deal of opportunity for Polanski to direct, although he did secure a position as assistant director to Andrzej Munk who was preparing a film to be titled BAD LUCK (1959). Barbara was cast in the role of the female lead, a seductress, and even Polanski had a role, that of a tutor whom at one point she seduces. A French producer, who wanted to cast Barbara in a film, spoke with Polanski over the telephone and had the mistaken impression that she could speak French. Arrangements were made for the two of them to travel to Paris. After some initial awkwardness, Barbara did get the role and her name was changed to Barbara Lass. By this time, Polanski had established with Barbara the lifestyle he would retain whether married or not. In his autobiography, Roman explained that marriage "didn't prevent me from having one-night stands when Barbara was away or I was on the road. I was attracted to other girls, and when I got the opportunity to do so, I slept with them. The frustration of remaining faithful at all times led, I still felt, to sub-conscious resentment. From my own point of view, these brief affairs didn't impair our relationship in the least."[16] However, when Barbara did eventually leave him for another man, he was bitterly resentful and it was a resentment he never really was able to overcome. In Paris, Polanski recalled, Barbara "was so happy just to be there, so utterly feminine in her reactions, so childishly delighted by all she saw, that my heart melted."[17]

The only directing jobs that came his way during this eighteen-month stay abroad resulted in just one short film, LE GROS ET LE MAIGRE [THE FAT AND THE LEAN] (French, 1961), in which he portrayed a servant tyrannized by actor André Katelbach playing his peasant master. If the Germans and Russians had taught him nothing else, they were adept instructors in the meaning and exercise of power in the modern world.

Assured that he would have an opportunity to direct a feature film if he returned to Poland, Polanski did so in 1961. Barbara was, according to Polanski, involved in an off-screen affair. W. Somerset Maugham once devised the maxim, "*il y a toujours un qui aime et un qui se laisse aimer*," and for Polanski, despite his admission of personal promiscuity, in his relationship with Barbara, it was he who loved her and she who allowed herself to be loved. "No one enters upon life without assumptions," C.G. Jung wrote in "*Die Lebenswende*" ["The Turnings of Life"]. "These assumptions are occasionally false, arising not from the external situations which one encounters. Often it is a matter of too great expectations or an underestimation of external difficulties or unjustified optimism or negativism."[18] We all seem to be prone to such assumptions, engendered by temperament or perhaps by some unconscious psychic predisposition. The aging process normally, if it isn't excessively hindered by neurosis, should in time divest us of at least some of the more untenable of our assumptions. Yet, what are we to make of the fixed idea that women are by nature promiscuous and unfaithful? I doubt that this can be accurately attributed to the category of unconscious assumptions about life which are more or less present at birth, but for some, and Polanski is definitely one of them, it is a notion that can achieve and maintain the intensity of an obsession.

Initially, Roman's collaborator for the screenplay to KNIFE IN THE WATER (Contemporary, 1962) was Jakub Goldberg, an assistant director working for Kamera at the time and a friend of Polanski's whom Roman had cast as one of the two men carrying the wardrobe in his earlier short film. The script idea met with approval but when it came time to develop it into a full shooting script nothing much happened until Jerzy Skolimowski joined the group. He was just beginning the five-year course at Lodz; he was also highly gifted. The two men locked themselves away in Goldberg's room and came up with a final screenplay that Roman subsequently credited more to Skolimowski than to himself.

While waiting for bureaucratic approval of this script, Polanski turned to another project, what would be his last short film, MAMMALS, which was actually financed independently of the government, a situation unique in Poland and highly unorthodox. The financial backing came from Wojciech Frykowski. Roman had known and liked Wojciech for some time. The son of a major supplier for the Polish black market, Roman chose not even to mention this connection in his autobiography, preferring instead to characterize Wojciech's father as one of the last independent small textile printers. The film, photographed against a dazzling background of white snow, was a parable about two men who bicker so much between themselves that they are unable to help each other across the frozen wastes. The short was completed but not yet edited when KNIFE IN THE WATER was approved for production. Roman values loyalty above all other attributes and he remained loyal to Wojciech in later years, even when his sources for money had evaporated and his prospects were bleak. Eventually he followed Roman to Los Angeles, was readily absorbed into the Southern California drug culture, and was there on Cielo Drive with Sharon Tate and the others the night the Manson "family" struck. Thought by his assailants to be Roman's younger brother, Wojciech had staggered out of the house and onto the front lawn, screaming for someone to help him. The drugs and the dreams would end abruptly for him in the smog-laden City of the Angels. His corpse showed that he had been shot twice, struck over the head with a blunt instrument thirteen times, and stabbed fifty-one times. Polanski would describe Wojciech to the press as " 'a man of little talent but immense charm.' "[19]

Of the three parts called for in the script of KNIFE IN THE WATER, only that of Andrzej was assigned to a professional actor, Leon Niemczyk. To play Andrzej's faithless wife, Polanski spent days at the Warsaw municipal swimming pool, interviewing talent in and out of the water. He finally came up with Jolanta Umecka, a music student, who seemed to fit exactly his idea of the woman he wanted. The role of the young man who seduces Umecka was one Roman wanted to play himself. Dissuaded from this idea, he cast Zygmunt Malanowicz, a drama school student, but dubbed his voice in the Polish version with his own, so he was there at least in part.

Production proceeded at a snail's pace—much of the story taking place aboard a boat in the Polish lake region—with Polanski sometimes getting ten seconds of film a day, sometimes nothing. To evoke a performance from the old woman in WHEN ANGELS FALL, another non-professional, Polanski had plied her with chocolate bon-bons. To overcome Umecka's anxiety before the camera, Polanski resorted to a similar device, feeding her chocolate biscuits. As her tension increased, so did her eating, until the curves restrained by her bathing suit threatened to become too opulent. Production was almost halted due to rumors, later proven groundless, of orgies in the boathouse.

There are two stories in KNIFE IN THE WATER. The primary story is the Œdipus conflict played out between an older man and his young wife when a hitchhiker intrudes on their lives and proceeds to challenge the older man sexually, finally succeeding in seducing his wife. The knife carried by the hitchhiker, which he can use dextrously, is obviously symbolic of his youthful virility. There is a reversal in that it is the hitchhiker who is supposedly murdered by the older man, but this is only a sham; and, while the husband is ashore, the hitchhiker rejoins the wife who is isolated on the boat and she welcomes his sexual advances. The secondary story is the tedium of conventional bourgeois married life and the pointlessness of existence for these three who vie between the poles of sexual interest and possessiveness. Upon release, the picture won rave reviews and, after being shown in the United States, was even nominated for an Academy Award. Polanski found himself famous, virtually overnight, and began referring to himself as "the great Polanski." What most impressed critics about KNIFE IN THE WATER was its intense concentration and they delighted in the opportunity it afforded them to discern Freudian undertones. However, other critics went so far as to read in the film an ambiguous political statement. Certainly Poland's Communist Party leader, Wladyslaw Gomulka, felt this way when he condemned the picture for its depiction of decadent behavior. The upshot was that Polanski, although acclaimed, was unable to secure further employment in Poland. While the preference for theme over story has long been a Slavic proclivity, KNIFE IN THE WATER, viewed objectively today, seems a trifle dull, especially if the political implication of depicting social ennui behind the Iron Curtain is not taken into account. Doubtless this had much to do with the film's popularity in the West.

By the time KNIFE IN THE WATER was completed, Polanski's marriage to Barbara was over. He returned to Paris and to Pierre Roustang, one of those involved in luring Barbara into French films. It was at a party thrown by Roustang that Roman met Gérard Brach, probably the single most important relationship in his life. After that initial meeting, the two became inseparable and would continue to collaborate on pictures on and off over the years. Brach had just emerged from a difficult divorce, as had Polanski, and the two decided to produce a screenplay which would embody their disillusionment in women. The character of Teresa in CUL-DE-SAC (Sigma III, 1966) was the result. Polanski and Brach shared an apartment and arrived at their basic cinematic ideas through animated discussions, punctuated by chess games when no new ideas were forthcoming, followed by Brach writing the scenes in French, Polanski criticizing what had been written, and Brach rewriting. They assembled a script out of scenes they felt they would like someday to see in a film, now that they had the female character, and called the finished product at first WHEN KATELBACH COMES.

Roman could find no backers for the project, but he did receive an offer to direct the Amsterdam episode of LES PLUS BELLES ESCROQUERIES DU MONDE [THE MOST BEAUTIFUL SWINDLES IN THE WORLD] (French, 1967). Brach collaborated with Polanski on the screenplay for his segment of this omnibus film, but as a whole it flopped when released. However, the picture did get Roman and Gérard to Cannes for the Film Festival and it was there that Polanski first made the acquaintance of Victor Lownes, an executive in Playboy Enterprises who was to manage the Playboy Club in London. He became a close friend for a while.

Polanski was also invited to attend the Academy Awards in Los Angeles. He had listed himself with the William Morris Agency. Although he never received an offer through the organization, while in Los Angeles one of the agents arranged a blind date for Polanski with Carol Lynley. "Beautiful, baby-faced Carol, who had a terrific sense of humor, remained a close friend of mine for years to come," Polanski later recalled. "She must have taken to me right away because she invited me home. So if William Morris never achieved anything else, it did at least get me laid."[20]

Gene Gutowski, a producer in London, was so impressed with KNIFE IN THE WATER that he invited Polanski to seek his fortune in that city. Polanski was interested still in CUL-DE-SAC, but the best that he and Gutowski could do was to attract financing from Michael Klinger's Compton Films to do an original horror picture. Klinger was primarily in the field of soft-core pornography and (as later Wolf Hartwig, Munich's porno king, with Sam Peckinpah) Klinger hoped to improve his company's image by producing and releasing a film of stature, provided it could be made inexpensively. For writing, directing, and producing the film, Polanski, Brach, and Gutowski were to share an initial payment of $5,000 and a percentage of the net profits. The original screenplay Polanski and Brach wrote was titled REPULSION (Royal Films International, 1965).

For the lead, Polanski hired Catherine Deneuve who had recently begun a film career in earnest with Roger Vadim's LE VICE ET LE VIRTU (French, 1962). She had hoped to marry Vadim but, due to his reluctance, had settled instead for having a child by him out of wedlock. Vadim had been taken with her adolescent figure, so reminiscent of a Colette heroine, and noted in his MEMOIRS OF THE DEVIL (1975) how, although she liked to laugh, she seemed enveloped in a persistent air of gloom. It was these qualities precisely which

Polanski felt made her ideal for the role of Carol Ledoux in REPULSION. After a somewhat moody build-up, Carol goes berserk, murdering one of her male admirers and the landlord before she is discovered by her sister and her sister's boyfriend cringing beneath her sister's bed. The highpoint of the film, according to its admirers, is the development of Carol's disintegratory hallucinations. It is on this basis that comparisons are drawn between REPULSION and Hitchcock's PSYCHO (Paramount, 1960).

Depending on to whom he was talking, Polanski gave out rather contradictory impressions concerning the film. In 1966 he told CAHIERS DU CINÉMA that "REPULSION . . . is not a Polish subject. . . . I do not mean that there are no neurotics in Poland, but no doubt there are fewer of them; in any case neurosis is not expressed that way. What is the reason? Maybe the solitude is less great there than elsewhere. . . . In any case, I wanted to show precisely a certain kind of disorder and not another. Therefore I had to do so where that disorder existed."[21] Some years later, when speaking at the American Film Institute in Los Angeles, Polanski observed that "the scripts which I wrote with Gérard Brach are not solely Anglo-Saxon, the subjects. Like REPULSION, it could happen anywhere."[22] When we talked in Paris, I asked Roman if Carol in the film was supposed to have repressed Lesbian tendencies, as suggested by some critics at the time. "Not at all," he replied. "She murders men out of a fear of sex. She's not a normal person to begin with; hence the photo of her at the end. She is a homicidal schizophrenic, yes, but not a blood-thirsty monster. The opposite is true. She is innocent. She's just fascinated by sex, by her sister's boyfriend's things in the bathroom."

Columbia Pictures acquired distribution rights for the United States. As a distribution tool to excite interest among exhibitors and the public, Columbia's publicity department leaked the rumor that in those scenes where Deneuve fantasizes she is being raped, because Polanski was such a fanatic for realism, he was supposed to have filmed the sexual act really in progress and lighted the participants' figures so as to cast revealing shadows on the wall. It was a lie and it did nothing to counteract the disappointing American box office. In fact, Deneuve had refused so much as to be filmed in the nude. It was only after the picture was completed and through Victor Lownes' influence that Polanski was able to persuade Deneuve to pose for some semi-nude photographs for PLAYBOY. He seemed pleased to note in ROMAN that Deneuve wound up marrying the PLAYBOY photographer who took the pictures.

European critics were quite positive, however, in their responses to the film and internationally REPULSION did much better than in the United States. If I have an objection, it has nothing to do with the heavy-handed special effects which are the best Polanski could make them on his limited budget. Rather, I am uncomfortable with the way he made Carol's descent into insanity so subjective an experience. The spectacle, as a consequence, is more alienating than empathetic, and empathy is what would most be needed to put across both the character and her situation. As it stands, REPULSION shocks without ever evoking our involvement; we are as much outsiders from Carol's personality as she is an outsider from those around her. No doubt, Polanski would counter that this was a horror film and empathy is not important. What is impressive to me about REPULSION is the use of sound to heighten every significant visual effect. Perhaps this represents his greatest debt to Orson Welles' early films. Polanski can at times become so enraptured with visual content that he utterly forsakes story, but his sense of the dramatic power of sound never deserts him. When he spoke at the American Film Institute, he took pains to illustrate how a composer working at a piano, by means of rigorous trial and error, comes to compose a faultless melody. I was affected by that same quality in him while at the Studios de Boulogne listening to his dubbing of THE TENANT.

The success of REPULSION was such that Polanski and Gutowski were able to get financial backing from the same source so he could proceed with CUL-DE-SAC. He was also better paid, receiving £10,000 for his services. For me, CUL-DE-SAC is the first film he made up to that time which proves consistently entertaining. The characters and the *comédie noir* situation never slacken. Donald Pleasence, later a nasty heavy in several Hollywood films, was cast as George, a man who leaves his first wife to live in a secluded castle with a second, younger, more attractive wife whom he genuinely loves and who is unfaithful to him. It ends with George sitting, bereft, on a rock in the midst of a promontory, calling out in his aloneness the name of his first wife. Françoise Dorleac, Catherine Deneuve's older sister and soon to die in an automobile crash while vacationing with Deneuve, plays the second wife (we never see the first one). Neither Pleasance nor Dorleac were in accord with Polanski's interpretation of their relationship. " 'She went for his money, of course,' " Pleasance later said, " 'but she liked him as well. This was an area where Roman and I disagreed. He was absolutely adamant that she did not find George attractive in any way.' "[23] Lionel Stander was at his most amusing portraying the bumbling American gangster who disrupts this idyllic, medieval romance (one-sided, according to Polanski) between Pleasance and Dorleac. " 'Of course she *is* bored,' " Pleasance went on, " 'but Françoise wanted the character to be more two-dimensional, whereas Roman wanted her to be simply sluttish. I don't think he ever really liked her performance very much, though I myself thought it was great.' "[24]

What came to affect Polanski's view of women, at least off-camera, was his meeting Sharon Tate prior to making his next picture, THE FEARLESS VAMPIRE KILLERS (M-G-M, 1967). Martin Ransohoff was the executive producer on the film, acting as liaison between M-G-M and the film's producer, Gene Gutowski, with Polanski directing from a script he had written with Gérard Brach. Tate was under contract to Ransohoff and he wanted Polanski to use her in the forthcoming film. Roman was first introduced to Tate at one of Ransohoff's parties.

In ROMAN, these early scenes with Sharon seem to have been condensed and altered in order to be consistent with the view Polanski chose to put forward of himself as well as of Sharon. In HELTER SKELTER (1974) by Vincent Bugliosi, the Los Angeles District Attorney who helped solve the puzzle of Sharon's murder, an account which Polanski himself termed "full and reasonably accurate,"[25] the transcript of Polanski's polygraph test is provided, evidence which he gave when he was very intent to help in any way he could in the apprehension of Sharon's assailants. This testimony is somewhat at odds with the later version in ROMAN. "I thought she was quite pretty," Polanski told Lieutenant Earl Deemer of LAPD, "but I wasn't at that time very impressed. But then I saw her again. I took her out. We talked a lot, you know. At that time I was really swinging. All I was interested in was to fuck a girl and move on. I had a very bad marriage, you know. Years before. Not bad; it was beautiful, but my wife dumped me. So I was feeling great, because I was a success with women and I just like fucking around."[26] According to the police investigation into Sharon's past, Bugliosi found that "though Sharon Tate looked the part of the starlet, she didn't live up to at least one portion of that image. She was not promiscuous. Her relationships were few, and rarely casual, at least on her part. She seemed attracted to dominant men."[27]

Polanski corroborated this view of Sharon in his testimony. "I remember I spent a night—I lost a key—and I spent a night in her house in the same bed, you know. And I knew there was no question of making love with her. That's the type of girl she was. I mean, that rarely happens to me! And then we went on location—it was about two or three months later. When we were on location shooting the film, I asked her, 'Would you like to make love with me?' and she said, very sweetly, 'Yes.' And then for the first time I was somewhat touched by her, you know. And we started sleeping regularly together. And she was so sweet and so lovely that I didn't believe it, you know. I'd had bad experiences and I didn't believe that people like that existed, and I was waiting a long time for her to show the color, right? But she was *beautiful*, without this phoniness. She was fantastic. She loved me. . . . And I said, 'You know how I am; I screw around.' And she said, 'I don't want to change you.' She was a *fucking angel*. She was a unique character, who I'll never meet again in my life."[28]

When asked about use of the drug LSD, Polanski admitted that he went on one trip with Sharon. It was toward the end of 1965, his third and her fifteenth or sixteenth. " '. . . In the morning she started flipping out and screaming and I was scared to death. And after that she said, "I told you I couldn't take it and this is the end."'[1] And it was the end, for me and for her.' "[29] The implication, from the way this is said, would seem to be that the trip was Polanski's idea, and not Sharon's.

In ROMAN, all of this is condensed into his version of their very first date together. They went to Polanski's house where they split a cube of LSD in sugar. "I suppose it was inevitable that we should go to bed together," Polanski wrote, "but we didn't do so till dawn was breaking. Not at all scary this time, the acid lent our lovemaking a touch of unreality. Afterward we talked some more until I had to leave for Heathrow to catch a plane. . . . "[30] Then followed a hiatus, broken only when they were on location during filming. "When I asked, rather haltingly, if she wanted me to come upstairs with her, she gave me one of her uniquely dazzling smiles and said yes. That marked the real beginning of our love affair."[31] I am inclined to accept the polygraph version and not what is written in ROMAN. For one thing, when Roman first met Sharon she was still involved with Jay Sebring and it would have been wholly inconsistent with what we know of her character for her to have been sleeping with two men at the same time. Later, when they were on location, the relationship with Sebring was virtually over, at least on Sharon's part, and her willingness to sleep with Roman is understandable. Even Roman admitted that Sharon was never promiscuous. "I'm the bad one," he testified during his polygraph examination. "I always screw around. That was Sharon's big hangup, you know."[32] This statement would also seem to indicate that, contrary to the impression Roman wished to put forward of her in his autobiography, Sharon was deeply hurt by Polanski's incessant philandering, even if she did not often say anything.

Yet, however much Sharon may have affected Roman in his personal life, she did nothing to alter his view of women in THE FEARLESS VAMPIRE KILLERS or in any of his subsequent films. According to Freud in "The Most Prevalent Form of Degradation in Erotic Life," "a fully normal attitude in love" comes about when the "two currents of feeling have to unite—we may describe them as the tender, affectionate feelings and the sensual feelings. . . . "[33] Not only does this never happen in any of the male/female relationships depicted in Polanski's films, but women were always pictured as flat, one-dimensional sources of sexual gratification. The exception is Carol in REPULSION, who becomes a castrating, murderous female, but in her sexual obsession she is related in spirit, if not in expression, to all of Polanski's other major female protagonists.

M. Esther Harding identified libido with the "daemon of sexuality" in PSYCHIC ENERGY: ITS SOURCE AND ITS TRANSFORMATION (1973) and wrote that "a human being who is still identified with the daemon of sexuality is able to live his sexuality only on an auto-erotic level. This is true whether the impulse finds its outlet in masturbation or whether it leads him to sexual relations with another person of either his own or the opposite sex. For as the interest and desires of the individual in this stage of development are concerned solely with his own sensations and bodily needs, his sexual instinct still lacks that degree of psychic modification which necessarily precedes any real concern with the object. Therefore almost any partner will serve for satisfaction on this level, provided the necessary stimulus is present to set off the physical mechanism of detumescence. Consequently, persons in this stage of development are usually promiscuous and fickle, and at times may be driven by a veritable daemon of desirousness, seemingly without regard for either the requirements of relationship or the fundamental decencies. To a man on this level, a woman is nothing but a sexual object, and one woman can be substituted for another with the greatest ease."[34] It would seem Polanski's view of women is embodied in a remark he made to PEOPLE MAGAZINE when he stated that " 'girls should accept their role as governed by biological realities.' "[35]

In THE NEED TO BE LOVED (1963), Theodor Reik observed that "whatever the deeper motives are for a woman's promiscuity, her behavior is inevitably accompanied by a loss of self-esteem and results in contempt for herself as an individual and for her sex. It corrupts her self-image when she is degraded to the position of a sexual object of the male. No woman with a high opinion of herself as a person and as a member of her sex will drift into promiscuity except in utter despair or under the pressure of dire need of money. The demoralizing effect of promiscuity is akin to that of a man who sells himself into slavery."[36] Hence, Françoise Dorleac's objection to the way Polanski insisted she portray Pleasence's wife. Polanski's female protagonists have no integrity because they are made to appear contemptible. "The fundamental situation is unchangeable," Ivan Butler commented on the conclusion of CUL-DE-SAC,"—all that changes is who orders whom."[37] It is an insight which deserves to be expanded to cover virtually all of Polanski's films: the power structures never change, only who occupies what position, and the image of woman remains always the same. It has also been quite that way in Roman Polanski's life. He lives much the same now in Paris as he did decades ago in Poland.

THE FEARLESS VAMPIRE KILLERS had an original running time of 128 minutes. Under Ransohoff's supervision, the American release version was recut to make a 98 minute film. Polanski was so incensed by this arbitrary treatment that he demanded his name be removed from the credits. This M-G-M and Ransohoff's Filmways company refused to do. Intended as a satire on vampire films (although it escapes me how any film in this genre can be regarded as anything less than a satire), THE FEARLESS VAMPIRE KILLERS was in the vanguard, whether as comedy or parody. It is dull at times, where Polanski became infatuated with visual imagery, but it was his first color film and he can perhaps be excused for luxuriating in it. This is especially true if we acknowledge Polanski for showing us scenes never photographed before, such as the Jewish vampire who isn't affected in the least by the sight of a crucifix or the *fagelah* vampire who is quite taken by Alfred, played by Polanski, arguing for sexual tolerance even in the realm of the occult. " 'I think he put more of himself into VAMPIRE KILLERS than into any other film,' " said Dennis Slocombe, cinematographer on the picture. " 'It brought to light the fairy-tale interest that he has. . . . The figure of Alfred is very much like Roman himself—a slight figure, young and a little defenseless—a touch of Kafka. It is very much a personal statement of his own humor. He used to chuckle all the way through.' "[38]

Between writing CUL-DE-SAC and REPULSION, Brach and Polanski wrote a script titled CHERCHEZ LA FEMME, telling the story of an American dentist who is weary of American women and embarks on a series of adventures through Europe in quest of a congenial wife. It was translated into English by Larry Gelbert. Polanski and Gutowski had formed a production company, Cadre Films,

and intended to put this script into production after the joint venture with Ransohoff's Filmways and M-G-M on THE FEARLESS VAMPIRE KILLERS.
However, the dispute over the cutting of the American version culminated in
the film never being produced and Polanski signing a contract with Robert Evans,
then head of world-wide production at Paramount since that studio's take-over
by Gulf & Western. There was nothing in Evans' background, from his being
rescued from haberdashery by Norma Shearer to play her first husband, Irving
Thalberg, in MAN OF A THOUSAND FACES (Universal, 1955) to Darryl
Zanuck's having Henry King cast him as a toreador in THE SUN ALSO RISES
(20th-Fox, 1957), to explain how he suddenly emerged in such an important
executive capacity.

While Ira Levin's novel ROSEMARY'S BABY (1968) was still in galleys,
his Hollywood agent sent a copy of it to Alfred Hitchcock and a second copy
to horror exploitation film producer and director William Castle. Castle was
excited and wanted to purchase screen rights but the asking price of a quarter
of a million dollars was too steep for him. After some haggling, Castle acquired
the rights for $100,000, plus an additional fifty thousand if it became a bestseller
and five per cent of the net profits of the film. Evans contacted Castle and had
him come to the Paramount lot in Los Angeles. Paramount wanted to finance
and distribute. Evans introduced Castle to Charles Bluhdorn, the mastermind
behind Gulf & Western. Bluhdorn negotiated terms with Castle and they agreed
on a figure of $250,000 and fifty per cent of the net profits. Neither Evans nor
Bluhdorn had read the novel, but Bluhdorn, probably at Evans' instigation,
wanted Roman Polanski to direct the film. Castle had wanted to direct ROSE-
MARY'S BABY himself, but he at least agreed to meet with Polanski.

Frequently Roman gives people a poor first impression and this was the case
with Castle. "On my first meeting with Roman Polanski," Castle recalled, "I
took an instant dislike to him. A short, stocky man, dressed in the Carnaby
Street fashion of the time, he seemed cocky and vain, continually glancing into
the mirror in my office. I had made up my mind that he would not direct
ROSEMARY'S BABY. I asked him to sit down, which he declined. He inso-
lently faced me, legs spread apart. It was useless trying to make small conversation with him, so I decided to make the meeting brief and get rid of him."[39]
Yet, in spite of Castle's resolve, Polanski, who *had* read the book, talked so
intelligently and knowingly about how to treat the property that Castle changed
his mind and called Bluhdorn at Paramount after the meeting to tell him so.

Polanski returned to London, completed a first screen treatment, and sent it
to Castle. He then telephoned Castle from London, told him he would be arriving
in a week, and said he would appreciate it if Castle would help find a house for
him to rent somewhere near the ocean. His fiancée, Sharon Tate, would be in
touch with Castle. When Castle met Sharon, he found her "beautiful" with an
"unaffected simplicity."[40] Castle showed her the house he had located, Brian
Aherne's home which was available because Aherne was going to Europe. " 'It's
perfect . . . Roman and I will be so happy here,' " she enthused when she saw

it.[41] On 20 January 1968, almost six months before ROSEMARY'S BABY (Paramount, 1968) was released, Roman and Sharon were married in London. Roman had sold semi-nude photographs of her to PLAYBOY to help promote THE FEARLESS VAMPIRE KILLERS and the wedding reception was held at the London Playboy Club. "The thought of marrying and raising a family scared me," Roman would later reflect, "not because it might encroach on my freedom—Sharon, I knew, would never let that happen—but because personal ties made me feel vulnerable. This fear was a hangover from my childhood, from the insecurity I'd experienced at the age of five or six, when my family began to disintegrate."[42]

Prior to their marriage, Sharon had landed a major role in VALLEY OF THE DOLLS (20th-Fox, 1967) and she and co-star Patty Duke became friends. Patty was breaking up with her first husband and, following Sharon's marriage, she rented her house to the newlyweds. Almost two decades later, talking to Patty about her recently published autobiography, I mentioned the fact that she had had very little to say about Sharon. She agreed and said that her reason had been that too many people who knew Sharon slightly, if at all, had written about her and she felt that as one of Sharon's closest friends she preferred to say very little. She had had somewhat negative feelings about Roman, whom she thought gnome-like, and was convinced that his incessant womanizing had been a torment which Sharon endured silently. Sharon had also been convinced that, once she was pregnant, the baby would bring her and Roman closer together.

"There were rumors of trouble in her marriage," Vincent Bugliosi recorded. "Several of [Sharon's] female friends told LAPD that she had waited to tell Roman of her pregnancy until it was too late to abort. If she was concerned that even after marriage Polanski remained the playboy, she hid it. Sharon herself often told a story then current in the movie colony, of how Roman was driving through Beverly Hills when, spotting a pretty girl walking ahead of him, he yelled, 'Miss, you have a bea-u-ti-ful arse.' Only when the girl turned did he recognize his wife. . . . No one who actually knew Sharon Tate said anything bad about her. Very sweet, somewhat naive—these were the words most often used."[43]

Gene and Judy Gutwoski lived for a time with the Polanskis. One weekend Sharon and Judy went out of town and Roman went to bed with a model who, he felt, had had her eye on him for weeks. Judy found out about it from Gene and told Sharon. According to Polanski in ROMAN, Sharon never mentioned this conversation, but Roman himself thought it was "venomous" and typical of those people who were trying to drive him and Sharon apart.

One night, with a video camera he had acquired while ROSEMARY'S BABY was in production, Polanski proposed to Sharon that he switch it on while they were making love. " 'Fine,' said Sharon, 'what characters shall we play?' The whole thing was frivolous rather than lewd and exhibitionistic."[44] After Sharon's death, the police found the video tape and it gave rise to rumors of orgies. "The film showed Sharon and Roman Polanski making love," Vincent Bugliosi wrote, adding in a footnote that "one writer would later claim that the police found a vast collection of pornography . . . , including numerous films and still shots of famous Hollywood stars engaged in various sexual acts. Aside from the above, and several unexposed rolls of video tape, the only photographs found anywhere . . . were a set of wedding pictures and a large number of publicity shots of Sharon Tate."[45] Bugliosi's book was published in 1974. When Barbara Leaming came to publish her biography of Polanski in 1981, she had obviously not bothered to consult Bugliosi's official account. "Sexual scenes were staged and taped," she wrote, "to be played and replayed. The tapes, eventually seized by police, depicted well-known Hollywood figures at play—including Roman and Sharon."[46]

ROSEMARY'S BABY, with its story of an innocent girl living in New York surrounded by a cult of devil-worshippers and impregnated by Satan, was the picture Roman made when, according to his own statements, he was happiest. It is filled with the tensions, suspense, suspicions, and hopelessly trapped feelings so typical of Polanski's European films, but added are strong logical and narrative story elements, a well-made plot, if you will, rather uncharacteristic of his previous efforts. In the novel, Satan is given credence. As an agnostic, Roman could not accept this view. Therefore, he left himself a loophole, the possibility that Rosemary only imagines all that presumably happens to her. He aptly cast Mia Farrow as Rosemary and achieved a degree of intimacy in the film by having her walk toward the camera or away from it or in front of it. If anything, the dream sequence is even more compelling than similar scenes in REPULSION. Polanski had in fact studied his own dreams in constructing such sequences. "The fact that the dream is frightening," he told students at the American Film Institute, "is because the subject of the dream is frightening. . . . I think the main thing about dreams is that everything constantly changes. Dreams are not static and, when you look at someone's face, his face imperceptibly changes. Like you start talking to your father and before you even realize, he's already Nixon for some reason. The other thing about dreams is that you are not aware of the background unless it plays some important role in the dream. . . . So in trying to translate a dream to a film, I try to make this background so that it is not so prominent, except when it has some particular meaning."[47]

Part of the way in which Polanski attempted to shed doubt on Rosemary's perceptions has to do with his use of sound. As Ivan Butler noted, in this he was using again techniques he had pioneered in REPULSION. "The ticking bedside clocks accompanying slow-mounting tension and the onset of nightmare: Rosemary gazing at her twisted reflection in a polished toaster as Carol did in a kettle: the forbidden door concealed behind a piece of furniture: the half-regarded television sets: the monotonous practising on a distant piano (scales in REPULSION, Beethoven's *Für Elise* in ROSEMARY'S BABY): the intrusive bells: the eye imagery—particularly one shot of Rosemary in the cupboard in which even the swinging light chord of REPULSION reappears—. . . they all bring to mind the earlier film (already present in the strong reminiscent setting), and add an extra edge to the unease felt from the very opening of ROSEMARY'S BABY.''[48]

Frank Sinatra, rather than marrying Lauren Bacall, married Mia Farrow instead and he was still married to her at the time production began on ROSEMARY'S BABY. "I couldn't fathom the Mia-Sinatra relationship," Polanski later reflected. "Sharon and I dined with them a couple of times. Good host and good company though he was, Sinatra never disguised that his was a man's world. What he liked best was man talk at the bar of his Beverly Hills home. Mia, on the other hand, was a sensitive flower child, a sucker for every conceivable cause from ecology to the rights of American Indians, and a committed opponent of the Vietnam War, which Sinatra supported. They didn't appear to have a single thing in common, yet it was apparent to all who saw them together that this was no marriage of convenience and that Mia was deeply in love with her husband.''[49] Polanski took longer than expected to complete the film and Sinatra became enraged because he wanted Mia free to appear in a picture with him. Finally, when she refused to walk off the film, Sinatra ''fired'' her by sending a flunkie to inform her on the set that he was filing for a divorce. The action reduced Farrow to tears and, although shattered by it, she did not quit, but rather continued in the role without being affected adversely in her portrayal.

The Polanskis went to Europe where Sharon was to appear in a film in Italy and Roman was to work on a screenplay for the DAY OF THE DOLPHIN. When her pregnancy began seriously to show, Roman found himself incapable of making love to Sharon. "In some very feminine way," Polanski wrote, "Sharon regarded this as proof of my continuing affection; as long as we made love, she felt nothing could go seriously wrong with our relationship.''[50] Sharon became distraught until she was able to rationalize Roman's behavior as induced by a fear that he might hurt the baby. In Los Angeles, the Polanskis had continued to change houses until 12 February 1969, when they moved into the house at 10050 Cielo Drive. It was to this house that Sharon returned during the eighth month of her pregnancy, leaving Roman in London working on his screen-play. Wojciech Frykowski who had taken Abigail Folger, the heiress, as his lover was living there and Jay Sebring stopped over to visit Sharon that night in August, 1969 when the murderers showed up. Sharon's assailant, a woman named Susan Atkins, claimed that by driving a knife into Sharon she was expressing her love for her. Sharon had pleaded to spare her for the sake of her baby when she and the other three were set upon, but was told by Susan that she had no mercy for her. Susan continued to stab Sharon until her screaming stopped. She had been stabbed a total of sixteen times. Had there been time, Susan had hoped to cut the dead baby, a boy, out of Sharon's corpse. A fifth victim, visiting the caretaker, was also murdered.

The violent and brutal world with which Polanski had been preoccupied in his films and which most Americans prefer not to see had now suddenly come to life and tapped Roman on the shoulder, as it had before when he was a child near Wysoka and a German soldier had started shooting at him as a convenient target and as it had again in the German bunker when he had been hit on the head. Returning to the United States, once he had been notified of the tragedy, Polanski gave a press conference and was interrogated by the police. He then went briefly into hiding on the Paramount lot. When William Castle visited him, Roman met Castle with tears in his eyes. " 'Sharon,' " he had said, " 'my poor Sharon . . . and our baby.' "[51]

For Polanski, the aftereffects have been unceasing. Indeed, with the passing years, Sharon has increasingly come to symbolize purity; his veneration of her memory is unbounded. In his autobiography he recorded how he is incapable of experiencing visual pleasure of any kind without telling himself how much Sharon would have loved it. Ever the playboy, he did concede that at least in this way, " . . . I shall remain faithful to her till the day I die."[52]

"One should not associate with people who lack shyness about what's personal," Nietzsche wrote in MENSCHLICHES ALLZUMENSCHLICHES [HUMAN ALL TOO HUMAN] (1878), "or inexorably put the handcuffs of convenience on them beforehand."[53] In Polanski's case, when he visited the death house for the first time, he was accompanied by a reporter and a photographer from LIFE, recording pictorially and verbally his reactions. He dramatically asked the question: Why? Because of the anguish the murder of Sharon brought into his life, he would continue for years to be dogged by the curious who wanted to know how he felt about it, while in print he became the subject of pseudo-psychoanalytic speculations. Yet, the most moving aspect of the tragedy was not Roman's public and private mourning, nor the willing and unwilling invasion of his personal life, but rather the senseless death of Sharon herself who, despite everything, was in those last months totally devoted to her marriage and her baby. Her bloody crucifixion reveals the constancy of barbarism below the surface among supposedly civilized people. "As an artist," Boleslaw Sulik reflected in his Introduction to the three film scripts we gave Polanski in Paris, "he seems to have been born with fixed and pessimistic conclusions about the human condition."[54] Sharon's murder did not so much confirm this posture as, in his words, "it reinforced my faith in the absurd."[55]

### III

It is in the fourth act of Puccini's LA BOHÈME that Mimi stumbles into Rudolfo's garret, dying of consumption, and the two of them lyrically sing of their past love which had once brought them so close and then drove them even more irresistibly apart. *"Che gelida manina . . . se la lasci riscaldar!"* Mimi recalls Rudolfo as having said, remembering the first time they met. It is this line at the conclusion of THE FEARLESS VAMPIRE KILLERS which Polanski gave himself in the character of Alfred, commenting to Sharon, "Your tiny hand is frozen . . . ," before she sinks her vampire's fangs into his neck.

Vicki and I attended a performance of LA BOHÈME at Covent Garden in which the soprano singing Mimi was competent but excessively overweight. Vicki objected. "How are we to believe Mimi is wasting away from tuberculosis when she comes bouncing on stage at a hundred and fifty pounds?" It was as ridiculous in its way as Lady Macbeth in Polanski's film, in her night of guilt and sorrow before her suicide, surrounded by murmurs concerning her madness, walking to and fro bare-assed in her bed chamber, her slender body lithe, youthful, sensuous, her red nipples erect (either with excitement or, more probably, in reaction to cold drafts on the set). Polanski justified this vision of Lady Macbeth on the basis of the fact that bedclothes were not worn in the Middle Ages. However, it is unlikely people pranced nude in damp castles and, surely, no one before Polanski thought to present the weird sisters as ugly hags engaging in their Corybantic antics also in the nude. According to Polanski, he had studied Shakespearean literature and staging exhaustively, always taking "the explanation that was the most visual, that was the most useful for our cinematographic adaptation. I also tried to translate to a visual whatever was possible, because often the language is so archaic that half the house doesn't understand what it's all about, but they shake their heads as they don't want to appear stupid." It apparently escaped Polanski's notice that nearly every student in the United Kingdom and the United States has read the play while an adolescent and knows what it is about.

While Sharon was still alive, Roman had worked together with Gérard Brach in scripting a film to be titled A DAY AT THE BEACH. Gene Gutowski wanted their company, Cadre Films, to produce it, and eventually Paramount agreed to co-finance the film in Denmark out of funds frozen there with Simon Hesera, one of Polanski's hangers-on, as the director. Polanski did not direct DAY OF THE DOLPHIN (Avco-Embassy, 1973). That assignment fell to Mike Nichols. Polanski toyed with ideas of making a film about Italian violinist and composer, Niccolò Paganini, or one about the ill-fated Donner party which, *en route* to California, got snowed in and resorted to cannibalism. What he did direct was MACBETH (Columbia, 1971) which was financed by Playboy Productions, largely through the influence of Victor Lownes. It was the commercial failure of this vehicle which came permanently between the two men. However, with Hugh Heffner of PLAYBOY personally involved, it is little wonder that Polanski would indulge in the nude scenes to keep up the interest in the story.

Shakespeare wasn't the least squeamish about blood-letting on stage, but it was due to his perspicacity as a dramatist, and not reticence, that he decided to have the rape and murder of MacDuff's wife and children take place *in camera*. Polanski insisted on showing it vividly in his film and made it incredibly gory. Unfortunately, the eruptions of violence and luscious, gorgeous photography are all his MACBETH has to offer. Polanski himself had no feeling for the sublimity of Shakespeare's English. There is so little emotion of any kind in his adaptation that Polanski's MACBETH might well have been a adaptation of a play by Jean Racine instead. When Lady Macbeth stands on a parapet and demands:

> Come, you spirits that tend on mortal thoughts,
> unsex me here; and fill me, from the crown to
> the toe, top-full of direct cruelty . . .

she has in the Polanski version merely the insouciant placidity of Racine's Bérénice when she stoically reflects:

> *Je l'aime, je le fuis; Titus m'aime; il me quitte.*
> *Portez loin de mes yeux vos soupirs et vos fers.*
> *Adieu. Servons tous trois d'exemple à l'univers.*[56]

Bald language with no expression cannot tell us what the characters feel nor what motivates them to act as they do, although Shakespeare's verbal imagery can always make us feel more than Racine's can. Having had to struggle during my teens reading Martin Luther's BIBEL when German was not my native language, I recognize the problems this assignment must have presented Polanski just in the effort to familiarize himself with Elizabethan English, but in Shakespeare, as in St. Jerome's Vulgate, the King James BIBLE, or Luther's BIBEL, words must carry the strongest emotional and dramatic conviction, for they arise from it as well as give expression to it. In translating MACBETH to the screen, Polanski never had his characters assault the heavens, as indeed they must. He satisfied himself instead with pretty images and hollow words.

Nor was Polanski's next undertaking any more successful. D Major!—the key in which Mozart composed such exquisite *Unterhaltungsmusik*, the key of the K.136 Divertimento, the second flute concerto, the "Coronation" piano concerto, two string quartets, a string quintet, so many serenades, the "Haffner" and "Prague" symphonies, and that minor masterpiece, the Sonata for Two Pianos. It may seem, this latter work, merely *"eine kleine klassische Bewegung"* in the Mozartean *oeuvre*, but I delight in it. Polanski obviously did, too, since it was no accident that D Major was the key he chose for WHAT? (Avco-Embassy, 1973).

Remember the scene at the end of LA TRAVIATA when Violetta, filled with the sudden strength of dying, whispers (*voce sotto*) to the Germonts, "*È strano!*" and the Germonts, straining forward to where she reclines on her sofa, enquire, "*Che?*" There is no word in Italian opera so rich in associations. Polanski knew it, and so did at least his Italian audience; but beyond that no one else could go, for ultimately only Polanski and Gérard Brach knew what was going on in WHAT?, a Carlo Ponti production filmed in Italy. Nor did anyone much care, apparently; the idea was to get a Roman Polanski film to follow in the wake of the success of ROSEMARY'S BABY.

Polanski was back at pool side, this time in Rome, interviewing females in and out of the water. He finally chose Sydne Rome, one of the first to be interviewed. She was to play "the girl" in WHAT?, to run around an Italian seaside villa with her naked breasts flapping, pursued by roués and social decadents, because for Polanski she symbolized in her appearance and personality something quintessentially American. When she sits down before the piano—

ah, it was Mozart, in D Major! Not once, but twice, she asks her accompanist: "Haven't we gone through this before?" As the D Major Sonata itself, the film also has its introspective and melancholy moods, juxtaposed with the vigorous, absurd, almost silly gaiety. Polanski went a step beyond FANTASIA (RKO, 1940) and set a story to music, rather than music to a story. He cast himself as Mosquito, a zany character flitting among such *comédie noir* characters as the old philosopher, impotent with age and dying, who can expire in ecstasy thanks to Rome's spreading her legs over his face so he can gaze one final time at *l'organe du transport delicieux*; or the amorous couple undulating beneath an animal skin with their minimal dialogue: He: "Take." She: "Give." He: "Take." She: "Give!" They sigh, I believe, when he does, and she does. What amusing nonsense when writing about it, but it is rather boring when viewing it. When we saw WHAT? again at a reissue house, retitled ROMAN POLANSKI'S FORBIDDEN DREAMS, the audience (fully aware at the time of Polanski's more recent difficulties) laughed harder at the trailer for THE TENANT (Paramount, 1976) than at WHAT?, with its narrative overlay announcing that, "No one does it to you like Roman Polanski!"

"I am sexually obsessed!" Polanski confided to CAHIERS DU CINÈMA.[57] Ralph Bellamy, who played Dr. Sapirstein in ROSEMARY'S BABY, had no doubt about that when we lunched together. "He's a brilliant director," Bellamy said, "and a perfectionist. You will go through a scene again and again until you hear this chuckle from behind the cameras. Then you know that Polanski liked it, that he got what he wanted. I was offered John Huston's role in CHINATOWN. I turned it down. I was sent a script that didn't look at all like the picture when Polanski finished it. It read like a porno film. They had me in an incestuous situation already on the third page." Obviously, Polanski stylized the treatment of sexuality in his filmed version, depending more on subtlety and delayed revelation. " 'Anjelica was with Jack and John knew it, but it wasn't yet so cemented, their relationship,' " Polanski told Lawrence Grobel when he was working on THE HUSTONS. " 'The only time that Anjelica came to visit us on the set was that scene with Jack Nicholson, when John asked him, "Mr. Gittes . . . do you sleep with my daughter? Come, come, you don't have to think about it to remember?" And Anjelica was watching the scene and she turned and walked away. She laughed later and told me that she was a bit embarrassed.' "[58]

I regard CHINATOWN as Polanski's most effective film and probably his finest because in it more than usually has been the case he was compelled to stick to a strong plot-line. "Whenever I was trying to do something interesting," he admitted, "I realized that it was a vain effort and I was going against the grain. It looked as though I was trying to jazz up certain things, so I just abandoned that approach and made it a straight suspense story." I suspect that is why the film works as well as it does. Polanski has never outgrown his love for the ambiguous and, whatever his dedication to discipline, he has always reacted disparagingly when, in conversation, I have confessed my preference for the compactness of the French in their penchant for a well-made plot. Yet it is to ROSEMARY'S BABY and to CHINATOWN, which have precisely such well-made plots, that Polanski owed his popularity with general audiences. These films, in fact, so enhanced his reputation as a bankable filmmaker that it was all too easy for some critics and producers to overlook that, notwithstanding, Roman *is* a European, with a European's sensibility and deep inner commitment to European culture and European music. When he completed CHINATOWN, Polanski went to Rome to direct the staging for a performance of Alban Berg's LULU. When he completed dubbing THE TENANT in Paris, he went to Munich to stage direct Verdi's RIGOLETTO. ROMAN opens with Polanski portraying Mozart in AMADEUS on stage in Warsaw.

I have mentioned the universal promiscuity of Polanski's female characters. They exist for the sexual pleasure of the male characters. This is no less true of the role played by Isabelle Adjani in THE TENANT than it was true for Jolanta Umecka's character at the beginning in KNIFE IN THE WATER. Conversely, Carol's descent into insanity is sexualized in REPULSION, as is that of Lady Macbeth. Women, in Polanski's cinematic world, are as driven to be sexual objects as men are desirous of having them be so; beyond this, they are capable of murder, or inducing another to murder, or being unfaithful. Faye Dunaway's character in CHINATOWN is sexually exploited by her father, has obviously been sexually promiscuous behind her husband's back, and is ultimately of no more use to Jake than as a convenient sexual partner. Depending on how you read the film, Rosemary is either a sexual object for Satan and, in her pregnancy, is of sexualized and diabolical significance for the others, or she imagines herself to be. In either case, by the fade she accepts her fate.

John Alan McCarty in an article titled "The Polanski Puzzle" (1970) made the point that "the theme of isolation is, in fact, the nucleus of all of Polanski's films."[59] This is true enough, as far as it goes, but McCarty did not get at the root of this sense of isolation. It is quite evidently sexual in origin. Male characters seem to be concerned either with material possessions or sexual conquests. The middle-aged husband in KNIFE IN THE WATER regards his young wife as among his belongings, much as his sailboat or his late-model car. The young hitchhiker is only interested in sexually experiencing Umecka's body before moving on—in Polanski's lexicon, he "just likes fucking around." Carol's sister's boyfriend in REPULSION is unhappily married but has no intention of getting a divorce. Her sister exists solely as a sexual distraction. Carol, unwilling to accept this role of a sexual object, retaliates but amid such erotic fantasies as to make her retaliation ultimately a lie. The male characters in CUL-DE-SAC may be searching for something, but it becomes apparent that it is not to be found in the company of a female and remains so ambiguous that we are no more certain of their motivations than we are of Trelkovsky's identification with the former female tenant of his apartment in THE TENANT. It may appear that J.J. Gittes is questing for truth; but, if he is, he is easily quieted by cynical despair at the ineradicable corruption of the social order of which he is only another corrupt part. Whether the setting is medieval Scotland, Southern California in the 'Thirties, or present-day Paris, the corruption and indifference of society remain essentially unassailable and the situations at the end of these films imply that they will repeat themselves, perhaps endlessly. In THE FEARLESS VAMPIRE KILLERS, the occult was eroticized for the sake of humor, but the vampires prey on ordinary mortals just as men and women use one another sexually for obscure and dubious ends. In these terms, the hot pursuits of the vampires are not really unrelated to the males sexually pursuing the females, above all Sydne Rome, in WHAT?

I should truthfully like to say in Polanski's behalf that when these images of men and women interacting together are juxtaposed they somehow constitute a commentary on the human condition, but I cannot. I do not think it is even possible to say that Polanski's films are a study in the vicissitudes of neurosis, since they strive to be more than a catalogue of psychopathologies; nor can they be said to exist primarily as vehicles for sheer entertainment. Rather, the conclusion to which I am drawn is that the isolation so many of Polanski's characters experience is based, as I have already hinted, in the consequences of their hopeless promiscuity. While I am certain this was never his conscious design, because of the regressive and infantile character of their promiscuity, Polanski's characters are incapable of rising to the occasion of a stable human relationship, much less entering upon the difficulties and challenges of maintaining such relationships. Freud, in the essay cited above, commented that "unrestrained sexual liberty from the beginning leads to no better result. It is easy to show that the value the mind sets on erotic needs instantly sinks as soon as satisfaction becomes readily obtainable. Some obstacle is necessary to swell the tide of the libido to its height; and at all periods of history, wherever natural barriers in the way of satisfaction have not sufficed, mankind has erected conventional ones in order to be able to enjoy love."[60] Polanski's characters, for the most part, exist without such barriers and, therefore, in a self-imposed vacuum which can know nothing of love and from which, seemingly, there is no escape.

We had all promised to see one another again when we parted in Paris but the opportunity did not avail itself until early in March, 1977, and then it had to be postponed. Roman had come to Hollywood accompanied by his assistant, Hercules Belville, whom we had met in Paris, and Belville's wife, Concepta, who was acting as Polanski's secretary. He had taken a suite at the Beverly-Wilshire Hotel and was at work on developing a screenplay based on a thriller by Lawrence Sanders which Columbia Pictures was to produce. On 11 March, Roman was arrested at the Beverly-Wilshire on six charges dealing with rape, drug-abuse, and sodomy. The victim, a thirteen-year-old girl, had presumably accompanied Polanski on the previous day to Jack Nicholson's Woodland Hills home, while Nicholson was out of the city, and the two had been observed by Anjelica Huston who was also arrested and charged with possession of cocaine. In her case, the charge would be dropped in exchange for her eye-witness testimony concerning Polanski and the girl. On 30 March, Polanski was indicted on all six counts, but his attorney, Douglas Dalton, was persuaded that plea-bargaining could reduce the severity of the charges. In the beginning, Polanski tended to be outspoken. For the news cameras covering his initial hearing, he commented succinctly: "I'm used to grief. This is a trifle." In an interview with PEOPLE MAGAZINE, he was less stoical. " 'If I had the choice to relive my life, I would not. Under no circumstances.' "[61] When he finally returned my call, he told me that his lawyer had given him strict orders to see no one and to say nothing, that he was already in worse trouble because of what he had said to the press. On the whole, however, he sounded cheerful and I responded in kind that Vicki and I had finally seen the uncut version of THE FEARLESS VAMPIRE KILLERS and that his version did indeed play better. I suggested, humorously, that perhaps he should hang garlic cloves all around him, as I was doing after seeing the film again, in order to ward off evil spirits.

Columbia Pictures removed him from THE FIRST DEADLY SIN and executives with whom we visited were fond of telling jokes about the "Polanski affair," such as that his latest picture was to be titled "Close Encounters of the Third Grade" after the new Steven Spielberg picture the studio was about to release, CLOSE ENCOUNTERS OF THE THIRD KIND (Columbia, 1977), and that the theme song for this new opus would be "Thank Heaven for Little Girls." Anatole France once remarked that the majestic equality of the law is such that it forbids the rich as well as the poor to steal bread or to sleep under bridges. In CHINATOWN, Polanski had one of Gittes' operatives remark, concerning the wealthy Mulrays, "Sue people like that and they're likely to be having lunch with the judge who's trying the case." Polanski found himself now identified in the public mind not with the underdog but with the rich and influential. Even when I mentioned to various parties who were familiar with the case that more than one beloved and venerable male screen idol had been cruising around Hollywood High School for the last twenty-five years seeking young girls looking for sexual experiences with the stars, I was only met with comments such as "He was stupid, that's all," or "He shouldn't have got caught."

By the time Polanski had another hearing before Santa Monica Superior Judge Laurence J. Rittenband, Dalton had succeeded in getting the counts against Roman reduced to a single charge of statutory rape. However, Judge Rittenband who had such personal antipathy for Polanski that he was not ever likely to be in the same company with him except in a courtroom ordered that the defendant must submit to examinations and mental tests to be administered by two court-appointed psychiatrists (notwithstanding the evidence to the contrary, courts persist in the belief that psychiatry is an exact science capable of precise measurements). When Polanski returned to court after the prescribed tests, Judge Rittenband was quoted as saying, despite the positive results and the recommendation for probation, " 'Although the victim was not an inexperienced and unsophisticated young girl, this fact was not a license to the defendant, a man of the world in his forties, to engage in an act of unlawful sexual intercourse with her, however submissive or uninhibited she might have been.' ''[62] The judge, after noting that the " 'prosecutrix was a well developed young girl, who looked older than her years, and regrettably was not unschooled in sexual matters,' " then " 'strongly condemned' the girl's mother for her role, saying, 'Her permitting her daughter to accompany the defendant to the Nicholson home, unchaperoned, was most unwise, irrespective of how it turned out.' ''[63]

Between the time that Columbia dropped Polanski and this latest hearing, Dino De Laurentiis hired Roman to direct a remake of HURRICANE (United Artists, 1937), originally directed by John Ford. In view of the fact that the court-appointed psychiatrists had declared that Roman was not a "mentally disordered sex offender," the judge granted him a stay of three months to complete work on HURRICANE, after which he was to report to the state prison at Chino, California for a maximum of ninety days of additional psychiatric study. When not even this examination seemed to satisfy the judge, Polanski and De Laurentiis arrived at an amicable agreement whereby Polanski surrendered the picture. After forty-two days at Chino, the psychiatric staff prepared its reports and recommended straight probation since Polanski was found to have no psychiatric problems and was not in need of psychotherapy. Unfortunately, Judge Rittenband announced before Roman's next hearing that he felt additional jail time was called for, an action which caused Dalton to request he be removed from the case on the grounds of excessive bias, an opinion which by this time was also shared by the district attorney prosecuting the case.

In ROMAN, Polanski claimed that in returning to Paris to direct THE TEN-ANT he "fell in love with the city all over again, realized, once and for all, that it was my true home and the place I wanted to live from now on."[64] Surely those words, if not a rationalization, were intended to impress French readers since as early as 9 August 1977 it was noted in THE LOS ANGELES TIMES that "Polanski, a native of Poland who holds French citizenship, also faces the possibility of deportation by federal authorities. Joseph Sureck, Immigration and Naturalization district director, said Polanski . . . had applied for status as a permanent U.S. resident."[65] Barbara Leaming in her biography concluded that "it is a testimonial to Polanski's ability to manipulate a situation that the probation report was so favorable to him."[66] Apparently making the effort in this instance, in contrast to her description of Polanski's video tape, to check the police reports, Leaming provided a description of what had happened on that fateful afternoon. "After performing cunnilingus," she wrote, "Polanski penetrated her vaginally, asking her, she recalled, if she used birth control pills and when she had last menstruated. She didn't know how long his penis had been in her vagina, 'but not a very long time.' He withdrew before ejaculating. Then Polanski penetrated her anally, climaxing in her rectum. At this point, Anjelica Huston returned and knocked at the bedroom door. Polanski got up and went to talk to her. When he returned to the bed, he tried once more to have intercourse with the child."[67] Not even Judge Rittenband, who did retire from the case, ever referred to the prosecutrix as a child. Polanski himself was more laconic in his description.

There was no doubt about the girl's "experience and lack of inhibition. She spread herself and I entered her. . . . Suddenly, though, Sandra [the pseudonym Roman gave the girl] froze. The light on the phone had come on, which meant there was someone else in the house. . . . That stopped us both in our tracks, but it didn't supress my desire for the girl. After whispered reassurances, Sandra gradually relaxed again. When it was all over, I opened the door a little and looked down the passage."[68] Leaming, contrary to the evidence in the case, claimed that Polanski found "a magnum of champagne" in the refrigerator which he opened to share with the girl.[69] Polanski correctly pointed out that it was a bottle and that it was half-full when they left. What I had a problem with at the time, and what still concerns me most of all, when it comes to this case is the fact that the sexual intercourse which resulted was not a matter of mutual attraction. Roman, in seducing the girl, gave her not only champagne but also a quaalude, a sedative-hypnotic drug which relaxes a person normally to a point where he is no longer in complete control of his faculties. Here, Roman's arguments that the girl was sexually experienced, even the claim that she was familiar with the effects of alcohol and quaaludes, break down and become a non sequitur.

As if his rape case were not enough, Polanski was again in the headlines, this time for grabbing a news photographer's camera and smashing it when the photographer had attempted to snap his picture while he knelt at Sharon's grave. After several telephone conversations, we finally did meet at the Beverly Hills Brown Derby for lunch. He was half an hour late and Concepta had telephoned to apologize and assure us that he was on the way. He appeared nervous and harried as he entered the front door. Vicki walked at once to him to guide him back to the table we had reserved. Although only two inches taller than Roman's five feet five inches, that day she made the mistake of wearing four-inch platform shoes and she sensed Roman's discomfort as they walked side by side.

"You look like you could really use a drink," I said as he slid into the booth.

"No, definitely not a drink," he said, fumbling with a packet of *Antonio y Cleopatra* cigars. I held out my lighter and he puffed at the cigar, finally taking the lighter tremblingly into his own hand to get the cigar going. "I'm hung over," he confessed. "It's the first time since last Christmas, when I went back to Poland to visit friends in Warsaw." He grinned. "Going to Poland always makes me want to drink, you know? Vodka. Sit around and talk and drink vodka."

"Have a drink," I urged. "It'll settle your stomach."

"What are *you* drinking?"

"Bloody Marys, but take my word for it, they're awful."

"A Coke. I'll have a Coke."

The waiter took our order. He did not seem to recognize Roman.

"You seem so upset," I said. "Last time we met you were very happy."

"Happy?"

"Yes. In Paris. You were happy in Paris."

He nodded to himself as much as he did to us. "That was a happy time, wasn't it?"

The drinks arrived and we decided from the menu.

"Maybe," I suggested, "you should try a Bromo-Seltzer and a couple of aspirins."

"Gaghch!" He shook his head vehemently. "Bromo-Seltzer!" He settled on chicken soup and ground sirloin. "This place is so noisy," he complained, looking around the dining room.

"Don't blame us. You wanted to come here."

"Well, yes, I haven't been here for years. It brings back memories."

"The food could be better. The only person I know who eats here regularly is George Raft. He has a table in the back dining room."

"George Raft? Who's he?"

"He used to play gangsters, especially at Warner Bros. You know who Alban Berg and Franz Kafka are, and not George Raft? Watch the late movies."

"Yes, I know. There are so many movies on at night out here. I've been watching them every chance I get."

"Good, because we have a movie question for you. Vicki and I saw THE TENANT again and we figure you didn't tell the whole story, did you? Trelkovsky is so fascinated by the girl who was the previous tenant in his room and is driven to suicide out of guilt. . . . "

"Yes," Roman interrupted, gazing at us pensively.

"We felt that perhaps he drove her to suicide," Vicki interjected. "Maybe he even pushed her out of the window himself and that's why she screams when he comes to visit her in the hospital. Like CRIME AND PUNISHMENT."

Roman was shaking his head in despair.

"You must have your Hollywood plot, mustn't you? Trelkovsky is just a hypersensitive person. When you're dealing with a hypersensitive person, you don't have to look for all manner of explanations. You always want to explain everything. Trelkovsky *imagines* he contributed to her death because he is sensitive. People who are lonely seem eccentric . . . you see them in every big city walking down the street muttering to themselves."

"The French didn't like the film," I said.

"That had nothing to do with the plot . . . it had to do with the French. I took them seriously, you see. You can make fun of a working man or a priest, but you must do it with tenderness. They like to laugh at themselves, but not if you do it critically. I was trying to show the typical French middle class."

Lunch was served. Polanski began nervously to spoon soup.

"Why are you here?" he asked. "Why didn't you stay in the East?"

"I hate California!" Vicki said.

"It wasn't the smog that attracted us," I said. "But places get bad. This place has gotten bad."

"Yes, yes," Polanski nodded. "The only way is if you have a house, you know, and have a few friends over. Then it's nice here . . . but not if you don't have your own place."

"PEOPLE MAGAZINE," I said, "quoted you as saying that if you could live your life over again, you wouldn't."

"No, I wouldn't."

"Why not? You have money."

"Money," he said scathingly.

"Yes, money. And you're making pictures, some of them very good pictures."

"Money is overrated." He pushed his empty soup cup aside. "You tell me? If you could live your life over again, would you really want to? You'd want to make a change here or there. I mean, with no changes? If I balance the good things that have happened to me with the bad, there's been more bad, and the bad has been more painful."

"And the good things?"

"You want my life?" he demanded accusingly. "Here!" He held out his cupped hands to me. "You want it? Take it! Me? I wouldn't live it over again."

The talk turned inevitably to the rape case. Roman was most concerned that he would be deported, even if he were to serve additional jail time. That fortuity would prevent him from doing the one thing he wanted to do at the moment, make films in the United States. He also was convinced that there would never have been a court case if he had paid the girl's mother fifty thousand dollars. He had refused to hear of it, believing he could beat the case in court. Now he was far less confident.

Even with a change in the judge hearing the case, deportation came to seem inevitable, following more jail time. Before he could be sentenced on 1 February 1978, Roman fled the United States, flying first to London and then on to Paris. It was a most prudent move for him to have made. In the treaty between France and the United States, statutory rape was not an offense subject to extradition. " 'My whole life is at stake—I don't know what I'm going to do,' " he told Al Albergate of THE LOS ANGELES HERALD-EXAMINER by transatlantic telephone. " ' . . . Please have sympathy with my problems.' "[70]

" 'He did something against the law and he skipped bail . . . ,' " John Huston remarked on Roman's flight. " 'I wish that he hadn't done that.' " When asked, even if it meant jail, Huston replied: " 'If necessary, sure. Why not?' "[71] It was possible John Huston had forgotten his own plight after that night of 25 September 1933 when he was drunk, driving a car, and hit and killed a woman named Tosca Roulien when she stepped off the curb at the corner of Gardner and Sunset Boulevard. John had gone to his father and Walter had gone to Louis B. Mayer at M-G-M, calling in all the favors he was owed. Mayer made a deal with the district attorney at the time which called for John to agree never to drive an automobile again in the State of California and to leave the country, which was the real reason he ended up in London working for Gaumont-British. When the Coroner's jury found in John's favor, Raoul Roulien sued him for

$250,525 in a civil suit for funeral expenses and damages. The suit took two years in the courts and a judgment was finally handed down against John in the sum of $5,000, which he had to pay and did pay. Huston only returned to Southern California once the suit was settled.

Perhaps, in retrospect, Namatian, the Gallic senator to Rome, said it best when he surveyed the ruin of his age: "*ordo renascendi est crescere posse malis*"—which, literally translated, means a rebirth of order can spring from misfortune but which I once found more freely, and pointedly, rendered as "it is the law of progress to advance by misfortune."[72] I prefer the latter in this context because I would have thought Roman might have followed this precept by coming to terms with what had happened to him by the time he wrote his autobiography. Granted, while his trial was still going on, he was photographed in the company of Nastassia Kinski with whom he had had a sexual relationship when she was fifteen, and this had upset a number of people including the judge who was hearing the case. However, when at last he came to write ROMAN, he was rather proud of the way he had had sexual relations with a number of young teenage girls attending finishing schools in the Gstaad district and assured his readers that at this age "they were more beautiful, in a natural, coltish way, than they would ever be again."[73] He did not mention if inducements, such as those he had used in his California episode, had been necessary or not.

> What Terrors round him wait?
> Amazement in his van, and Flight combined,
> And Sorrow's faded form, and Solitude behind.

These words appear on the title page of James Fenimore Cooper's THE DEER-SLAYER (1841). There is no question that the spectre of what happened to him haunted him, at least as far as his career was concerned, and that it did indeed curtail his mobility as a director, notwithstanding the defiance combined with special pleading which characterize his own account of his life.

What he did was direct TESS (Columbia, 1980), the most expensive and elaborate film ever produced in France, based on Thomas Hardy's novel, TESS OF THE D'URBERVILLES (1891), a book Sharon had read and loved and left behind when they parted for the last time. Although slow paced, with the camera literally making love to Nastassia Kinski as Tess, Roman did direct a film which with the exception of CHINATOWN shows him at the height of his powers and truly, given the right property and the most powerful motivation, a master filmmaker. What was ultimately of the greatest consequence, however, was not the artistic triumph of TESS but its commercial success, particularly in the United States. More than anything, this proved that Polanski was bankable, despite his personal difficulties, and he was finally given the opportunity to make PIRATES (Cannon, 1986), based on a screenplay that he had written with Gérard Brach after the completion of CHINATOWN and which, until then, had been unable to attract financing.

Basically, PIRATES is a film in the vein of CUL-DE-SAC, a *comédie noir* in which Walter Matthau is a peg-legged pirate. When we first see him, he is on a raft in the middle of the ocean, accompanied by Frog, played by Cris Campion. Matthau eats a little fish, hook and all, and then, still hungry, he tries to eat Frog. Numerous adventures befall these two, most of them absurd and many of them grotesque, before they end up again adrift in the ocean.

PIRATES lasted only three days in most of the American theatres where it played. It was by far Polanski's most expensive film, with a negative cost of $31,000,000, and it had a domestic gross of only $600,000. Unfortunately, the foreign gross wasn't much better. Following this debacle, to save what he could of his reputation as a commercially viable filmmaker, Polanski got together again with Brach and wrote the screenplay for what was clearly intended to be a commercial thriller.

FRANTIC (Warner's, 1988), as the film was titled, starred Harrison Ford as Dr. Richard Walker, an American heart surgeon, who travels to Paris with his wife, played by Betty Buckley, to attend a medical convention. Once in their Paris hotel room, the couple discovers that one of their suitcases does not belong to them. While Walker is taking a shower, his wife is kidnapped. The kidnappers want the suitcase returned. Walker then sets out to get his wife back and his search brings him into contact with the owner of the suitcase, a young Parisian woman played by a new Polanski screen discovery, Emmanuelle Seigner. Compared to the ineluctable logic of the plot of CHINATOWN, FRANTIC is incredibly flawed. As a French citizen returning to France, Seigner's luggage would have had to pass through customs and the error in suitcases would have been discovered then. Further, why is Walker's wife kidnapped when the suitcase the kidnappers wanted was right there in the room with her? There are genuine moments of tension and suspense, but the film does not build, the way a Hitchcock thriller builds, and Ford, while competent in his role, is not ever really "frantic." In the final analysis, there is too little suspense and too little action in FRANTIC and matters are not helped much by Emmanuelle Seigner who is shown to have a very attractive body but who is a less than capable actress. FRANTIC, as PIRATES, is visually interesting—no Polanski film is ever lacking in visual interest—but without cogent story values, this alone is never enough to sustain a film.

Roman Polanski passed for a time into folk culture, although for all the wrong reasons, but now even that is fading, and these days his name, when it is recognized, is more likely to inspire dismissal or indifference rather than sympathy. A career which once held so much promise has increasingly threatened to retreat finally into the full circle which characterizes the situations experienced by so many of Polanski's cinematic characters. In summing up his life in RO-MAN, he asked some rhetorical questions about his own motivations. No one reading his narrative, as he wrote it, would have suggested, as he did, that it was a sexual impulse that drove him, asking himself if it was "that I would never have met all the women I dreamed of possessing had I remained an undersize inhabitant of the Cracow ghetto or a peasant boy from Wysoka?"[74]

What Polanski concluded instead was that he was primarily motivated by an impulse to please, to entertain, to startle others, or to make them laugh. I cannot accept that entirely and the reason that I cannot is that Roman Polanski never struck me as a person sufficiently able to step outside of himself and his own ego so as to experience life through the eyes and sensibility of another. Rather he remains sealed in that state of aloneness so common to his screen characters but without the depth of sensitivity to be found in those lines of Rilke's which I recalled while walking down a street with him in Paris. True, he is above all a survivor, but one who has, it would seem, been singularly without internal and spiritual growth, one whom suffering could not stop but also one sealed off from his own depths, as if that was the price he had to pay in order to survive. In his case, sadly, there seems to have very little, if any, advance by misfortune.

# Sam Peckinpah

## I

It is rare, if not unique, that two major Western films are in production a mile apart at the same time. Yet that was the case in December, 1972 when Sam Peckinpah was in Durango, Mexico to film what then was titled BILLY THE KID AND PAT GARRETT and John Wayne with his unit including director Andrew McLaglen was also there to film what was called WEDNESDAY MORNING but which became CAHILL, U.S. MARSHAL (Warner's, 1973) upon release. Lorraine Gauguin, who was a contributing editor to VIEWS & REVIEWS Magazine which I then edited and published, felt it was too fine an opportunity to be missed. In this I concurred. We also agreed that she should cover the two sets in a brace of articles for VIEWS & REVIEWS as well as for PHOTOPLAY Magazine, while I would reserve my impressions for use in my book THE FILMING OF THE WEST. Access to Durango was many times more complicated than flying from Dallas to Puerto Vallarta would prove years later with only one stop on the way. The flight from Los Angeles to Durango on a Mexican DC-9 made rather long and very leisurely stops at Tijuana, La Paz, and Mazatlán before arriving hours late at the destination. It was dark and a studio car was available for those bound to the two production areas. Visitors were to be housed at The Campo Mexico Court.

"Lots of *gringos* in there for smoking marijuana," the driver said, laughing, as the car passed a new state prison on the right side, lit up with floodlights directed toward the turrets. "Ha, ha, better not touch any *grifa*. Those guys don't get out for years—*años*, ha, ha."

The Campo Mexico Court was a run-down string of sixty bungalows which formed a semicircle around a dining room inappropriately called El Dorado and furnished in plastic, naugahyde, and formica. At breakfast time the next day, the dining room would be filled with cast and crew members from the two productions, smelling of leather and old sweat, stale cigar smoke and last night's booze, many of them chewing tobacco or smoking while waiting for their food; but now, at a late hour, on the night of our arrival Sam Peckinpah was sitting quietly at a corner table playing poker with Kris Kristofferson, Jack Elam, and some stuntmen. Although I did not know it then, it was Sam's custom when on a picture to dress in one outfit, consisting in this case of old blue jeans, leather boots, and a jean jacket. On the whole, you would think that everyone at Sam's table would be in high spirits on this night since a soccer game had just been held that afternoon and the M-G-M team won, getting a trophy in the bargain for beating the Batjac team and with a lot of money changing hands. However, the truth of the matter was that Sam's mood was dour and Sam set the tone for the evening. Even the afternoon's triumph palled, according to the unit publicist, once Sam learned that Rona Barrett had called him a drunk. Now, drinking heavily, he was pissed off and everyone knew it. "He insists that he does *not* have a drinking problem," the unit publicist disclosed. Sam remained intent on the game and talk was kept at the level of a murmur. He glowered beneath the red bandanna headband he wore, graying hair spurting out above and below it.

Certainly the most elegant diner at El Dorado was Emilio Fernández. He was an enormous man who, it was whispered, had shot more than one man. He was dressed in a black suit, a wide black sombrero with red, hand-tooled boots and wore a loaded Colt's .45 strapped to his hip. This was how he always dressed except when he was in character. He had been cast as a sheepherder named Paco in Sam's picture. Once perhaps Mexico's top director, constant disputes with his producers had led him presently to turn increasingly to acting. He played the general Mapache in THE WILD BUNCH (Warner's, 1969). He seemed to terrify everyone other than Sam. Sam liked him. With Fernández at the customary Mexican dinner hour of ten o'clock was a stunningly attractive Indian girl with raven hair hanging loosely to her hips. She wore a long Indian dress and an intricate Mexican pelisse of bright colors. She listened stoically as Fernández condemned Hollywood. He was obviously drunk and tended to sway on his heels as he arose to express his anger. The girl's indifference was genuine. Fernández was bellowing in English and she did not understand a word he was saying. Besides, she was only nine years old, which is not as strange as it might seem when it is recalled that Fernández' last wife was a mere fourteen. The substance of Fernández' harangue was how Hollywood had ruined John Steinbeck's THE RED PONY (Republic, 1949).

"John was my close friend, my *compadre*," Fernández fumed. "I directed THE PEARL and he loved it. Those gutless *maricones*, those *cabrones* ruined a masterpiece. I'm glad John's dead. I'm glad John's dead and he won't have to see that crap!"

THE RED PONY would be remade for television the next year and Lorraine's father, Julian Rivero, a Mexican character actor, would have a role in that production which would star Henry Fonda. It was almost with relief that I wandered over to Sam's table. Fernández was still raving when I introduced myself. I suggested the possibility of an interview.

"I don't give any fucking interviews," Sam snapped.

There was silence after that, broken only by the slurred ranting from Fernández.

"What do you think?" Sam asked suddenly. "Listen to him. And he's never even seen the fucking picture."

I had to laugh and that broke the ice. When he heard that I intended to visit the Wayne camp the next day, he became confidential.

"Do me a favor," he said. "It's funny, you know, but I've never met him. I'd like to."

"I'll see what I can do," I assured him.

I did not know it then and, in fact, I would not really realize it until many years later, but this was a test. It was Sam's way to test just about everyone that he ever met.

The next morning George Kennedy, Jack Elam, Neville Brand, Gene Lyons, Elisha Cook, Jr., R.G. Armstrong, L.Q. Jones, and a number of wranglers and stuntmen were standing around waiting to be transported to their various sets, whether on the Wayne picture or the Peckinpah picture. Dub Taylor who claimed he had a part in both pictures was having breakfast. At the time of initial release, both parts would be edited out and he would be credited in neither film.

"Pigshit parts is the kind I play," he remarked, attacking his *huevos rancheros* with a tamale. "Pigshit is what they play, too. All of us is pigshits and the pigshittier we are the more money we make and the audience loves us." He waved his hands around to indicate the waiting actors and crew members.

Lorraine then asked Taylor if Peckinpah was trying to make a hero out of Billy the Kid, the role being played by Kris Kristofferson. Taylor thought for a moment and then squinted his eyes.

"Yeah, I suppose you could say that. But I'll tell you this. After Sam gets through nobody will ever make a picture about Billy the Kid again. *This is it!* They'll never touch Billy again!"

In the interim Neville Brand had wandered over to the table and loomed over Taylor, his hair down to his shoulders. He was wearing a heavy wool sweater and faded jeans. Time had passed since he presumably relieved himself on a bus load of tourists at Universal City Studios. He hadn't had a drink in two years. However, he carried a pipe, had a cigarette in his mouth, and packed a huge cigar around with him at all times. Taylor was quick to note that Brand had become a changed man.

"Hell," Brand said, "I only gave up drinkin', none of my other vices."

"I went into this bean parlor out yonder and ordered some *cabrito*," Taylor said, changing the subject.

"What's *cabrito*?" Brand asked him.

"Hell, man, it's goat," Taylor said, gulping his *huevos rancheros*. "Well, it didn't taste like no *cabrito* to me. I asked the guy runnin' the place what it was. 'This ain't no *cabrito*,' I tells him. He goes into the kitchen and comes back and says, 'I'm sorry, seenyor, we was all out of *cabrito*. That's dog!' "

"How'd it taste?" Brand asked.

"Not bad, but it wasn't *cabrito*," Taylor replied, squeezing out of his chair, his breakfast finished.

"You know," Brand said, sitting down in the chair Taylor had just vacated, "you're sleepin' in the other half of my room and there's only a little rickety latch on the door." He laughed with an evil grin while grinding out his cigarette. He lit up the cigar. "Yeah, it used to be one big room when John Wayne used it. He used it for four or five pictures, but now he rents a house. I've got the huge, enormous bed flown down from Hollywood for big Duke on my side. Your side's just got a tiny fold-out couch." Again he laughed.

A studio car was provided to take us to the Batjac set located at an old stone granary that Warner Bros. had converted into a sound stage. In the distance the town of Durango could be seen and on the edge of it, atop a mountain set in sharp relief against lazily moving clouds, was the white church of El Calvario.

"Sam Peckinpah lives up near there," the studio driver observed.

Brand, who had hitched a ride this morning with all the visiting journalists, frowned as he looked around at his fellow passengers.

"Dumb liberal yo-yos," he snarled, and suddenly there was no more conversation. Into the vacuum, Brand began to sing an old stagecoach song he had evidently learned for his part in the Wayne picture. "The ladies are compelled to sit," he sang off key, "their dresses in tobacco spit. The gentlemen don't seem to care, but talk on politics and swear."

On the whole, this was not an auspicious beginning for the day, much less any indication that it was going to be easy to arrange a meeting between Sam and Duke. Once at the location, Michael Wayne, who has proven a tremendous source of information to me over the years about his father's activities, was only too ready to stress how the majority of the members of the Batjac crew had come from Hollywood and had worked with Duke for years.

"We use very few Mexicans on our crew," he said, "only what the government demands. When you go over to the M-G-M picture, ask them how many Americans are working on their picture. Very few."

Warner Bros. spent a half million dollars in constructing a Western street that was an almost exact replica of an old Texas town, including a railroad station. Andrew McLaglen had apparently fallen victim to what everyone termed *el charro*, a particularly virulent form of influenza. Wayne had to take over directing scenes in his own picture, something which he tended to want to do even without such justification. Once the journalists were introduced to him, they began to bait him with questions of a political cast. It was then that I learned that the only reason they were here at all was that Peckinpah had refused to give any interviews to anyone and they had to get some kind of story.

"What do you think of Kissinger?" one of them asked Wayne.

"There is a very fine dust in here," Wayne remarked, coughing and ignoring the question. It was a dry cough; there was no phlegm. Wayne was living on part of only one lung. "Can you see the dust up there, a fine, white dust?"

I couldn't see any dust, but the granary was damp and cold.

"Do you smoke very much?" another reporter asked.

"Only three cigars a day. I try to keep it down."

He would smoke more than that just while answering questions.

"What do you think of Kissinger?"

"Do you inhale?"

"I try not to but . . . that's hard for an inveterate smoker, but I try not to."

Wayne spoke very slowly; he was relaxed. He did not give the impression of being a complicated man.

"Did your doctor tell you about the cancer right away?"

"No, he didn't have the guts. He wouldn't tell me. I was going through the pictures [X-rays] with an intern. He showed me the latest one of my lungs. 'This is the cancer,' he said. Then he looked at me. 'Didn't your doctor tell you?' "

"How did you feel when you found out?"

"Like somebody had hit me in the stomach with a baseball bat."

"What did you think about?"

"Well, I have enough faith in that Man up there. I thought about my family, about what they would do without me, about getting my things in order."

"Have you met Kissinger?"

This reporter had been at it for an hour. Wayne had answered others' questions. He did not become irritated.

"Yes."

"What did you think of him?"

Wayne was cautious.

"I felt he was a nice man."

"Why did you start smoking again?" another asked.

"I used to chew, but it began to affect my voice."

"What do you think of Kissinger?"

It continued this way for some time. When I finally got a chance to have a word alone with him, I didn't waste any time bringing up Sam's proposal.

"I wouldn't let that Commie son-of-a-bitch within six feet of me," he said, displaying more anger than he had at any time when he was being baited by the reporters.

"Does that mean no, absolutely?" I asked.

I got such a hard stare in return that I shut up.

M-G-M had done almost the same thing that Warner Bros. had where Sam was filming. The studio had built a town set near Chupaderos, a fort once used by Pancho Villa who had come from Durango. The fort had been rebuilt to appear as Fort Sumner, New Mexico, the place at which the Kid was gunned down by Pat Garrett. In the center of the street a scaffold had been erected and around it a group of extras were congregated, dressed in period costume. Most

of the women and children had blond hair since they were actually wives and
offspring of the crew which was British when it wasn't Mexican. Michael Wayne
had it right. Sam employed very few Americans. James Coburn, dressed in his
black coat and Stetson to typify Garrett the nemesis, was also on the set, smoking
a cigar and occasionally spitting. He was recovering from *el charro* and, according to him, Sam actually had a severe case. So far Kristofferson had not
been affected, something he attributed to the liberal intake of alcohol. Rumor
on the set had it that he had actually cut back to two quarts a day, but who was
counting, especially with Sam around? Coburn ambled up a narrow staircase to
a small room where Sam would be shooting the jailhouse sequence with Kristofferson, Coburn, and R.G. Armstrong and Matt Clark cast as Garrett's two
deputies, assigned to watch over the Kid. No one but cast members and necessary
crew were allowed on this small, indoor set.

Peckinpah, identically attired as the previous night, was now standing next
to Gordon Carroll, a tall, lanky, retiring man who was trying to explain to the
few visitors allowed this far that in Sam's picture Billy the Kid had been made
into a contemporary figure. Espying me, Sam walked over.

"Any luck?"

I shook my head, no, and told him what Wayne had said.

"You might as well pack it in, Sam. To Pauline Kael you're a Fascist and
to Duke a Commie. You can't win."

If he was surprised by the outcome, his weathered face didn't show it.

"Is this true, about your making Billy the Kid a contemporary figure?" I
gestured around at the Nineteenth-century set and the period costumes.

"That's bullshit," Sam said. "This is the *real* fucking story."

Lorraine, who had been listening to this conversation and who thought highly
of John Wayne and very little of Sam, took this opportunity to get in a question.
Her mini tape-recorder was no doubt turned on for Sam's answer.

"Isn't this a rewrite of ONE-EYED JACKS which you wrote for Marlon
Brando in 1957 and which you said in PLAYBOY magazine was the definitive
work on Billy the Kid?"

"*This* is the definitive work on Billy the Kid," Sam said, glaring at her before
turning on his heel and disappearing up the narrow staircase.

Sam originally hired Katy Haber when in the United Kingdom filming STRAW
DOGS (Cinerama, 1971). I did not know at the time that he had let her go after
completing THE GETAWAY (National General, 1972), or rather as she said in
a subsequent interview with Garner Simmons, " 'On GETAWAY Sam, of
course, had married Joie so there wasn't a whole lot of room for me, was
there?' "[1] Sam was marrying for the fifth and final time when he tied the knot
with Joie Gould and it didn't last very long. After THE GETAWAY, Katy
returned to the United Kingdom to see her mother and then was hired to work
on a Sam Fuller picture which Warner Bros. closed down after five weeks.
Coincidentally, Katy was out of a job on the same day that Sam's new secretary
quit while this film was in production. " 'Sam called Camille Fielding in Cal-

ifornia and told her he needed a secretary,' '' Katy had continued in her interview with Simmons. Camille Fielding was the wife of composer Jerry Fielding who scored many of Sam's pictures. Camille had said, " ' ''What about Katy?'' And Sam said, ''That bitch is working for Sam Fuller in Spain.'' And Camille said, ''No, she isn't. She just called, and the picture's been cancelled.'' . . . So I packed my bags and flew to Mexico. But PAT GARRETT was by far the most emotionally draining experience I have ever been involved with. I think I'm a fairly placid person, but after PAT GARRETT I was as close to a nervous breakdown as I ever hope to come. It was awful.' ''[2] There was no indication of any of that as she and Rudy Wurlitzer joined Gordon Carroll on the town street. Katy was dark-haired, attractive, with nobly etched features. Wurlitzer, who had written the original screenplay and who would later denounce the entire production, wore jeans and a straw hat. He had a long, red beard. Wurlitzer commented to Katy that he hoped that Bob Dylan, who had a small role in the film, would write the musical score and that Kris would sing it.

"Jesus," Katy responded. "Everybody in the world will buy it."

"Everybody in the world will come to see the picture," Carroll chimed in.

"You can always tell when you have a winner," Katy rejoined. "There is a feel to it and this one is a winner. I just know it."

What none of them could know was that PAT GARRETT AND BILLY THE KID (M-G-M, 1973) would not earn back half its cost upon theatrical release, that M-G-M itself would close its exchanges before the film had even finished making the theatrical rounds, and that Sam would sue the studio for butchering the film he had made. For him, as he had said, this was the definitive story of Billy the Kid, but in reality the film he was making was the torment of Pat Garrett and how he had to sell out in order to survive and prosper. The only hint of that change in perspective that was kept intact upon initial release was the alteration in title: from BILLY THE KID AND PAT GARRETT, as it was called by everyone connected with the film when it was being shot, to PAT GARRETT AND BILLY THE KID.

A short while later Gary Combs rode up on a strawberry roan. He was Kristofferson's stunt double. The previous day he had been thrown from a horse and knocked unconscious, but he had since been X-rayed and was found to be uninjured. He talked about his wife's probable reaction when he finally got home. He had lost an eye on LITTLE BIG MAN (National General, 1971) when he got shot by an arrow. In his first picture following that accident, SOLDIER BLUE (Avco-Embassy, 1971), he had been nearly burned alive in the asbestos suit he had been wearing. He struck me as a shy man, but he was willing to talk about his work on THE GETAWAY.

"I doubled Steve McQueen," he said. "I did all that driving. I just stomped on the gas, then the brakes and skidded a lot. It looked dangerous but it wasn't. Fortunately with one eye my eyesight is pretty good. Everything looks flat but most people don't know I lost an eye."

Combs appeared to be encouraged by his audience. He went on to tell about the three Los Angeles hookers Sam had imported to play prostitutes in this picture.

"They had the room beneath me at the Durango Hotel," he recalled, "and, man, the noise down there kept me awake. There was traffic in there all night."

A publicist, almost as if on cue, came up with a stack of stills of nude scenes of James Coburn being bathed by the hookers. There were stills of Coburn in bed, lolling amid the naked pudenda, and in their very midst was Sam Peckinpah, the same beat-up clothes, the headband, and the wrap-around mirrored sunglasses. The scene would be cut from the final release print and is not even to be found in Peckinpah's ultimate cut of the film, save for a brief shot of Coburn in bed with the four women.

"The same day they took those scenes I did a stunt," Combs went on. "I went to see the rushes and they were looking at those raunchy bath and bed scenes. Finally I shouted, 'I just came in to see my stunt, can I leave now?' They would have dinner with us every night and one gal had a lot of personal problems. The writer on the John Wayne picture felt real sorry for her and he would sit and listen to her. But we couldn't take it any more when she kept going on and on about her hemorrhoids. L.Q. Jones finally hollered at her to go soak in a tub of hot water and let us eat in peace."[3]

I had begun my preliminary work on THE FILMING OF THE WEST in 1966 which was to screen and take notes on every surviving Western film that was ever made. At this time, when I was at my apartment in Milwaukee, Wisconsin, I would customarily screen two Westerns a night and between seven and nine over the week-ends. I was still in the very late 'Fifties, trying my best to keep the films in chronological order, at least by decade, and so I had actually not seen any of Sam's Westerns, including THE WILD BUNCH. I was far more interested in John Wayne and learning what I could from him about his career and the people with whom he had worked. Sam was, at best, a curiosity. Eventually, in late 1973 I did get to Sam's earlier Western films and Films, Inc. sent me a print of PAT GARRETT AND BILLY THE KID as soon as one arrived from M-G-M. I was overwhelmed by what I saw on the screen. It had been a Sam Peckinpah week culminating with PAT GARRETT AND BILLY THE KID and I felt a physical nausea and repulsion combined with an abject fascination. Nothing in the history of the Western film prior to Sam Peckinpah had prepared me for the images, the violence, and the power of his films. I recounted my impressions of what had occurred while in Durango in Chapter 20. The penultimate chapter I had decided to title "Sam Peckinpah and the Western with Only Villains." Now I had all manner of questions I wanted to put to Sam and no opportunity to do so. Doubleday and Company, which was to publish my book, wanted the complete manuscript to be in house by the beginning of September, 1974 at the latest.

I was in not only a bad marriage, but a foolish one. In fact, had it not been for Ruth's parents, I seriously doubt that we would have been married. We met while we were both students at Marquette University and I hired her to do cover illustrations for the FINE ARTS REVIEW, the program guide which I edited for WFMR-FM where I also worked hosting programs of classical music. Ruth began telling me the most horrendous stories about how she had been ill-treated by her parents and how desperately she wanted to escape from them. She was engaged to a young man of whom her parents approved and when she broke that engagement her parents blamed me. She was living on campus in a dormitory and did not wish to return home when the semester ended. I made arrangements for her to live the summer months with a woman teacher I knew. This proved the last straw. Her parents committed her to an asylum. I remember going out one night, creeping on the grounds, and managing to see her long enough for her to slip me a note pleading to get her released. I hired an attorney to represent her on the outside. On the inside, although she was of age, she would have to undergo two psychiatric examinations before she could win her freedom. Her former fiancé's father was a doctor and he had been a signatory to her commital. Ruth failed the first examination and was moved to a special ward of the county asylum for the insane, and out of the private sanitarium where she had first been held. I could visit her at least at the county institution. She passed the second examination and by court order was released on her own recognizance. I married her to prevent such a terrible thing ever happening again to her but even the day it happened I had regrets over my action.

As the years passed, Ruth's mental state worsened, but her experience with court-appointed psychiatrists at the time of her sanity hearing made any suggestion that she seek therapy less than useless. She would become incensed. I began working in the private employment agency business in 1968 and by 1974 owned and operated two employment agencies in Milwaukee as well as publishing VIEWS & REVIEWS and working on my books. My nights were spent screening films and I would rise at four o'clock in the morning in order to write. I have no valid excuse for how I behaved. I was young, ambitious, obsessed with what I wanted to do, and I allowed myself to ignore Ruth's worsening condition. My bankers could see the sorry mental state she was in and insisted that I remove her physically from the premises of my office suites. I owed their bank a lot of money and I was not in a position to argue. Ruth was convinced that her removal had been because I wished to conduct affairs with various female employees. I hired Rosemary Ingham to assist Ruth on VIEWS & REVIEWS and they were headquartered at our apartment. More and more Rosemary did all the work while Ruth became increasingly dysfunctional. Ruth would hide behind the apartment door when I would come home at night, suddenly jumping out at me and claiming that she had been counting the orgasms of the woman I had supposedly been with that day. She built an altar and claimed that she could hear the thoughts of everyone who lived in our high-rise apartment building. Rosemary had felt from the beginning that Ruth was harmlessly batty but she became somewhat alarmed when Ruth announced one day that she intended to open her own art gallery. Ruth dragged Rosemary to see a vacant store that was to let and then shocked her by saying that she would not be able to rent the space because she had heard voices in the walls and they told her that, if she did rent that space, it would be destroyed by fire. Rosemary came to me with her concerns and I was in an quandary.

One day Ruth was taken with the notion that an entire issue of VIEWS & REVIEWS must be devoted to Sam Peckinpah. She shot off a letter to Sam, telling him about the book I was writing, the special issue, and how she wanted to do sketches of him while on the set directing a picture. I was under tremendous pressure from Doubleday to get my book in because the firm was planning a major promotion of it. Also, United Films in Tulsa, Oklahoma wanted me to prepare a series of video episodes based on the book. When Sam agreed to see Ruth, I talked the matter over with Rosemary and we agreed that a little time away might do her good. I prepared twenty or so questions for her to ask Sam and also made a list of photo illustrations I hoped she could acquire in Los Angeles from either still shops or at the Academy library.

Ruth was gone for several days. When she did return, I met her at the airport and she said she did not want to talk. Once back at the apartment, she told me that she had no answers to my questions for Sam, she had no stills, she had nothing. However, she had seen him, she said, and they had gone to bed together. She gave me a most detailed description of what they had done together.

"Do you love him?" I asked her, mostly in exhaustion and resignation.

"I don't know," she said, "but he said not to be surprised if he shows up here some day on my door step."

I was not so much angry or jealous as nonplussed. I decided that no matter what might come, I must finish my book. The Labor Day week-end was approaching and I planned to work all day and all night for three days straight. I could possibly finish. That Friday night, Ruth left our apartment and disappeared. No one knew where she was. Rosemary came over and started making calls, including contacting Sam and Katy Haber, and Sam promised her he would call if Ruth showed up in Los Angeles. When Ruth did surface, some six days later, she claimed she had been in Los Angeles, that she had left because I had threatened to kill her, and that she wanted a divorce instantly. I discussed the matter with people I thought ought to know better than I did how to deal with this crisis and, finally, persuaded Ruth to enter into a legal separation which would automatically become a divorce after a year's time. In the meantime, she would return to Los Angeles and I would continue to support her until she found a job there.

THE FILMING OF THE WEST was completed, a little late but not too much. Rosemary typed the final manuscript and she proofed it with Vicki who worked as my business secretary. Then one delay after another came from the publisher's end and the book that I had struggled with so to make my deadline finally appeared in March, 1976. To justify paying Ruth a salary from my employment agencies, I had given her one job to do: at the end of each month she had to pick up from my accountant the statement of withholding taxes that had to be paid, make out a check, and deposit this check at the bank. On a trip to Los

Angeles a year before to see Jane Fonda, who had recently returned from North Vietnam, Ruth had fallen into a conversation with Fonda and was mortified to learn how much of each tax dollar was being used to promote the war. Without telling anyone, she decided to make her own protest and simply not to pay in any withholding taxes. Now that she was gone, the IRS came for a visit and wanted, with penalties and interest, a great deal of money, and at once. All this while, Rosemary pressed ahead as the managing editor of VIEWS & REVIEWS and, although delayed, she did want to have a Sam Peckinpah issue. She had talked on the telephone and corresponded a lot with Katy in an effort to get answers out of Sam and to complete the comprehensive filmography which Karl Thiede, our research editor, wanted to include in the special issue. Katy through it all was truly a champion. Rosemary had purchased a fine article on Sam's career to headline the issue. When I signed a three-book contract with the Scarecrow Press to edit collections of career studies of film directors, I decided that I wanted to write one on Sam myself. Katy had originally sent Ruth copies of every interview Sam had ever given, but they had been lost in the subsequent turmoil and Rosemary had had to ask Katy for a new set. THE MILWAUKEE JOURNAL ran a feature story by Robert Kerwin that had been syndicated. It described Sam on the set of his latest picture, THE KILLER ELITE (United Artists, 1975). "San Francisco is cold and foggy," Kerwin wrote. "Sam is depressed and blue. He looks gray, bent—a slouching death wish. He reddens, coughs, spits away part of a hangover. Above the worn, gray face, pulled over the yellow-gray hair is a black wool watch cap. His shades are one-way silver mirror: You don't see him but he sees all. The hands are jammed into the pockets as if that's all the warmth left in the world. Peckinpah is about 50 but looks— in the A.M.—an enfeebled 20 years older."[4]

Vicki had since become my personal secretary. We had to go to Los Angeles for a number of reasons and I arranged with Katy to visit with Sam. He was on the Culver City M-G-M lot. THE KILLER ELITE was being edited. Sam thought it was "a piece of shit." He was also suing M-G-M for two million dollars for having butchered PAT GARRETT AND BILLY THE KID upon release. We might have missed him entirely had he not just been released from jail for slugging a Continental Airlines employee after drunkenly attempting to board a plane bound for Hawaii. Sam was sitting in one of the screening rooms in the basement of the Irving Thalberg building when we walked in, screening CABARET (Allied Artists, 1972) in an effort to find a suitable music track for the piece of shit. I had told him over the telephone that I intended to accomplish the impossible and was bringing Vicki along for the purpose of recording an "intelligent" interview. Sam chuckled and said he would try to remember all the Polish jokes he ever knew.

"Hello, Jon," Sam called out of the darkness as we entered. "Sit down. Have you seen this picture?"

"No."

Vicki sat down next to me. Katy nudged us from behind.

"Want a drink?" she asked.

"What are you drinking?" Vicki inquired.

"Vodka and quinine water."

"Try it," Sam urged. "It tastes like monkey piss."

Katy handed us each a paper cup filled to the brim.

"Sorry," she said, "but there's no ice."

"How do you like it?" Sam asked. "Katy puts salt in it. That does something."

"It's not Scotch," I said.

"Monkey piss's better," Sam assured me.

When the lights came up, Sam saluted me with his cup.

"Want another?" Katy asked.

"Of course he'll have another," Sam said gruffly.

We had another, and another, and another. Sam seldom was ever alone. As I came to realize later, he was running too hard ever to be alone. A screenwriter and his wife were sitting on Sam's far side. Sam engaged them in a game of imaginary poker and lost a dollar.

"I ask myself why the fuck I make movies," Sam said, turning toward me, "and then I look at television and I know why."

He grinned. The lines in his face were deeper than I had remembered them as being. His hair was sparser, iron-gray and natted. His face had been described as a battlefield but, if it was, by this time the losses were far exceeding the wins. He was dressed in white jeans, a plain shirt open at the neck, and a white jean jacket. His mirrored sunglasses dangled from an elastic cord around his neck.

"Why the fuck do you want to interview me?" Sam asked morosely. "I sent you copies of all the interviews I've ever given. Use them. I never say anything new."

"Maybe that's why."

"Want to see rushes from KILLER ELITE?"

I shrugged. As we walked out of the screening room, up the steps and outside into the afternoon sunlight, Sam fell in beside me. We lagged behind the others, Katy in the lead.

"You've bought yourself a divorce," Sam said, stopping.

"Yeah." It was not something I wanted very much to talk about. I did not know how much of what Ruth had claimed happened, had happened. Both Rosemary and Vicki had been inclined to dismiss it. There was no question that Ruth had seen him, however, and that she had been in touch with him subsequently. Sam unzipped his fly and proceeded to relieve himself. There was silence until he finished and had zipped his jeans.

"I've bought myself five of them," he said, holding up a hand with five fingers outstretched. His look seemed to reflect genuine concern, if not compassion.

"That's not in any of your interviews," I said.

We resumed walking.

"There's a big difference between pussy and a good woman," he said.

"I've heard that from you before."

"What's wrong with it?"

"Sam, you're drunk."

"I haven't been sober in twenty years."

"Could it be that twenty years of drinking is affecting the way you make pictures?"

"Could be. My doctor told me I had to quit drinking when I started BRING ME THE HEAD OF ALFREDO GARCIA [United Artists, 1974]."

"So?"

"I quit. I started smoking marijuana. I didn't know what I was even doing any more. So . . . I've gone back to drinking."

We stepped into the editing room.

"This is my editor, Garth Craven," Sam said, introducing me to a young, modish Englishman standing near a movieola. I had read in several film journals about the expertise with which Peckinpah always edited his films. I suspected he would even edit while shooting, and I know for a fact that until the making of BRING ME THE HEAD OF ALFREDO GARCIA he could recall every little bit of film he had shot on a picture.

"This son-of-a-bitch has cut my pictures since GARRETT. How you coming?"

"I'm on the second reel," Craven said.

There were several cases of Scotch set in a corner. One was open. Everyone was sitting around on easy chairs that had once been props, except for Vicki; she was perched on a high editor's stool.

"Let's have a drink, Jon," Sam suggested. "Katy, get some ice."

Sam poured Scotch into a paper cup for each of us, filling it to the top so we had to drink it down to make room for the ice. He looked at Vicki. She shook her head.

"One of us is going to have to stay sober if anyone is going to get this interview," she retorted to his unspoken inquiry.

"Hey," Sam said, trying to focus on her short, fluffy brown-blonde hair and bronzed skin, "you ever been in pictures?" He collapsed into an easy chair in front of the stool on which she was perched, grinning foolishly.

"Yeah, I know," she told him, "I'd be perfect if you ever get a part for a girl with small breasts."

Sam frowned, grabbed her arm, and began chewing on it.

"Sit down here beside me," he addressed me as he let go of Vicki's arm. He rubbed his cut and bruised knuckles. He had pleaded guilty to the charge of battery and had been fined and put on probation. "If I had it to do over," he observed, "I'd have hit him harder."

"That's just playacting," I said. But Sam, I knew, did upon occasion hit people, usually friends.

"Garth!" Sam shouted. "Start those fucking rushes."

The movieola began to turn film. We watched scenes shot from several different camera angles. Sam had the whiskey bottle beside him. He refilled our paper cups.

"You see what's up there?" he asked, staring gloomily at the small screen. "Every fucking thing I am is up there. There isn't anything else."

"Maybe there should be."

We watched another scene.

"Here," Sam demanded. "Give me your cup." He poured more whiskey into his cup and then mixed the contents of the two cups together, as if he were preparing a Bromo-Seltzer. He handed back my cup.

"There," he said, "now we're friends, *real* friends."

He grabbed onto my hand and held me fixed with his eyes.

"I mean that."

"Listen, Sam, what about the interview?"

"Fuck the interview. What about me? Drink up."

"I haven't eaten all day."

"Then for sure, drink up. You'll feel better."

I drank up. Sam let go shaking my hand. The reel ended.

"Put on another reel, God damn it."

"I've read Max Evans' book about you."

"How did you like it?"

"I was rather disappointed. You never came to life in it."

"What did you expect? Evans was a chickenshit. He didn't dare tell the truth about that picture because he was afraid of his wife."

The book was titled SAM PECKINPAH: MASTER OF VIOLENCE (1972). It narrated what had happend while Sam had been directing THE BALLAD OF CABLE HOGUE (Warner's, 1970), a picture in which Evans had a small part. Years later, Garner Simmons in PECKINPAH: A PORTRAIT IN MONTAGE (1982) would clarify in just what way Evans had been a chickenshit. As on GARRETT, Sam had imported a number of whores to come to the hotel near the Valley of Fire location in Nevada and one of them had a social disease that some crew member rechristened "apple valley fever." Simmons had asked Evans about the episode and why he had omitted it. " 'Sure there were whores on CABLE HOGUE. But the reason I didn't write that in my book is that I've got a wife that'll kill ya, and that ain't no joke. When you're writin' with a .45 cocked in your ear, well, you write somethin' else! . . . There was also some "apple valley fever" that ran absolutely rampant on the picture. I think myself and two others missed it out of the whole crew, and that includes the waitresses, the cooks, the goddamn bartenders, and the gardener. And the few that didn't have it were so weak with worry, they could barely operate anyway.' "[5] Frankly, I do not believe that including that episode would have much mitigated my overall disappointment.

"I have to go check on the cat," Katy said, getting up. Sam caught her around the hips and began caressing her backside. She leaned over and kissed him. Then he let her go.

"Do you like cats, Jon?"

"No."

"I don't like 'em either, but I'm getting to like this cat. Katy and I will be sleeping and this cat will jump on my shoulder and bury his face under my arm."

The next reel started and we watched rushes. James Caan was blowing up a building, the scene, in fact, with which the film opened upon release. The shots had about them the intensity Sam could always get, but somehow, even in rough cut, this picture lacked fire. It was the way Garrett's wife had described him when they argued before he left her to hunt for the Kid: it was dead inside. That scene is in Sam's first cut of GARRETT but even he left it out, as had the official release version, when he made his ultimate cut. Sam pulled out a couple of crumpled cigarettes and handed one to me. I lit them both.

"We've got to smoke a joint after this," he said.

"You can forget the interview," I said. "I've forgotten all the questions I wanted to ask."

"Good, then we can have a joint."

"I'm too sick now. I can't mix liquors when I'm drinking."

"Do you want to see another reel, Sam?" Garth asked.

"No, we've seen enough." Sam turned to me. "I liked John Ford. Did you ever meet him?"

"Yes."

"I never did, but I watch his pictures over and over."

Subsequently, Sam would tell Garner Simmons that he had met Ford, only once, on the steps of the Irving Thalberg building we had just left. " 'People spend a lot of time comparing my work to his. Most of that's bullshit. In the first place, I don't like most of his later films. . . . His best Western was MY DARLING CLEMENTINE. Fonda was sensational in that. I hated THE SEARCHERS. I loved the book, but I thought the movie was shit. But I suppose he didn't like much of what I did, either. I think we're very different.' ' '[6] At the time of our conversation, I recalled to myself how Sam had disrupted the testimonials to Ford the night Ford was to receive the Medal of Freedom. He rose from his seat and announced to all the luminaries present that they should edit their remarks to a two-reeler and get on with the show. He was very nearly ejected.

"I wish I didn't have to catch a fucking plane for Madrid tomorrow," Sam said, clutching again at my hand. "They want me to make a picture in Europe. Friends?"

"Friends," I said.

"The joint?"

"No, home."

"I only wish I knew where I was going to be. Since my home burned down, I don't have any place to live any more."

"You sound like a Peckinpah character."

"You'll be back?"

"Yes, I'll be back."

"When?"

"I don't know."

I got unsteadily to my feet. Vicki slid off the stool. Sam shook my hand some more.

"Christ, I'm tired," he said, letting go and dropping back into the easy chair.

# II

Peckinpah detested intellectualizing about his films, quite probably because as he would often say what's there is on the screen. David Foster, the producer of THE GETAWAY, said it best when he observed that " 'Sam relies almost entirely on his emotional responses. If you take him deadly serious every single moment, he'll drive you crazy. But if you keep it in perspective, and allow him to apply those instincts to the picture, there's no problem. And he gets some terrific things on film.' "[7] In Peckinpah's best work there is such a primitive force and disturbing emotional quality as to be impervious and commanding. Max Evans in a sketch of remembrance he wrote after Sam's death had it right: "Once he touched your life, even briefly, he became unforgettable; and so are many of his films."[8] The very best of his films were very personal vehicles and the world they reveal was very much an expression of the personality and beliefs of their creator. I have always questioned his rationalizations for frequently evoking violence and blood-letting, but there is no denying that he was right in believing that we must not live by half-truths. Yet he himself spent the better part of his adult life in all-out flight from his own consciousness. He was sentimental about children but I question how much he really was able to love them. One need only recall some of his most striking images: the children dropping the scorpion into the ant heap at the beginning of THE WILD BUNCH or the look on the child's face at the end as he shoots down Pike; the children following after Cable Hogue and heckling him; the children swinging on the noose which will hang Billy the Kid and the young boy, repudiating the closing images of SHANE (Paramount, 1953), throwing stones at Garrett's horse when Garrett rides out of Fort Sumner after having killed the Kid; the children at the beginning of CROSS OF IRON (Avco-Embassy, 1977) and the children's voices which open THE KILLER ELITE while the explosive charges are being put in place. Sam's view of children as little adults exulting in cruelty was one of his fixed ideas, as was his profound misogyny, and he stubbornly clung to it. I doubt that he would have been moved to change his mind even had he stood within the confines of Dachau and been able to study the simple drawings of flowers, birds, and crude houses drawn by thousands of children as they waited unknowingly to be herded into the collective gas chambers. For all the stylized violence in his films, Sam Peckinpah obstinately refused ever to look very deeply into the soul of human cruelty just as he never stepped—perhaps because he never dared to step—outside the parameters of his own fantasies.

Sam's ancestors came from the Frisian Islands, off the coast of the Netherlands, and settled in Madeira County in the San Joaquin Valley in Nineteenth-century California. Peckinpah Mountain in Madeira County was named after Sam's paternal grandfather. Sam's maternal grandfather, Denver Samuel Church, was a rancher, a Congressman, and a judge. Sam's father went to work for Denver Church as a common ranch hand before falling in love with his daughter. David Peckinpah and Fern Church were married in December, 1915. Louise Church felt her daughter had married beneath her station and, according to Sam, so, too, at times did his mother. Denver Charles Peckinpah was born on 23 September 1916 and was named for his grandfathers. Denver Church had put David Peckinpah in charge of the ranch after his marriage. While serving his third term in the House, Denver Church brought David, Fern, and young Denver to Washington so David could begin his studies at the National University Law School. Church did not seek re-election and, following his admission to the California bar, David joined in private practice the firm of Church, Church, and Peckinpah which lasted until 1924 and Denver's election to the Superior Court at Fresno. On 21 February 1925 David Samuel Peckinpah was born. His mother said, upon seeing the infant, "Oh, no, not another black Peckinpah." The reference had to do with his family and not with the infant since, at the age of one in a photograph of "D. Sam" sitting on Denver Church's knee, we see a baby with blond hair and light green eyes. David Peckinpah, known intimately by the family as "the Boss," became in turn a Superior Court judge as eventually would Sam's brother, Denver. As a youth, Sam proved unruly and, as a disciplinary measure, he was sent to San Rafael Military Academy. Upon graduation, Sam entered the U.S. Marine Corps and was sent to China, even though the war was ending. He saw no action. When he was discharged from his four-year hitch, his family urged Sam to pursue the law. Sam was confused and uncertain. He went for a time to Mexico, as he would frequently later when bewildered or at a loss in life, and then, upon his return, enrolled at Fresno State College. He renewed his acquaintance with Marie Selland, whom he had known in earlier years. She was a drama major at the college. After accompanying Marie to one of her classes in stage direction, Sam knew he had found his vocation. Later that same year, 1947, Sam and Marie were married.

Sam was early attracted to Tennessee Williams' plays and adapted THE GLASS MENAGERIE as a one-hour production for his senior project. Graduating from Fresno State, Sam enrolled at the University of Southern California to pursue a Master's degree in drama. He had completed most of his course work but left school without writing his thesis when Sharon Peckinpah was born on 30 July 1949. His first job out of school was with the Huntington Park Theatre, near Los Angeles, where he produced and directed nearly all the theatre's stage productions for two seasons. During the summer months, Sam directed summer stock in Albuquerque, New Mexico, taking Marie and Sharon with him. Sam was determined to direct films and to get him closer to his objective he next went to work for KLAC-TV in Los Angeles as a stage hand. He wrote his thesis while working his way up the ladder at KLAC-TV. It was titled "An Analysis of the Method Used in Producing and Directing a One Act Play for the Stage and Closed Circuit Television Broadcast." The play Sam chose was Tennessee Williams' PORTRAIT OF A MADONNA in which he cast his wife in the leading role. It was both produced for the stage for presentation at USC's Stop Gap Theatre on 8 July 1953 and on 27 July Sam directed a version for closed circuit television using the facilities of KLAC-TV.

Sam continued to make short, experimental films in his spare time and he also tried his hand at writing scripts. On 16 November 1953 Kristen Peckinpah was born. Also, as the year closed, Sam lost his job at KLAC-TV. When told by an executive that he was being paid to do what he was told and not to think, he reputedly told the executive to take his job and shove it up his ass. Later Pat Garrett would utter a similar line to business executives who want to advance him money to kill the Kid, his one moment of rebellion against the Establishment as he goes about his dire mission. By camping outside Walter Wanger's office, Sam managed to convince the veteran producer to hire him in some capacity and he was employed in a minor position on RIOT IN CELL BLOCK 11 (Allied Artists, 1954) directed by Don Siegel and starring Neville Brand. Siegel could see the talent radiating from the young Peckinpah and he became his mentor, employing him as his dialogue director on a number of films. Siegel even asked Sam to do a rewrite on the script for INVASION OF THE BODY SNATCHERS (Allied Artists, 1956). Sam wrote in some parts for himself but he looked so different in those days as to be unrecognizable to modern audiences seeing the film now.

In 1955, he landed a job writing scripts for television's GUNSMOKE, then a half hour series. Ten of these scripts were adaptations of previous radio episodes from the years before the show had moved to the small screen. The two original scripts that Sam wrote were both rejected by the show's producer, Charles Marquis Warren. For the next three years, Sam worked steadily writing scripts for a number of television Westerns, including BROKEN ARROW and TALES OF WELLS FARGO. He found writing to be necessarily a solitary occupation, at times even painful, and at odds with his gregarious temperament. He hired Nancy Galloway to be his typist. On 15 February 1956 Melissa Peckinpah was born. Sam at the time housed his family in a Quonset hut at Malibu. He would live mostly in Malibu in future decades, usually in some kind of trailer—as he called it—although more commonly known as mobile homes, at least by those buying and selling them. Finally, in 1958 he rewrote one of his original GUN-SMOKE scripts and managed to interest Four Star Productions in using it as the basis for a new television series to be titled THE RIFLEMAN. Dick Powell produced the pilot for this series and ran it as an episode in his network anthology,

ZANE GREY THEATRE. Sam's basic concept for the series was that a sharp-shooter and his young son would encounter various adventures, each of which would in some way contribute to the boy's growing awareness of the world and his own values. Dick Powell, one of the "good guys" according to Sam, gave him his first chance to direct by assigning him several installments in the series once it was purchased by the ABC network.

Powell then proposed to Peckinpah that he try conceiving a new half-hour pilot, which he could direct, to be included in the ZANE GREY THEATRE anthology for the 1959 season and Sam came up with the notion for THE WESTERNER. Dave Levy of NBC liked Peckinpah's previous work and, primarily through his influence, the network bought this new pilot and Dick Powell scheduled thirteen episodes. Sam was the producer for the series in addition to writing and directing some of the episodes himself. Many of Sam's entries stressed comic and hyperbolic elements and perhaps the most carefully drawn Peckinpah character was one he borrowed from James Edward Grant's screenplay for HONDO (Warner's, 1953) which was based on a Louis L'Amour short story which L'Amour subsequently novelized under this same title. The character was Brown, series-star Brian Keith's dog. It wasn't really Keith's dog. Keith would insist that Brown was "nobody's dog." But, as Hondo and *his* dog, the two of them traveled together and watched out for each other. After the initial complement of thirteen shows, THE WESTERNER was cancelled due to the controversial nature of some of the material. This early already Sam was intent on projecting his image of the whore as the only really honest woman. In his personal life, he was irrationally jealous, convinced in a way from which he could not be persuaded that when Marie wanted to go out at night it had to be for the purpose of a clandestine rendezvous. As Sam once put it, "most married women fuck for the money that's in it."[9] Marie in her relative inexperience was driven to distraction battling Sam's phantoms. The torment of writing was eased by excessive drinking. Sam's routine would often consist of persisting straight through, regardless of the passage of time, until a script was completed. Both he and Marie were nocturnal creatures so turning the clock around proved no great hardship. However, in departing from the air waves, THE WESTERNER did manage to win a nomination from the Screen Producers' Guild as the "Best Filmed TV Series."

Brian Keith, who was slated to star in THE DEADLY COMPANIONS (Pathé-American, 1961), was instrumental in getting Sam hired to direct the film. It was being produced by Charles B. FitzSimmons, brother of the film's female co-star, Maureen O'Hara. Brian Keith's role is that of a Civil War veteran on the trail of a Confederate renegade who seven years earlier at Chickamauga tried to scalp him. Keith, known as Yellowleg, has a scar across his hairline and his gun arm is crippled. Very early in the picture, in trying to stop a bank robbery, Yellowleg's trick arm throws off his aim and by accident he kills O'Hara's young son. She is a prostitute and decides to journey across the desert to bury the boy next to his father at Siringo. Yellowleg saves Turk, played by Chill Wills, from a scrape caused by his cheating at cards, realizing that Turk is the man he has been hunting. Turk is accompanied by his young protégé, a gunslinger named Billy played by Steve Cochrane. The three accompany O'Hara in her trek to Siringo, Billy lusting for O'Hara. The script called for Turk to kill Billy at the end and for Yellowleg, surrendering his *idée fixe* of revenge, to ride off into the sunset with the heroine-whore. Sam wanted to change this, to let Yellowleg have the satisfaction of vengeance, at least by displacement, by himself killing Billy. FitzSimmons vetoed this idea. Had Sam been able to film it his way, THE DEADLY COMPANIONS would have been almost a reprise of THE BALLAD OF CABLE HOGUE, with the exception of its having the conventional happy ending.

What the film does have in common with later Peckinpah Westerns is the notion of redemption as a consequence of undergoing a physical ordeal and trial by violence. During the trip across the desert, once Turk and Billy have dropped back from the buckboard driven by O'Hara whose character name is Kit, she and Yellowleg see a stagecoach on a high crest, silhouetted against the sky, careening at full speed. The stage comes closer into the frame and then tips over, so that the viewer sees that within it are Indians dressed in shawls and bonnets, being chased by other braves in a drunken parody imitating their recent act of brigandage. From the very beginning, the only use Peckinpah had for Indians was to further his dramatic purposes. Otherwise, they were non-persons. Yellowleg steals an Indian's horse. The brave sets out after him, the pursuit a matter of personal honor. I suppose it is ironic that, in terms of the thematic concerns of the film, Yellowleg, the hunter, becomes himself the hunted; but, mostly, this sub-plot is employed to create a savage, lustful, primeval image. Hiding in a cave, Kit is terrified when the figure of the brave looms over her, and she shoots him down. This reinforces the ideology that, under the proper circumstances, women are as capable of violence as men and that through violence Kit herself is somehow cleansed.

What peaks the lust directed toward Kit is her decision, midway through the film, to bathe in the nude. A female in a Western environment is viewed, according to the screenplay, as a distraction, a danger, and an object when sufficiently attractive and physically well endowed likely to arouse almost uncontrollable sexual heats. Sam is not entirely to be blamed for this image since he was prohibited from making any changes at all in the Kit character once production began. In fact, O'Hara refused so much as to speak to him save when it was absolutely necessary. Notwithstanding, I believe this element was one of the things which attracted Sam to this picture and Kit does serve in her way as a prototype for all the subsequent heroine-whores who consistently populate Peckinpah's films and who in their ways embody Sam's ideal of woman: extraordinarily good-looking prostitutes who can perform domestic functions, who come to prefer sexual relations with the protagonists (whom they genuinely enjoy servicing), but who are finally irrelevant in the lives of the protagonists because the ritual ideology of the stories prohibits a protagonist from ever developing a permanent relationship with anyone of the opposite sex. Sam later disowned THE DEADLY COMPANIONS. Just how little Sam had to do with the screen story becomes more apparent with the films that followed. Sam often spoke of Ernest Hemingway as a major influence. One thing he did have in common with Hemingway was the notion that the proper conclusion to a story is for the protagonist to die.

On 30 November 1960, just about the time that THE WESTERNER was still going strong, David Peckinpah died from a sudden heart attack. During the nadir of the Depression, David and Fern had adopted a young girl whom they named Fern Lea. She tried to get in touch with Sam to inform him of what had happened but found it difficult because Sam and Marie had separated. Despite the birth of Sam's only son, Matthew Peckinpah on 8 January 1962, Sam and Marie would be divorced that year. For Marie, the jealousy, suspicion, rage, and Sam's belief that women enjoy pain had become intolerable. " 'Sam loved Marie,' " Garner Simmons quoted one observer. " 'But he wanted a storybook marriage, and they [ideal marriages] just don't exist.' "[10] Sam was equally laconic about it, if not very original. " 'You clothe the object of your own needs in the vestments of your own desires. When you wake up to the fact that it just ain't there, that's when you've got to go.' "[11] I say that it was not very original because Flaubert once made a remarkably similar confession to the Goncourts: " 'Toutes les femmes qu'il a eu n'ont jamais été que les matelas d'une autre femme rêvée.' "[12] In RIDE THE HIGH COUNTRY (M-G-M, 1962) Sam would have an opportunity to put forth his view of the roles of the sexes at the same time as he paid tribute to the passing of "the Boss."

This would be Randolph Scott's first picture after his series directed by Budd Boetticher, ending with COMANCHE STATION (Columbia, 1960). "In every one of the Scott pictures," Boetticher later said, "I felt that I could have traded Randy's part with the villain's."[13] That is precisely what Sam did in making RIDE THE HIGH COUNTRY. In the script as originally written, both Joel McCrea and Scott are former lawmen who are hired to transport a gold shipment; the Scott character was to try and steal the shipment; and, at the end, he was to die. Sam altered that. The Scott character still tries to steal the gold shipment, still fails, but in the shootout with the Hammonds it is the McCrea character who dies and, in dying, inspires the Scott character to transport the gold shipment the rest of the way, his honor restored by the McCrea character's faith in him, that he will do the right thing, that only momentarily did he desert the code by which both men have lived so long. Had the McCrea character lived and the Scott character proved himself and regained his integrity, the plot would have been as dozens of others: reform and redemption through the example set by the hero. Had the Scott character proved himself and regained his integrity only to die in the process, it would have been a severe judgment: do not fall from grace even for a moment if you hope to be among the elect. Had it been a Boetticher film, the Scott character would have been an outlaw who would decide in the course of the journey either to do the right thing, because of the hero's example, or the wrong thing and be killed by the hero. But this is a Peckinpah ending. He was not about to let the Scott character, at the end, ride off to Mexico with the gold. He was not then sufficiently bitter and disillusioned. "My father said it all one day," he related in his PLAYBOY interview. "He gave me Steve Judd's great line in RIDE THE HIGH COUNTRY: 'All I want is to enter my house justified.' "[14] McCrea's character does. Randolph Scott as Gil Westrum also enters his house justified, if only finally and only after Judd's death. It would not be that way for Sam.

On the way to Coarsegold to pick up the shipment, Judd, Westrum, and Westrum's protégé, Heck Longtree played by Ronald Starr, stop at the Knudsen ranch. When a child, Peckinpah had been taught passages from the Bible by rote by his father. In casting R.G. Armstrong as Knudsen, Sam initiated the prototype of the religious fanatic who runs as a thread through all of his Westerns, becoming an ever darker figure until he emerges as Bob Ollinger played by R.G. Armstrong in PAT GARRETT AND BILLY THE KID. Sam put his own frustration at married life into the mouth of Judge Tolliver, the drunken Justice of the Peace in Coarsegold played by Edgar Buchanan: "A good marriage is difficult to find. It is almost impossible to keep. People change . . . the glory of a good marriage don't come right away. It comes later on . . . it's hard work." Neither the judge's sermonizing nor Knudsen's quoting of the scriptures means a damned thing: what matters is personal loyalty to an ideal, the sense of one's own honor and integrity. They can, so the film tells us, even make a bad man good.

Mariette Hartley made her screen debut as Knudsen's daughter. She wants to escape from her father's tyranny, run off to Coarsegold, and marry one of the Hammond brothers, Billy, played by James Drury. She joins up with the trio. On the trail, she comments to Judd: "My father says there's only right and wrong, good and evil, nothing in between. It isn't that simple, is it?" "No, it isn't," he replies. "It should be, but it isn't." Jean-Louis Rieupeyrout in LA GRANDE AVENTURE DU WESTERN who saw in this film "a perfect and very personal synthesis of the moral instruction dispensed by the best part of the contemporary Western, films directed by Ford, Mann, and Aldrich," after quoting this dialogue between McCrea and Hartley, found he had to add: "Isn't that a response worthy of being applied to this contemporary Western so rich in intentions as in contents? We surrender to the evidence: the course that since 1950 we have traveled via successive stages of the genre has already marked the truth of these words. . . . "[15] As willing as I am to concede this point, I would have expected it to have been made in reference to THE WILD BUNCH. What makes the statement particularly impressive is that Rieupeyrout made it fully five years before THE WILD BUNCH and, therefore, saw RIDE THE HIGH COUNTRY as continuing a trend toward moral ambiguity which for him had already been discernible in Westerns for a long time.

Heck and the girl fall in love. Thus there is fulfilled romance and restored honor, but the prevailing tone is sad. Judd and Westrum are old men; most of the gold mined in Coarsegold ends up at the brothel; the amount to be transported is less than it was estimated to be and in a way Westrum is a fool since, although his honor is saved, he will likely return to the artificial life of being a showman, pretending to be someone he is not, where he was when we first see him. Peckinpah obstinately retained one more fantasy. He was paid $15,000 to direct this film while its stars, whatever their roles, from investments they made with money earned playing make-believe heroes were multi-millionaires. Scott, indeed, was one of the ten wealthiest men in the State of California. There was an irony in this, a greater irony than Sam's romantic vision permitted him to show.

" 'Sam, in my estimation, is one of the top directors—the upper echelon of directors,' " Randolph Scott said later. " 'I would have liked to have worked on other films with him. I wish that he had come along earlier in my career, which is not to say that I was dissatisfied with the many men I did work with. But Sam is a great trouble-shooter on a film. He has an innate instinct and talent for dealing with a script that many others just do not have. Sometimes, you know, a scene doesn't play well as it's written, and Sam had the ability to take something that didn't work and alter it in such a way that it would work.' "[16] Frank Santillo was the film editor on the picture and he observed something which I have seen over the years in the rushes Sam showed me. " 'The thing that's really difficult in cutting for Sam,' " he said, " 'is that he shoots a lot of film, but it's all good. That makes it difficult to decide what to keep and what to throw away.' "[17]

RIDE THE HIGH COUNTRY was released on the bottom half of a double bill yet it was voted the "Best American Film" of 1962 by NEWSWEEK magazine. It was listed among the "Ten Best" by TIME, beat out Fellini's 8½ for the "*Grand Prix*" at the Belgian Film Festival, and it was awarded the "*Diosa del Plato*" for best direction by the Mexican film critics. " ' . . . When it was over,' " Sam's sister, Fern Lea, recalled after first seeing the film, " 'I went into the ladies' room and cried and cried because the character played by Joel McCrea reminded me so much of my father who had just died the year before.' "[18] In the film, R.G. Armstrong as Knudsen is seen for the last time kneeling and dead before his dead wife's grave stone which bears the inscription: "Wherefore, O Harlot, I will judge thee as women that break wedlock and shed blood are judged. . . . " It does not bode well for the future of Heck and Elsa Knudsen. Sam, his personal life in a shambles, undertook to alter completely the life-style he had known. He sought reconciliations periodically with Marie, but his life-style became more and more nomadic. He tried living in houses, then shacks, then in trailers, then on studio lots, and finally nowhere before he moved into a trailer again. He rejected material possessions but he retained every scrap of paper on which he had ever scribbled anything he thought he might use someday. Money became meaningless to him and he supported a number of hangers-on when he could.

Sam was not above borrowing. When he scripted "The Losers" for the DICK POWELL THEATRE, he took the characters, some scenes, and even the dialogue at the close from Max Evans' THE HI-LO COUNTRY (1961), although he later paid Evans a good sum of money to option rights to the book. Dick Powell died and shortly after his production company folded. Sam was hired to direct MAJOR DUNDEE (Columbia, 1964), but as soon as production started producer Jerry Bresler shaved the shooting schedule from seventy-two days to sixty and the budget by a million dollars—primarily because Columbia was highly cost-conscious. Sam ignored Bresler's dictates, however, as soon as he was on location in Mexico. He had taken increasingly to prefer the company of whores. He felt that while married women fucked for what they could get you never knew how much that would be. A whore set her price in the beginning. He had a role for a Mexican girl and he wanted to cast a Mexican actress who was intimate at the time with Budd Boetticher who was then in Mexico working on his very long-term film ARRUZA. Budd wouldn't let her take the part so Sam cast Mexican actress and flamenco dancer Begonia Palacios instead. Sam fell in love with her and they were married. Over the years, he would marry and divorce her a total of three times, twice marrying in civil ceremonies and once in a Roman Catholic church for which service he even temporarily converted to Catholicism (although he had been raised a Christian Scientist and found himself coming back to its tenets as his moods would shift in life). Between marriages to Begonia, Sam would tell Boetticher, when he saw him, " ' "Man, you really know how to fuck a guy up!" ' "[19]

Sam had long been a heavy drinker but these days and for many years to come he was never really sober. It was his intention to hold the production schedule on MAJOR DUNDEE at the seventy-two days allotted initially, but even at that he ran way over. He got constant flack from Columbia which only made him angry. Perhaps the drinking somewhat distorted his personality. He had worked amicably enough with Dick Powell and other producers in the past. Henceforth, his attitude toward producers and producing companies was strictly one of per-petual warfare. He felt he needed this tension to get a good picture. Over the years, his hatred of and anger at producers became almost pathological. If his intemperate jealousy finally drove Marie from him, his attitude toward producers curtailed his freedom to create for the rest of his life. Sam was convinced that he was getting a good picture in MAJOR DUNDEE, even an epic picture. Charlton Heston and Richard Harris were the stars, Heston cast as a Yankee, Harris as a Confederate, with the plot joining them together in an uneasy alliance against the war-like Apaches. Heston said he was willing to return his salary on the picture to Columbia if Sam could just continue production, and he did. Columbia sent a field man to Mexico City, presumably to close down the set. Sam met him at the airport and stripped his clothes off him. From this point on Bresler and Columbia waited somewhat impatiently until he was done and then, systematically, in the editing process cut the thirty-five pages of script that Peckinpah had been ordered to excise. During production, Sam would custom-arily use the toilet in James Coburn's camper. Coburn, who was working for Sam for the first time, used this opportunity to talk about the character he was supposed to be playing as well as the motivation behind Dundee's dissipation. He wanted to know what the picture was about, what Dundee was about. " ' "Because he continues," ' " Sam told Coburn of Dundee. " ' "I mean through all the shit, through all the lies, through all the drunkeness and the bullshit that Major Dundee goes through, he survives and continues!" ' "[20] In addition to Coburn, the cast also included others who would become Peckinpah regulars: L.Q. Jones, Slim Pickens, and R.G. Armstrong. When MAJOR DUNDEE was released, it proved a commercial and critical disaster. When Sam was fired on THE CINCINNATI KID (M-G-M, 1965) after only four days, his career in Hollywood was at a virtual stand-still. Many claimed that he was all washed up.

Sam's first marriage to Begonia failed and he blamed it on his unemployability. He continued to see his children and over the years Marie was always very cooperative in allowing him generous visitation. He tried writing scripts under five different pseudonyms. He adapted James A. Michener's CARAVANS (1963) and contributed a script to M-G-M for a film to be titled READY FOR THE TIGER. He borrowed money. Everything he attempted went nowhere and he was miserable. He drank more heavily than ever. He worked on the screenplay for THE GLORY GUYS (United Artists, 1966) and he was hired to script VILLA RIDES (Paramount, 1968) which was to star Yul Brynner. The actor didn't like Sam's script and had it changed during production. Sam even applied for a job at UCLA lecturing on television production.

Finally, Daniel Melnick of Talent Associates contacted Sam. He wanted him to adapt and direct an ABC network presentation of Katherine Anne Porter's only well-plotted short novel, NOON WINE. In his script Peckinpah added several scenes. Katherine Anne was a long-time correspondent of mine and I can say she was not anything if not contradictory. She wrote to Sam after the telecast that she was very unhappy with the changes that had been made and that she felt the short novel was superior as she wrote it. Yet, years later, she wrote to me that she regretted that Sam Peckinpah was not to direct the screen version of her only novel, SHIP OF FOOLS (1962). Sam was befuddled when I told him that she had said he had understood her characters with an unfailing insight, given what she had written to him. Sam cast Jason Robards, Jr., and Olivia de Havilland as the leads, with Ben Johnson and L.Q. Jones in support. The teleplay won critical acclaim across the country and the Screen Directors' Guild voted Sam one of the ten best television directors for the 1966–1967 season. Daniel Melnick who was responsible for giving Sam this decisive break in his career was also an uncannily accurate judge of character. " 'There are personal qualities he has that make those of us who have spent a great deal of time with him think of him as a very good friend and care for him a great deal,' " he said once of Sam. " 'I have those feelings. He also has the ability to make you want to kill him a good deal of the time. He's an enormously exploitative, manipulative person. And he has the ability to convince almost anybody of anything. He's very charming while seeming to disdain charm as a bourgeois artifice. He has the ability to make almost everybody who works with him believe that he's the last person in the movie business left with integrity and guts. . . . The strange thing is, Sam doesn't really believe that he's as talented as he is, which is one of the problems he has in life. I think he's an enormously talented person who has dissipated himself.' "[21]

The vote from the Guild won Sam the opportunity to direct a segment of BOB HOPE'S CHRYSLER THEATRE, but he was in despair until he established a liaison with Phil Feldman, an independent producer who had offices at what was then known as Warner Bros.-Seven Arts following Jack L. Warner's sale of the Burbank studio to Seven Arts. Feldman wanted Sam to direct THE WILD BUNCH, based on a story by Walon Green. Sam liked the property because it gave him a suitable chance to vent the pent-up frustration and violence he had experienced in his own life since MAJOR DUNDEE and because he could incorporate into it his pervasive suspicion of the Establishment which forced men who wanted freedom into ostracism and finally self-annihilation. "I liked the period I grew up in, the 'Thirties," Sam once said. "It was a different America. We hadn't run out of ground."[22] Now, in THE WILD BUNCH, even though the period was set in the last century, Sam could tell the story of men "who ran out of territory and they know it, but they're not going to bend, either; they refuse to be diminished by it. They play their string out to the end."[23] There are no bad guys and good guys in the traditional sense in THE WILD BUNCH, only men destined by fate to extirpate their oppressions and play out against each other an ineluctable dance of death. Men are corrupted by the system and, regardless of the odds, a man owes it to himself to stand with his companions.

In truth, Sam's Westerns have to be viewed in the context of other Westerns. If THE DEADLY COMPANIONS and RIDE THE HIGH COUNTRY share certain parallels and plot ingredients with Budd Boetticher's Randolph Scott Westerns, MAJOR DUNDEE in terms of theme and structure resembles Hawks' RED RIVER (United Artists, 1948), Ford's FORT APACHE (RKO, 1948), Anthony Mann's THE LAST FRONTIER (Columbia, 1955), and most of all Ford's version of a military filibuster into Mexico in pursuit of Apaches, RIO GRANDE (Republic, 1950). Dundee is joined by a complement of Confederate prisoners in a mission to pursue Charriba and his Apache renegades and to destroy them. The recruits give their word that they will remain under Dundee's command until the Apaches are taken. When O.W. Hadley, played by Warren Oates, deserts and is brought back, Dundee orders him off his horse in the same words that John Wayne as Tom Dunson uses in RED RIVER when he is confronted by deserters who are brought back to face him: "I don't want to have to look up to him." Dundee is filled with the same kind of bitterness over being stationed at a distant Western outpost as a disciplinary measure and his inner sense of humiliation fires his ambition just as happens to Henry Fonda's Colonel Thursday in FORT APACHE and Robert Preston's Colonel Marston in THE

LAST FRONTIER. Unlike either, however, Major Dundee is ultimately successful, as is John Wayne's Lieutenant Colonel Kirby Yorke in RIO GRANDE.

Paul Seydor in an uncharacteristic moment in a book that is often an extraordinary exercise in the art of apologetics remarked in PECKINPAH: THE WESTERN FILMS (1980) that in filming MAJOR DUNDEE what got Peckinpah "into trouble [was] that too many elements and aspects of the materials, especially their historicity, resisted being developed in the way he wanted to develop them; and the one element that was needed to unify them all, the character of Dundee, both caused many of the problems and suffered most from them."[24] Black troopers were not used by the Union to fight Indians during the Civil War, but Sam ignored this and included several under Dundee's command to raise a racial issue with the Confederates. Peckinpah's expeditionary force treats a village of Mexican peasants as callously as do the French and the *Juaristas* who are fighting between themselves for control of Mexico. In the midst of his pursuit, in fact shortly after O.W. Hadley is executed, Dundee has sexual intercourse with Teresa Santiago, played by Senta Berger, a woman who prior to this time in the film was an object sought after by both Dundee and Harris' Captain Benjamin Tyreen. Following the episode, Dundee rides into Durango alone, despite Teresa's warning that the French are "*tres fort*" there, and goes on a long drunk. Peckinpah, as Ford before him but even more emphatically, presents lovingly scenes of brawling and carousing which do nothing for the film story other than tediously illustrate Dundee's degradation. Just before Tyreen rescues him so the company can get back to business, Dundee does avail himself of an opportunity to express his contempt for women in a scene with Teresa and a prostitute with whom he has spent some time. In its way, this was an anticipation in fantasy of a scene Sam himself would play out in future years with women who deeply loved him.

"We still haven't isolated exactly what this picture's *about . . . ,*" Charlton Heston recorded in his diary at the time, "maybe because we can't agree, or just don't know . . . but we have to decide."[25] He probably should have also used the toilet in Coburn's camper. Since the film was so badly truncated before release, critics such as Paul Seydor or Jim Kitses in HORIZONS WEST (1970) have undertaken to reconstruct the film as Peckinpah originally intended it and to judge it on the basis of what it might have been, or should have been, rather than on what it is, although even so avid an advocate as Seydor had to admit that "if the film in its present form suggests that Peckinpah may have been unprepared at the conceptual level to tackle a project of this size and scope when he did, it is nevertheless an impressive demonstration of his ability to handle, so relatively early in his career, the logistical side of a really *big* production."[26] Kitses, on the other hand, was far more positive: "The recurrent features of this form are familiar: an undermanned company (or settlement), while torn by internal conflicts, functions as the heroic unit in achieving the group objective, the defeat of the faceless hostile. If the form has been brilliantly inflected by both Ford and Mann . . . to make deeply ambiguous statements, nowhere has it been so relentlessly undermined as in Peckinpah's hands.''[27] I think Kitses was absolutely right. MAJOR DUNDEE's chief characteristic is to undermine the very idea of an heroic fighting unit. ''What Sam had in mind was, I think, THE WILD BUNCH,'' Heston subsequently concluded, ''and what the studio had in mind was a film that made a lot of money and was about cowboys and Indians.''[28] Peckinpah himself once commented: ''They cut it in DUNDEE. I did it in THE WILD BUNCH.''[29] What was it Peckinpah tried to do in MAJOR DUNDEE? In Kitses' words, MAJOR DUNDEE depicts ''the blood-bath from which America is born.''[30] So much, really, for those who are inclined to feel that Peckinpah made THE WILD BUNCH in reference to the Vietnam War. That war may have helped the controversy and popularity of THE WILD BUNCH, but the underlying vision in the later film was already being worked through in MAJOR DUNDEE before the Vietnam War had become truly an issue of national dissension. Michael Pate was cast as Sierra Charriba, leader of the Apaches, and in the graphic spirit of Ford the trap set by the ragtail whites and blacks in Dundee's campaign, once it is sprung, brings about a blood-bath for the Indians. Then there is a second blood-bath when Dundee's troops try to cross the Rio Grande, hacking and butchering their way through a company of French lancers, a battle in which Tyreen loses his life but not his honor and in which Dundee supposedly saves his life while regaining his honor. If there is a theme in all this violence, it is not a new one, just one more vividly realized in terms of on-camera bloodshed: the old foolishness about redemption through violence. This is also the principal theme of THE WILD BUNCH.

William R. Meyer in THE MAKING OF THE GREAT WESTERNS (1979) included a breakdown chart for Howard Hawks' Westerns in which the chief roles are hero, second lead, young man, female, old man, and villain. In RED RIVER, for example, the hero role is played by John Wayne who also played the villain role (just as there is a similar duality in Heston's role as Major Dundee). The second lead is played by John Ireland. The young man is played by Montgomery Clift, the female by Joanne Dru, and the old man by Walter Brennan. In RIO BRAVO, the hero is John Wayne, the second lead Dean Martin, the young man Ricky Nelson, the female Angie Dickinson, the old man Walter Brennan, and the villain John Russell. In MAJOR DUNDEE the second lead is Richard Harris, the young man Jim Hutton, the female Senta Berger, the villain Michael Pate, and Coburn's portrayal of Potts functions in the role of the old man who, as in a Hawks film, is at the center of the action, even a participant, without ever himself being an initiating force. In THE WILD BUNCH the hero is William Holden as Pike, leader of the bunch. The second lead is split between Ernest Borgnine, as Dutch, who still rides with Pike, and Robert Ryan as Thornton, who used to ride with the bunch but who has sold out to the Establishment and leads the pursuit. The female—an extremely limited role in any Peckinpah Western with the exception of THE BALLAD OF CABLE HOGUE—is played by Aurora Clavel, the unfaithful wife who had an affair with Pike and was killed by her cuckolded husband, an event which leaves Pike with a painful memory.

The young man is Angel, played by Jaime Sanchez, and the old man is Sykes, played by Edmond O'Brien. The villain is played by Emilio Fernández who, as Mapache, the leader of a band of cutthroat Mexican revolutionaries is the equivalent of Sierra Charriba in MAJOR DUNDEE. Although many scenes and individual shots in MAJOR DUNDEE adumbrate scenes and individual shots in THE WILD BUNCH, what in particular is different is that the violence in the latter picture becomes so intensified that the protagonists as well as the villains are consumed in the final bloody holocaust.

There are two Mexicos in THE WILD BUNCH, the Mexico of the *Mapachistas* (*mapache* in Spanish means raccoon) and the *Méjico lindo* to be found in Angel's village which the bunch visits in the course of the film. The latter, Peckinpah felt at the time, was a viable alternative to the United States and commented in an interview that "everything important in my life has been linked to Mexico in one way or another. The country has a special effect on me. . . . In Mexico it's all out front—the color, the life, the warmth. If a Mexican likes you, he'll touch you. It's direct. It's real. . . . Here in this country, everybody is worried about stopping the war and saving the forests and all that, but these same crusaders go out the door in the morning forgetting to kiss their wives and water the flowers. In Mexico they don't worry so goddamned much about saving the human race or about the wheeling and dealing that's poisoning us. In Mexico they don't forget to kiss each other and water the flowers."[31] More of a disavowal of THE WILD BUNCH as an anti-war film would be difficult to imagine. The *Méjico lindo* of Angel's village is a place so pastoral and calm that even the Gorch brothers, played by Warren Oates and Ben Johnson, dangerous rapists normally, help an attractive *señorita* draw water rather than attacking her. *Méjico lindo* is a Peckinpah fantasy. As such, it is pleasant; but, as a realistic statement, if it had been so intended (and I doubt that it was), it can only be considered patent nonsense.

"Scorpions struggle in a sea of killer ants, children gaily watching," Kitses wrote of the opening image of THE WILD BUNCH. " . . . While dramatically preparing us for the action to follow, the image also describes the relationship between Peckinpah's characters and the society through which they move. And we must not forget the children: above all, the moment introduces a network of detail that is crucial in the film, a structure in which innocence and cruelty, laughter and barbarity, idealism and blood-lust, exist side by side."[32] This is perhaps the most basic fantasy in Peckinpah's vision of the American West and of Western society in the broadest sense: individual criminals are supplanted by a society that is itself criminal.

When he was scouting locations in Mexico, Sam became engaged to Begonia for the second time. He later recalled in an interview how he came up with the idea of the scorpions and the killer ants. "In Mexico you must have a stand-by director. Mine was a very good friend of mine named Emilio Fernández. We were talking about the script. He said, 'You know for me, the Wild Bunch is like a scorpion on an ant hill.' And I said, 'Wait a minute, what's that?' And my fiancée phoned to see when I was coming for supper and I told her, 'Madam, I am with Emilio Fernández and the pimple on his ass is worth more to me at the moment than our future.' And I said to Emilio, 'Let's talk.' "[33]

When Tector Gorch (Ben Johnson) wants to get rid of old Sykes, Pike tells him: "You're not getting rid of anybody. We're going to stick together, just like it used to be. When you side a man you stay with him, and if you can't do that you're like some animal. You're finished. *We're* finished. All of us." Of course, Pike has not always lived up to this code in the past, which is how Thornton ended up on the other side. He is shown to have fallen short of his ideal on more than one occasion, but, it turns out, the bloody carnage at the end holds the balm of salvation. Pike also abandoned Aurora long ago to her husband just as he fled a brothel leaving Thornton behind to be captured and imprisoned. Maybe it is for this reason that he is shot twice in the back, once by a whore and once by a child in military regalia. Angel learns about women when his village sweetheart gives herself sexually to Mapache because Mapache has money and power. Angel shoots her and it is her mother who betrays Angel to Mapache and who triggers his capture, torture, and, finally, execution by Mapache precipitating, in turn, the bunch's revenge. Women may not have a big role to play in this film, as in Peckinpah's vision of the world, but they cause most of the trouble, at least indirectly, and these images do add up to a distrust, and even a dislike, of women. While I reject Paul Seydor's attempts to deny Peckinpah's misogyny, I do agree with him that "Thornton becomes . . . both Pike's nemesis and the touchstone by which Pike's own failings and compromises are thrown into fuller relief . . . ; and inasmuch as Thornton's dogged pursuit symbolizes Pike's past, it is obvious that far from searching for that past, Pike has been trying all along to escape it."[34] As Gil Westrum in RIDE THE HIGH COUNTRY, however much Pike may have failed to live up to his own code, the path of redemption opens for him; while, unlike Pat Garrett in PAT GARRETT AND BILLY THE KID, who has sold out to the Establishment and has forever lost a part of himself, Thornton is saved: at the end he joins Sykes and a band of revolutionaries.

The racial implications of THE WILD BUNCH are very clear. When the bunch succeeds in its theft of arms and ammunition coveted by the *Mapachistas*, their front man, Herrera, played by Alfonso Arau, meets the bunch on the trail and, as Arthur G. Pettit put it, "insisting that he brings love and affection from his generals, points to the *Mapachista* troops that line the horizon and declares: 'We are friends—*all* of us.' Pike, lighting a fuse and threatening to blow up the shipment, along with the bunch and Herrera, cuts the odds from six Americans and several hundred Mexicans to a personal face-down between himself and Herrera. Screwing his dark, toothy face into the comical grimace of a cakewalk darky, Herrera whines: 'Ple-ee-ze, cot de foose.' Pike cuts the fuse and the perspiring Herrera retreats in disgrace, showing once again that Mexican cowardice and treachery are no match for the straight-talking, fast-acting bunch."[35] The scenes of carnage and butchery when the bunch destroys Mapache and all his followers, so striking at the time because of the slow-motion photography of gushing blood and shattered bodies intercut into the choreography of slaughter, carry a clear message. The four remaining members of the bunch, even though it means their own death, show the power and glory of their race as they kill hundreds of the brown-skinned foe. "The Wild Bunch is America," Jim Kitses wrote. The film is an exultation of racism and this undoubtedly contributed to its popularity at the time of its release. It is also an angry film, and killing becomes a form of final release, a romantic immolation in blood and bullets and torn flesh. Nor is it really possible to enjoy THE WILD BUNCH without to some extent accepting its racial ideology. The film represents the logical extension of white supremacy which has traditionally informed so much of the Western mythos. Peckinpah was not objectifying the phenomenon. By returning to a final image of the bunch riding out triumphantly from Angel's village, he was providing them and what they did with legendary status, as Ford earlier had Colonel Thursday and his Regulars in FORT APACHE in a similar closing scene. "This concept of cutting together film shot at a variety of speeds ranging from normal to extreme slow motion is a key element in the power of the violence in THE WILD BUNCH as well as in subsequent Peckinpah films," Garner Simmons wrote. "Slow motion alone merely elongates time. However, by placing shots of different speeds in juxtaposition as the moment of violence is revealed, an internal tension is created within that sequence of shots. This tension has become the distinctive trademark of Peckinpah's screen violence."[36] Peckinpah's apologists argue that in his conclusion to THE WILD BUNCH he was treating racial genocide with irony, while his critics claim that he was indulging in a Fascist fantasy. My own view is that he was doing both, and more: he solved the problem, in Paul Seydor's words, of "winning an audience's assent to a vision in which violence is part of the very essence" by getting audiences to watch his film.[37]

When Warner Bros. initially released the film in the United States, the flashbacks were cut, that of Pike's affair with a married woman who is killed and that of Pike and Thornton simultaneously recalling the episode in the brothel where Pike gains his freedom and Thornton is captured. Sam felt at the time that by allowing this to happen, Phil Feldman was permitting to be cut precisely " 'the things which humanized the characters. I couldn't believe it. Here people are screaming for my head on a platter because I have too much violence in the film, and Feldman makes certain that's all anybody sees.' "[38] The way the film now exists, three different versions can be seen: one with the flashbacks cut, one with only the flashback of the brothel scene restored, and one with both flashbacks restored. More to the point was Peckinpah's meticulous concern for dialogue which had him looping a lot of dialogue later after principal photography had been completed. " ' . . . Sam is always concerned with the audience's being able to hear every word,' " Lou Lombardo said, who was the film editor on THE WILD BUNCH. " 'If you lose a word, you lose meaning.' "[39]

"Well, there are two kinds of women," Sam said in his PLAYBOY interview.

"There are women and then there's pussy. A woman is a partner. If you can go a certain distance by yourself, a good woman will triple it." In his next two films, Sam illustrated his basic notion of the two kinds. Hildy, the prostitute played by Stella Stevens in THE BALLAD OF CABLE HOGUE, is a woman. Dustin Hoffman's wife in STRAW DOGS, played by Susan George, is the other kind. "To start out with, she asked for the rape," Sam said about George's character in the film. "But later she could barely bring herself to pull the trigger to save his [Hoffman's] life. . . . She is basically pussy."[40]

In THE BALLAD OF CABLE HOGUE, Jason Robards, Jr., as Hogue is left out in the desert to die by his two partners, Taggart and Bowen, played respectively by L.Q. Jones and Strother Martin. Wandering around the desert, nearly dead, Hogue discovers water. He meets a self-proclaimed preacher, played by David Warner, goes to town and files on his claim, tries without success to interest R.G. Armstrong, as the local manager of the stage line, in a half interest, borrows a hundred dollars from a friendly banker to make improvements, and sees Hildy toward whom he is at once attracted. When Hildy is driven out of town by the so-called "good people," she comes to stay with Hogue at his water hole before continuing on to San Francisco. Sam had cast Dub Taylor as a temperance lecturer in THE WILD BUNCH many of whose followers are gunned down during the abortive robbery at the beginning of the film. In THE BALLAD OF CABLE HOGUE, Hogue's antics with Hildy outrage the temperance league which is meeting in a tent and it is this incident which probably precipitates Hildy's forced exodus. Hogue wants revenge and Hildy wants to marry a rich man. Hildy is up front about it. Unlike Gene Evans' wife, played by Susan O'Connell, who enjoys days and nights frolicking with the preacher, she admits she fucks for what she can get out of it. The one exception is Hogue, but she will not stay with him. "Of all the whores I've been with—American, Chinese, English, Mexican, any nationality—I've failed to end up in some kind of warm personal relationship with only about ten percent," is how Sam put it in his PLAYBOY interview. "I've *lived* with some good whores. They've taken me home or I've taken them home. We've been human beings together. I never thought of these women as objects to be used. I put a lot of the relationships I've had with whores into the love story of Cable Hogue and his whore, Hildy. They had a relationship that was truer and more tender than that between most husbands and wives. The fact that she was a whore and went to bed with men for money didn't change anything."[41] Hogue's idyll with Hildy lasts three weeks before the preacher returns, in flight from Evans, whose wife has confessed everything. Evans' wife is pussy. "Most of us marry pussy at one time or another," Sam went on. "A smart, unscrupulous cunt can always use her looks to get some poor slob to marry her. And in marriage, so often, especially if the man is lonely, he will clothe her in the vestments of his own needs—and if she's young, she'll do the same to him. . . . All of a sudden the illusion wears off and they really see each other. . . ."[42]

The preacher eludes Evans without a confrontation. Peckinpah actually did shoot a sequence in which Evans and Warner fought it out with Hogue stepping in and getting an injured wrist, but all that is left of it in release prints of the film is the dirty bandage Hogue wears in the scene which follows and which he never has on again. The next day, Hildy goes on her way, Hogue in the meanwhile continuing to wait for Taggart and Bowen to show up. The stage line has given him a contract to function as a way station and over the next few years he accumulates a fair amount of money. When Taggart and Bowen do show up, Hogue tricks them into digging what may well be their own grave, throws snakes in the hole after them, and plugs Taggart when Taggart goes for his gun. Bowen begs for mercy and Hogue makes him a partner. Hildy then returns, in an automobile driven by a black chauffeur, and asks Hogue if he is ready to join her. Hogue is ready, but he is run over by the automobile after pushing Bowen aside when the vehicle begins rolling down an incline. The preacher returns in time to read a eulogy over him.

The picture has been called one of Peckinpah's gentler moments and that it is, although no less a fantasy than THE WILD BUNCH. In a dozen ways, Peckinpah gave tribute to John Ford's West, in the love shown the American flag (recalling a similar moment in Ford's DRUMS ALONG THE MOHAWK [20th-Fox, 1939]), the yellow ribbon Susan O'Connell wears in her hair (reminiscent of Ford's SHE WORE A YELLOW RIBBON [RKO, 1949]), the attitude of the righteous townspeople toward Hildy (harking back to the scene in STAGECOACH [United Artists, 1939] when Claire Trevor's Dallas is forced to leave town), and a reversal from nearly all Westerns and especially Ford's in showing a compassionate banker willing to take a chance and make a character loan.

> *Hildy*: You've been awful nice to me, Hogue. Ain't it never bothered you none, what I am?
>
> *Hogue*: No, it never bothered me. I enjoyed it. Well, what the hell are you? A human being. We try the best we can. We all got our own ways of living.
>
> *Hildy*: And loving?
>
> *Hogue*: Gets mighty lonesome without it.

The implication here is plain. Hildy is a prostitute because it is her way of living *and* loving. It seems incredible to me that Sam could have preserved such a hopelessly sentimental notion about prostitutes considering the number with whom he associated. Hogue tells Hildy that he lives in the desert because in the desert he is someone. It would be different if he lived in town. "In town," he says, "I'm nothing. I've been that before. I don't like being nothing."

When Hildy leaves him to find her rich man, Hogue goes on about his business. The preacher knows what Hogue is feeling inside. "Funny thing," he says. "It doesn't matter how much or how little you've wandered around, how many women you've been with. Every once in a while one of them cuts right through, right straight into you." Hogue is bewildered. "Well, what do you do about it?" he asks. "I suppose, maybe, when you die you get over it," the preacher tells him. One gets the impression from this that the "way to salvation" is for Hogue to abandon his hopes for revenge and go off with Hildy. If so, it is an even more absurdly romantic proposition than what Hogue actually does: he remains in the desert until he revenges himself on Taggart and forgives Bowen. While I happen to be entertained by THE BALLAD OF CABLE HOGUE, unlike Paul Seydor and other critics, I cannot take the premises of the film in earnest and discuss them as if they represented some profound perspective on life. I regard it instead as a male reverie. Hildy is an imaginative projection of Peckinpah's definition of a good woman. " 'CABLE HOGUE is possibly my best film,' " Sam once said. " ' . . . I still cry when he says to her, "Now, there is a picture." And she says, "You've seen it before, Hogue." And Jason replies, "Lady, nobody's ever seen you before." Talk about a love scene. They were sensational.' "[43] I agree that the love scenes are extraordinarily well done. However, it does not follow, as Seydor insisted, that "if Peckinpah really were the misogynist he has been called, scenes like this would be inconceivable."[44] To the contrary, what is misogynistic in the film is its limiting women to two basic kinds: the good prostitute who admits up front what she is and what she wants and pussy which is ready to romp in bed with one man while married to another.

Linda Rosenbaum was Sam's secretary at the time of THE BALLAD OF CABLE HOGUE. They had one of their typical disagreements and Sam fired her just before the unit was to leave Echo Bay in the Valley of Fire in Nevada and go to Phoenix for final shooting. When Sam got to Phoenix, he started looking for her. She could not be found. "Sam lamented, 'I fire her twice a week,' " Max Evans recorded. " 'She knows I don't mean it.' " Before Evans left Echo Bay, Rosenbaum had joined him and some others for breakfast. "When asked what we should tell Sam when he inquired about her she said, 'Just tell him I'm somewhere on the North American continent.' She hesitated a moment, looked off somewhere and spoke softly, 'Poor Sam.' "[45] The women who tried to get closest to Sam were usually even more romantic than he could be upon occasion.

On 4 July 1961 Jason Robards, Jr., and Lauren Bacall were married in Ensanada, Mexico. Bacall was pregnant with their child. Bacall had sold the mansion she had lived in with Bogart and by then lived in an apartment in The Dakota in New York, the location where Roman Polanski would film ROSEMARY'S BABY (Paramount, 1968) and outside which John Lennon would be killed. The eleven rooms of this apartment had almost as much space as had the home in Holmby Hills. After her marriage to Robards, although there were photographs everywhere, the only visible reminder of the past was a leatherbound script of KEY LARGO that had imprinted in gold the words, "The Bogarts—Betty and Humphrey." Filming on THE BALLAD OF CABLE HOGUE was concluded near the end of March, 1969. Evans wrote that "Jason . . . was always . . . giving all he had and more. And never once during all the turmoil did he even mention all the marital difficulties he was having with his wife. . . . ''[46] What had really soured everything was that Bogart, after his death, became an even bigger star than he had been alive and increasingly Bacall came to bask in his reflected glory. She worked, yes, but even more she was pursued by many wanting to know more about Bogart. After eight years of marriage, Bacall divorced Robards on 11 September 1969. Robards did not contest the action. All he would say was: "I am tired of being Mrs. Bogart's second husband.''[47]

Charles Silver in THE WESTERN FILM (1976) raised an interesting point when he noted that "a problem with Peckinpah's later and lesser films arises from the uncertainty as to whether he is chronicling decadence or is, in fact, decadent. In THE WILD BUNCH he is able to fall back on the old Hawksian virtues of togetherness, men united by a cause. He freezes the last happy frame, as if to preserve a time when there were causes to unite behind. Peckinpah's THE BALLAD OF CABLE HOGUE . . . contains a hopefulness of a kind, embodied in its lyrical theme song, 'Tomorrow.' Jason Robards' striking it rich represents the ultimate, if all too brief, triumph of the grizzled sidekick. His success is the success of all the Walter Brennans of the West who have lusted in frustration after all the Stella Stevens types. Peckinpah is aware of the decadence inherent in Robards' redemption through hedonism, and he must finally kill him off.''[48] I do not know if Sam was consciously aware of why he had to have Hogue die, but there is no denying that redemption through hedonism leads to the same result as redemption through violence. Pauline Kael was wrong to call him a Fascist, but she was right on the mark when she accused him of nihilism. The viewer is assured of Hogue's virility when, in his eulogy, the preacher remarks, "But, Lord, he was a man," with Hildy chiming in, "Amen to that!" The preacher also says—it *is* a moving eulogy, however ridiculous— "He built his empire, but was man enough to give it up for love when the time came." This would imply that there was a "right" time, an appeal to ritual behavior; but when that "right" time comes all Hogue has time to do is to die. " . . . I think dying well has a lot to do with living well," Sam said within months of his own death. "I think that Cable died well.''[49]

In those scenes where Hogue captures snakes with his bare hands and makes a stew from toads, grasshoppers, rabbits, squirrels, gophers, and prairie dogs (with wild onions for seasoning), the metaphor of turning a desert into a garden is newly invoked, and the wasteland is seen to be bountiful. The values are clearly those of *Méjico lindo*, Hogue and Hildy "don't forget to kiss each other and water the flowers." Matthew Peckinpah was with his father during the filming of the picture and Sam even gave him a small part, as a young boy eating Hogue's desert concoction whose mother, once she finds out what is in it, screams at him, "Matthew, stop eatin' that stuff!" When Matthew returned home to Marie, he told her that he was absolutely certain that he *never* wanted to be an actor.

THE BALLAD OF CABLE HOGUE cost almost three million to make, far over budget primarily because of the persistent bad weather the company had encountered at Echo Bay. "Bankers have believed in me," Sam once remarked when we were talking quietly, "producers have, releasing companies, the people who work for me—and then you believe that the picture you've made is the very best you possibly could have made, and it doesn't gross. It's very hard, sometimes." Sam had grown so fond of Cable's shack that for a time he contemplated bringing it back to Malibu so he could live in it permanently. He wanted to live out his string as Cable had. What plunged him into despair was that Warner Bros. was convinced that THE BALLAD OF CABLE HOGUE was not commercial and consigned it to a quick obscurity.

ABC Films, with Cinerama distributing theatrically, contracted Peckinpah for what would prove a brace of films, commencing with STRAW DOGS which was to be filmed on location in the United Kingdom. Sam felt that the original novel on which the film was based had nothing to offer except its final scene, the raid on the farm, and so had the story completely reworked for the screenplay. There is a dual theme in STRAW DOGS: the recognition on the part of the protagonist played by Dustin Hoffman that the woman he is married to is basically pussy and that every man harbors in his soul the capacity for a violent outburst leading to the slaughter of his fellow man given the right provocation. Feeling Hollywood had mistreated him, Sam thought for a while that he might want to live in England. His third attempt at marriage to Begonia had failed and so he engaged Joie Gould as his secretary and carried on an intermittent romance with her. He also hired Katy Haber as his production assistant. One consolation was that Daniel Melnick, who had hired him to direct NOON WINE, was the producer.

Susan George as Hoffman's wife is raped twice in a row, once by a man with whom she used to be intimate and then she is taken from the rear by a man she cannot stand. For Sam, the double rape gave her a little bit more than what she had wanted. Pauline Kael claimed the second rape was sodomy. Sam insisted that it wasn't, merely rear entry, and that Kael must have an anal complex. All of this notwithstanding, the rape sequence is totally unbelievable, with Susan George vascillating back and forth during the first rape, enjoying it and then hating it. This attitude simply does not work given how the painful flashbacks then haunt her for the rest of the picture, especially in view of Sam's declaration that as pussy she had wanted the rape to happen. The picture concludes with more loose ends than any Peckinpah picture ever has with the exception of BRING ME THE HEAD OF ALFREDO GARCIA. The final scene finds Hoffman and David Warner, playing the village idiot who has inadvertently killed a girl who was obviously pussy but whose family raided the farm where Hoffman was living to get him and getting killed in the process, sitting together in Hoffman's car. Hoffman knows he must leave his wife, but he has lost his way. To simulate fog, Sam had several smudge pots lit along the roadside. A fire broke out and had to be put out. When he tried the scene again, still with smudge pots but more judiciously placed, it was Hoffman who came up with the last line in the picture. He responds to David Warner's remark that he doesn't know his way home that he doesn't, either. The lurching of the car as Hoffman says this was caused by Katy Haber, as she once told me, bouncing her derrière on the trunk. Yet, where does this leave the viewer? Is Hoffman going to take Warner into town? The magistrate has been killed, but Warner has also committed at least accidental manslaughter. And what of the old man whose foot was shot with his shotgun? He's still outside somewhere and Susan George, terrified, without communications of any kind, is left isolated in the death house. It was not on any of the problems with the story that critics dwelt, however, in attacking the film, but rather on the unmitigated violence of the latter half of the picture during the siege.

Viewed today, by the standards established by slasher films in the 1980s, THE WILD BUNCH and STRAW DOGS are almost muted in their violence. We have become indifferent, or perhaps immune, to screen violence, or maybe our tolerance level has increased. Mr. Scogan in Aldous Huxley's CHROME YELLOW (1922), reflecting on the carnage of the First World War, noticed how we are less and less amazed by real violence. " 'Today,' " he says, " 'we are no longer surprised at these things. The Black and Tans harry Ireland, the Poles maltreat the Silesians, the bold Fascisti slaughter their poor countrymen: we take it all for granted. Since the war we wonder at nothing.' "[50] In various interviews, Sam would customarily defend what he was doing with a number of arguments. It was his misfortune that LIFE had called him the "Master of Violence" and even a friend such as Max Evans used the sobriquet in the subtitle to his book on the making of THE BALLAD OF CABLE HOGUE. Sam's violent films grossed and his gentler films did not. All right, then violence must be what Sam must do. If Hitchcock was the master of suspense, that was because he always made suspense films. Now Sam must make violent films.

STRAW DOGS was very successful. The same cannot be said of JUNIOR BONNER (Cinerama, 1972) which came next and which was to be in a gentle mood. Lucien Ballard, who had been Sam's cinematographer on THE WILD BUNCH and THE BALLAD OF CABLE HOGUE, was hired again. Steve McQueen was to be the star. There was insufficient conflict in the film to create much interest and the characters were not strong enough to carry the storyline which was about rodeo life. Robert Preston and Ida Lupino handed in the best performances as McQueen's separated parents who come to accept each other's weaknesses and each other, caring about each other even though they know they cannot live together.

When McQueen asked for Sam to direct THE GETAWAY it was because he had worked well with Sam. However, since his production company was involved in this film, he did not want to see a repetition of JUNIOR BONNER which lost a great deal of money. Sam's drinking had intensified, but starting with STRAW DOGS he began getting Vitamin B shots to compensate for the effects of the alcohol. Sam conceived of THE GETAWAY as a combination picture, an essay in violence that would embody a poignant love story. McQueen plays a man betrayed by a murderous, violent element on his trail, intent on killing him. The chase is played out against a contrast of the two kinds of women. Ali McGraw is the good woman, working with McQueen, accepting his dominance, tripling his distance and carrying him through to safety when, by herself, she would be lost and fumbling in the world. Sally Struthers was cast as a particularly lurid personification of pussy. Critics complained that the entire Struthers episode detracted from the central tension of the plot. Yet Sam doubtless delighted in showing Jack Dodson, Sally's husband, tied up in hotel rooms while Al Lettieri, playing a killer who is after McQueen, ravishes Struthers in front of him, both relishing every passionate minute of it. By comparison, Ali McGraw is colorless and dull. McQueen oversaw some changes made in the release version, and the film became the second top-grossing picture that year.

While in production, Sam hired Sharon Peckinpah to assist him and then fired her, most probably for justified cause. Sam always took his work very seriously. It was also during this picture that he married Joie Gould. He had converted to Roman Catholicism for his third and final marriage to Begonia. For Joie, he converted to Judaism. " 'We had gotten into an argument, and I slapped her with my open hand,' " Sam later said. " 'I really felt bad about it. So in a moment of remorse I agreed to marry her.' " He also said: " '. . . She took all the money I got on GETAWAY and took a trip around the world at my expense. We were not exactly what you might call star-crossed lovers.' "[51] This was simply not the truth. Sam gave her a settlement many times smaller than his salary on THE GETAWAY, not to mention his residual income from the picture after it was released. However, to dramatize the event he henceforth had a matrimonial clause inserted in his picture contracts whereby should he marry while the film was in production he would automatically forfeit all income from it. With or without that clause, and including a number of years during which he did not work much at all, Sam never did marry again.

Sam was occupying an office at what was then known as the Samuel Goldwyn lot on Santa Monica Boulevard and living in a house trailer in Malibu when the deal was set for him to direct PAT GARRETT AND BILLY THE KID for M-G-M. Max Evans stopped at his office and, after showing Max THE GET-AWAY which was in the editing stage, Sam remarked, " 'You know how I throw away money. Well, I thought I should be sure to leave my four kids *something* so, I bought each one of them a Picasso the other day.' "[52] Once production had begun in Durango, to counteract Rona Barrett's accusation, Sam ran a full page ad in DAILY VARIETY showing himself with cast and crew members with drinks in their hands raised in a toast. The caption read: "Dear Sirs: With reference to the rumor that seems to be spreading around Hollywood that on numerous occasions Sam Peckinpah has been carried off the set taken with drink. This is to inform you that those rumors are totally unfounded. However, there have been mornings. . . . "[53] All the research Sam had done on the Kid's life could now be put to good use, including the framing device he had wanted to use in ONE-EYED JACKS which was to open with a shot of the Kid's coffin and then flash back to how he had ended up there. Sam felt he could tell the story of Billy the Kid's clash with Pat Garrett as if it were Greek tragedy or a Bible story, where everyone knew how the story ended so the emphasis could instead be placed on *why* it had to end that way.

There now exist four versions of this film: Sam's original director's cut which was never released, the M-G-M release version, the version that was prepared for syndicated television release, and the version that Sam personally edited for Daniel Melnick in late 1974 when Melnick was a vice president at M-G-M and which opportunity Melnick offered Sam to placate him in his law suit against the company. It is, therefore, even questionable at this point in time which of Sam's two versions, the earlier one or the later one, is the one he intended to be his *final* version. All I can do is to narrate how they differ.

First, there is the mood, which is more or less the same in all versions. There is no optimistic spirit of the land in PAT GARRETT AND BILLY THE KID, no new frontier, only the sense of a vast wasteland, a desert punctuated by silvery, surrealistic realistic lakes and streams. Much of the film is photographed in shadow, at dusk, in hazy light, or at night. The hopelessness of the terrain is reflected in the agonized loneliness of the principals who are engaged in a frustrated quest for identity, a bitter confrontation with futility, and, moving through it all, desperately erupting, there is a sustaining violence, a lewd intimacy with death. Second, and there is no way to put this charitably, there is an added dimension of almost alcoholic despair—to use consciously an oxymoron: a blurred clarity—combined with a depth of disquiet, a sorrowful, resigned, fated inevitability. This dimension is as intrinsic to the picture as the variously barren and occasionally luxuriant landscape. Finally, there is no regard for historical truth. Patrick Floyd Garrett—referred to only once in the film, by Chill Wills, and then incorrectly, as Patrick J. Garrett—was shot to death while urinating on a lonely road in New Mexico on 28 February 1908. Billy the Kid was shot to death by Pat Garrett in the dark of Pete Maxwell's bedroom at Fort Sumner on 14 July 1881, armed at the time only with a butcher knife.

Sam's first and second versions of the film open to a scene dated 1909, near Las Cruces, New Mexico. Garrett is an old man, riding in a buggy, telling Poe, the man who had been a special deputy during the hunt for the Kid, that he is a son-of-a-bitch and that he must get his sheep off the land that Garrett has leased to him. A man is seen crawling beneath a bush to take aim. As his rifle bullet hits Garrett, Garrett stands up in the buggy and then Poe plugs Garrett in the back. As Garrett's body falls, there is intercut with the bullets ripping him apart shots of bullets tearing off the heads of chickens buried in the ground. The location is identified as Fort Sumner, 1887. Garrett, accompanied by J.W. Bell, is riding in while the Kid and his gang are engaged in target practice. Music is played under the credits which are intercut with shots, but no ballad is sung. In fact, in both his first and second versions, Sam used the ballad composed by Bob Dylan who was given the role of Alias in the film only twice as opposed to both the release version and the television version which use the ballad constantly. There is a quick shot of Maria, played by Rita Coolidge, walking while Garrett and Bell approach the Kid and his gang after Garrett has shot off the head of a chicken as well. Provision must have been made during filming for the television version which pictures the tops of liquor bottles rather than chickens being shot off, since the footage matches otherwise. Garrett lets Billy know the reason he has come to Fort Sumner is that Chisum and the other big ranchers have hired him to be sheriff of Lincoln County and that they want the Kid gone. "Now, are they tellin' me, or are they askin' me?" the Kid inquires. "I'm askin' yuh," Garrett replies, "but in five days I'm makin' yuh when I take over sheriffin' Lincoln County." At this point, Sam's credit appears: Directed by Sam Peckinpah. "It feels like times have changed," Pat tells the Kid, and this will become his refrain throughout the film. "Times, maybe, but not me," the Kid says. In many places the dialogue in the release version is shortened and, actually, is more effective. For example, as Garrett is heading out the door, Bell has a gratuitous line, which he delivers to the Kid and his gang: "You boys are playin' a losing game. I'm figurin' on staying alive." While it is true that this line foreshadows another line when Bell is guarding the Kid in jail in a later scene and the Kid asks him if he thinks the Kid is going out a loser, it takes away from the power of that scene. The release version concludes the scene with the Kid, when asked why he doesn't shoot Garrett, responding: "Why? He's my friend." In both of Sam's versions, one of the gang then says: "He ain't no more." "I reckon," Billy says, and then there is a fade to black. The release version is better, I think, with the fade to black after the line, "He's my friend."

Cut to a scene of an isolated shack being surrounded by Garrett and a posse. Billy is inside with Rudolph Wurlitzer as O'Folliard and Charles Martin as Bowdre. The first thing O'Folliard does when getting up is to have a drink. The Kid remarks that he cannot stand a son-of-a-bitch who pours himself full of it right off. Then, he takes the bottle from O'Folliard, takes a slug himself. In the release version, he proceeds to spit it out. In Sam's two versions, he swallows the whiskey without comment.

In the jail sequence, it is obvious in all four versions that Garrett is the one who plants the six-gun in the outhouse. It opens to the Kid playing poker with Garrett and Bell, with R.G. Armstrong as Bob Ollinger watching and holding his shotgun close to himself. A scaffold is being erected outside in the street. The Ollinger character is the standard Peckinpah religious fanatic. Angry at the Kid, holding the shotgun to the Kid's chest, he yells at him: "Repent, you son-of-a-bitch." "Jesus," the Kid says, "I repent." Garrett leaves to collect some taxes. It is at this time, presumably, that he hides the six-gun which the Kid uses to kill Bell. Ollinger, who has been across the street, runs back toward the jail only to see the Kid standing on the second story porch with his own shotgun filled with fourteen thin dimes pointed at him. In the two Peckinpah versions, the Kid shoots Ollinger twice, once with each barrel, saying after the second shot: "Keep the change, Bob." In the release version, the Kid fires only once and is actually more sympathetic as a result.

In both of Sam's versions, the ballad is played for the first time as the Kid rides out of town. When Garrett returns, he hires Jack Elam as a deputy to help him hunt for the Kid. In the barber shop, Garrett tells a boy to tell his wife that he will be home for dinner and then to contact the men standing around at the courthouse. In the first Peckinpah version, Garrett is followed to his house, where he pauses at the gate. Cut to the Kid riding, the ballad being sung, and then the Kid sawing off his leg irons, only finally to ride in twilight around a pool in which his mounted figure is reflected darkly. This all is intercut with Garrett's visit with his wife, a Mexican woman played by Aurora Clavel who Sam had previously cast as the unfaithful wife with whom Pike had had the single romance in his life. She tells Garrett that he has become all empty inside. In a parallel scene, the Kid is shown, now at Fort Sumner, walking behind Maria, while a group of children heckle him. In Sam's second cut, all of this was deleted. Garrett pauses at the gate and we never see him in conversation with his wife. This conversation was also absent in the release version, although it was restored for the television version to compensate for time lost due to other scenes deleted because of visual violence.

Stopping at the military governor's mansion, Garrett refuses an additional reward offered for the Kid's capture by two capitalist investors. Jason Robards, Jr., cast as Governor Wallace, is sympathetic with Garrett's sentiments. There is a brief shot of Poe. For viewers of Sam's cuts, he is familiar as the man riding with Garrett when he is shot; in the other versions, his inclusion is confusing. The Kid, in the meantime, shoots down some bounty hunters at Fort Sumner and then is seen running off the cattle he claims Chisum owes him from when he was riding for him. Meanwhile, Garrett hires Slim Pickens as Sheriff Baker and Katy Jurado as his wife to help him confront Black, played by L.Q. Jones. Pickens is mortally wounded in the fracas in all four versions. In Sam's two, he dies without Dylan's ballad, "Knocking at Heaven's Door," which is used in the release and television versions. It is after this sequence that Garrett is joined by Poe in Sam's two versions, something that does not happen in the others until much later. Together with Poe, Garrett rides to the Chisum ranch in Sam's versions. Chisum, played by Barry Sullivan, wants the Kid. Garrett thanks him for the loan. Obviously, this loan is connected with the land that will later lead to the conflict with Poe and Garrett's death. In order properly to understand Garrett's character, the framing story, the conversation with his wife, and this talk with Chisum are vital to the film and never should have been removed.

"This country's gettin' old," Garrett tells Poe when they are back on the trail, "an' I aim to get old with it. The Kid don't want it that way, an' maybe he's a better man for it."

Although the actual sequences are altered in the release version and the television version from what they are in Sam's versions, Garrett proceeds at this point to kill off more of the Kid's friends, all in an effort to put off a confrontation with the Kid and to give the Kid a clear message that he must leave the Territory. Paco, played by Emilio Fernández, leaves Fort Sumner with his young wife and intends to cross Chisum's land. The Kid, too, decides that the time has come for him to ride to Mexico. On the way, he sees Paco being whipped to death, tied to a wheel of his wagon, and his wife being stripped and raped by Chisum's men. He shoots the men down and tries to comfort the dying Paco. It is this event which makes him decide to return to Fort Sumner and meet whatever fate has in store for him. In Sam's two versions, it is on the way back to Fort Sumner that the Kid runs into Jack Elam at the Horrell ranch. Horrell is played by Gene Evans. The Kid goes up against Elam, back to back, both to take ten paces. The Kid turns with gun drawn at the count of one, Elam at the count of eight. Both cheat, but the Kid cheats better. None of the Horrell children, lined up to watch the standoff, comments about the unfairness. In Sam's two versions, Poe and Garrett now split up at Chill Wills' saloon. Garrett kills more of the Kid's cronies. In Sam's first cut and in the release version, it is while Garrett is at a brothel run by Walter Kelley as Rupert that he has Ruthie Lee, played by Rutanya Alda, sent to his room. She has been with the Kid more than a few times and Garrett slaps out of her where the Kid is hiding: at Fort Sumner. In Sam's second cut, this sequence is deleted. Instead, Poe shows up at a shack occupied by Dub Taylor and two cronies. It is a stupid, drunken sequence in which, finally, Taylor tells Poe that the Kid is at Fort Sumner. While the Ruthie Lee sequence makes Garrett less sympathetic, it works better. The sequence is also in the release version. In both Peckinpah versions, Rupert tells Garrett, upon his entrance, "Last time you had to have four to get it up and five to get it down." Needless to say, this line is not in the television version, nor is it in the release version. Also deleted from those versions is much of the drunken romping with the four whores. In Sam's first cut, Garrett knows where the Kid is, in his second cut it is Poe who tells him, having learned it from Taylor.

The Kid, finally back at Fort Sumner, knows Garrett is coming, but he relaxes his vigilance to make love to Maria—women are dangerous: they can betray a man (Ruthie Lee) or they can distract a man (Maria). On his way to Pete Maxwell's place where the Kid has taken Maria, Garrett happens upon Will, the coffinmaker, played by Sam. Later, Sam joked to me that this was the only time he ever turned down a drink, obviously a reference again to Rona Barrett's comment. Will is putting the finishing touches on a coffin and claims that when he is finished with it he will put his belongings in it and leave the Territory for good. "Finally figured it out, eh?" he says to Garrett, turning down the flask Garrett holds out to him. "Well, go get him. You don't even trust yourself any more, do you Garrett?" This is all that is in the release and television versions and it plays well. In Sam's cuts, in a voice that sounds angry and drunk, he continues: "You can't trust anybody, Garrett, you chicken-shit, badge-wearing son-of-a-bitch." This added line destroys the menace of Garrett's presence and distracts from concern over the Kid. Garrett has plugged too many people for saying less, or saying nothing at all, for him to put up with this without at least pistol-whipping old Will.

Garrett shoots the Kid, who is barechested but armed with his gun which he does not fire, and then shoots his own reflection in a mirror. He pistol-whips Poe when Poe would cut off the Kid's trigger finger, telling him: "What you want and what you get are two different things." This line was cut in the release version and, frankly, it is delivered so badly by Coburn that it needed to be cut. The next day Garrett rides off alone, a boy throwing stones after him. This is how the release and television versions end. In Sam's two cuts, this scene is intercut with a replay of Garrett's assassination. The whole film story was only a flashback in Garrett's last fleeting moments alive.

There is no question in my mind that Sam was finished as a filmmaker when PAT GARRETT AND BILLY THE KID was taken out of his hands by M-G-M. Never again would he be able to sustain his magic throughout an entire film. If the truth be told, he was unable to provide as effective a second cut for PAT GARRETT AND BILLY THE KID as he had a first cut. Ironically, his next film, BRING ME THE HEAD OF ALFREDO GARCIA, would be his first chance to make a film exactly the way he wanted to make it without interference, without it being taken away from him. Some time before production even began, Sam fell apart. "Katy Haber . . . and I were having to lead and half carry him to the bathroom," Max Evans recalled. "Day after day he lay in bed throwing up, refusing whatever food Katy served him. He was living on vodka and little red, hardkicking pills, either one enough to wipe out the average man in his condition. He became so weak, we had to totally carry him. . . .

"Katy said, 'My god, Max, we gave him our word we'd not take him to the hospital, but what are we going to do?'

" 'We've got to find something he'll eat,' I told her.

"She left instantly for the supermarket and returned with the makings for a huge pot of chicken soup. She sat by his bed day and night spoon feeding him. Sometimes he'd take only a sip an hour, but she gradually got him walking. She cut the vodka, hid the pills, and put up with a madness that was even unnatural for him. Yes, Katy saved his life and put him going once more."[54]

James Coburn had said after PAT GARRETT AND BILLY THE KID, that Sam could "create an atmosphere, whether's he drunk, sober, pissed off or in a rage, or whatever. I mean, for about three or four hours a day, he's a fucking genius. But the rest of the time he spends wallowing in a kind of emotional reaction to either good or bad memories."[55] Henceforth, those three or four hours a day would be harder and harder to come by. The original story for BRING ME THE HEAD OF ALFREDO GARCIA had been by Frank Kowalski, a long-time associate of Sam's, but the screenplay had failed to realize any of the story's potential. "Someone else wrote the screenplay, which Sam, during and after his illness, turned into an almost impossible, unshootable script," Max Evans wrote. "I told him it would be a disaster. He said, 'Fix it.' I worked continuously for two and a half days on it. When I handed it to him, he gave it an instant trip to the wastebasket without reading a line."[56]

Sharon came to live with Katy and her father while BRING ME THE HEAD OF ALFREDO GARCIA was in production, residing in a house Sam leased for six months in Mexico City. Begonia showed up one day. Although she had not been able to conceive during their three marriages, out of wedlock she had been impregnated by Sam. Sharon and Katy moved out and Begonia moved in. Their daughter, Lupita, was born prematurely in October, 1973, and Sam included her in his final will and testament. When Begonia suggested that they marry for the fourth time, Sam kicked her out.

Upon release, BRING ME THE HEAD OF ALFREDO GARCIA revealed a script that was confused, direction that was uncertain, and the film even became the object of industry boycotts. Sam once told me that Erwin Ezzies, then chairman of the board of United Artists, would call him twice a day to tell him what the picture was losing as the grosses were reported. He also said: " 'I did ALFREDO GARCIA, and I did it exactly the way I wanted to. Good or bad, like it or not, that was my film.' "[57]

That is something he could not say about THE KILLER ELITE. He just did not like the film, although it has its moments and a stylish performance from Robert Duvall. Vicki and I wanted to try again for an interview that would be of substance. Since by this time, according to his accountant, Sam was in Yugoslavia for from one to three years, Yugoslavia it would be.

## III

"He's not the same man any more," Billy says about Pat Garrett. I was thinking that might well be true of Sam as we waited in our hotel room in the ancient part of Rome in May, 1976 for the international operator to call me back. Sharon had preceded Sam to Yugoslavia to help him on the picture. When Sam arrived, he was engulfed by journalists plying him with questions in the four national languages of the country which he invariably answered in Spanish, the only foreign language he knew. Sam had rented a villa a short distance outside Portoroz, a seaside resort town on the Adriatic, and his daughter Kristen had also come to spend some time with him. The cast and crew, including Katy, were staying at the Metropol Hotel in Portoroz. The picture, CROSS OF IRON, was being financed by Wolf Hartwig, the former porno king of Munich. I had placed my call to Katy because, unlike Sam, she was always easy to find, but on the Continent you could wait up to four hours just to get a connection.

THE FILMING OF THE WEST had finally appeared earlier that year after numerous delays on the part of the production people at Doubleday. I had sent a copy of it to Sam. John C. Mahoney, in his review of it for THE HOLLYWOOD REPORTER, had commented on what I had written about Sam's Westerns that "Tuska can say that he believes Sam Peckinpah is the most important director to emerge since World War II, but he reports truths which do less to document his conviction than they do to demonstrate damaging abuses to that talent."[58] I didn't know how Sam would react to what I had said. The telephone rang. I picked up the receiver and got Katy right away.

"Where are you?" she asked.

"In Rome. We'll be there day after tomorrow."

"Good. Sam won't be shooting. I'll tell him you've arrived . . . almost. He'll be glad to see you."

The connection was fading, so I quit while I was ahead.

Shortly after Vicki and I arrived and checked into the Hotel Metropol, Sam called me from his villa and suggested lunch. He would send a car for us. We met at an outdoor restaurant located on a cliff overlooking the Adriatic sea. Sam was with Lucky, a native Serbian who was acting as his guide and interpreter. Dressed in blue jeans and a jean jacket, despite the location Sam insisted that he was just an old, broken-down cowboy. It was sunny, but, for once, Sam wasn't wearing his mirrored sunglasses.

Vicki handed him the packet of mail Katy had given us at the hotel. Sam began tearing open envelopes. There was a letter from Melissa telling him how she was doing at school. She addressed him as "Dear Father."

"That's a nice letter," Sam said, putting it aside.

The next letter was from one of the many children he had adopted financially through a Big Brother program. The third letter was from his Los Angeles attorney, advising him that he was being sued for a quarter of a million dollars for having committed battery.

"How long are you over here?" I asked.

"I'm not over here, Jon. I'm in exile." He squinted his gray eyes at me. "Have some wine. It's good Yugoslavian white wine."

"Mr. Sam is right," Lucky assured us.

"See," Sam said, holding out a hand that trembled with a quiet palsy, "if you drink to a certain point in your life, you don't get the shakes any more." He grinned. Later he would injure himself on this film and the attending physician would tell him that his liver was dangerously enlarged.

"You're looking better than you did in the States," Vicki said.

"Yeah," Sam replied, "but I got a little gut now."

He patted his midriff. We had lunch and Sam ordered fish. He asked Lucky to keep the head and tail for the cat.

"You still have the cat?" I asked.

"Yeah," Sam said, "only it's a different cat. I find it good company. When we're done shooting here, Lucky—who by trade is a sailor; he quit the merchant service to work with us—is going to take me scuba diving all through the Adriatic. Then I would like to make a porn flick. I've always wanted to make a porn flick."

We had cognac. After several rounds, Sam suggested we go down to the seashore to the editing shack so we could watch rushes. He had the car brought around.

While we were waiting, Sam leaned close to me.

"You know," he said quietly, "I never had anything to do with that wife of yours, but I can tell you one thing: she's one crazy lady."

"It doesn't matter, Sam," I assured him, suprised at how much I wanted to change the subject. It did not matter, but somehow I continued to blame myself for having permitted her condition to get to the point it had without at least having tried to do something about it.

On the way to the editing shack, we passed the garden patch which Sam was using for the battlefield.

"James Coburn says this new picture is about the violence men commit on themselves," I said.

"That's right in part," Sam agreed. "This is Jim's third picture with me. CROSS OF IRON is about a group of German soldiers retreating from the Eastern front. They're finished and they're running, but they don't stop fighting. Coburn is the leader. You can see what a job Wolf Hartwig is doing financing this picture just by looking at that exterior. You've got to meet him while you're here. I can't tell you what it's been like: delays, halts in shooting, no rushes, no film sometimes. Wolf says it's all due to trouble at the border. I asked him if not paying the crew was because of trouble at the border. He's a Prussian. He was on the Eastern front and has lead in his butt, so you know what direction he was going."

Sam cackled. His contract with Hartwig called for a $400,000 salary and ten per cent of the gross revenues. The technical crew was international, although predominantly British. The coffee was a day old, but we drank it anyway. Sam sat on an editor's stool and had rushes run. There were battle scenes and battle scenes. Somehow there was more loving care and feeling in these clips and splices of film than, upon release, there was anywhere in the picture. Yet, there was no denying the anguished power of the last thirty minutes of the European version and I could understand later why Orson Welles would write to Sam to tell him that it was the finest anti-war film he had ever seen.

"Ach, excuse me," a man said, standing in the doorway. He was of medium height, wearing a red shirt and red trousers with a white belt, and he had a bullet-shaped head.

"This," drawled Sam, punching me in the shoulder and grinning, "is our producer, Wolf Hartwig."

Sam introduced me as Hartwig goose-stepped into the room.

"Ja, I know you," he said accusingly. "You're just like Pauline Kael."

"He's not like Pauline Kael, Wolf," Sam said slowly, correcting him. "He only writes about pictures after they're made, and he never reviews them."

"Ach, ja, an historian. I tell you I know him."

Wolf began pacing back and forth, his head pressed down against his chest, hands clenched behind him.

"Vell, I'm glad you're here. I don't vant you writing about dis picture unless I am included."

"Oh, he'll be sure to include you, Wolf, won't you?" Sam said, punching me again in the shoulder.

"Sure."

"*Ja!*" Wolf said, standing and nodding his head.

"Hello, Sam," Veronique Vendell said from the doorway. She was dressed in a tight red sweater that clung to her ample breasts and that matched her red stretch pants. She entered the room, smiling. In the picture her part was biting off Arthur Brauss' penis, which would be among the sequences edited from the American release version in order to give the picture an "R" rating. This was unfortunate because it was integral to the story and to understanding the point that was being made about human beings when at the center of a war.

"This," Wolf introduced her to us, "iss my former secretary, then star of my sex films, and now my vife."

"Hello," she said to everyone in the room, rubbing the flat of her hand against her mound of Venus as more teeth came into her smile.

"Vell, now to get back," Wolf said, resuming his pacing, "I know dat Sam has probably toldt you of the difficulties ve'ff been haffing on dis picture."

"No difficulties, Wolf," Sam said, "just minor things like running out of film, or not getting paid. Another of the crew just quit."

"*Ja*, qvidt! Vell, I tell you Sam, anybody who vants to can qvidt, budt not you. *You* can't qvidt. I own you, Sam, until you finish dis picture. You and I are like brudders, like dis." Wolf wound his arms around himself and gave himself a tight squeeze. "You are my property, Sam. I own you." Wolf paused suddenly in his pacing and glared at me. "Und vot do you tink of dis picture so far?"

"I haven't seen enough of it to tell."

"*Ja*, vell I vill tell you von ting, it had better be very gudt. Do you know vhy? Because I got die great Sam Peckinpah to direct it for me. It had better be gudt. Do you hear dat, Sam? It had *better* be gudt!" Wolf started pacing again. "Ve haff a story to tell here, die story of how die German soldier feldt vhen die var vas lost. Dere haff been no pictures sympathetic to the Germans in die last var. Vell, dis vill be a first. A first!" He stopped to stare at me. "I haff to go now, budt I vant you to put in vot I haff said, exactly die vay I haff said it. Understand? Exactly!"

"Don't worry, Wolf," Sam said, "he will."

Hartwig said *Auf Wiederseh'n* all around and shook my hand, and then Sam's.

"I luff dis man," he said, holding onto Sam's hand and looking at me. "He'd better make a gudt picture, dat's all I got to say."

"I'll make your fucking picture, Wolf," Sam said.

Once he was gone, Veronique with him, Sam clapped me on the back and recommended we all go to the hotel for a drink. Again he sent for the car.

"I get this fucking Mercedes," Sam remarked as we came out of the editing shack, "but Wolf drives an American Cadillac. The streets are too narrow and there's a lot of places he can't go with it, but it's the only car he'll drive, just so everyone knows it's Wolf Hartwig driving through."

At the hotel bar, we were joined by most of the cast and crew who were congregating for dinner prior to ascending to the casino on the roof to gamble. Katy was among them and she came over to join us. Arthur Brauss, the Nazi party man whom Veronique does in, strolled up. Sam introduced him to Vicki.

"When are your bosoms going to grow?" he asked, leering and scratching his crotch. "Turn around and let me see your ass." Vicki turned around. "You've got a beautiful ass." He was scratching again. "I should apologize, but the uniforms Wolf got us to wear are full of crabs. We're all scratching."

"I'll bet it was the uniforms," Vicki quipped.

"Just one Polish joke," Sam said to Vicki. "Come on. I'm the only one here other than Katy who doesn't have trouble pronouncing your last name."

"Okay, but just one."

"Ah," Sam sighed with pleasure. "Do you know what a Polish air conditioner is like?"

"No," Vicki said.

"It's one Polack sitting on top of a high stool flapping his arms while four other Polacks turn him around and around, each holding onto a leg of the stool."

Brauss slapped the bar, laughing. Vicki smiled.

"All right, Jon, now I have one for you," Sam said, turning to me. "Did I ever show you how to masturbate a dinosaur?"

"No."

"Okay," Sam shouted down the bar, "clear the way."

He held his hands together and formed a large circle with his arms. He then ran, holding his arms in this position, to the very end of the long barroom and disappeared out the door. In a moment he returned, still running and holding his arms in a circle. He stopped where we were standing, puffing.

"That's how!" he wheezed. He was grinning happily. "I thought you'd like it. Now let me have another of those Irish cigarettes you're smoking."

They were Sweet Aftons. I gave him the box.

"Let me send you a carton when I get back to London," I said.

"You're on."

Sam ordered all of us triple whiskeys. He was dispensing with the polite drinking. For every drink we had, Sam had three.

"Did you guys finally get the interview finished?" Katy asked.

"I don't give any fucking interviews any more," Sam said.

"No," I told her.

"My God," she said, "how long is it going to take?"

"Probably the next twenty-five years," I replied.

Sam tipped his head back and thought for a moment.

"Yup," he said then, picking up his drink, "that's just about right."

The more he drank, the angrier he became. Finally he decided he wanted to work on the script. Katy said she hadn't typed the new changes as yet, and Sam began cursing. He wanted to make more changes right away. He said he was very pissed off. He didn't get into the elevator as we stood in front of it. Katy did, and she was crying.

I knew then it would be impossible for me ever to interview Sam, because while he stood there talking to us, suddenly no one could touch him. He was isolated and alone and glowering, and I had come to love him too much, as sometimes men come to love each other no matter how beaten up they have been by life. Over the years, Vicki has accused me of having an especially soft place in my heart for Sam. No one could entirely approve of the way he treated Katy, considering all she had tried to be and had been to him. Sam could be generous to a fault. I could personally forgive him anything. Yet, he could also be more cruel to those who loved him most than anyone I have known. He left much pain and sorrow in his wake which the passage of time may never entirely heal.

Following CROSS OF IRON, which opened to mixed reviews, Sam was hired to direct CONVOY (United Artists, 1978) which starred Kris Kristofferson and Ali MacGraw. Only it wasn't old home week. " 'The difficulty was that Kristofferson had undergone a number of personal changes including quitting booze,' " Garth Craven recalled. " 'He was a totally different figure with whom Sam had little rapport. As for Ali MacGraw, I think Sam always knew she was no actress. . . . So fairly early on, I think Sam realized he was stuck with these two people sitting in the cab of a truck with three or four basic camera angles he couldn't deviate from.' "[59] Sam's paranoia, if anything, had intensified to the point where one time, while on location in Albuquerque, he summoned Max Evans to his trailer. With the radio blaring, he told Evans that he was being bugged and he wanted Max to find out who was bugging him so he could return the favor.

Following CONVOY, Sam withdrew from filmmaking for a time. He bought a small parcel of land in Montana from Warren Oates who had a ranch there and, with the help of neighbors, he erected a cabin for himself and took to living a life much as Hogue had. " 'Love it there,' " Sam later told Roderick Mann of THE LOS ANGELES TIMES. " 'It's heavy game country, you know. You chop your own wood, make your own fire—you'd better or you'll freeze your ass. I can't tell you how good the food tastes when you cook it yourself over a wood fire. . . . There's no electricity, no running water. I live at the top of the road. Four-and-a-half miles away, at the bottom, is my closest neighbor, Warren Oates. If I want a hot bath I have to go down to him. Sometimes he even lets me have soap and a towel.' "[60]

In late 1977, Sam flew to Rome to play a character based on Ned Buntline in CHINA 9, LIBERTY 37 (Lorimar, 1984) which starred Warren Oates. While there, he also appeared in a low-budget science fiction film titled THE VISITOR (International, 1979) in which John Huston also had a small role. Sam had once said that he was a greater admirer of Huston's screen work. "Every picture of Huston's has tried not only to tell a story but to make some kind of statement. The perfect films of this kind are THE MALTESE FALCON and THE TREASURE OF THE SIERRA MADRE. I wish I could make a film that good."[61] His role in THE VISITOR was that of a seedy gynecologist. He was filmed in silhouetted profile only and his voice was dubbed.

Sam suffered his first heart attack on 15 May 1979. He underwent surgery in a hospital in Livingston, Montana where he had a pacemaker implanted. His brother, Denver, who had had a similar heart attack was at Sam's bedside. Back in Los Angeles in December, 1979, Sam gave out an interview in which he commented that he was developing two properties, one a contemporary Western called THE TEXANS and another called SNOWBLIND. The latter was " 'about that old Peruvian remedy. . . . Cocaine. A great story. It tells a lot about the subculture of the United States in the late '60s and early '70s. I may do it.' "[62] I wrote to him that same month to tell him about my work on IMAGES OF INDIANS and how it had effectively altered my view of what Western films had done to Native Americans. I believe he watched the series. Shortly before his death, he said that "I would like to do a good Western concerning the story of the Indians, particularly in the Montana area, and what happened to some of the great tribes and people. I don't think it's been portrayed correctly."[63]

In 1980, Sam was given the John Ford Award for his contributions to Western filmmaking by the National Cowboy Hall of Fame and Western Heritage Center in Oklahoma City. Denver and Denver's son David accompanied Sam to receive the award. It was ironical, in a way, in view of how Sam had once behaved at the ceremony honoring Ford with the Medal of Freedom. Continued heart trouble made Sam decide even to give up port wine and champagne to which he had confined himself after his first heart attack. He also gave up smoking. Describing his first period of inactivity following MAJOR DUNDEE, Sam had said: " . . . If you're a director and you don't get a chance to direct you start to die a little bit."[64] It must have been even harder for him during this period. Don Siegel hired him to direct the second unit on JINXED (United Artists, 1982), a Bette Midler picture with her even choosing the camera angles. It died at the box office. It did, however, lead to a chance for Sam to direct on his own when he was hired to make THE OSTERMAN WEEKEND (20th-Fox, 1983). The producers wanted Sam because they wanted an extremely violent film and were convined that he could deliver. What they got was a very confused film, in many ways a caricature of what had once been his best work. His last directorial work was on two music videos featuring Julian Lennon. To this his career had come at the end.

In the latter part of 1985, Sam had dinner with Max Evans at The Mikado, a Japanese restaurant in North Hollywood. "About half way through," Evans recalled, "he raised his glass of water and said, 'Nobody's ever gonna believe that you and I are sitting here together stone sober, nothing but water in any of these glasses and not even a cigarette in our pockets.'

" 'No, Sam,' I agreed, 'they won't believe it.'

"Carol O'Connor, a lady friend he went to see later that night, said he'd talked about our odd dinner at least twenty times over his last few months."[65]

O'Connor was a young woman about Matthew's age with whom Sam had an on-again/off-again relationship. As Hogue with Hildy, she would occasionally come to stay at Sam's trailer in Malibu, but she would also leave. Apparently, she wanted to marry. Sam was not sure. Matthew had decided to enter the Marine

Corps, although he insisted to his mother that the decision had nothing to do with what his father had done at a similar age. During his last months, Sam and Matthew began to talk to each other. Being the only son among Sam's five children had been a considerable burden to him growing up. Nancy Galloway returned to perform secretarial duties for Sam, a link with his early years living in the Quonset hut with Marie.

The Christmas season, in those early years when the children were still young, had been very important to Sam and he had always gone all out for it. Later, that time only made him sad. In December, 1985 he made up his mind to spend the holidays in Puerto Vallarta. Once there, he telephoned Begonia in Mexico City and asked her to come to see him, even though she had since remarried. She came. Sam suffered a blood clot on his lung, complicated if not actually induced by the use of cocaine, and a desperate Begonia had to overcome great difficulties to arrange for Sam's transportation back to the States. He was taken in his stricken condition to the Centinela Hospital Medical Center in Inglewood. His children were summoned. Sharon was the closest. While he had been drinking, she had forbidden him to see his grandchildren. She came now but felt she had to leave. He had played this death scene for her one too many times. Sam had two heart attacks and died.

Recently in Portland, Oregon, where we live, Marie Selland and I met over coffee. Ruth had since remarried the son of silent screen actor Wallace Reid, who died in 1923. Marie had remarried, eighteen years after her divorce from Sam, and happily. Vicki and I had married and I told Marie how much our daughter, Jenni, loves Marie's bread sticks which can be purchased at a deli in our neighborhood. Marie now has her own catering service.

"Do you think Sharon has any regrets that she did not stay until the end?" I asked her.

"She says she doesn't, but you know how that is."

I could not help repeating Oscar Wilde's line: "Children begin by loving their parents; as they grow older they judge them; sometimes they forgive them."[66]

"Yes," she said, very quietly. "Sharon admits she still has trouble with forgiveness."

"You knew him," I said, "before he even knew that he wanted to be a director. You knew him when he was starting out, so full of hope and energy and ambition. You knew him when he was finally at that point where he could devote an entire film to conveying his very personal message. What would he have felt had he been able then to foresee his end?"

Her eyes suddenly welled up with tears.

"It is difficult for me to talk about him sometimes, about his dying."

I was sorry I had asked. For much of his life, Sam had so desensitized himself that he probably did not know that he was not living well. He had always been delicate physically and his body finally could hold out no longer. I can only wonder if he had an intimation that he was not dying well. Surely it occurred to him that he was not entering his house justified. Maybe it no longer mattered.

There were two qualities Sam had in common with John Ford. No one else I know of, not even John Huston, could paint so vividly with a camera as Sam could, except for Ford; and no one approached his work at such a gut level that talking about it in an intellectual fashion after a film was completed was virtually impossible. Talking to Ford had been, in its way, as frustrating as talking to Sam, because I had had too great expectations. Neither could verbalize what he had tried to do the way Hawks could, but then Howard could never pack the emotional wallop that Ford or Sam could when they were at their finest. Sam had once said of Ernest Hemingway: " 'That man was my bible.' "[67] As John Huston, he seemed to accept Hemingway's confusion of machoism with courage. Unlike Huston, he did not create a persona with which to woo those around him.

Sam's assumptions about women were something he already possessed when he courted Marie and he held fast to them to the end. His nihilism was more subtle in origin but finally, I suspect, it went back to the sad fact that he never realized how very fine a director he really was. " 'I'm a student of violence,' " he said in his defense, " 'because I'm a student of the human heart.' "[68] No image of violence in any of his films can compare with the violence he committed against himself. He ultimately lacked the Nietzschean courage to attack his own convictions. It was his sterling, monumental talent instead which he doubted. Yet, I do not wish to appear harsh. C.G. Jung once counseled that "we must not forget that very few human beings are artists in life and that the art of living is the most distinguished and rarest of all the arts—to empty the cup ever gracefully, who has attained it?"[69]

Sam Peckinpah died on 28 December 1985. Originally he had had a codicil to his will leaving a sum of money behind for his friends to throw a bash after his death. When he stopped drinking, he removed the codicil. He had already been cremated and his ashes disposed of in the Pacific Ocean off Malibu when a memorial service was held for him at the Directors' Guild Theater on Sunday morning 13 January 1986. Some family members were there and a number of friends and associates. Richard Gillis sang his ballad "Butterfly Morning" which Sam had incorporated in THE BALLAD OF CABLE HOGUE and Kris Kristofferson sang a song he had especially written for Sam. "It was quite a production . . . ," Max Evans wrote, "a fitting tribute in high style and beauty."[70] The Sam I knew and loved best, had he been able to attend, would have disrupted the whole thing and probably have been evicted for causing a ruckus.

Life goes on. I was pleased to learn from Marie that Kristen gave birth to a son in 1986. She named him Sam. I found myself reversing what Sam's mother had said at his birth—this time *not* oh, no—but oh, yes, another black Peckinpah.

# Notes

## INTRODUCTION

1. Durgnat, Raymond, "The Strange Case of Alfred Hitchcock, Part Three" in FOCUS ON ALFRED HITCHCOCK (Englewood Cliffs: Prentice-Hall, 1972) edited by Albert J. LaValley, p.91.

2. Truffaut, François, HITCHCOCK (New York: Simon and Schuster, 1967), p.240.

3. Wood, Robin, "Why We Should Take Hitchcock Seriously" in FOCUS ON ALFRED HITCHCOCK, *op.cit.*, p.76.

4. *Ibid.*, p.85.

5. Hesse, Hermann, "Klein und Wagner" in GESAMMELTE DICHTUNGEN Dritter Band (Frankfurt am Main: Suhrkamp Verlag, 1958), p.494. The translation is mine.

## H. BRUCE HUMBERSTONE

1. Tuska, Jon, THE FILMING OF THE WEST (New York: Doubleday, 1976), p.110.

2. Orwell, George, "Benefit of Clergy: Some Notes on Salvador Dali" in THE COLLECTED ESSAYS, JOURNALISM, AND LETTERS OF GEORGE ORWELL, Volume 3 (New York: Harcourt Brace Jovanovich, Inc., 1968) edited by Sonia Orwell and Ian Angus, p.156.

3. A detailed history of the Philo Vance films can be found in my book IN MANORS AND ALLEYS: A CASEBOOK ON THE AMERICAN DETECTIVE FILM (Westport: Greenwood Press, 1988).

4. Letter from H. Bruce Humberstone to Jon Tuska dated 15 June 1976.

## HENRY KING

1. Brownlow, Kevin, THE PARADE'S GONE BY . . . (New York: Bonanza Books, 1968), p.107.

2. Gish, Lillian, THE MOVIES, MR. GRIFFITH, AND ME (Englewood Cliffs: Prentice-Hall, 1969), p.254.

3. Denton, Clive, "Henry King" in THE HOLLYWOOD PROFESSIONALS VOLUME TWO (New York: A.S. Barnes, 1974), p.8.

4. Gussow, Mel, DON'T SAY YES UNTIL I FINISH TALKING: A BIOGRAPHY OF DARRYL F. ZANUCK (1971; New York: Pocket Books, 1972), p.146.

5. Denton, Clive, op.cit., p.27.

6. For a further discussion of this phenomenon see my book THE AMERICAN WEST IN FILM: CRITICAL APPROACHES TO THE WESTERN (Westport: Greenwood Press, 1985), pp.133–148 and pp.211–219.

7. King, Henry, "The Actor-Director's Viewpoint" in MOTOGRAPHY Volume 15, No.23 (4 December 1915), p.1170.


## ALFRED HITCHCOCK

1. Jung, C.G., ZWEI SCHRIFTEN ÜBER ANALYTISCHE PSYCHOLOGIE (Zurich and Stuttgart: Rascher Verlag, 1964), p.217. The translation is mine. In the original text, the words are italicized.

2. Quoted in Truffaut, François, HITCHCOCK, op.cit., p.27.

3. Taylor, John Russell, HITCH: THE LIFE AND TIMES OF ALFRED HITCHCOCK (1978; New York: Berkley Books, 1980), p.21.

4. Spoto, Donald, THE DARK SIDE OF GENIUS: THE LIFE OF ALFRED HITCHCOCK (Boston: Little, Brown, 1983), p.67.

5. Taylor, John Russell, op.cit., p.61.

6. Truffaut, François, op.cit., p.59.

7. Spoto, Donald, op.cit., p.551.

8. Ibid., p.550.

9. Hitchcock, Alfred, "Direction" in FOCUS ON ALFRED HITCHCOCK, op.cit., p.34.

10. Jung, C.G., op.cit., p.213. The translation is mine.

11. Spoto, Donald, op.cit., p.264.

12. Keyes, Evelyn, SCARLETT O'HARA'S YOUNGER SISTER: MY LIFE IN AND OUT OF HOLLYWOOD (Secaucus: Lyle Stuart, 1977), p.27.

13. Truffaut, François, op.cit., p.104.

14. Ibid., p.105.

15. Quoted in Spoto, Donald, op.cit., p.259.

16. Ibid., p.299.

17. Higham, Charles, and Roy Moseley, CARY GRANT: THE LONELY HEART (San Diego: Harcourt Brace Jovanovich, 1989), pp.172–173.

18. Quoted in MacShane, Frank, THE LIFE OF RAYMOND CHANDLER (New York: Dutton, 1976), pp.174–175.

19. Ibid., p.177.

20. Spoto, Donald, op.cit., p.349.

21. Higham, Charles, and Roy Moseley, op.cit., p.242.

22. Ibid., p.246.

23. Quoted in Spoto, Donald, op.cit., p.455.

24. Quoted in ibid., p.491.

25. Quoted in *ibid.*, p.500.

26. *Ibid.*, p.516.

## HOWARD HAWKS

1. Rivette, Jacques, "Genie de Howard Hawks," CAHIERS DU CINÉMA (May, 1953), p.17. The translation is mine.

2. Bacall, Lauren, BY MYSELF (New York: Knopf, 1978), p.83.

3. *Ibid.*, p.101.

4. Mast, Gerald, HOWARD HAWKS, STORYTELLER (New York: Oxford University Press, 1982), p.14.

5. Quoted in Blotner, Joseph, "Faulkner in Hollywood" contained in MAN AND THE MOVIES (Baton Rouge: Louisiana State University Press, 1967) edited by W.R. Robinson, p.272.

6. Bacall, Lauren, *op.cit.*, p.85.

7. Thompson, Verita, BOGIE AND ME: A LOVE STORY (New York: St. Martin's Press, 1982) with Donald Shepherd, pp.52–53.

8. Warner, Jack L., MY FIRST HUNDRED YEARS IN HOLLYWOOD (New York: Random House, 1965) with Dean Jennings, p.105.

9. Mast, Gerald, *op.cit.*, p.55.

10. *Ibid.*, pp.245–246.

11. *Ibid.*, p.248.

12. McBride, Joseph, HAWKS ON HAWKS (Berkeley: University of California Press, 1982), p.95.

13. Hotchner, A.E., PAPA HEMINGWAY: A PERSONAL MEMOIR (New York: Random House, 1966), p.49.

14. McBride, Joseph, *op.cit.*, p.96.

15. Warner, Jack L., *op.cit.*, p.106.

16. *Ibid.*, p.106.

17. McBride, Joseph, *op.cit.*, p.26.

18. Mast, Gerald, *op.cit.*, p.108.

19. *Ibid.*, pp.54–55.

20. McBride, Joseph, *op.cit.*, p.61.

21. Mast, Gerald, *op.cit.*, pp.206–207.

22. McBride, Joseph, *op.cit.*, p.96.

23. Quoted in Marx, Arthur, GOLDWYN: A BIOGRAPHY OF THE MAN BEHIND THE MYTH (New York: Norton, 1976), p.225.

24. Mast, Gerald, *op.cit.*, p.184.

25. Quoted in Higham, Charles, and Roy Moseley, *op.cit.*, p.94.

26. McBride, Joseph, *op.cit.*, p.80.

27. Mast, Gerald, *op.cit.*, pp.30–31.

28. Belton, John, THE HOLLYWOOD PROFESSIONALS VOLUME Three (New York and London: A.S. Barnes/Tantivy, 1974), p.11.

29. *Ibid.*, p.10.

30. Mast, Gerald, *op.cit.*, p.253.

31. *Ibid.*, p.268.

32. McBride, Joseph, *op.cit.*, p.90.

33. Mast, Gerald, *op.cit.*, p.283.

34. McBride, Joseph, *op.cit.*, p.144.

35. Aurelius, Marcus, [TO HIMSELF], III:5.

36. Quoted in Rieupeyrout, Jean-Louis, LA GRANDE AVENTURE DU WESTERN (Paris: Éditions du cerf, 1964), p.318.

37. Chase, Borden, RED RIVER [BLAZING GUNS ON THE CHISHOLM TRAIL] (New York: Bantam Books, 1948), p.147. Hawks bought the rights to this novel prior to its serialization in THE SATURDAY EVENING POST and tried to get the POST to change the title to RED RIVER. This the POST would not do, but when it came time for the paperback to appear Chase and Bantam were only too happy to have both titles appear with the former title in brackets!

38. Willis, Donald C., THE FILMS OF HOWARD HAWKS (Metuchen: Scarecrow Press, 1975), p.49.

39. Mast, Gerald, *op.cit.*, p.303.

40. Rieupeyrout, Jean-Louis, *op.cit.*, p.319. The translation is mine.

41. Mast, Gerald, *op.cit.*, p.301.

42. Eliot, T.S., "The Love Song of J. Alfred Prufrock" contained in THE COMPLETE POEMS AND PLAYS: 1909–1950 (New York: Harcourt, Brace, 1958), p.6.

43. Guthrie, A.B., Jr., "The Historical Novel" contained in WESTERN WRITING (Albuquerque: University of New Mexico Press, 1974) edited by Gerald R. Haslam, p.58.

44. *Ibid.*, p.51.

45. Wollen, Peter, SIGNS AND MEANING IN THE CINEMA (Bloomington: Indiana University Press, 1969), p.88.

46. Brackett, Leigh, "Working with Hawks" contained in WOMEN AND THE CINEMA: A CRITICAL ANTHOLOGY (New York: Dutton, 1977) edited by Karyn Kay and Gerald Peary, p.196.

47. McBride, Joseph, *op.cit.*, p.114.

48. *Ibid.*, p.67.

49. Quoted in Parkinson, Michael, and Clyde Jeavons, A PICTORIAL HISTORY OF WESTERNS (London: Hamlyn Publishing Group, 1972), p.182.

50. Willis, Donald C., *op.cit.*, p.57.

51. Quoted in Wood, Robin, "Rio Bravo" contained in FOCUS ON HOWARD HAWKS (Englewood Cliffs: Prentice-Hall, 1972) edited by Joseph McBride, p.129.

52. *Ibid.*, pp.123–124.

53. Bogdanovich, Peter, "El Dorado" contained in FOCUS ON HOWARD HAWKS, *op.cit.*, p.147

54. Ford, Gregg, "Mostly on RIO LOBO" contained in FOCUS ON HOWARD HAWKS, *op.cit.*, p.153.

55. *Ibid.*, p.160.

56. McBride, Joseph, *op.cit.*, pp.82–83.

57. Higham, Charles, and Roy Moseley, *op.cit.*, pp.192–193.

58. Blotner, Joseph, *op.cit.*, p.299 and p.303.

59. Mast, Gerald, *op.cit.*, p.16.

60. This article is contained in Bogdanovich, Peter, JOHN FORD (Berkeley: University of California Press, 1978), pp.109–112.

61. Belton, John, *op.cit.*, p.43.

62. Kobal, John, PEOPLE WILL TALK (New York: Knopf, 1985), p.486.

## JOHN HUSTON

1. Huston, John, AN OPEN BOOK (New York: Knopf, 1980), p.12.
2. *Ibid.*, p.28.
3. *Ibid.*, p.46.
4. Keyes, Evelyn, *op.cit.*, p.146.
5. Huston, John, *op.cit.*, p.62.
6. Bacall, Lauren, *op.cit.*, p.218.
7. Huston, John, *op.cit.*, p.63.
8. Nolan, William F., JOHN HUSTON: KING REBEL (Los Angeles: Sherbourne Press, 1965), p.38.
9. Thompson, Verita, *op.cit.*, pp.36–37.
10. Kaminsky, Stuart, JOHN HUSTON: MAKER OF MAGIC (Boston: Houghton Mifflin, 1978), p.21.
11. Hammett, Dashiell, THE MALTESE FALCON in THE NOVELS OF DASHIELL HAMMETT (New York: Knopf, 1965), p.439.
12. Goodman, Ezra, THE FIFTY-YEAR DECLINE AND FALL OF HOLLYWOOD (New York: Simon and Schuster, 1961), p.204.
13. Quoted in Greenberger, Howard, BOGEY'S BABY: A BIOGRAPHY (New York: St. Martin's Press, 1978), p.49.
14. *Ibid.*, p.40.
15. Thompson, Verita, *op.cit.*, p.33.
16. Greenberger, Howard, *op.cit.*, p.60.
17. *Ibid.*, p.75.
18. *Ibid.*, p.74.
19. *Ibid.*, p.75. Bacall, describing her attraction to Frank Sinatra after Bogart's death, recalled that "Bogie had always paid an overabundance of physical attention to me— he had incredible energy—he was life. I was used to it, and I needed it." Bacall, Lauren, *op.cit.*, p.307.
20. Keyes, Evelyn, *op.cit.*, p.82.
21. *Ibid.*, p.89.
22. *Ibid.*, p.95.
23. *Ibid.*, p.97.
24. Greenberger, Howard, *op.cit.*, p.103.
25. Thompson, Verita, *op.cit.*, p.25.
26. Keyes, Evelyn, *op.cit.*, p.127.
27. Quoted in Nolan, William F., p.20.
28. Bacall, Lauren, *op.cit.*, p.172.
29. Quoted in Benson, Sheila, " 'Huston' Does the Man Proud," in THE LOS ANGELES TIMES Wednesday, 7 June 1989, Part 6, p.7.
30. Quoted in Nolan, William F., *op.cit.*, p.64.
31. Keyes, Evelyn, *op.cit.*, pp.108–109.
32. Quoted in Nolan, William F., *op.cit.*, p.66.
33. *Ibid.*, p.67.
34. Huston, John, *op.cit.*, p.146.
35. Quoted in Nolan, William F., *op.cit.*, p.69.
36. Bacall, Lauren, *op.cit.*, p.173.

37. Keyes, Evelyn, *op.cit.*, p.114.
38. Huston, John, *op.cit.*, p.144.
39. Quoted in Nolan, William F., *op.cit.*, p.74.
40. Keyes, Evelyn, *op.cit.*, p.117.
41. Kaminsky, Stuart, *op.cit.*, p.60.
42. Nolan, William F., *op.cit.*, p.74.
43. *Ibid.*, p.75.
44. Greenberger, Howard, *op.cit.*, p.94.
45. *Ibid.*, p.96.
46. Huston, John, *op.cit.*, p.159.
47. Keyes, Evelyn, *op.cit.*, p.146 and p.150.
48. Huston, John, *op.cit.*, p.206.
49. Nolan, William F., *op.cit.*, pp.80–81.
50. *Ibid.*, p.26.
51. Greenberger, Howard, *op.cit.*, p.111.
52. Nolan, William F., *op.cit.*, p.89.
53. Bacall, Lauren, *op.cit.*, p.196.
54. Nolan, William F., *op.cit.*, p.103.
55. Keyes, Evelyn, *op.cit.*, p.134.
56. Huston, John, *op.cit.*, p.166.
57. Kaminsky, Stuart, *op.cit.*, pp.96–97.
58. Huston, John, *op.cit.*, p.269.
59. *Ibid.*, p.246.
60. Thompson, Verita, *op.cit.*, p.210.
61. Huston, John, *op.cit.*, p.249.
62. Bacall, Lauren, *op.cit.*, p.250.
63. Gussow, Mel, *op.cit.*, p.188.
64. Huston, John, *op.cit.*, p.283. Huston also felt that the overall tone was "bombastic and over-inflated. Everybody in it is bigger than life." (p.284). It is interesting to contrast this assessment with Tony Thomas' in THE WEST THAT NEVER WAS (Secaucus: Citadel Press, 1989): "It is Lancaster at his best, giving a shaded portrayal of a tough, leathery man who lives by a simple code of honesty, who will not compromise, and whose seemingly unemotional nature hides a streak of tenderness. This is a classic figure in American film and Lancaster always performed it with conviction." (p.214).
65. Huston, John, *op.cit.*, p.228.
66. Keyes, Evelyn, *op.cit.*, pp.298–299.
67. Quoted in Nolan, William F., *op.cit.*, p.22.
68. Quoted in Grobel, Lawrence, THE HUSTONS (New York: Scribner's, 1989), p.708.
69. Huston, John, *op.cit.*, p.344.
70. Quoted in Grobel, Lawrence, *op.cit.*, p.732.
71. Huston, John, *op.cit.*, p.372.
72. Amory, Cleveland, "If I Had My Life to Live Over Again," PARADE MAGAZINE (2 August 1987), p.7.
73. Phillips, Gene D., "Talking with John Huston," FILM COMMENT, Vol.9, No.3, May-June, 1973, p.18.
74. Quoted in Grobel, Lawrence, *op.cit.*, p.736.
75. Quoted in *ibid.*, p.44.

76. Quoted in *ibid.*, p.641.
77. *Ibid.*, p.726.
78. Quoted in *ibid.*, pp.384–385.
79. *Ibid.*, p.165.
80. Quoted in *ibid.*, p.271.
81. *Ibid.*, p.513.
82. Quoted in *ibid.*, p.506.
83. Quoted in *ibid.*, p.553.
84. *Ibid.*, p.230.
85. Quoted in *ibid.*, p.32.
86. Quoted in *ibid.*, p.33.
87. Quoted in *ibid.*, p.779.
88. Quoted in Amory, Cleveland, *op.cit.*, p.4.
89. Quoted in *ibid.*, p.4.

## ORSON WELLES

1. Letter from Orson Welles to Jon Tuska dated 10 March 1980.
2. Rosenbaum, Jonathan, "Orson Welles' HEART OF DARKNESS," FILM COMMENT, Vol.8, No.4, November-December, 1972, p.31.
3. Quoted in Brady, Frank, CITIZEN WELLES: A BIOGRAPHY OF ORSON WELLES (New York: Scribner's, 1989), p.vii.
4. Tynan, Kenneth, "Orson Welles," in FOCUS ON ORSON WELLES (Englewood Cliffs: Prentice-Hall, 1976) edited by Ronald Gottesman, p.10.
5. *Ibid.*, p.24.
6. Brady, Frank, *op.cit.*, p.451.
7. Quoted in Higham, Charles, ORSON WELLES: THE RISE AND FALL OF AN AMERICAN GENIUS (New York: St. Martin's Press, 1985), p.229.
8. Castle, William, STEP RIGHT UP (New York: Putnam's, 1976), p.98.
9. *Ibid.*, p.98.
10. Quoted in Kobal, John, RITA HAYWORTH: THE TIME, THE PLACE, AND THE WOMAN (New York: Norton, 1977), p.211.
11. Higham, Charles, *op.cit.*, p.229.
12. Naremore, James, THE MAGIC WORLD OF ORSON WELLES (New York: Oxford University Press, 1978), p.186.
13. Review in DAILY VARIETY, 16 October 1985, p.195.
14. Delson, James, "Heston on Welles," in FOCUS ON ORSON WELLES, *op.cit.*, p.60.
15. Johnson, William, "Orson Welles: Of Time and Loss," in FOCUS ON CITIZEN KANE (Englewood Cliffs: Prentice-Hall, 1971) edited by Ronald Gottesman, p.27.
16. Leaming, Barbara, ORSON WELLES: A BIOGRAPHY (New York: Viking, 1985), p.13.
17. Higham, Charles, *op.cit.*, p.44.
18. Leaming, Barbara, *op.cit.*, p.22.
19. *Ibid.*, p.79.
20. Brady, Frank, *op.cit.*, p.74.
21. Leaming, Barbara, *op.cit.*, p.81.
22. Higham, Charles, *op.cit.*, p.102.

23. Quoted in Brady, Frank, *op.cit.*, p.226.

24. Quoted in *ibid.*, p.225.

25. Houseman, John, RUN-THROUGH (1972; New York: Curtis Books, 1972), pp.459–460.

26. Toland, Gregg, "How I Broke the Rules in CITIZEN KANE," in FOCUS ON CITIZEN KANE, *op.cit.*, p.75.

27. Brady, Frank, *op.cit.*, pp.259–260.

28. Tynan, Kenneth, *op.cit.*, p.22.

29. Quoted in Brady, Frank, *op.cit.*, p.361.

30. Higham, Charles, *op.cit.*, p.176.

31. Truffaut, François, "Foreword" to Bazin, André, ORSON WELLES: A CRITICAL VIEW (New York: Harper's, 1979) translated by Jonathan Rosenbaum, p.13.

32. Quoted in Higham, Charles, *op.cit.*, p.198.

33. Quoted in a separate, unpaginated "Epilogue: A Meeting" accompanying John Kobal's biography.

34. Hill, James, RITA HAYWORTH: A MEMOIR (New York: Simon and Schuster, 1983), p.15.

35. *Ibid.*, p.100.

36. Kobal, John, RITA HAYWORTH: THE TIME, THE PLACE, AND THE WOMAN, *op.cit.*, p.79.

37. Kobal, John, PEOPLE WILL TALK, *op.cit.*, p.596.

38. *Ibid.*, p.487.

39. *Ibid.*, p.491.

40. Hill, James, *op.cit.*, p.21.

41. Kobal, John, RITA HAYWORTH: THE TIME, THE PLACE, AND THE WOMAN, *op.cit.*, p.130.

42. Hill, James, *op.cit.*, p.108.

43. *Ibid.*, p.219.

44. Quoted in Leaming, Barbara, IF THIS WAS HAPPINESS: A BIOGRAPHY OF RITA HAYWORTH (New York: Viking, 1989), p.107.

45. Quoted in Kobal, John, RITA HAYWORTH: THE TIME, THE PLACE, AND THE WOMAN, *op.cit.*, p.188.

46. Leaming, Barbara, IF THIS WAS HAPPINESS: A BIOGRAPHY OF RITA HAYWORTH, *op.cit.* p.117.

47. Kobal, John, RITA HAYWORTH: THE TIME, THE PLACE, AND THE WOMAN, *op.cit.*, pp.185–187.

48. Quoted in Leaming, Barbara, ORSON WELLES: A BIOGRAPHY, *op.cit.*, p.298.

49. Truffaut, François, *op.cit.*, p.14.

50. Brady, Frank, *op.cit.*, p.380.

51. Quoted in Kobal, John, RITA HAYWORTH: THE TIME, THE PLACE, AND THE WOMAN, *op.cit.*, p.218.

52. Borde, Raymond, and Etienne Chaumeton, PANORAMA DU FILM NOIR AMÉRICAIN (Paris: Éditions D'Aujourd'hui, 1955), p.75. The translation is mine.

53. Higham, Charles, and Joel Greenberg, HOLLYWOOD IN THE FORTIES (Cranbury and London: Barnes/Tantivy, 1968), p.30.

54. A more detailed discussion of Welles' contribution to *film noir* is to be found in my book, DARK CINEMA: AMERICAN *FILM NOIR* IN CULTURAL PERSPECTIVE (Westport: Greenwood Press, 1984).

55. Naremore, James, *op.cit.*, p.162.

56. Bazin, André, *op.cit.*, p.94.

57. Quoted in Cobos, Juan, Rubio, Miguel, and J.A. Pruneda, "A Trip to Don Quixote-land: Conversations with Orson Welles," in FOCUS ON CITIZEN KANE, *op.cit.*, p.10.

58. Johnson, William, *op.cit.*, p.27.

59. Kobal, John, "The Time, The Place, and The Girl: Rita Hayworth," FOCUS ON FILM (Summer, 1972), p.22.

60. Quoted in Kobal, John, RITA HAYWORTH: THE TIME, THE PLACE, AND THE WOMAN, *op.cit.*, p.220. It was at Rita's suggestion that Kobal changed "girl" to "woman" in the title of his biography.

61. Leaming, Barbara, ORSON WELLES: A BIOGRAPHY, *op.cit.*, p.264.

62. Leaming, Barbara, IF THIS WAS HAPPINESS: A BIOGRAPHY OF RITA HAY-WORTH, *op.cit.*, p.17.

63. *Ibid.*, p.18.

64. *Ibid.*, p.117.

65. Quoted in Kobal, John, RITA HAYWORTH: THE TIME, THE PLACE, AND THE WOMAN, *op.cit.*, p.226.

66. *Ibid.*, p.226.

67. Quoted in Chambers, Andrea, and Lee Powell, "Out of the Past," in PEOPLE MAGAZINE Vol.32, No.20 (14 January 1990), p.132.

68. Quoted in Leaming, Barbara, IF THIS WAS HAPPINESS: A BIOGRAPHY OF RITA HAYWORTH, *op.cit.*, p.189.

69. *Ibid.*, p.236. Even the very title of Leaming's biography is derived from a remark that Orson made to her about his marriage to Rita, "If this was happiness, imagine what the rest of her life had been."

70. *Ibid.*, p.283.

71. "Walter Scott's Personality Parade," PARADE (14 January 1990), p.2.

72. Quoted in Kobal, John, RITA HAYWORTH: THE TIME, THE PLACE, AND THE WOMAN, *op.cit.*, p.279.

73. Leaming, Barbara, IF THIS WAS HAPPINESS: A LIFE OF RITA HAYWORTH, *op.cit.*, p.134.

74. Higham, Charles, ORSON WELLES: THE RISE AND FALL OF AN AMERI-CAN GENIUS, *op.cit.*, p.244.

75. Quoted in Brady, Frank, *op.cit.*, p.427.

76. Quoted in Higham, Charles, ORSON WELLES: THE RISE AND FALL OF AN AMERICAN GENIUS, *op.cit.*, p.253.

77. Quoted in Brady, Frank, *op.cit.*, p.440.

78. Quoted in Leaming, Barbara, ORSON WELLES: A BIOGRAPHY, *op.cit.*, p.391.

79. Quoted in Delson, James, *op.cit.*, p.55.

80. Quoted in Brady, Frank, *op.cit.*, p.508.

81. Quoted in Higham, Charles, ORSON WELLES: THE RISE AND FALL OF AN AMERICAN GENIUS, *op.cit.*, p.296.

82. Cowie, Peter, THE CINEMA OF ORSON WELLES (New York/London: Barnes/Tantivy, 1973), p.154.

83. McBride, Joseph, "Chimes at Midnight," in FOCUS ON ORSON WELLES, *op.cit.*, p.186.

84. Brady, Frank, *op.cit.*, p.539.

85. Leaming, Barbara, ORSON WELLES: A BIOGRAPHY, *op.cit.*, p.472.

86. Silver, Charles, "The Immortal Story," in FOCUS ON ORSON WELLES, *op.cit.*, p.188.

87. Bazin, André, *op.cit.*, p.132.

88. Brady, Frank, *op.cit.*, p.547.

89. Higham, Charles, ORSON WELLES: THE RISE AND FALL OF AN AMERICAN GENIUS, *op.cit.*, p.332.

90. Brady, Frank, *op.cit.*, p. 595.

## ROMAN POLANSKI

1. Butler, Ivan, THE CINEMA OF ROMAN POLANSKI (New York: Barnes, 1970) pp.177–178.

2. Rilke, Rainer Maria, "*Die Einsamkeit*" [Loneliness] from DAS BUCH DER BILDER [THE BOOK OF IMAGES, written in 1902 and published first in 1906.] In my translation, it reads:

> Raining down in the hour of twilight,
> as all the streets turn toward the dawn,
> and when bodies, sad in unfulfillment,
> disillusioned leave one another,
> and when, hating each other, they must sleep
> together in one bed:
> > then loneliness merges with the flow . . .

3. Hemingway, Ernest, TO HAVE AND HAVE NOT (1937; New York: P.F. Collier, n.d.), p.225.

4. Wilmington, Mike, "Roman Polanski's CHINATOWN" in THE VELVET LIGHT TRAP No.13 (Fall, 1974), p.13.

5. *Ibid.*, p.13.

6. Sarris, Andrew, "The Facts, Ma'am" in THE NEW YORK TIMES BOOK REVIEW (26 March 1978), p.9.

7. Nietzsche, Friedrich, MENSCHLICHES, ALLZUMENSCLICHES [HUMAN, ALL TOO HUMAN] (1886) in Volume One of WERKE IN DREI BÄNDEN (Munich: Carl Hanser Verlag, 1955) edited by Karl Schlechta, p.830.

8. Butler, Ivan, *op.cit.*, p.13.

9. Polanski, Roman, ROMAN BY POLANSKI (1984; New York: Ballantine Books, 1985), p.1.

10. *Ibid.*, p.23.

11. Leaming, Barbara, POLANSKI: A BIOGRAPHY OF THE FILMMAKER AS VOYEUR (1981; New York: Simon and Schuster, 1983), p.16.

12. Polanski, Roman, *op.cit.*, p.27.

13. Grant, Lee, "The Tormented Life of Roman Polanski" in THE MILWAUKEE JOURNAL (15 May 1977), p.3.

14. "In Trouble" in PEOPLE MAGAZINE Vol.7 No.12 (28 March 1977), p.56.

15. Butler, Ivan *op.cit.*, p.18.

16. Polanski, Roman, *op.cit.*, p.142.

17. *Ibid.*, p.143.

18. Jung, C.G., *"Die Lebenswende"* in DIE DYNAMIK DES UNBEWUSSTEN, Volume Eight of the GESAMMELTE WERKE (Zurich and Stuttgart: Rascher Verlag, 1967), p.448. The translation is mine. Although the title of this essay, one of Jung's finest, means literally "The Turnings of Life," it has been somewhat ineptly translated using a concept alien to its essential meaning as "The Stages of Life" in Jung, C.G., MODERN MAN IN SEARCH OF A SOUL (New York: Harcourt, Brance, 1933) translated by W.S. Dell and Cary F. Baynes.

19. Bugliosi, Vincent, with Curt Gentry, HELTER SKELTER (1974; New York: Bantam Books, 1975), p.45.

20. Polanski, Roman, *op.cit.*, p.194.

21. Delahaye, Michael, and Jean-André Fieschi, "Landscape of a Mind," CAHIERS DU CINÉMA in English, No.3, February, 1966, reprinted in POLANSKI: THREE FILM SCRIPTS (New York: Harper's, 1975), p.207.

22. "Dialogue on Film: Roman Polanski" published in Los Angeles by the American Film Institute, Volume 3, Number 8 (August, 1974), p.15.

23. Quoted in Butler, Ivan, *op.cit.*, p.108.

24. Quoted in *ibid.*, p.110.

25. Polanski, Roman, *op.cit.*, p.295.

26. Bugliosi, Vincent, *op.cit.*, p.80.

27. *Ibid.*, p.36.

28. *Ibid.*, p.81.

29. *Ibid.*, p.84.

30. Polanski, Roman, *op.cit.*, p.235.

31. *Ibid.*, p.238.

32. Bugliosi, Vincent, *op.cit.*, p.82.

33. Freud, Sigmund, "Contributions to the Psychology of Love. The Most Prevalent Form of Degradation in Erotic Life" translated by Joan Riviere in Volume 4 of COLLECTED PAPERS (New York: Basic Books, 1959), p.204.

34. Harding, M. Esther, PSYCHIC ENERGY: ITS SOURCE AND ITS TRANSFORMATION (1963; Princeton: Princeton University Press, 1973), p.125.

35. "In Trouble" in PEOPLE MAGAZINE, *op.cit.*, p.54.

36. Reik, Theodor, THE NEED TO BE LOVED (New York: Farrar, Straus, and Giroux, 1963), p.97.

37. Butler, Ivan, *op.cit.*, p.101.

38. Quoted in *ibid.*, p.142.

39. Castle, William, STEP RIGHT UP, *op.cit.*, p.193.

40. *Ibid.*, p.194.

41. Quoted in *ibid.*, p.195.

42. Polanski, Roman, *op.cit.*, p.275.

43. Bugliosi, Vincent, *op.cit.*, p.40.

44. Polanski, Roman, *op.cit.*, p.298.

45. Bugliosi, Vincent, *op.cit.*, p.30.

46. Leaming, Barbara, POLANSKI: A BIOGRAPHY, *etc.*, *op.cit.*, p.100.

47. "Dialogue on Film: Roman Polanski," *op.cit.*, p.17.

48. Butler, Ivan, *op.cit.*, p.167.

49. Polanski, Roman, *op.cit.*, p.253.

50. *Ibid.*, p.286.

51. Castle, William, *op.cit.*, p.229.

52. Polanski, Roman, *op.cit.*, p.308.

53. Nietzsche, Friedrich, *op.cit.*, p.831.

54. Sulik, Boleslaw, Introduction to POLANSKI: THREE FILM SCRIPTS, *op.cit.*, p.13.

55. Polanski, Roman, *op.cit.*, p.427.

56. Racine, Jean, BÉRÉNICE contained in THÉÂTRE DE JEAN RACINE (Paris: Éditions de Cluny, 1950), p.260. In my translation, it reads: "I love him, I flee from it. Titus loves me; he would be quit of me. Take your sighs and your armor far from my eyes. Farewell. All three of us serve as examples to the universe."

57. Delahaye, Michael, and Jean-André Fieschi, *op.cit.*, p.211.

58. Grobel, Lawrence, *op.cit.*, p.678.

59. McCarty, John, "The Polanski Puzzle" in TAKE ONE, Vol.2, No.5, May-June, 1970, p.19.

60. Freud, Sigmund, *op.cit.*, p.213.

61. "In Trouble" in PEOPLE MAGAZINE, *op.cit.*, p.56.

62. Quoted from Farr, Bill, "Mental Tests for Polanski" in THE LOS ANGELES TIMES (19 September 1977), p.1.

63. *Ibid.*, p.1.

64. Polanski, Roman, *op.cit.*, p.349.

65. Quoted from Farr, Bill, "Polanski Pleads Guilty on 1 Count" in THE LOS ANGELES TIMES (9 August 1977), p.6.

66. Leaming, Barbara, POLANSKI: A BIOGRAPHY, *etc.*, *op.cit.*, p.181.

67. *Ibid.*, p.166.

68. Polanski, Roman, *op.cit.*, p.369.

69. Leaming, Barbara, POLANSKI: A BIOGRAPHY, *etc.*, *op.cit.*, p.165.

70. Quoted from Albergate, Al, "Polanski: My Whole Life is at Stake" in THE LOS ANGELES HERALD-EXAMINER (3 February 1978), p.1.

71. Grobel, Lawrence, *op.cit.*, p.701.

72. Translated thus by Dawson, Christopher, THE MAKING OF EUROPE (1932; Cleveland: World Publishing, 1956), p.40.

73. Polanski, Roman, *op.cit.*, p.312.

74. *Ibid.*, p.426.

## SAM PECKINPAH

1. Quoted in Simmons, Garner, PECKINPAH: A PORTRAIT IN MONTAGE (Austin: University of Texas Press, 1982), p.177.

2. *Ibid.*, p.177.

3. Lorraine Gauguin's two articles were "With Duke Down Mexico Way: December, 1972" in VIEWS & REVIEWS Magazine, Volume 5, Issue 1, September, 1973, pp.4–8 and "One Size Fits All: December, 1972" in VIEWS & REVIEWS Magazine, Volume 5, Issue 2, December, 1973, pp.10–16. My version and impressions were given in my book THE FILMING OF THE WEST, *op.cit.*, pp.203–208 and pp.566–574.

4. Kerwin, Robert, "Hollywood's Guru of Guts and Gore: On Location with Sam Peckinpah," THE MILWAUKEE JOURNAL SUNDAY MAGAZINE, 26 October 1975, p.7.

5. Quoted in Simmons, Garner, *op.cit.*, p.115.

6. Quoted in *ibid.*, p.194. Notwithstanding, Peckinpah's screenplay for THE GLORY

GUYS (United Artists, 1965) has many similarities with Ford's FORT APACHE (RKO, 1948).

7. Quoted in *ibid.*, p.158.

8. Evans, Max, "Sam Peckinpah: A Very Personal Remembrance" contained in SUPER BULL (Albuquerque: University of New Mexico Press, 1986), p.3.

9. "PLAYBOY Interview: Sam Peckinpah," PLAYBOY, Vol.19, No.8, August, 1972, p.71.

10. Quoted in Simmons, Garner, *op.cit.*, p.40.

11. Quoted in *ibid.*, p.40.

12. Quoted in Lucas, F.L., THE DECLINE AND FALL OF THE ROMANTIC IDEAL (New York: Macmillan, 1936), p.24. In my translation, it reads: "All the women which one has had have been nothing but mattresses for the woman of one's dreams."

13. Sherman, Eric, and Martin Rubin, THE DIRECTOR'S EVENT (New York: Atheneum, 1970), p.49.

14. "PLAYBOY Interview: Sam Peckinpah," *op.cit.*, p.76.

15. Rieupeyrout, Jean-Louis, LA GRANDE AVENTURE DU WESTERN, *op.cit.*, p.358. The translation is mine.

16. Quoted in Simmons, Garner, *op.cit.*, pp.46–47.

17. *Ibid.*, p.50.

18. *Ibid.*, p.54.

19. *Ibid.*, p.64.

20. *Ibid.*, p.67.

21. *Ibid.*, p.130.

22. "PLAYBOY Interview: Sam Peckinpah," *op.cit.*, p.72.

23. *Ibid.*, p.72.

24. Seydor, Paul, PECKINPAH: THE WESTERN FILMS (Urbana: University of Illinois Press, 1980), p.56.

25. Heston, Charlton, THE ACTOR'S LIFE (New York: Dutton, 1978), p.190.

26. Seydor, Paul, *op.cit.*, p.69.

27. Kitses, Jim, HORIZONS WEST (Bloomington: Indiana University Press, 1970), p.146.

28. Quoted in Seydor, Paul, *op.cit.*, p.54.

29. *Ibid.*, p.54.

30. Kitses, Jim, *op.cit.*, p.151.

31. "PLAYBOY Interview: Sam Peckinpah," *op.cit.*, p.74.

32. Kitses, Jim, *op.cit.*, p.161.

33. "Sam Peckinpah Lets It All Hang Out," TAKE ONE, Vol.2, No.3, January-February, 1969, p.20.

34. Seydor, Paul, *op.cit.*, p.97.

35. Pettit, Arthur G., "The Polluted Garden: Sam Peckinpah's Double Vision of Mexico," contained in WESTERN MOVIES (Albuquerque: University of New Mexico Press, 1979) edited by William T. Pilkington and Don Graham, p.101.

36. Simmons, Garner, *op.cit.*, p.85.

37. Seydor, Paul, *op.cit.*, p.79.

38. Quoted in Simmons, Garner, *op.cit.*, p.107.

39. Quoted in *ibid.*, p.119.

40. "PLAYBOY Interview: Sam Peckinpah," *op.cit.*, p.71.

41. *Ibid.*, p.71.

42. *Ibid.*, p.71.

43. Quoted in Simmons, Garner, *op.cit.*, pp.119–120.

44. Seydor, Paul, *op.cit.*, p.152.

45. Evans, Max, SAM PECKINPAH: MASTER OF VIOLENCE (Vermillion: University of South Dakota Press, 1972), p.65.

46. *Ibid.*, p.61.

47. Quoted in Greenberger, Howard, *op.cit.*, p.205.

48. Silver, Charles, THE WESTERN FILM (New York: Pyramid Books, 1976), p.133.

49. "Straight Shootin' Sam," SOUTHWEST MEDIA REVIEW, Spring, 1985, p.17.

50. Huxley, Aldous, CROME YELLOW, contained in GREAT SHORT WORKS OF ALDOUS HUXLEY (New York: Harper's, 1969) edited by Bernard Bergonzi, p.71.

51. Quoted in Simmons, Garner, *op.cit.*, pp.162–163.

52. Evans, Max, SAM PECKINPAH: MASTER OF VIOLENCE, *op.cit.*, p.92.

53. Quoted in Simmons, Garner, *op.cit.*, pp.179–180.

54. Evans, Max, "Sam Peckinpah: A Very Personal Remembrance," *op.cit.*, p.15.

55. Leydon, Joseph, "James Coburn: His Life and HARD TIMES," TAKE ONE, Vol.4, No.12, July-August, 1974, p.7.

56. Evans, Max, "Sam Peckinpah: A Very Personal Remembrance," *op.cit.*, p.15.

57. Quoted in Simmons, Garner, *op.cit.*, p.208.

58. Mahoney, John C., "Browsing the Book Stalls," THE HOLLYWOOD REPORTER, 19 March 1976, p.23.

59. Quoted in Simmons, Garner, *op.cit.*, p.233.

60. Mann, Roderick, THE LOS ANGELES TIMES CALENDAR, 9 December 1979, p.47.

61. "PLAYBOY Interview: Sam Peckinpah," *op.cit.*, p.73.

62. Mann, Roderick, *op.cit.*, p.47.

63. "Straight Shootin' Sam," *op.cit.*, p.17.

64. "Sam Peckinpah Lets It All Hang Out," *op.cit.*, p.20.

65. Evans, Max, "Sam Peckinpah: A Very Personal Remembrance," *op.cit.*, p.22.

66. Wilde, Oscar, THE PICTURE OF DORIAN GRAY contained in THE COMPLETE WORKS OF OSCAR WILDE (London: Collins, 1966), p.61.

67. Quoted in Seydor, Paul, *op.cit.*, p.86.

68. Quoted in the Sam Peckinpah obituary, NEWSWEEK, 7 January 1985, p.65.

69. Jung, C.G., *"Die Lebenswende,"* *op.cit.*, p.457. The translation is mine.

70. Evans, Max, "Sam Peckinpah: A Very Personal Remembrance," *op.cit.*, p.21.

# Filmographies

## Karl Thiede

The basic format for the entries is title, release date (domestic), distributor, director, cast, type of film (color, scope, silent, sound), running time, production dates, costs, grosses, and notes. For the TV shows the format is the same with the name of the series preceding the episode title.

Throughout these filmographies, the following abbreviations have been used:

| | |
|---|---|
| ADP | Adaptation |
| AHC | Alfred Hitchcock's cameo |
| AHP | Alfred Hitchcock Presents |
| BUD | Budget of the show |
| C | Cast |
| D | Director |
| DD | Dialogue Director |
| DG | Domestic Gross (in film rental U.S. and Canada) |
| FG | Foreign Gross (in film rental all countries except U.S. and Canada) |
| FT | Feet |
| GFS | General Film Service |
| KSF | Knickerbocker Star Features |
| M | Minutes |
| NC | Negative Cost |
| OS | Original Screenplay |
| PP | Principal Photography (the show was shot from one date to another date) |
| PRD | Produced |

| PS | Production Start (the date Principal Photography started) |
| R | Reels (35mm) |
| SC | Screenplay |
| T.S. | Trade Show to Exhibitor |
| TV | Television |
| WT | Working Title |
| WWG | Worldwide Gross (Domestic plus Foreign Gross in film rental) |

All films are in black and white (B&W) unless otherwise indicated. Profit and loss statements on films, given where known, are based on studio records. Various accounting procedures from allocation to charge-back of overhead are implied in these figures and the profit and/or loss statement is according to computations made by the producing and/or releasing company. Accordingly, a film may be seen to gross more than it cost and still incur a loss. All films are listed, whenever possible, in chronological order according to U.S. release. Dates are given in the European style of day/month/year. When TV film rental is included to yield the WWG figure, this is to be taken as the figure current with the publication of this book and one that is still accumulating.

## H. BRUCE HUMBERSTONE

1. THE CITY OF STARS   (1925) Universal   D: H. Bruce Humberstone
   C: Gene Hersholt, Norman Kerry, William Desmond
   Silent/22M/2R

**Assistant Director Credits**

2. BEN-HUR   (30/12/1925) M-G-M   D: Fred Niblo
   C: Ramon Navarro, Francis X. Bushman, May McAvoy
   Silent/B&W and 2 Color Technicolor/11,693FT/12R
   1925 Release NC: $3,967,000.   DG: $4,359,000.
   FG: $5,027,000.   WWG: $9,386,000.   Loss = $968,000.
   1932 Rerelease NC: $36,000.   DG: $199,000.
   FG: $1,153,000.   WWG: $1,352,000   Profit = $779,000.

3. PARIS   (24/5/26) M-G-M   D: Edmund Goulding
   C: Charles Ray, Joan Crawford, Douglas Gilmore
   Silent/5,580FT/6R
   PP: 8/3/1925–17/4/1925.
   NC: $198,191.68.   DG: $275,000.
   FG: $92,000.   WWG: $367,000.   Profit = $33,000.

4. THE TEMPTRESS   (3/10/26)   D: Mauritz Stiller/Fred Niblo
   C: Greta Garbo, Antonio Moreno, Roy D'Arcy
   Silent/8,221FT/8R
   PP: 29/3/1926–19/6/1926
   NC: $669,216.87.   DG: $587,000.
   FG: $378,000.   WWG: $965,000.   Loss = $43,000.

5. VALENCIA   (18/12/26) M-G-M   D: Dimitri Buchowetzki
   C: Mae Murray, Lloyd Hughes, Roy D'Arcy
   Silent/5,680FT/6R
   PP: 28/8/1926–17/10/1926
   NC: $276,762.79.   DG: $419,000.
   FG: $156,000.   WWG: $575,000.   Profit = $101,000.

6. CAMILLE   (21/4/27) First National   D: Fred Niblo
   C: Norma Talmadge, Gilbert Roland, Lilyan Tashman
   Silent/8,700FT/9R
   DG: $894,109.   FG: $450,000.   WWG: $1,344,109.

7. TOPSY AND EVA   (16/6/27) United Artists   D: Del Lord
   C: Rosetta Duncan, Vivian Duncan, Gibson Gowland
   Silent/7,456FT/8R
   NC: $341,310.   DG: $350,071.

8. MY BEST GIRL   (31/10/27) Pickford-United Artists   D: Sam Taylor
   C: Mary Pickford, Charles Rogers, Sunshine Hart
   Silent/7,460FT/9R
   NC: $483,104.   DG: $1,027,757.

9. THE DEVIL DANCER   (3/11/27) Goldwyn-United Artists   D: Fred Niblo
   C: Gilda Gray, Clive Brook, Anna May Wong
   Silent/7,600FT/8R
   NC: $457,850.   DG: $526,851.

10. THE GAUCHO   (1/1/28) Fairbanks-United Artists   D: F. Richard Jones
    C: Douglas Fairbanks, Lupe Velez, Eve Southern
    Silent/9,358FT/10R
    NC: $1,147,881.   DG: $1,396,963.   Profit = $363,268.

11. TWO LOVERS   (23/3/28) Goldwyn-United Artists   D: Fred Niblo
    C: Ronald Coleman, Vilma Banky, Noah Beery, Sr.
    Silent/8,817FT/9R
    NC: $720,357.   DG: $779,127.   Profit = $44,937

12. THE WOMAN DISPUTED   (21/10/28) United Artists   D: Henry King/Sam Taylor
    C: Norma Talmadge, Gilbert Roland, Arnold Kent
    Silent/8,129FT/9R
    NC: $660,740.   DG: $793,877.   Profit = $93,919

13. THE IRON MASK   (21/2/29) Fairbanks-United Artists   D: Alan Dwan
    C: Douglas Fairbanks, Gino Gorrado, Belle Bennett
    Part Sound/10,157FT/10R
    NC: $1,495,603.   DG: $1,512,535.

14. COQUETTE   (12/4/29) Pickford-United Artists   D: Sam Taylor
    C: Mary Pickford, John Mack Brown, Matt Moore
    Sound/6,993FT/9R
    NC: $813,108.   DG: $1,403,762.

15. BIG NEWS   (7/9/29) Pathé   D: Gregory La Cava
    C: Robert Armstrong, Carole Lombard, Tom Kennedy
    Sound/6,028FT/7R

16. TAMING OF THE SHREW   (26/10/29) Pickford-Fairbanks-United Artists
    D: Sam Taylor

C: Mary Pickford, Douglas Fairbanks, Edwin Maxwell
Sound/10,157FT/10R
NC: $649,319.   DG: $1,135,228

17. CONDEMNED   (3/11/29) Goldwyn-United Artists   D: Wesley Ruggles
C: Ronald Coleman, Ann Harding, Dudley Diggs
Sound/83M
NC: $608,450.   DG: $940,762.

18. RAFFLES   (26/7/30) Goldwyn-United Artists   D: Harry D'Abbadie D'Arrast/ George Fitzmaurice
C: Ronald Coleman, Kay Francis, Bramwell Fletcher
Sound/6,509/8R
NC: $685,469.   DG: $869,764.

19. WHOOPEE!   (7/9/30) Goldwyn-United Artists   D: Thornton Freeland
C: Eddie Cantor, Eleanor Hunt, Paul Gregory
Sound/2 Color Technicolor/8,393FT/12R
NC: $1,023,972.   DG: $1,636,772.

20. ONE HEAVENLY NIGHT   (10/1/31) Goldwyn-United Artists   D: George Fitzmaurice
C: Evelyn Lane, John Boles, Leon Errol
Sound/82M
NC: $810,165.   DG: $685,968.

21. THE DEVIL TO PAY   (31/1/31) Goldwyn-United Artists   D: George Fitzmaurice
C: Ronald Coleman, Loretta Young, Florence Britton
Sound/74M
NC: $628,432.   DG: $685,856.

22. STREET SCENE   (5/9/31) United Artists   D: King Vidor
C: Sylvia Sidney, William Collier, Jr., Estelle Taylor
Sound/80M
NC: $532,017.   DG: $836,968.

23. THE UNHOLY GARDEN   (10/10/31) Goldwyn-United Artists   D: George Fitzmaurice
C: Ronald Coleman, Fay Wray, Estelle Taylor
Sound/85M
NC: $614,494.   DG: $534,054.

24. ARROWSMITH   (1/12/31) Goldwyn-United Artists   D: John Ford
C: Ronald Coleman, Helen Hayes, A.E. Anson
Sound/108M
NC: $692,890.   DG: $796,980.

25. THE GREEKS HAD A NAME FOR THEM   (13/2/32) United Artists   D: Lowell Sherman
C: Ina Claire, Madge Evans, Joan Blondell
Sound/79M
NC: $555,064.   DG: $397,867.

26. BIRD OF PARADISE   (15/7/32) RKO   D: King Vidor
C: Dolores Del Rio, Joel McCrea, John Halliday
Sound/80M
PP: 6/2/1927–27/4/1927 NC: $752,000. DG: $503,000.
FG: $249,000.   WWG: $752,000.   Loss = $240,000.

**Directing Credits**

27. STRANGERS OF THE EVENING    (15/6/32) Tiffany    D: H. Bruce Humberstone
C: Zasu Pitts, Eugene Pallette, Lucien Littlefield
Sound/70M

28. THE CROOKED CIRCLE    (25/9/32) Worldwide    D: H. Bruce Humberstone
C: Ben Lyon, Zasu Pitts, James Gleason
Sound/70M

29. IF I HAD A MILLION (Forger Sequence)    (11/32) Paramount    D: H. Bruce
Humberstone
C: Gary Cooper, Wynne Gibson, George Raft
Sound/95M

[Other sequences and directors: Raspberry—Ernst Lubitsch; Prologue and Epilogue—Norman Taurog; Violet, Grandma—Stephan Roberts; Road Hog, China
Shop—Norman McLeod; Death Cell—William A. Seiter.]

30. KING OF THE JUNGLE    (10/3/33) Paramount    D: H. Bruce Humberstone
C: Buster Crabbe, Frances Dee, Douglas Dumbrille
Sound/74M

31. GOODBYE LOVE    (10/11/33) RKO    D: H. Bruce Humberstone
C: Charles Ruggles, Verree Teasdale, Mayo Methot
Sound/66M

32. MERRY WIVES OF RENO    (12/5/34) Warner Bros.    D: H. Bruce Humberstone
C: Margaret Lindsay, Glenda Farrell, Donald Woods
Sound/64M
NC: $101,000.    DG: $220,000.
FG: $103,000.    WWG: $426,000.    Profit = $141,250.

33. THE DRAGON MURDER CASE    (24/8/34) First National    D: H. Bruce
Humberstone
C: Warren William, Margaret Lindsay, Lyle Talbot
Sound/68M
NC: $201,000.    DG: $285,000.
FG: $141,000.    WWG: $426,000.    Profit = $118,500.

34. LADIES LOVE DANGER    (3/5/35) Fox    D: H. Bruce Humberstone
C: Mona Barrie, Gilbert Roland, Donald Cook
Sound/69M

35. SILK HAT KID    (19/7/35) Fox    D: H. Bruce Humberstone
C: Lew Ayers, Mae Clarke, Paul Kelly
Sound/69 1/2M

36. THREE LIVE GHOSTS    (10/1/36) M-G-M    D: H. Bruce Humberstone
C: Richard Arlen, Beryl Mercer, Dudley Diggs
Sound/5,576FT/62M
PP: 7/11/1935–6/12/1935
NC: $194,467.23.    DG: $238,000.
FG: $161,000.    WWG: $399,000.    Profit = $57,000

37. CHARLIE CHAN AT THE RACE TRACK    (7/8/36) 20th-Fox    D: H. Bruce
Humberstone
C: Warner Oland, Keye Luke, Helen Wood
Sound/70M

38. CHARLIE CHAN AT THE OPERA (8/1/37) 20th-Fox D: H. Bruce Humberstone
C: Warner Oland, Boris Karloff, Keye Luke
Sound/68M

39. BREEZING HOME (31/1/37) Universal D: Milton Carruth/H. Bruce Humberstone
C: William Gargan, Binnie Barnes, Wendy Barrie
Sound/64M
WT: I HATE HORSES
BUD: $167,500.    NC: $183,269.87.
[Humberstone began directing this film on 23 November 1936 at $500 a week for ten weeks. Although he received his guaranteed $5,000, he was replaced by Milton Carruth who received credit as the sole director.]

40. CHARLIE CHAN AT THE OLYMPICS (7/5/37) 20th-Fox D: H. Bruce Humberstone
C: Warner Oland, Katherine DeMille, Pauline Moore
Sound/71M

41. IN OLD CHICAGO (15/4/38) 20th-Fox D: Henry King
C: Tyrone Power, Alice Faye, Don Ameche
Sound/110M
[Humberstone directed only the burning of Chicago sequence.]
NC: $1,550,000.    DG: $2,000,000.
[This film was rereleased 19 October 1943 at 94M.]

42. CHECKERS (11/2/38) 20th-Fox D: H. Bruce Humberstone
C: Jane Withers, Stuart Erwin, Una Merkel
Sound/78M

43. RASCALS (20/5/38) 20th-Fox D: H. Bruce Humberstone
C: Jane Withers, Rochelle Hudson, Robert Wilcox
Sound/77M

44. TIME OUT FOR MURDER (23/9/38) 20th-Fox D: H. Bruce Humberstone
C: Gloria Stuart, Michael Whalen, Chick Chandler
Sound/60M

45. WHILE NEW YORK SLEEPS (6/1/39) 20th-Fox D: H. Bruce Humberstone
C: Michael Whalen, Jean Rogers, Chick Chandler
Sound/61M

46. CHARLIE CHAN IN HONOLULU (13/1/39) 20th-Fox D: H. Bruce Humberstone
C: Sidney Toler, Phyllis Brooks, Victor Sen Young
Sound/68M

47. PARDON OUR NERVE (24/2/39) 20th-Fox D: H. Bruce Humberstone
C: Lynn Bari, June Gale, Guinn Williams
Sound/68M

48. PACK UP YOUR TROUBLES (20/10/39) 20th-Fox D: H. Bruce Humberstone
C: Jane Withers, The Ritz Brothers, Lynn Bari
Sound/75M

49. LUCKY CISCO KID (28/6/40) 20th-Fox D: H. Bruce Humberstone
C: Cesar Romero, Mary Beth Hughes, Evelyn Venable
Sound/66M

50. THE QUARTERBACK   (4/10/40) Paramount   D: H. Bruce Humberstone
C: Wayne Morris, Virginia Dale, Lillian Cornell
Sound/69M

51. TALL, DARK, AND HANDSOME   (24/1/41) 20th-Fox   D: H. Bruce Humberstone
C: Cesar Romero, Virginia Gilmore, Milton Berle
Sound/78M

52. SUN VALLEY SERENADE   (29/8/41) 20th-Fox   D: H. Bruce Humberstone
C: Sonja Henie, John Payne, Milton Berle
Sound/86M
NC: $1,300,000.   [Rereleased in September, 1946.]

53. I WAKE UP SCREAMING   (14/11/41) 20th-Fox   D: H. Bruce Humberstone
C: Betty Grable, Victor Mature, Carole Landis
Sound/82M
WT and T.S.: HOT SPOT

54. TO THE SHORES OF TRIPOLI   (10/4/42) 20th-Fox   D: H. Bruce Humberstone
C: John Payne, Maureen O'Hara, Randolph Scott
Sound/Technicolor/86M
NC: $1,000,000.   DG: $2,300,000.

55. ICELAND   (2/10/42) 20th-Fox   D: H. Bruce Humberstone
C: Sonja Henie, Jack Oakie, John Payne
Sound/79M
NC: $1,120,000.   DG: $1,700,000.

56. HELLO FRISCO, HELLO   (26/3/43) 20th-Fox   D: H. Bruce Humberstone
C: Alice Faye, Jack Oakie, John Payne
Sound/Technicolor/98M
NC: $1,665,000.   DG: $3,400,000.

57. PIN-UP GIRL   (5/44) 20th-Fox   D: H. Bruce Humberstone
C: Betty Grable, John Harvey, Martha Raye
Sound/Technicolor/83M
NC: $1,615,000.

58. WONDER MAN   (8/6/45) Goldwyn-RKO   D: H. Bruce Humberstone
C: Danny Kaye, Virginia Mayo, Vera-Ellen
Sound/Technicolor/98M
NC: $1,450,000

59. WITHIN THESE WALLS   (7/45) 20th-Fox   D: H. Bruce Humberstone
C: Thomas Mitchell, Mary Anderson, Edward Ryan
Sound/71M

60. THREE LITTLE GIRLS IN BLUE   (10/46) 20th-Fox   D: H. Bruce Humberstone
C: June Haver, George Montgomery, Vivian Blaine
Sound/Technicolor/90M
NC: $2,335,000.   DG: $3,000,000.

61. THE HOMESTRETCH   (5/47) 20th-Fox   D: H. Bruce Humberstone
C: Cornel Wilde, Maureen O'Hara, Glenn Langan
Sound/Technicolor/96M
NC: $2,649,801.26.   DG: $2,429,682.

62. FURY AT FURNACE CREEK   (5/48) 20th-Fox   D: H. Bruce Humberstone
C: Victor Mature, Coleen Gray, Glenn Langan

Sound/88M
NC: $1,518,269.09.   DG: $1,414,629.

63. SOUTH SEA SINNER   (1/50) Universal-International   D: H. Bruce Humberstone
C: Shelley Winters, MacDonald Carey, Helena Carter
Sound/7,944FT/88M

64. HAPPY GO LOVELY   (18/7/51) RKO   D: H. Bruce Humberstone
C: David Niven, Vera-Ellen, Cesar Romero
Sound/Technicolor/88M

65. SHE'S WORKING HER WAY THROUGH COLLEGE   (12/7/52) Warner
Bros.   D: H. Bruce Humberstone
C: Virginia Mayo, Ronald Reagan, Gene Nelson
Sound/Technicolor/101M
NC: $1,360,000.   DG: $2,320,000.
FG: $673,000.   WWG: $2,993,000.   Profit = $884,750

66. THE DESERT SONG   (30/5/53) Warner Bros.   D: H. Bruce Humberstone
C: Kathryn Grayson, Gordon MacRae, Steve Cochran
Sound/Technicolor/110M
NC: $1,812,000.   DG: $1,413,000.
FG: $1,001,000.   WWG: $2,414,000.   Loss = $101,500.

67. TEN WANTED MEN   (2/55) Columbia   D: H. Bruce Humberstone
C: Randolph Scott, Jocelyn Brando, Richard Boone
Sound/Technicolor/80M
DG: $1,000,000.

68. THE PURPLE MASK   (7/55) Universal-International   D: H. Bruce Humberstone
C: Tony Curtis, Colleen Miller, Gene Barry
Sound/Technicolor/Cinemascope/7,361FT/82M

69. TARZAN AND THE LOST SAFARI   (3/5/57) M-G-M   D: H. Bruce
Humberstone
C: Gordon Scott, Robert Beatty, Yolande Donlan
Sound/Technicolor/7,237FT/80M
DG: $981,444.   FG: $1,938,561.   WWG: $2,920,005.

70. TARZAN'S FIGHT FOR LIFE   (11/7/58) M-G-M   D: H. Bruce Humberstone
C: Gordon Scott, Eve Brent, Carl Benton Reid
Sound/Eastman Color/7,766FT/87M
PS: 10/2/58
DG: $784,498.   FG: $1,741,041.   WWG: $2,525,539.

71. MADISON AVENUE   (10/1/62) 20th-Fox   D: H. Bruce Humberstone
C: Dana Andrews, Eleanor Parker, Jeanne Crain
Sound/Cinemascope/94M
DG: $264,721.

## HENRY KING

### Acting Credits

1. A FALSE FRIEND   (3/4/13) Lubin   D: Wilbert Melville
Silent/1R

2. THE SPLIT NUGGET   (11/4/13) Lubin   D: Wilbert Melville
Silent/1R

3. THE BIRTHMARK    (26/4/13) Lubin    D: Bertram Bracken
Silent/1R

4. THE PADRE'S STRATEGY    (13/5/13) Lubin    D: Wilbert Melville
Silent/1R

5. A PERILOUS RIDE    (22/5/13) Lubin    D: Wilbert Melville
Silent/1R

6. A ROMANCE OF THE OZARKS    (29/5/13) Lubin    D: ?
Silent/1R

7. A WOMAN'S HEART    (2/6/13) Lubin    D: Bertram Bracken
Silent/1R

8. THE LEGEND OF LOVER'S LEAP    (9/6/13) Lubin    D: Bertram Bracken
Silent/1R

9. THE MYSTERIOUS HAND    (7/7/13) Lubin    D: Bertram Bracken
Silent/1R

10. THE APACHE KIND    (14/7/13) Lubin    D: Bertram Bracken
Silent/1R

11. JIM'S REWARD    (19/7/13) Lubin    D: Wilbert Melville
Silent/1R

12. AN ACTOR'S STRATEGY    (21/7/13) Lubin    D: Wilbert Melville
Silent/1R

13. THE MESSAGE OF THE ROSE    (2/8/13) Lubin    D: Wilbert Melville
Silent/1R

14. THE CAMERA'S TESTIMONY    (7/8/13) Lubin    D: Wilbert Melville
Silent/1R

15. THE OUTLAW'S GRATITUDE    (11/8/13) Lubin    D: Bertram Bracken
Silent/1R

16. BLACK BEAUTY    (19/8/13) Lubin    D: ?
Silent/1R

17. THE TENDERFOOT HERO    (23/8/13) Lubin    D: Bertram Bracken
Silent/1R

18. HIS LAST CROOKED DEAL    (30/8/13) Lubin    D: Bertram Bracken
Silent/1R

19. PLAYING WITH FIRE    (9/9/13) Lubin    D: Wilbert Melville
Silent/1R

20. THE MEDAL OF HONOR    (13/9/13) Lubin    D: Bertram Bracken
Silent/1R

21. TO LOVE AND CHERISH    (15/9/13) Lubin    D: Bertram Bracken
Silent/1R

22. A MEXICAN TRAGEDY    (23/9/13) Lubin    D: Bertram Bracken
Silent/1R

23. FOR HER BROTHER'S SAKE    (4/10/13) Lubin    D: Bertram Bracken
Silent/1R

24. THE MATE OF THE SCHOONER SADIE    (17/10/13) Lubin    D: Bertram
Bracken
Silent/1R

25. MAGIC MELODY   (4/11/13) Lubin   D: Bertram Bracken
Silent/1R

26. WHEN THE CLOCK STOPPED   (14/11/13) Lubin   D: Bertram Bracken
Silent/1R

27. TURNING THE TABLES   (29/11/13) Lubin   D: Bertram Bracken
Silent/1R

28. MELITA'S SACRIFICE   (1/12/13) Lubin   D: ?
Silent/1R

29. HER FATHER   (6/12/13) Lubin   D: Bertram Bracken
Silent/1R

30. LIFE, LOVE AND LIBERTY   (12/12/13) Lubin   D: Bertram Bracken
Silent/1R

31. WHEN HE SEES   (16/12/13) Lubin   D: Bertram Bracken
Silent/1R

32. THE ETERNAL DUEL   (19/1/14) Lubin   D: Bertram Bracken
Silent/1R

33. THE MEASURE OF A MAN   (10/2/14) Lubin   D: Paul Powell
Silent/1R

34. BY IMPULSE   (19/11/13) Balboa-Pathé   D: ?
Silent/1R
[Balboa, which Henry King joined in July, 1913, was an independent producing company which sold its films to any distributor that would take them.]

35. YOU'VE GOT TO PAY   (10/12/13) Balboa-Pathé   D: ?
Silent/932FT/1R

36. THE MOTH AND THE FLAME   (27/12/13) Balboa-Pathé   D: ?
Silent/1,565FT/2R

37. THE POWER OF PRINT   (29/1/14) Balboa-Pathé   D: ?
Silent/1,653FT/2R

38. ABIDE WITH ME   (11/3/14) Balboa-Pathé   D: ?
Silent/1R

39. THE PATH OF SORROW   (5/14) Balboa-Warner   D: Bertram Bracken
Silent/3R

40. A WILL O' THE WISP   (21/9/14) Balboa-Boxoffice   D: ?
Silent/4R

41. SANDS OF LIFE   (9/14) Balboa-Boxoffice   D: ?
Silent/2R

42. NERVE   (10/14) Balboa-Boxoffice   D: ?
Silent/1R

43. THE RAT   (10/14) Balboa-Boxoffice   D: ?
Silent/2R

44. THE TEST OF MANHOOD   (13/10/14) Balboa-Boxoffice   D: ?
Silent/3R

45. SACRIFICIAL FIRES   (10/14) Balboa-Boxoffice   D: ?
Silent/3R

46. THE CRUISE OF THE HELLSHIP   (10/14) Balboa-Boxoffice   D: ?
Silent/3R

47. SAVED FROM HIMSELF   (1/2/15) Balboa-Pathé   D: ?
Silent/3R

48. THE ACID TEST   (1/3/15) Balboa-Pathé   D: ?
Silent/3R

49. THE BLISS OF IGNORANCE   (29/3/15) Balboa-Pathé   D: ?
Silent/3R

50. THE PRICE OF FAME   (17/4/15) Balboa-Pathé   D: Harry Harvey
Silent/3R
[This was the first of a series of twelve short films in the WHO PAYS? series which starred Ruth Roland and Henry King playing different characters in each. They are #s50–58, 60, 61, and 63.]

51. THE PURSUIT OF PLEASURE   (24/4/15) Balboa-Pathé   D: Harry Harvey
Silent/3R

52. WHEN JUSTICE SLEEPS   (1/5/15) Balboa-Pathé   D: Harry Harvey
Silent/3R

53. THE LOVE LIAR   (8/5/15) Balboa-Pathé   D: Harry Harvey
Silent/3R

54. UNTO HERSELF ALONE   (15/5/15) Balboa-Pathé   D: Harry Harvey
Silent/3R

55. HOUSES OF GLASS   (22/5/15) Balboa-Pathé   D: Harry Harvey
Silent/3R

56. BLUE BLOOD AND YELLOW   (29/5/15) Balboa-Pathé   D: Harry Harvey
Silent/3R

57. TODAY AND TOMORROW   (5/6/15) Balboa-Pathé   D: Harry Harvey
Silent/3R

58. FOR THE COMMONWEALTH   (12/6/15) Balboa-Pathé   D: Harry Harvey
Silent/3R

59. LETTERS ENTANGLED   (14/6/15) Balboa-Selig-GFS   D: ?
Silent/2R

60. THE POMP OF THE EARTH   (19/6/15) Balboa-Pathé   D: Harry Harvey
Silent/3R

61. THE FRUIT OF FOLLY   (26/6/15) Balboa-Pathé   D: Harry Harvey
Silent/3R

62. THE TOMBOY   (28/6/15) Balboa-Pathé   D: ?
Silent/2R

63. TOIL AND TYRANNY   (3/7/15) Balboa-Pathé   D: Harry Harvey
Silent/3R

64. THE BUTTERFLY   (7/15) Balboa-Pathé   D: ?
Silent/2R

65. THE BIG BROTHER   (11/2/16) Balboa-KSF-GFS   D: ?
Silent/3R

66. WHO KNOWS?   (25/2/16) Balboa-KSF-GFS   D: ?
Silent/3R

67. THE OATH OF HATE    (5/5/16) Balboa-KSF-GFS   D: ?
Silent/3R

68. THE STAINED PEARL    (9/6/16) Balboa-KSF-GFS   D: Fred Huntley
Silent/3R

69. THE CROOKED ROAD    (7/7/16) Balboa-KSF-GFS   D: ?
Silent/3R

70. THE SAND LARK    (28/7/16) Balboa-KSF-GFS   D: ?
Silent/3R

71. THE POWER OF EVIL    (1/10/16) Balboa-B.S. Moss   D: ?
Silent/5R

72. VENGEANCE OF THE DEAD    (3/17) Balboa-Fortune Photoplay-GFC   D: Harry Harvey
Silent/4R

73. THE DEVIL'S BAIT    (4/17) Balboa-Fortune Photoplay-GFC   D: Harry Harvey
Silent/4R

## Directing Credits

1. THE NEMESIS    (31/5/15) Balboa-Pathé   D: Henry King
Silent/2R
WT: THE BRAND OF MEN
[At this point in his career, Henry King directed his own productions with Bert Ensminger as assistant director, Joseph Brotherton as chief cameraman, and Jackie Blake as assistant cameraman. Although I can find no proof of it, I believe that the following titles listed above as acting credits were also directed by Henry King: THE OATH OF HATE, THE CROOKED ROAD, THE SAND LARK, and THE POWER OF EVIL.]

2. SHOULD A WIFE FORGIVE?    (8/11/15) Balboa-Equitable-World   D: Henry King
C: Lillian Lorraine, Mabel Van Buren, Henry King
Silent/5R

3. A GENTLEMAN'S AGREEMENT    (22/11/15) Balboa-Pathé   D: Henry King
C: Edith Reeves, Ruth Lackage, William Lampe
Silent/3R

4. LITTLE MARY SUNSHINE    (3/3/16) Balboa-Pathé-Gold Rooster   D: Henry King
C: Baby Marie Osborne, Henry King, Andrew Arbuckle
Silent/5R

5. PAY DIRT    (18/6/16) Balboa-KSF-GSF   D: Henry King
C: Henry King, Marguerite Nichols, Gordon Sackville
Silent/5R

6. FAITH'S REWARD    (25/8/16) Balboa-KSF-GSF   D: Henry King
C: Henry King, Marguerite Nichols, Ida Van Tine
Silent/3R

7. SHADOWS AND SUNSHINE    (12/11/16) Balboa-Pathé   D: Henry King
C: Baby Marie Osborne, Lucy Payton, Daniel Gilfether
Silent/5R

8. JOY AND THE DRAGON    (31/12/16) Balboa-Pathé    D: Henry King
C: Baby Marie Osborne, Henry King, Mollie McConnell
Silent/5R

9. TWIN KIDDIES    (28/1/17) Balboa-Pathé    D: Henry King
C: Baby Marie Osborne, Henry King, Ruth Lackaye
Silent/5R

10. TOLD AT TWILIGHT    (25/3/17) Balboa-Pathé    D: Henry King
C: Baby Marie Osborne, Daniel Gilfether, Henry King
Silent/5R

11. SUNSHINE AND GOLD    (29/4/17) Balboa-Pathé    D: Henry King
C: Baby Marie Osborne, Henry King, Daniel Gilfether
Silent/5R

12. THE MAINSPRING    (17/8/17) Balboa-Falcon Feature-GFC    D: Henry King
C: Henry King, Ethel Pepperell, Bert Ensminger
Silent/4R

13. THE LOCKED HEART    (27/7/18) Balboa-GFC    D: Henry King
C: Gloria Joy, Henry King, Vola Vale
Silent/4,750FT/5R

14. THE CLIMBER    (28/9/17) Balboa-Falcon Feature-GFC    D: Henry King
C: Henry King, T.H. Gibson Gowland, Lucille Pietz
Silent/4R

15. SOULS IN PAWN    (6/8/17) American-Mutual    D: Henry King
C: Gail Kane, Robert Klein, Ruth Everdale
Silent/5R
WT: THE WOMAN IN BLACK
[According to MOTION PICTURE NEWS of 19 May 1917, Henry King, after being with Balboa for four years, signed to direct films for the American Film Company which, as Balboa, sold the productions to other companies to distribute. This change in affiliations explains the discrepancies in the release of various films from Balboa and American.]

16. THE BRIDE'S SILENCE    (10/9/17) American-Mutual    D: Henry King
C: Gail Kane, Ashton Dearholt, Henry A. Barrows
Silent/5R
WTs: THE UNAFRAID and THE SPECTER OF SUSPICION

17. SOUTHERN PRIDE    (8/10/17) American-Mutual    D: Henry King
C: Gail Kane, Cora Drew, Jack Vosburgh
Silent/5R

18. A GAME OF WITS    (5/11/17) American-Mutual    D: Henry King
C: Gail Kane, George Periolat, Spottiswoode Aitken
Silent/5R

19. THE MATE OF THE SALLY ANN    (26/11/17) American-Mutual    D: Henry King
C: Mary Miles Minter, Alan Forrest, George Periolat
Silent/5R
[Rereleased in July, 1920 as PEGGY REBELS by the American Film Company itself.]

20. BEAUTY AND THE ROGUE    (28/1/18) American-Mutual    D: Henry King
C: Mary Miles Minter, Alan Forrest, Orral Humphrey
Silent/5R
WTs: MADEMOISELLE TIPTOES and BOBBY

21. POWERS THAT PREY    (4/3/18) American-Mutual    D: Henry King
    C: Mary Miles Minter, Alan Forrest, Harvey Clark
    Silent/5R
    WT: EXTRA! EXTRA!

22. HEARTS OR DIAMONDS?    (29/4/18) Mutual    D: Henry King
    C: William Russell, Charlotte Burton, Howard Davies
    Silent/5R

23. SOCIAL BRIAR    (13/5/18) American-Mutual    D: Henry King
    C: Mary Miles Minter, Alan Forrest, Anne Schaefer
    Silent/5R

24. UP ROMANCE ROAD    (24/6/18) Mutual    D: Henry King
    C: William Russell, Charlotte Burton, John Burton
    Silent/5R

25. HOBBS IN A HURRY    (6/10/18) American-Pathé    D: Henry King
    C: William Russell, Henry Barrows, Winifred Westover
    Silent/6R

26. ALL THE WORLD TO NOTHING    (1/12/18) American-Pathé    D: Henry King
    C: William Russell, Winifred Westover, J. Morris Foster
    Silent/6R

27. WHEN A MAN RIDES ALONE    (19/1/19) American-Pathé    D: Henry King
    C: William Russell, Carl Stockdale, Luke Warrenton
    Silent/5R

28. WHERE THE WEST BEGINS    (2/3/19) American-Pathé    D: Henry King
    C: William Russell, Eileen Percy, J. Cullen Landis
    Silent/4,785FT/5R

29. BRASS BUTTONS    (30/3/19) American-Pathé    D: Henry King
    C: William Russell, Eileen Percy, Frank Brownlee
    Silent/4,685FT/5R

30. SOME LIAR    (18/5/19) American-Pathé    D: Henry King
    C: William Russell, Eileen Percy, Haywood Mack
    Silent/5R

31. A SPORTING CHANCE    (29/6/19) American-Pathé    D: Henry King
    C: William Russell, Fritzi Brunette, J. Farrell MacDonald
    Silent/4,670FT/5R

32. THIS HERO STUFF    (10/8/19) American-Pathé    D: Henry King
    C: William Russell, Winifred Westover, J. Barney Sherry
    Silent/5R

33. SIX FEET FOUR    (15/9/19) American-Pathé    D: Henry King
    C: William Russell, Vola Vale, Clarence Burton
    Silent/6R

34. 23½ HOURS' LEAVE    (16/11/19) Thomas Ince-Famous Players-Lasky    D: Henry King
    C: Douglas MacLean, Doris May, Thomas Guise
    Silent/4,838FT/5R

35. A FUGITIVE FROM MATRIMONY    (23/11/19) Robertson-Cole    D: Henry King
    C: H.B. Warner, Seena Owen, Adele Farrington
    Silent/4,979FT/5R

36. HAUNTING SHADOWS (11/1/20) Robertson-Cole   D: Henry King
C: H.B. Warner, Edward Piel, Charles Hill
Silent/5R

37. THE WHITE DOVE (28/3/20) Robertson-Cole   D: Henry King
C: H.B. Warner, James O. Barrows, Clare Adams
Silent/5R

38. UNCHARTED CHANNELS (6/6/20) Robertson-Cole   D: Henry King
C: H.B. Warner, Kathryn Adams, Sam de Grasse
Silent/5R

39. ONE HOUR BEFORE DAWN (1/8/20) Pathé   D: Henry King
C: H.B. Warner, Anna Q. Nilsson, Augustus Phillips
Silent/4,696FT/5R

40. HELP WANTED—MALE (26/9/20) Pathé   D: Henry King
C: Blanche Sweet, Henry King, Frank Leigh
Silent/6R

41. DICE OF DESTINY (5/12/20) Pathé   D: Henry King
C: H.B. Warner, Lillian Rich, Howard Davis
Silent/5R

42. WHEN WE WERE TWENTY-ONE (16/1/21) Pathé   D: Henry King
C: H.B. Warner, Claire Anderson, James Morrison
Silent/5R

43. THE MISTRESS OF SHENSTONE (27/2/21) Robertson-Cole   D: Henry King
C: Pauline Frederick, Roy Stewart, Emmett C. King
Silent/5,900FT/6R

44. SALVAGE (5/6/21) Robertson-Cole   D: Henry King
C: Pauline Frederick, Ralph Lewis, Milton Sills
Silent/5,745FT/6R

45. THE STING OF THE LASH (11/9/21) Robertson-Cole   D: Henry King
C: Pauline Frederick, Clyde Fillmore, Lawson Butt
Silent/5,485FT/6R

46. TOL'ABLE DAVID (21/11/21) Inspiration-First National   D: Henry King
C: Richard Barthelmess, Gladys Hulette, Walter P. Lewis
Silent/7,118FT/7R
[Inspiration Pictures had a distribution deal with First National. The first four pictures were
to be budgeted at no more than $100,000 each, the next four at no more than $110,000 each,
and the next four at no more than $125,000 each.]

47. THE SEVENTH DAY (6/2/22) Inspiration-First National   D: Henry King
C: Richard Barthelmess, Frank Losse, Leslie Stone
Silent/5,335FT/6R

48. SONNY (22/5/22) Inspiration-First National   D: Henry King
C: Richard Barthelmess, Margaret Seddon, Pauline Garon
Silent/6,968FT/7R

49. THE BOND BOY (9/10/22) Inspiration-First National   D: Henry King
C: Richard Barthelmess, Charles Hill Mailes, Ned Sparks
Silent/6,902FT/7R

50. FURY (1/1/23) Inspiration-First National   D: Henry King
C: Richard Barthelmess, Tyrone Power, Sr., Pat Hartigan
Silent/8,709FT/9R

51. THE WHITE SISTER   (5/9/23) Inspiration-Metro   D: Henry King
C: Lilian Gish, Ronald Coleman, Gail Kane
Silent/13,147FT/13R
[M-G-M bought the negative and remake rights from Inspiration for $150,000. M-G-M then rereleased the film on 2 February 1929 to a DG: $140,000.   FG: $146,000. WWG: $286,000.   Profit = $16,000.]

52. SACKCLOTH AND SCARLET   (22/3/25) Paramount   D: Henry King
C: Alice Terry, Orville Caldwell, Dorothy Sebastian
Silent/6,752FT/7R

53. ANY WOMAN   (4/5/25) Paramount   D: Henry King
C: Alice Terry, Ernest Gillen, Margarita Fisher
Silent/5.963FT/6R

54. ROMOLA   (30/8/25) Inspiration-Metro-Goldwyn   D: Henry King
C: Lillian Gish, Dorothy Gish, William H. Powell
Silent/12,974FT/12R

55. STELLA DALLAS   (19/11/25) Goldwyn-United Artists   D: Henry King
C: Ronald Coleman, Belle Bennett, Alice Joyce.
Silent/10,157FT/10R
NC: $363,265.   DG: $1,189,668.

56. PARTNERS AGAIN   (14/2/26) Goldwyn-United Artists   D: Henry King
C: George Sidney, Alexander Carr, Betty Jewel
Silent/5,562FT/6R
DG: $309,532.

57. THE WINNING OF BARBARA WORTH   (26/9/26) Goldwyn-United Artists   D: Henry King
C: Ronald Coleman, Vilma Banky, Charles Lane
Silent/8,757FT/9R
NC: $732,002.   DG: $993,571.

58. THE MAGIC FLAME   (14/8/27) Goldwyn-United Artists   D: Henry King
C: Ronald Coleman, Vilma Banky, Augustino Borgato
Silent/8,308FT/9R
NC: $596,128.   DG: $814,551.

59. THE WOMAN DISPUTED   (21/10/28) United Artists   D: Henry King/Sam Taylor
C: Norma Talmadge, Gilbert Roland, Arnold Kent
Silent/8,129FT/9R
NC: $660,740.   DG: $793,877.   Profit = $93,919.

60. SHE GOES TO WAR   (8/6/29) Inspiration-United Artists   D: Henry King
C: Eleanor Boardman, John Holland, Edmund Burns
Part Sound/9,500FT/9R
NC: $628,052.   DG: $485,428.   Loss = $303,060.

61. HELL HARBOR   (22/3/30) Inspiration-United Artists   D: Henry King
C: Lupe Velez, Jean Hersholt, John Holland
Sound/8,354FT/10R
NC: $601,185.   DG: $458,139.

62. THE EYES OF THE WORLD   (30/8/30) United Artists   D: Henry King
C: Una Merkel, Nance O'Neil, John Holland

Sound/7,272FT/8R
NC: $317,700.   DG: $266,494.

63. LIGHTNIN'   (28/11/30) Fox   D: Henry King
C: Will Rogers, Joel McCrea, Louise Dresser
Sound/8,500FT/10R

64. MERELY MARY ANN   (6/9/31) Fox   D: Henry King
C: Janet Gaynor, Charles Farrell, Beryl Mercer
Sound/75M

65. OVER THE HILL   (29/11/31) Fox   D: Henry King
C: Mae Marsh, James Kirkwood, James Dunn
Sound/89M

66. THE WOMAN IN ROOM 13   (15/5/32) Fox   D: Henry King
C: Elissa Landi, Ralph Bellamy, Neil Hamilton
Sound/69M

67. STATE FAIR   (10/2/33) Fox   D: Henry King
C: Janet Gaynor, Will Rogers, Lew Ayres
Sound/94M
DG: $1,800,000.   [Rereleased on 1 August 1936.]

68. I LOVE YOU WEDNESDAY   (16/6/33) Fox   D: Henry King
C: Warner Baxter, Elissa Landi, Victor Jory
Sound/75M

69. CAROLINA   (2/2/34) Fox   D: Henry King
C: Janet Gaynor, Lionel Barrymore, Robert Young
Sound/82M

70. MARIE GALANTE   (25/10/34) Fox   D: Henry King
C: Spencer Tracy, Ketti Gallian, Ned Sparks
Sound/88M

71. ONE MORE SPRING   (15/2/35) Fox   D: Henry King
C: Janet Gaynor, Warner Baxter, Walter King
Sound/87M

72. WAY DOWN EAST   (25/10/35) Fox   D: Henry King
C: Rochelle Hudson, Henry Fonda, Slim Summerville
Sound/84M

73. THE COUNTRY DOCTOR   (6/3/36) 20th-Fox   D: Henry King
C: Dionne Quintuplets, Jean Hersholt, June Lang
Sound/94M

74. RAMONA   (25/9/36) 20th-Fox   D: Henry King
C: Loretta Young, Don Ameche, Kent Taylor
Sound/Technicolor/84M
DG: $1,000,000.

75. LLOYDS OF LONDON   (25/11/36) 20th-Fox   D: Henry King
C: Freddie Bartholomew, Madeleine Carroll, Sir Guy Standing
Sound/117M

76. SEVENTH HEAVEN   (26/3/37) 20th-Fox   D: Henry King
C: Simone Simon, James Stewart, Jean Hersholt
Sound/102M

77. IN OLD CHICAGO   (15/4/38) 20th-Fox   D: Henry King
C: Tyrone Power, Alice Faye, Don Ameche
Sound/110M
NC: $1,550,000.   DG: $2,000,000.
[H. Bruce Humberstone directed only the burning of Chicago sequence. The film was rereleased on 19 October 1943 at 94M.]

78. ALEXANDER'S RAGTIME BAND   (19/8/38) 20th-Fox   D: Henry King
C: Tyrone Power, Alice Faye, Don Ameche
Sound/106M
NC: Over $1,000,000.   DG: $2,000,000.   FG: $1,700,000.
[Rereleased in March, 1947 with a DG: $542,246.]

79. JESSE JAMES   (27/1/39) 20th-Fox   D: Henry King
C: Tyrone Power, Henry Fonda, Nancy Kelly
Sound/Technicolor/106M
BUD: $1,165,242.72.   NC: $1,191,752.45.   DG: $2,600,000.
[Rereleased in February, 1946 in B&W.]

80. STANLEY AND LIVINGSTONE   (18/8/39) 20th-Fox   D: Henry King
C: Spencer Tracy, Nancy Kelly, Richard Greene
Sound/101M
[Rereleased January, 1947.]

81. LITTLE OLD NEW YORK   (9/2/40) 20th-Fox   D: Henry King
C: Alice Faye, Fred MacMurray, Richard Greene
Sound/100M
NC: $1,000,000.

82. MARYLAND   (19/7/40) 20th-Fox   D: Henry King
C: Walter Brennan, Fay Bainter, Brenda Joyce
Sound/Technicolor/90M

83. CHAD HANNA   (27/12/40) 20th-Fox   D: Henry King
C: Henry Fonda, Dorothy Lamour, Linda Darnell
Sound/Technicolor/88M

84. A YANK IN THE R.A.F.   (3/10/41) 20th-Fox   D: Henry King
C: Tyrone Power, Betty Grable, John Sutton
Sound/95M
NC: $1,200,000.   DG: $2,650,000.

85. REMEMBER THE DAY   (2/1/42) 20th-Fox   D: Henry King
C: Claudette Colbert, John Payne, John Sheppard
Sound/84M
DG: $1,100,000.

86. THE BLACK SWAN   (4/12/42) 20th-Fox   D: Henry King
C: Tyrone Power, Maureen O'Hara, Laird Cregar
Sound/Technicolor/85M
DG: $3,000,000.

87. THE SONG OF BERNADETTE   (12/43) 20th-Fox   D: Henry King
C: Jennifer Jones, William Eythe, Charles Bickford
Sound/158M
DG: $5,000,000. [General release was in April, 1945 at 156M.]

88. WILSON   (1/8/44) 20th-Fox   D: Henry King
C: Alexander Knox, Charles Coburn, Geraldine Fitzgerald

Sound/Technicolor/154M
NC: $3,000,000.    DG: $4,250,000.

89.  A BELL FOR ADANO   (5/7/45) 20th-Fox    D: Henry King
C: Gene Tierney, John Hodiak, William Bendix
Sound/103M

90.  MARGIE   (11/46) 20th-Fox    D: Henry King
C: Jeanne Crain, Glenn Langan, Lynn Bari
Sound/Technicolor/90M
DG: $4,000,000.

91.  CAPTAIN FROM CASTILE   (1/1/48) 20th-Fox    D: Henry King
C: Tyrone Power, Jean Peters, Cesar Romero
Sound/Technicolor/140M
BUD: $3,631,000.   NC: $6,504,280.   DG: $3,608,275.   [Shot in 112 days.]

92.  DEEP WATERS   (7/48) 20th-Fox    D: Henry King
C: Dana Andrews, Jean Peters, Cesar Romero
Sound/85M
BUD: $1,559,972.   NC: $1,498,099.   DG: $1,176,915.   [Shot in 59 days.]

93.  PRINCE OF FOXES   (12/49) 20th-Fox    D: Henry King
C: Tyrone Power, Orson Welles, Wanda Hendrix
Sound/107M
DG: $2,608,750.

94.  TWELVE O'CLOCK HIGH   (12/49) 20th-Fox    D: Henry King
C: Gregory Peck, Hugh Marlowe, Gary Merrill
Sound/132M
DG: $3,269,380. [Rereleased in January, 1955.]

95.  THE GUNFIGHTER   (7/50) 20th-Fox    D: Henry King
C: Gregory Peck, Helen Westcott, Millard Mitchell
Sound/84M
DG: $1,897,741.

96.  I'D CLIMB THE HIGHEST MOUNTAIN   (2/51) 20th-Fox    D: Henry King
C: Susan Hayward, William Lundigan, Rory Calhoun
Sound/Technicolor/88M
DG: $2,241,790.

97.  DAVID AND BATHSHEBA   (8/51) 20th-Fox    D: Henry King
C: Gregory Peck, Susan Hayward, Raymond Massey
Sound/116M
DG: $4,720,000.   [Rereleased in May, 1960.]

98.  WAIT TILL THE SUN SHINES, NELLIE   (7/52) 20th-Fox    D: Henry King
C: Jean Peters, David Wayne, Hugh Marlowe
Sound/Technicolor/108M
DG: $1,203,424.

99.  O. HENRY'S FULL HOUSE (Gift of the Magi)   (9/52) 20th-Fox    D: Henry King
C: Jeanne Crain, Farley Granger, Sig Ruman
Sound/117M
NC: $945,000.   DG: $883,323.
[Other episodes were directed by Henry Koster, Henry Hathaway, Jean Negulesco, and Howard Hawks.]

100. **THE SNOWS OF KILIMANJARO**   (7/52) 20th-Fox   D: Henry King
C: Gregory Peck, Susan Hayward, Ava Gardner
Sound/Technicolor/117M
DG: $5,601,807.

101. **KING OF THE KHYBER RIFLES**   (12/53) 20th-Fox   D: Henry King
C: Tyrone Power, Terry Moore, Michael Rennie
Sound/Technicolor/99M
DG: $2,518,293.

102. **UNTAMED**   (3/55) 20th-Fox   D: Henry King
C: Tyrone Power, Susan Hayward, Richard Egan
Sound/Deluxe Color/Cinemascope/111M
DG: $2,229,313.

103. **LOVE IS A MANY-SPLENDORED THING**   (8/55) 20th-Fox   D: Henry King
C: Jennifer Jones, William Holden, Torin Thatcher
Sound/Deluxe Color/Cinemascope/102M
DG: $3,132,758.

104. **CAROUSEL**   (2/56) 20th-Fox   D: Henry King
C: Gordon MacRae, Shirley Jones, Cameron Mitchell
Sound/Deluxe Color/Cinemascope/127M
DG: $3,004,000.
[Also in 1956 Henry King and Tyrone Power appeared in a U.S. Air Force documentary on the work of the Civil Air Patrol in their capacity as flyers, entitled SKY SENTINELS. The documentary was directed by Robert Friend.]

105. **THE SUN ALSO RISES**   (9/57) 20th-Fox   D: Henry King
C: Tyrone Power, Ava Gardner, Mel Ferrer
Sound/Deluxe Color/Cinemascope/129M
DG: $2,068,619.

106. **THE BRAVADOS**   (7/58) 20th-Fox   D: Henry King
C: Gregory Peck, Joan Collins, Stephen Boyd
Sound/Deluxe Color/Cinemascope/98M
DG: $1,840,000.

[THE OLD MAN AND THE SEA (Warner's, 1958) with Spencer Tracy has been listed as a Henry King film. It is not. Fred Zinneman started tests in Cuba on 7 February 1956. Principal photography started on 27 April 1956 and continued under Zinneman until 19 June 1956. Don Page, Zinneman's assistant director, shot four more days, from 20 to 23 June 1956 while Zinneman was in New York. Zinneman did not return. Art Rosson shot twenty-four days, from 25 June to 31 July 1956, in Nassau. By 13 July 1956 John Sturges became involved in the production. The following year on 11 June 1957 preproduction was started under Sturges in Hawaii with principal photography going from 17 June until 29 June 1957 in Hawaii. Fifty-four days were then shot in Burbank from 5 July 1957 until 30 August 1957.]

107. **THIS EARTH IS MINE**   (7/59) Universal   D: Henry King
C: Rock Hudson, Jean Simmons, Dorothy McGuire
Sound/Technicolor/Cinemascope/124M
DG: $3,400,000.

108. **BELOVED INFIDEL**   (11/59) 20th-Fox   D: Henry King
C: Gregory Peck, Deborah Kerr, Eddie Albert
Sound/Deluxe Color/Cinemascope/123M
DG: $1,402,556.

109.  TENDER IS THE NIGHT    (19/1/62) 20th-Fox    D: Henry King
C: Jennifer Jones, Jason Robards, Jr., Joan Fontaine
Sound/Deluxe Color/Cinemascope/146M
DG: $1,195,887.

# ALFRED HITCHCOCK

1. NUMBER THIRTEEN    Woolf and Freedman Film Service    D: Alfred Hitchcock
C: Clare Greet, Ernest Thesiger
[Begun in 1922 but uncompleted and never released.]

## Assistant Director Credits

2. ALWAYS TELL YOUR WIFE    (T.S. 2/23)    Woolf and Freedman Film
Service    D: Hugh Croise/Alfred Hitchcock
C: Sir Seymour Hicks, Gertrude McCoy
Silent/2R
[After assisting, Hitchcock took over as director when Croise fell ill.]

3. WOMAN TO WOMAN    (T.S. 11/23) Bacon-Saville-Freedman    D: Graham Cutts
C: Betty Compson, Josephine Earle, Marie Ault
Silent/7,455FT

4. THE WHITE SHADOW    (T.S. 2/24) Bacon-Saville-Freedman    D: Graham Cutts
C: Betty Compson, Clive Brook, Henry Victor
Silent/5,047FT

5. THE PRUDE'S FALL    (T.S. 5/24) Bacon-Saville-Freedman    D: Graham Cutts
C: Jane Novak, Julanne Johnstone, Warwick Ward
Silent/5,675FT

6. THE PASSIONATE ADVENTURE    (3/11/24) Gainsborough    D: Graham Cutts
C: Alice Joyce, Clive Brook, Marjorie Daw
Silent/7,923FT

7. THE BLACKGUARD    (26/10/25) Gainsborough-UFA    D: Graham Cutts
C: Walter Rilla, Bernard Goetzke, Jane Novak
Silent/6,016FT

## Directing Credits

8. THE PLEASURE GARDEN    (24/1/27)    Gainsborough-Emelka    D: Alfred
Hitchcock
C: Virginia Valli, Carmelita Geraghty, Miles Mander
Sound/7,058FT

9. THE MOUNTAIN EAGLE    (23/5/27)    Gainsborough-Emelka    D: Alfred
Hitchcock
C: Bernard Goetzke, Nita Naldi, Malcolm Keen
Silent/7,503FT
[The U.S. title was FEAR O'GOD]

10. THE LODGER    (14/2/27) Gainsborough    D: Alfred Hitchcock
C: Ivor Novello, Marie Ault, Malcolm Keen
Silent/7,685FT
[AHC: His back to camera in an office scene and one of the crowd at the arrest.]
[ The U.S. title was THE CASE OF JONATHAN DREW.]

11. DOWNHILL   (24/10/27) Gainsborough   D: Alfred Hitchcock
C: Ivor Novello, Ben Webster, Robin Irvine
Silent/7,853FT
[The U.S. title was WHEN BOYS LEAVE HOME.]

12. EASY VIRTUE   (5/3/28) Gainsborough   D: Alfred Hitchcock
C: Isabel Jeans, Franklyn Dyall, Bransby Williams
Silent/7,392FT
[At this point, Hitchcock signed with British International Pictures to direct twelve pictures over three years for £13,000 ($80,000) a year.]

13 THE RING   (14/1/28) B.I.P.   D: Alfred Hitchcock
C: Carl Brisson, Lillian Hall-Davies, Ian Hunter
Silent/8,454FT

14. THE FARMER'S WIFE   (8/3/28) B.I.P.   D: Alfred Hitchcock
C: Jameson Thomas, Lillian Hall-Davies, Gordon Harker
Silent/8,775FT

15. CHAMPAGNE   (9/8/28) B.I.P.   D: Alfred Hitchcock
C: Betty Balfour, Gordon Harker, Jack Trevor
Silent/8,038FT

16. THE MANXMAN   (1/30) B.I.P.   D: Alfred Hitchcock
C: Carl Brisson, Malcolm Keen, Anny Ondra
Silent/8,163FT

17. BLACKMAIL   (25/11/29) B.I.P.   D: Alfred Hitchcock
C: Anny Ondra, John Longden, Sara Allgood
Sound/7,136FT/8R
[AHC: Reading a newspaper on a subway while a little boy annoys him.]

18. JUNO AND THE PAYCOCK   (22/9/30) B.I.P.   D: Alfred Hitchcock
C: Sara Allgood, Edward Chapman, Maire O'Neill
Sound/8,751FT/97M

19. ELSTREE CALLING   (29/9/30)   D: Alfred Hitchcock
C: Will Fyffe, Tommy Handler, Gordon Harker
Sound/95M
[Other directors who contributed to this compendium film were Adrian Bunel, Andre Chevlot, Paul Murray, and Jack Hulbert. The U.S. title was HELLO, EVERYBODY.]

20. MURDER   (27/3/31) B.I.P.   D: Alfred Hitchcock
C: Herbert Marshall, Norah Baring, Phyllis Konstam
Sound/9,700FT
[AHC: On a street.]

21. MARY   (1931) B.I.P.   D: Alfred Hitchcock
C: Alfred Abel, Olga Tchakowa, Paul Graetz
[This film was the German language version of MURDER.]

22. THE SKIN GAME   (19/10/31) B.I.P.   D: Alfred Hitchcock
C: Edmund Gwenn, Jill Esmond, John Longden
Sound/7,933FT

23. RICH AND STRANGE   (13/6/32) B.I.P.   D: Alfred Hitchcock
C: Henry Kendall, Joan Barry, Betty Amann
Sound/8,300FT
[The U.S. title was EAST OF SHANGHAI.]

24. NUMBER SEVENTEEN    (7/11/32) B.I.P.    D: Alfred Hitchcock
C: Leon M. Lion, Anne Grey, John Stuart
Sound/5,766FT.

25. WALTZES FROM VIENNA    (30/4/34) Tom Arnold    D: Alfred Hitchcock
C: Jessie Matthews, Esmond Knight, Frank Vosper
Sound/7,300FT/80M
[AHC: As a cook wearing a toque climbing up a ladder to peek into what appears to be a bedroom window. The U.S. title was STRAUSS' GREAT WALTZ.]

26. THE MAN WHO KNEW TOO MUCH    (14/2/35) Gaumont-British    D: Alfred Hitchcock
C: Leslie Banks, Peter Lorre, Edna Best
Sound/84M
PP: 29/5/1934-12/8/1934

27. THE THIRTY-NINE STEPS    (18/11/35) Gaumont-British    D: Alfred Hitchcock
C: Robert Donat, Madeleine Carroll, Lucy Mannheim
Sound/7,821FT/87M
PP: 11/1/1935–18/3/1935
[AHC: Man in hat passing on the street.]

28. THE SECRET AGENT    (14/5/36) Gaumont-British    D: Alfred Hitchcock
C: Madeleine Carroll, John Gielgud, Peter Lorre
Sound/7,816FT/87M

29. SABOTAGE    (6/2/37) Gaumont-British    D: Alfred Hitchcock
C: Sylvia Sidney, Oscar Homolka, Desmond Tester
Sound/6,917FT/77M
[The U.S. title was A WOMAN ALONE.]

30. YOUNG AND INNOCENT    (5/2/38) Gainsborough-Gaumont-British    D: Alfred Hitchcock
C: Derrick de Marney, Nova Pilbeam, Percy Marmount
Sound/80M
[AHC: A photographer outside a courtroom. The U.S. title was THE GIRL WAS YOUNG.]

31. THE LADY VANISHES    (5/10/38) Gainsborough-Gaumont-British    D: Alfred Hitchcock
C: Margaret Lockwood, Michael Redgrave, Paul Lukas
Sound/8,650FT/96M
[AHC: Quick shot of him walking in railway station.]

32. JAMAICA INN    (20/5/39) Mayflower    D: Alfred Hitchcock
C: Maureen O'Hara, Charles Laughton, Robert Newton
Sound/9,540FT/106M

33. REBECCA    (12/4/40) Selznick-United Artists    D: Alfred Hitchcock
C: Laurence Olivier, Joan Fontaine, George Sanders
Sound/11,756FT/131M
PP: 8/9/1939–20/11/1939
BUD: $800,000.   NC: $1,280,000.   DG: $1,846,000.
FG: $981,000.   WWG: $3,270,000.   Profit = $700,000.
[AHC: Near a phone booth as George Sanders makes a call. The picture was rereleased on 26 April 1946 with a DG: $544,000.   FG: $981,000.   WWG: $1,525,000.   Profit = $1,000,000.]

34. FOREIGN CORRESPONDENT   (16/8/40)  Wanger-United Artists   D: Alfred Hitchcock
C: Joel McCrea, Laraine Day, Herbert Marshall
Sound/10,798FT/120M
NC: $1,478,000.   DG: $1,218,000.
FG: $855,000.   WWG: $2,073,000.   Loss = $55,000.
[AHC: Passing Joel McCrea on the street.]

35. MR. AND MRS. SMITH   (31/1/41) RKO   D: Alfred Hitchcock
C: Carole Lombard, Robert Montgomery, Gene Raymond
Sound/8,510FT/95M
PP: 5/9/1940–2/11/1940
NC: $743,000.   DG: $980,000.
FG: $415,000.   WWG: $1,395,000.   Profit = $73,000.
[AHC: Passing Robert Montgomery on the street. PICTURE PEOPLE Number 4, released at ten minutes in length by RKO on 20 October 1940 includes a scene of Carole Lombard directing Hitchcock's cameo for this film.]

36. SUSPICION   (14/11/41) RKO   D: Alfred Hitchcock
C: Cary Grant, Joan Fontaine, Cedric Hardwicke
Sound/99M
PP: 10/2/1941–16/5/1941
NC: $1,102,000.   DG: $1,305,000.
FG: $895,000   WWG: $2,200,000.   Profit = $425,000.
[AHC: In village near a mailbox. The working title for this film was BEFORE THE FACT.]

37. SABOTEUR   (24/4/42) Universal   D: Alfred Hitchcock
C: Robert Cummings, Priscilla Lane, Otto Kruger
Sound/108M
DG: $1,250,000.
[AHC: At a newsstand.]

38. SHADOW OF A DOUBT   (15/1/43) Universal   D: Alfred Hitchcock
C: Joseph Cotten, Teresa Wright, MacDonald Carey
Sound/9,766FT/108M
NC: $813,000.   DG: $1,200,000.
[AHC: On a train, back to the camera, he holds a bridge hand consisting of thirteen cards of the same suit.]

39. LIFEBOAT   (28/1/44) 20th-Fox   D: Alfred Hitchcock
C: Tallulah Bankhead, William Bendix, Walter Slezak
Sound/96M
NC: $1,590,000.
[AHC: Pictured in a newspaper held by William Bendix showing the effects of Reduco before and after.]

40. THE FIGHTING GENERATION   (11/44) National Screen Service   D: Alfred Hitchcock
C: Jennifer Jones
Sound/1R
[A short produced by David O. Selznick as a trailer for the sixth War Bond drive 20/11/1944–16/12/1944.]

41. AVENTURE MALGACHE [MADAGASCAR LANDING]   (1944) British Ministry of Information   D: Alfred Hitchcock
C: The Moliere Players

Sound/31M
PP: Between 20/1/1944 and 25/2/1944

42. BON VOYAGE   (1944) British Ministry of Information   D: Alfred Hitchcock
C: John Blythe, The Moliere Players
Sound/25M
PP: Between 20/1/1944 and 25/2/1944

43. SPELLBOUND   (25/12/45) Selznick-United Artists   D: Alfred Hitchcock
C: Ingrid Bergman, Gregory Peck, Rhonda Fleming
Sound/10,022FT/111M
PP: 7/7/1944–13/10/1944
BUD: $1,250,000.   NC: $1,696,000.   DG: $4,971,000.
FG: $2,256,000.   WWG: $7,227,000.   Profit = $3,062,900.
[AHC: Getting off elevator in hotel. The working title for this film was THE HOUSE OF
DR. EDWARDS.]

44. NOTORIOUS   (6/9/46) RKO   D: Alfred Hitchcock
C: Ingrid Bergman, Cary Grant, Claude Rains
Sound/9,136FT/101 1/2M
PP: 15/10/1945–17/1/1946
NC: $2,300,000.   DG: $4,800,000.
FG: $2,300,000.   WWG: $7,100,000.   Profit = $2,000,000.
[AHC: Drinking champagne at a party.]

45. THE PARADINE CASE   (31/12/47) Selznick   D: Alfred Hitchcock
C: Gregory Peck, Ann Todd, Charles Laughton
Sound/125M
PP: 23/12/1946–13/3/1947
BUD: $3,000,000.   NC: $4,000,000.
[AHC: Carrying a cello case.]

46. ROPE   (25/9/48) Warner Bros.   D: Alfred Hitchcock
C: James Stewart, John Dall, Farley Granger
Sound/Technicolor/80M
PP: 22/1/1948–21/2/1948
NC: $1,510,000.   DG: $2,028,000.
FG: $720,000.   WWG: $2,748,000.   Profit = $331,000.
[AHC: Hitchcock promoting Reduco in the skyline of New York.]

47. UNDER CAPRICORN   (8/10/48) Warner Bros.   D: Alfred Hitchcock
C: Ingrid Bergman, Joseph Cotten, Michael Wilding
Sound/Technicolor/117M
NC: $2,500,000.   DG: $1,210,000.
FG: $1,458,000.   WWG: $2,668,000.   Loss = $699,000.
[AHC: At the Governor's reception and on the stairs of Government House.]

48. STAGE FRIGHT   (15/4/50) Warner Bros.   D: Alfred Hitchcock
C: Marlene Dietrich, Jane Wyman, Michael Wilding
Sound/110M
NC: $1,437,000.   DG: $1,012,000.
FG: $896,000.   WWG: $1,908,000.   Loss = $206,000.
[AHC: Staring at Jane Wyman in the street.]

49. STRANGERS ON A TRAIN   (30/6/51) Warner Bros.   D: Alfred Hitchcock
C: Robert Walker, Farley Granger, Laura Elliott
Sound/101M

NC: $1,568,000.   DG: $1,788,000.
FG: $1,144,000.   WWG: $2,932,000.   Profit = $431,000.
[AHC: Boarding train carrying a double bass.]

50.  I CONFESS   (28/2/53) Warner Bros.   D: Alfred Hitchcock
C: Montgomery Clift, Anne Baxter, Karl Malden
Sound/95M
NC: $1,671,000.   DG: $1,471,000.
FG: $1,742,000.   WWG: $3,213,000.   Profit = $539,000.
[AHC: Crossing the top of a long staircase.]

51.  DIAL M FOR MURDER   (29/5/54) Warner Bros.   D: Alfred Hitchcock
C: Ray Milland, Grace Kelly, Robert Cummings
Sound/Warnercolor 3-D/105M
NC: $1,341,000.   DG: $2,390,000.
FG: $2,059,000.   WWG: $4,449,000.   Profit = $1,776,000.
[AHC: Pictured in reunion photo on a wall.]

52.  REAR WINDOW   (4/8/54) Paramount   D: Alfred Hitchcock
C: James Stewart, Grace Kelly, Thelma Ritter
Sound/Technicolor/112M
DG: $9,812,000.
[AHC: Seen winding a clock.]

53.  TO CATCH A THIEF   (15/9/55) Paramount   D: Alfred Hitchcock
C: Cary Grant, Grace Kelly, Jessie Royce Landis
Sound/Technicolor/Vistavision/106M
DG: $4,500,000.
[AHC: Next to Cary Grant on a bus.]

54.  THE TROUBLE WITH HARRY   (17/10/55) Paramount   D: Alfred Hitchcock
C: Edmund Gwenn, John Forsythe, Shirley MacLaine
Sound/Technicolor/Vistavision/99M
DG: Less than $1,000,000.
[AHC: Walking past John Forsythe's outdoor exhibit.]

55.  THE MAN WHO KNEW TOO MUCH   (30/5/56) Paramount   D: Alfred Hitchcock
C: James Stewart, Doris Day, Christopher Olsen
Sound/Technicolor/Vistavision/120M
DG: $5,100,000.
[AHC: In the Morocco market place.]

56.  THE WRONG MAN   (27/1/57) Warner Bros.   D: Alfred Hitchcock
C: Henry Fonda, Vera Miles, Anthony Quayle
Sound/105M
NC: $1,968,000.   DG: $1,167,000.
FG: $1,000,000.   WWG: $2,167,000.   Loss = $642,750.
[AHC: Narration of the Prologue.]

57.  VERTIGO   (6/58) Paramount   D: Alfred Hitchcock
C: James Stewart, Kim Novak, Barbara Bel Geddes
Sound/Technicolor/Vistavision/127M
DG: $5,306,000.
[AHC: Crossing a street.]

58.  NORTH BY NORTHWEST   (17/7/59) M-G-M   D: Alfred Hitchcock
C: Cary Grant, Eva Marie Saint, James Mason

Sound/Metrocolor/Vistavision/12,254FT/136M
PP: 27/8/1958–18/12/1958
BUD: $3,071,000.   NC: $4,350,000.   DG: $6,703,000.
FG: $5,830,000.   WWG: $12,533,000.   Profit = $2,407,000.
[AHC: Running to catch bus.]

59. PSYCHO   (1/8/60) Paramount   D: Alfred Hitchcock
C: Anthony Perkins, Janet Leigh, Vera Miles
Sound/109M
NC: $800,000.   DG: $11,200,000.
[AHC: Man in cowboy hat standing outside realty office. Hitchcock also directed and appeared in a trailer running 6:17M to promote this film, by giving a sardonic guided tour of the Bates Motel and the Bates house.]

60. THE BIRDS   (8/4/63) Universal   D: Alfred Hitchcock
C: Tippi Hedron, Rod Taylor, Jessica Tandy
Sound/Technicolor/10,800FT/120M
DG: $5,045,000.
[AHC: Walking two dogs out a pet store. Hitchcock also directed and appeared in a trailer running 5M, this time in color, sitting down to a bird dinner and talking about the film.]

61. MARNIE   (22/7/64) Universal   D: Alfred Hitchcock
C: Tippi Hedron, Sean Connery, Diane Baker
Sound/Technicolor/11,675FT/130M
BUD: $3,400,000.   DG: $2,841,000.
[AHC: Leaving a hotel room.]

62. TORN CURTAIN   (2/8/66) Universal   D: Alfred Hitchcock
C: Paul Newman, Julie Andrews, Lila Kedrova
Sound/Technicolor/11,482FT/128M
DG: $6,601,000.
[AHC: Sitting in a hotel lobby holding a baby.]

63. TOPAZ   (3/1/70) Universal   D: Alfred Hitchcock
C: Frederick Stafford, John Forsythe, Dany Robin
Sound/Technicolor/126M
NC: $4,000,000.   DG: $3,017,000.
[AHC: In a wheelchair at the airport.]

64. FRENZY   (20/6/72) Universal   D: Alfred Hitchcock
C: Jon Finch, Barry Foster, Barbara Leigh-Hunt
Sound/Technicolor/115M
NC: $2,000,000.   DG: $6,382,000.
[AHC: Spectator at the opening rally.]

65. FAMILY PLOT   (9/4/76) Universal   D: Alfred Hitchcock
C: Karen Black, Bruce Dern, Barbara Harris
Sound/Technicolor/120M
DG: $6,621,000.
[AHC: Shadow silhouetted behind glass door of Vital Statistics office.]

## Television Shows

1. ALFRED HITCHCOCK PRESENTS: BREAKDOWN   (13/11/55)   CBS   D: Alfred Hitchcock
C: Joseph Cotten, Raymond Bailey, Forrest Stanley
26M

[Hitchcock acted as the host introducing this and all of the television shows listed below with the exception of Nos. 8 and 16.]
PP: 7/9/1955–10/9/1955

2. AHP: REVENGE   (1/10/55) CBS   D: Alfred Hitchcock
C: Ralph Meeker, Vera Miles, Francis Bavier
26M
PP: 15/9/1955–17/9/1955

3. AHP: THE CASE OF MR. PELHAM   (4/12/55) CBS   D: Alfred Hitchcock
C: Tom Ewell, Raymond Bailey, Kirby Smith
26M
PP: 7–8/9/1955–10/9/1955

4. AHP: BACK FOR CHRISTMAS   (4/3/56) CBS   D: Alfred Hitchcock
C: John Williams, Isobel Elsom, A.E. Gould-Porter
26M
PP: 13–14/1/1956–16/1/1956

5. AHP: WET SATURDAY   (30/9/56) CBS   D: Alfred Hitchcock
C: Sir Cedric Hardwicke, John Williams, Kathryn Givney
26M
PP: 22/8/1956–24/8/1956

6. AHP: MR BLANCHARD'S SECRET   (23/12/56) CBS   D: Alfred Hitchcock
C: Mary Scott, Robert Horton, Dayton Lummis
26M
PP: 18–19/10/1956–22/10/1956

7. AHP: ONE MORE MILE TO GO   (7/4/57) CBS   D: Alfred Hitchcock
C: David Wayne, Steve Brodie, Louise Larabee
26M
PP: 9/1/1957–11/9/1957

8. SUSPICION: FOUR O'CLOCK   (30/9/57) NBC   D: Alfred Hitchcock
C: E.G. Marshall, Nancy Kelly, Richard Long
52M
PP: 29/7/1957–2/8/1957

9. AHP: THE PERFECT CRIME   (20/10/57) CBS   D: Alfred Hitchcock
C: Vincent Price, James Gregory
26M
PP: 17/7/1957–19/7/1957

10. AHP: LAMB TO THE SLAUGHTER   (13/4/58) CBS   D: Alfred Hitchcock
C: Barbara Bel Geddes, Allan Lane, Harold J. Stone
26M
PP: 18/2/1958–19/2/1958

11. AHP: A DIP IN THE POOL   (1/6/58) CBS   D: Alfred Hitchcock
C: Keenan Wynn, Fay Wray, Louise Platt
26M
PP: 15/4/1958–16/4/1958

12. AHP: POISON   (5/10/58) CBS   D: Alfred Hitchcock
C: James Donald, Wendell Corey, Arnold Moss
26M
PP: 21/8/1958–22/8/1958

13. AHP: BANQUO'S CHAIR   (3/5/59) CBS   D: Alfred Hitchcock

C: John Williams, Kenneth Haigh, Reginald Gardiner
26M
PP: 25/3/1959–26/3/1959

14. AHP: ARTHUR   (27/9/59) CBS   D: Alfred Hitchcock
C: Laurence Harvey, Hazel Court, Robert Douglas
26M
PP: 7/7/1959–9/7/1959

15. AHP: THE CRYSTAL TRENCH   (4/10/59) CBS   D: Alfred Hitchcock
C: James Donald, Patricia Owens, Werner Klemperer
26M
PP: 25/8/1959–27/8/1959

16. FORD STARTIME: INCIDENT AT A CORNER   (5/4/60) NBC   D: Alfred
Hitchcock
C: Vera Miles, Paul Hartman, George Peppard
52M
PP: 8–12/2/1960–15–17/2/1960

17. AHP: MRS. BIXBY AND THE COLONEL'S COAT   (27/9/60) CBS   D: Alfred
Hitchcock
C: Audrey Meadows, Les Tremayne, Stephen Chase
26M
PP: 17/8/1960–19/8/1960

18. AHP: THE HORSEPLAYER   (14/3/61) CBS   D: Alfred Hitchcock
C: Claude Rains, Ed Gardner, Percy Helton
26M
PP: 4/1/1961–6/1/1961

19. AHP: BANG! YOU'RE DEAD!   (17/10/61) CBS   D: Alfred Hitchcock
C: Billy Mummy, Biff Elliott, Lucy Prentiss
26M
PP: 25/7/1961–27/7/1961

20. Alfred Hitchock Hour: I SAW THE WHOLE THING!   (11/10/62) CBS   D: Alfred
Hitchcock
C: John Forsythe, Kent Smith, Evans Evans
52M
PP: 23/7/1962–27/7/1962

## Credits as Producer

1. LORD CAMBER'S LADIES   (7/11/32) B.I.P.   D: Benn W. Levy
C: Gertrude Lawrence, Sir Gerald du Maurier, Benita Hume
Sound/94M

# HOWARD HAWKS

## Writing Credits

1. QUICKSANDS   (28/2/23) American Releasing Corp.   D: Jack Conway
C: Helen Chadwick, Richard Dix, Alan Hale, Sr.
Silent/4,593FT/5R
[Hawks produced this film as well as wrote the story. It was rereleased by Paramount on 21
May 1927.]

2. TIGER LOVE   (30/6/24) Paramount   D: George Melford
C: Antonio Moreno, Estelle Taylor, Raymond Nye
Silent/5,325FT/6R

3. THE DRESSMAKER FROM PARIS   (30/3/25) Paramount   D: Paul Bern
C: Leatrice Joy, Ernest Torrence, Allan Forrest
Silent/7,080FT/8R

4. HONESTY—THE BEST POLICY   (8/8/26) Fox   D: Chester Bennett
C: Rockcliffe Fellowes, Pauline Starke, Johnnie Walker
Silent/4,200FT/15R

## Directing Credits

1. THE ROAD TO GLORY   (7/2/26) Fox   D: Howard Hawks
C: May McAvoy, Leslie Fenton, Ford Sterling
Silent/6,038FT/6R

2. FIG LEAVES   (22/8/26) Fox   D: Howard Hawks
C: George O'Brien, Olive Borden, Phyllis Haver
Silent/2 Color Sequences/6,498FT/7R

3. THE CRADLE SNATCHERS   (28/5/27) Fox   D: Howard Hawks
C: Louise Fazenda, J. Farrell MacDonald, Ethel Wales
Silent/6,281FT/7R

4. PAID TO LOVE   (23/7/27) Fox   D: Howard Hawks
C: George O'Brien, Virginia Valli, J. Farrell MacDonald
Silent/6,888FT/7R

5. A GIRL IN EVERY PORT   (26/2/28) Fox   D: Howard Hawks
C: Victor McLaglen, Maria Casajuana, Natalie Joyce
Silent/5,500FT/6R

6. FAZIL   (4/6/28) Fox   D: Howard Hawks
C: Charles Farrell, Greta Nisson, Mae Busch
Silent with Music & Effects/7,217FT/7R

7. THE AIR CIRCUS   (30/9/28) Fox   D: Howard Hawks
C: Louise Dresser, David Rollins, Arthur Lake
Part Sound/7,702FT/8R

8. TRENT'S LAST CASE   (31/3/29) Fox   D: Howard Hawks
C: Donald Crisp, Raymond Griffith, Raymond Hatton
Silent with Music & Effects/5,834FT/6R

9. THE DAWN PATROL   (10/7/30) First National   D: Howard Hawks
C: Richard Barthelmess, Douglas Fairbanks, Jr., Neil Hamilton
Sound/9,500FT/12R
NC: $729,000.   DG: $1,061,000.
FG: $563,000.   WWG: $1,624,000.   Profit = $400,000.

10. THE CRIMINAL CODE   (3/1/31) Columbia   D: Howard Hawks
C: Walter Huston, Phillips Holmes, Constance Cummings
Sound/100M
PP: 23/9/1930–10/11/1930

11. SCARFACE   (9/4/32) United Artists   D: Howard Hawks
C: Paul Muni, Ann Dvorak, Karen Morley
Sound/95M

NC: $711,379.92.    DG: $691,499.

12. THE CROWD ROARS    (16/4/32) Warner Bros.    D: Howard Hawks
C: James Cagney, Ann Dvorak, Joan Blondell
Sound/84M
NC: $265,000.    DG: $524,000.
FG: $245,000.    WWG: $769,000.    Profit = $261,750.

13. TIGER SHARK    (24/9/32) First National    D: Howard Hawks
C: Edward G. Robinson, Richard Arlen, Zeta Johann
Sound/80M
NC: $375,000.    DG: $436,000.
FG: $443,000.    WWG: $879,000.    Profit = $49,750.

14. TODAY WE LIVE    (21/4/33) M-G-M    D: Howard Hawks
C: Joan Crawford, Gary Cooper, Franchot Tone
Sound/10,300FT/114M
PP: 5/12/1932–3/3/1933
NC: $659,710.94.    DG: $590,000.
FG: $445,000.    WWG: $1,035,000.    Loss = $23,000.

15. THE PRIZEFIGHTER AND THE LADY    (10/11/33) M-G-M    D: Howard
Hawks, W. S. VanDyke
C: Max Baer, Sr., Primo Carnera, Myrna Loy
Sound/9,345FT/104M
PP: 17/8/1933–29/9/1933
NC: $680,084.73.    DG: $432,000.
FG: $501,000.    WWG: $933,000.    Loss = $105,000.

16. VIVA VILLA!    (27/4/34) M-G-M    D: Howard Hawks/Jack Conway
C: Wallace Beery, Leo Carrillo, Fay Wray
Sound/10,284FT/114M
PP: 30/10/1933–12/1/1934
NC: $1,017,400.33.    DG: $941,000.
FG: $934,000.    WWG: $1,875,000.    Profit = $87,000.

17. TWENTIETH CENTURY    (11/5/34) Columbia    D: Howard Hawks
C: John Barrymore, Carole Lombard, Walter Connolly
Sound/91M
PP: 22/2/1934–24/3/1934 DG: $308,000.

18. BARBARY COAST    (27/9/35) Goldwyn-United Artists    D: Howard Hawks
C: Miriam Hopkins, Edward G. Robinson, Joel McCrea
Sound/90M
NC: $778,468.92.    DG: $851,620.
FG: $429,489.    WWG: $1,281,109.    Profit = $82,363.

19. CEILING ZERO    (25/1/36) First National    D: Howard Hawks
C: James Cagney, Pat O'Brien, June Travis
Sound/95M
NC: $448,000.    DG: $926,000.
FG: $331,000.    WWG: $1,257,000.    Profit = $294,750.

20. SUTTER'S GOLD    (11/4/36) Universal    D: James Cruze
C: Edward Arnold, Lee Tracy, Binnie Barnes
Sound/95M
BUD: $693,750.    NC: $785,068.69.
[Hawks was hired to direct this film for a flat fee of $10,000, but he did not actually direct.

He also received $20,000 for work on the script. Gene Fowler and William Faulkner also worked on the script, for which Fowler was paid $22,500 and Faulkner $2,000. The final credits read Jack Kirkland (paid $7,150), Walter Woods (paid $3,275), and George O'Neil (paid $7,250).]

21. THE ROAD TO GLORY   (4/9/36) 20th-Fox   D: Howard Hawks
C: Fredric March, Warner Baxter, Lionel Barrymore
Sound/101M

22. COME AND GET IT   (13/11/36) Goldwyn-United Artists   D: Howard Hawks
C: Edward Arnold, Joel McCrea, Frances Farmer
Sound/99M
NC: $1,291,934.27.   DG: $876,436.
FG: $439,658.   WWG: $1,316,094.   Loss = $454,863.

23. BRINGING UP BABY   (18/2/38) RKO   D: Howard Hawks
C: Katharine Hepburn, Cary Grant, Charles Ruggles
Sound/102M
PP: 23/9/1937–6/1/1938
NC: $1,074,543.   DG: $715,000.
FG: $394,000.   WWG: $1,109,000.   Loss = $365,000.

24. ONLY ANGELS HAVE WINGS   (25/5/39) Columbia   D: Howard Hawks
C: Cary Grant, Jean Arthur, Richard Barthelmess
Sound/121M
PP: 20/12/1938–24/3/1939   DG: $980,000.

25. HIS GIRL FRIDAY   (18/1/40) Columbia   D: Howard Hawks
C: Cary Grant, Rosalind Russell, Ralph Bellamy
Sound/92M
PP: 27/9/1939–21/11/1939   DG: $1,057,000.

26. SERGEANT YORK   (27/9/41) Warner Bros.   D: Howard Hawks, Sam Woods
C: Gary Cooper, Walter Brennan, Joan Leslie
Sound/134M
NC: $2,393,000.   DG: $6,120,885.
FG: $2,653,000.   WWG: $8,773,885.   Profit = $3,687,413.

27. BALL OF FIRE   (9/1/42) Goldwyn-RKO   D: Howard Hawks
C: Gary Cooper, Barbara Stanwyck, Oscar Homolka
Sound/111M
NC: $800,000.   DG: $1,856,000.
FG: $785,000.   WWG: $2,641,000.   Profit = $1,030,750.

28. THE OUTLAW   (5/2/43) Howard Hughes   D: Howard Hawks/Howard Hughes
C: Jane Russell, Walter Huston, Jack Buetel
Sound/121M
BUD: $1,250,000.
[The original release length was 121M. When it was released a second time on 8 February 1946 at 116M by United Artists, it had a DG: $3,050,000.   FG: $1,149,904.   WWG: $4,199,904. When it was released a third time on 11 February 1950 at 103M by RKO, it had a DG: $1,960,000.]

29. AIR FORCE   (20/3/43) Warner Bros.   D: Howard Hawks
C: John Garfield, Gig Young, Harry Carey, Sr.
Sound/124M
NC: $2,646,000.   DG: $2,616,000.
FG: $1,513,000.   WWG: $4,129,000.   Profit = $150,000.

30. TO HAVE AND HAVE NOT    (20/1/45) Warner Bros.    D: Howard Hawks
    C: Humphrey Bogart, Lauren Bacall, Walter Brennan
    Sound/100M
    NC: $1,664,307.    DG: $3,652,000.
    FG: $1,605,000.    WWG: $5,257,000.    Profit = $1,778,443.

31. THE BIG SLEEP    (31/8/46) Warner Bros.    D: Howard Hawks
    C: Humphrey Bogart, Lauren Bacall, Martha Vickers
    Sound/114M
    NC: $1,561,563.    DG: $3,493,000.
    FG: $1,346,000.    WWG: $4,839.000.    Profit = $1,567,687.

32. RED RIVER    (17/9/48) United Artists    D: Howard Hawks
    C: John Wayne, Montgomery Clift, Joanne Dru
    Sound/11,422FT/127M
    NC: $2,800,000.    DG: $3,976,474.    FG: $1,300,000.    WWG: $5,276,474.
    [When RED RIVER was rereleased on 6 June 1952, it had a DG: $485,459.    FG: $691,210.    WWG: $1,176,669.]

33. A SONG IS BORN    (6/11/48) RKO    D: Howard Hawks
    C: Danny Kaye, Virginia Mayo, Benny Goodman
    Sound/Technicolor/113M
    NC: $2,800,000.    DG: $2,400,000.

34. I WAS A MALE WAR BRIDE    (9/49) 20th-Fox    D: Howard Hawks
    C: Cary Grant, Ann Sheridan, William Neff
    Sound/105M
    NC: $3,330,000.    DG: $4,036,948.

35. THE BIG SKY    (8/52) RKO    D: Howard Hawks
    C: Kirk Douglas, Elizabeth Threatt, Dewey Martin
    Sound/122M
    PP: 25/7/1951–12/11/1951    DG: $1,650,000.

36. O. HENRY'S FULL HOUSE (Ransom of Red Chief)    (9/52) 20th-Fox    D: Howard Hawks
    C: Fred Allen, Oscar Levant, Lee Aaker
    Sound/117M
    NC: $945,000.    DG: $883,323.
    [Other episodes were directed by Henry Koster, Henry Hathaway, Jean Negulesco, and Henry King.]

37. MONKEY BUSINESS    (9/52) 20th-Fox    D: Howard Hawks
    C: Cary Grant, Ginger Rogers, Charles Coburn
    Sound/97M
    NC: $1,615,000.    DG: $1,882,544.

38. GENTLEMEN PREFER BLONDES    (8/53) 20th-Fox    D: Howard Hawks
    C: Marilyn Monroe, Jane Russell, Charles Coburn
    Sound/Technicolor/Cinemascope/91M
    NC: $2,260,000.    DG: $4,744,374.

39. LAND OF THE PHARAOHS    (2/7/55) Warner Bros.    D: Howard Hawks
    C: Jack Hawkins, Joan Collins, Dewey Martin
    Sound/Warnercolor/Cinemascope/105M
    NC: $3,150,000.    DG: $2,044,000.
    FG: $2,685,000.    WWG: $4,729,000.    Loss = $1,003,250.

40. RIO BRAVO    (4/4/59) Warner Bros.    D: Howard Hawks

C: John Wayne, Dean Martin, Ricky Nelson
Sound/Technicolor/141M
NC: $3,061,000.   DG: $5,498,000.
FG: $4,550,000.   WWG: $10,048,000.   Profit = $3,000,000.

41. HATARI!   (20/6/62) Paramount   D: Howard Hawks
C: John Wayne, Elsa Martinelli, Hardy Kruger
Sound/Technicolor/149M
DG: $7,000,000.

42. MAN'S FAVORITE SPORT   (29/1/64) Universal   D: Howard Hawks
C: Rock Hudson, Paula Prentiss, Maria Perschy
Sound/Technicolor/10,796FT/120M
DG: $2,351,173.

43. RED LINE 7000   (9/11/65) Paramount   D: Howard Hawks
C: Gail Hire, James Caan, Laura Devon
Sound/Technicolor/110M
DG: $1,946,000.

44. EL DORADO   (7/6/67) Paramount   D: Howard Hawks
C: John Wayne, Robert Mitchum, Charlene Holt
Sound/Technicolor/126M
DG: $5,424,742.

45. RIO LOBO   (16/12/70) National General   D: Howard Hawks
C: John Wayne, Mike Henry, Bill Williams
Sound/Technicolor/114M
DG: $4,460,117.

## Credits as Producer

1. CORVETTE K-225   (1/10/43) Universal   D: Richard Rosson
C: Randolph Scott, Noah Beery, Jr., Ella Raines
Sound/8,861FT/98M
BUD: $736,670.   NC: $1,031,630.   DG: $1,000,000.

2. THE THING   (4/51) RKO   D: Christian Nyby
C: Kenneth Tobey, Margaret Sherman, James Arness
Sound/87M
PP: 25/10/1950–3/3/1951   DG: $1,950,000.

# JOHN HUSTON

## Acting Credits

1. TWO AMERICANS   (22/6/29) Paramount   D: Joseph Santley
Silent/2R

2. THE CARDINAL   (12/12/63) Columbia   D: Otto Preminger
Sound/Technicolor/Panavision/175M

3. CANDY   (17/12/68) Cinerama   D: Christian Marquand
Sound/Technicolor/126M

4. DE SADE   (27/8/69) American-International   D: Cy Enfield
Sound/Pathé Color/113M

5. MYRA BRECKINRIDGE    (23/6/70) 20th-Fox    D: Michael Sarne
Sound/Deluxe Color/Panavision/94M

6. THE OTHER SIDE OF THE WIND    Unreleased/Unfinished    D: Orson Welles
Sound/Eastman Color
[Production on this film without a script began in 1970 and continued sporadically through 1984 at which time Welles surrendered the negative, the film incomplete. Filming commenced on 23 August and fourteen years later the cost was at least $750,000.]

7. THE BRIDGE IN THE JUNGLE    (1971) United Artists    D: Pancho Kohner
Sound/Color/86M
[This film was unreleased theatrically. Very limited release occurred in 16mm and it had a foreign television gross of $74,000.]

8. THE DESERTER    (7/4/71) Paramount    D: Burt Kennedy
Sound/Technicolor/Panavision/99M

9. MAN IN THE WILDERNESS    (11/71) Warner Bros.    D: Richard C. Sarafian
Sound/Technicolor/105M

10. BATTLE FOR THE PLANET OF THE APES    (6/73) 20th-Fox    D: J. Lee Thompson
Sound/Deluxe Color/Panavision/86M

11. CHINATOWN    (20/6/74) Paramount    D: Roman Polanski
Sound/Technicolor/Panavision/131M

12. BREAKOUT    (5/75) Columbia    D: Tom Greis
Sound/Eastman Color/96M

13. THE WIND AND THE LION    (22/5/75) M-G-M/United Artists    D: John Milius
Sound/Color/Cinemascope/119M

14. SHERLOCK HOLMES IN NEW YORK    (18/10/76) 20th-Fox/NBC    D: Boris Sagal
Sound/Color/100M
[This film was made for television.]

15. TENTACLES    (25/2/77) American-International    D: Oliver Hellman
Sound/Color/90M

16. THE RHINEMAN EXCHANGE    (10,17,24/3/77) Universal/NBC    D: Burt Kennedy
Sound/Color/250M
[A television mini-series.]

17. ANGELA    (4/78) Embassy    D: Boris Sagal
Sound/Pathé Color/91M

18. THE WORD    (12–15/11/78) Charles Fries    D: Richard Lang
Sound/Color/400M
[A television mini-series.]

19. WINTER KILLS    (18/5/79) Avco-Embassy    D: William Richert
Sound/Color/Panavision/97M

20. JAGUAR LIVES!    (31/8/79) American-International    D: Ernest Pintoff
Sound/90M

21. THE VISITOR    (10/79) International    D: Michael J. Paradise
Sound/Color/90M

22. THE BIGGEST BATTLE  (1979)  D: ?
[A French film, also known as THE GREATEST BATTLE.]

23. HEAD ON  (1979) Summa Vista  D: Michael Grant
Sound/98M

24. THE RETURN OF THE KING  (1980)  D: ?
[This film was made for television.]

25. CANNERY ROW  (12/2/82) M-G-M United Artists  D: David S. Ward
[Huston Narrated this film]
Sound/Metrocolor/120M

26. LOVESICK  (18/2/83) Warner Bros.  D: Marshall Brickman
Sound/Technicolor/97M

27. A MINOR MIRACLE  (26/8/83) Jensen Farley  D: Terrell Pannen
Sound/Color/?

28. MOMO  (3/87)  D: Johannes Schaaf
Sound/Color/100M
[This was an Italian/West German co-production.]

29. MR. CORBETT'S GHOST  (date unknown)  D: Danny Huston
Sound/Color/?

## Writing Credits

1. A HOUSE DIVIDED  (5/12/31) Universal  D: William Wyler
C: Walter Huston, Helen Chandler, Vivian Oakland
Sound/70M
[WT: HEART AND HAND. John Huston worked on the dialogue.]

2. LAW AND ORDER  (7/2/32)Universal  D: Edward L. Cahn
C: Walter Huston, Harry Carey, Russell Hopton
Sound/73M
[John Huston worked on the adaptation and the dialogue.]

3. MURDERS IN THE RUE MORGUE  (21/2/32) Universal  D: Robert Florey
C: Bela Lugosi, Sidney Fox, Bert Roach
Sound/61M
[John Huston worked on the dialogue.]

4. JEZEBEL  (26/3/38) Warner Bros.  D: William Wyler
C: Bette Davis, Henry Fonda, George Brent
Sound/104M
[Screenplay by Clement Ripley, Abem Finkel, and John Huston. Between this film and MURDERS IN THE RUE MORGUE, Huston may have contributed in some form to the two British films, DEATH DRIVES THROUGH (Gaumont-British, 1935) and RHODES OF AFRICA (Gaumont-British, 1936).]

5. THE AMAZING DR. CLITTERHOUSE  (30/7/38) First National  D: Anatole Litvak
C: Edward G. Robinson, Claire Trevor, Humphrey Bogart
Sound/87M
[Screenplay by John Wexley and John Huston.]

6. JUAREZ  (10/6/39) Warner Bros.  D: William Dieterle
C: Paul Muni, Bette Davis, Brian Aherne
Sound/127M

[Screenplay by John Huston, Aeneas MacKenzie, and Wolfgang Reinhardt.]

7. THE STORY OF DR. EHRLICH'S MAGIC BULLET    (2/3/40) Warner Bros.    D: William Dieterle
    C: Edward G. Robinson, Ruth Gordon, Otto Kruger
    Sound/103M
    [Screenplay by John Huston, Heinz Herald, and Norman Burnside. Between JUAREZ and this film, John Huston may have contributed in some way to the film WUTHERING HEIGHTS (Goldwyn-United Artists, 1939).]

8. HIGH SIERRA    (25/1/41) First National    D: Raoul Walsh
    C: Ida Lupino, Humphrey Bogart, Alan Curtis
    Sound/100M
    [Screenplay by John Huston and W.R. Burnett.]

9. SERGEANT YORK    (27/9/41) Warner Bros.    D: Howard Hawks, Sam Woods
    C: Gary Cooper, Walter Brennan, Joan Leslie
    Sound/134M
    [Screenplay by Abem Finkel, Harry Chandlee, Howard Koch, and John Huston.]

10. THE STRANGER    (25/5/46) RKO    D: Orson Welles
    C: Edward G. Robinson, Loretta Young, Orson Welles
    Sound/85M
    [Anthony Veiller was credited with the screenplay although both John Huston and Orson Welles also worked on it.]

11. THREE STRANGERS    (16/2/46) Warner Bros.    D: Jean Negulesco
    C: Sydney Greenstreet, Geraldine Fitzgerald, Peter Lorre
    Sound/92M
    [Screenplay by John Huston and Howard Koch.]

12. THE KILLERS    (30/8/46) Universal    D: Robert Siodmak
    C: Ava Gardner, Edmond O'Brien, Burt Lancaster
    Sound/9,206FT/102M
    [Anthony Veiller was credited with the screenplay although John Huston also worked on it.]

13. MR. NORTH    (22/7/88) Goldwyn    D: Danny Huston
    C: Anthony Edwards, Robert Mitchum, James Costigan
    Sound/Metrocolor/92M
    [Screenplay by Janet Roach, John Huston, and James Costigan. Huston also contributed without credit to Tony Huston's screenplay REVENGE (Columbia, 1989).]

## Directing Credits

1. THE MALTESE FALCON    (18/10/41) Warner Bros.    D: John Huston
    C: Humphrey Bogart, Mary Astor, Gladys George
    Sound/100M
    NC: $375,000.    DG: $967,000.
    FG: $805,000.    WWG: $1,772,000.    Profit = $854,000.
    [John Huston was credited with the screenplay.]

2. IN THIS OUR LIFE    (16/5/42) Warner Bros.    D: John Huston
    C: Bette Davis, Olivia DeHavilland, George Brent
    Sound/97M
    NC: $713,000.    DG: $1,651,000.
    FG: $1,143,000.    WWG: $2,794,000.    Profit = $1,282,500.

3. ACROSS THE PACIFIC    (5/9/42) Warner Bros.    D: John Huston/Vincent Sherman

C: Humphrey Bogart, Mary Astor, Sydney Greenstreet
Sound/97M
NC: $576,000.   DG: $1,381,000.
FG: $994,000.   WWG: $2,375,000.   Profit = $1,105,250.

4. REPORT FROM THE ALEUTIANS   (30/7/43) U.S. Signal Corps   D: John Huston
Sound/Technicolor/47M
[John Huston also wrote the narration which was read by Walter Huston.]

5. BATTLE OF SAN PIETRO   (3/5/45) U.S. Signal Corps   D: John Huston
Sound/30M
[John Huston also wrote and read the narration.]

6. LET THERE BE LIGHT   (1/81) U.S. Signal Corps   D: John Huston
[Charles Kaufman and John Huston wrote the narration which was read by Walter Huston. Technically, although this film was made available for public viewing in 1981, it has never been officially released.]
Sound/60M

7. THE TREASURE OF THE SIERRA MADRE   (24/1/48) Warner Bros.   D: John Huston
C: Humphrey Bogart, Walter Huston, Tim Holt
Sound/126M
NC: $2,474,000.   DG: $2,746,000.
FG: $1,349,000.   WWG: $4,095,000.   Profit = $397,250.
[John Huston was credited for the screenplay and also had a cameo role.]

8. KEY LARGO   (31/7/48) Warner Bros.   D: John Huston
C: Humphrey Bogart, Edward G. Robinson, Lauren Bacall
Sound/101M
NC: $1,763,000.   DG: $3,219,000.
FG: $1,150,000.   WWG: $4,369,000.   Profit = $1,313,750.
[Screenplay by John Huston and Richard Brooks. Between THE TREASURE OF THE SIERRA MADRE and this film, John Huston contributed as a director but without credit to the film ON OUR MERRY WAY (United Artists, 1948) which credited directors King Vidor, Leslie Fenton, and George Stevens.]

9. WE WERE STRANGERS   (5/49) Columbia   D: John Huston
C: Jennifer Jones, John Garfield, Pedro Armendariz
Sound/106M
PP: 30/8/1948–26/10/1948   DG: over $900,000.   DG: $1,361,000.
[Screenplay by John Huston and Peter Viertel. John Huston also had a cameo role.]

10. THE ASPHALT JUNGLE   (2/6/50) M-G-M   D: John Huston
C: Sterling Hayden, Louis Calhern, Jean Hagen
Sound/10,086FT/112M
PP: 25/10/1949–21/12/1949   NC: $1,232,000.   DG: $1,325,000.
FG: $1,065,000.   WWG: $2,390,000.   Profit = $180,000.
[Screenplay by John Huston and Ben Maddow.]

11. THE RED BADGE OF COURAGE   (28/9/51) M-G-M   D: John Huston
C: Audie Murphy, Bill Mauldin, John Dierkes
Sound/6,203FT/69M
PP: 25/8/1950–11/10/1950   NC: $1,673,000.   DG: $790,000.
FG: $295,000.   WWG: $1,085,000.   Loss = $1,014,000.
[Screenplay by John Huston.]

12. THE AFRICAN QUEEN   (21/3/52) United Artists   D: John Huston
C: Humphrey Bogart, Katharine Hepburn, Robert Morley
Sound/Technicolor/104M
[Screenplay by John Huston and James Agee.] DG: $4,130,000.

13. MOULIN ROUGE   (6/3/53) United Artists   D: John Huston
C: Jose Ferrer, Colette Marchand, Suzanne Flon
Sound/Technicolor/118M
NC: $1,500,000.   DG: $4,245,000.
[Screenplay by Anthony Veiller and John Huston.]

14. BEAT THE DEVIL   (6/3/54) United Artists   D: John Huston
C: Humphrey Bogart, Jennifer Jones, Gina Lollobrigida
Sound/82M
NC: over $1,000,000.   DG: $975,000.
FG: $155,000.   WWG: $1,130,000.
[Screenplay by John Huston and Truman Capote with Anthony Veiller and Peter Viertel.]

15. MOBY DICK   (30/6/56) Warner Bros.   D: John Huston
C: Gregory Peck, Richard Basehart, Leo Glenn
Sound/Technicolor/116M
NC: $4,200,000.   DG: $4,718,000.
FG: $2,601,000.   WWG: $7,319,000.   Profit = $989,250.
[Screenplay by John Huston and Ray Bradbury.]

16. HEAVEN KNOWS, MR. ALLISON   (3/57) 20th-Fox   D: John Huston
C: Deborah Kerr, Robert Mitchum
Sound/Color/Cinemascope/107M
NC: $2,905,000.   DG: $3,624,000.
[Screenplay by John Huston and John Lee Mahin.]

17. THE BARBARIAN AND THE GEISHA   (10/58) 20th-Fox   D: John Huston
C: John Wayne, Eiko Ando, Sam Jaffe
Sound/Color/Cinemascope/104M
NC: $3,495,000.   DG: $1,416,000.

18. THE ROOTS OF HEAVEN   (11/58) 20th-Fox   D: John Huston
C: Errol Flynn, Juliette Greco, Eddie Albert
Sound/Color/Cinemascope/125M
NC: $3,300,000.   DG: $942,000.

19. THE UNFORGIVEN   (16/4/60) United Artists   D: John Huston
C: Burt Lancaster, Audrey Hepburn, Audie Murphy
Sound/Color/Panavision/125M
NC: $5,000,000.   DG: $2,423,000.
FG: $4,340,000.   WWG: $6,763,000.

20. THE MISFITS   (1/2/61) United Artists   D: John Huston
C: Clark Gable, Marilyn Monroe, Montgomery Clift
Sound/124M
NC: $4,000,000.   DG: $3,905,000.
FG: $1,945,000.   WWG: $5,850,000.

21. FREUD   (12/12/62) Universal   D: John Huston
C: Montgomery Clift, Susannah York, Larry Parks
Sound/10,807FT/120M
DG: $664,000.

22. THE LIST OF ADRIAN MESSENGER   (29/5/63) Universal   D: John Huston

C: George C. Scott, Dana Wynter, Clive Brook
Sound/8,820FT/98M
NC: $3,000,000.   DG: $1,559,000.

23. THE NIGHT OF THE IGUANA   (10/7/64) M-G-M   D: John Huston
C: Richard Burton, Ava Gardner, Deborah Kerr
Sound/Cinemascope/10,576FT/117M
NC: $3,232,000.   DG: $4,350,000.
FG: $2,550,000.   WWG: $6,900,000.   Profit = $340,000.
[Screenplay by John Huston and Anthony Veiller.]

24. THE BIBLE   (28/9/66) 20th-Fox   D: John Huston
C: Michael Parks, Ulla Bergryd, Richard Harris
Sound/Deluxe Color/175M
NC: $18,000,000.   DG: $13,406,000.
[John Huston also acted the role of Moses and was the voice of God.]

25. CASINO ROYALE   (28/4/67) Columbia   D: John Huston
C: David Niven, Peter Sellers, Ursula Andress
Sound/Technicolor/Panavision/130M
NC: $12,000,000.   DG: $10,200,000.
[Other directors who collaborated on this picture were Ken Hughes, Val Guest, Robert Parrish, and Joe McGarth.]

26. REFLECTIONS IN A GOLDEN EYE   (11/10/67) Warner Bros.   D: John Huston
C: Elizabeth Taylor, Marlon Brando, Brian Keith
Sound/Technicolor/Panavision/109M
DG: $2,867,000.

27. SINFUL DAVEY   (5/3/69) United Artists   D: John Huston
C: John Hurt, Pamela Franklin, Nigel Davenport
Sound/Deluxe Color/Cinemascope/94M
NC: $3,000,000.   DG: $172,000.
FG: $449,000.   WWG: $621,000.   Loss = $3,100,000.

28. A WALK WITH LOVE AND DEATH   (5/10/69) 20th-Fox   D: John Huston
C: Anjelica Huston, Assaf Dayan, Anthony Corlan
Sound/Deluxe Color/90M
DG: $112,000.

29. THE KREMLIN LETTER   (1/2/71) 20th-Fox   D: John Huston
C: Bibi Andersson, Richard Boone, Dean Jagger
Sound/Deluxe Color/Panavision/113M
DG: $837,000.
[Screenplay by John Huston and Gladys Hill.]

30. THE LAST RUN   (30/6/71) M-G-M   D: John Huston/Richard Fleischer
C: George C. Scott, Tony Musante, Trish Van Devere
Sound/Metrocolor/Panavision/95M
NC: $1,842,000.   DG: $2,108,000.
FG: $1,163,000.   WWG: $3,271,000.   Loss = $807,000.
[Filming began in Spain on 4 January 1971 with Huston directing. On 18 January 1971 Huston, Tina Aumont, who had been cast as the leading lady, and several crew members left the set. Huston was replaced.]

31. FAT CITY   (2/72) Columbia   D: John Huston
C: Stacy Keach, Jeff Bridges, Candy Clark
Sound/Color/100M

DG: $500,000.

32. THE LIFE AND TIMES OF JUDGE ROY BEAN    (12/72) National General    D:
John Huston
C: Paul Newman, Ava Gardner, Victoria Principal
Sound/Color/120M
NC: $4,000,000.    DG: $6,166,000.    [John Huston had a cameo role.]

33. THE MACKINTOSH MAN    (8/73) Warner Bros.    D: John Huston
C: Paul Newman, Dominique Sanda, James Mason
Sound/Technicolor/105M
DG: $2,064,477.

34. THE MAN WHO WOULD BE KING    (12/75) Allied Artists    D: John Huston
C: Sean Connery, Michael Caine, Christopher Plummer
Sound/Technicolor/Panavision/129M
BUD: $8,000,000. DG: $6,500,000.
[Screenplay by Gladys Hill and John Huston.]

35. INDEPENDENCE    (1976) 20th-Fox    D: John Huston
C: William Atherton, Pat Hingle, Ken Howard
Sound/Eastman Color/Panavision/28M
[A special film made for the National Park Service and shown thirty-two times a day at two
specially built theatres in Independence Hall, Philadelphia.]

36. WISE BLOOD    (17/2/80) New Line Cinema    D: John Huston
C: Brad Dourif, Ned Beatty, Harry Dean Stanton
Sound/Color/108M
BUD: $2,000,000.
[Between INDEPENDENCE and this film, John Huston was signed to direct LOVE AND
BULLETS (A.F.D., 1979) starring Charles Bronson, but he was hospitalized and Stuart
Rosenberg directed it instead. John Huston had a cameo role in WISE BLOOD.]

37. PHOBIA    (26/9/80) Paramount    D: John Huston
C: Paul Michael Glaser, John Colicos, Susan Hogan
Sound/Color/94M
DG: $21,000.

38. VICTORY    (31/7/81) Paramount    D: John Huston
C: Michael Caine, Sylvester Stallone, Pele
Sound/Metrocolor/Panavision/117M
DG: $4,176,000.

39. ANNIE    (21/5/82) Columbia    D: John Huston
C: Albert Finney, Aileen Quinn, Carol Burnett
Sound/Metrocolor/Panavision/128M
NC: $51,000,000.    DG: $37,240,000.

40. UNDER THE VOLCANO    (13/6/84) Universal    D: John Huston
C: Albert Finney, Jacqueline Bisset, Anthony Andrews
Sound/Technicolor/112M
DG: $1,402,000.

41. PRIZZI'S HONOR    (14/6/85) 20th-Fox    D: John Huston
C: Jack Nicholson, Anjelica Huston, Kathleen Turner
Sound/Deluxe Color/Panavision/129M
DG: $13,652,000.

42. THE DEAD    (17/12/87) Vestron    D: John Huston

Sound/Color/83M
DG: $1,589,000

# ORSON WELLES

## Acting Credits

1. SWISS FAMILY ROBINSON   (16/2/40) RKO   D: Edward Ludwig
   Sound/91M
   [Welles was the narrator.]

2. JANE EYRE   (2/44) 20th-Fox   D: Robert Stevenson
   Sound/96M

3. FOLLOW THE BOYS   (5/5/44) Universal   D: Edward Sutherland
   Sound/122M
   [Welles appeared as himself.]

4. TOMORROW IS FOREVER   (20/2/46) RKO   D: Irving Pichel
   Sound/105M

5. DUEL IN THE SUN   (30/12/46) Selznick   D: King Vidor
   Sound/Technicolor/126M
   [Welles was the narrator.]

6. BLACK MAGIC   (19/8/49) United Artists   D: Gregory Ratoff
   Sound/105M

7. PRINCE OF FOXES   (12/49) 20th-Fox   D: Henry King
   Sound/107M

8. THE THIRD MAN   (1/50) Eagle Lion   D: Carol Reed
   Sound/108M

9. THE BLACK ROSE   (9/50) 20th-Fox   D: Henry Hathaway
   Sound/Technicolor/120M

10. THE LITTLE WORLD OF DON CAMILLO   (13/1/53) Rizzoli/Amato/IFE
    Releasing   D: Julien Duvivier
    Sound/96M
    [Welles was the narrator.]

11. L'UMO, LA BESTIA E LA VIRTÙ   (1953)   D: Steno (Stefano Vanzina)

12. TRENT'S LAST CASE   (1/1/54) Republic   D: Herbert Wilcox
    Sound/90M

13. RETURN TO GLENASCUAL   (2/54) Mayer-Kingsley   D: Hilton Edwards
    Sound/26M

14. TROUBLE IN THE GLEN   (1/12/54) Republic   D: Herbert Wilcox
    Sound/Trucolor/91M

15. OUT OF DARKNESS   (1955)   D: Albert Wassermann
    [Welles was the narrator of this documentary.]

16. THREE CASES OF MURDER   (3/55) Associate Artists   D: George More
    O'Ferrall
    Sound/99M

17. SI VERSAILLES M'ETAIT CONTE   (3/55) Times   D: Sacha Guitry

Sound/Technicolor/152M

18. NAPOLEON   (5/4/55) Cinedis   D: Sacha Guitry
Sound/190M

19. MOBY DICK   (30/6/56) Warner Bros.   D: John Huston
Sound/Technicolor/116M

20. MAN IN THE SHADOW   (1/58) Universal   D: Jack Arnold
Sound/Cinemascope/80M

21. THE LONG HOT SUMMER   (3/58) 20th-Fox   D: Martin Ritt
Sound/Deluxe Color/Cinemascope/113M

22. THE VIKINGS   (28/6/58) United Artists   D: Richard Fleischer
Sound/Deluxe Color/116M

23. SOUTH SEAS ADVENTURE   (16/7/58) Stanley Warner   D: Francis D. Lyon
Sound/Technicolor/Cinerama/120M
[Welles was the narrator.]

24. THE ROOTS OF HEAVEN   (11/58) 20th-Fox   D: John Huston
Sound/Deluxe Color/Cinemascope/131M

25. LES SEIGNEURS DE LA FORÊT   (1959) Belgian   D: Heinz Sielmann/Henry Brandt
Sound/Deluxe Color/Cinemascope/88M
[Welles was the narrator along with William Warfield. The film was released in the U.S. by 20th-Fox under the title MASTERS OF THE CONGO JUNGLE in May, 1960.]

26. HIGH JOURNEY   (1959) French   D: Peter Baylis
[Welles was the narrator.]

27. COMPULSION   (4/59) 20th-Fox   D: Richard Fleischer
Sound/Cinemascope/103M

28. CRACK IN THE MIRROR   (5/60) 20th-Fox   D: Richard Fleischer
Sound/Cinemascope/97M

29. AUSTERLITZ   (28/6/60) French/Lux   D: Abel Gance
Sound/Eastman Color/83M

30. FERRY TO HONG KONG   (22/2/61) 20th-Fox   D: Lewis Gilbert
Sound/Deluxe Color/Cinemascope/103M

31. DAVID AND GOLIATH   (4/61) Allied Artists   D: Richard Pottier/Ferdinando Baldi
Sound/Eastman Color/Totalscope/95M

32. KING OF KINGS   (11/10/61) M-G-M   D: Nicholas Ray
Sound/Technicolor/Technirama 70mm/161M
[Welles was the narrator.]

33. THE TARTARS   (20/6/62) M-G-M   D: Richard Thorpe
Sound/Technicolor/83M

34. DESORDE   (1962)   D: Jacques Baratier
[Welles narrated the English language version of this documentary short.]

35. DER GROSSER ATLANTIK   (1962) West German   D: Peter Baylis
[Welles narrated the English language version of this documentary released as RIVER OF THE OCEAN.]

36. LAFAYETTE   (10/4/63) Maco Film   D: Jean Dreville
Sound/Technicolor/Technirama 70mm/110M

37. ROGOPAG   (9/63) Italian   D: Pier Paolo Pasolini
Sound/125M

38. THE V.I.P.S   (13/9/63) M-G-M   D: Anthony Asquith
Sound/Metrocolor/Panavision/119M

39. THE FINEST HOURS   (10/64) Columbia   D: Peter Baylis
Sound/Color/114M
[Welles was the narrator of this documentary.]

40. MARCO THE MAGNIFICENT   (24/8/66) M-G-M   D: Denys de la Patelliere/
Noel Howard
Sound/Eastman Color/Franscope/101M

41. IS PARIS BURNING?   (10/11/66) Paramount   D: Rene Clement
Sound/Panavision/138M

42. A MAN FOR ALL SEASONS   (12/12/66) Columbia   D: Fred Zinnemann
Sound/Technicolor/120M

43. THE SAILOR FROM GIBRALTER   (24/4/67) Lopert   D: Tony Richardson
Sound/89M

44. CASINO ROYALE   (28/4/67) Columbia   D: Joseph McGrath/Val Guest/John
Huston/Ken Hughes/Robert Parrish
Sound/Color/Panavision/130M

45. A KING'S STORY   (24/5/67) Continental   D: Harry Booth
Sound/100M
[Welles was the narrator along with Flora Robson and Patrick Wymark of this documentary.]

46. KAMPF UM ROM   (1968)   D: Robert Siodmak

47. I'LL NEVER FORGET WHAT'S 'IS NAME   (22/6/68) Regional   D: Michael
Winner
Sound/Technicolor/99M

48. OEDIPUS THE KING   (21/12/68) Universal   D: Philip Saville
Sound/Technicolor/8,760FT/97M

49. BARBED WATER   (1969)   D: Adrian J. Wensley-Walker
[Welles was the narrator of this documentary.]

50. TWELVE PLUS ONE [UNA SU TREDICI]   (1969)   D: Nicolas Gessner

51. MICHAEL THE BRAVE [MIHAI VITEAZU]   (1969)   D: Sergiu Nicolaescu

52. HOUSE OF CARDS   (24/5/69) Universal   D: John Guillerman
Sound/Technicolor/98M

53. THE SOUTHERN STAR   (28/5/69) Columbia   D: Sidney Hayers
Sound/Technicolor/Techniscope/104M

54. UPON THIS ROCK   (1970)   D: Harry Rasky

55. TO BUILD A FIRE   (1970)   D: David Cobham
Sound/Color/approx. 30M
[Welles was the narrator of this documentary short.]

56. THE KREMLIN LETTER   (1/2/70) 20th-Fox   D: John Huston
Sound/Deluxe Color/Panavision/113M

57. START THE REVOLUTION WITHOUT ME   (4/2/70) Warner Bros.   D: Bud Yorkin
Sound/Technicolor/98M
[Welles was the narrator.]

58. CATCH–22   (24/6/70) Paramount   D: Mike Nichols
Sound/Technicolor/Panavision/121M

59. JULIUS CAESAR   (22/9/70)   D: Stuart Rosenburg
Sound/Color/117M

60. TO KILL A STRANGER   (1971)   D: Peter Collinson

61. SENTINELS OF SILENCE   (1971)   D: Robert Amran
[Welles was the narrator of this documentary.]

62. BATTLE OF NERETVA   (2/71) American International   D: Veljko Bulajic
Sound/Technicolor/Panavision/112M

63. WATERLOO   (31/3/71) Paramount   D: Sergei Bondarchuk
Sound/Technicolor/Panavision/123M

64. DIRECTED BY JOHN FORD   (15/9/71) Films, Inc.   D: Peter Bogdanovich
Sound/Color/95M
[Welles was the narrator of this documentary.]

65. A SAFE PLACE   (10/71) Columbia   D: Henry Jaglom
Sound/Color/94M

66. THE LAST ROMAN   (1972) Constantin   D: ?
Sound/Color/92M

67. THE CRUCIFIXION   (1972)   D: Robert Guenette
[Welles was the narrator of this documentary.]

68. LA DECADE PRODIGIEUSE [TEN DAYS' WONDER]   (4/72) Levitt-Pickman   D: Claude Chabrol
Sound/Technicolor/101M

69. MALPERTUIS   (9/5/72) United Artists   D: Harry Kumel
Sound/Color/110M

70. GET TO KNOW YOUR RABBIT   (6/72) Warner Bros.   D: Brian de Palma
Sound/Technicolor/93M

71. NECROMANCY   (8/72) Cinerama   D: Bert I. Gordon
Sound/Color/82M

72. THE CANTERBURY TALES   (2/9/72) United Artists   D: Pier Paolo Pasolini
Sound/Color/111M

73. TREASURE ISLAND   (10/72) National General   D: John Hough
Sound/Eastman Color/92M

74. SUTJESKA   (8/73) Yugoslavian   D: Stipe Delic
[Welles also received a credit for contributing to the screenplay for this film.]

75. BROTHER, CAN YOU SPARE A DIME?   (8/75)   D: Philippe Mora
Sound/106M
[Welles was the narrator of this documentary.]

76. BUGS BUNNY SUPERSTAR   (12/75) Hare Raising Films   D: Larry Jackson
Sound/Color/90M
[Welles was the narrator of this documentary.]

77. VOYAGE OF THE DAMNED   (2/77) Avco-Embassy   D: Stuart Rosenberg
Sound/Eastman Color/Panavision/155M

78. THE CHALLENGE   (10/77) New Line   D: Herbert Klein
Sound/Color/104M
[Welles was the narrator of this documentary.]

79. THE LATE GREAT PLANET EARTH   (12/77) Pacific International   D: Robert
Amram/Rolf Forsberg
Sound/Color/90M
[Welles was the narrator of this documentary along with Hal Lindsey.]

80. HOT TOMORROWS   (4/78) American Film Institute   D: Martin Brest
Sound/Color/73M

81. NEVER TRUST AN HONEST THIEF   (1979)   D: ?

82. THE MUPPET MOVIE   (6/79) Associated Film Distributors   D: James Frawley
Sound/Color/98M

83. BLOOD AND GUNS [VIVA LA REVOLUCION]   (11/79) Movietime   D: Giulio
Petroni
Sound/Color/96M

84. THE SECRET OF NIKOLA TESLE   (1980) Yugoslavian   D: Krsto Papio
Sound/Eastman Color/120M

85. THE SHAH OF IRAN   (1/80) British   D: Walter Ellaby
Sound/Color/111M
[Welles was the narrator of this documentary.]

86. THE MAN WHO SAW TOMORROW   (1/81) Warner Bros.   D: Robert Guenette
Sound/Technicolor/83M

87. HISTORY OF THE WORLD, PART I   (6/81) 20th-Fox   D: Mel Brooks
Sound/Deluxe Color/Panavision/93M
[Welles was the narrator.]

88. BUTTERFLY   (2/82) Analysis   D: Matt Cimber
Sound/Color/107M

89. GENOCIDE   (21/3/82) Simon Wiesenthal Center/United Artists Classics   D: Ar-
nold Schwartzman
Sound/B&W and Color/82M
[Welles was the narrator of this documentary along with Elizabeth Taylor.]

90. SLAPSTICK OF ANOTHER KIND   (3/84) International   D: Steven Paul
Sound/Metrocolor/87M

91. WHERE IS PARSIFAL?   (22/5/84) British   D: Henri Helman
Sound/Rankcolor/84M

92. THE MUPPETS TAKE MANHATTAN   (13/7/84) Tri-Star   D: Frank Oz
Sound/Color/94M

93. ORSON WELLES Á LA CINÉMATIQUE   (14/9/84) Cinématique Françiase   D:
Pierre-Andre Boutang
Sound/Color/97M
[An interview/discussion with Welles.]

94. ALMONDS AND RAISINS   (8/85) TeleCulture   D: Russ Karel
Sound/90M

[Welles was the narrator.]

95. THE TRANSFORMERS: THE MOVIE   (8/8/86) DeLaurentiis   D: Nelson Shin
Sound/Color/86M
[An animated feature.]

96. SOMEONE TO LOVE   (28/3/87) International Rainbow Pictures   D: Henry Jaglom
Sound/Deluxe Color/109M
[Welles appeared as himself.]

## Directing Credits

1. THE HEARTS OF AGE   (1934)   D: Orson Welles/William Vance
C: Orson Welles, Virginia Nicholson, William Vance
Silent/4M
[A short filmed in 16mm.]

2. TOO MUCH JOHNSON   (1938)   D: Orson Welles
C: Joseph Cotten, Virginia Nicholson, Edgar Barrier
Silent/40M
[Filmed segments in 16mm never shown but intended to accompany the stage production by this name.]

3. CITIZEN KANE   (1/5/41) RKO   D: Orson Welles
C: Orson Welles, Joseph Cotten, Dorothy Comingore
Sound/119M
PP: 30/7/1940–20/10/1940
BUD: $723,800.   NC: $839,727.   DG: $990,000.
FG: $290,000.   WWG: $1,280,000.   Loss = $154,000.
[Screenplay by Herman J. Mankiewicz and Orson Welles.]

4. THE MAGNIFICENT AMBERSONS   (10/7/42) RKO   D: Orson Welles
C: Joseph Cotten, Dolores Costello, Anne Baxter
Sound/88M
PP: 28/10/1941–22/1/1942
BUD: $853,950.   NC: $1,125,000.   DG: $648,000.
FG: $165,000.   WWG: $813,000.   Loss = $674,000.
[Screenplay by Orson Welles with additional scenes directed by Freddie Fleck and Robert Wise.]

5. JOURNEY INTO FEAR   (12/2/42) RKO   D: Norman Foster/Orson Welles
C: Joseph Cotten, Dolores Del Rio, Orson Welles
Sound/71M
PP: 6/1/1942–12/3/1942
NC: $602,000.   DG: $391,000.
FG: $213,000.   WWG: $604,000.   Loss = $195,000.

6. IT'S ALL TRUE   (1942)   Uncompleted/Unreleased   D: Orson Welles
C: Jesús Vasquez, Domingo Solera, José Olimpio "Jacre" Meira
PS: 8/2/1942
[The money lost on this venture, before Welles was taken off the project by RKO, was somewhere between $600,000 and $1,000,000. Taking the lower figure, at this point he had cost RKO $1,623,000.]

7. THE STRANGER   (25/5/46) International/RKO   D: Orson Welles
C: Edward G. Robinson, Loretta Young, Orson Welles
Sound/85M

DG: $2,000,000   FG: $935,000.   WWG: $2,935,000.

8. THE LADY FROM SHANGHAI   (14/4/48) Columbia   D: Orson Welles
C: Rita Hayworth, Orson Welles, Everett Sloane
Sound/87M
PP: 2/10/1946–11/3/1947   DG: $1,253,000.
[Screenplay by Orson Welles.]

9. MACBETH   (10/48)   D: Orson Welles
C: Orson Welles, Jeanette Nolan, Dan O'Herlihy
Sound/107M
BUD: $884,367.
[Screenplay by Orson Welles.]

10. OTHELLO   (3/12/55) United Artists   D: Orson Welles
C: Orson Welles, Michael MacLiammoir, Suzanne Cloutier
Sound/92M
DG: $40,000.   FG: $19,000.   WWG: $59,000.
[Screenplay by Orson Welles.]

11. MR. ARKADIN   (11/11/62)   D: Orson Welles
C: Orson Welles, Michael Redgrave, Patricia Medina
Sound/99M
[The reason this film appears here out of chronological sequence is that it was first released in Great Britain under the title CONFIDENTIAL REPORT on 11 August 1955 by Warner Bros., having been filmed in 1954. It took seven more years before Welles could interest an American distributor, probably because of the film's poor showing internationally. Screenplay by Orson Welles.]

12. TOUCH OF EVIL   (2/58)   D: Orson Welles
C: Charlton Heston, Janet Leigh, Orson Welles
Sound/8,573FT/95M
[Screenplay by Orson Welles.]

13. THE TRIAL   (20/2/63) Astor   D: Orson Welles
C: Anthony Perkins, Jeanne Moreau, Romy Schneider
Sound/118M
PP: 26/3/1962–2/6/1962
[Screenplay by Orson Welles.]

14. FALSTAFF   [CHIMES   AT   MIDNIGHT]   (2/67)   Peppercorn-Wormser-Saltzman   D: Orson Welles
C: Orson Welles, Jeanne Moreau, Keith Baxter
Sound/115M
BUD: $800,000.
[Screenplay by Orson Welles.]

15. THE IMMORTAL STORY   (8/69) Altura Films   D: Orson Welles
C: Orson Welles, Jeanne Moreau, Roger Coggio
Sound/Eastman Color/93M
[Screenplay by Orson Welles. This film, as FILMING OTHELLO listed below, is included among Welles' screen credits because while produced for television it did have theatrical release.]

16. F FOR FAKE   (2/77) Specialty Films   D: Orson Welles
C: Orson Welles, Oja Kodar, Elmyr de Hory
Sound/Color/90M

[Welles was the narrator and appeared as himself in this documentary on fakery. Screenplay by Orson Welles.]

17. FILMING OTHELLO    (7/79) Independent Images/Film Forum    D: Orson Welles
C: Orson Welles, Micheal MacLiammoir, Suzanne Cloutier
Sound/B&W and Color/90M
[Welles was the narrator and appeared as himself in this documentary on the making of his film. Screenplay by Orson Welles.]

## Writing Credits

[According to Welles, he wrote the Abraham episode for THE BIBLE (20th-Fox, 1966).]

## Uncompleted Films

[The following films were actually put into production at some point although they were never finished, as was also the case with IT'S ALL TRUE listed above.]

1. DON QUIXOTE    D: Orson Welles
C: Francisco Reiguera, Akim Tamiroff, Patty McCormack
[In production in 1955 and occasionally thereafter.]

2. THE DEEP    D: Orson Welles
C: Orson Welles, Jeanne Moreau, Laurence Harvey
[In production intermittently 1967–1969.]

3. THE OTHER SIDE OF THE WIND    D: Orson Welles
C: John Huston, Peter Bogdanovich, Joseph McBride
[Production began on 23 August 1970 and continued sporadically until 1984 when Welles was compelled to surrender the elements which had cost at that point approximately $750,000.]

## Television Shows

1. COLGATE THEATRE: FOUNTAIN OF YOUTH    (16/9/58) NBC    D: Orson Welles
C: Ben Jobin, Joi Lansing, Rick Jason
Sound/30M
[Welles spent thirty days, instead of the allotted ten, directing this pilot for Desilu and went seriously over budget with an expensive wrap party.]

# ROMAN POLANSKI

1. ROWER [THE BIKE]    Uncompleted/Unreleased    D: Roman Polanski
[A short film begun in Poland in 1955 photographed in color.]

2. ROZBIJEMY ZABAWE [BREAK UP THE DANCE]    (1957)    D: Roman Polanski
Sound
[Screenplay for this short film by Roman Polanski.]

3. TWO MEN AND A WARDROBE    (1958) Polish    D: Roman Polanski
C: Jakub Goldberg, Henryk Kluba, Roman Polanski
Sound/Color/15M
[Screenplay by Roman Polanski.]

4. WHEN ANGELS FALL    (1959) Polish    D: Roman Polanski

C: Barbara Kwiatkowska, Jakub Goldberg, Henryk Kluba
Sound/Black & White and Color/approximately 12M
[Screenplay by Roman Polanski.]

5. LAMPA [THE LAMP]   (1959) Polish   D: Roman Polanski
[Screenplay by Roman Polanski.]

6. THE FAT AND THE LEAN   (1961) French   D: Roman Polanski
C: André Katelbach, Roman Polanski
Sound/Color/16M
[Screenplay by Roman Polanski and Jean-Pierre Rousseau.]

7. MAMMALS   (1962)   D: Roman Polanski
C: Henryk Kluba, Michal Zolnierkiewicz, Roman Polanski
Sound/Color/11M
[Screenplay by Roman Polanski and Andrzej Kondratiuk.]

8. KNIFE IN THE WATER   (23/10/62) Contemporary   D: Roman Polanski
C: Leon Niemczyk, Jolanta Umecka, Zygmunt Malanowicz
Sound/8,460FT/94M
[Screenplay by Roman Polanski, Jerzy Skolimowksi, and Jakub Goldberg.]

9. THE MOST BEAUTIFUL SWINDLES IN THE WORLD (River of Dia-
monds)   (12/9/63) Jack Ellis   D: Roman Polanski/Ugo Gregoretti/Claude Chabrol/
Jean-Luc Goddard
C: Nicole Karen, Jan Teulings, Arnold Gelderman
Sound/90M
[The French title for this film was LES PLUS BELLES ESCROQUERIES DU MONDE (THE
MOST BEAUTIFUL SWINDLES IN THE WORLD), a four-part film. Screenplay for the
Polanski segment by Roman Polanski and Gérard Brach.]

10. REPULSION   (2/10/65) Royal Films   D: Roman Polanski
C: Catherine Deneuve, Ian Hendry, John Fraser
Sound/9,360FT/104M
[Screenplay by Roman Polanski and Gérard Brach.]

11. CUL-DE-SAC   (7/11/66) Sigma III   D: Roman Polanski
C: Donald Pleasence, Françoise Dorléac, Lionel Stander
Sound/9,990FT/111M
[Screenplay by Roman Polanski and Gérard Brach.]

12. THE FEARLESS VAMPIRE KILLERS, OR: PARDON ME, BUT YOUR TEETH
ARE IN MY NECK   (13/11/67) M-G-M   D: Roman Polanski
C: Jack MacGowran, Roman Polanski, Sharon Tate
Sound/Metrocolor/Panavision/98M
PP: 21/2/1966–29/7/1966   NC: $1,987,000.   DG: $398,000.
FG: $5,841,000.   TV: $569,000.   WWG: $6,808,000.   Profit = $2,053,000.
[Screenplay by Roman Polanski and Gérard Brach. The film was titled DANCE OF THE
VAMPIRES in foreign release and was uncut at 9,654FT/107M. Based on the FG figure
above contrasted with the DG for the cut version, the film was significantly more successful
in its uncut version.]

13. ROSEMARY'S BABY   (12/6/68) Paramount   D: Roman Polanski
C: Mia Farrow, John Cassavetes, Ruth Gordon
Sound/Technicolor/12,290FT/137M
DG: $13,814,000.
[Screenplay by Roman Polanski.]

14. MACBETH   (12/71) Columbia   D: Roman Polanski
C: John Finch, Francesca Annis, Martin Shaw
Sound/Color/140M
BUD: $3,000,000.   NC: $3,600,000.   DG: $345,000.
[Screenplay by Kenneth Tynan and Roman Polanski.]

15. WHAT?   (10/73) Avco-Embassy   D: Roman Polanski
C: Marcello Mastrioni, Sydne Rome, Hugh Griffith
Sound/Technicolor/112M
DG: $17,445.

16. CHINATOWN   (20/6/74) Paramount   D: Roman Polanski
C: Jack Nicholson, Faye Dunaway, John Huston
Sound/Technicolor/Panavision/131M
DG: $12,547,000.

17. THE TENANT [LE LOCATAIRE]   (20/6/76) Paramount   D: Roman Polanski
C: Roman Polanski, Isabelle Adjani, Shelley Winters
Sound/Eastman Color/124M
DG: $987,000.
[Screenplay by Roman Polanski and Gérard Brach.]

18. TESS   (12/12/80) Columbia   D: Roman Polanski
C: John Collin, Tony Church, Nastassia Kinski
Sound/Eastman Color/Panavision/170M
DG: $9,843,000.
[Screenplay by Roman Polanski and Gérard Brach.]

19. PIRATES   (18/7/86) Cannon   D: Roman Polanski
C: Walter Matthau, Cris Campion, Damien Thomas
Sound/Color/Panavision/124M
NC: $31,000,000.   DG: $600,000.
[Screenplay by Roman Polanski and Gérard Brach.]

20. FRANTIC   (26/2/88) Warner Bros.   D: Roman Polanski
C: Harrison Ford, Emmanuelle Seigner, Betty Buckley
Sound/Color/120M
PS: 21/4/87   NC: $17,000,000.   DG: $8,919,000.
[Screenplay by Roman Polanski and Gérard Brach.]

## SAM PECKINPAH

### Acting Credits

1. THE VISITOR   (10/79) International   D: Michael J. Paradise
Sound/Color/90M
[Paradise's real name is Giulio Paradisi.]

2. CHINA 9, LIBERTY 37   (30/11/84) Lorimar   D: Monte Hellman
Sound/Color/Cinemascope/105M
[This film was made in Italy in 1978.]

### Writing Credits

1. THE GLORY GUYS   (7/7/65) United Artists   D: Arnold Laven
C: Tom Tyron, Harve Presnell, Senta Berger
Sound/Color/Cinemascope/112M

DG: $568,000.   FG: $1,574,000.   WWG: $2,142,000.
[Screenplay by Sam Peckinpah.]

2. VILLA RIDES   (29/5/68) Paramount   D: Buzz Kulick
C: Yul Brynner, Robert Mitchum, Grazia Buccella
Sound/Technicolor/125M
DG: $1,122,000.
[Screenplay by Robert Towne and Sam Peckinpah.]

## "Gopher" Credit

1. RIOT IN CELL BLOCK 11   (28/2/54) Allied Artists   D: Don Siegel
C: Neville Brand, Emile Meyer, Frank Faylen
Sound/80M

## Dialogue Director Credits

1. PRIVATE HELL 36   (9/54) Filmmakers   D: Don Siegel
C: Ida Lupino, Steve Cochran, Howard Duff
Sound/81M

2. AN ANNAPOLIS STORY   (10/4/55) Allied Artists   D: Don Siegel
C: John Derek, Diana Lynn, Kevin McCarthy
Sound/81M

3. INVASION OF THE BODY SNATCHERS   (5/2/56) Allied Artists   D: Don Siegel
C: Kevin McCarthy, Dana Wynter, Larry Gates
Sound/Superscope/80M

4. GREAT DAY IN THE MORNING   (16/5/56) RKO   D: Jacques Tourneur
C: Virginia Mayo, Robert Stack, Ruth Roman
Sound/Superscope/92M

5. CRIME IN THE STREETS   (10/6/56) Allied Artists   D: Don Siegel
C: James Whitmore, John Cassavetes, Sal Mineo
Sound/91M

## Second Unit Director Credit

6. JINXED   (22/10/82) United Artists   D: Don Siegel
C: Bette Midler, Ken Wahl, Rip Torn
Sound/Color/103M
BUD: $13,285,000.   NC: $13,767,000.   DG: $1,224,000.
FG: $128,000.   TV: $2,950,000.   WWG: $4,300,000.   Loss = $19,562,000.

## Directing Credits

7. THE DEADLY COMPANIONS   (6/6/61) Pathé-American   D: Sam Peckinpah
C: Maureen O'Hara, Brian Keith, Steve Cochran
Sound/Pathé Color/Panavision/90M
NC: $400,000.

8. RIDE THE HIGH COUNTRY   (9/5/62) M-G-M   D: Sam Peckinpah
C: Randolph Scott, Joel McCrea, Ronald Starr
Sound/Metrocolor/Cinemascope/8,562FT/94M
PP: 16/10/1961–21/11/1961   BUD: $768,000.   NC: $855,000.
DG: $669,000.   FG: $1,474,000.   WWG: $2,143,000.   Profit = $101,000.

9. MAJOR DUNDEE   (22/6/64) Columbia   D: Sam Peckinpah
   C: Charlton Heston, Richard Harris, Jim Hutton
   Sound/Eastman Color/Cinemascope/11,204FT/16R/124M
   DG: $1,600,000.
   [Screenplay by Harry Julian Fink, Oscar Saul, and Sam Peckinpah.]

10. THE CINCINNATI KID   (15/10/65) M-G-M   D: Sam Peckinpah/Norman
    Jewison
    C: Steve McQueen, Edward G. Robinson, Ann-Margaret
    Sound/Metrocolor/9,450FT/105M
    PP: 21/12/1964–15/3/1965   BUD: $3,158,000.   NC: $3,843,000.
    DG: $3,885,000.   FG: $2,542,000.   TV: $2,609,000.
    WWG: $9,036,000.   Profit = $1,359,000.
    [Peckinpah was fired off this picture after four days and replaced by Jewison.]

11. THE WILD BUNCH   (18/6/69) Warner Bros.   D: Sam Peckinpah
    C: William Holden, Ernest Borgnine, Robert Ryan
    Sound/Color/Cinemascope/152M
    DG: $5,375,000. [Screenplay by Walon Green and Sam Peckinpah.]

12. THE BALLAD OF CABLE HOGUE   (18/3/70) Warner Bros.   D: Sam Peckinpah
    C: Jason Robards, Jr., Stella Stevens, David Warner
    Sound/Color/Cinemascope/120M
    DG: $1,264,000.

13. STRAW DOGS   (12/71) Cinerama   D: Sam Peckinpah
    C: Dustin Hoffman, Susan George, Peter Vaughan
    Sound/Color/113M
    NC: $2,200,000.   DG: $8,000,000.   FG: $3,500,000.   WWG: $11,500,000
    Profit = $1,425,000.   [Screenplay by David Z. Goodman and Sam Peckinpah.]

14. JUNIOR BONNER   (6/72) Cinerama   D: Sam Peckinpah
    C: Steve McQueen, Robert Preston, Ida Lupino
    Sound/Color/103M
    NC: $3,200,000.   DG: $1,900,000.
    FG: $900,000.   WWG: $2,800,000.   Loss = $2,820,000.

15. THE GETAWAY   (12/72) National General   D: Sam Peckinpah
    C: Steve McQueen, Ali McGraw, Ben Johnson
    Sound/Color/122M
    DG: $15,976,000.

16. PAT GARRETT AND BILLY THE KID   (23/5/73) M-G-M   D: Sam Peckinpah
    C: James Coburn, Kris Kristofferson, Richard Jaeckel
    Sound/Metrocolor/Cinemascope/9,680FT/12R/106M
    PP: 13/11/1972–6/2/1973   BUD: $3,229,000.   NC: $4,404,000.
    DG: $2,996,000.   FG:$3,060,000.   TV:$1,700,000.
    WWG: $7,756,000.   Profit = $504,000.

17. BRING ME THE HEAD OF ALFREDO GARCIA   (7/8/74) United Artists   D:
    Sam Peckinpah
    C: Warren Oates, Isela Vega, Gig Young
    Sound/Deluxe Color/112M
    NC: $1,997,000.   DG: $837,000.   FG: $1,685,000.
    TV: $798,000.   WWG: $3,320,000.   Loss = $1,817,000.

18. THE KILLER ELITE   (17/12/75) United Artists   D: Sam Peckinpah
    C: James Caan, Robert Duvall, Arthur Hill

Sound/Color/Cinemascope/14R/123M
NC: $5,235,000.   DG: $4,128,000.   FG: $2,525,000.
TV: $3,665,000.   WWG: $10,318,000.   Loss = $2,340,000

19. CROSS OF IRON   (5/77) Avco-Embassy   D: Sam Peckinpah
    C: James Coburn, Maximilian Schell, James Mason
    Sound/Technicolor/133M
    DG: $1,495,000.

20. CONVOY   (28/6/78) United Artists   D: Sam Peckinpah
    C: Kris Kristofferson, Ali McGraw, Ernest Borgnine
    Sound/Deluxe Color/Panavision/12R/111M
    BUD: $3,775,000.   NC: $3,800,000.   DG: $9,403,000.
    FG: $252,000.   TV: $6,083,000.   WWG: $15,738,000.   Profit = $3,500,000.

21. THE OSTERMAN WEEKEND   (14/10/83) 20th-Fox   D: Sam Peckinpah
    C: Rutger Hauer, John Hurt, Craig T. Nelson
    Sound/Deluxe Color/102M
    DG: $2,726,000.

## Music Video Directing Credit

1. VALOTTE   (1985)   D: Sam Peckinpah
   C: Julian Lennon

2. TOO LATE FOR GOODBYES   (1985)   D: Sam Peckinpah
   C: Julian Lennon

## Television Shows

1. GUNSMOKE: THE QUEUE   (28/11/55) CBS   D: Charles Marquis Warren
   C: James Arness, Keye Luke, Sebastian Cabot
   26M
   [Peckinpah adapted John Meston's radio script for television.]

2. GUNSMOKE: YORKY   (31/12/55) CBS   D: Charles Marquis Warren
   C: James Arness, Jeff Silva, Howard Petrie
   26M
   [Peckinpah adapted John Meston's radio script for television.]

3. GUNSMOKE: COOTER   (19/5/56) CBS   D: Robert Stevenson
   C: James Arness, Strother Martin, Vinton Hayworth
   26M
   [Peckinpah adapted John Meston's radio script for television.]

4. GUNSMOKE: HOW TO DIE FOR NOTHING   (23/6/56) CBS   D: Ted Post
   C: James Arness, Larry Dobkin, Mort Mills
   26M
   [Peckinpah adapted John Meston's radio script for television.]

5. GUNSMOKE: THE GUITAR   (18/7/56) CBS   D: Harry Horner
   C: James Arness, Aaron Spelling, Jacques Aubuchon
   26M
   [Peckinpah adapted John Meston's radio script for television.]

6. GUNSMOKE: THE ROUNDUP   (25/9/56) CBS   D: Ted Post
   C: James Arness, Michael Hinn, Jacques Aubuchon
   26M
   [Peckinpah adapted John Meston's radio script for television.]

7. GUNSMOKE: LEGAL REVENGE    (13/11/56) CBS    D: Andrew McLaglen
C: James Arness, Cloris Leachman, Philip Bourneuf
26M
[Peckinpah adapted John Meston's radio script for television.]

8. GUNSMOKE: POOR PEARL    (19/12/56) CBS    D: Andrew McLaglen
C: James Arness, Denver Pyle, Constance Ford
26M
[Peckinpah adapted John Meston's radio script for television.]

9. BROKEN ARROW: THE ASSASSIN    (23/4/57) ABC    D: ?
C: John Lupton, Michael Ansara, Tom Fadden
26M
[OS: Sam Peckinpah.]

10. TALES OF WELLS FARGO: APACHE GOLD    (23/9/57) NBC    D: ?
C: Dale Robertson
26M
[OS: Sam Peckinpah.]

11. BROKEN ARROW: THE TEACHER    (19/11/57) ABC    D: ?
C: John Lupton, Michael Ansara, Phyllis Avery
26M
[OS: Sam Peckinpah.]

12. GUNSMOKE: HOW TO KILL A WOMAN    (29/11/57) CBS    D: John Rich
C: James Arness, Robert Brubaker, Barry Atwater
26M
[Peckinpah adapted John Meston's radio script for television.]

13. TRACKDOWN: THE TOWN    (13/12/57) CBS    D: Donald McDougall
C: Robert Culp
26M
[OS: Sam Peckinpah.]

14. HAVE GUN, WILL TRAVEL: THE SINGER    (8/2/58) CBS    D: ?
C: Richard Boone
26M
[OS: Sam Peckinpah.]

15. TOMBSTONE TERRITORY: JOHNNY RINGO'S LAST RIDE    (19/2/58)
ABC    D: ?
C: Pat Conway, Myron Healy, Bob Bice
26M
[OS: Sam Peckinpah.]

16. GUNSMOKE: DIRT    (28/2/58) CBS    D: Ted Post
C: James Arness, June Lockhart, Wayne Morris
26M
[Peckinpah adapted John Meston's radio script for television.]

17. MAN WITHOUT A GUN: THE KIDDER    (26/5/58) 20th-Fox/NTA    D: ?
C: Rex Reason
26M
[OS: Sam Peckinpah.]

18. BROKEN ARROW: TRANSFER    (24/6/58) ABC    D: ?
C: John Lupton, Michael Ansara, Tex Foster
26M

[OS: Sam Peckinpah.]

19. THE RIFLEMAN: THE SHARPSHOOTER   (30/9/58) ABC   D: Arnold Laven
    C: Chuck Connors, Johnny Crawford, Sidney Blackmer
    26M
    [OS: Sam Peckinpah. This pilot segment for the subsequent series ran as a part of ZANE GREY THEATRE for the first time on CBS on 7 March 1958.]

20. THE RIFLEMAN: HOME RANCH   (7/10/58) ABC   D: Sam Peckinpah
    C: Chuck Connors, Johny Crawford, Lee Farr
    26M

21. THE RIFLEMAN: THE MARSHAL   (21/10/58) ABC   D: Sam Peckinpah
    C: Chuck Connors, Johnny Crawford, Paul Fix
    26M
    [OS: Sam Peckinpah.]

22. THE RIFLEMAN: THE BOARDING HOUSE (24/2/59) ABC D: Sam Peckinpah
    C: Chuck Connors, Johnny Crawford, Katy Jurado
    26M
    [OS: Sam Peckinpah.]

23. ZANE GREY THEATRE: TROUBLE AT TRES CRUCES   (26/3/59) CBS   D: Sam Peckinpah
    C: Brian Keith, Neville Brand, Ted de Corsica
    26M
    [OS: Sam Peckinpah.]

24. THE RIFLEMAN: THE MONEY GUN   (12/5/59) ABC   D: Sam Peckinpah
    C: Chuck Connors, Johnny Crawford, Bert Freed
    26M
    [OS: Sam Peckinpah and Bruce Geller.]

25. ZANE GREY THEATRE: LONESOME ROAD   (19/11/59) CBS   D: Sam Peckinpah
    C: Edmond O'Brien, Rita Lynn, Tom Gilson
    26M
    [OS: Sam Peckinpah.]

26. THE RIFLEMAN: THE BABY SITTER   (15/12/59) ABC   D: Sam Peckinpah
    C: Chuck Connors, Johnny Crawford, Phyllis Avery
    26M
    [OS: Sam Peckinpah and Jack Curtis.]

27. ZANE GREY THEATRE: MISS JENNY   (7/1/60) CBS   D: Sam Peckinpah
    C: Vera Miles, Ben Cooper, Jack Flam
    26M
    [OS: Sam Peckinpah and Robert Heverly.]

28. KLONDIKE: KLONDIKE FEVER   (10/10/60) NBC   D: William Conrad
    C: Ralph Taeger, Mari Blanchard, Joi Lansing
    26M
    [ADP: Sam Peckinpah and Carey Wilbur.]

29. KLONDIKE: SWOGER'S MULES   (21/11/60) NBC   D: Sam Peckinpah
    C: Ralph Taeger, Mari Blanchard, Joi Lansing
    26M
    [OS: Sam Peckinpah, Jack Gariss, and Elliott Lewis.]

30. THE WESTERNER: JEFF   (30/9/60) NBC   D: Sam Peckinpah
    C: Brian Keith, Diana Millay, Geoffrey Toone
    26M
    [OS: Sam Peckinpah, Bruce Geller, Cyril Hume, and Robert Heverly. This series was produced at Republic Pictures' lot for Four Star Films by Sam Peckinpah.]

31. THE WESTERNER: THE OLD MAN   (7/10/60) NBC   D: Andre de Toth
    C: Brian Keith, Sam Jaffe, John Dehner
    26M
    [OS: Sam Peckinpah and Jack Curtis.]

32. THE WESTERNER: THE TREASURER   (14/10/60) NBC   D: Ted Post
    C: Brian Keith
    26M

33. THE WESTERNER: BROWN   (21/10/60) NBC   D: Sam Peckinpah
    C: Brian Keith, John Dehner, Harry Swoger
    26M

34. THE WESTERNER: MRS. KENNEDY   (28/10/60) NBC   D: Bernie Kowalski
    C: Brian Keith, Jean Allison, Paul Richards
    26M
    [OS: Sam Peckinpah and John Dunkel.]

35. THE WESTERNER: SCHOOL DAYS   (4/11/60) NBC   D: Andre de Toth
    C: Brian Keith, Richard Rust, R.G. Armstrong
    26M
    [OS: Sam Peckinpah and Robert Heverly.]

36. THE WESTERNER: THE COURTING OF LIBBY   (11/11/60) NBC   D: Sam Peckinpah
    C: Brian Keith, John Dehner, Joan O'Brien
    26M

37. THE WESTERNER: LINE CAMP   (18/11/60) NBC   D: Tom Gries
    C: Brian Keith, Robert Culp
    26M

38. THE WESTERNER: DOS PIÑOS   (25/11/60) NBC   D: Donald McDougall
    C: Brian Keith, Red Morgan, Malcolm Atterbury
    26M

39. THE WESTERNER: GOING HOME   (2/12/60) NBC   D: Elliot Silverstein
    C: Brian Keith, John Brinkley, Mary Murphy
    26M

40. THE WESTERNER: HAND ON THE GUN   (9/12/60) NBC   D: Sam Peckinpah
    C: Brian Keith, Ben Cooper, Michael Ansara
    26M

41. THE WESTERNER: GHOST OF A CHANCE   (23/12/60) NBC   D: Bruce Geller
    C: Brian Keith
    26M

42. THE WESTERNER: THE PAINTING   (30/12/60) NBC   D: Sam Peckinpah
    C: Brian Keith, John Dehner, Madlyn Rhue
    26M

43. PONY EXPRESS: THE STORY OF JULESBURG   (28/6/61) NBC   D: Sam Peckinpah

C: Grant Sullivan
26M

44. ROUTE 66: MON PETIT CHOW   (24/11/61) CBS   D: Sam Peckinpah
C: Martin Milner, George Maharis, Lee Marvin
52M

45. DICK POWELL THEATRE: PERICLES ON 31ST STREET   (4/12/62) NBC   D: Sam Peckinpah
C: Theodore Bikel, Arthur O'Connell, Carroll O'Connor
52M

[OS: Sam Peckinpah and Harry Mark Petrakis.]

46. DICK POWELL THEATRE: THE LOSERS   (15/1/63) NBC   D: Sam Peckinpah
C: Lee Marvin, Keenan Wynn, Rosemary Clooney
52M

[OS: Bruce Geller and Sam Peckinpah.]

47. ABC STAGE 67: NOON WINE   (23/11/66) ABC   D: Sam Peckinpah
C: Jason Robards, Jr., Olivia de Havilland, Per Oscarsson
Color/52M

[ADP: Sam Peckinpah.]

48. BOB HOPE'S CHRYSLER THEATRE: THAT LADY IS MINE   (1/2/67) NBC   D: Sam Peckinpah
C: Jean Simmons, Bradford Dillman, Alex Cord
Color/52M

# Bibliography

## BOOKS

Bacall, Lauren, BY MYSELF (New York: Knopf, 1978).

Bazin, André, ORSON WELLES: A CRITICAL VIEW (New York: Harper's, 1979) translated by Jonathan Rosenbaum.

Belton, John, THE HOLLYWOOD PROFESSIONALS VOLUME THREE (New York and London: Barnes/Tantivy, 1974).

Bessy, Maurice, ORSON WELLES (Paris: Éditions Seghers, 1970).

Bogdanovich, Peter, JOHN FORD (Berkeley: University of California Press, 1978).

Borde, Raymond, and Etienne Chaumeton, PANORAMA DU FILM NOIR AMÉRICAIN (Paris: Éditions D'Aujourd'hui, 1955).

Brady, Frank, CITIZEN WELLES: A BIOGRAPHY OF ORSON WELLES (New York: Scribner's, 1989).

Brownlow, Kevin, THE PARADE'S GONE BY . . . (New York: Bonanza Books, 1968).

Bugliosi, Vincent, HELTER SKELTER (1974; New York: Bantam Books, 1975) with Curt Gentry.

Butler, Ivan, THE CINEMA OF ROMAN POLANSKI (New York: Barnes, 1970).

Castle, William, STEP RIGHT UP! (New York: Putnam's, 1976).

Chase, Borden, RED RIVER (New York: Bantam Books, 1948).

Dawson, Christopher, THE MAKING OF EUROPE (1932; Cleveland: World Publishing, 1956)

Denton, Clive, "Henry King" in THE HOLLYWOOD PROFESSIONALS VOLUME TWO (New York and London: Barnes/Tantivy, 1974).

Eliot, T.S., THE COMPLETE POEMS AND PLAYS: 1909–1950 (New York: Harcourt, Brace, 1958).

Evans, Max, SAM PECKINPAH: MASTER OF VIOLENCE (Vermillion: University of South Dakota Press, 1972).

———, SUPER BULL (Albuquerque: University of New Mexico Press, 1986).

Freud, Sigmund, COLLECTED PAPERS IN FIVE VOLUMES (New York: Basic Books, 1959).

Gish, Lillian, THE MOVIES, MR. GRIFFITH, AND ME (Englewood Cliffs: Prentice-Hall, 1969).

Goodman, Ezra, THE FIFTY-YEAR DECLINE AND FALL OF HOLLYWOOD (New York: Simon and Schuster, 1961).

Gottesman, Ronald, editor, FOCUS ON CITIZEN KANE (Englewood Cliffs: Prentice-Hall, 1971).

————, editor, FOCUS ON ORSON WELLES (Englewood Cliffs: Prentice-Hall, 1976).

Greenberger, Howard, BOGEY'S BABY: A BIOGRAPHY (New York: St. Martin's Press, 1978).

Grobel, Lawrence, THE HUSTONS (New York: Scribner's, 1989).

Gussow, Mel, DON'T SAY YES UNTIL I FINISH TALKING: A BIOGRAPHY OF DARRYL F. ZANUCK (1971; New York: Pocket Books, 1972).

Hammett, Dashiell, THE NOVELS OF DASHIELL HAMMETT (New York: Knopf, 1965).

Harding, M. Esther, PSYCHIC ENERGY: ITS SOURCE AND ITS TRANSFORMA-TION (1963; Princeton: Princeton University Press, 1973).

Haslam, Gerald R., editor, WESTERN WRITING (Albuquerque: University of New Mexico Press, 1974).

Hemingway, Ernest, TO HAVE AND HAVE NOT (1937; New York: P.F. Collier, n.d.).

Hesse, Hermann, GESAMMELTE DICTUNGEN IN SIEBEN BÄNDEN (Frankfurt am Main: Suhrkamp Verlag, 1958).

Heston, Charlton, THE ACTOR'S LIFE (New York: Dutton, 1978).

Higham, Charles, and Roy Moseley, CARY GRANT: THE LONELY HEART (San Diego: Harcourt Brace Jovanovich, 1989).

————, and Joel Greenberg, HOLLYWOOD IN THE FORTIES (Cranbury and London: Barnes/Tantivy, 1968).

————, ORSON WELLES: THE RISE AND FALL OF AN AMERICAN GENIUS (New York: St. Martin's Press, 1985).

Hill, James, RITA HAYWORTH: A MEMOIR (New York: Simon and Schuster, 1983).

Hotchner, A.E., PAPA HEMINGWAY: A PERSONAL MEMOIR (New York: Random House, 1966).

Houseman, John, RUN-THROUGH (1972; New York: Curtis Books, 1972).

Huston, John, AN OPEN BOOK (New York: Knopf, 1980).

Huxley, Aldous, GREAT SHORT WORKS OF ALDOUS HUXLEY (New York: Harper's, 1969) edited by Bernard Bergonzi.

Jung, C.G., DIE DYNAMIK DES UNBEWUSSTEN (Zurich and Stuttgart: Rascher Verlag, 1967).

————, ZWEI SCHRIFTEN ÜBER ANALYTISCHE PSYCHOLOGIE (Zurich and Stuttgart: Rascher Verlag, 1964).

Kaminsky, Stuart, JOHN HUSTON: MAKER OF MAGIC (Boston: Houghton Mifflin, 1978).

Kay, Karyn, and Gerald Peary, editors, WOMEN AND THE CINEMA: A CRITICAL ANTHOLOGY (New York: Dutton, 1977).

Keyes, Evelyn, SCARLETT O'HARA'S YOUNGER SISTER: MY LIFE IN AND OUT OF HOLLYWOOD (Secaucus: Lyle Stuart, 1977).

Kitses, Jim, HORIZONS WEST (Bloomington: Indiana University Press, 1970).

Kobal, John, PEOPLE WILL TALK (New York: Knopf, 1985).

———, RITA HAYWORTH: THE TIME, THE PLACE, AND THE WOMAN (New York: Norton, 1977).

LaValley, Albert J., editor, FOCUS ON ALFRED HITCHCOCK (Englewood Cliffs: Prentice-Hall, 1972).

Leaming, Barbara, IF THIS WAS HAPPINESS: A BIOGRAPHY OF RITA HAYWORTH (New York: Viking, 1989).

———, ORSON WELLES: A BIOGRAPHY (New York: Viking, 1985).

———, POLANSKI: A BIOGRAPHY OF THE FILMMAKER AS VOYEUR (1981; New York: Simon and Schuster, 1983).

Lucas, F.L., THE DECLINE AND FALL OF THE ROMANTIC IDEAL (New York: Macmillan, 1936).

MacShane, Frank, THE LIFE OF RAYMOND CHANDLER (New York: Dutton, 1976).

Marx, Arthur, GOLDWYN: A BIOGRAPHY OF THE MAN BEHIND THE MYTH (New York: Norton, 1976).

Mast, Gerald, HOWARD HAWKS, STORYTELLER (New York: Oxford University Press, 1982).

McBride, Joseph, editor, FOCUS ON HOWARD HAWKS (Englewood Cliffs: Prentice-Hall, 1972).

———, HAWKS ON HAWKS (Berkeley: University of California Press, 1982).

———, ORSON WELLES (New York: Viking, 1972).

Naremore, James, THE MAGIC WORLD OF ORSON WELLES (New York: Oxford University Press, 1978).

Nietzsche, Friedrich, WERKE IN DREI BÄNDEN (Munich: Carl Hanser Verlag, 1955) edited by Karl Schlechta.

Nolan, William F., JOHN HUSTON: KING REBEL (Los Angeles: Sherbourne Press, 1965).

Orwell, George, THE COLLECTED ESSAYS, JOURNALISM, AND LETTERS OF GEORGE ORWELL IN FOUR VOLUMES (New York: Harcourt Brace Jovanovich, 1968) edited by Sonia Orwell and Ian Angus.

Parkinson, Michael, and Claude Jeavons, A PICTORIAL HISTORY OF WESTERNS (London: Hamlyn Publishing Group, 1972).

Pilkington, William T., and Don Graham, WESTERN MOVIES (Albuquerque: University of New Mexico Press, 1979).

Polanski, Roman, POLANSKI: THREE FILM SCRIPTS (New York: Harper's, 1975).

———, ROMAN BY POLANSKI (1984; New York: Ballantine Books, 1985).

Racine, Jean, THÉATRE DE JEAN RACINE (Paris: Éditions de Cluny, 1950).

Reik, Theodor, THE NEED TO BE LOVED (New York: Farrar, Straus, and Giroux, 1963).

Rieupeyrout, Jean-Louis, LA GRANDE AVENTURE DU WESTERN (Paris: Éditions du cerf, 1964).

Robinson, W.R., editor, MEN AND THE MOVIES (Baton Rouge: Louisiana State University Press, 1967).

Seydor, Paul, PECKINPAH: THE WESTERN FILMS (Urbana: University of Illinois Press, 1980).

Sherman, Eric, and Martin Rubin, THE DIRECTOR'S EVENT (New York: Atheneum, 1970).

Silver, Charles, THE WESTERN FILM (New York: Pyramid Books, 1976).

Simmons, Garner, PECKINPAH: A PORTRAIT IN MONTAGE (Austin: University of Texas Press, 1982).

Spoto, Donald, THE DARK SIDE OF GENIUS: THE LIFE OF ALFRED HITCHCOCK (Boston: Little, Brown, 1983).

Taylor, John Russell, HITCH: THE LIFE AND TIMES OF ALFRED HITCHCOCK (1978; New York: Berkley Books, 1980).

Thomas, Tony, THE WEST THAT NEVER WAS (Secaucus: Citadel Press, 1989).

Thompson, Verita, BOGIE AND ME: A LOVE STORY (New York: St. Martin's Press, 1982).

Truffaut, François, HITCHCOCK (New York: Simon and Schuster, 1967).

Tuska, Jon, THE AMERICAN WEST IN FILM: CRITICAL APPROACHES TO THE WESTERN (Westport: Greenwood Press, 1985).

————, DARK CINEMA: AMERICAN FILM NOIR IN CULTURAL PERSPECTIVE (Westport: Greenwood Press, 1984).

————, THE DETECTIVE IN HOLLYWOOD (New York: Doubleday, 1978).

————, THE FILMING OF THE WEST (New York: Doubleday, 1976).

————, IN MANORS AND ALLEYS: A CASEBOOK ON THE AMERICAN DETECTIVE FILM (Westport: Greenwood Press, 1988).

Warner, Jack L., MY FIRST HUNDRED YEARS IN HOLLYWOOD (New York: Random House, 1965) with Dean Jennings.

Wilde, Oscar, THE COMPLETE WORKS OF OSCAR WILDE (London: Collins, 1966).

Willis, Donald C., THE FILMS OF HOWARD HAWKS (Metuchen: Scarecrow Press, 1975).

Wollen, Peter, SIGNS AND MEANING IN THE CINEMA (Bloomington: Indiana University Press, 1969).

## ARTICLES

Albergate, Al, "Polanski: My Whole Life is at Stake," THE LOS ANGELES HERALD-EXAMINER (3 February 1978).

Amory, Cleveland, "If I Had My Life to Live Over Again," PARADE MAGAZINE (2 August 1987).

Benson, Sheila, " 'Huston' Does the Man Proud," THE LOS ANGELES TIMES (7 June 1989).

Chambers, Andrea, and Lee Powell, "Out of the Past," PEOPLE MAGAZINE, Vol.32, No.20 (14 January 1990).

Delahaye, Michael, and Jean-André Fieschi, "Landscape of a Mind," CAHIERS DU CINÉMA (February, 1966).

Farr, Bill, "Mental Tests for Polanski," THE LOS ANGELES TIMES (19 September 1977).

————, "Polanski Pleads Guilty on 1 Count," THE LOS ANGELES TIMES (9 August 1977).

Gauguin, Lorraine, "One Size Fits All," VIEWS & REVIEWS Magazine, Vol.5, Is.2 (December, 1973).

————, "With Duke Down Mexico Way: December, 1972," VIEWS & REVIEWS Magazine, Vol.5, Is.1 (September, 1973).

Grant, Lee, "The Tormented Life of Roman Polanski," THE MILWAUKEE JOURNAL (15 May 1977).

Kerwin, Robert, "Hollywood Guru of Guts and Gore: On Location with Sam Peckinpah,"
     THE MILWAUKEE JOURNAL (26 October 1975).
King, Henry, "The Actor-Director's Viewpoint," MOTOGRAPHY, Vol.5, No.23
     (4 December 1915).
Kobal, John, "The Time, The Place, and The Girl: Rita Hayworth," FOCUS ON FILM
     (Summer, 1972).
Leydon, Joseph, "James Coburn: His Life and HARD TIMES," TAKE ONE, Vol.4,
     No.12 (July-August, 1974).
Mahoney, John C., "Browsing the Book Stalls," THE HOLLYWOOD REPORTER
     (19 March 1976).
Mann, Roderick, THE LOS ANGELES TIMES CALENDAR (9 December 1979).
McCarty, John, "The Polanski Puzzle," TAKE ONE, Vol.2, No.5 (May-June, 1970).
Peckinpah, Sam, "PLAYBOY Interview," PLAYBOY, Vol.19, No.8 (August, 1972).
———, "Sam Peckinpah Lets It All Hang Out," TAKE ONE, Vol.2, No.3 (January-
     February, 1969).
———, "Straight Shootin' Sam," SOUTHWEST MEDIA REVIEW (Spring, 1985).
Phillips, Gene D., "Talking with John Huston," FILM COMMENT, Vol.9, No.3 (May-
     June, 1973).
Polanski, Roman, "Dialogue on Film," American Film Institute in Los Angeles, Vol.3,
     No.8 (August, 1974).
Rivette, Jacques, "Genie de Howard Hawks," CAHIERS DU CINÉMA (May, 1953).
Rosenbaum, Jonathan, "Orson Welles' HEART OF DARKNESS," FILM COMMENT,
     Vol.8, No.4 (November-December, 1972).
Sarris, Andrew, "The Facts, Ma'am," THE NEW YORK TIMES BOOK REVIEW
     (26 March 1978).
Scott, Walter, "Walter Scott's Personality Parade," PARADE MAGAZINE (14 January
     1990).
Wilmington, Mike, "Roman Polanski's CHINATOWN," THE VELVET LIGHT TRAP,
     No.13 (Fall, 1974).

# Index

ACROSS THE PACIFIC (Warner's, 1942), 150, 212

Adjani, Isabelle, 266

Adler, Buddy, 59, 60, 61, 172

AFRICAN QUEEN, THE (United Artists, 1952), 164, 165–166, 168, 177

Agee, James, 164

AIR FORCE (Warner's, 1943), 116

Albert, Eddie, 61, 173

Alda, Rutanya, 318

Aldrich, Robert, 298

ALEXANDER'S RAGTIME BAND (20th-Fox, 1938), 40, 53–54

Altman, Robert, 191, 244

Ambler, Eric, 210

Ameche, Don, 40, 53

Anderson, Maxwell, 159

ANNIE (Columbia, 1982), 182

Aristotle, 68

Armstrong, R. G., 279, 298, 299, 301, 308, 316

ARROWSMITH (United Artists, 1931), 16, 18

Arthur, Jean, 114

ASPHALT JUNGLE, THE (M-G-M, 1950), 162, 163

Astor, Mary, 140, 141, 149, 150, 186

Aurelius, Marcus, 121

*Auteur* theory, 1–2

Bacall, Lauren, 96, 97, 98, 99, 100, 114, 118, 119, 120, 129, 134, 149, 152, 153, 155, 156, 158, 159, 160, 161, 165, 166, 169, 170, 171, 177, 261, 310, 311

Balcon, Michael, 66, 67, 69, 72, 73, 77, 146

Ball, Lucille, 16, 213

BALLAD OF CABLE HOGUE, THE (Warner's, 1970), 290, 292, 296, 304, 308–310, 311, 312, 313, 328

Ballard, Lucien, 313

BALL OF FIRE (RKO, 1942), 131–132

BARBARIAN AND THE GEISHA, THE (20th-Fox, 1958), 172

BARBARY COAST, THE (United Artists, 1935), 112, 122–123, 131

Barrett, Rona, 278, 314

Barrymore, John, 110, 111, 170, 198, 208

Barrymore, Lionel, 48, 159

Barthelmess, Richard, 42, 104, 114

BATTLE OF SAN PIETRO, THE (1943), 151

Bazin, André, 222, 226, 234

BEAT THE DEVIL (United Artists, 1954), 168, 169, 170, 172

Bellamy, Ralph, 115, 265

Belton, John, 116, 136
Belville, Concepta, 267, 270
Belville, Hercules, 267
BEN-HUR (M-G-M, 1925), 12, 19, 44
Berg, Alban, 271
Berger, Senta, 303, 304
Bergman, Ingrid, 83, 84
Bernard of Chartres, 239
Bessy, Maurice, 228, 233, 235
BIBLE. . .IN THE BEGINNING, THE
    (20th-Fox, 1966), 177–178
BIG SKY, THE (RKO, 1952), 126–128,
    130, 131, 133
BIG SLEEP, THE (Warner's, 1946), 97,
    99, 119–120
BIRD OF PARADISE, THE (RKO,
    1932), 17–18, 21
BIRDS, THE (Universal, 1963), 90–91
Bischoff, Sam, 18, 19
BLACKMAIL (British International,
    1929), 70–71
Blanke, Henry, 147, 149, 155, 156, 157,
    158
Blitzstein, Marc, 147, 204
Boetticher, Budd, 33, 297, 300, 302
Bogart, Humphrey, 97, 98, 99, 100, 117,
    118, 119, 141, 147, 148, 150, 152,
    153, 154, 155, 156, 157, 158, 159,
    160, 161, 165, 166, 168, 169, 170,
    171, 175, 179, 184, 196, 243, 244,
    310, 311
Bogdanovich, Peter, 102, 129, 130, 136,
    199, 236
Borde, Raymond, 221
Borgine, Ernest, 304
Boyer, Charles, 99
Brach, Gérard, 251, 252, 254, 257, 263,
    264, 273
Brackett, Leigh, 119, 121, 128
Bradbury, Ray, 170
Brady, Frank, 195, 203, 206, 208, 219,
    230, 234, 236
Brand, Neville, 109, 279, 280, 294
Brando, Marlon, 282
Brauss, Arthur, 323, 324
BREAK UP THE DANCE (Polish,
    1957), 248

Brennan, Walter, 55, 112, 122, 123–124,
    129, 304, 311
Brent, George, 150
Bresler, Jerry, 300
BRINGING UP BABY (RKO, 1938),
    113–114, 133
BRING ME THE HEAD OF ALFREDO
    GARCIA (United Artists, 1974), 289,
    312, 319, 320
Brownlow, Kevin, 42
Bruce, Nigel, 72, 80
Bryant, Donald S., 189, 191, 192
Brynner, Yul, 301
Buchan, John, 75
Buchanan, Edgar, 298
Buchowetzki, Dimitri, 13
Buckley, Betty, 274
Bugliosi, Vincent, 255, 259, 260
Burnett, W. R., 148, 162
Burton, Richard, 176, 177
Butler, Ivan, 239, 245, 248, 257, 260

Caan, James, 291
Cagney, James, 107, 112
CAHILL, U.S. MARSHAL (Warner's,
    1973), 277
CAMILLE (First National, 1927), 13
Campion, Cris, 274
Capa, Robert, 167, 169
Capone, Al, 106, 107
Capote, Truman, 154, 168
Capra, Frank, 2, 114, 135, 182
Carrington, Margaret, 198, 202
Carroll, Gordon, 282, 283
Carroll, Leo G., 80
Carroll, Madeline, 76
CASABLANCA (Warner's, 1942), 96–
    97, 118, 129, 141, 152
Castle, William, 196, 197, 258, 262
Chabrol, Claude, 4, 5
CHAMPAGNE (British International,
    1928), 69–70
Chandler, Raymond, 85, 119, 193, 197,
    198, 244, 245
Chaplin, Charles, 222
CHARLIE CHAN AT THE OLYMPICS
    (20th-Fox, 1937), 24, 26

CHARLIE CHAN AT THE OPERA
(20th-Fox, 1937), 9, 24, 26
CHARLIE CHAN AT THE RACE
TRACK (20th-Fox, 1936), 24, 27, 50
CHARLIE CHAN IN HONOLULU
(20th-Fox, 1939), 26
Chase, Borden, 123, 124, 125, 130
Chaumeton, Etienne, 221
CHECKERS (20th-Fox, 1938), 24
CHIMES AT MIDNIGHT (Peppercorn-
Wormser-Saltzman, 1967), 232, 233
CHINA 9, LIBERTY 37 (Lorimar,
1984), 325
CHINATOWN (Paramount, 1974), 139,
143, 150, 159, 180, 182, 242, 243,
244, 245, 265, 266, 268, 273
Church, Denver Samuel, 293
Church, Fern, 293
Cicero, 39, 239
CINCINNATI KID, THE (M-G-M,
1965), 301
CITIZEN KANE (RKO, 1941), 85, 190,
195, 199, 200, 206, 207–208, 210,
212, 221, 229, 233, 236
Clark, Matt, 282
Clavel, Aurora, 304, 317
Clift, Montgomery, 86, 123, 124, 125,
127, 129, 175, 176, 185, 304
CLOSE-UP: THE CONTRACT DIREC-
TOR (Scarecrow Press, 1976), 36
Coburn, James, 282, 284, 300, 301, 303,
304, 319, 322
Cochrane, Steve, 296
Cohn, Harry, 19, 20, 21, 101, 105, 109,
110, 114, 196, 197, 216, 217, 220
Coleman, Ronald, 14, 15, 16, 43, 44,
45, 47
Combs, Gary, 283, 284
COME AND GET IT (United Artists,
1936), 112, 113, 114
CONDEMNED (United Artists, 1929),
15
Connery, Sean, 91, 179
Conrad, Joseph, 76, 77, 192, 193, 198,
207
CONVOY (United Artists, 1978), 325
Coolidge, Rita, 315

Cooper, Gary, 44, 45, 80, 115, 116,
124, 129, 131, 132
Cooper, James Fenimore, 273
COQUETTE (United Artists, 1929), 14
Cortez, Stanley, 210
Cotten, Joseph, 82, 210
COUNTRY DOCTOR, THE (20th-Fox,
1936), 51
Coward, Noel, 69
Cowie, Peter, 231
Crane, Stephen, 162
Craven, Garth, 289, 291, 325
Crawford, Joan, 13, 109
CRIMINAL CODE, THE (Columbia,
1931), 105–106, 110, 145
CROOKED CIRCLE, THE (WorldWide,
1932), 20, 36
CROSS OF IRON (Avco-Embassy,
1977), 292, 325
CROWD ROARS, THE (Warner's,
1932), 107, 121
CUL-DE-SAC (Sigma III, 1966), 252,
254, 257, 266, 273
Cummings, Robert, 81, 86
Curtiz, Michael, 21, 97

D'Abbadie D'Arrast, Harry, 13
Dali, Salvador, 83
Davies, Marion, 207
Davis, Bette, 140, 150
DAWN PATROL, THE (Warner's,
1930), 58, 104–105, 106, 112, 116
DEAD, THE (Vestron, 1987), 183, 184,
234
DEADLY COMPANIONS, THE (Pathé-
American, 1961), 295–297, 302
DEAD RECKONING (Columbia, 1946),
196, 197
De Haviland, Olivia, 150, 186, 301
Delahaye, Michael, 240
De Laurentiis, Dino, 177, 269
Del Rio, Dolores, 18, 208, 209, 210,
211, 217
DeMille, Cecil B., 21, 43
Deneuve, Catherine, 252, 253, 254
DETECTIVE IN HOLLYWOOD, THE
(documentary), 180, 189, 244

DETECTIVE IN HOLLYWOOD, THE
    (Doubleday, 1978), 4, 179, 181, 244
DEVIL DANCER, THE (United Artists,
    1927), 14
DIAL M FOR MURDER (Warner's,
    1954), 81, 82
Dickinson, Angie, 129, 134, 304
Dieterle, William, 147
Dietrich, Marlene, 231
Dinesen, Isak, 232–233, 234
Disney, Walt, 77
Dmytryk, Edward, 60, 154, 163, 175,
    189, 190, 191, 212
Donat, Robert, 76
Dorleac, Françoise, 254, 257
Douglas, Kirk, 127, 176
Douglas, Melvyn, 240
DRAGON MURDER CASE, THE (First
    National, 1934), 9, 21–22
Dru, Joanne, 126, 128, 304
DRUMS ALONG THE MOHAWK
    (20th-Fox, 1939), 309
Drury, James, 298
Duke, Patty, 259
Dunaway, Faye, 242, 243, 244, 266
Durgnat, Raymond, 5
Duvall, Robert, 320
Dwan, Allan, 14
Dylan, Bob, 283, 315, 317

Eason, B. Reaves "Breezy," 11, 12, 13,
    29
EASY VIRTUE (Gainsborough, 1928),
    69
Elam, Jack, 278, 279, 317, 318
EL DORADO (Paramount, 1967), 130,
    131
Eliot, T. S., 126
Euripides, 68, 90, 236
Evans, Gene, 308, 318
Evans, Max, 290, 292, 300, 310, 313,
    314, 315, 325, 326, 328
Evans, Robert, 61, 242, 258
Ezzies, Erwin, 320

Fairbanks, Douglas, Sr., 14, 15, 23
FAMILY PLOT (Universal, 1976), 69,
    73, 93

FAREWELL TO ARMS, A (20th-Fox,
    1957), 171–172
Farmer, Frances, 112
FARMER'S WIFE, THE (British Interna-
    tional, 1928), 69
Farrow, Mia, 260, 261
Faulkner, William, 96, 98, 109, 112,
    115, 116, 119, 135, 143
Faye, Alice, 30, 40, 53
FEARLESS VAMPIRE KILLERS, THE
    (M-G-M, 1967), 254, 256, 257, 258,
    259, 262, 267
Feldman, Phil, 302, 307
Fellini, Federico, 299
Fernández, Emilio, 177, 278, 279, 305,
    306, 317
Ferrer, José, 166
Fielding, Camille, 283
Fielding, Jerry, 283
Fieschi, Jean-André, 240
FILMING OF THE WEST, THE (Dou-
    bleday, 1976), 179, 181, 277, 284,
    286, 320
FILMING OTHELLO (Independent Im-
    ages, 1979), 193, 235
Finch, Jon, 92
Finney, Albert, 182
F IS FOR FAKE (Specialty Films, 1977),
    234
Fitzgerald, F. Scott, 61
Fitzgerald, Michael, 235
Fitzmaurice, George, 15
Fitzsimmons, Charles B., 295, 296
Flaubert, Gustave, 248, 297
Fleming, Victor, 110, 121, 122, 145
Flon, Suzanne, 167, 168
Flynn, Errol, 61, 173, 174
Fonda, Henry, 49, 54, 88, 279, 291, 302
Fonda, Jane, 287
Fontaine, Joan, 5, 6, 80, 81, 82
Ford, Gregg, 130–131
Ford, Harrison, 274
Ford, John, 2, 11, 16–17, 21, 40, 46,
    48, 49, 50, 59, 62, 120, 123, 126,
    127, 130, 131, 134, 136, 137, 172,
    182, 207, 269, 291, 298, 302, 303,
    304, 307, 309, 326, 328

FOREIGN CORRESPONDENT (United
   Artists, 1940), 6, 80–81, 212
Forester, C. S., 165
FORT APACHE (RKO, 1948), 302, 307
Foster, David, 292
Foster, Norman, 48, 141, 211
FRANTIC (Warner's, 1988), 274
FRENZY (Universal, 1972), 92
Freud, Sigmund, 4, 256, 267
FREUD (Universal, 1962), 168, 175,
   176, 185
Freund, Karl, 75
FROM HERE TO ETERNITY (Colum-
   bia, 1953), 6
FRONT PAGE, THE (Columbia, 1940),
   114
Frykowski, Wojciech, 250, 261
Fuller, Sam, 282, 283
FURY (Inspiration, 1923), 42–43
FURY AT FURNACE CREEK (20th-
   Fox, 1948), 32

Gable, Clark, 52, 53, 96, 164, 174, 175,
   179
Gabor, Zsa Zsa, 166–167
Galloway, Nancy, 294, 327
Galsworthy, John, 72
Garbo, Greta, 13, 169
Gardner, Ava, 60, 177, 178
Garfield, John, 156, 160, 161
GAUCHO, THE (United Artists, 1928),
   14
Gauguin, Lorraine, 277, 278, 279, 282
Gauthier, Suzanne, 73
GENTLEMEN PREFER BLONDES
   (20th-Fox, 1953), 134
George, Susan, 308, 312
GETAWAY, THE (National General,
   1972), 282, 292, 313, 314
Gibson, Hoot, 11, 12
Gide, André, 71
Gielgud, John, 76
Gillette, William, 205
GIRL IN EVERY PORT, A (Fox, 1928),
   102, 107, 108, 127
Gish, Lillian, 42, 43, 49
Gleason, James, 20, 31

GLORY GUYS, THE (United Artists,
   1966), 301
Goddard, Paulette, 16, 183
Goetz, William, 23, 30, 32, 56, 219, 220
Goldwyn, Samuel, 14, 15, 16, 17, 23,
   30, 37, 44, 45, 46, 51, 103, 112, 113,
   132, 145–146, 314
Gomulka, Wladyslaw, 251
Goodman, Ezra, 150
Gorky, Maxim, 3
Goulding, Edmund, 9, 13, 17, 31–32,
   42, 43, 48
Grable, Betty, 16, 28–29, 30
Grant, Cary, 5, 6, 81, 83, 84, 88, 89,
   90, 91, 113, 114, 115, 124, 133
Grant, James Edward, 295
Greco, Juliette, 61, 173
GREEKS HAD A WORD FOR THEM,
   THE (United Artists, 1932), 17
Green, Walon, 302
Greenberg, Joel, 221
Greenberger, Howard, 161
Greene, Graham, 195
Greenstreet, Sidney, 149, 150, 151
Grey, Zane, 46, 124
Griffith, D. W., 13, 23, 42, 43, 49, 51,
   145, 147
Grobel, Lawrence, 184, 185, 186, 265
GROS ET LE MAIGRE, LE (French,
   1961), 249
GUNFIGHTER, THE (20th-Fox, 1950),
   40, 50, 58–59
Guthrie, A. B., Jr., 126, 127
Gutowski, Gene, 252, 254, 257, 259,
   263

Haber, Katherine, 282, 283, 286, 287,
   288, 289, 290–291, 312, 313, 319,
   320, 321, 324, 325
Hammett, Dashiell, 118, 119, 120, 142,
   143, 149, 151, 179, 180, 181, 182,
   198, 244, 245
HAPPY GO LOVELY (RKO-British,
   1951), 33
Haran, Shifra, 218, 219
Harding, M. Esther, 256
Hardy, Thomas, 273
Harlan, Russell, 133

Harris, Richard, 300, 303, 304
Hartley, Mariette, 298
Hartwig, Wolf, 252, 320, 322, 323
HATARI! (Paramount, 1962), 121, 128
Hawks, Howard, 2, 58, 60, 61, 95–137,
    145, 148, 152, 162, 164, 182, 187,
    215, 216, 243, 244, 302, 304, 328
Hayworth, Rita, 114, 196, 197, 200,
    213, 214–226, 232
Hearst, William Randolph, 207, 209
HEAVEN KNOWS, MR. ALLISON
    (20th-Fox, 1957), 171
Hecht, Ben, 83, 106, 109, 110, 114,
    115, 133, 171
Hedren, Tippi, 91, 92
Heffner, Hugh, 263
Hellman, Lillian, 142, 179, 180, 181,
    182
HELLO FRISCO, HELLO (20th-Fox,
    1943), 30
Hemingway, Ernest, 40, 59, 60, 61, 96,
    97, 98, 102–103, 108, 118, 120, 151,
    165, 167, 171, 172, 243, 297, 328
Hepburn, Katharine, 113, 165, 166
Heraclitus, 7
Herrmann, Bernard, 89, 92, 206
Hesse, Hermann, 7
Heston, Charlton, 200, 230, 300, 303,
    304
Higham, Charles, 83, 132, 197, 200,
    205, 227, 231, 234
HIGH NOON (United Artists, 1952), 58,
    118, 128, 129
Hill, Gladys, 144, 175, 180, 181, 185
Hill, James, 214, 216, 217
Hitchcock, Alfred, 2, 4, 5, 6, 63, 65–93,
    101, 112, 146, 212, 230, 253, 274,
    313
Hitchcock, Patricia, 73, 79
Hoffman, Dustin, 308, 312, 313
Holden, William, 60, 173, 304
Holt, Tim, 156
HONDO (Warner's, 1953), 295
Horace, 187
Houseman, John, 147, 190, 193, 195,
    197, 199, 202, 203, 204, 205, 206,
    207, 209, 212
Howard, Leslie, 148, 166

Hughes, Howard, 26, 98, 104, 106, 114,
    115, 116, 117, 126, 133
Humberstone, H. Bruce "Lucky," 1, 2,
    9–37, 45, 50, 52–53
Huston, Anjelica, 168, 178, 183, 265,
    267, 269
Huston, John, 2, 71, 100, 118, 120, 122,
    139–187, 198, 212, 219, 230, 234,
    242, 243, 244, 265, 272, 325, 328
Huston, Walter, 105, 143, 144, 145,
    147, 148, 150, 154, 156, 157, 158,
    163, 170, 272
Hutchison, Fred, 180, 181, 182, 189,
    191, 194
Huxley, Aldous, 313

I CONFESS (Warner's, 1953), 86, 87
IMAGES OF INDIANS (PBS, 1980),
    191, 192, 326
IMMORTAL STORY, THE (Altura
    Films, 1968), 233
Ince, Thomas, 41, 42
Ingham, Rosemary, 285, 286, 287, 288
IN MANORS AND ALLEYS: A CASE-
    BOOK ON THE AMERICAN DE-
    TECTIVE FILM (Greenwood Press,
    1988), 4
IN OLD CHICAGO (20th-Fox, 1938),
    25, 30, 33, 52–53
IN THIS OUR LIFE (Warner's, 1942),
    150, 212
INVASION OF THE BODY SNATCH-
    ERS (Allied Artists, 1956), 294
IRON MASK, THE (United Artists,
    1929), 14
Irving, Amy, 235
IT'S ALL TRUE (documentary), 210,
    213, 220
I WAKE UP SCREAMING (20th-Fox,
    1941), 28–29
I WAS A MALE WAR BRIDE (20th-
    Fox, 1949), 132

Jaglom, Henry, 199, 235, 236
JAMAICA INN (Mayflower, 1939), 78,
    79, 84
JESSE JAMES (20th-Fox, 1939), 54–55
JINXED (United Artists, 1982), 326

Johnson, Ben, 301, 305, 306
Johnson, Nunnally, 51, 58
Johnson, William, 200, 222, 229
Jones, Jennifer, 56, 60, 62, 82, 160,
  168, 172
Jones, L. Q., 279, 284, 301, 308, 317
JOURNEY INTO FEAR (RKO, 1942),
  210, 211, 212
Joyce, James, 145, 183
Jung, C. G., 4, 66, 79, 249, 328
JUNIOR BONNER (Cinerama, 1972),
  313
JUNO AND THE PAYCOCK (British
  International, 1930), 71
Jurado, Katy, 317

Kael, Pauline, 206, 233, 282, 311, 312,
  322
Kafka, Franz, 231, 257, 271
Kaminsky, Stuart, 139–140, 149
Kaye, Danny, 30, 132, 159
Keith, Brian, 295
Kelly, Grace, 81, 86, 88, 91
Kennedy, Joseph P., 17
Kerr, Deborah, 61, 171, 177
Keyes, Evelyn, 80, 154, 155, 156, 157,
  158, 159, 160, 161–162, 163, 167,
  168, 169, 177, 179, 183
KEY LARGO (Warner's, 1948), 159–
  160, 310
Khan, Yasmin Aga, 223
KILLER ELITE, THE (United Artists,
  1975), 287, 288, 292, 320
King, Henry, 2, 14, 21, 25, 39–63, 103,
  136, 137, 177, 227, 258
KING OF THE JUNGLE (Paramount,
  1933), 21
KING OF THE KHYBER RIFLES (20th-
  Fox, 1953), 59
Kinski, Nastassia, 273
Kipling, Rudyard, 171, 179
Kissinger, Henry, 280, 281
Kites, Jim, 303, 304, 305, 307
Klinger, Michael, 252
KNIFE IN THE WATER (Contemporary,
  1962), 250–251
Kobal, John, 137, 196, 197, 214, 215,
  216, 217, 218, 223, 224

Koch, Howard, 147, 149, 150, 151, 205
Kodar, Oja, 225, 232–233, 234, 235,
  236
Komeda, Krzysztof, 248
Korda, Alexander, 81, 220
Kristofferson, Kris, 278, 279, 325, 328
Kwiatkowska, Barbara, 248, 249

LaCava, Gregory, 15
LADIES LOVE DANGER (Fox, 1935),
  22, 23
LADY FROM SHANGHAI, THE (Co-
  lumbia, 1948), 196, 197, 217, 220,
  221, 222, 223, 224, 226, 229, 236–
  237
LADY VANISHES, THE (Gainsborough,
  1938), 78
Laemmle, Carl, 11
L'Amour, Louis, 295
LAMP, THE (Polish, 1959), 248
Lancaster, Burt, 174
LAND OF THE PHARAOHS (Warner's,
  1955), 134
Lang, Fritz, 54, 74
Lasky, Jesse L., 101, 115, 116
Lass, Barbara, 248, 249
LAST FRONTIER, THE (Columbia,
  1955), 302, 303
Laughton, Charles, 78, 79, 84
LAW AND ORDER (Universal, 1932),
  58, 146
Lea, Fern, 297, 299
Leaming, Barbara, 199, 200, 203, 206,
  207, 217, 218, 223, 224, 225, 226,
  229, 232, 233, 246, 260, 269, 270
Leigh, Janet, 90, 230–231
Leigh, Vivien, 121, 122
LeMay, Alan, 174
Lennon, John, 310
Lennon, Julian, 326
LET THERE BE LIGHT (documentary),
  151
Levin, Ira, 258
Levine, Nat, 214–215
LIFE AND TIMES OF JUDGE ROY
  BEAN, THE (National General, 1972),
  178–179, 184
LIFEBOAT (20th-Fox, 1944), 82, 84, 87

LIGHTNIN' (Fox, 1930), 46
Lockwood, Margaret, 78
LODGER, THE (Gainsborough, 1927), 67–69, 70, 92
Lombard, Carole, 81, 110, 111, 112
Lombardo, Lou, 307
LONG GOODBYE, THE (United Artists, 1973), 244
Lord, Del, 13
Lorre, Peter, 73, 74, 75, 76, 84, 88, 93, 140, 141, 150, 151, 169
LOST PATROL, THE (RKO, 1934), 21
LOVE IS A MANY-SPLENDORED THING (20th-Fox, 1955), 59–60
Lubitsch, Ernst, 20
LUCKY CISCO KID (20th-Fox, 1940), 27, 36
Lukas, Paul, 74
Luke, Keye, 9, 26
Lupino, Ida, 148, 313
Luther, Martin, 264
Lyon, Ben, 20, 36

MACBETH (Republic, 1948), 226–227
MACBETH (Columbia, 1971), 93, 263–264
MacDonald-Wright, Stanton, 144, 181, 182
MAGNIFICENT AMBERSONS, THE (RKO, 1942), 209, 210, 211, 212, 236
Mahoney, John C., 320
MAJOR DUNDEE (Columbia, 1964), 300–301, 302, 303, 304, 305, 326
MALTESE FALCON, THE (Warner's, 1941), 118, 122, 140–143, 148, 149, 150, 168, 169, 180, 182, 212, 244, 245, 325
MAMMALS (Polish, 1962), 250
Mankiewicz, Herman J., 206, 207, 210
Mann, Anthony, 298, 302, 303
MAN WHO KNEW TOO MUCH, THE (Gaumont-British, 1935), 72, 73, 74, 75
MAN WHO KNEW TOO MUCH, THE (Paramount, 1956), 88
MAN WHO WOULD BE KING, THE (Allied Artists, 1975), 179, 180

MANXMAN, THE (British International, 1930), 70
Marlowe, Christopher, 204
MARNIE (Universal, 1964), 89, 91–92
Marshall, Herbert, 71, 72, 81
Martin, Charles, 316
Martin, Dean, 117, 129, 304
Martin, Strother, 308
Marxism, 4, 247
Mason, Edith, 201
Mast, Gerald, 97, 101, 102, 106, 108, 111, 115, 118, 123, 126, 136
Matthau, Walter, 274
Maugham, W. Somerset, 49, 75, 193, 249
Maurier, Daphne du, 79, 91
Mayer, Louis B., 23, 32, 109, 110, 163, 164, 209, 219, 272
McBride, Joseph, 103, 105, 109, 112, 114, 121, 232, 233, 234, 236
McCarty, John Alan, 266
McCrea, Joel, 18, 46, 80, 122, 123, 297, 298, 299
McGraw, Ali, 314, 325
McLaglen, Victor, 102
McQueen, Steve, 283, 313, 314
Melnick, Daniel, 30, 312, 315
Melville, Herman, 170, 184
Mencken, H. L., 145
Meredith, Burgess, 183, 184, 187
MERELY MARY ANN (Fox, 1931), 46–47
MERRY WIVES OF RENO (Warner's, 1934), 21
Methot, Mayo, 99, 148, 153
Meyer, William R., 304
Michener, James A., 301
Miles, Vera, 89, 90
Milestone, Lewis, 26, 104, 106, 114, 170
Milland, Ray, 86, 87
Miller, Arthur, 174
MISFITS, THE (United Artists, 1961), 174, 183
MR. AND MRS. SMITH (RKO, 1941), 81, 212
MR. ARKADIN (Talbot, 1962), 200, 229–230

Mitchum, Robert, 131, 171
Mix, Tom, 12, 46, 47, 146
MOBY DICK (Warner's, 1956), 168,
    169–170, 171, 184, 230
MONKEY BUSINESS (20th-Fox, 1952),
    95–96, 133–134
Monroe, Marilyn, 133, 134, 162, 174,
    175, 184, 199
Montgomery, Robert, 192
Moorehead, Agnes, 210
MOULIN ROUGE (United Artists,
    1953), 166, 167, 168
Mozart, W. A., 264, 265, 266
Muni, Paul, 106, 107, 147
MURDER (British International, 1931),
    71, 72, 81
Murnau, F. W., 67, 101
Murphy, Audie, 164
MY BEST GIRL (United Artists, 1927),
    13–14
MY DARLING CLEMENTINE (20th-
    Fox, 1946), 50
"Mystery of Marie Rogêt, The," 4

Namatian, 273
Naremore, James, 197, 222
Newman, Paul, 92, 179
Niblo, Fred, 12, 13, 14, 44, 45
Nichols, Mike, 263
Nicholson, Jack, 151, 159, 160, 183,
    242, 243, 245, 265, 267
Nietzsche, Friedrich, 185, 245, 262, 328
NIGHT AFTER NIGHT (Paramount,
    1932), 20
NIGHT OF THE IGUANA, THE (M-G-
    M, 1964), 176–177, 180
Nixon, Richard M., 260
Nolan, William F., 139, 179
NORTH BY NORTHWEST (M-G-M,
    1959), 67, 89
NOTORIOUS (RKO, 1946), 83–84
Novak, Kim, 89
Nyby, Christian, 126, 133

Oates, Warren, 302, 305, 325
O'Brien, Edna, 181
O'Casey, Sean, 71
O'Connell, Susan, 308, 309

O'Hara, Maureen, 79, 295, 296
Oland, Warner, 9, 23, 24, 26
Ondra, Anny, 70–71
ONE HEAVENLY NIGHT (United Art-
    ists, 1930), 15
O'Neill, Eugene, 144
ONLY ANGELS HAVE WINGS (Co-
    lumbia, 1939), 114, 129, 215, 216
Orwell, George, 12
OSTERMAN WEEKEND, THE (20th-
    Fox, 1983), 326
OTHELLO (United Artists, 1955), 193,
    227, 228, 229
OTHER SIDE OF THE WIND, THE,
    178, 233, 234, 235, 236
OUTLAW, THE (RKO, 1943), 116, 122

PACK UP YOUR TROUBLES (20th-
    Fox, 1939), 26, 27
Padovani, Lea, 199, 227–228
Paganini, Niccolò, 263
Palacios, Begoniâ, 300, 301, 305, 312,
    314, 320, 327
Pallette, Eugene, 19, 22, 36
PARADINE CASE, THE (Selznick Inter-
    national, 1947), 84
PARDON OUR NERVE (20th-Fox,
    1939), 26
Pate, Michael, 304
PAT GARRETT AND BILLY THE KID
    (M-G-M, 1973), 277, 283, 284, 287,
    289, 291, 292, 298, 306, 314, 315–
    319
Peck, Gregory, 57, 58, 59, 61, 84, 162,
    163, 184
Peckinpah, David, 293, 297
Peckinpah, Denver Charles, 293, 326
Peckinpah, Kristen, 294, 320, 328
Peckinpah, Lupita, 320
Peckinpah, Matthew, 297, 311, 326, 327
Peckinpah, Melissa, 294, 321
Peckinpah, Sam, 2, 10, 128, 177, 252,
    277–328
Peckinpah, Sharon, 293, 294, 314, 319,
    320, 327
Perry, Lincoln, 48–49
Pettit, Arthur G., 306
Picasso, Pablo, 314
Pickens, Slim, 391, 317

Pickford, Mary, 14, 15, 23
Piekarski, Vicki, 8, 10, 14, 18, 19, 23, 27, 34, 35, 36, 37, 53, 65, 73, 75, 93, 135, 136, 139, 180, 181, 190, 191, 239, 240, 241, 242, 262, 263, 268, 270, 271, 286, 287, 288, 289, 292, 320, 321, 324, 325, 327
PIN-UP GIRL (20th-Fox, 1944), 30, 36
PIRATES (Cannon, 1986), 273, 274
Pitts, Zasu, 19
Pleasence, Donald, 254, 257
PLEASURE GARDEN, THE (Gainsborough, 1927), 66–67
Poe, Edgar Allan, 3, 4, 146, 192
Polanski, Roman, 2, 4, 93, 143, 150, 159, 208, 227, 239–275, 310
Ponti, Carlo, 264
Porter, Katherine Anne, 301
Powell, Dick, 294, 295, 299, 300
Powell, William, 21, 44, 101
Power, Tyrone, 52, 53, 54, 59, 61
Preston, Robert, 302, 313
PRIZZI'S HONOR (20th-Fox, 1985), . 183
PSYCHO (Paramount, 1960), 68, 90, 92, 253
Puccini, Giacomo, 262

Racine, Jean, 263, 264
RAFFLES (United Artists, 1930), 15
Raft, George, 20, 100, 106, 140–141, 148, 150, 158, 172, 271
RAMONA (20th-Fox, 1936), 51
Ransohoff, Martin, 254, 257, 258
Rathvon, N. Peter, 190, 212
REAR WINDOW (Paramount, 1954), 87, 88
REBECCA (United Artists, 1940), 6, 79, 80, 81, 82, 83, 212
RED BADGE OF COURAGE, THE (M-G-M, 1951), 162, 163, 164, 165
RED PONY, THE (Republic, 1949), 278
RED RIVER (United Artists, 1948), 102, 122, 123–126, 127, 129, 130, 131, 133, 135, 148, 302, 304
Reed, Sir Carol, 195
Reid, Wallace, 327
Reik, Theodor, 257

REPORT FROM THE ALEUTIANS (1943), 151
REPULSION (Royal Films International, 1965), 252, 253, 254, 257, 260, 266
Reville, Alma, 6, 66, 71, 72, 77, 84
RICH AND STRANGE (British International, 1932), 67, 72
RIDE THE HIGH COUNTRY (M-G-M, 1962), 297–299, 302, 306
Rieupeyrout, Jean-Louis, 125, 298
Rilke, Rainer Maria, 241, 275
RING, THE (British International, 1928), 69
RIO BRAVO (Warner's 1959), 117, 118, 122, 128, 129, 130, 131, 134
RIO GRANDE (Republic, 1950), 302, 303
RIO LOBO (National General, 1970), 121, 130, 131
RIOT IN CELL BLOCK 11 (Allied Artists, 1954), 294
Rivero, Julian, 278
Rivette, Jacques, 95–96, 122, 130
ROAD TO GLORY, THE (Fox, 1926), 101
ROAD TO GLORY, THE (20th-Fox, 1936), 112
Robards, Jason, Jr., 301, 308, 310, 311
Robinson, Edward G., 108, 122, 123, 147, 159, 160
Rockefeller, Nelson, 210, 211
Rogers, Ginger, 133, 134
Rogers, Will, 46, 47, 48, 49
Rohmer, Eric, 4, 5
Roland, Gilbert, 13, 22, 160
Rome, Sydne, 264, 265, 267
Romero, Cesar, 27, 33
ROMOLA (Inspiration-M-G-M, 1924), 44
Roosevelt, Franklin Delano, 57, 159, 218
ROOTS OF HEAVEN, THE (20th-Fox, 1958), 173–174
ROPE (Warner's, 1948), 84
ROSEMARY'S BABY (Paramount, 1968), 258, 259, 260–261, 264, 266, 310
Rosenbaum, Jonathan, 193
Rosenbaum, Linda, 310
Ruggles, Wesley, 15, 32

Russell, Jane, 115, 116, 134
Russell, Rosalind, 115
Ryan, Robert, 304

SABOTAGE (Gaumont-British, 1937), 76
SABOTEUR (RKO, 1942), 81, 82
St. Jerome, 264
Sanders, George, 80, 81, 178
Sarris, Andrew, 7
Sartre, Jean-Paul, 151–152, 176
SCARFACE (United Artists, 1932), 98, 106–107, 120
Schaefer, George J., 207, 209, 212, 213
Schary, Dore, 162, 163, 164, 165
Schenck, Nicholas, 23, 44, 163, 164
Schopenhauer, Arthur, 7
Scott, Lizabeth, 196
Scott, Randolph, 30, 33, 297, 298, 299, 302
SECRET AGENT, THE (Gaumont-British, 1936), 75, 76
Seigner, Emmanuelle, 274
Selland, Marie, 293, 294, 295, 297, 299, 300, 311, 327, 328
Selznick, David O., 17, 18, 21, 23, 25, 41, 51, 56, 62, 77, 78, 79, 80, 82, 83, 84, 109, 163, 168, 169, 170, 171, 172, 173
Selznick, Myron, 13, 77, 87, 140
Sen Young, Victor, 26
SERGEANT YORK (Warner's, 1941), 115–116, 118, 148, 164
Seydor, Paul, 303, 306, 307, 310
SHADOW OF A DOUBT (Universal, 1943), 81–82, 83, 219
Shakespeare, William, 201, 204, 227, 232, 263, 264
SHANE (Paramount, 1953), 58, 292
Shaw, George Bernard, 81
SHE DONE HIM WRONG (Paramount, 1933), 20
Sheridan, Ann, 132, 134
Sherman, Lowell, 17, 20
SHE WORE A YELLOW RIBBON (RKO, 1949), 309
Siegel, Don, 294, 326
SILK HAT KID (Fox, 1935), 23

Silver, Charles, 233, 311
Simmons, Garner, 282, 283, 290, 291, 297, 307
Sinatra, Frank, 169, 170, 171, 177, 261
Skolimowsky, Jerzy, 250
Sloane, Everett, 221
Slocombe, Dennis, 257
SNOWS OF KILIMANJARO, THE (20th-Fox, 1952), 57, 59
SOMEONE TO LOVE (International Rainbow Pictures, 1987), 236
SONG IS BORN, A (RKO, 1948), 132
SONG OF BERNADETTE, THE (20th-Fox, 1943), 43, 56–57
Sophocles, 68
SPELLBOUND (United Artists, 1945), 83
Spiegel, Sam, 160, 163, 164, 165, 166, 219, 220
Spielberg, Stephen, 235
Spoto, Donald, 6, 65–66, 67, 73, 79, 83, 87, 93
STAGECOACH (United Artists, 1939), 123, 309
Stander, Lionel, 254
STANLEY AND LIVINGSTONE (20th-Fox, 1939), 40, 55
Stanwyck, Barbara, 132
Stark, Ray, 182
Starr, Ronald, 298
STATE FAIR (Fox, 1933), 40, 47–48
Steinbeck, John, 278
STELLA DALLAS (United Artists, 1925), 44, 47
Sternberg, Josef von, 20, 75
Stevens, Stella, 308, 311
Stewart, James, 84, 87, 88, 89
Stokowski, Leopold, 169
STRANGER, THE (RKO, 1946), 160, 219, 220
STRANGERS OF THE EVENING (Tiffany, 1932), 19, 20, 36
STRANGERS ON A TRAIN (Warner's, 1951), 73, 84, 85–86, 87
STRAW DOGS (Cinerama, 1971), 282, 308, 312–313
STREET SCENE (United Artists, 1931), 16

Struthers, Sally, 314
Sulik, Boleslaw, 262
Sullivan, Barry, 317
SUN ALSO RISES, THE (20th-Fox, 1957), 40, 59, 60, 61, 62, 102–103, 173, 177
SUN VALLEY SERENADE (20th-Fox, 1941), 28, 30
SUSPICION (RKO, 1941), 5, 6, 81, 212

TALL, DARK, AND HANDSOME (20th-Fox, 1941), 27
TAMING OF THE SHREW, THE (United Artists, 1929), 15
Tarkington, Booth, 210
Tate, Sharon, 250, 254, 255–256, 258, 259, 261, 262, 263, 264, 273
Taylor, Dub, 279, 280, 318
Taylor, Elizabeth, 162, 176
Taylor, John Russell, 67, 68
Taylor, Sam, 13, 14, 15, 16, 45
Temple, Shirley, 47, 48, 49
TEMPTRESS, THE (M-G-M, 1926), 13
TENANT, THE (Paramount, 1976), 239, 240, 245, 254, 265, 266, 269, 271
TENDER IS THE NIGHT (20th-Fox, 1961), 62
TESS (Columbia, 1980), 273
Thalberg, Irving, 61, 80, 108, 112, 165, 258, 287, 291
THEY WENT THAT-AWAY (PBS, 1970), 189
Thiede, Karl, 8, 287
THING, THE (RKO, 1951), 133
THIRD MAN, THE (Eagle-Lion, 1950), 195, 228
THIRTY-NINE STEPS, THE (Gaumont-British, 1935), 75–76, 81
Thompson, Verita, 99–100, 148, 152, 154–155, 169
THREE LITTLE GIRLS IN BLUE (20th-Fox, 1946), 31
THREE LIVE GHOSTS (M-G-M, 1936), 23
THREE STRANGERS (Warner's, 1945), 146, 147, 151

TIGER SHARK (Warner's, 1932), 107–108, 109
TIME OUT FOR MURDER (20th-Fox, 1938), 26
TO CATCH A THIEF (Paramount, 1955), 88, 91
TODAY WE LIVE (M-G-M, 1933), 98, 109
Todd, Mike, 30, 175, 176, 220
TO HAVE AND HAVE NOT (Warner's, 1944), 96, 97, 100, 102, 114, 117, 118, 119, 120, 129, 149, 152, 161, 243
TOL'ABLE DAVID (First National, 1921), 40, 42
Toland, Gregg, 95, 112, 132, 190, 206, 207, 210
Toler, Sidney, 26
TOPAZ (Universal, 1969), 92
TOPSY AND EVA (United Artists, 1927), 13
TORN CURTAIN (Universal, 1966), 68, 92
TO THE SHORES OF TRIPOLI (20th-Fox, 1942), 29, 30
TOUCH OF EVIL (Universal, 1958), 197, 230–231, 237
Towne, Robert, 244
Tracy, Spencer, 55, 163, 164
Traven, B., 155–156, 157
TREASURE OF THE SIERRA MADRE, THE (Warner's, 1948), 146, 155, 160, 174, 177, 212, 325
TRENT'S LAST CASE (Fox, 1929), 103
Trevor, Claire, 159, 309
TRIAL, THE (Astor, 1963), 231–232
TROUBLE WITH HARRY, THE (Paramount, 1955), 88
Truffaut, François, 5, 73, 85, 122, 210, 219
Turner, Kathleen, 183
Turner, Ted, 186
Tuska, Jenni, 327
Tuska, Ruth, 284, 285, 286, 287, 288
Tuska, Vicki. See Piekarski, Vicki
TWELVE O'CLOCK HIGH (20th-Fox, 1949), 50, 57–58, 59, 63

TWENTIETH CENTURY (Columbia, 1934), 110–112, 115

TWO LOVERS (United Artists, 1928), 14

TWO MEN AND A WARDROBE (Polish, 1958), 248

Tynan, Kenneth, 195, 208

Umecka, Jolanta, 250, 251, 266

UNDER THE VOLCANO (Universal, 1984), 182–183, 187, 235

UNFORGIVEN, THE (United Artists, 1960), 174

UNIVERSAL IN 1925 (Universal, 1925), 12

Vadim, Roger, 252

VALENCIA (M-G-M, 1926), 13

Van Dine, S. S., 21, 28, 144

Vendell, Veronique, 323

Verdi, Giuseppe, 266

Verne, Jules, 220

VERTIGO (Paramount, 1958), 89, 90

Vidor, King, 16, 17, 18, 19

Viertel, Peter, 165, 167, 168, 171, 177

VILLA RIDES (Paramount, 1968), 301

VISITOR, THE (International, 1979), 325

Wallis, Hal B., 21, 22, 25

Wanger, Walter, 80, 294

Warner, David, 308, 312

Warner, Jack L., 22, 98, 99, 100, 101, 104, 105, 107, 109, 111, 115, 116, 119, 120, 140, 148, 156, 157, 158, 160, 161, 302

Wasserman, Lew, 32, 87, 92

WAY DOWN EAST (Fox, 1935), 49

Wayne, John, 96, 97, 121, 123, 124, 126, 129, 130, 131, 136, 148, 172, 173, 277, 279, 280–281, 282, 284, 302, 303, 304

Wayne, Michael, 280, 282

Weissberger, L. Arnold, 191–192, 193, 200, 203, 205, 208, 209, 233

Welles, Orson, 133, 147, 160, 173, 174, 178, 181, 182, 184, 185, 189–237, 244, 245, 254, 322

Wellman, William, 30, 104

Wells, H. G., 204

Werfel, Franz, 56–57

West, Mae, 20

WE WERE STRANGERS (Columbia, 1949), 160–161, 162, 165, 167

WHAT? (Avo-Embassy, 1973), 243, 264–265, 267

WHEN ANGELS FALL (Polish, 1959), 248–249, 251

WHILE NEW YORK SLEEPS (20th-Fox, 1939), 26

WHITE SISTER, THE (Inspiration-M-G-M, 1923), 43, 44

WHOOPEE! (United Artists, 1930), 15

WILD BUNCH, THE (Warner's, 1969), 128, 278, 284, 292, 298, 304, 305–307, 309, 311, 313

Wilde, Oscar, 327

Wilder, Billy, 85, 131, 133

Williams, Tennessee, 177, 293, 294

Willis, Donald C., 123, 129

Wills, Chill, 295, 315

WILSON (20th-Fox, 1944), 55, 57

WINNING OF BARBARA WORTH, THE (United Artists, 1926), 44–45

Wise, Robert, 190, 206

Wollen, Peter, 127–128

WOMAN DISPUTED, THE (United Artists, 1928), 45

WONDER MAN (RKO, 1945), 30

Wood, Robin, 5, 6, 130

Woolrich, Cornell, 28, 87

Wright, Teresa, 82, 83

Wright, Willard Huntington, 21, 28, 144

WRONG MAN, THE (Warner's, 1957), 88–89

Wurlitzer, Rudolph, 283, 316

Wurtzel, Sol, 22, 24, 25, 26, 27, 46, 47, 101

Wyler, William, 13, 112, 113, 142, 147, 159

Yates, Herbert J., 226
YOUNG AND INNOCENT (Gainsborough, 1938), 77

Zanuck, Darryl F., 1, 9, 23, 24, 25, 27, 28, 29, 30, 31, 37, 49, 50, 51, 52, 54, 55, 56, 57, 58, 59, 60, 61, 62, 82, 103, 134, 149, 173, 174, 193, 213, 214, 219, 258
Ziegfeld, Florenz, 15, 213
Zukor, Adolph, 115, 241
ZYKOVS, THE, 3

**About the Author**

JON TUSKA is a filmmaker and a writer on film and popular culture. He is the author of many books, including the Greenwood Press titles *Billy the Kid: A Bio-Bibliography* (1983); *Dark Cinema: American Film Noir in Cultural Perspective* (1984); *The American West in Film: Critical Approaches to the Western* (1985); and *In Manors and Alleys: A Casebook on the American Detective Film* (1988).